world development report 2006

Equity and Development

world development report 2006

Equity and Development

A copublication of The World Bank
and Oxford University Press

©2005 The International Bank for Reconstruction and Development / The World Bank
1818 H Street NW
Washington DC 20433
Telephone: 202-473-1000
Internet: www.worldbank.org
E-mail: feedback@worldbank.org

1 2 3 4 08 07 06 05

A copublication of The World Bank and Oxford University Press.

Oxford University Press
198 Madison Avenue
New York NY 10016

This volume is a product of the staff of the International Bank for Reconstruction and Development / The World Bank. The findings, interpretations, and conclusions expressed in this paper do not necessarily reflect the views of the Executive Directors of The World Bank or the governments they represent.

The World Bank does not guarantee the accuracy of the data included in this work. The boundaries, colors, denominations, and other information shown on any map in this work do not imply any judgement on the part of The World Bank concerning the legal status of any territory or the endorsement or acceptance of such boundaries.

ISBN-10: 0-8213-6249-6
ISBN-13: 978-0-8213-6249-5
ISSN: 0163-5085
eISBN: 0-8213-6250-X
DOI: 10.1596/978-0-8213-6249-5

Cover image: *Dream of a Sunday Afternoon in Alameda Park* 1947–48 (fresco) by Diego Rivera. The mural is located in Museo Mural Diego Rivera, Mexico City. Reproduction authorized by the Instituto Nacional de Bellas Artes y Literatura–Mexico; Copyright © Photograph by Francisco Kochen.

Library of Congress Cataloging-in-Publication Data has been applied for.

Contents

Boxes

Figures

Tables

Foreword

We live in a world of extraordinary inequalities in opportunity, both within and across countries. Even the basic opportunity for life itself is disparately distributed: whereas less than half of 1 percent of children born in Sweden die before their first birthday, nearly 15 percent of all children born in Mozambique fail to reach that milestone. Within El Salvador, the infant mortality rate is 2 percent for children of educated mothers but 10 percent for those whose mothers have no schooling. In Eritrea, immunization coverage is close to 100 percent for children in the richest fifth of the population but only 50 percent for the bottom fifth.

These children cannot be blamed for the circumstances into which they were born, yet their lives—and their ability to contribute to the development of their nations—are powerfully shaped by them. That is why the *World Development Report 2006*, the 28th in this annual series, focuses on the role of equity in the process of development. *Equity* is defined in terms of two basic principles. The first is *equal opportunity*: a person's life achievements should be determined primarily by his or her talents and efforts, rather than by predetermined circumstances such as race, gender, social and family background, or country of birth. The second principle is the *avoidance of deprivation in outcomes*, particularly in health, education, and consumption levels.

For many, if not most, people, equity is intrinsically important as a development goal in its own right. But this Report goes further, by presenting evidence that a broad sharing of economic and political opportunities is also instrumental for economic growth and development.

Broadening opportunities strongly supports the first pillar of the Bank's development strategy, namely, improving the investment climate for everyone. The interdependence of the economic and political dimensions of development also reinforces the importance of the second strategic pillar, empowerment. This Report shows that the two pillars are not independent from each other in supporting development but instead reinforce each other. It is my hope that this Report will influence strongly the way that we and our development partners understand, design, and implement development policies.

Paul D. Wolfowitz
President
The World Bank

Acknowledgments

This Report has been prepared by a core team led by Francisco H.G. Ferreira and Michael Walton, and comprising Tamar Manuelyan Atinc, Abhijit Banerjee, Peter Lanjouw, Marta Menéndez, Berk Özler, Giovanna Prennushi, Vijayendra Rao, James Robinson, and Michael Woolcock. Important additional contributions were made by Anthony Bebbington, Stijn Claessens, Margaret Ellen Grosh, Karla Hoff, Jean O. Lanjouw, Xubei Lou, Ana Revenga, Caroline Sage, Mark Sundberg, and Peter Timmer. The team was assisted by Maria Caridad Araujo, Andrew Beath, Ximena del Carpio, Celine Ferre, Thomas Haven, Claudio E. Montenegro, and Jeffery C. Tanner. The work was conducted under the general guidance of François Bourguignon.

Extensive and excellent advice was received from Anthony B. Atkinson, Angus Deaton, Naila Kabeer, Martin Ravallion, and Amartya Sen, to whom the team is grateful without implication. Many others inside and outside the World Bank also provided helpful comments; their names are listed in the Bibliographical Note. The Development Data Group contributed to the data appendix and was responsible for the Selected World Development Indicators. Much of the background research was supported by a multidonor programmatic trust fund, the Knowledge for Change Program, funded by Canada, the European Community, Finland, Norway, Sweden, Switzerland, and the United Kingdom.

The team undertook a wide range of consultations for this Report, which included workshops in Amsterdam, Beirut, Berlin, Cairo, Dakar, Geneva, Helsinki, Hyderabad, London, Milan, Nairobi, New Delhi, Oslo, Ottawa, Paris, Rio de Janeiro, Stockholm, Tokyo, Venice, and Washington, D.C.; videoconferences with sites in Bogota, Buenos Aires, Mexico City, and Tokyo; and an on-line discussion of the draft Report. The team wishes to thank participants in these workshops, videoconferences, and discussions, which included researchers, government officials, and staff of nongovernmental and private-sector organizations.

Rebecca Sugui served as executive assistant to the team, Ofelia Valladolid as program assistant, Madhur Arora and Jason Victor as team assistants. Evangeline Santo Domingo served as resource management assistant.

Bruce Ross-Larson was the principal editor. Book design, editing, and production were coordinated by the World Bank's Office of the Publisher under the supervision of Susan Graham and Monika Lynde.

Abbreviations and Data Notes

Abbreviations

The following abbreviations are used in this Report:

AA	Affirmative action	NGO	Nongovernmental organization
AIDS	Acquired immune deficiency syndrome	ODA	Official development assistance
CCP	Chinese Communist Party	OECD	Organisation for Economic Co-operation and
DAC	Development Assistance Committee		Development
DHS	Demographic and Health Survey	PPA	Participatory Poverty Assessment
ECD	Early child development	PPP	Purchasing-power parity
EPL	Employment protection legislation	PROMESA	Promoción y Mejoramiento de la Salud
FDI	Foreign direct investment	SMEs	Small and medium enterprises
GDP	Gross domestic product	TAC	Treatment Action Campaign
GHG	Greenhouse gas	TIMSS	Third International Mathematics and Science
GNI	Gross national income		Study
HIPC	Heavily Indebted Poor Countries	TRIPs	Trade-related aspects of intellectual property
HIV	Human immunodeficiency virus		rights
ICOR	Incremental Capital-Output Ratio	U.N.	United Nations
ICRISAT	International Crop Research Institute in the Semi-Arid Tropics	UNCTAD	United Nations Conference on Trade and Development
IDA	International Development Association	UNDP	United Nations Development Programme
ILO	International Labour Organization	UNAIDS	Joint United Nations Programme on HIV/AIDS
IMF	International Monetary Fund	UNICEF	United Nations International Children's
IMS	Intercontinental Marketing Services		Emergency Fund
KDP	Kecamatan Development Project	VAT	Value added tax
MDG	Millennium Development Goals	WHO	World Health Organization
MMM	Movement Militant Mauricien	WTO	World Trade Organization
MSF	Médecins Sans Frontières	WWII	World War II
NAFTA	North American Free Trade Agreement		

Data notes

The countries included in regional and income groupings in this Report are listed in the Classification of Economies table at the beginning of the Selected World Development Indicators. Income classifications are based on GNP per capita; thresholds for income classifications in this edition may be found in the Introduction to Selected World Development Indicators. Group averages reported in the figures and tables are unweighted averages of the countries in the group, unless noted to the contrary.

The use of the word *countries* to refer to economies implies no judgment by the World Bank about the legal or other status of a territory. The term *developing countries* includes low- and middle-income economies and thus may include economies in transition from central planning, as a matter of convenience. The term *advanced countries* may be used as a matter of convenience to denote high-income economies.

Dollar figures are current U.S. dollars, unless otherwise specified. *Billion* means 1,000 million; *trillion* means 1,000 billion.

Overview

Consider two South African children born on the same day in 2000. Nthabiseng is black, born to a poor family in a rural area in the Eastern Cape province, about 700 kilometers from Cape Town. Her mother had no formal schooling. Pieter is white, born to a wealthy family in Cape Town. His mother completed a college education at the nearby prestigious Stellenbosch University.

On the day of their birth, Nthabiseng and Pieter could hardly be held responsible for their family circumstances: their race, their parents' income and education, their urban or rural location, or indeed their sex. Yet statistics suggest that those predetermined background variables will make a major difference for the lives they lead. Nthabiseng has a 7.2 percent chance of dying in the first year of her life, more than twice Pieter's 3 percent. Pieter can look forward to 68 years of life, Nthabiseng to 50. Pieter can expect to complete 12 years of formal schooling, Nthabiseng less than 1 year.[1] Nthabiseng is likely to be considerably poorer than Pieter throughout her life.[2] Growing up, she is less likely to have access to clean water and sanitation, or to good schools. So the opportunities these two children face to reach their full human potential are vastly different from the outset, through no fault of their own.

Such disparities in opportunity translate into different abilities to contribute to South Africa's development. Nthabiseng's health at birth may have been poorer, owing to the poorer nutrition of her mother during her pregnancy. By virtue of their gender socialization, their geographic location, and their access to schools, Pieter is much more likely to acquire an education that will enable him to put his innate talents to full use. Even if at age 25, and despite the odds, Nthabiseng manages to come up with a great business idea (such as an innovation to increase agricultural production), she would find it much harder to persuade a bank to lend her money at a reasonable interest rate. Pieter, having a similarly bright idea (say, on how to design an improved version of promising software), would likely find it easier to obtain credit, with both a college diploma and quite possibly some collateral. With the transition to democracy in South Africa, Nthabiseng is able to vote and thus indirectly shape the policy of her government, something denied to blacks under apartheid. But the legacy of apartheid's unequal opportunities and political power will remain for some time to come. It is a long road from such a (fundamental) political change to changes in economic and social conditions.

As striking as the differences in life chances are between Pieter and Nthabiseng in South Africa, they are dwarfed by the disparities between average South Africans and citizens of more developed countries. Consider the cards dealt to Sven—born on that same day to an average Swedish household. His chances of dying in the first year of life are very small (0.3 percent) and he can expect to live to the age of 80, 12 years longer than Pieter, and 30 years more than Nthabiseng. He is likely to complete 11.4 years of schooling—5 years more than the average South African. These differences in the quantity of schooling are compounded by differences in quality: in the eighth grade, Sven can expect to obtain a score of 500 on an internationally comparable math test, while the average South African student will get a score of only 264—more than two standard deviations below the Organisation for Economic Co-operation and Development (OECD) median.

Nthabiseng most likely will never reach that grade and so will not take the test.[3]

These differences in life chances across nationality, race, gender, and social groups will strike many readers as fundamentally unfair. They are also likely to lead to wasted human potential and thus to missed development opportunities. That is why World Development Report 2006 analyzes the relationship between equity and development.

By equity we mean that individuals should have equal opportunities to pursue a life of their choosing and be spared from extreme deprivation in outcomes. The main message is that equity is complementary, in some fundamental respects, to the pursuit of long-term prosperity. Institutions and policies that promote a level playing field—where all members of society have similar chances to become socially active, politically influential, and economically productive—contribute to sustainable growth and development. Greater equity is thus doubly good for poverty reduction: through potential beneficial effects on aggregate long-run development and through greater opportunities for poorer groups within any society.

The complementarities between equity and prosperity arise for two broad sets of reasons. First, there are many market failures in developing countries, notably in the markets for credit, insurance, land, and human capital. As a result, resources may not flow where returns are highest. For example, some highly capable children, like Nthabiseng, may fail to complete primary schooling, while others, who are less able, may finish university. Farmers may work harder on plots they own than on those they sharecrop. Some efficient developing-country producers of agricultural commodities and textiles are shut out of some OECD markets, and poor unskilled workers have highly restricted opportunities to migrate to work in richer countries.

When markets are missing or imperfect, the distributions of wealth and power affect the allocation of investment opportunities. Correcting the market failures is the ideal response; where this is not feasible, or far too costly, some forms of redistribution—of access to services, assets, or political influence—can increase economic efficiency.

The second set of reasons why equity and long-term prosperity can be complementary arises from the fact that high levels of economic and political inequality tend to lead to economic institutions and social arrangements that systematically favor the interests of those with more influence. Such inequitable institutions can generate economic costs. When personal and property rights are enforced only selectively, when budgetary allocations benefit mainly the politically influential, and when the distribution of public services favors the wealthy, both middle and poorer groups end up with unexploited talent. Society, as a whole, is then likely to be more inefficient and to miss out on opportunities for innovation and investment. At the global level, when developing countries have little or no voice in global governance, the rules can be inappropriate and costly for poorer countries.

These adverse effects of unequal opportunities and political power on development are all the more damaging because economic, political, and social inequalities tend to reproduce themselves over time and across generations. We call such phenomena "inequality traps." Disadvantaged children from families at the bottom of the wealth distribution do not have the same opportunities as children from wealthier families to receive quality education. So these disadvantaged children can expect to earn less as adults. Because the poor have less voice in the political process, they—like their parents—will be less able to influence spending decisions to improve public schools for their children. And the cycle of underachievement continues.

The distribution of wealth is closely correlated with social distinctions that stratify people, communities, and nations into groups that dominate and those that are dominated. These patterns of domination persist because economic and social differences are reinforced by the overt and covert use of power. Elites protect their interests in subtle ways, by exclusionary practices in marriage and kinship systems, for instance, and in ways that are less subtle, such as aggressive political manipulation or the explicit use of violence.

Such overlapping political, social, cultural, and economic inequalities stifle mobility. They are hard to break because they are so closely tied to the ordinary business of life. They are perpetuated by the elite, and often internalized by the marginalized or oppressed groups, making it difficult for the poor to find their way out of poverty. Inequality traps can thus be rather stable, tending to persist over generations.

The report documents the persistence of these inequality traps by highlighting the interaction between different forms of inequality. It presents evidence that the inequality of opportunity that arises is wasteful and inimical to sustainable development and poverty reduction. It also derives policy implications that center on the broad concept of leveling the playing field—both politically and economically and in the domestic and the global arenas. If the opportunities faced by children like Nthabiseng are so much more limited than those faced by children like Pieter or Sven, and if this hurts development progress in the aggregate, then public action has a legitimate role in seeking to broaden the opportunities of those who face the most limited choices.

Three considerations are important at the outset. First, while more even playing fields are likely to lead to lower observed inequalities in educational attainment, health status, and incomes, the policy aim is not equality in outcomes. Indeed, even with genuine equality of opportunities, one would always expect to observe some differences in outcomes owing to differences in preferences, talents, effort, and luck.[4] This is consistent with the important role of income differences in providing incentives to invest in education and physical capital, to work, and to take risks. Of course outcomes matter, but we are concerned with them mainly for their influence on absolute deprivation and their role in shaping opportunities.

Second, a concern with equality of opportunity implies that public action should focus on the distributions of assets, economic opportunities, and political voice, rather than directly on inequality in incomes. Policies can contribute to the move from an "inequality trap" to a virtuous circle of equity and growth by leveling the playing field—through greater investment in the human resources of the poorest; greater and more equal access to public services and information; guarantees

on property rights for all; and greater fairness in markets. But policies to level the economic playing field face big challenges. There is unequal capacity to influence the policy agenda: the interests of the disenfranchised may never be voiced or represented. And when policies challenge privileges, powerful groups may seek to block reforms. Thus, equitable policies are more likely to be successful when leveling the economic playing field is accompanied by similar efforts to level the domestic political playing field and introduce greater fairness in global governance.

Third, there may be various short-run, policy-level tradeoffs between equity and efficiency. These are well recognized and extensively documented. The point is that the (often implicit) cost-benefit calculus that policymakers use to assess the merits of various policies too often ignores the long-term, hard-to-measure but real benefits of greater equity. Greater equity implies more efficient economic functioning, reduced conflict, greater trust, and better institutions, with dynamic benefits for investment and growth. To the extent that such benefits are ignored, policymakers may end up choosing too little equity.

By the same token, however, those interested in greater equity must not ignore the short-term tradeoffs. If individual incentives are blunted by income redistribution schemes that tax investment and production too steeply, the result will be less innovation, less investment, and less growth. The history of the twentieth century is littered with examples of ill-designed policies pursued in the name of equity that seriously harmed—rather than spurred—growth processes by ignoring individual incentives. A balance must be sought, taking into account both the immediate costs to individual incentives and the long-term benefits of cohesive societies, with inclusive institutions and broad opportunities.

While careful assessment of policy design in local contexts is always important, equity considerations need to be brought squarely into the center of both diagnosis and policy. This is not intended as a new framework. It means integrating and extending existing frameworks: equity is central both to the investment environment and to the agenda of empowerment, working through the impact on institutions and specific policy designs. Some may value equity for its own sake, others primarily for its instrumental role in reducing absolute poverty, the World Bank's mission.

This report recognizes the intrinsic value of equity but aims primarily to document how a focus on equity matters for long-run development. It has three parts.

- Part I considers the evidence on inequality of opportunity, within and across countries. Some attempts to quantify inequality of opportunity are reviewed but, more generally, we rely on evidence of highly unequal outcomes across groups defined by predetermined circumstances—such as gender, race, family background, or country of birth—as markers for unequal opportunities.
- Part II asks why equity matters. It discusses the two channels of impact (the effects of unequal opportunities when markets are imperfect, and the consequences of inequity for the quality of institutions a society develops) as well as intrinsic motives.
- Part III asks how public action can level the political and economic playing fields. In the domestic arena, it makes the case for investing in people, expanding access to justice, land, and infrastructure, and promoting fairness in markets. In the international arena, it considers leveling the playing field in the functioning of global markets and the rules that govern them—and the complementary provision of aid to help poor countries and poor people build greater endowments.

The remainder of this overview provides a summary of the principal findings.

Inequity within and across nations

From an equity perspective, the distribution of opportunities matters more than the distribution of outcomes. But opportunities, which are potentials rather than actuals, are harder to observe and measure than outcomes.

Within-country inequities have many dimensions

Direct quantification of inequality of opportunity is difficult, but one analysis of Brazil provides an illustration (chapter 2). Earnings inequality in 1996 was divided into one share attributable to four predetermined circumstances that lie beyond the control of individuals—race, region of birth, parental education, and paternal occupation at birth—and a residual share. These four circumstances account for around one-quarter of overall differences in earnings between workers. Arguably, other determinants of opportunity are equally predetermined at birth but not included in this set—for example, gender, family wealth, or the quality of primary schools. Because such variables are not included in the inequality "decomposition," the results here can be seen as lower-bound estimates of inequality of opportunity in Brazil.

Unfortunately, predetermined (and thus morally irrelevant) circumstances determine much more than just future earnings. Education and health are of intrinsic value and affect the capacity of individuals to engage in economic, social, and political life. Yet children face substantially different opportunities to learn and to lead healthy lives in almost all populations, depending on asset ownership, geographic location, or parental education, among others. Consider how access to a basic package of immunization services differs for the rich and the poor across countries (figure 1).

There is substantial inequality in access between, for example, Egypt, where almost everyone is covered (on the left), and Chad, where more than 40 percent of children are excluded (on the right). Yet the disparities can be as large within some countries as they are across all nations in the sample. In Eritrea, for instance, the richest fifth enjoys almost complete coverage, but almost half of all children in the poorest fifth are excluded.

Significant gender differences also persist in many parts of the world. In parts of East and South Asia, notably in certain areas in rural China and northwest India, the opportunity to life itself can depend on one single predetermined characteristic: sex. These regions have significantly more boy

Figure 1 Wealth matters for the immunization of children

Percentage not covered

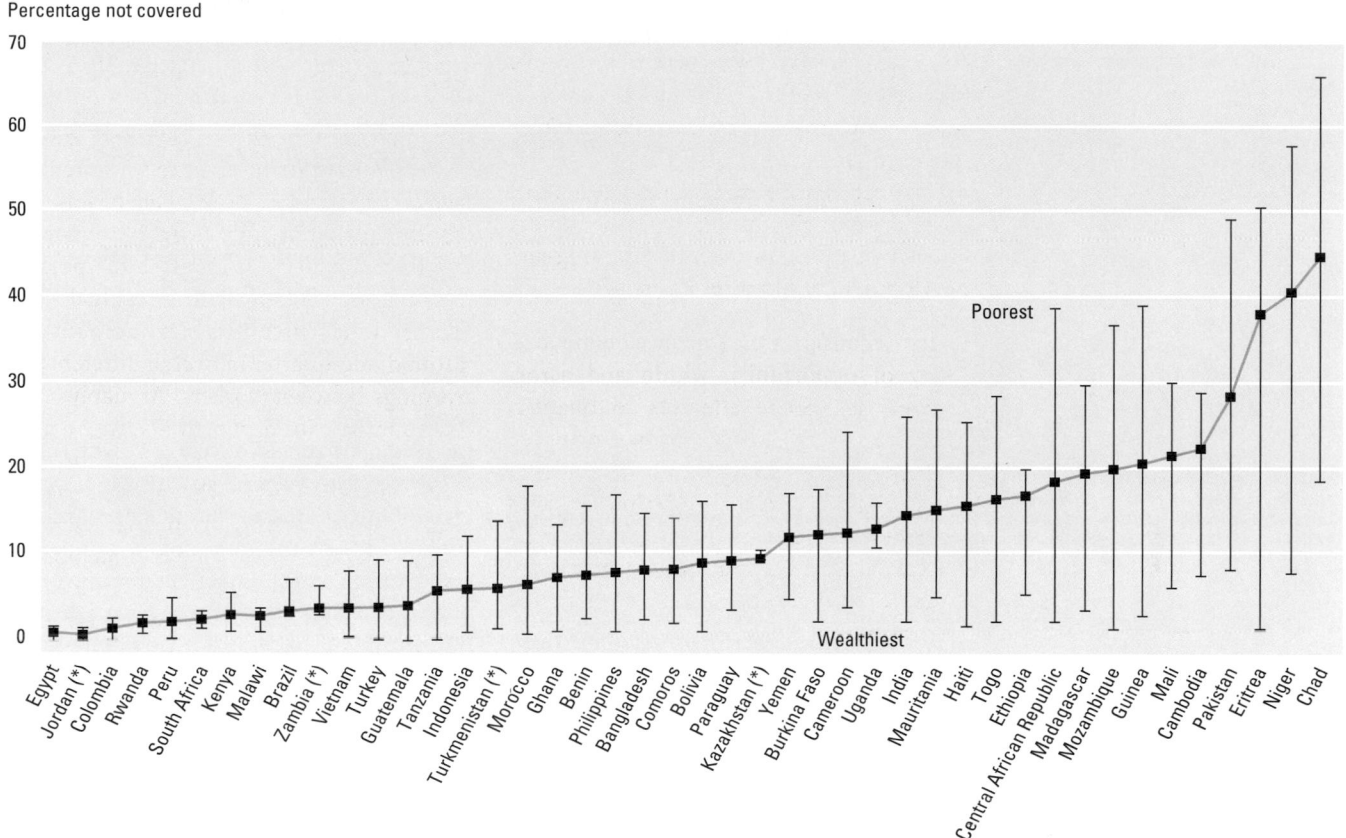

Source: Authors' own calculations from Demographic Health Survey (DHS) data
Note: * indicates that the poorest quintile have higher access to childhood immunization services than the wealthiest quintile.
The continuous orange line represents the overall percentage of children without access to a basic immunization package in each country,
while the endpoints indicate the percentages for the top and the bottom quintile of the asset ownership distribution.

infants than girls, in part because of sex-selective abortion and differential care after birth. And in many (though not all) parts of the world, more boys than girls attend school. The hundreds of millions of disabled children across the developing world also face very different opportunities than their able-bodied peers.

These inequities are usually associated with differences in an individual's "agency"— the socioeconomically, culturally, and politically determined ability to shape the world around oneself. Such differences create biases in the institutions and rules in favor of more powerful and privileged groups. This is seen in realities as diverse as the low chances for mobility of scheduled castes in a village in rural India and the frequent episodes of discrimination against the Quichua people in Ecuador. Persistent differences in power and status between

groups can become internalized into behaviors, aspirations, and preferences that also perpetuate inequalities.

Inequalities of opportunity are also transmitted across generations. The children of poorer and lower-status parents face inferior chances in education, health, incomes, and status. This starts early. In Ecuador, three-year-old children from all socioeconomic groups have similar test scores for vocabulary recognition and are close to a standard international reference population. But by the time they are five, all have faltered relative to the international reference group, except for those in the richest groups and with the highest levels of parental education (figure 2). Such pronounced differences in vocabulary recognition between children whose parents had 0 to 5 years of schooling and those whose parents had 12 or more years are likely to

Figure 2 Opportunities are determined early
Cognitive development for children ages three to five in Ecuador differs markedly across family backgrounds

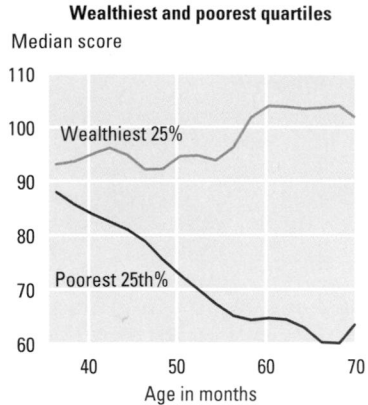

Wealthiest and poorest quartiles
Median score

Wealthiest 25%

Poorest 25th%

Age in months

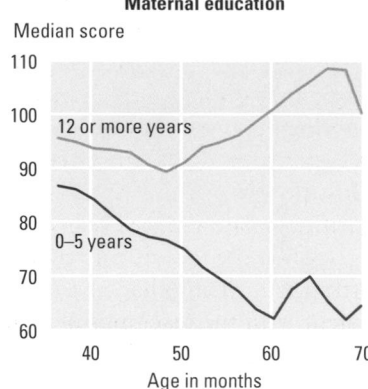

Maternal education
Median score

12 or more years

0–5 years

Age in months

Source: Paxson and Schady (2005).
Note: Median values of the test of vocabulary recognition (TVIP) score (a measure of vocabulary recognition in Spanish, standardized against an international norm) are plotted against the child's age in months. The medians by exact month of age were smoothed by estimating fan regressions of the median score on age (in months), using a bandwidth of 3.

carry over to their performance once they enter primary school, and will likely persist thereafter. Intergenerational immobility is also observed in rich countries: new evidence from the United States (where the myth of equal opportunity is strong) finds high levels of persistence of socioeconomic status across generations: recent estimates suggest that it would take five generations for a family that earned half the national average income to reach the average.[5] Immobility is particularly pronounced for low-income African Americans.

Global inequities are massive

If unequal opportunities are large within many countries, they are truly staggering on a global scale. Chapter 3 shows that cross-country differences begin with the opportunity for life itself: while 7 of every 1,000 American babies die in the first year of their lives, 126 of every 1,000 Malian babies do. Babies who survive, not only in Mali but in much of Africa and in the poorer countries of Asia and Latin America, are at much greater nutritional risk than their counterparts in rich countries. And if they go to school—more than 400 million adults in developing countries never did—their schools are substantially worse than those attended by children in Europe, Japan, or the United States. Given lower school qual-

Figure 3 Life expectancy improved and became more equal—until the onset of the AIDS crisis

Population-weighted international distribution of life expectancy, 1960–2000

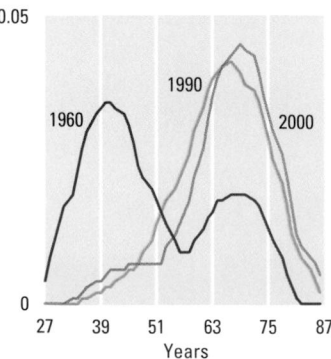

1960
1990
2000

Years

Source: Schady (2005).

ity, undernutrition, and the earnings a child can generate by working instead of studying, many children leave school early. The average person born between 1975 and 1979 in Sub-Saharan Africa has only 5.4 years of schooling. In South Asia, the figure rises to 6.3 years; in OECD countries, it is 13.4 years.

With such differences in education and health, compounded by large disparities in access to infrastructure and other public services, it is not surprising that opportunities for the consumption of private goods differ vastly between rich and poor countries. Mean annual consumption expenditures range from Purchasing Power Parity (PPP) $279 in Nigeria to PPP $17,232 in Luxembourg. This means that the average citizen in Luxembourg enjoys monetary resources 62 times higher than the average Nigerian. While the average Nigerian may find it difficult to afford adequately nutritious meals every day, the average citizen of Luxembourg need not worry too much about buying the latest generation cell phone on the market. Because of the much greater restrictions on the movement of people between countries than within countries, these inequalities in outcomes among countries are likely to be much more closely associated with inequalities in opportunities than within countries.

Global inequality trends have varied. Between 1960 and 1980 there was a pronounced decline in the inequality in life expectancy across countries, driven by major increases in the poorest countries in the world (figure 3). This welcome development was due to the global spread of health technology and to major public health efforts in some of the world's highest mortality areas. Since 1990, however, HIV/AIDS (predominantly in many African countries) and a rise in mortality rates in transition economies (largely in Eastern Europe and Central Asia) have set back some of the earlier gains. Because of the AIDS crisis, life expectancy at birth has fallen dramatically in some of the world's poorest countries, sharply increasing the differences between them and richer societies.

Inequality in access to schooling has also been falling around the world, within most

Figure 4 A long-run diverging trend in income inequality begins to reverse because of growth in China and India

Mean log deviation

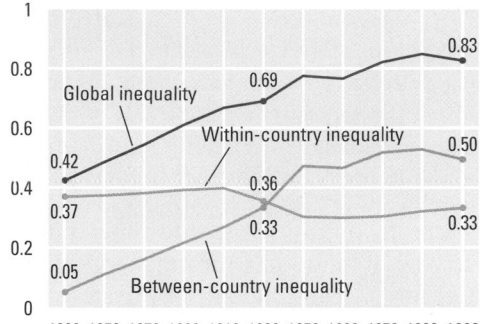

Source: Authors' manipulation of data from Bourguignon and Morrisson (2002).

countries as well as across them, as average schooling levels rise in the vast majority of countries. This too is a welcome development, although concerns over the quality of schooling provide reasons for guarding against complacency.

While our primary concern is with inequality of opportunities, the large differences in income or consumption across countries surely affect the life chances faced by children born today in those different nations. Trends in life expectancy at birth and years of schooling were converging, at least until 1990, but a different picture emerges for income and consumption. While the recent trends depend greatly on the specific concept chosen (discussed in great detail in chapter 3), global income inequality has steadily increased over the long run until the onset of rapid economic growth in China and India in the 1980s (figure 4).

It is possible to decompose total inequality across individuals in the world into differences among countries and differences within countries. Between-country differences were relatively small early in the nineteenth century, but they came to account for a larger part of total inequality toward the end of the twentieth century. If China and India are excluded, global inequalities have continued to rise, owing to the continuing divergence between most other low-income countries and rich countries.

Why does equity matter for development?

Why do these persistent inequalities—both within and across countries—matter? The first reason is that the interconnections and resilience of these inequalities imply that some groups have consistently inferior opportunities—economic, social, and political—than their fellow citizens. Most people feel that such egregious disparities violate a sense of fairness, particularly when the individuals affected can do little about them (chapter 4). This is consistent with the teachings of much political philosophy and with the international system of human rights. The core moral and ethical teachings of the world's leading religions include a concern for equity, although many have also been sources of inequities and historically have been linked to unequal power structures. There is also experimental evidence suggesting that many—but not all—people behave in ways consistent with a concern for fairness, in addition to caring about how they fare individually.

Important as these intrinsic reasons are for caring about inequality of opportunities and unfair processes, the primary focus of this report is on the instrumental relationship between equity and development, with particular emphasis on two channels: the effects of unequal opportunities when markets are imperfect, and the consequences of inequity for the quality of institutions a society develops.[6]

With imperfect markets, inequalities in power and wealth translate into unequal opportunities, leading to wasted productive potential and to an inefficient allocation of resources. Markets often work imperfectly in many countries, whether because of intrinsic failures—such as those associated with asymmetric information—or because of policy-imposed distortions. Microeconomic case studies suggest that an inefficient allocation of resources across productive alternatives is often associated with differences in wealth or status (chapter 5).

If capital markets worked perfectly, there would be no relation between investment and the distribution of wealth: anyone with a profitable investment opportunity would be able to either borrow money to finance it, or to sell equity in a firm set up to undertake it. But capital markets in just about every country (developed and developing) are very far from perfect: credit is rationed across prospective clients, and interest rates differ considerably across borrowers, and between lenders and borrowers, in ways that cannot be linked to default risk or other economic factors affecting expected returns to lenders. For example, interest rates decline with loan size in Kerala and Tamil Nadu in India, and across trading groups in Kenya and Zimbabwe, in ways not explained by risk differences.[7] In Mexico, returns to capital are much higher for the smallest informal sector firms than for larger ones.

Land markets also have imperfections associated with a lack of clear titling, histories of concentrated land ownership, and imperfect rental markets. In Ghana, lower security of tenure among women leads to an inefficiently low frequency of land fallowing and, hence, to progressive declines in land productivity.

The market for human capital is also imperfect, because parents make decisions on behalf of their children and because the expected returns to investment are influenced by location, contacts, and discrimination—on grounds of gender, caste, religion, or race. Discrimination and stereotyping—mechanisms for the reproduction of inequality between groups—have been found to lower the self-esteem, effort, and performance of individuals in the groups discriminated against. This reduces their potential for individual growth and their ability to contribute to the economy.

Striking evidence of the impact of stereotyping on performance comes from a recent experiment in India. Children from different castes were asked to complete simple exercises, such as solving a maze, with real monetary incentives contingent on performance. The key result of the experiment is that low-caste children perform on par with high-caste children when their caste is not publicly announced by the experimenter but significantly worse when it is made public (figure 5). If a similar inhibition of talent occurs in the real world, this implies a loss of potential output owing to social stereotyping.

Economic and political inequalities are associated with impaired institutional development. The second channel through which inequity affects long-run processes of development is the shaping of economic and political institutions (chapter 6). Institutions determine the incentives and constraints people face and provide the context in which markets function. Different sets of institutions are the outcome of complex historical processes that reflect the interests and structure of political influence of different individuals and groups in a society. From this perspective, market imperfections may arise not by accident but because they distribute income or power in particular ways. In this view, there will be social conflict over the institutions of society and incentives for people who control power to shape institutions in ways that benefit them.

The central argument here is that unequal power leads to the formation of institutions that perpetuate inequalities in power, status, and wealth—and that typi-

Figure 5 Children's performance differs when their caste is made salient

Average number of mazes solved, by caste, in five experimental treatments

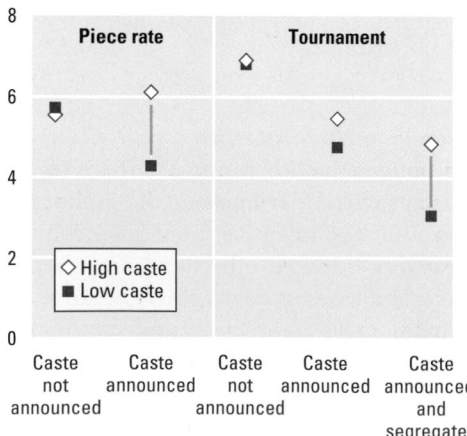

Source: Hoff and Pandey (2004).
Note: The figure depicts the number of mazes correctly completed by low-caste and high-caste children from a set of Indian villages in a number of different experiments. The difference between the first two and the last three columns refers to payouts: whether children are paid per correct maze completed (piece rate) or only if they complete the most mazes (tournament).

cally are also bad for the investment, innovation, and risk-taking that underpin long-term growth. Good economic institutions are equitable in a fundamental way: to prosper, a society must create incentives for the vast majority of the population to invest and innovate. But such an equitable set of economic institutions can emerge only when the distribution of power is not highly unequal and in situations in which there are constraints on the exercise of power by officeholders. Basic patterns in cross-country data and historical narratives support the view that countries moving onto institutional paths that promoted sustained prosperity did so because the balance of political influence and power became more equitable.

One example comes from a comparison of the early institutions and of the long-term development paths of European colonies in North and South America. The abundance of unskilled labor prevalent in the South American colonies—where either native Americans or imported African slaves were available in large numbers—combined with the technology of mining and large plantation agriculture to provide the economic base for hierarchical and extractive societies, in which land ownership and political power were highly concentrated. In North America, by contrast, similar attempts to introduce hierarchical structures were foiled by the scarcity of labor—except where agro-climatic conditions made slavery economically feasible, such as in the southern region of the United States. Competition for free labor in the northern areas of North America led to the development of less unequal land ownership patterns, a faster expansion of the franchise, and rapid increases in literacy and basic education. The resulting economic and political institutions persisted over time, with positive consequences for long-run economic development.

Leveling the economic and political playing fields

So a portion of the economic and political inequalities we observe around the world is attributable to unequal opportunities. This inequality is objectionable on both intrinsic and instrumental grounds. It contributes to economic inefficiency, political conflict, and institutional frailty. What are the implications for policy, and do they give rise to an agenda that is different from the poverty reduction agenda already embraced by the World Bank, other multilateral institutions, and many governments?

We argue that an equity lens enhances the poverty reduction agenda. The poor generally have less voice, less income, and less access to services than most other people. When societies become more equitable in ways that lead to greater opportunities for all, the poor stand to benefit from a "double dividend." First, expanded opportunities benefit the poor directly, through greater participation in the development process. Second, the development process itself may become more successful and resilient as greater equity leads to better institutions, more effective conflict management, and a better use of all potential resources in society, including those of the poor. Resulting increases in economic growth rates in poor countries will, in turn, contribute to a reduction in global inequities.

One manifestation of the greater participation of the poor in economic growth is the fact that the growth elasticity of poverty reduction falls with greater income inequality. In other words, the impact of (the same amount of) growth on poverty reduction is significantly greater when initial income inequality is lower. On average, for countries with low levels of income inequality, a 1 percentage point growth in mean incomes leads to about a 4 percentage-point reduction in the incidence of $1 per day poverty. That power falls to close to zero in countries with high income inequality.[8] Policies that lead to greater equity thus lead to lower poverty—directly through expanding the opportunities of the poor and indirectly through higher levels of sustained development.

An equity lens adds three new—or at least often neglected—perspectives to development policymaking:

- *First, the best policies for poverty reduction could involve redistributions of influence, advantage, or subsidies away from dominant groups.* Highly unequally distributed wealth associated with unduly concentrated political power can prevent institutions from enforcing broad-based personal and property rights, and lead to skewed provisioning of services and functioning of markets. This is unlikely to change unless voice and influence, and public resources, shift away from the dominant group toward those with fewer opportunities.[9]

- *Second, while such equity-enhancing redistributions (of power, or access to government spending and markets) can often be efficiency-increasing, possible tradeoffs need to be assessed in the design of policy.* At some point, higher tax rates to finance spending on more schools for the poorest will create so much disincentive to effort or investment (depending on how the taxes are raised), that one should stop raising them. When making a policy choice along such tradeoffs, the full value of the benefits from equity enhancement should be considered. If greater spending on schools for lower-caste children means that, over the long term, stereotyping will decline in society, with attendant increases in performance that are additional to the specific gains from greater schooling today, these gains should not be ignored.

- *Third, the dichotomy between policies for growth and policies specifically aimed at equity is false.* The distribution of opportunities and the growth process are jointly determined. Policies that affect one will affect the other. This does not mean that each policy needs to take equity into account individually: for example, the best way to deal with inequitable effects of a particular trade reform is not always through fine-tuning trade policy itself (which might make it more susceptible to capture) but through complementary policies for safety nets, labor mobility, and education. The overall package and the fairness of the underlying process are what matter.

The analysis of development experience clearly shows the centrality of overall political conditions—supporting the emphasis on governance and empowerment in recent years. However, it is neither the mandate nor the comparative advantage of the World Bank to engage in advice on issues of political design. In turning to policy implications, we focus instead on the core areas of development policy, while recognizing that policy design needs to take account of the broader social and political context, and that accountability mechanisms influence development effectiveness.

Because economic policies are determined within a sociopolitical reality, *how* policies are designed, introduced, or reformed matters as much as which specific policies are proposed. Policy reforms that result in losses for a particular group will be resisted by that group. If the group is powerful, it will usually subvert the reform. The sustainability of reforms, therefore, may depend on making information about its distributional consequences publicly available and, perhaps, forming coalitions of middle and poorer groups that stand to gain from them to "empower," directly or indirectly, relatively disadvantaged members of society.

How policies are implemented has a technical aspect as well. Just as we emphasize that the full long-term benefits of redistributions need to be taken into account when making policy choices, so must all their costs. A focus on equity does not change the facts that asset expropriations—even in instances of historical grievances—may have adverse consequences for subsequent investment, that high marginal tax rates create disincentives to work, or that inflationary financing of budget deficits tends to lead to regressive implicit taxation, economic disorganization, and reduced investment and growth. In short, a focus on equity must not be an excuse for poor economic policy.

The report discusses the role of public action in leveling the economic and political playing field under four main headings. Three of the headings concern domestic policies: investing in human capacities; expanding access to justice, land, and infrastructure; and promoting fairness in markets. The fourth turns to policies for greater global equity, in terms of access to markets, resource flows, and governance.

Throughout the discussion, the report weighs a desire to be specific and practical against the fact that the best specific policy mix is a function of country context. The educational challenges facing Sudan are different from those facing Egypt. The optimal sequencing of reform in the public sectors of Latvia and Bolivia are unlikely to be the same. The capacity for implementing health finance reform in China and Lesotho are also different. So the detailed, specific policy advice always needs to be developed at the country—or even subnational—level. Everything that is said below therefore retains some level of generality and should be interpreted accordingly, and cautiously.

Human capacities

Early childhood development. In many developing countries, the actions of the state in providing services magnify—rather than attenuate—inequalities at birth. A guiding principle is to shape public action so that the acquisition of human capacities is not driven by circumstances of their birth, although it can reflect people's preferences, tastes, and talents.

Because differences in cognitive development start to widen from a very early age (see figure 2), early childhood development initiatives can be central to more equal opportunities. Evidence supports the view that investing in early childhood has large impacts on children's health and readiness to learn and can bring important economic returns later in life—often greater than investments in formal education and training.

An experiment in Jamaica focused on undersized children (ages 9 to 24 months) and found that they suffered from lower levels of cognitive development than those of normal height. Nutritional supplements and a program of regular exposure to mental stimulation, helped offset this disadvantage. After 24 months, kids who received both better nutrition and more stimulation had virtually caught up developmentally

Figure 6 Catching up through early interventions

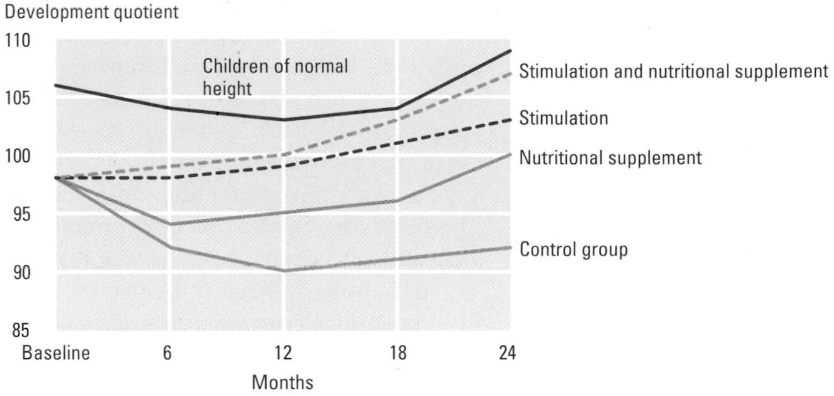

Source: Grantham-McGregor and others (1991).
Note: The development quotient is an index of progress on four behavioral and cognitive indicators of childhood development. Number of months refers to the time after entry into the program—generally at an age of nine months.

with children who started life at a normal height (figure 6). This illustrates how decisive and well-designed public action can substantially reduce the opportunity gaps between those least privileged and the societal norm. Investing in the neediest people early in their childhoods can help level the playing field.

Schooling. The process continues throughout the school system. Actions to equalize opportunities in formal education need to ensure that all children acquire at least a basic level of skills necessary to participate in society and in today's global economy. Even in such middle-income countries as Colombia, Morocco, and the Philippines, most children completing basic education lack an adequate level of achievement, as measured by internationally comparable test scores (chapters 2 and 7).

Access to schooling matters—especially in very poor countries—but, in many countries, it is only a small part of the problem. Greater access needs to be complemented by supply-side policies (to raise quality) and demand-side policies (to correct for the possibility that parents may underinvest in the education of their children for various reasons). There are no magic bullets for this, but increasing teachers' incentives, enhancing the basic quality of the school's physical infrastructure, and researching and implementing teaching methods to increase the learning performance of students who do not do well when left to their own devices are some of the suggestions on the supply side.

On the demand side, there is now a considerable body of evidence showing that scholarships conditional on attendance have significant impacts. Such transfers work in countries from Bangladesh to Brazil, with the impacts often greater for girls. There are also promising approaches to bring in excluded groups—as in the Vidin model of reaching Roma in Bulgaria—and to bring up those left behind through remedial education—as in the Balsakhi program using young women as para-teachers in 20 cities in India. As argued in World Development Report 2004, developing the accountability of schools and teachers to students, parents, and the broader community can help ensure effective service provider behavior.

Health. Two areas stand out in reducing inequity and tackling economic distortions in the provision of health services. First, there are many cases when the benefits spill over beyond the direct beneficiary in a range of areas of service provision: for immunization, for water and sanitation, and for information on hygiene and child care. Public assurance of provisioning makes sense in these areas. Demand-side subsidies to provide incentives for maternal and child health increase use, offsetting possible information problems as in Mexico's *Oportunidades* program.

Second, insurance markets for catastrophic health problems are beset with failures. (Here "catastrophic" is in relation to the capacity of the household to deal with the direct costs and the loss in earnings.) The traditional supply-side model of relying on public hospitals works badly, especially for poor and excluded groups. What can work better is public provisioning or regulation that provides some insurance for all. Examples include risk pooling in Colombia, health cards in Indonesia and Vietnam, and Thailand's "30-baht" universal coverage scheme. As with education, these interventions need to be combined with incentives for providers to be responsive to all groups.

Risk management. Social protection systems shape opportunities by providing peo-

ple with a safety net. In addition to ill health, macroeconomic crises, industrial restructuring, weather, and natural disasters can constrain investment and innovation. The poor, with the lowest capacity to manage shocks, generally are the least well covered by risk-management structures, although in most countries many among the non-poor risk falling into poverty. Broader social protection systems can help prevent today's inequalities—sometimes generated by bad luck—from becoming entrenched and leading to tomorrow's inequities. Just as safety nets can spur households to engage in riskier activities that can yield higher returns, they can also help complement reforms that produce losers.

Safety nets typically target three groups: the working poor, people viewed as unable to work or for whom work is undesirable, and special vulnerable groups. If safety nets are designed in a manner appropriate to the local realities on the ground in each country, individual targeted interventions in these three categories can be combined to provide an effectively universal public insurance system. In such a system, each household that suffers a negative shock, and falls below some predetermined threshold of living standards, would qualify for some form of state support.

Taxes for equity. Successful interventions to level the playing field require adequate resources. The main aim of good tax policy is to mobilize sufficient funding, while distorting incentives and compromising growth as little as possible. Because taxes impose efficiency costs by altering individual choices between labor and leisure and consumption and savings, most developing countries are likely to be best served by avoiding high marginal taxes on income and relying on a broad base, especially for taxes on consumption. Public spending should play the primary role in actively furthering equity. Nevertheless, there is some scope for making the overall tax system moderately progressive without large efficiency costs. Societies that desire such an outcome can consider simple exemptions for basic foodstuffs, and an expanded role for property taxation, for example.

While the capacity of the tax administration and the structure of the economy influence the ability to raise revenues, the quality of institutions and the nature of the social compact are also critical. When citizens can rely on services actually being provided, they likely are more willing to be taxed. Conversely, a corrupt or kleptocratic state engenders little citizen trust in authority and little incentive to cooperate. As a general rule, a more legitimate and representative state may be a prerequisite to an adequate tax system, even as the notion of adequacy varies from country to country.

Justice, land, and infrastructure

The development of human capacities will not broaden opportunities if some people face unfair returns on those capacities and unequal protection of their rights, and have unequal access to complementary factors of production.

Building equitable justice systems. Justice systems can do much to level the playing field in the political, economic, and sociocultural domains, but they can also reinforce existing inequalities. The report pays attention to both codified law and the ways in which the law is applied and enforced in practice. Legal institutions can uphold the political rights of citizens and curb the capture of the state by the elite. They can equalize economic opportunities by protecting property rights for all and ensuring nondiscrimination in the market. They underpin and reflect the rules of the game in society and thus are central to fair process—and to the broad-based property rights and unbiased dispute resolution mechanisms so important for investment.

The law can also accelerate shifts in norms, and justice systems can serve as a progressive force for change in the social domain by challenging inequitable practices. For example, the U.S. Civil Rights Act of 1964 and Medicare in 1965 enforced the desegregation of hospitals and led to large reductions in infant mortality for African Americans. Affirmative action programs have also been shown to reduce group-based differences in earnings and education. But they can become politically entrenched and limited to helping the better-off among disadvantaged groups.

Equity in laws and fairness in their implementation involve striking a balance between strengthening the independence of justice systems and increasing accountability—especially to counter the risk that the powerful and wealthy might corrupt, influence, or ignore the law. Measures to make the legal system more accessible—mobile courts, legal aid, and working with customary institutions—all help reduce the barriers that excluded groups face. Customary institutions raise complex issues and may incorporate inequities (for example, with respect to gender), but they are too important to be ignored. South Africa is an example of a country that is pursuing a policy that balances recognition of customary practices with the rights and responsibilities in state law.

Toward greater equity in access to land. Broader access to land does not necessarily have to come through ownership (chapter 8). Instead, improving the functioning of land markets and providing greater security of tenure for poorer groups may be a more fruitful area for policy—as in rural Thailand and in urban Peru. Redistributive land reform can make sense in some circumstances in which land inequalities are extreme and the institutional context allows for designs that effectively redistribute land to smaller farms and support this with complementary services, without large transitional costs. But this can be difficult, and tradeoffs may be large when property rights have a high degree of legitimacy.

Expropriating land (with compensation) is probably the most disruptive redistribution instrument. Divesting state lands and recuperating illegal settlements, possibly in exchange for titling a portion of the settlement, may be two cost-effective alternatives. Market or community-based approaches that allow community members to obtain subsidized credit for land rentals or purchases according to the willing-buyer-willing-seller principle, as in Brazil and South Africa, appear promising. A land tax can be a useful complement, generating revenues to purchase land to redistribute or encouraging redistribution by disproportionately taxing large or underused plots.

Providing infrastructure equitably. Access to infrastructure—roads, electricity, water, sanitation, telecoms—is typically highly unequal across groups. For many people in developing countries, lack of access to affordable infrastructure services means living in isolation from markets and services and having intermittent or no supply of power or water for productive activities and daily existence. This often results in a significant curtailment of economic opportunities.

While the public sector will in many cases remain the main source of funds for infrastructure investments aimed at broadening opportunities for those who have the fewest, the efficiency of the private sector can also be harnessed. Although utility privatizations have often been attacked for having unequal effects, the evidence indicates a more complex reality. Privatizations in Latin America typically led to expansions in access to services, particularly in electricity and telecommunications. In some cases, however, postprivatization increases in prices more than outweighed gains from quality and coverage, leading to widespread popular discontent.

Privatizations are therefore a classic case of a policy that may or may not make sense, depending on the local context. If the public system is highly corrupt or inefficient, and one expects postprivatization regulatory capacity to be adequate, it can be a useful tool. In other cases, poorly designed privatizations may be captured, transferring public assets, at excessively low prices, into private hands.

Experience suggests that whether infrastructure services are provided by private operators or public utilities seems less important for equity than the structure of incentives facing providers and how accountable these providers are to the general public. We argue that policymakers can improve the equitable provision of infrastructure services by focusing on expanding affordable access for poor people and poor areas—which often means working with informal providers and targeting subsidies—and strengthening the governance of the sector through the greater accountability of providers and the stronger voice of beneficiaries.

Markets and the macroeconomy

Markets are central to shaping the potential for people to convert their assets into outcomes. When market transactions are influenced by the wealth or status of participants, they are both inequitable and inefficient—and can also influence the incentives for different groups to expand their assets (chapter 9).

Financial markets. Captured banking systems exchange favors: market power is protected for a few large banks, which then lend favorably to a few selected enterprises, which may not be those with the highest expected risk-adjusted returns. This may lie behind a cross-country association between greater financial depth and lower income inequality. Achieving more equal access to finance by broadening financial systems thus can help productive firms that were previously beyond the reach of formal finance.

These relations are only suggestive, however, so the report draws on case studies from middle-income economies, such as the Republic of Korea, Malaysia, Mexico, and the Russian Federation, and poorer economies, including Indonesia and Pakistan, to provide more concrete evidence. These studies suggest an apparent paradox. Societies with extensive inequalities in power and wealth, weak institutions, and controlled financial systems typically suffer from narrow financial sectors that are oriented to the influential and hide weak asset quality. Opening the financial system would seem to be an obvious solution. Liberalization, however, has also often been captured by the influential or wealthy, in countries ranging from Mexico (in the early 1990s) to transition economies such as the Czech Republic and Russia.

Gradual deepening and broadening thus needs to be combined with stronger horizontal accountability (in regulatory structures), greater openness to societal accountability, and, where feasible, external commitment devices (such as the entry of Central European and Baltic states to the European Union). Programs targeted to the poor—such as microcredit schemes—can help but are no substitute for the overall broadening of access.

Labor markets. Leveling the playing field in labor markets consists of seeking the right (country-specific) balance between flexibility and protection to provide more equal access to equal employment conditions to as many workers as possible. Many countries have fairly extensive regulations and provisions for formal sector workers, and far fewer for "outsiders" in the unregulated (and often less safe) informal sector. There is usually a degree of voluntary movement between the sectors, and great diversity within the informal sector itself, ranging from microentrepreneurs and some of the self-employed with incomes above formal sector workers to many with much worse employment conditions. This mix leads to inadequate protection for poorer workers, while regulations for formal workers can reduce the flexibility of employment and often are a poor deal for the workers themselves, such as when job-related social security systems are inefficient.

Two broad labor market approaches are relevant for equity. First, interventions in the labor market should ensure effective application of the core labor standards across the whole market, implying no slave or indentured work, no dangerous forms of child labor, and no discrimination. Workers should be free to assemble and form associations, and their unions should be free to have an active role in bargaining. Second, in all areas the policy mix needs to be assessed in ways that balance protection (for all workers) with allowances for the restructuring so central to dynamic growth and employment creation.

Worker security is often provided by various excessively stringent forms of employment protection legislation, which, in general make it costly to hire and, in some cases, make it even costlier to hire unskilled, young, and female workers—exactly those the laws seek to protect. For many countries, less distortionary and more inclusive policy alternatives are available, which may make the playing field more even in labor markets. These alternatives include unemployment insurance schemes (more likely in middle-income countries) and low-wage employment schemes (ideally with an employment guarantee), which can be applied successfully even in poor countries or states.

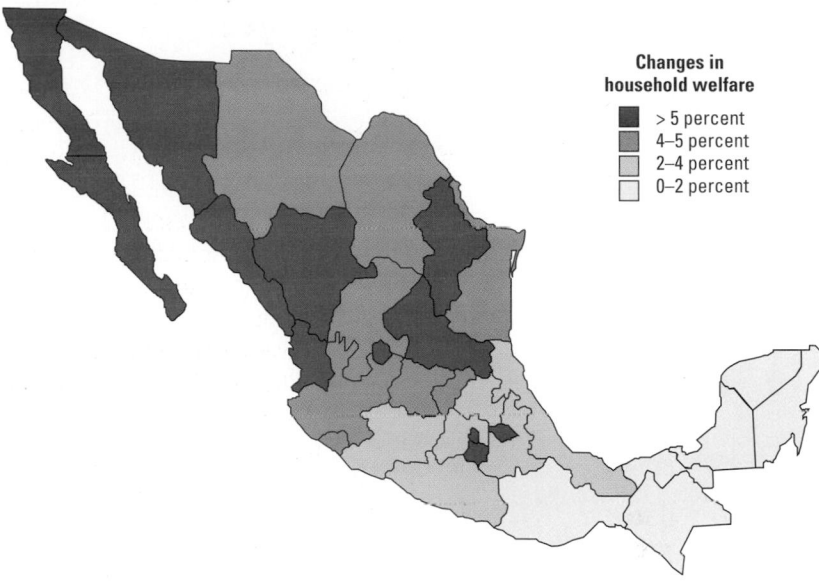

Figure 7 Better to be close to economic opportunities
Changes in household welfare in Mexico, following trade liberalization in the 1990s

Changes in
household welfare

■ > 5 percent
■ 4–5 percent
▨ 2–4 percent
□ 0–2 percent

Source: Nicita (2004).

Product markets. There is substantial heterogeneity in the effects of opening a country's product markets to trade, at least in the short to medium term. This can be due to geographic location, as illustrated by the varying impact of trade liberalization in Mexico (figure 7). This illustrates the importance of interactions between domestic product markets and patterns of infrastructure provision. There are also often strong interactions with skills in the labor market. In many countries, opening to trade (often coinciding with opening to foreign direct investment) has been associated with rising inequality in earnings in the past two decades. This is especially so for middle-income countries, notably in Latin America. Opening to trade often boosts the premium on skills as firms modernize their production processes (skill-biased technical change, in the jargon of economists). This is bad for equity if the institutional context restricts the capacity of workers to shift into new work—or limits future cohorts' access to education.

Macroeconomic stability. This report argues that there are two-way relationships between inequitable institutions and macroeconomic crises, with mostly bad effects for equity and long-run growth. Weak and captured institutions are associated with a greater propensity for countries to experience macroeconomic crises. When crises occur, they can be costly for the poor, who have weaker instruments to manage shocks. In addition, crisis resolution is often regressive, through a variety of mechanisms (most of them not captured in traditional household survey instruments): declines in the labor share, at least for formal workers; capital gains for those who get their money out; and fiscal workouts that bail out the influential at substantial cost. Such bailouts must be paid for through some combination of higher taxes and lower spending. Because taxes are typically proportional and spending is often progressive at the margin (notably in Latin America), the cost of bailouts is borne disproportionately by poorer groups. High inflation has also been found to be both bad for growth and regressive in its impact.

A concern for equity would lead, in general, to a highly prudent stance on macroeconomic management and financial regulation. Populist macroeconomic policy, sooner or later, is bad for equity and bad for growth. Policy design can increase equity through the pursuit of countercyclical fiscal policy, building safety nets before a crisis, reducing risky lending, and supporting only smaller depositors in bailouts. But, as in other policy areas, these responses need to be underpinned by institutional designs that combine greater institutional freedom from political influence (such as independent central banks and autonomous financial regulatory agencies) with greater information and debate in society.

The global arena

One predetermined circumstance that most powerfully determines a person's opportunities for leading a healthy and productive life is his or her country of birth. Global inequities are massive. Reducing them will depend primarily on domestic policies in poor countries through their impact on growth and development. But global action can change external conditions and affect the impact of domestic policies. In this sense, global and domestic actions are complementary.

We live in an integrated world in which people, goods, ideas, and capital flow across countries. Indeed, most policy advice given to poor countries over the last several decades—including that by the World Bank—has emphasized the advantages of participating in the global economy. But global markets are far from equitable, and the rules governing their functioning have a disproportionately negative effect on developing countries (chapter 10). These rules are the outcome of complex negotiating processes in which developing countries have less voice. Moreover, even if markets worked equitably, unequal endowments would limit the ability of poor countries to benefit from global opportunities. Leveling the global economic and political playing fields thus requires more equitable rules for the functioning of global markets, more effective participation of poor countries in global rule-setting processes, and more actions to help build and maintain the endowments of poor countries and poor people.

The report documents some of the many inequities in the functioning of global markets for labor, goods, ideas, and capital. Unskilled workers from poor countries, who could earn higher returns in rich countries, face great hurdles in migrating. Developing-country producers face obstacles in selling agricultural products, manufactured goods, and services in developed countries. Patent protection restricts access to innovations (particularly drugs) for poor countries, while new research is strongly oriented to the diseases of richer societies. Rich-country investors often get better deals in debt crises. In most cases, more equitable rules would bring benefits to developed- and developing-country citizens. Benefits vary across markets and countries, with those from greater legal migration likely to be greatest (and to accrue directly to migrants) and those from trade likely to accrue mostly to middle-income rather than the least developed countries.

The report discusses options to reduce inequities in the functioning of global markets, including the following: allowing greater temporary migration into OECD countries, achieving ambitious trade liberalization under the Doha Round, allowing poor countries to use generic drugs, and developing financial standards more appropriate to developing countries.

The international laws that govern global markets are the product of complex negotiations. In some cases, as for human rights covenants, the processes generating the laws are perceived to be fair. In other cases, processes and outcomes are perceived as unfair, even though the formal regulations are equitable. Within the World Trade Organization (WTO), for example, each country has a vote and each can block proceedings. Even so, WTO processes are at times perceived as unfair because of the underlying power imbalance between strong commercial interests and the public interest, in both developed and developing countries. These imbalances manifest themselves, for instance, in the number of staff employed in Geneva by different WTO members. More effective representation of poor countries in global institutions would help improve processes and may lead to more equitable rules.

The impact of reducing imperfections in global markets varies by country. The larger and fast-growing developing countries stand to benefit significantly from freer global trade, migration, and capital flows, helping them sustain fast growth (while equitable domestic policies both help underpin long-run growth and the broad internal sharing of this growth). Countries left behind in the global economy stand to benefit much less from global markets in the short run and will continue to rely on aid. For them, global action that helps compensate for unequal endowments is truly essential. Action to build endowments is primarily domestic, through public investments in human development, infrastructure and governance structures. But global action can support domestic policies through resource transfers in the form of aid, which is not offset by debt repayments, and investments in global public goods, particularly global commons.

Aid levels need to be bolstered in line with the commitments rich countries made at the 2002 Monterrey Conference and concrete plans should be made to reach the target of devoting 0.7 percent of gross national income to aid. Larger volumes of aid will only help, however, if aid is effective in alleviating constraints and spurring development in the recipient countries. Greater effectiveness can be achieved by emphasizing results, moving away from ex ante conditionality, and progressively shifting design and management from donors to recipients. Aid should not be undermined by debt, for debt reduction that is not financed by additional resources can actually undercut effective aid programs. Innovative mechanisms to expand development assistance should be explored, including global taxes and private contributions.

Equity and development

Bringing equity to the center of development builds on and integrates the major emphases in development thinking of the past 10 to 20 years—on markets, on human development, on governance, and on empowerment. It is noteworthy that this year equity is the focus of both this World Development Report and the Human Development Report of the United Nations Development Programme. The plea for a more level playing field in both the politics and the economies of developing countries serves to integrate the World Bank's twin pillars of building an institutional climate conducive to investment and empowering the poor. By ensuring that institutions enforce personal, political, and property rights for all, including those currently excluded, countries will be able to draw on much larger pools of investors and innovators, and be much more effective in providing services to all their citizens. Greater equity can, over the long term, underpin faster growth. This can be helped by greater fairness in the global arena, not least through the international community's meeting its commitments made at Monterrey. Faster growth and human development in poorer countries are essential to reducing global inequity and to reaching the Millennium Development Goals.

Introduction

Nthabiseng and Pieter—the hypothetical South African children who opened the report's overview—are not unusual examples of people who face highly disparate initial opportunities. A girl born to a lower-caste family of nine in the slums of Dhaka has vastly different opportunities from a boy born to well-educated and affluent parents in the well-heeled neighborhoods. An AIDS orphan in rural Zimbabwe is almost certain to have fewer chances and choices in life than a compatriot born to healthy and well-educated parents in Harare. Those differences are even greater across borders: an average Swiss, American, or Japanese child born at the same instant as Nthabiseng will have incomparably superior life chances.

Such staggering inequalities in opportunity are intrinsically objectionable, and almost every culture, religion, and philosophical tradition has developed arguments and beliefs that place great value on equity for its own sake. In addition, Part II of this report will argue that we now have considerable evidence that equity is also instrumental to the pursuit of long-term prosperity in aggregate terms for society as a whole. But before one can describe inequity, or assess its impact on growth and development, a clear definition of the term is needed.

This introductory chapter presents our working definition of equity and briefly discusses its main component—equality of opportunity. It then turns from our central normative concepts to one of the report's key positive concepts: inequality traps. An inequality trap encapsulates the mutually reinforcing nature of various inequalities, which leads to their persistence and to an inferior development trajectory.

Equity and inequality of opportunity: the basic concepts

What is equity? As with any normative concept, the word "equity" means different things to different people. It is a difficult concept, with a history of different interpretations, varying by country and academic discipline. Economists link equity to questions of distribution. Lawyers tend to think of principles meant to correct the strict application of the law, which may lead to an outcome judged to be unfair in specific circumstances. Philosophers have produced the most headway in the thinking about equity. Indeed, the attributes that would characterize a just and fair society lie at the foundation of Western political philosophy, from Plato's *Republic* and Aristotle's *Politics* onward. Equity is also central to most of the world's great religions, including Buddhism, Christianity, Hinduism, Islam, and Judaism, as well as to most other faith traditions. More recently, social choice theory, and the closely related domain of welfare economics, have been concerned with the aggregation of preferences into some form of "social optimum."

Summarizing such long-standing and nuanced characterizations is perilous, but the common denominator of these many different views is that equity relates to fairness, whether locally in families and communities, or globally across nations. We do not dwell on the different approaches to equity here, but we do elaborate on them in chapter 4, which reviews various categories of evidence in support of the intrinsic importance of equity. For this report, we think of equity as being defined in terms of two basic principles:

- *Equal opportunity.* The outcome of a person's life, in its many dimensions, should reflect mostly his or her efforts and talents, not his or her background. Predetermined circumstances—gender, race, place of birth, family origins—and the social groups a person is born into should not help determine whether people succeed economically, socially, and politically.[1]

- *Avoidance of absolute deprivation.* An aversion to extreme poverty, or indeed a Rawlsian[2] form of inequality aversion in the space of outcomes, suggests that societies may decide to intervene to protect the livelihoods of its neediest members (below some absolute threshold of need) even if the equal opportunity principle has been upheld. The road from opportunities to outcomes can be tortuous. Outcomes may be low because of bad luck, or even because of a person's own failings. Societies may decide, for insurance or for compassion, that its members will not be allowed to starve, even if they enjoyed their fair share of the opportunity pie, but things somehow turned out badly for them.

The equal opportunity principle is conceptually simple: circumstances at birth should not matter for a person's chances in life. But to measure inequality of opportunities is much harder. Chapter 2 briefly discusses one approach, which decomposes observed income inequality into one part that can be attributed, in a statistical sense, to predetermined circumstances—such as race, place of birth, and parental background—and one part that cannot. The first component captures a lower bound value for the opportunity share of income or earnings inequality. But it is generally very difficult to measure things like family background precisely: years of schooling and broad occupational categories are imperfect proxies for a family's endowments of human, physical, and social capital.

A superior approach would be to capture the inherently multidimensional and group-based nature of inequality of opportunity. How do the factors that determine a person's chances in life—the access to health and educational opportunities, the ability to connect to the rest of the world, the quality of the services available, the way institutions treat them—relate to one another? And how do these factors vary across groups? Such an approach would require a focus not only on the dispersion of univariate distributions (such as income inequality or life expectancy) but also on the correlations among them (how do health outcomes vary across socioeconomic groups?). This is the approach taken in most of chapter 2, which summarizes information on inequalities (with emphasis on the plural) in the various building blocks of opportunity and on their interrelationships.

In taking this route, the report recognizes that predetermined circumstances, or membership in prespecified groups, affect opportunities in two ways:

- The circumstances of one's birth affect the endowments one starts with, including all kinds of private assets, such as physical wealth (including land and financial assets), family background (the human, social, and cultural capital of one's parents), and access to public services and infrastructure (sometimes referred to as geographic capital).

- Group membership and initial circumstances also affect how one is treated by the institutions with which one must interact. Two individuals may both live in areas where formal labor markets exist, where courts are agile, and where a police force is present. But if these two (otherwise identical) people, because of their gender, race, religion, sexual orientation, political beliefs, residential address, or any other morally irrelevant reason, are differently rewarded for the same work in the labor market, are discriminated against by the court of law, or are treated with bias by the police force, then the rules are not being applied fairly. Therefore, these two people do not have the same opportunity sets. Equity also requires fairness in processes.

Endowments that are less unequal, processes that are fair, and protection from deprivation are not always mutually consistent. At the policy level, there may be tradeoffs among them. Indeed, some policies or institutions developed to further one of the principles may compromise the other.

For example, a policy of affirmative action that seeks to correct past inequities in the access to educational opportunities for one group—to equalize endowments—may imply that individuals of greater merit (but from another group) are excluded, creating unfair processes. For another example, the taxes needed to raise government revenues to make transfers to poor individuals (desirable to avoid deprivation) expropriate some fruits of the efforts of hardworking men and women. This might be seen as violating property rights or the rights to appropriate the fruits of one's own labor, again creating unfair processes.

Whenever such tradeoffs exist—which is most of the time—no textbook policy prescription can be provided. Each society must decide the relative weights it ascribes to each of the principles of equity and to the efficient expansion of total production (or other aggregate). This report will not prescribe what is equitable for any society. That is a prerogative of its members to be undertaken through decision-making processes they regard as fair.

Inequality traps

If people care about equity, and if political systems aggregate people's views into social preferences, why don't the distributions we observe represent optimal choices? Why do inequalities of opportunity persist, if they are both unfair and inimical to long-term prosperity? And how do these inequalities reproduce themselves? The short answer is that political systems do not always assign equal weights to everyone's preferences. Policies and institutions do not arise from a benign social planner who aims to maximize the present value of social welfare. They are the outcomes of political economy processes in which different groups seek to protect their own interests. Some groups have more power than others, and their views prevail. When the interests of dominant groups are aligned with broader collective goals, these decisions are for the common good. When they are not, the outcomes need be neither fair nor efficient.

Figure 1.1 The interaction of political, economic, and sociocultural inequalities

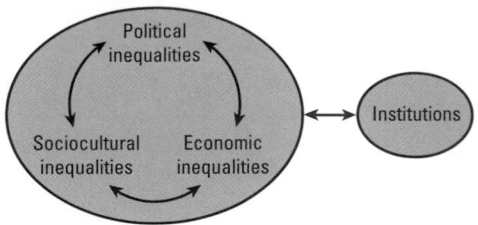

The interaction of political, economic, and sociocultural inequalities shapes the institutions and rules in all societies. The way these institutions function affects people's opportunities and their ability to invest and prosper. Unequal economic opportunities lead to unequal outcomes and reinforce unequal political power. Unequal power shapes institutions and policies that tend to foster the persistence of the initial conditions (figure 1.1).

Consider the status of women in patriarchal societies. Women are often denied property and inheritance rights. They also have their freedom of movement restricted by social norms that create separate "inside" and "outside" spheres of activity for women and men. These social inequalities have economic consequences: girls are less likely to be sent to school; women are less likely to work outside the home; women generally earn less than men. This reduces the options for women outside marriage and increases their economic dependence on men. The inequalities also have political consequences: women are less likely to participate in important decisions within and outside the home.

These unequal social and economic structures tend to be readily reproduced. If a woman has not been educated and has grown up to believe that "good, decent" women abide by existing social norms, she is likely to transmit this belief to her daughters and to enforce such behavior among her daughters-in-law. An inequality trap may thus prevent generations of women from getting educated, restrict their participation in the labor market, and reduce their ability to make free, informed choices and to realize their potential as individuals. This reinforces gender differences in power that tend to persist over time.

Similarly, the unequal distribution of power between the rich and the poor—between dominant and subordinate groups—helps the rich maintain control over resources. Consider an agricultural laborer working for a powerful landlord. Illiteracy and malnourishment may prevent him from breaking out of the cycle of poverty. But he is also likely to be heavily indebted to his employer, which puts him under the landlord's control. Even if laws were in place that would allow him to challenge his landlord's dictates, being illiterate, he would find it difficult to navigate the political and judicial institutions that might help him assert his rights. In many parts of the world, this distance between landlords and laborers is compounded by entrenched social structures: landlords typically belong to a dominant group defined by race or caste, tenants and laborers to a subordinate group. Because members of these groups often face severe constraints from social norms against intermarrying, group-based inequalities are perpetuated across generations.

Poor individuals in geographically isolated regions and racial and ethnic minorities also have less political power and less voice in many countries. This affects their ability to propose and implement policies that would reduce their disadvantage, even if such policies might be growth-enhancing for the country.[3] The correlations between the unequal distribution of assets, opportunities, and political power give rise to a circular flow of mutually reinforcing patterns of inequality. Such a flow, and its associated feedback loops, help inequalities persist over long periods—even if they are inefficient and deemed unfair by a majority of the population.[4]

Economic and political inequalities are themselves embedded in unequal social and cultural institutions.[5] The social networks that the poor have access to are substantially different from those the rich can tap into. For instance, a poor person's social network may be geared primarily toward survival, with limited access to networks that would link him or her to better jobs and opportunities. The rich, by contrast, are bequeathed with much more economically productive social networks that maintain economic rank. Rich parents can use their social connections to ensure that their child gets into a good school, or they can call a few good friends to make sure that their son gets a good job. Conversely, poor parents are more subject to chance. Connections open doors and reduce constraints.

Social networks are closely allied with culture. (By "culture" we mean aspects of life that deal with relationships among individuals within groups, among groups, and between ideas and perspectives). Subordinate groups may face adverse "terms of recognition," the framework within which they negotiate their interactions with other social groups.[6] One obvious expression is explicit discrimination that can lead to an explicit denial of opportunities and to a rational choice to invest less at the margin.

But the process may also be less overt. A person born into a low social class or a socially excluded group may adopt the dominant group's value system.[7] Religious beliefs may propel this: women may take on gendered beliefs about their economic and social role, and low castes may absorb the upper castes' view of their "inferior" status. In schools, a stigmatized group may face a "stereotype threat," adopting the dominant group's view of their ability to perform in cognitive tests or in occupations historically controlled by dominant groups.[8] This can affect a discriminated group's "capacity to aspire."[9] It also implies that "voice," the capacity of individuals to influence the decisions that shape their lives, is also unequally distributed and that "effort" and "ability" are not necessarily exogenous (predetermined).[10]

The existence of these inequality traps—with mutually reinforcing inequalities in the economic, political, social, and cultural domains—has two main implications for this analysis. The first implication is that, because of market failures and of the ways in which institutions evolve, inequality traps can affect not only the distribution but also the aggregate dynamics of growth and development. This in turn means that, in the long run, equity and efficiency may be complements, not substitutes.[11]

Capital, land, and labor markets in developing countries are imperfect. Informational asymmetries and contract enforcement problems imply that some people with good project ideas (and thus a potentially high marginal product of capital) end up constrained in their access to capital. This, even as other people earn a lower return on their (more abundant) capital. In agriculture, land market failures mean that some farmers exert too little effort on some plots (where they are sharecropping), and too much effort on other plots (which they own).[12] Investment in human capital can also be allocated inefficiently, because of intrahousehold disputes, because credit-constrained households lack the resources to keep their children healthy and in school, or because discrimination in the labor market reduces the expected returns to schooling for some groups. What do such diverse market failures have in common? They cause differences in initial endowments—such as family wealth, race, or gender—to make investment less efficient.

There also are political and institutional reasons why equity and efficiency are long-term complements. Markets are not the only institutions in society. The functioning of states, legal systems, and regulatory agencies—indeed, of all the institutions that assign and enforce property rights and mediate conflicts among citizens—is influenced by the distribution of political power (or influence, or voice) in society. Unequal distributions of control over resources and of political influence perpetuate institutions that protect the interests of the most powerful, sometimes to the detriment of the personal and property rights of others.[13]

Those whose rights are not protected have little incentive to invest, perpetuating poverty and reproducing inequality. Conversely, good institutions that protect and enforce personal and property rights for all citizens have led to higher sustained economic growth and long-term prosperity. Equity can, once again, help societies grow and develop.

This does *not* mean, of course, that efficiency-equity tradeoffs have somehow been abolished. In some cases, equity enhancements bring immediate—as well as long-run—benefits for efficiency. If we reduce discrimination against women in one segment of the labor market, such as management, and if this brings a new pool of talent into that segment, efficiency is likely to increase even in the short run.[14] In other cases, however, expanding the opportunity sets for the disadvantaged may require more costly redistribution. To finance better-quality schooling for those who have the least educated parents, and who attend the worst schools, it may be necessary to raise taxes on other people. The basic economic insight that such taxation distorts incentives remains valid. Such policies should be implemented only to the extent that the (present) value of the long-run benefits of greater equity exceed the efficiency costs of funding them.[15]

The point is that some of these long-term benefits of pursuing greater equity are ignored in the conceptual calculus of policy design. The fact that better-schooled children who are poor and from a racial minority will be more productive is usually taken into account. But the fact that they may acquire greater political voice and help make social institutions more inclusive—which, in turn, may increase the stake of that group in society, potentially leading to greater trust, less conflict, and more investment—may not be. To the extent that such indirect (but important) benefits of equity-enhancing policies are ignored, too few of them are pursued—even assuming a purely benevolent government.

By placing equity and fairness as central elements of an efficient development strategy, developing countries will be better able to reach sustainable growth and development trajectories. Such equitable growth paths are likely to lead to faster reductions in the many dimensions of poverty, the central objective of development everywhere.[16]

The second implication of the existence of inequality traps is that no real-life policy or institution is entirely exogenous: no existing organization or application of a policy idea has been implemented on a purely technocratic basis. All policies and institutions exist because the political system has brought them into being or allowed them to survive. The political system reflects the distribution of power and voice attained at a particular time and place. This distribution is, in turn, influenced by the distribution of wealth, income, and other assets and outcomes in that society. Such "circular causality" for wealth, income, social and cultural capital, and power, mediated through institutions, evolves throughout time and history.

Acknowledging history and social and political institutions is crucial to avoid policy mistakes. But a fatalistic view of the world is not only wrong, but also counterproductive. To propose policies without understanding history, or the specific context for developing these policies, often leads to failure. But this acknowledgment is not equivalent to the view that no policies should be suggested at all. Such a view fails to recognize how purposeful social and political action can achieve significant policy and institutional changes—and would result in fatalistic inaction.

History is *not* endlessly repetitive and, as this report documents, many countries have taken on the challenge of breaking inequality traps with some success. Groups have also changed their circumstances or changed social and political institutions. Consider the civil rights movement in the United States, the democratic overthrow of apartheid in South Africa, the more participatory budgeting practices in some Brazilian cities, and the reforms in access to land, education, and local government in the Indian state of Kerala. The challenge for policy is to ask when and how such changes can be supported.

A brief preview of the Report

Part I summarizes evidence on inequity within and across countries. Part II asks why equity matters for development, both intrinsically and instrumentally. Part III turns to the policy implications. If unequal opportunities and absolute deprivation are inimical to long-term prosperity—as well as intrinsically objectionable—there is scope for policy and institutional reform aimed at leveling the economic and political playing fields.

An equity lens and the focus on leveling the playing field add three basic points. First, redistributions from richer and more powerful groups to poorer groups that face more limited opportunities are sometimes necessary and should be pursued. Second, when considering policy tradeoffs between equity and efficiency, the full long-term benefits of equity—including on the development of better and more inclusive institutions—need to be taken into account. Third, all categories of economic policy—macro and micro—have effects on both efficiency (and growth) and equity (and distribution). Because our ultimate goal is the reduction of poverty through the equitable pursuit of prosperity, the policy suggestions in these chapters are consistent with good poverty-reduction policies, which the World Bank has been advocating since at least the publication of the World Development Report 1990.[17] These suggestions are also in line with the 2000 World Development Report's three pillars of opportunity, empowerment, and security.[18]

Inequity within and across countries

PART *I*

Inequality traps stifle economic development in a north Indian village

Villagers differ markedly from one another in the opportunities they have to improve their welfare and in their abilities to use the assets and endowments available to them. Mirrored in village economic and social institutions—and in the political processes for seeking change—these deep-seated inequalities have prevented the village from improving human development and accelerating economic growth.

The village of Palanpur, in the north Indian state of Uttar Pradesh, has been the subject of intensive study by a group of development economists between the late 1950s and early 1990s.[1] Researchers visited the village repeatedly and collected detailed quantitative and qualitative information. While a single village study covering a specific period of time cannot be used to draw inferences about development in rural India as a whole, it does provide a distinct window into the kind of processes that can shape growth and equity over time.

The study documents modest economic progress over time with slow growth in per capita incomes and some declines in income poverty. But alongside this sluggish growth is evidence of stagnation and even deterioration along other dimensions of well-being.

Different groups of villagers, defined by such predetermined characteristics as caste or gender, face radically different opportunities for economic and social mobility. Their economic endowments differ markedly, as do their education, health, occupational mobility, and capacity to influence and shape social and political institutions in the village. Disadvantage in one dimension of opportunity is generally reinforced by disadvantage in others, combined in a way that perpetuate the stark inequities over generations.

These deep-seated inequalities of opportunity shape, and are shaped by, market imperfections in the village, resulting in suboptimal investments and impeding growth. Inequalities are also mirrored in village institutions. State and central government policies that were introduced in the village were inevitably filtered through a highly unequal distribution of power and influence. Rather than stimulating broad economic and social progress, public policy has simply reproduced the prevailing patterns of inequality.

Caste

Caste in Palanpur defines opportunities and determines the activities villagers pursue, even independent of occupation, education, and other standard household characteristics. The three largest castes in Palanpur are Thakurs, Muraos, and Jatabs.

At the top is a martial caste known as the Thakurs, which accounted for about a quarter of the population in 1993. Thakurs are disproportionately represented in jobs such as the army and police that accord well with their martial past. They are typically averse to wage employment in the village, because this would place them in a subordinate position. Alert to nonfarm employment opportunities outside the village, they are well placed to take advantage of them, thanks to stronger information and social networks.

Just below the Thakurs is a cultivating caste, the Muraos, also accounting for a quarter of the population. Muraos are traditional cultivators who have continued to specialize in agriculture. Very hardworking, they have seen a rapid rise in wealth and economic status in the village. While they may still not enjoy the same social status as Thakurs, they have become more prosperous and now challenge the previously unquestioned political and economic dominance of the Thakurs.

At the bottom are the scheduled castes known as Jatabs, accounting for 12 percent of the population. Traditionally "untouchable" leather workers who now engage primarily in agricultural wage labor, Jatabs have not seen any of the social mobility of the Muraos. They remain a caste apart, with little or no land, poor education, and little access to nonfarm employment outside the village. Despite some slight improvement over the years, Jatabs continue to endure many forms of discrimination, including that from government officials.

Gender

Gender inequalities in Palanpur are pronounced. In 1993 there were 84 females for every 100 males, strikingly lower than in most parts of the world (where the ratio is usually greater than one). Child mortality rates are much higher among girls than among boys. As the researchers reported, "We witnessed several cases of infant girls who were allowed to wither away and die in circumstances that would undoubtedly have prompted more energetic action in the case of a male child."[2]

Young girls leave their village to join their husband's family. Marriage is "the gift of a daughter." In the new household, the girl is acutely vulnerable with no income-earning opportunities, no property, no possibility of returning home permanently. Giving birth to a child improves her status—particularly if it's a boy. But family planning practices are limited, leading to high fertility rates and short birth-spacing. Repeated pregnancies take an enormous toll on women's general health and put their lives at risk at the time of delivery. Old age is strongly associated with widowhood, in part because of the typically large age difference between husbands and wives. To survive, widows depend overwhelmingly on adult sons.

The participation of women in the labor force in Palanpur is extremely low. Of 313 women age 15 or older in 1993, only 14 had anything other than domestic work as their primary or secondary occupation. This low female participation in the labor force and society, more generally, has extensive consequences. For example, the survival disadvantage of girls compared with boys tends to narrow only when adult women have wider opportunities for gainful employment. Similarly, the virtual exclusion of women from most representative institutions in Palanpur has limited the focus and quality of local politics and public action.

Schooling

Inequalities in education are wide, declining only slowly. In the late 1950s, just under 20 percent of males age seven or older, and only 1 percent of females, were literate. By 1993, male literacy had risen to 37 percent and female literacy to just below 10 percent. Yet education is clearly of great value in Palanpur. Years of schooling strongly increase the likelihood that an individual will find employment in a regular job outside the village. Among farmers, too, direct observation strongly suggests that better-educated farmers in Palanpur have been crucial in technological innovation and diffusion.

The perceived value of female education is quite different from that for boys, because girls are expected to spend most of their adult life in domestic work. Although there is good evidence of the benefits of education in domestic activities, it is not clear that the effects of maternal literacy on child health, for example, are recognized. Even if benefits are correctly perceived, they might not be of direct interest to the parents, because daughters are "transferred" from the village when they marry. Those who bear the costs of female education thus share little in the benefits.

The upper-caste Thakurs have a view (adopted by many others) that education is not important or even suitable for the lower castes. Blatant forms of discrimination against children from disadvantaged castes have disappeared from the schooling system, but subtler forms of discrimination have remained—for example, the high-caste teacher considered any form of contact with Jatab children as "repulsive," which likely affected his or her rapport with them and probably discouraged their attendance.

Work

Occupational divisions in Palanpur have widened as the village has shifted from an overwhelmingly agricultural economy to one in which nonagricultural activities have come to account for 30 to 40 percent of village income. In 1957–58 some 13 villagers (of 528) were employed in regular or semi-regular nonfarm jobs. By 1993, this number had increased more than four times to 57 jobs (the total population had only doubled).

Outside jobs are associated with higher and more stable incomes, and the work is often less strenuous and demanding than in agriculture. Access to nonfarm jobs is far from equal, however. Workers who wish to obtain a regular job generally have to pay bribes and, more important, get a recommendation or introduction from a friend or relative. Such rationing by personal contacts and influence implies that people with low social status tend to be at a disadvantage in the competition for nonfarm jobs, even for given education levels, skills, and endowments.

The least advantaged segments of the labor force in Palanpur are highly represented in agricultural wage labor. Casual wage labor in agriculture can be described as a "last-resort" occupation, one taken up by those who have no significant alternative. Agricultural wage rates have risen over time, but slowly, and there are prolonged periods of seasonal unemployment.

Econometric analysis indicates that—controlling for a large number of household characteristics (caste, demographic characteristics, education, land, and so on)—the probability of engagement in agricultural labor is 50 to 60 percent higher for households that had engaged in this occupation a decade earlier. Occupational inequalities thus result in income inequality, and they persist over long periods.

Incomes, assets, and liabilities

Per capita incomes in Palanpur have grown at around 2 percent a year between 1957–8 and 1983–4 and income poverty fell from around 47 to 34 percent during this period. Incomes in the village are distributed about as unequally as they are in India as a whole, and income inequality has remained relatively stable over time.

An assessment of economic inequalities based on *wealth* provides a different picture. Ownership of durables has expanded, and the value of land and other productive assets has grown, implying a significant rise in gross wealth. But there has also been a dramatic and uneven expansion of liabilities. Inequality in the distribution of *net* wealth has widened in Palanpur from a Gini of around 0.46 in 1962–3 to a conservatively estimated 0.55 in 1990.

Many of the liabilities come from publicly provided and subsidized credit sources that have expanded sharply over time, but that have been associated with pervasive corruption. Disadvantaged groups, such as the Jatabs, are the principal targets of fraudulent accounting practices that have resulted in a dizzying accumulation of debts and dramatically raised the cost of borrowing for such households. Those without access to cheap formal credit have to fall back on private moneylenders, at high interest rates.

Collective inaction

The different bases of social division in Palanpur have led to multiple solidarities and oppositions. The village society is highly fragmented, with few solid rallying points for collective action, whether cooperative or adversarial. The limited reach of collective action, in turn, is responsible for some of the most serious failures of its development. For example, the village assembly (panchayat) is constituted every few years, but it rarely meets. In 1984 it was made obligatory that at least one woman participant be selected, but in Palanpur she is never consulted and has never attended any panchayat meetings. All decisions and responsibilities are effectively taken by a village headman, who has always come from one of the privileged groups. There also is ample scope for self-serving patronage and fraud. Modern arrangements (elections, reserved seats for low castes, and women on the panchayat) have not profoundly altered the elitist and nonparticipatory character of local politics in the village.

The dominance of privileged groups over collective institutions has had far-reaching consequences. Between the late 1950s and early 1990s, no fewer than 18 types of government-provided programs were introduced to the village: a public works road-building program, free schooling, free basic health care, old-age pensions, a fair-price shop, a farmer's cooperative, and so on. Most of them remained nonfunctional, particularly when there was a redistributive component. Only programs that enjoyed strong backing from the politically advantaged in the village were allowed to succeed. The authors of the study conclude, "There is little prospect of major improvement in the orientation and achievements of government intervention without a significant change in the balance of political power, both at the state and at the local level."[3]

Source: Drèze, Lanjouw, and Sharma (1998).

Inequity within countries: individuals and groups

Across the world, individuals and groups face highly unequal opportunities to better themselves economically and socially. Inequalities, as such, might not be of particular concern if outcomes varied for reasons that had to do mainly with individual efforts. But, taking our cue from the first chapter, we are concerned here with systematic differences in opportunities for individuals and groups who differ only in skin color, caste, gender, or place of residence, predetermined characteristics that can be argued to be "morally irrelevant." As illustrated in focus 1, on the Indian village of Palanpur, when such inequalities of opportunity are pronounced, they are often reproduced over time and not only affect welfare directly but also act to stifle human development and economic growth.

On the basis of what predetermined characteristics should groups be defined such that we would not want to see systematic differences in their opportunities? Clearly there is no single answer. Roemer (1998) argues that society has to make this choice through some kind of ethical and political process. The circumstances could include social origin variables outside an individual's control, such as sex, race, ethnicity, caste, parental education and occupation, wealth, or place of birth. Cogneau (2005) notes that a society's choice of circumstances establishes a direct link between equality of opportunities and the intergenerational transmission of outcomes. In this chapter, we are largely compelled to let data availability dictate the group definitions we consider. We can thus present only a partial, and often rudimentary, picture of the full range of inequity that might exist in a country. Because we wish not only to look within a country but also to compare across countries, we use group definitions of broad relevance.

Although economic inequalities are clearly part of the story, this chapter goes beyond incomes to emphasize inequalities in key dimensions of opportunity, such as health, education, and the freedom and capacity of people to participate in and shape society. There is a special concern with inequalities that tend to perpetuate differences across individuals and groups over time, within and across generations. These result in "inequality traps" that are pervasive in many countries. Such inequality traps reinforce our concern with equity on intrinsic grounds, but they can also be particularly detrimental to the development process, because they act to curtail economic dynamism.

A key objective here is to show how inequalities combine, interact, and are reproduced through interlinked economic, political, and sociocultural processes. Individuals and groups differ markedly in their power to influence these processes; indeed, they differ even in their capacity to aspire to such influence. The report emphasizes that such "agency" is a dimension of opportunity, alongside education, health, and wealth. And inequalities of agency are central in explaining how inequalities of opportunity are transmitted over time (box 2.1).

This chapter presents evidence of a high degree of inequality of opportunity in many developing countries—inequalities manifest in a variety of dimensions, such as health, education, and income. It then focuses on the specific dimension of inequality of power, or agency. Throughout the chapter, we emphasize that inequalities in different dimensions can interact with, and reinforce, one another over time. To highlight these connections, we end by focusing on the specific case of gender inequity.

Inequalities in health

Alongside the intrinsic importance of health as a dimension of welfare, poor health can directly influence an individual's opportunities—his or her earnings capacity, performance at school, ability to care for children, participation in community activities, and so on. This important instrumental function of health implies that inequalities in health often translate into inequalities in other dimensions of welfare. And these inequalities are reproduced over time. We focus here on children, while recognizing that differences in social status, wealth, and health also matter for adults.

Demographic and Health Survey (DHS) data indicate that health status varies sharply across population groups. To what extent does it vary across population groups defined by characteristics that are predetermined and arguably have no moral relevance? We draw on DHS data from 60 countries to examine how the health of children varies across population groups defined by mother's education, rural or urban residence, and parent's economic status, proxied by an index of household ownership of consumer durables. (We look further at cross-country differences in health in chapter 3.)

Infant mortality. For these countries, infant mortality rates vary markedly—from a low of around 25 per 1,000 live births in Colombia and Jordan, to more than 125 in Mali, Niger, and Mozambique (figure 2.1). But even where overall infant mortality rates are high, the figures for children whose mothers have a secondary education or higher are dramatically lower. The risk of death among children with well-educated mothers in Mali, for example, is about the same as that for the average child in Indonesia. And while the overall infant mortality rate in Brazil lies

---

BOX 2.1 *Unequal opportunities persist across generations in Brazil*

As a prelude to the themes in this chapter, we describe one attempt to quantify the level and persistence of inequalities of opportunity in Brazil, based on nationally representative household survey data. Brazil was selected for a reason. With a Gini coefficient of per capita incomes just below 0.6 and persistent over time, it is generally perceived to be one of the world's most unequal countries.*

Brazil's main household survey, the *Pesquisa Nacional por Amostra de Domicilios* (PNAD), included in 1996 a set of supplemental questions on the parents of respondents. This permitted an analysis of the intergenerational persistence in inequalities. Using four circumstance variables (parental schooling, father's occupation, race, and region of birth), Bourguignon, Ferreira, and Menendez (2005) investigated how inequalities of opportunity generate inequality in current earnings across different cohorts of adult individuals. Applying a conceptual framework closely related to that in chapter 1, they decomposed earnings inequality into a lower bound component attributable to the inequality of opportunity—to the effect of the four observed circumstance variables—and a residual component, which would account for personal effort, luck, measurement error, transitory income, and other unobservable characteristics. They found that the four variables accounted for more than a fifth of the total earnings inequality within gender cohorts. Of the four, family background was most important.

This distribution of certain opportunities and outcomes has persisted across generations. When the authors estimated econometrically the relationship between schooling and race, region of origin, parental education, and father's occupation, only the coefficient on parental education seems to have fallen across cohorts. In other words, race, region of origin, and father's occupation continue to predict an individual's education level. And even for education, mechanisms are at work to reproduce schooling levels across generations, especially at the lower end of the distribution.

Brazil underscores the need to look at a range of outcomes (of which incomes are only one, with education, health and services also of great concern). It also underscores the need to look at a range of processes—of which income and economic wealth-based mechanisms form only part, and for which group-based interactions are as central as household and individual conditions, behaviors, and characteristics.

Source: Bourguignon, Ferreira, and Menendez (2005).
* The perception of particularly high inequality in Brazil may to some extent be a result of the way income is measured there. Alternative approaches to measuring inequality, based on other welfare indicators, indicate that Brazil may be less of an outlier in Latin America than previously believed. See box 2.5 and also De Ferranti and others (2004).

---

below 50 (estimates from 1996), the rate for children whose mothers have not been educated is roughly twice as high. Further analysis, not reported here, indicates that infant mortality rates are also sharply differentiated across population groups defined by rural-urban residence and economic status, proxied by asset ownership.

Stunting. Another dimension of health, extreme stunting (with height-for-age below three standard deviations from the reference population), also varies markedly across countries. Overall rates are as high as 30 percent in Pakistan and the Republic of Yemen, but negligible in Trinidad and Tobago and very low in Jordan, Armenia, Brazil, and Kazakhstan (figure 2.2).

Figure 2.1 Infant mortality varies across countries but also by mother's education within countries

Infant mortality rate per 1,000 live births

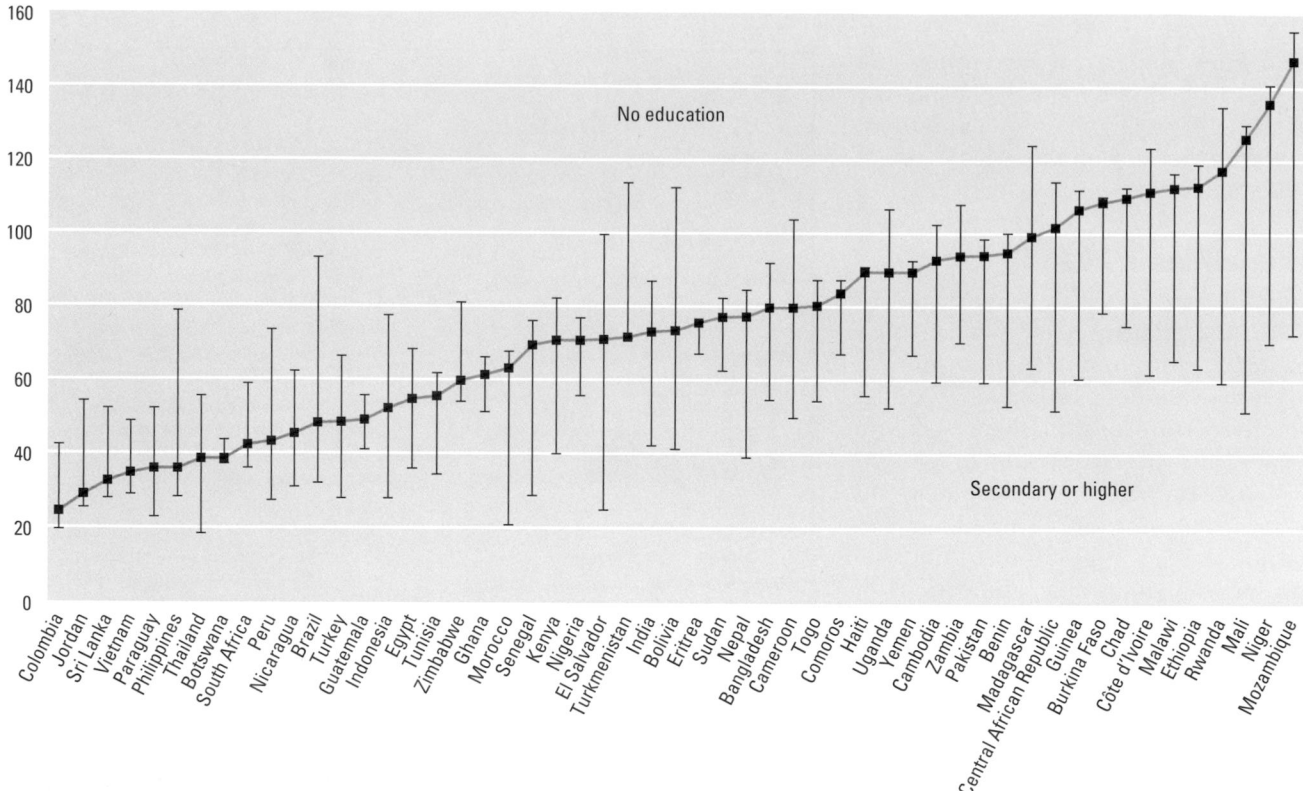

Source: Authors' calculations from Demographic Health Survey (DHS) data.
Note: The continuous dark line represents the mean infant mortality rate in each country, while the endpoints of the whiskers indicate the infant mortality rates by different levels of mother's education.

Figure 2.2 Stunting levels of children born in rural versus urban areas are far from the same

Percentage of children severely stunted (z-score < 3)

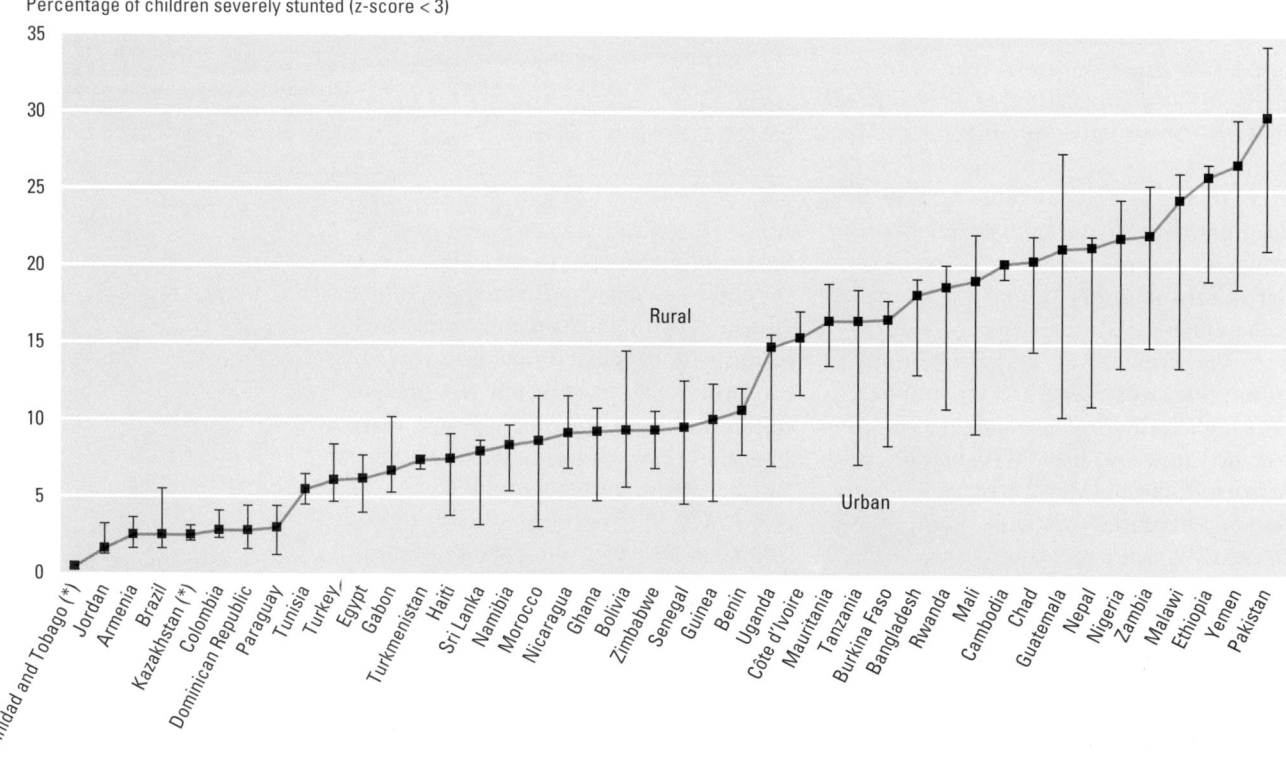

Source: Authors' calculations from Demographic Health Survey (DHS) data.
Note: The continuous dark line represents the percentage of severely stunted children in each country, while the endpoints of the whiskers indicate the percentages for urban and rural areas.
* Indicates stunting level in urban areas are higher than in rural areas.

Figure 2.3 Access to childhood immunization services depends on parents' economic status

Percentage not covered

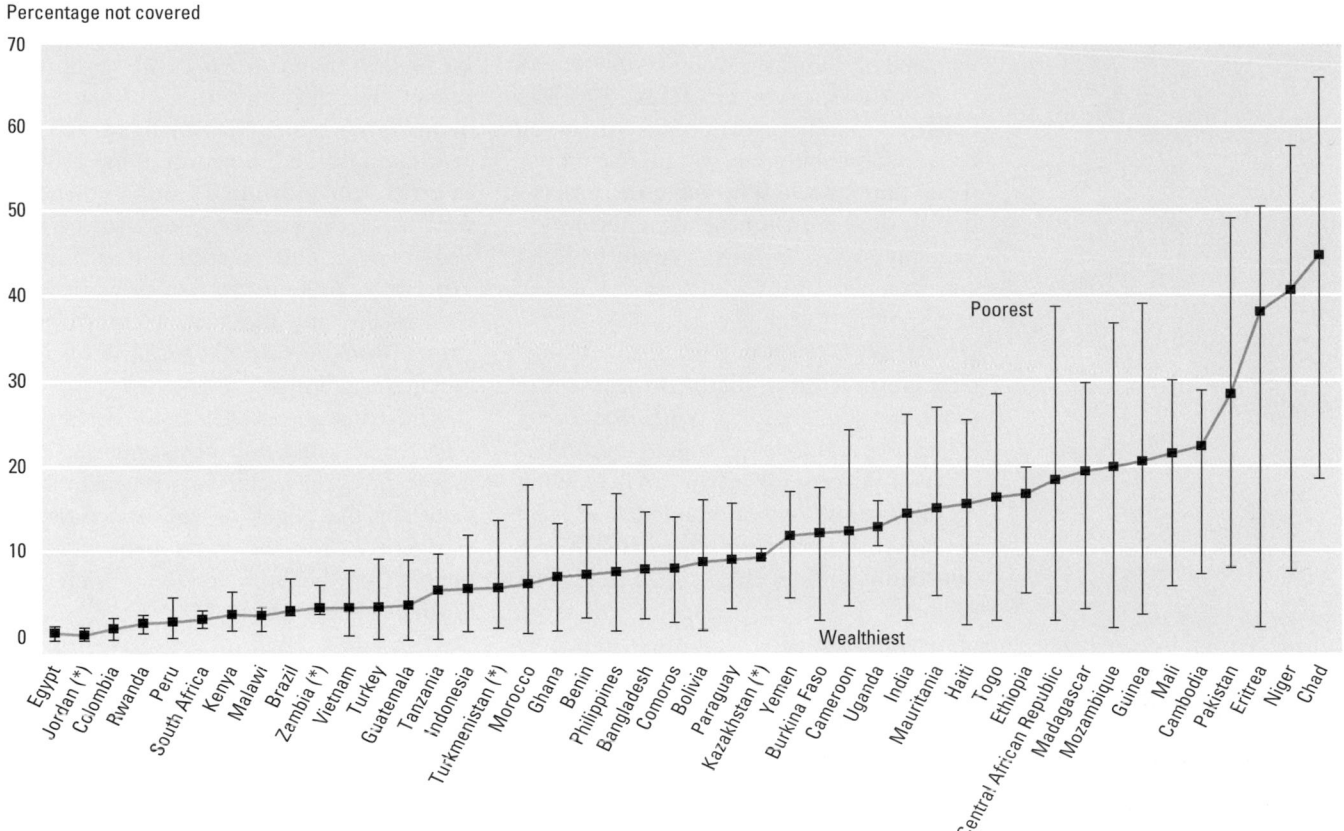

Source: Authors' calculations from Demographic Health Survey (DHS) data.
Note: The continuous dark line represents the percentage of children without access to a basic immunization package in each country, while the endpoints of the whiskers indicate the percentages for the top and the bottom quintile of the asset ownership distribution.
* Indicates that the poorest quintile have higher access to childhood immunization services than the wealthiest quintile.

The difference between children born in rural and urban areas can be dramatic, particularly at higher overall stunting levels. In Guatemala, stunting rates for children in urban areas are around 10 percent, but in rural areas they are as much as three times higher. Children in Guatemala clearly have no choice in deciding whether they are born in the countryside or the city, but their opportunities to achieve good health are clearly much less assured in rural than in urban areas. As for infant mortality rates, stunting among children is also sharply differentiated by mother's education and household economic status.

Access to immunization. Children born in families whose asset ownership places them in the top quintile of the distribution of economic status have a high probability of access to health services, proxied here as having received at least one of three key childhood vaccinations—bacille Calmette-Guérin; diptheria, pertussis, and tetanus; or measles (figure 2.3). This is so even in countries where the overall percentage of children without any coverage is as high as 40 percent. Conversely, children whose parents are in the bottom quintile are much more likely to lack access to such basic health care. In Morocco, where roughly 5 percent of children have not received even one of these three vaccinations, the proportion for children in the poorest quintile is well above 15 percent.

High-impact health services. The World Bank (2003j), drawing on DHS data from 30 low- and middle-income countries, finds that the poor are considerably less likely than the non-poor to have access to high-impact health services, such as skilled delivery care, antenatal care, and complementary feeding. Similarly, Wodon (2005) draws on household survey data from 15 African countries to indicate that, while virtually all urban households are within one hour's travel time to a health center, the proportion in rural areas is generally only around half, and as low as 35–38 percent in Niger and Ethiopia.

Disability. Data from a number of countries suggest that disabled people are much more likely to be poor. Hoogeveen (2003) reports that in Uganda the probability of poverty for urban dwellers living in a household with a disabled head is 38 percent higher than for those who live in a household with an able-bodied head. The Serbian Poverty Reduction Strategy reports that 70 percent of disabled people are unemployed. In a study drawing on 10 household surveys in eight countries, self-reported disability was found to be more correlated with nonattendance at school than other characteristics, including gender or rural residence.[1] Sen (2004) emphasizes that the disabled face not only an "earnings handicap," associated with a lower probability of employment and lower compensation for their work, but also a "conversion handicap." By this he means that a physically disabled person requires more income than an able-bodied person to achieve the same living standard.

Social inequalities damaging health. Not only are health outcomes correlated with inequalities in other dimensions, but such social inequalities can be argued to be detrimental to individual health outcomes.[2] In his comprehensive review of the literature, Deaton (2003) argues that, while it is certainly plausible that various inequalities (such as those in power) cause bad health, it is not clear that inequality of income is the main culprit. He provides evidence suggesting that, after controlling for an individual's income, income inequality at the group level does not matter independently for individual health. Thus,

the main inequalities that affect health may not be in the income space. He cites examples of other key dimensions of inequality: land ownership, women's agency (health and fertility in India), and democratic rights (in England in the 1870s and in the U.S. South in the 1960s). In general, an individual's rank in the relevant hierarchy has been found to be important to health in animal and human experiments. Repeated stress associated with insults and the lack of control that comes from low rank has a well-developed biochemical basis.[3]

The consequences of poor health are reflected in education achievements, economic prosperity, and future generations. Consider the plight of AIDS orphans in southern Africa, the stark inequalities of opportunity they face, and the possible role for public action (box 2.2).

DHS data (figures 2.1–2.3) provide detailed insights into the relationship between inequalities in health and some key circumstance variables. But they are not particularly well suited to capturing the contribution of detailed spatial factors, such as place of birth, in overall inequality, because of the limited sample size. In one attempt to get around this problem, child height in Cambodia was estimated at the commune level based on a statistical procedure to combine DHS data with population census data.[4] The study documents considerable heterogeneity across Cambodia's more than 1,600 communes in the prevalence of stunting and being underweight among children under the age of five (figure 2.4). The analysis provides clear evidence that in Cambodia a child's opportunities for good health have a strong spatial dimension to them. Yet clearly, no child is able to determine in which locality he or she is born.

Trends

Average health in most countries improved in the twentieth century (chapter 3). Deaton (2004) documents that improvements in health are likely to have accompanied economic growth, but he also emphasizes the globalization of knowledge, facilitated by local political, eco-

---

BOX 2.2   *Unequal assets, unequal opportunities: AIDS orphans in Southern Africa*

It is hard to imagine people with fewer assets, through absolutely no fault of their own, than AIDS orphans. Left to fend for themselves on the death of one or both parents from a progressively debilitating, heavily stigmatized, and costly-to-treat disease, their plight would be of concern even if they numbered but a few. In southern Africa, however, the United Nations Children's Fund (UNICEF) estimates that there were 12.3 million AIDS orphans in 2003, a veritable demographic group in their own right. By 2010, UNICEF projects that there will be 1.5 million AIDS orphans in South Africa; by 2014, 1 million in Zambia.

An entire generation of Africans is emerging who will have been raised, if they are lucky, by grandparents or extended family members (themselves likely to be impoverished, overwhelmed, and suffering from the disease). At worst, they will grow up in child-headed households or in situations in which their basic rights to food, clothing, shelter, and adequate care are routinely denied.

Wills and schooling

Beginning to overcome the huge disadvantages that AIDS orphans start life with requires special attention on numerous fronts (box 7.11 considers a variety of policy options). From a legal standpoint, parents who know their death is imminent and who have young children need to be encouraged (even if they are illiterate) to prepare enforceable wills that will protect the inheritance rights of their children to ensure that surviving adults do not just forcibly take their land,

savings, or other valuables. From an education standpoint, it is vital to keep children in school, where the acquisition of even basic skills can give them some viable prospect of being able to move out of poverty. Where a child is the head of a household and perhaps its sole income earner, however, the pressures to drop out of school are enormous. Numerous studies document significantly higher dropout rates of AIDS orphans. In Kenya, one extreme example found that "52 percent of the children orphaned by AIDS were not in school, compared to 2 percent of non-orphans" (UNAIDS 2002, 135).

Attending school is also important from a civic perspective: it socializes children into the norms and mores of society, and gives them the confidence and capacity to participate more fully in it. Without such socialization, vulnerable young children are easy targets for those offering them security and status through membership in a street gang, criminal network, or militia movement. If AIDS orphans continue to stay from school at their current rate, comments one senior U.N. official, "you will have a society where kids haven't been to school and therefore can't fulfill even basic jobs...a society where a large proportion can have antisocial instincts because their lives have been so hard. You [will] have a generation of children who will be more vulnerable to exploitation and to disease because they won't have the same sense of self-worth" (cited in Fleshman 2001, 1). Such children face the dismal prospect of failing to accumulate assets because of the extreme burdens thrust on them

in their most formative years and the paucity of opportunities available to them thereafter.

Avoiding infection

The most immediate priority, however, is ensuring that AIDS orphans do not themselves become infected with the disease, thereby increasing the likelihood that they will perpetuate the cycle. AIDS orphans face precisely such a risk, however, because the stigma of HIV/AIDS means that people often assume that the children of parents who died from AIDS must be infected, shunning, shaming, or exploiting them accordingly. Some AIDS orphans have even been denied access to schools and health clinics because of the fear their very presence generates. Children grieving the loss of a parent are also vulnerable to the sexual predations of those putatively claiming to offer them comfort. Indeed, the desperation and apparent hopelessness of their circumstances—all the more so if it coincides with a natural disaster such as drought—can drive AIDS orphans into prostitution.

The plight of AIDS orphans provides a graphic illustration of how cycles of disadvantage can perpetuate themselves, and how social isolation and exclusion (especially at a young age) can preclude the acquisition of assets and undermine the capacity to sustain participation in the institutions that provide the best path out of poverty.

Sources: Avert.org (2004) http://www.avert.org/aidsorphans.htm. Accessed December 14, 2004. Fleshman (2001). Hargreaves and Glynn (2002), Lewis (2003), UNAIDS (2002), UNICEF (2003), USAID, UNAIDS, and UNICEF (2004).

---

nomic, and educational conditions. In the 1980s and 1990s, however, progress slowed—a result of the worldwide HIV/AIDS epidemic and rises in cardiovascular mortality in Eastern Europe and former Soviet Union countries.

How have inequalities in health evolved *within* countries? Data from DHS provide some clues. For a subset of countries, multiple rounds of DHS data are available to document changes in infant mortality over time. Of some 36 "spells" of health change that could be identified, roughly 25 corresponded to improved health outcomes in the form of lower infant mortality rates. Although overall health improved in these 25 cases, the gaps between urban and rural areas, between groups defined by mother's education, and between groups defined by durable asset ownership did not universally decline alongside the overall declines

Figure 2.4 Stunting and underweight in Cambodia

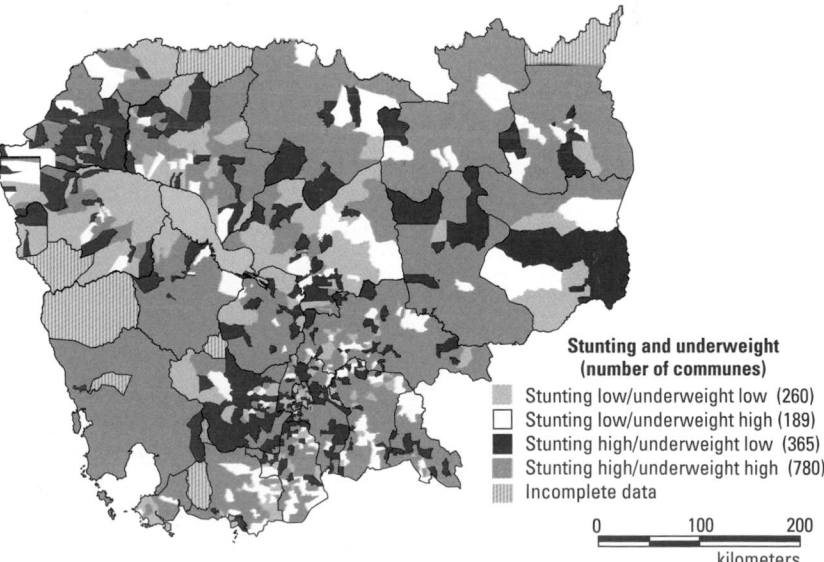

Stunting and underweight (number of communes)

- Stunting low/underweight low (260)
- Stunting low/underweight high (189)
- Stunting high/underweight low (365)
- Stunting high/underweight high (780)
- Incomplete data

0   100   200
kilometers

Source: Fujii (2005).

BOX 2.3 *Health improvements and greater health equity in Peru*

Paxson and Schady (2004), drawing on multiple rounds of DHS data, document the declining infant mortality rate in Peru between the late 1970s and late 1990s. A general downward trend exhibited a sharp setback during the major economic crisis between 1988 and 1992, but resumed after the crisis. The downward trend remained evident even after adjusting for age of mother, recall period, education, and urban status—indicating that the overall trend decline in infant mortality was not attributable only to general improvements in education, an aging population, or urbanization. In addition, the fact that infant mortality rose sharply around 1990, even after these adjustments, supports the notion that the decrease in household income and the collapse of public expenditures on health as a result of the crisis were important.

Infant mortality rates in Peru varied markedly with the education level of the mother in late 1970s and the 1980s (see figure below). During the economic crisis, increases in mortality were largest among infants born to women with less education. After the crisis, the gap between infant mortality rates associated with different maternal education levels declined steadily, suggesting an overall decline in inequality in mortality alongside the decline in overall mortality rates.

There is some support for the view that changes in the amount and composition of public expenditures on social programs drove these improvements. Real total expenditures increased two and a half times between 1991 and 2000, and such public spending did not bypass the poor.

Adjusted infant mortality rates by maternal education

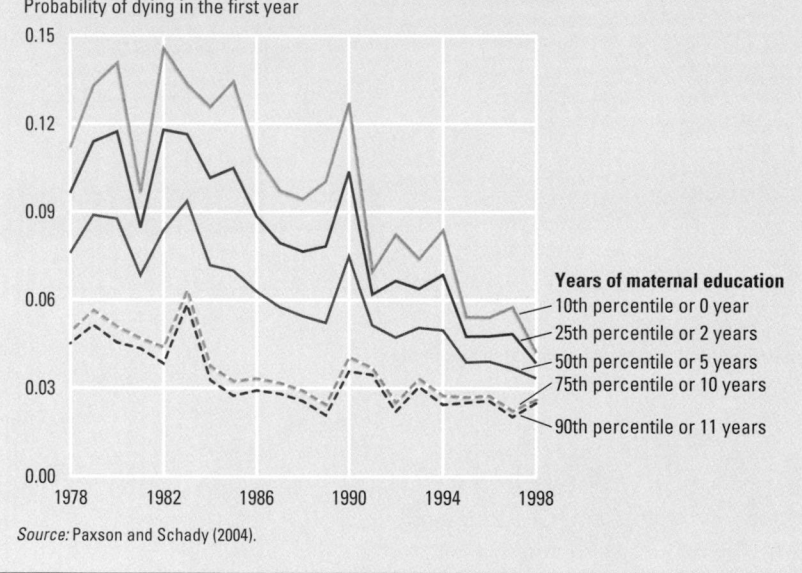

Source: Paxson and Schady (2004).

1990s, the overall decline in the infant mortality rate to 7.9 in 1994 was accompanied by an increase in the ratio of black to white infant mortality rates from 1.6 in 1950 to 2.2 in 1991. Inequality in health does not inevitably fall as overall health improves, but such a virtuous process is possible (box 2.3).

Inequalities in education

Education is of great intrinsic importance when assessing inequalities of opportunity. It is also an important determinant of individuals' income, health (and that of their children), and capacity to interact and communicate with others. Inequalities in education thus contribute to inequalities in other important dimensions of well-being.

Measuring inequality in education is not easy. Census and survey data in most countries can generally yield statistics on, for example, years of schooling. But such information does not capture well the quality of education and how that might vary across individuals. Nor is it easy to compare years of schooling across countries, because those years might mean something quite different from country to country.

Test results. Despite the measurement difficulties, there is considerable evidence of inequalities of opportunity in education in the developing world. Consider the differences in test performance among Ecuadorian children ages three to six years across population groups defined by parental education, region of residence, and wealth (box 2.4).

Test results among very young children capture well the inequality in opportunity in education, but such data are not readily available for large numbers of developing countries. So we look instead at the percentage of household heads with no education by gender and by urban-rural residence.

Male and female household heads. The overall percentage of household heads without any education varies dramatically across our sample of 60-odd countries (figure 2.5). In the high-income countries, the percentage rates are negligible. But at

in infant mortality.[5] The improvements in health were not necessarily shared across all groups in the population.

As Cornia and Menchini (2005) note, mortality differentials across groups tend to narrow with an improvement of the average only if policies focus explicitly on equity. Without such a focus, improvements in the average may not translate to declining group differences. For example, in the United States between the 1950s and

the other extreme, in Burkina Faso and Mali, for example, the overall percentage is more than 80 percent. What is similarly striking is that, in most countries, the likelihood that the household head is uneducated is dramatically higher than average when she is a woman. In the Laos People's Democratic Republic, for example, although the overall percentage of household heads with no education is about 20 percent, the rate is closer to 70 percent for female household heads.

Rural and urban household heads. Similar patterns can be observed for rural and urban areas (figure 2.6). In general, household heads are far more likely to have no education when they are based in rural areas than in urban areas. Even in countries where the overall percentage without education is very high, the rate in urban areas can be dramatically lower. For example, in Burundi, the percentage of household heads with no education in urban areas compares with the national average in Mexico, the Dominican Republic, and Brazil.

Access to teachers. A recent study of primary schools and health clinics in Bangladesh, Ecuador, India, Indonesia, Peru, and Uganda has identified teacher absenteeism as an important, common, problem. The study found that higher income areas generally have lower teacher absentee rates than poorer areas.[6] It also found that higher paid teachers, generally more educated and experienced, appear equally or more likely to be absent than contract or less remunerated instructors, perhaps because these instructors sense a lower risk of being fired for their absence. And although salaries in rural areas were often higher than in urban areas, teacher attendance in these areas was typically lower than in urban areas. In most surveyed countries, the quality of infrastructure and the frequency of monitoring appeared to contribute to lower absenteeism.

Trends

Another way to assess inequalities of opportunity in education is to calculate an overall index of inequality for years of edu-

---

BOX 2.4 *Child test scores in Ecuador: the role of wealth, parental education, and place of residence*

That education achievements vary markedly by population groups—and that this can have profound implications—is brought out forcefully in a recent study by Paxson and Schady (2005). They show that cognitive development of Ecuadorian children ages three to six years, as measured by a test of vocabulary recognition (TVIP), varies significantly depending on the wealth of their household, their place of residence, the education of their mother, and that of their father. The extent to which these circumstance variables are associated with performance on cognitive tests is typically more pronounced for the older children in their sample.

These socioeconomic characteristics are significantly associated with cognitive development even after controlling for child health and home environment. The researchers point to the striking evidence that, in Ecuador, the youngest children, irrespective of wealth quintile or education of their parents, perform broadly as well as their comparators. But as children in Ecuador get older, their cognitive development, relative to this benchmark, falters significantly. Only children in the top half of the wealth distribution and with highly educated parents maintain their performance relative to their comparators. By the time they are six years old, most children in the sample are so far behind in their cognitive development that it is uncertain whether and how they could ever catch up.

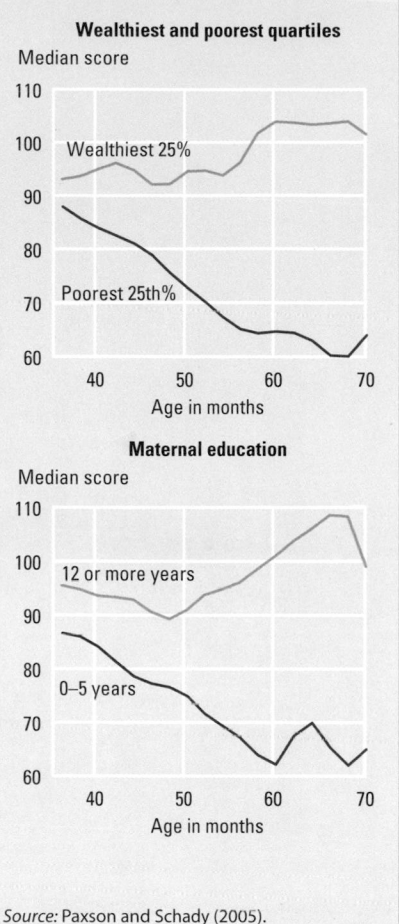

Source: Paxson and Schady (2005).

---

cation and to assess how much overall inequality of education can be attributed to mean differences between "morally irrelevant" groups. Araujo, Ferreira, and Schady (2004) find that the inequality of adult education, measured by years of schooling for 124 countries, can be pronounced. They also find that it is strongly (and inversely) correlated with mean years of schooling across countries.[7]

The data assembled by these authors also indicate that the inequality of education for specific subgroups of the population can change. While female schooling achievements relative to male achievements were dramatically lower among the oldest cohorts, particularly in Sub-Saharan Africa, South

Figure 2.5 Education levels vary across countries, but they also depend on gender of household head

Percentage of household heads with no education

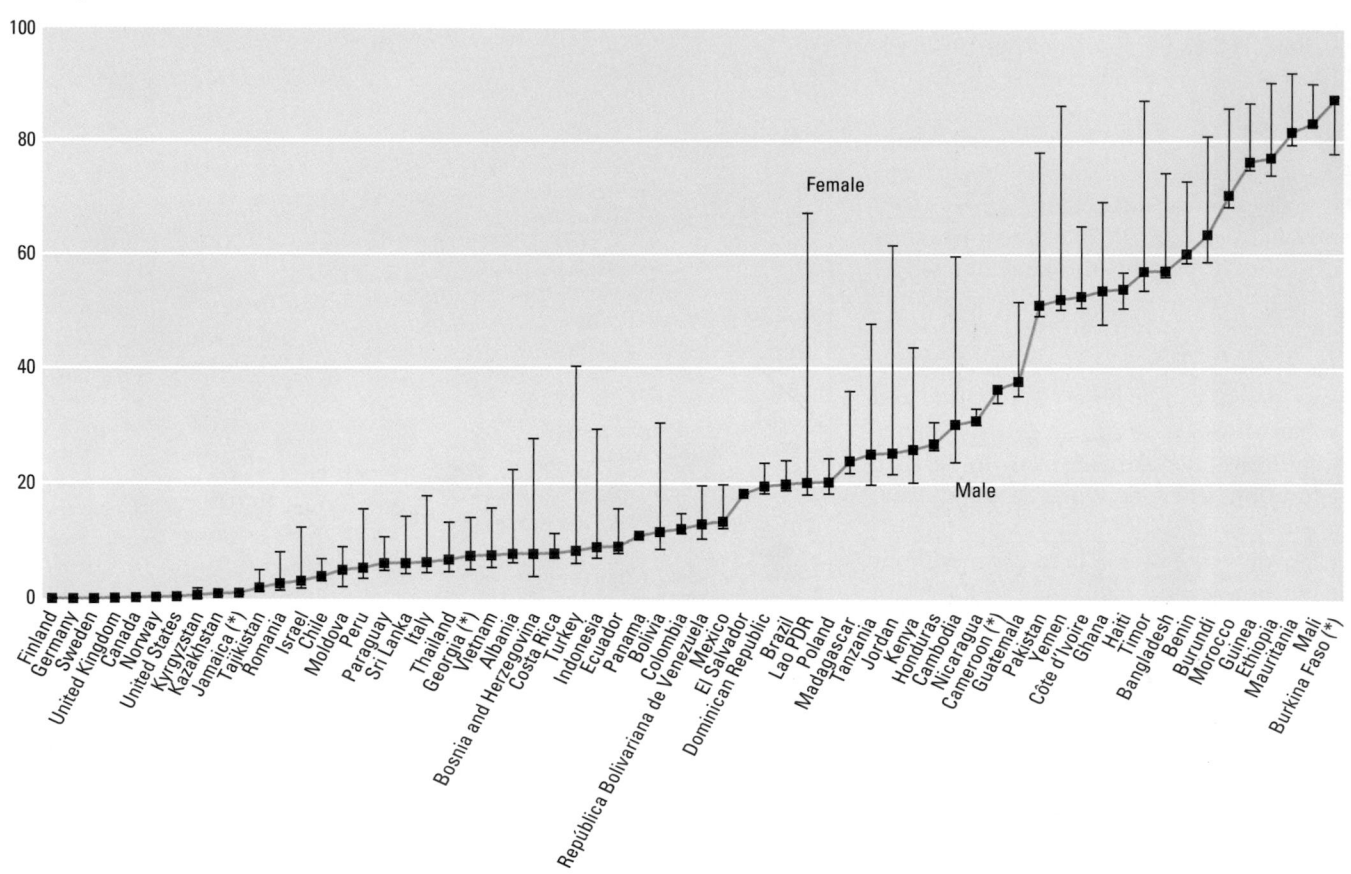

Source: Authors' calculations from household survey data.
Note: The continuous dark line represents the percentage of household heads with no education in each country, while the endpoints of the whiskers indicate the percentages for male and female-headed households.
* Indicates that female-headed households have higher average levels of education than male-headed households.

Asia, and to a lesser extent the Middle East and North Africa, these disparities are noticeably lower for the younger cohorts, particularly in Sub-Saharan Africa (figure 2.7). Additionally, disparities in years of schooling between urban and rural areas have been falling in some regions, most strikingly in the Middle East and North Africa and in Eastern Europe and Central Asia. But in Sub-Saharan Africa there has been little, if any, change. The (urban-rural) between-group contribution to inequality in this region has hovered at around 30 percent across all the cohorts examined.

Economic inequalities

An individual's consumption, his or her income, or his or her wealth have all been used as indicators of the command of an individual over goods and services that can be purchased in the market and that contribute directly to well-being. It is clear too, that individuals' economic status can determine and shape in many ways the opportunities they face to improve their situations. Economic well-being can also contribute to improved education outcomes and better health care. In turn, good health and good education are typically important determinants of economic status.

An ideal measure of economic well-being for assessing inequality will capture an individual's long-term economic status. But it is difficult to produce such a comprehensive indicator accurately. In practice, it is common to work with measures of current income or consumption compiled from household survey data. While consumption

Figure 2.6 Education levels vary by country and between rural and urban sectors

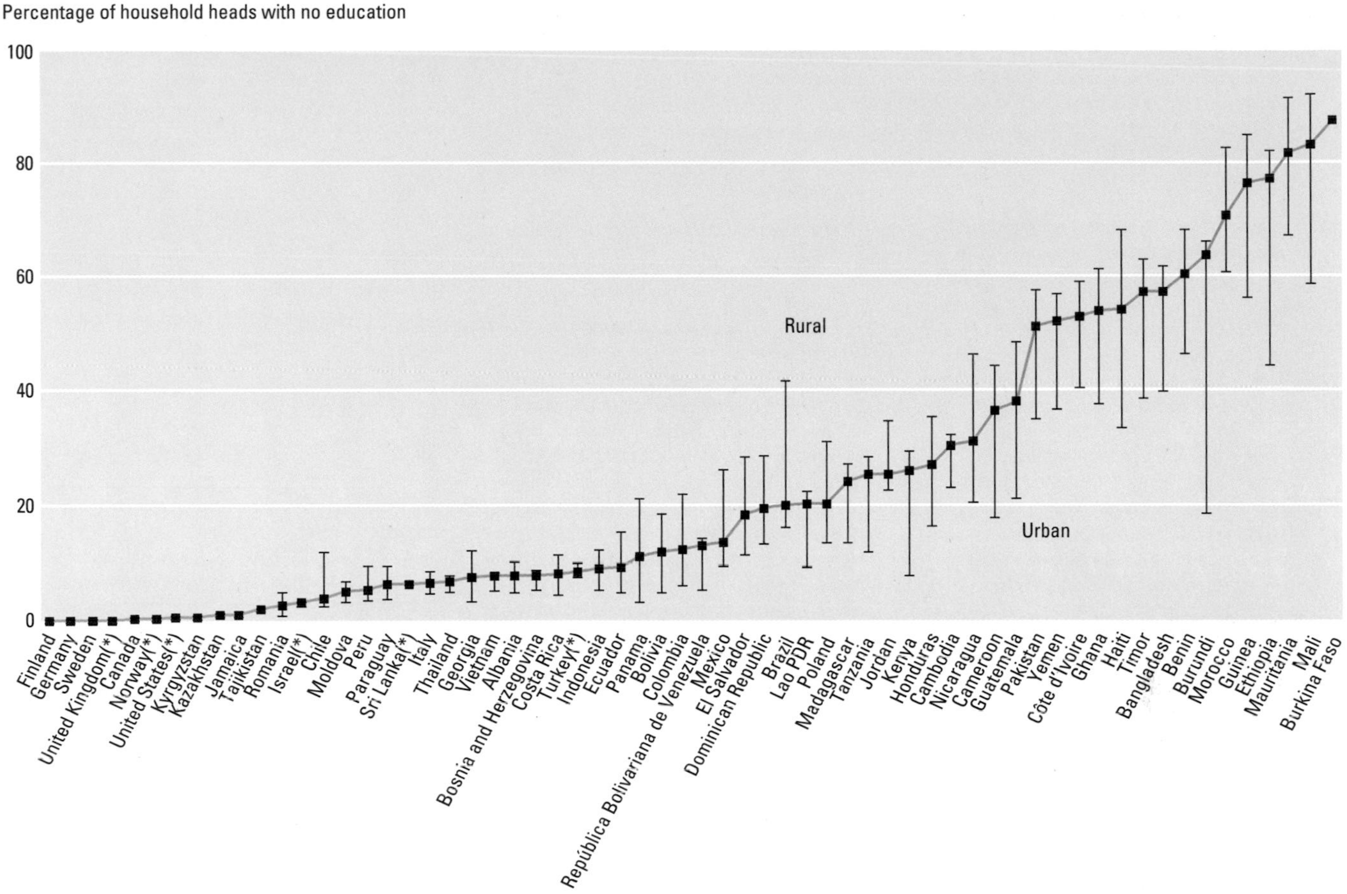

Percentage of household heads with no education

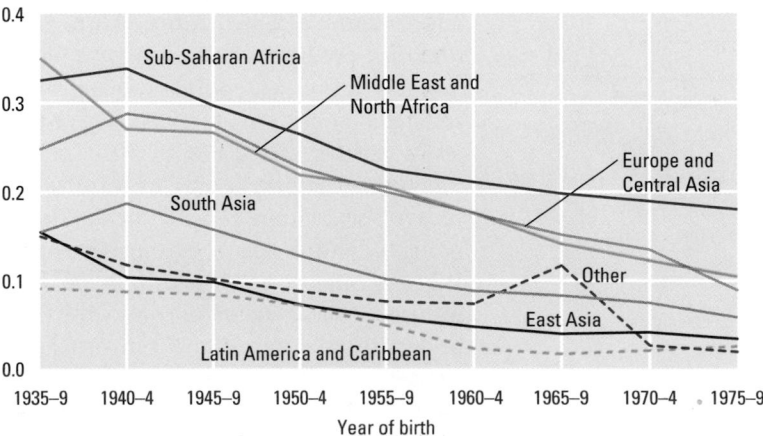

Rural

Urban

Source: Authors' calculations from household survey data.
Note: The continuous dark line represents the percentage of household heads with no education in each country, while the endpoints of the whiskers indicate the percentages for urban and rural households.
* Indicates that rural households have higher average levels of education than urban households.

and income inequality are expected to correlate reasonably well with long-term well-being, it is unclear exactly how well they actually do. And different measures of economic welfare—based on income, consumption, or wealth—can yield quite different assessments of inequality (see also box 2.5).

For example, Sudjana and Mishra (2004), drawing on evidence produced by Claessens, Djankov, and Lang (2000), argue that wealth inequality in Indonesia is far more concentrated than suggested by comparable figures based on consumption (figure 2.8). In 1996 more than 57 percent of the stock market capitalization in Indonesia was controlled by 10 families. This is in stark contrast to neighboring countries, such as Singapore and Malaysia, but it is

Figure 2.7 The share of inequality in years of schooling attributable to differences between males and females has been declining

Between-group contribution to total inequality
(proportion)

Sub-Saharan Africa

Middle East and
North Africa

Europe and
Central Asia

South Asia

Other

East Asia

Latin America and Caribbean

Year of birth

Source: Araujo, Ferreira, and Schady (2004).

BOX 2.5 *Beware of intercountry comparisons of inequality!*

Because countries differ in their data collection systems, cross-country data on economic inequality are generally based on a variety of indicators that are treated interchangeably. The lack of a uniform basis for measuring economic inequality in different countries has serious implications for comparability.

One of the main sources of noncomparability of inequality is that some countries use household income as indicator of well-being while others use consumption expenditures (Atkinson and Brandolini 2001). These two indicators capture different aspects of economic welfare, with the former perhaps seen better as a measure of welfare opportunity and the latter as a measure of welfare achievement. In most countries, measured inequality based on income is higher than if it is based on consumption. But this is not inevitable, and the degree to which the two indicators disagree varies from country to country (see table to the right).

The problem of comparability is not confined to the choice of welfare indicator. An important but underappreciated additional issue is that, even for a given indicator, its definition varies considerably across countries and even within countries over time. Consumption inequality based on different definitions of consumption can vary markedly, and will depend on a variety of factors, including the following:

- The length of the recall period over which consumption is recorded.

- The degree of disaggregation of consumption items.
- The methods for imputation of housing and durables consumption.

Similarly, income inequality can vary depending on whether income—

- Is intended to capture pre- or post-tax income,
- Includes actual and implicit transfers, and
- Refers to full income or earnings only.

Additional factors confounding comparability include differences in survey nonresponse rates across countries (which are likely to affect measured inequality—see Korinek, Mistiaen, and Ravallion forthcoming). Differences across countries in the availability of spatial price indexes can also affect conclusions. Thomas (1987) demonstrates that adjusting for spatial price variation can affect conclusions about the degree of income or consumption inequality. Across countries there tends to be little uniformity in whether, and how, spatial price variation is accommodated.

Cross-country datasets on economic inequality generally incorporate some attempts to improve comparability, but they typically fall far short of achieving strict comparability. Without a concerted effort to harmonize data collection across countries, it is unlikely that such global databases can be relied on to provide more than a tentative picture of differences in inequality across countries.

Inequality: summary measures in a selection of countries: consumption versus income

		Gini coefficient	
	Year	Consumption	Income
Panama	1997	0.468	0.621
Brazil	1996	0.497	0.596
Thailand	2000	0.428	0.523
Nicaragua	1998	0.417	0.534
Peru	1994	0.446	0.523
Morocco	1998	0.390	0.586
Vietnam	1998	0.362	0.489
Nepal	1996	0.366	0.513
Albania	1996	0.252	0.392
Bulgaria	1995	0.274	0.392
Russian Federation	1997	0.474	0.478
Bangladesh	2000	0.334	0.392

Source: Authors' creation.

Figure 2.8 Market capitalization controlled by the top 10 families in selected countries, 1996

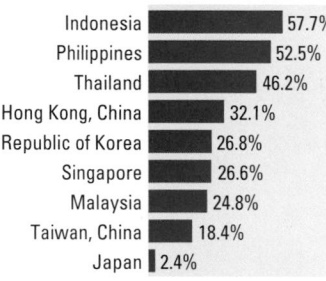

Indonesia	57.7%
Philippines	52.5%
Thailand	46.2%
Hong Kong, China	32.1%
Republic of Korea	26.8%
Singapore	26.6%
Malaysia	24.8%
Taiwan, China	18.4%
Japan	2.4%

Source: Claessens, Djankov, and Lang (2000).

only marginally higher than the figure for the Philippines. More generally, Davies and Shorrocks (2005) report estimates published by Merrill Lynch and Forbes that some 20 percent of the world's millionaires come from the developing world. Similarly, Morck, Stangeland, and Yeung (2000) find a higher ratio of billionaire wealth to gross domestic product (GDP) in Latin America and the Caribbean, and East Asia, but not India and South Africa (see chapters 6 and 9 for further discussion). These figures imply that the distribution of wealth may, on average, be more concentrated in developing countries than in the developed. When wealth is associated with political influence, such inequalities also translate into political capture and can provide a window on this added dimension of opportunity.

Bearing in mind the warnings offered in box 2.5, figure 2.9 provides an approximate

picture of how economic inequality is distributed across countries. The highest levels of recorded inequality occur in Africa, the second highest in Latin America. But inequality measures for Latin America come largely from income data, while those in other regions, such as South Asia, come mainly from consumption data. As box 2.5 illustrated, income data tend to produce higher measured inequality. Within regions, the data suggest that inequality can vary markedly between countries: consumption inequality in South Africa is extremely high, while in Mauritius it is lower even than in OECD countries.

How much overall economic inequality within countries is attributable to differences across population groups? Unlike health and education inequalities, the systematic decomposition of income inequality by population groups has long been subject to analysis in the economics literature.

Figure 2.9 Africa and Latin America have the world's highest levels of inequality
Income and expenditure Gini coefficients

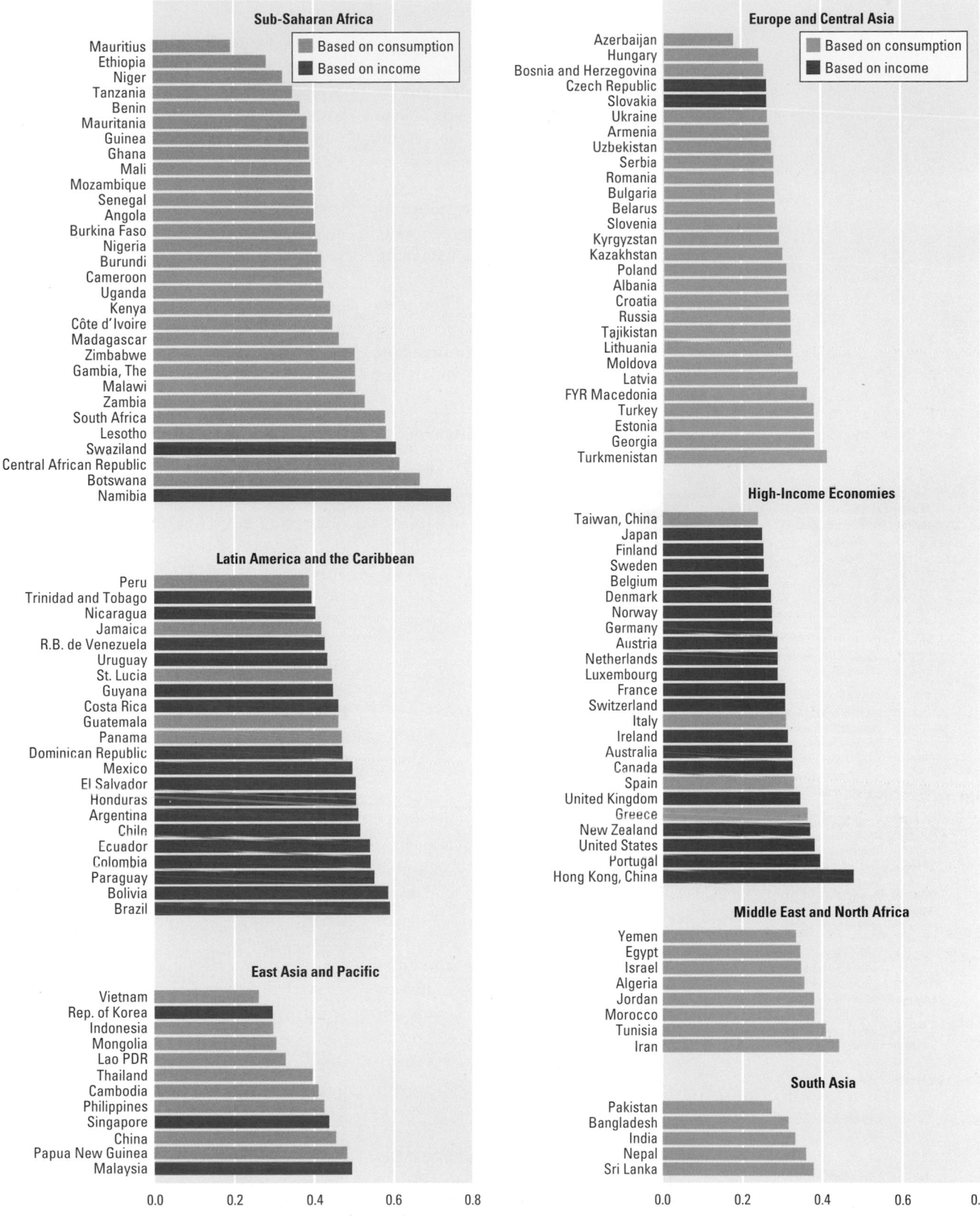

Source: Authors' calculations from household survey data.

These decomposition exercises seek to understand what share of inequality can be attributed to differences between groups and what to inequality within groups. There are several attractions to studying certain population groups in this way and to comparing findings across countries.

Our interest here is to define groups by circumstances we might consider "morally irrelevant," thereby gaining a window on the importance of inequality of opportunity in the economic sphere. Additionally, decomposition results generally are far less sensitive to differences in definitions of underlying welfare indicators than are measured levels of inequality. In that sense, some of the difficulties with cross-country comparisons described in box 2.5 are attenuated by subgroup decompositions.

Between-group shares of total inequality

While the "between-group" share of overall inequality is an appealing indicator of the salience of differences across groups in the overall assessment of inequality, there are concerns about its interpretation.[8] In particular, empirical measures of between-group shares are generally found to be quite low (see figures 2.10 and 2.11).[9] The conventional presentation of between-group inequality is relative to total inequality. Elbers and others (2005), however, note that total inequality can be viewed as the between-group inequality that would be observed if every household in the population constituted a separate group. Clearly, against such a benchmark, one would rarely observe a high share of between-group inequality.

Elbers and his colleagues propose an alternative, comparing the actual between-group inequality with the maximum possible inequality that would be obtained by keeping the number of groups and their sizes at actual levels. For example, an assessment of the contribution of gender differences to inequality compares actual between-gender inequality with the hypothetical between-gender inequality that would be obtained by sorting the income distribution so that all males appeared at one end of the distribution and all females at the other. This ratio provides a measure of how far actual between-group inequality lies below the maximum between-group inequality that is feasible given the existing configuration of groups.

Economic inequality can be decomposed in a large sample of countries based on several population breakdowns, two of which are presented in figures 2.10 and 2.11: social group and education of household head. Such decompositions can follow the conventional decomposition methodology, complemented by the Elbers and others (2005) measure of feasible group decomposition.

Figure 2.10 Between-group inequality decompositions: social group of the household head

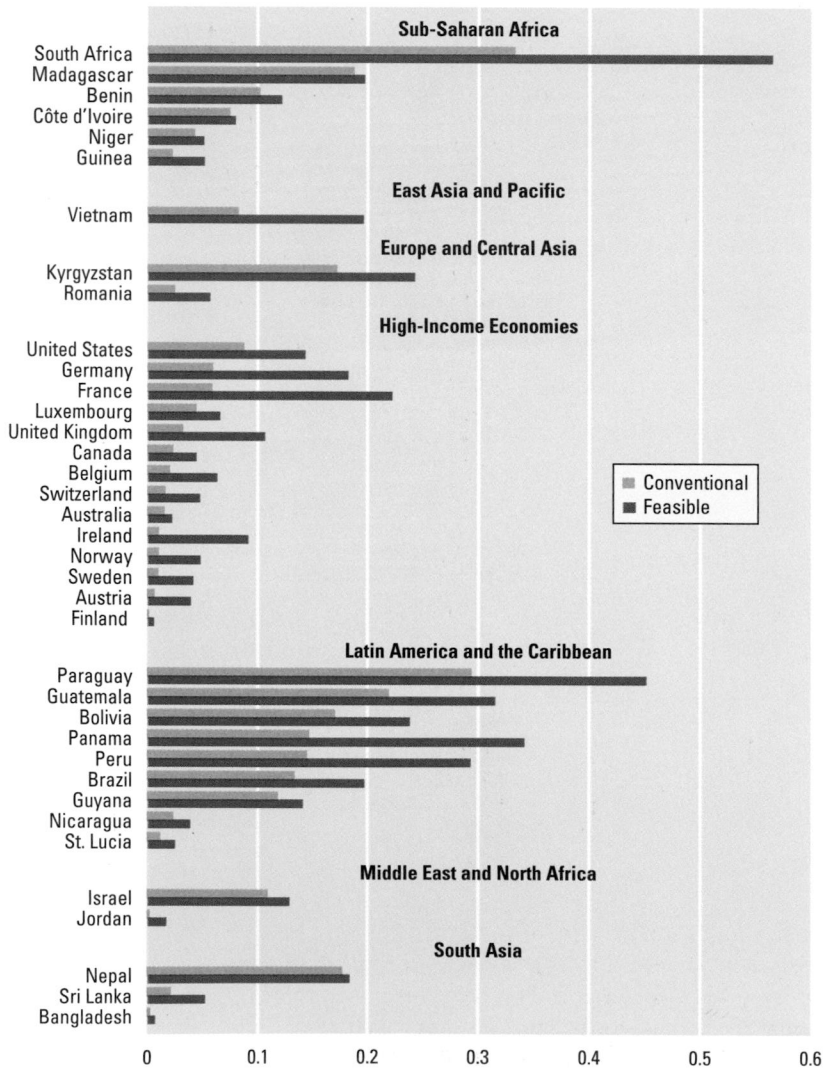

Source: Authors' calculations from household survey data.

Figure 2.11 Between-group inequality decompositions: education of the household head

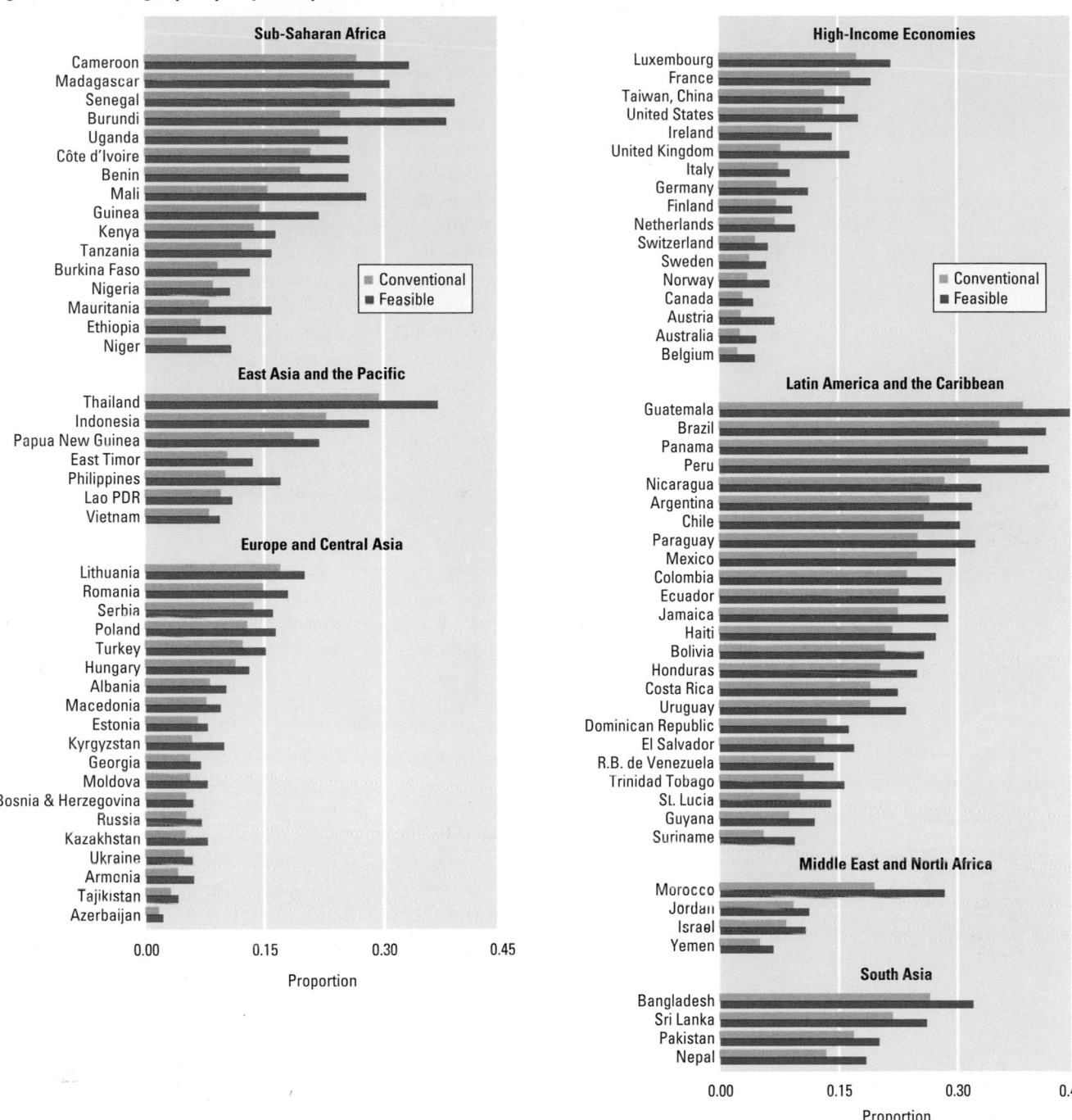

Source: Authors' calculations from household survey data.

Different population breakdowns contribute to differing extents to overall inequality. In general, the conventional calculation of the between-group contribution points to a fairly low share attributable to between-group differences. But in some countries even the conventional share is high. For example, in Paraguay, when inequality is decomposed between groups by language spoken at home, the conventional between-group share is approximately 30 percent (figure 2.10). And when inequality is decomposed for five broad education groups in Guatemala, the between-group contribution is above 40 percent (figure 2.11).

In most countries, the between-group share is noticeably higher for decompositions based on the alternative, "feasible" calculation. Based on this approach, observed between-group differences are indeed substantial in many countries—for the group definitions here. To the extent that these circumstances are judged "morally irrelevant," the findings suggest that in economic life, just as in health and education, a substantial portion of observed inequality in many developing countries can be linked to inequalities of opportunity.

Spatial differences

As with inequalities in health, conventional survey data cannot say much about the contribution of finely detailed spatial heterogeneity to overall inequality—because of the limited sample size. In an exercise analogous to that for health in Cambodia (figure 2.4), a variety of studies have applied statistical techniques to combine survey data with population census data to produce tentative estimates of inequality at the community and district levels. Elbers and others (2004) document the contribution to overall estimated inequality of differences in mean consumption for subdistricts in Ecuador, Madagascar, and Mozambique. They demonstrate that the between-subdistrict contribution to total estimated inequality ranges from a low of 22 percent in Mozambique to more than 40 percent in Ecuador (table 2.1). Based on a similar approach, World Bank (2004e) reports between-commune differences in Morocco, accounting for 40 percent of overall estimated consumption inequality. The general impression is that spatial differences across locali-

ties account for a larger share of total inequality as the number of localities increases. The analysis confirms that for some countries the spatial dimension of inequality is of considerable importance. This conclusion carries over even more powerfully at the global level, where the between-country contribution to global inequality is dramatic (chapter 3).

Other studies and methodologies corroborate the finding that spatial differences within countries are important. Using farm-household data for rural China, Jalan and Ravallion (1997) identify "spatial poverty traps," where poorer areas have lower provisions of essential public goods (such as roads) and, as a result, households in the area experience lower productivity on their investments. Various studies find spatial effects on living standards, even after controlling for nongeographic household characteristics. Ravallion and Wodon (1999) demonstrate that place of residence is an important determinant of poverty in Bangladesh. They also note that important spatial differences can be discerned even within urban areas—households in the district of Dhaka are markedly better off than their counterparts in other urban districts.

Many studies suggest that spatial differences in incomes are driven by policy. In China, Kanbur and Zhang (2001) find a measurable polarization between inland and coastal regions where factors unrelated to physical geography—development of heavy industry in certain provinces, trade openness, and government investment in coastal regions—are associated with widening interregional inequality. Escobal and Torero (2003) compare coastal Peru with the highlands and find that average per capita expenditures vary markedly and that this variance is associated with fewer and weaker infrastructure services in the highlands.

The role of infrastructure is thus central. Although it is not disputed that physical geography can also influence poverty directly, the association between geographic variation in poverty and geographic variation in infrastructure access is typically strong. Accordingly, it is argued that the influence of regional geographic location on inequality will diminish as access to transport and

Table 2.1   Decomposition of inequality between and within communities

Level of decomposition	Number of communities	Within-group inequality (percent)	Between-group inequality (percent)
Ecuador	1,579	58.8	41.2
Madagascar	1,248	74.6	25.4
Mozambique	424	78.0	22.0

Source: Elbers and others (2004).
Note: Our communities in Ecuador are zonas in urban areas and parroquias in rural areas. Communities in Madagascar are firiasana (communes) and in Mozambique they are administrative posts. The decompositions are performed using the conventional methodology.

communications services improve; being geographically isolated will matter less because infrastructure improvements will help compensate for distance.[10]

The relationship between group differences and inequality

As is clear from the discussion here, our interest in the contribution of group differences to total inequality extends beyond normative considerations of fairness and justice. Differences between groups are also thought to explain overall inequality outcomes, particularly the reproduction of inequalities over time. The basic idea is that between-group differences in income inequality, for example, will tend also to be mirrored in between-group differences in health and education inequalities—and in the agency of groups in influencing their circumstances (see below). These group differences will then reinforce one another. Group differences in education, for example, will translate into differences in incomes and in political voice and participation. These inequalities will, in turn, affect health inequalities between groups, which are passed on to education inequalities and so on. "Inequality traps" are the result. A corollary of this idea is that efforts to moderate overall inequality levels might require a focus on reducing between-group differences.

It is difficult to systematically document this instrumental role of group differences. Figure 2.12 illustrates one attempt. Overall inequality is correlated with the between-group share for the sample of countries in figures 2.10 and 2.11, controlling for region and whether the underlying welfare indicator is income or consumption. Nothing in the mechanics of the calculation forces overall inequality to be correlated with the share attributable to between-group differences. Yet, for this sample of countries, higher overall inequality is associated with a larger between-group share of overall inequality, which is attributable to the rural-urban breakdown, to differences across social groups, to differences in education, and (weakly) to differences in broad occupation class of the household head.[11]

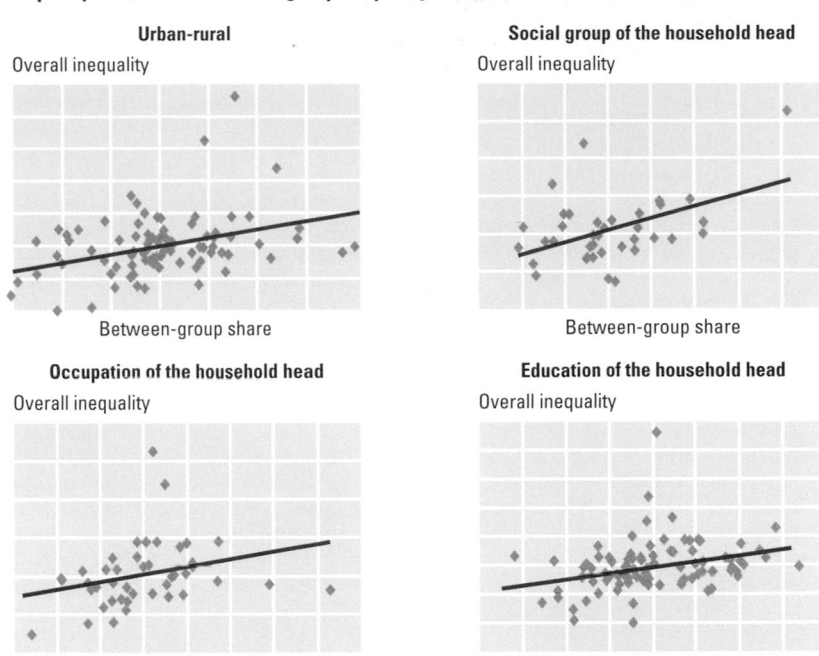

Figure 2.12 Location, education, and social groups can make a difference: regressions of total inequality on shares of between-group inequality of different household characteristics

Source: Authors' calculations from household survey data.
Note: Regressions include as controls (X) regional area dummies and a welfare measure (Y/C) dummy. The shares of the between component of inequality across gender and age of the household head, and regions within the country were not significant.

One interpretation of these findings is that between-group differences account for, and possibly explain, a non-negligible portion of overall inequality. This is consistent with the broader theme of this report: that group differences reinforce one another and in this way contribute to the replication of inequality over time. But these simple correlations, while suggestive, could also be pointing to other processes and on their own cannot exclude other competing explanations.

Inequality and growth, economic structure, and trade

Systematic exploration of the impact of between-group shares on overall inequality has not, to date, been a major topic of empirical investigation. A longer-standing question in economics has been how inequality evolves with economic growth more generally. Pioneering work by Kuznets in the 1950s launched an enormous amount of empirical work on this question, stimulating much debate. There is still no

BOX 2.6 *Revisiting the Kuznets hypothesis for economic growth and inequality*

The starting point of the literature linking economic development and income inequality dates to the well-known works of two Nobel Prize winners, W. Arthur Lewis (1954) and Simon Kuznets (1955). Lewis, in his classic 1954 article "Economic Development with Unlimited Supplies of Labor," developed a theoretical model in which growth and accumulation in a dual economy would start in the modern industrial sector, where capitalists would hire at a given wage and reinvest a share of their profits. The number of traditional agricultural laborers willing to move to this high-productivity, high-wage sector was assumed to be unlimited. In this process of development, and as long as these assumptions would prevail, inequality in the distribution of income would increase as average incomes rose. There would be a turning point after which inequality would fall again as the surplus labor phase ends and the dualistic economy becomes a single-sector, fully industrialized economy.

Although Kuznets did not explicitly model the intersectoral shifts of population as part of the development process, he did build on them to articulate his basic idea of an inverted-U relationship between economic growth and income inequality (the "Kuznets curve"). In his presidential address at the Annual Meeting of the American Economic Association in 1954, he hypothesized that in the process of growth and industrialization, inequality would first increase, because of the shift from agriculture and the countryside to industry and the city, and then decrease as returns across sectors equalized. The data Kuznets used to make this statement came

from a long-run series of inequality indicators for England, Germany, and the United States, and from a single observation in time for three developing countries—India, Ceylon (Sri Lanka today), and Puerto Rico. These were the data available at that time, and Kuznets was well aware of the limitations of the empirical backing of his argument, in his own words, on "5 percent of empirical information and 95 percent speculation, some of it possibly tainted by wishful thinking."

Kuznets based his speculation primarily on longitudinal data and called for in-depth case studies of the economic growth of nations. But many subsequent studies simply used aggregate cross-country data (often of not particularly high quality) and reduced-form models to explore and support the hypothesis of an inevitable tradeoff between development and equality. The Kuznets curve became one of the most quoted stylized facts of the study of income distribution for nearly four decades.

Cross-country data can be misleading for dynamic processes
With the development of much larger data sets, such as the Deininger and Squire (1996) international inequality database (following on from Fields 1989), empirical "tests" of the Kuznets curve were widely conducted. But it has become understood that the use of cross-country data to analyze what are essentially dynamic processes can be strongly misleading. Moreover, numerous studies have shown that the evidence in favor of the Kuznets curve is not at all robust to econometric specifications, sample

composition, and period of observation. See, among others, Bourguignon and Morrisson (1989), Fields and Jakubson (1994), Deininger and Squire (1998), and Bruno, Ravallion, and Squire (1998). Bruno, Ravallion, and Squire (1998), while drawing in part on cross-country data, also analyzed one country—India—for which relatively long time-series data had become available, and again found no sign that growth increased inequality.

Why the Kuznets curve does not hold in practice probably has to do with the fact that developing countries do not generally satisfy the assumptions on migration processes and sectoral development underlying the Kuznets hypothesis. To explain international differences in inequality of incomes, it is important that the link between economic inequalities and other factors, such as economic dualism, land, education, and regional differences, be more carefully analyzed.

No straightforward relationship between income and inequality
To conclude, there is today something of a consensus that no straightforward relation between income and inequality can be established. As argued by Kanbur (2000) in his exhaustive review of the Kuznets curve literature in the *Handbook of Income Distribution:* "it seems to us far better to focus directly on policies, or combination of policies, which will generate growth without adverse distributional effects, rather than rely on the existence or nonexistence of an aggregative, reduced form relationship between per capita income and inequality."

Source: Authors' creation.

consensus on a systematic relationship between the long-term growth processes of industrialization and urbanization—and overall inequality (box 2.6).

Cross-country studies have also analyzed the relationship between inequality and economic structure. Bourguignon and Morrison (1990), for example, argue that "developing countries which are comparatively endowed with mineral resources and land (climate) tend to be less egalitarian than others, although the effect of the agricultural comparative advantage may be offset by the distribution of land." They also find that the labor productivity difference between agriculture and the rest of the economy is a powerful explanatory factor for differences in income inequality in a number of developing countries in the 1970s and 1980s.[12]

A large body of literature has also explored the relationship between trade openness and inequality but has not reached a consensus. For example, Dollar and Kraay (2002) and Dollar and Kraay (2004) find no effect of trade openness on inequality, but Lundberg and Squire (2003) do find such an effect. Ravallion (2001) and Milanovic (2002) report that at low incomes openness may be inequality-increasing, but that this effect reverses at higher incomes.

Trends

The discussion above highlights the many mechanisms for hypothesizing how aggregate economic growth, and the evolution of different sectors of the economy, can influence economic inequality. Popular lines of argument have emphasized Lewis-Kuznets type processes, the race between relative supply and demand for skills along with household adjustments to participation, education, and fertility; the transitions from controlled to market-oriented economic systems; and various forms of power and bargaining-related views of the world. In the end, and perhaps not surprisingly, it is difficult to identify a single overarching explanation. Until recently, this did not seem to matter much because there was a general perception that inequality does not vary markedly over short periods.[13] In earlier studies, few countries having data on inequality over multiple time periods indicated sharp changes.

For countries and regions. Empirical investigation of how inequality evolves in a country is subject to concerns similar to those for comparisons of levels (see box 2.5). But there is a growing sense that the impression of stable, unchanging income inequality may well be misleading. A few recent examples of changing inequality bear mentioning. First, careful work by Atkinson (2003) has documented the evolution of inequality in OECD countries during the second half the twentieth century. He finds that inequality in the United States has been rising steadily since the early 1970s (after seeing little change, and possibly some decline, in the preceding decades) and has risen dramatically in the United Kingdom since 1980. Between 1984 and 1990, the Gini coefficient in the United Kingdom rose by 10 percentage points (but then did not increase further)—an unprecedented increase over such a short time. Elsewhere in the OECD, inequality changes have been less marked. But to the extent that the early and middle decades of the twentieth century were associated with declining inequality in these countries, this trend seems to have halted by the century's later decades.

Second, inequality in China was markedly higher at the end of the 1990s than it had been in the early part of the 1980s. In general, the recent evidence in East Asia suggests that inequality has risen faster in the second round of high growth Asian economies—such as China and Vietnam—than had been observed in the first

round—Hong Kong (China), Republic of Korea, Malaysia, Singapore, and Taiwan (China). A complete picture of the factors behind this process is as yet unclear. Although it is likely that at least part of the story is linked to intersectoral transfers, as emphasized by Lewis (box 2.6), Ravallion and Chen (2004) indicate that inequality in China grew fastest during periods when economic growth and poverty reduction were slow. They argue that China provides little support for the view that rising inequality is inevitable with rapid economic growth and poverty reduction.

Third, South Asia has generally been perceived as a region with relatively low inequality. This probably is due, in part, to inequality being measured by consumption. In this region, too, the prevailing view has been that inequality changes little over time. But the stylized fact of low and stable inequality in South Asia has also been challenged. In India, the largest country in the region, some uncertainty remains over how inequality has evolved, because of well-publicized issues concerning data comparability over time.[14] The best available estimates suggest that inequality in India has been rising, but with no solid assessment of by how much.[15]

In Bangladesh, Nepal, and Sri Lanka, however, recent and reliable data show very large increases of inequality in the late 1980s and 1990s. In Bangladesh, income inequality (as opposed to consumption inequality) has been documented to have risen from a Gini of 0.30 to 0.41 between 1991 and 2000.[16] In Sri Lanka, the increase in consumption inequality has been very similar, from 0.32 to 0.40 between 1990 and 2002.[17] And, in Nepal, the Planning Commission has produced estimates suggesting that consumption inequality rose from 0.34 to 0.39 between 1995–6 and 2003–4.[18] Only in Pakistan is the evolution of inequality not clear, because of difficulties with data comparability.

In other regions of the world, the recent picture on inequality trends is more difficult to summarize. For Latin America, De Ferranti and others (2004) indicate that inequality increased in most countries, by a sizable margin, during the "lost decade" of the 1980s. But during the 1990s, inequality continued to rise in only about half of the countries in the region, and less rapidly. The authors note that, in Argentina, inequality has risen sharply in the growth period and during the crisis years. In Brazil and Mexico, the 1990s witnessed some small declines. In Eastern Europe and Central Asia, changes in inequality during the early 1990s, associated with the transition to the market economy, have been difficult to document systematically because of data problems, according to World Bank (2000c). Between 1998 and 2003, consumption inequality declined in the former Soviet Union countries (with the exception of Georgia and Tajikistan), while there was no clear trend in eastern and southern European countries (World Bank, 2005a). In Africa and the Middle East, it is difficult to point to broad trends, largely because of concerns with data comparability over time.

To what extent does our examination of levels and trends in income inequality bear on the themes of this report? This report is most concerned about changes in inequalities in incomes, and other specific dimensions, if these dimensions are associated with changes in underlying inequalities of opportunities. Rising income inequality in Russia during the 1990s, for example, is of concern precisely because of its strong association with rising political influence and state capture.

But this is not inevitably the case. A recent study of income distribution dynamics in six East Asian and Latin American countries by Bourguignon, Ferreira, and Lustig (2005) decomposes income distribution dynamics into the underlying driving forces. They show that complex and country-specific interactions between powerful underlying social and economic phenomena imply that distributional experiences must be assessed country by country. For example, improvements in education (equalizing opportunities) may be associated in one case with falling income inequality—Brazil or Taiwan, China—but in another country with rising inequality—Indonesia or Mexico. Our assessment of the equity implications of changes in income inequality will thus differ across countries.

Across generations. Our assessment will also depend on the degree to which inequalities are transmitted across generations. The study of intergenerational transmission of welfare is not straightforward, because of the scarcity of datasets containing information on various generations of adults in the same family. Data from long panels are rare, and questions about family background of individuals are not always asked in surveys (the Brazil data described in box 2.1 are a rare exception). Information about education or occupation for various generations can be captured relatively easily in recall questionnaires. But information about other dimensions, such as the incomes, earnings, or even health status of earlier generations, is not easily remembered by individuals (not least because they often change during a lifetime). The scarcity of intergenerational data is particularly striking in developing countries. Even though the persistence of inequalities across generations is often thought to be much more acute in developing countries, studies on intergenerational mobility in the developing world remain few and far between.

Even when the data exist, differences in methodologies and data often limit the scope for comparisons across countries. The most widespread measure of intergenerational mobility in the economics literature is the intergenerational earnings elasticity, or the elasticity of sons' earnings with the earnings of their parents. This measure generally comes from a log-linear regression of sons' earnings (although it could also be income or years of schooling) on fathers' observed earnings (or its predicted value using such other information as education or occupation). The closer the elasticity is to zero, the more mobile the society is supposed to be. This elasticity has been widely used in the U.S. literature, where longitudinal data are relatively abundant. And for comparability, it has also been calculated in most other countries' recent studies.[19]

Until recently, estimates of the intergenerational elasticity of earnings were thought to be around 0.4 in the United States, suggesting a reasonably mobile society in incomes.[20] More recently, however, Mazumder (2005) uses new data and recent econometric techniques to correct for transitory fluctuations in earnings—he shows that the previous estimates of intergenerational elasticity were biased downward by about 30 percent. He argues that the true estimate is somewhere around 0.6 for the United States.

> An intergenerational elasticity of 0.6 compared to 0.4 paints a dramatically different picture of mobility in American society. For example, it implies that a family whose earnings are half the national average would require five generations instead of three before it substantially closed the gap. Obviously a difference of two generations, or about fifty years, is quite substantial and suggests the need to examine policies that foster greater mobility.[21]

In parallel analyses, estimates of intergenerational mobility in Canada, Finland, or Sweden, among others, have tended to report elasticities closer to 0.2 or lower, suggesting that these societies are considerably more mobile than the United States. A relatively early study of mobility in the United Kingdom (Atkinson, Maynard, and Trinder 1983) reports an elasticity of 0.43, while a more recent study by Dearden, Machin, and Reed (1997) estimates an elasticity of 0.57. These studies indicate that people in the United Kingdom are about as mobile as those in the United States. Because of the data limitations, only a few exceptional studies on intergenerational earnings elasticities for less-developed countries have been carried out. These provide evidence of relatively low mobility.[22]

In another literature review of cross-country differences in intergenerational earnings mobility, Solon (2002) asks whether there is any link between cross-sectional inequality within a generation and the intergenerational transmission of inequality. Although there is greater cross-sectional inequality in the United States and the United Kingdom than in Sweden or Finland, Canada also has relatively high inequality. The evidence needed to provide a clear answer to this question is therefore still fragmentary, and only "con-tinuing research (on international evidence of intergenerational mobility) will improve our understanding of why the intergenerational transmission of economic status is strong in some countries and weak in others."[23]

The intergenerational transmission mechanisms of inequalities will differ across countries and within countries across different population groups. As described above, Mazumder (2005) points to rather low levels of intergenerational mobility in the United States. He also highlights an important racial dimension to this limited mobility and finds evidence of substantial immobility at the ends of the distribution. He shows that of the individuals whose fathers were in the bottom decile of the earnings distribution, 50 percent will be below the thirtieth percentile and 80 percent below the sixtieth percentile. He finds the evidence to be consistent with the hypothesis that such immobility "might be due to the inability of families to invest in their children's human capital due to the lack of resources." By contrast, more than 50 percent of the individuals whose parents were in the top decile will remain above the eightieth percentile and two-thirds will be above the median.

In another U.S. study, Hertz (2005) confirms the findings of Mazumder (and others) on the size of the intergenerational elasticity. He then shows evidence that it is largely driven by the especially low rate of mobility of black families from the bottom of the income distribution. While only 17 percent of whites born to the bottom decile of family income remain there as adults, the corresponding figure is 42 percent for blacks. He also finds that "rags-to-riches" transitions from the bottom quartile to the top were less than half as likely for black as for white families. He further provides evidence that the black-white mobility gap is not "appreciably altered by controlling for parents' years of schooling." Last, he provides evidence that the incomes of black children are unresponsive to small changes in parents' incomes at the bottom of the distribution.

To recap, summary measures suggest that even in such developed countries as the

United States and United Kingdom there is rather limited intergenerational mobility across generations. Research in these countries has highlighted important heterogeneities in the patterns of reproduction of different inequalities across populations groups. For most developing countries, relatively little is known about intergenerational income mobility. But given the acute group-based inequalities in many developing countries, there appears to be little basis for expecting much intergenerational mobility.

Agency and equity: inequalities of power

The foregoing discussion has raised explicitly the question of how inequalities are determined and reproduced. It has pointed to the potentially important role of group differences in this process. This focus on process and the factors that account for the persistence of inequality over time puts the spotlight on how much inequality is rooted in deeper institutions in society—institutions of governance, access to land, control of labor, market regulation. Chapter 6 deals with the emergence and effects of such institutions in more detail. Here we turn to different kinds of evidence—and traditions of analysis—to discuss the unequal capacity of people to influence the form taken by these institutions and the consequences of unequal institutions for continuing inequality in such capacities. For poverty the inequalities in capacity to forge the institution or society can be as important as inequalities in health, income, and education.[24]

A recent study of inequalities in governance in four slums of Delhi found that access to formal government by slum dwellers is more available to the better off and to those who have good contact networks.[25] Community leaders in these slums facilitate access primarily to their caste members, and slum dwellers are more likely to delegate custodianship of their interests to better-educated community leaders. The study concludes that because access to bureaucracy and political representation for slum dwellers in Delhi is largely the preserve of the better off and better connected, decisions of formal policymakers do not seek to represent slum interests as a whole, producing interventions that do not target those in most need. The lack of broadly distributed "voice" thus results in patterns of resource allocation, and income generation, that are far from egalitarian.

The nature of this unequal capacity can be captured through the sociological concept of agency. Agency refers to people's capacity to transform or reproduce such societal institutions. Some of this capacity is conscious—for example, when interest groups lobby for a change in land tenure legislation, or when women refuse to accept laws around marriage that systematically disadvantage them. Some of it is uncon-

---

BOX 2.7 *Inequitable agencies and institutions in Pakistan*

A recently completed Human Development Report for Pakistan provides rich documentation of the skewed distributional impact of corruption (United Nations Development Programme 2003). The report notes that corruption raises the costs of getting things done—for setting up a new business, for crossing borders, for obtaining a driver's license. In Pakistan these costs fall most heavily on those least able to afford them: the poor. According to the Pakistan Human Development Report, 16.7 percent of the extremely poor reported paying a bribe to run their business enterprise, handing over an average of 6,800 rupees. Only 6.7 percent of the non-poor paid a bribe, of 9,300 rupees. In rural areas, the contrast is even starker: 20 percent of

the extremely poor paid a bribe, while only 4.3 percent of the non-poor had to do so. In urban areas, the extremely poor paid on average 8,700 rupees in bribes, while the non-poor paid only 1,200 rupees.

Similar patterns emerge for mediating disputes. The extremely poor not only pay a higher price to seek a resolution than the non-poor, but also they are less likely to receive a satisfactory outcome (38.5 percent versus 80.8 percent). Indeed, the fee the extremely poor must pay is often higher than their annual household income, leaving many to choose to suffer the consequences of a dispute even when they are clearly in the right. In addition, the extremely poor receive less assistance from the police (the

most immediate representatives of the formal justice system), who are involved in only 1 percent of their disputes but nearly 5 percent of the disputes of the non-poor. The poor perceive that the police will be slow and inefficient in handling their cases, and they frequently experience outright harassment and intimidation. Even to register a case of kidnapping with the police requires paying a bribe. In these situations, it is hardly surprising that the poor find it more expedient to take the law into their own hands, creating in many urban areas a host of new problems related to gang violence and vigilantism.

Source: United Nations Development Programme (2003).

BOX 2.8 *Legacies of discrimination and the reproduction of inequalities and poverty among the Batwa in Uganda*

The Batwa, who are described in many parts as pygmy peoples, live in Eastern Uganda, eastern Democratic Republic of Congo, and Rwanda. Batwa have been subject to negative stereotypes since at least 1751, when Edward Tyson concluded that pygmies were not human but rather apes or monkeys. They suffer multiple asset depletion and wide ranging forms of discrimination, a situation that public actions have at times made worse. Though longstanding forest dwellers, the British sought to expel them to create forest reserves in the 1930s. In 1991, the Uganda National Park authorities increased efforts to enforce this exclusion from forest areas. Although the World Bank—which was funding some of the park authorities' work—required that the government assess the impact on indigenous communities and follow defined compensation procedures, these did not take sufficient account

of power differences among Batwa and other affected groups, nor consider Batwa preferences. All communities were viewed as uniform, a practice that the authorities later recognized "did not take into account Batwa realities and left them with nothing" (Zaninka (2003), 170).

Non-Batwa locals have resisted efforts to provide more appropriate compensation to the Batwa. A Participatory Poverty Assessment (PPA) highlighted persistent discrimination, describing the Batwa as a "group of people who are despised" and who "have no means of production such as land, credit and training. They are regarded by other ethnic groups in Kisoro as a people with no rights." This leads to everyday and institutionalized forms of exclusion, with the Batwa suffering discrimination in access to both public spaces and services. While some Batwa respond to this by organizing themselves, others

respond in ways that—however rational and self-protecting—often reproduce the extent to which they are excluded. The same PPA reports some Batwa children saying that they did not attend school because it was so unfriendly to them. When asked what they wanted to do upon completing school, one child replied that she wished to be "a cleaner." Discrimination and prejudice diminish the capacity to aspire to and imagine a different future.

Repudiation and discrimination can also lead the Batwa to self-exclude from the public sphere. The PPA notes that no Batwa attended PPA exercises. Non-Batwa locals explained: "Batwa would never come to such meetings, so there is no point in mobilizing them."

Source: Moncrieffe (2005), citing Participatory Poverty Assessment reports.

---

scious—for example, when people engage in land transactions without questioning them, they reproduce the institutions of land tenure and the markets in land. When a disadvantaged group accepts its disadvantage as "taken for granted," the effect is to allow the continuing existence of the relationships that create such disadvantage.

The internalization of disadvantage leads to pernicious forms of agency that perpetuate inequalities. From inequalities in agency come inequalities in power, voice, and self-confidence—a major part of our story (box 2.7). Inequalities of agency are as much products of dominant institutions as sources of those institutional arrangements. Maintaining these arrangements both reflects and produces the distribution of power among people. As for health, education, and income, though, this distribution can change—and it has. Indeed, it has often changed in relation to changes in these other distributions.

Internalization of disadvantage and inequalities of agency

Recent work on urban slum dwellers in India[26] (and elsewhere)[27] suggests that a key form of powerlessness for the poor involves living with "negative terms of recognition." This concept highlights the conditions and constraints under which the poor negotiate

the very norms that frame their social lives. Being so routinely treated with contempt by government officials, employers, and fellow citizens—and encountering such enormous obstacles to advancement—means that excluded groups can, over time, come to subscribe to norms about themselves and their situation "whose social effect is to further diminish their dignity, exacerbate their inequality, and deepen their lack of access to material goods and services."[28]

In these circumstances, the poor are not only persistently and overtly discriminated against. Their problems are further compounded and consolidated by their apparent complicity in it, their revealed "adaptive preference"[29] for menial occupations and ascription to norms and subservient behaviors that only legitimize and perpetuate their powerlessness. Dire material circumstances, rational expectations about their limited prospects for upward mobility, and strong beliefs about the legitimacy and immutability of their situation conspire to create a vicious circle from which it may be very difficult for the poor to escape (see box 2.8).[30]

Inequality traps may cause crime and violence. First, people who perceive their poverty as permanent may be driven by hostile impulses rather than rational pursuit of their interests. Second, sensitivity to inequality, especially by those feeling trapped at the bottom, may lead to higher-risk tactics like crime, when the expected payoffs from socially legitimate activities are poor. Third, people may be particularly sensitive to group-based inequalities. If, for example, racial heterogeneity and income inequality are correlated and consolidate status distinctions in a society, this could spell potential for violence. Finally, as Merton (1938) elegantly states,

> . . . when a system of cultural values emphasizes, virtually above all else, certain *common* symbols of success *for the population at large* while its social structure rigorously restricts or completely eliminates access to approved modes of acquiring these symbols *for a considerable part of the same population,* . . . antisocial behavior ensues on a considerable scale. (italics reflect original emphasis)

A lack of upward mobility in a society, combined with a high premium on economic affluence, results in anomie—a breakdown of standards and values.[31]

Changing between-group inequalities of agency and institutional power

Inequality of agency often leads to institutions that reproduce such inequality. But these relationships are not immutable. There are ample cases in which interventions—by civil society, reformist public officials, external actors, religious institutions, and others—have given more self-confidence and assertiveness to disadvantaged groups, worked against the internalization of disadvantage, and created new channels for excluded groups to exercise voice with greater effect. These changes improve the terms of recognition for the powerless: they become recognized by more powerful groups who otherwise would not acknowledge them at all, leading to empowerment of disadvantaged groups in economic, social, and political realms.

Empowerment can occur in many ways.[32] Change typically occurs through the interaction between the opportunities for action created by dominant political structures and the capacity of poorer or middle groups to engage. The "political opportunity structure"—that shapes the possibilities for action—is itself a function of the openness of political institution, the coherence and

positions of elites, and the effectiveness of governments to implement approved courses of action. The capacity of subordinate groups is influenced by their "economic" capital—their education and economic resources—their "capacity to aspire," and the closely associated capacity to organize.[33]

In Indonesia, the Kecamatan Development Project (KDP) illustrates change occurring through action from above and below: it aims to improve the terms of recognition and the political agency of marginal groups, and to create new institutions for greater agency to lead to material changes in patterns of public investment. Consistent with the ongoing process of democratization in Indonesia, the source of change comes from public policy rather than nongovernmental action, allowing the project to operate on a large scale (see also focus 4 for examples of change occurring at the local level).

A recent study[34] of the efficacy of the KDP on challenging and changing the terms of recognition of participants suggests that it does provide villagers with a set of deliberative routines for more equitably managing the conflicts it inevitably triggers.[35] These routines introduce marginal actors to more equitable spaces of engagement with more organized and influential actors. But building this conflict management capacity among marginal groups depends on more than just forging collaborative routines. It also requires a set of rules—defined by the KDP—that limit the unfair exercise of power by dominant groups. With the KDP cultivating collaboration and tangible points of political power for marginalized groups, the results include a well-functioning school or medical clinic but equally important a style of group (re)definition and defense.

Changes in the agency of indigenous peoples in Ecuador since the 1960s provide another example in which mobilization from below came to change national and local structures. These changes are clear at both local and national levels. In the 1960s in the Andean province of Chimborazo, the indigenous *Quichua* people suffered multiple deprivations. They were subject to everyday forms of violence and to domination and racism in their interactions with other ethnic groups and with authorities.[36] Power was concentrated in the triumvirate of landowner, priest, and local government authority. Much indigenous labor was tied to large rural estates on which labor relations were sometimes violent and returns to labor manifestly unfair. Life expectancy was short, alcoholism severe, and children's access to education and health acutely constrained.

At the start of this twenty-first century, indigenous people now occupy several county mayorships and have a majority of councilors in several counties. The provincial prefect is also Quichua. Similarly at a national level, former leaders of national indigenous people's organizations are now ministers. And the national Confederation of Indigenous Nationalities of Ecuador has control of the directorate of bilingual education, the indigenous development council, and the office of indigenous health. It also played a big part in negotiating and administering a World Bank and International Fund for Agricultural Development–supported national Program for the Development of Indigenous and Afro-Ecuadorian Peoples. By any calculation, power relationships have changed in Ecuador, becoming more equitable, with indigenous people participating more completely (and more equitably) in their society.

The inequality trap for women

Unequal opportunities in health, education, economic welfare, and political agency can be readily observed in most developing countries. The preceding sections have emphasized that these different manifestations of inequity are not generally independent from one another and that this interdependence can replicate inequalities over time. This interrelationship can be vividly illustrated by examining the nature and implications of the inequality that traps many women in developing countries.

Men and women around the world have starkly different access to assets and opportunities, reinforced by unequal norms and social structures, perpetuating gender differences over centuries. Gender inequity directly affects the well-being of women and deci-

---

BOX 2.9   *Sex ratios and "missing women"*

Gender inequity causes many societies to display some preference for male children. But the "son preference" is strong enough to result in substantial excess female child mortality in parts of East and South Asia—leading to the phenomenon of what Amartya Sen calls "missing women." (Sen, 1990). In China and India the practice of female infanticide was noted at least a century ago, and in the Republic of Korea and India high juvenile sex ratios (the proportion of male to female children below the age of 4) have been documented since the first modern censuses were taken. By contrast there seems to be little son preference in Southeast Asia or in most other parts of the developing world.

The reasons for this seem to stem from rigid patrilineal inheritance systems. While most societies deny women inheritance rights, in other parts of the world there is some flexibility in these rules. In peasant Europe and Japan, for instance, women could inherit land if their parents had no sons. Despite egalitarian laws, customary practices in China, the Republic of Korea, and northwest India permit a man, if he does not have sons, to adopt one from other male kin. In the past, it would also have been possible to take another wife. The driving motivation is to use whatever means possible to continue the male family line. Thus, girl children are undervalued.

During pregnancy, sex-selection may lead to aborting female fetuses, reflected in sex ratios at birth that are more masculine than the biological rate of 105 boys for every 100 girls. Sex-selection can also happen through infanticide, although the data make it difficult to distinguish between selective abortion and infanticide. The third, and most common, mechanism is the neglect and other practices that result in higher mortality rates for girls than boys during early childhood.[37]

In China, intense efforts by the government resulted in a brief improvement in the sex ratio during 1953–64 (see figure to the right). But since the 1980s it has steadily

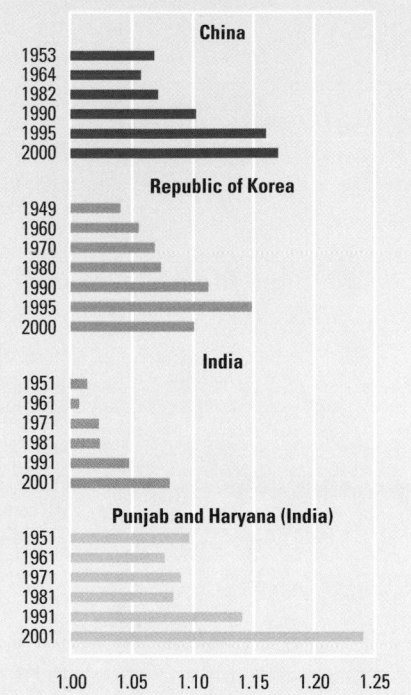

Juvenile (newborn to four years old) sex ratios in China, the Republic of Korea, India, and Punjab and Haryana, 1950–2000

risen. In the Republic of Korea stark declines have become only apparent in the last decade—perhaps because of improvements in labor market opportunities for women. India, as a whole, does not have juvenile sex ratios that are far different from many other parts of the world. But northwest India has seen some particularly worrying trends, with sex ratios sharply rising between 1981 and 2001, much attributable to the higher incidence of sex-selection in abortion. Other parts of India, especially the south, have more equitable labor markets and fewer restrictions on women's mobility and inheritance.

Source: Das Gupta and others (2003).

---

sions in the home, affecting investments in children and household welfare (box 2.9).

Gender inequity is the archetypical "inequality trap." Most societies have norms that preserve the prevalent social order, delineating different roles and spheres of influence for men and women. The male sphere is typically outside the home in market work and social interactions that enhance the family's status and power. The female sphere is usually inside the home—looking after household work, rearing children, and contributing to the stability of the household. So, women's activities serve primarily as inputs into the household's collective well-being, while men are ostensibly at its center—its breadwinners and its link to the larger world where economic and social status are determined.

Marriage and kinship systems preserve these structures of patriarchy. Most societies are "patrilocal," with women moving from their parents to their husband's home after marriage. Marriage can therefore be thought of as a framework that serves to exchange women between households, and marriage decisions are made with a view toward ensuring that this exchange of women promises the maximum gain to both households. The man's household is the point of reference—while the woman is simply an input into the processes for households controlled by men to generate economic and social returns.[38]

Inheritance tends to be consistent with this pattern. Most societies are not just patrilocal—they are also patrilineal, with inheritance and property rights primarily passed on to men. The majority of countries, outside of Europe and Central Asia and Latin America and Caribbean, restrict inheritance rights to women.[39] Some countries have legislation that guarantees equality in inheritance laws. But these laws often are not enforced, and real authority over decisions on inheritance rests in the hands of village elders and chiefs, who follow customary practices that discriminate against women.

Most countries that have unequal inheritance laws also have unequal property rights regimes.[40] Indeed, the vast majority of land owners are men.[41] Many societies compound this by denying women the right to divorce. This inequality in property rights regimes persists even in countries where agricultural production depends heavily on women's labor, such as many in Sub-Saharan Africa. In Cameroon, women make up more than 51 percent of the population and do more than 75 percent of the agricultural work, but they are estimated to hold fewer than 10 percent of all land certificates.[42] So, if women work on farms, they are usually working on farms owned by men.

In addition to being denied inheritance and property rights, women in many societies face restrictions on their mobility. For example, in the state of Uttar Pradesh in northern India close to 80 percent of women require their husband's permission to visit a health center, and 60 percent have to seek permission before stepping outside their house.[43] These mobility restrictions may be socially imposed, as with *gunghat* among Hindus—or have religious sanctions, as with *purdah* among Muslims. Such practices are not just socially enforced, they can be internalized by women who treat them as marks of honorable behavior. These norms are transmitted by parents to their children, ensuring their continuity over generations; in many societies, they are enforced by older women in the community.[44]

Restrictions on mobility and rules of kinship and inheritance help shape social perceptions about women's roles. If women are socially and economically directed to focus their attention and energy on activities in the home, this is not just what men expect of them—it is also what other women expect of them. In much of the developing world, women's participation in the labor market is more a function of adversity than active choice—because husbands cannot earn an adequate income or because of an unanticipated shock, such as a child's illness. Bangladeshi women described it this way, "Men work to support their families, women work because of need."[45] Women around the world participate in a fair amount of market-based activity for a wage, but they have to continue to perform most household chores (figure 2.13). They thus face a time squeeze, spending more time at work, both in and out of the home, than men do.

Because social and economic factors determine women's life chances more in marriage than in labor markets, parents invest less in their human capital. Throughout the developing world, women are much less likely to be enrolled in secondary school or university than men.[46] So, they typically work in less lucrative occupations. Moreover, labor markets may themselves be discriminatory, paying women less than men for the same work. For these reasons, even when women participate in the labor market, they earn less than men. Low earnings are a further disincentive for women to enter the labor market, perpetuating traditional social roles.

Inequality in the home

For a long time, economists did not adequately recognize that gender inequity has an impact in the home, and models of the household assumed that decisions were taken by one person—with no room for different choices across spouses. The consequence of this world view is not just academic. It suggests, for instance, that policy interventions that attempt to alleviate poverty should not bother with targeting by gender—or suggests that taxes on a household will not affect the allocation of resources within it.

Economists now question this view, developing models of household decision making that allow for inequality between spouses. The new models start with the assumption that households are efficient, in the sense that they make decisions that maximize the use of the household's resources. With this assumption, the models show that a spouse's share in household resources is determined by two factors. The first is the fallback option for the spouse in the event of divorce—laws of inheritance, property, and divorce would matter here. Second is the relative size of the spouse's contribution to the household's income, which is determined by their opportunities in the labor market.[47] If husbands and wives have different preferences, an increase in a woman's outside options or in her labor market opportunities should reflect consumption choices more in line with her preferences.

Econometric work confirms that an increase in a woman's relative worth and an improvement in her fallback options have effects on consumption patterns.[48] The health of Brazilian children improves when additional nonlabor income is in the hands of women.[49] In the United Kingdom, when legislation ensured that child support payments were made directly to mothers, expenditures on children's clothing tended to rise.[50] In Bangladesh and South Africa, women bringing more assets into the marriage increase household expenditures on children's education.[51] The patterns seem to indicate that, when women are better off, children seem to

Figure 2.13 Women work longer hours than do men

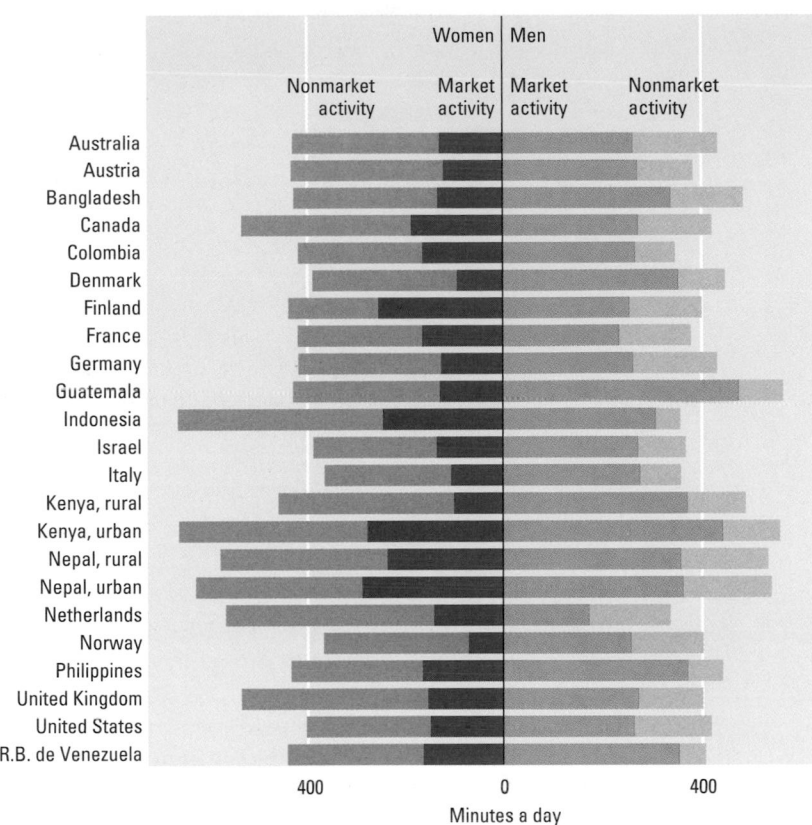

Source: United Nations Development Programme (1995).
Note: Data refers to rural Bangladesh in 1990, urban Colombia 1983, rural Guatemala 1977, urban Indonesia 1992, rural Kenya 1988, urban Kenya 1986, rural Nepal 1978, urban Nepal 1978, rural Philippines 1975–77, urban Venezuela 1983, Australia 1992, Austria 1992, Canada 1992, Denmark 1987, Finland 1987-88, France 1985–86, Germany 1991–92, Israel 1991–92, Italy 1988–89, the Netherlands 1987, Norway 1990–91, the United Kingdom 1985, and the United States 1985.

benefit more than when men are better off. The most obvious way to explain bargaining and sharing is to assume that women intrinsically care more about children than men do, but this risks being tautological.

Perhaps the explanation can benefit from understanding that social and economic differences outside the household can matter not only for determining bargaining power but also for socially determined perceptions of what men and women consider important. If men and women occupy different "outside" and "inside" spheres of influence, it seems to make sense that improvements in women's incomes would have a greater impact on investments in the household. Improvements in the income of men, by contrast, are more likely to result in socializing activities outside the home and in purchases that reflect social status.

Another consequence of this separation between inside and outside roles is that

Table 2.2 Percentage of women who have ever experienced physical or sexual violence by an intimate partner

	Physical violence	Sexual violence
Bangladesh, rural	42	
Brazil, urban	27	10
Ethiopia, rural	49	59
Namibia, urban	31	17
Peru, rural	62	47
Samoa	41	20
Serbia and Montenegro	23	6
Tanzania, urban	33	23
Thailand, rural	34	29

Source: Unpublished data from the WHO Multi-Country Study on Women's Health and Domestic Violence Against Women obtained from a presentation by Claudia Garcia-Moreno at the World Bank's Conference on Gender-Based Violence. The final published comparative report is forthcoming.
Note: Data refer to different time periods. Brazil, Peru, and Thailand refer to 2000. Reference period for Bangladesh, Ethiopia, Namibia, Samoa, Serbia and Montenegro, and Tanzania are unknown.

inequalities in the home are also manifested in differences in access to information, which can be used to manipulate intra-household bargaining. In an ethnographic study of Bangladeshi garment workers, Kabeer (1997) found that men and women tried to control information about their incomes from their spouses so that they could make purchases without consulting them. Women may also hesitate to share information with their husbands, or to collaborate efficiently in farming their plots of land, to retain control over their property. In studying the farms owned by men and those owned by women in Ghana, Udry (1996) found, keeping other things constant, that women-owned farms were less productive than those owned by men. When wives and husbands are not sharing information, or manipulating the flow of information, they clearly are not using their resources optimally. In other words, intrahousehold behavior is not efficient—contradicting an important assumption in economic models.

The widespread domestic violence in the family is another type of inefficiency. Recent World Health Organization (WHO) data show that both physical and sexual violence are widespread in diverse parts of the world (table 2.2). An important reason for domestic violence is that it allows husbands to institute a regime of terror to control their wives' behavior. In India, Bloch and Rao (2002) find that husbands systematically use violence as a means of extracting a larger dowry from their wives. This "instrumental" use of violence has widespread acceptance among both men and women. Surveys have found that large percentages of respondents in developing countries report that men have the right to beat their wives when they answer back or disobey them.[52]

Gender inequity is thus the result of an overlapping set of economic, social, cultural, and political inequalities that reinforce each other. They cause women to have less access to property rights, wealth, and education—and limit their access to labor markets and to spheres of activity outside the home. This, in turn, constrains their ability to influence household decisions. Also limiting this influence are asymmetries of information in the household and the use of violence to control women's behavior. All of this maintains a clear demarcation between the roles of women and men, readily reproduced across generations.

There are some signs that changes in labor markets and interventions by the state can break this inequality trap. The development of the garment industry in Bangladesh has resulted in a sharp and visible increase in women's access to a lucrative labor market, expanding their ability to influence household choices.[53] Higher wages for women seem to compensate for restrictive practices, such as purdah, by reducing limits on women's physical mobility, and increasing their say in household decision making.[54] Globalization has expanded opportunities for women in Mumbai and increased their access to schooling.[55] A comparative study of the Philippines, Sumatra, and Ghana found that patterns of land inheritance and investments in schooling have became more egalitarian because of changes in labor market opportunities for women.[56] And although China, Republic of Korea, and India started out with similar discriminatory social structures, intervention by the state has improved gender equity much more in China than in Republic of Korea or India.[57]

Equity from a global perspective

In examining the inequality of opportunities within countries, the previous chapter emphasized people's "predetermined circumstances," or life chances beyond their control, as distinct from their "efforts" and "talents" as individuals. One of these circumstances is a person's place of birth. In many countries, access to basic public health services, for example, is significantly lower in rural areas than in urban areas. That can mean much for surviving the first year of life—the infant mortality rate in Rio de Janeiro was 3.3 percent in 1996, less than half the 7.4 percent in northeast Brazil.

But, just as being born in a village or a city is one circumstance that should be irrelevant to a person's chances in life, being born in a specific country is another. Why is it objectionable for, say, Turkish women to have inferior opportunities and outcomes compared with Turkish men, but not so objectionable if the comparison is between Turkish men and English women? After all, in many dimensions of well-being, major differences in opportunities and outcomes exist between citizens of different countries, in some cases differences larger than those between various groups within countries.

This chapter tries to answer two questions. First, how much does one's country of birth determine one's opportunities in life? Second, does one's country of birth mean less for life chances today than in the near or distant past? To answer these questions, we discuss inequalities in health, education, income, and power in the global arena. We show that the inequalities between countries are staggering despite some improvements over time.

Examples and concepts

There is no doubt that we live in a world with massive inequalities in the opportunities to live a free, healthy, and fulfilled life. As Angus Deaton writes,

> We are living with appalling inequalities, in which the poor of the world die of AIDS, and, more broadly, where poor people around the world die of diseases that are *readily preventable* elsewhere, including in the first-world hospitals and clinics that serve the rich in poor countries.[1]

In 2000 the life expectancy of a child born in Sierra Leone (37 years) or Botswana (39 years) was less than half that for a child born in the United States (77 years).[2] The average educational attainment (unconditional on quality of schooling) of an individual born in a Sub-Saharan country between 1975 and 1979 is less than 6 years, but more than 12 years in OECD countries. Inequalities in income are also high among individuals in different parts of the world.[3]

How do we view large average improvements in the world, set against this picture of unacceptable inequalities between countries? Sen (2001) describes the current state of the world while making the case for a fairer distribution of the fruits of globalization: "Even though the world is incomparably richer than ever before, ours is also a world of extraordinary deprivation and staggering inequality." He argues that whether there have been some gains for all is not as important as whether the distribution of gains has been fair. Inequalities in affluence—and in political, social, and economic power among countries—are central to the debate on globalization. As long as the sharing of potential gains from globalization is viewed as unfair by many, the inequalities described in this chapter will be deemed unacceptable. This, despite the fact that absolute poverty has declined in the last two decades—though by no means uniformly.

To put global inequalities in well-being in perspective, it helps to examine two countries at opposite ends of the spectrum—Mali, one of the world's poorest countries, and the United States, one of the richest. A baby born in Mali in 2001 had an approximately 13 percent chance of dying before reaching age one, with this chance declining only slightly (to 9 percent) even if the baby were born to a family in the top quintile of the asset distribution. By contrast, a baby born in the United States the same year had a less than 1 percent chance of dying in its first year. The picture for under-five mortality is even more egregious: 24 percent of children will not reach age five in Mali, compared with less than 1 percent of American children. Even a child born into the richest quintile in Mali is more than 16 times likely to die before age five than an average American child.

The picture does not improve for education. The average American born between 1975 and 1979 has completed more than 14 years of schooling (roughly the same for men and women, and in urban and rural areas), while the average school attainment for the same cohort in Mali is less than two years, with women's attainment less than half that for men, and virtually zero in rural areas. If one considers the quality of the education received, the inequalities in learning achievement are possibly much larger.

It is not surprising, then, that many citizens of Mali, having survived immense hardships as children and without much education, can barely eke out a living as adults, on average living on less than $2 a day ($54 a month) in 1994. By comparison, the average American earned $1,185 a month, more than 20 times that for the average Malian.

While there is probably some consensus that inequalities in health, education, income, and voice are large globally, there is much less agreement on whether things have been getting better or worse. Is one's country of origin more or less pertinent today to the life chances that she faces at birth than it was 20, 50, or 200 years ago?

The debate on inequalities in various dimensions of well-being and their relation to globalization rages on as you read this report.[4] It is indeed harder to assert whether inequalities increased or decreased over time. Various questions have to be answered first: inequality of what, over which time period, using which concept of inequality? While there is some evidence of convergence in opportunities in health and education and some divergence in incomes (or at least lack of convergence), these results cannot be stated without many qualifications and caveats. Box 3.1 introduces some underlying concepts that need to be clarified.

Global inequalities in health

The unweighted and weighted international distributions of life expectancy at birth (ignoring the distribution of life expectancy at birth within countries) both show a clear "twin-peakedness" in 1960.[7] Data show that 50 countries had life expectancies between 35 and 45 years, 41 countries had life expectancies between 65 and 75 years, and there was relatively little mass in the middle of the distribution.

By 1980 the left-hand mode of the distribution had decreased considerably in size. The distributions began to look more right-skewed, unimodal, especially in the weighted international distribution: 73 countries had a life expectancy between 65 and 75, compared with 31 countries between 55 and 65, and 35 countries between 45 and 55. But by 2000 the two modes become evident once again, especially in the unweighted distribution, although there is more mass in the right mode of the distribution.

In 1980, the average life expectancy in four regions—Middle East and North Africa, East Asia (excluding China and Japan), South Asia, and Sub-Saharan Africa—was below the world average.[8] Between 1980 and 2000, rapid increases in life expectancy in the first three of these regions were globally inequality-reducing, while the decline of life expectancy in Sub-Saharan Africa in the 1990s boosted inequality by stretching the bottom tail of the distribution. By 2000, only South Asia and Sub-Saharan Africa were below the world average, with the difference in life expectancy at birth between

BOX 3.1 *Three competing concepts of inequality: global, international, and intercountry*

On the welfare gains from globalization, the two sides of the debate often make statements that are diametrically opposed, all the while examining the same data. While there are some differences in and problems with data, the wide discrepancy in views on the topic seems to stem from the fact that the two sides do not share the same values about what constitutes a just distribution of the gains from globalization.

Considered here are three different concepts of inequality, drawing from Milanovic (2005) and Ravallion (2004a). Both authors, and the globalization debate in general, discuss these "competing concepts" in the domain of incomes. But these concepts can be extended to other dimensions, such as health and education (especially for inequality between countries). The conclusions one would draw in each of these dimensions of well-being then depend on the concept of inequality adopted. It is impossible for the two sides to communicate without first making these concepts clear.

Has global income inequality increased or not? Before we can answer this, we have to define what we mean by *global* inequality and how that differs from what we will call *international* and *intercountry* inequality.

Global inequality: forget country boundaries, each person has his or her real income
Global inequality is easy to define: simply forget countries, line up all citizens of the world, and calculate the inequality in the distribution of their real incomes, adjusted for purchasing power parity.[5] The global inequality measures that belong to the general entropy class, such as a mean log deviation or Theil's index, can be neatly decomposed into inequality attributable to inequalities between persons within each country and the mean differences of income between countries (Shorrocks 1980).

Within-country inequality is what the overall inequality in the world would be if there were no differences in mean consumption across countries but each country had its actual inequality level. Between-country inequality can be interpreted as measuring what the level of inequality in the world would be if everyone within each country had the same (the country-average) consumption level. Total inequality in the world is the sum of these two parts, and the ratios of the respective parts to total inequality provide a measure of the percentage contribution of between-country and within-country inequality to total inequality.

International inequality: each person has his or her country's mean income
Throughout the rest of the report, we will refer to this between-country inequality as interna-

tional inequality, the inequality in the distribution of all of the world's citizens, but with each person assigned the mean income of his/her country instead of his/her own income. Global inequality is calculated by simply adding international inequality to within-country inequality.

Intercountry inequality: each country has one representative at its mean income
These two concepts, however, are not enough to settle the debate. Think of the following statement in support of the argument that inequality in the world has been increasing: "The GDP per capita of the richest country in the world was about 9 times that of the poorest around 1870 compared with 45 times by 1990."[6] Notice that while this statement seems to be referring to something akin to international inequality, there is a subtle but very important difference: the size of the richest or the poorest country plays no role in this statement. The statement remains the same whether the richest country is Palau and the poorest country is Jamaica, or whether they are China and India.

This is why a third concept is needed. In this concept, all countries of the world (instead of all citizens) line up together, and each of them is assigned her mean income. We will call the inequality in this distribution (of roughly 200 or so countries of the world) intercountry inequality. Milanovic (2005) refers to our intercountry, international, and global inequality concepts as Concept 1, Concept 2, and Concept 3 inequality, respectively (see figure below).

Why use intercountry inequality
The implicit value judgment in using intercountry inequality instead of international inequality is that countries, not people, should get equal weight in assessing the fairness of

the division of the gains from globalization. The measures most widely quoted by the critics of globalization treat each country as one observation, while decompositions of world inequality into between-country and within-country components described above give people equal weight, whether they live in China or Chad.

Note that in the globalization debate, the choice of the measure of inequality can also depend on the question one is trying to answer. If one is interested in the impact of some "globalizing" policies on growth or distributional outcomes at the country level, it might be preferable to use a measure of intercountry inequality.

Why use international inequality— as we do in this report?
Alternatively, if we are trying to determine whether world poverty or inequality decreased as a result of "globalizing" policies, then we might be more inclined to examine measures of international inequality.

No right or wrong choice
Arguments can be made in favor of each of these two concepts when assessing trends in inequality between countries. This choice is not a matter of what is right or wrong. When it comes to judging inequality, intelligent people can disagree about whether countries or people should be weighted equally—something that Ravallion (2004a) argues in detail. The point: the judgments (or the questions of interest) that affect the choice of the inequality concept employed in empirical work matter greatly to the assessment one can make about the distributive justice of current globalization processes.

Three concepts of inequality illustrated

Intercountry inequality:
Three countries and three representatives with mean incomes (height)

International inequality:
Entire population included, but with mean incomes

Global inequality:
All individuals with their actual income

Sources: Milanovic (2005) and Ravallion (2004a).

Figure 3.1 Vanishing twin peaks in life expectancy at birth

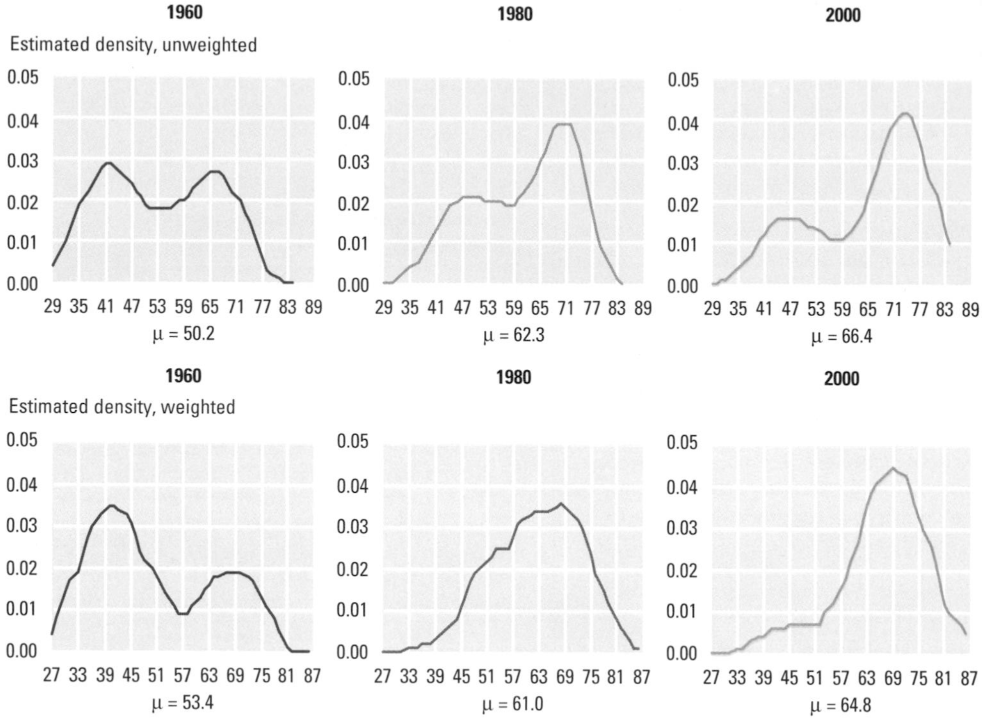

Source: Schady (2005).

these two regions having increased from 5.8 years to 15.6. Between-country inequality declined until the early 1990s and then increased back to its 1980 level by 2000. The large decline in life expectancy at birth in Sub-Saharan Africa more than offset the inequality-reducing effect of growth in South Asia in the 1990s.

Over a longer period (1820–1992) Bourguignon, Levin, and Rosenblatt (2004a) show tremendous gains in life expectancy at birth (rising from approximately 27 years to 61 years), unequally distributed at first, then equalizing in three waves between late nineteenth century and 1990. Decades of

consistent improvements in life expectancy at birth came to a screeching halt in the 1990s (table 3.1). Between-country inequality among developing countries is as high as it has ever been since 1960.

So, there is some convergence in life expectancy at birth over a long period, although there are significant losses in the 1990s in Sub-Saharan Africa, mainly caused by AIDS, and in some European and Central Asian countries.[9] With the developed countries reaching a biological limit at the top of the distribution and many regions catching up to them, the inequality of life expectancy in the world will become more a function of changes in health and population growth in Sub-Saharan Africa—barring a major health catastrophe elsewhere in the world. (We revisit this issue at the end of the chapter.) But for now there remain two worlds with significantly different life expectancies: the gap in life expectancy between Sub-Saharan Africa and Europe and North America in 2000 is higher than it was in 1950.[10]

Health outcomes of even the rich citizens in poor countries remain well below

Table 3.1 Increases in life expectancy at birth slowed down dramatically in the 1990s

	1960	1970	1980	1990	2000
Mean	53.4	57.4	61.0	64.0	64.8
Coefficient of variation	0.233	0.203	0.183	0.173	0.194
Theil-T	0.027	0.021	0.017	0.016	0.020
Theil-L	0.028	0.022	0.018	0.017	0.021

Source: Schady (2005).
Note: Theil-L and Theil-T are two inequality measures that belong to the general entropy class, with parameters 0 and 1, respectively (unweighted).

ment in Sub-Saharan Africa and South Asia remain low even for the youngest cohorts.

While significant disparities remain in educational attainment across countries despite evidence of significant catch-up by poorer countries in the past half century, there is also large variation within countries (chapter 2). In fact, less than 20 percent of the inequality in educational attainment between adults born between 1935 and 1979 is attributable to that between countries, a share that has been steadily declining over time. While both inequality within and between countries is declining, the rate of convergence in country means has been faster.

The story remains the same when decomposing inequality in educational attainment into inequalities between men and women. Roughly a quarter of global inequality in educational attainment is attributable to differences between men and women, but this gap is again declining over time, from 31 percent in the oldest cohort in our sample, to 16 percent in the youngest. But there are large differences in this convergence by region (figure 3.5). While Latin America and the Caribbean, East Asia, and Europe and Central Asia seem to have reached gender parity in education, along with other developed countries, the progress in South Asia, Sub-Saharan Africa, and the Middle East and North Africa has been slower. Women still lag far behind men in educational attainment.

It should not be assumed that high attainment necessarily implies high achievement, and vice versa. An analysis of the relationship between attainment (measured by the percentage of 25 to 34 year olds with upper-secondary education) and achievement (measured by reading proficiency of 15 year olds) in 27 OECD countries (plus Brazil) shows a rank correlation coefficient between these two variables of 0.57. It is clear that the rankings of countries according to these two indicators are not the same. The Republic of Korea and Japan (at the top of the OECD distribution) and Mexico, Portugal, and Turkey (at the bottom) have similar ranks for both attainment and achievement. But the Czech Republic, Norway, and the United States do worse in achievement than attainment. And achievement rankings

of Australia, Finland, and Ireland are much higher than their rankings in attainment.

Achievement differences between developing countries and OECD countries remain strikingly large. Using internationally comparable assessments of reading, mathematics, and science, Pritchett (2004b) shows that developing countries do not just constitute the lower tail of the learning distribution, but that most actually do far worse than the poorest performing OECD countries. For example, children in Argentina, Mexico, and Chile perform about two (OECD) standard deviations below children in Greece—one of the poorest performing countries in the OECD. In reading competence (based on PISA 2001), the

Table 3.2 Mean years of schooling increased continuously while inequality declined

	1960	1970	1980	1990	2000
Mean	3.38	3.82	4.67	5.55	6.30
Coefficient of variation	0.739	0.705	0.612	0.518	0.461
Theil-T	0.281	0.259	0.195	0.143	0.115
Theil-L	0.392	0.365	0.250	0.179	0.144

Source: Schady (2005).
Note: Theil-L and Theil-T are two inequality measures that belong to the general entropy class, with parameters 0 and 1, respectively (unweighted).

Figure 3.5 Gender disparities in years of schooling declined but remained significant in some regions

Male to female schooling ratio

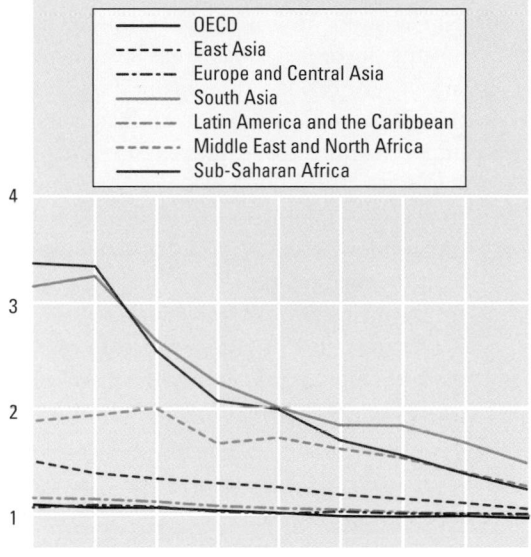

Source: Araujo, Ferreira, and Schady (2004).

average Indonesian student performed at the level of a French student at the seventh percentile. Considering children who have never attended school, those who enrolled but dropped out, and those who completed grade nine but whose test scores remain more than one standard deviation below the OECD mean in mathematics, Pritchett finds that 96 percent of 15 to 19 year olds in Morocco lack achievement in "adequate learning."[19]

Global inequalities in income and expenditure

The answers to basic questions—such as whether income inequality has been increasing or decreasing—depends, among other things, on which concept of inequality is under the microscope: intercountry inequality (in the distribution of unweighted country means), international inequality (in the distribution of country means weighted by their population size), or global inequality (in the distribution of individual incomes).

We start the discussion by presenting the median and mean incomes of selected countries by region for a range of years between 1997 and 2002, as well as the dispersion of those incomes within each country (figure 3.6). Large differences across countries and across people within countries are striking. For example, an individual in the tenth percentile in the U.S. distribution enjoys a level of income higher than an individual earning the mean income in Brazil or Argentina.[20] While a Chinese individual living in a rural area has a mean income similar to an average Cambodian, an urban Chinese enjoys a similar income to an average Brazilian.[21] A South African at the bottom of the income distribution in her country earns as much as the average individual in Mali while a South African at the ninetieth percentile of that income distribution enjoys a standard of living (in income) comparable to that of a median Irish individual.

The difference in the evolution of intercountry (unweighted) and international (weighted) inequality between 1950 and 2000—borrowing from Milanovic (2005), who calls this the "mother of all inequality disputes"—could hardly be more dramatic (figure 3.7). When countries are the unit of

Figure 3.6 Incomes range broadly across countries and individuals

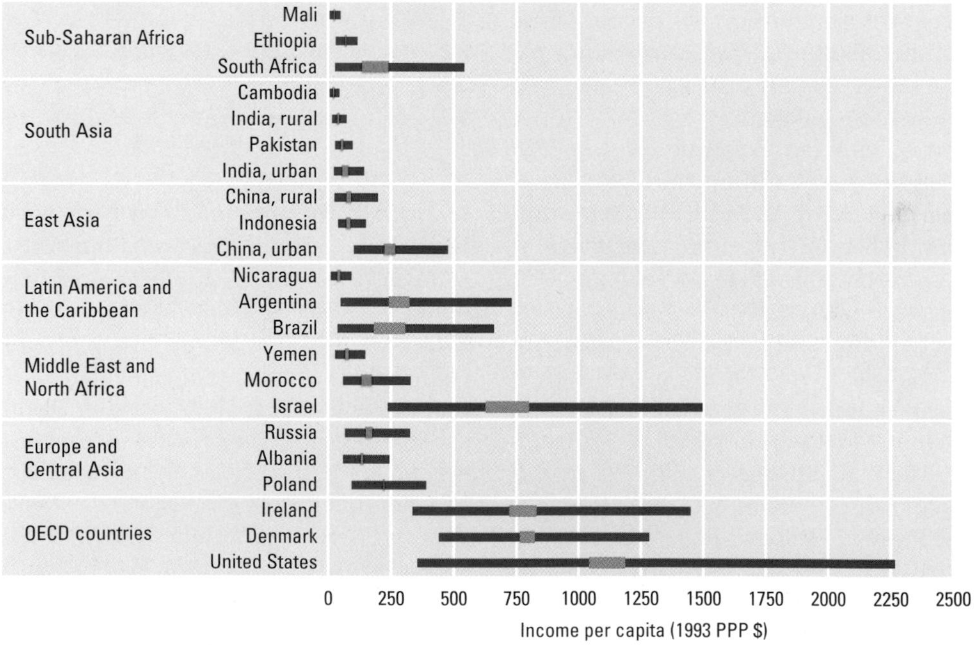

Source: Authors' calculations.
Note: Years range from 1997 to 2002 as measured by adjusted (1993 PPP $) monthly per capita income (blue box) or consumption (orange box). The lowest point of each line represents the income level at the tenth percentile, followed by that at the median, the mean (the two edges of each box), and the ninetieth percentile (top of each line).

Figure 3.7 Since 1950, intercountry inequality increased, while international inequality declined

Gini index

Source: Milanovic (2005).

Figure 3.8 Unlike relative inequality, absolute inequality has been steadily increasing

Indexes, 1970 = 100

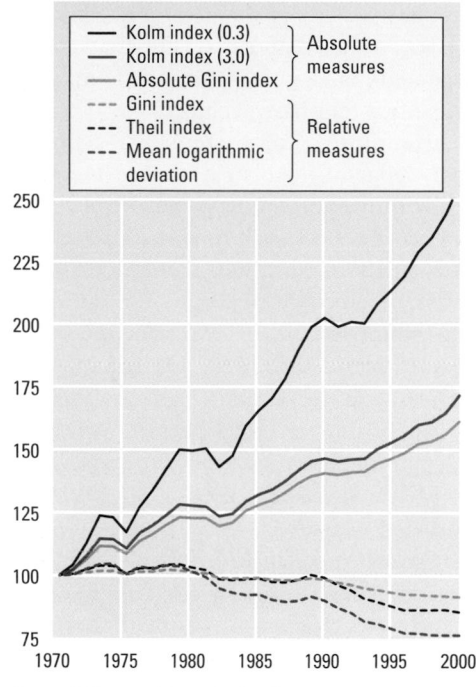

Source: Atkinson and Brandolini (2004).

observation, (intercountry) inequality has been undeniably increasing, especially since the 1980s. But international inequality has been steadily declining, thanks mostly to the income growth in some populous countries, mainly China and India. Note that intercountry inequality and international inequality without China and India track each other quite closely from 1980 onward, coinciding with the period of rapid growth in these two countries, the slower average growth in other developing countries, and the declines in measured output in Eastern Europe and former Soviet Union countries.

If Luxembourg and Nicaragua, at opposite ends of the world income distribution, grew at the same annual rate of 2 percent per capita a year for the next 25 years, the per capita yearly incomes in Luxembourg would increase from $17,228 (PPP-adjusted) to $28,264, an increase of more than $10,000 dollars. That of Nicaragua, by contrast, would increase by a mere $375, from $573 to $940, during the same period. Atkinson and Brandolini (2004) note that "with annual per capita growth rates of 5 percent in China and 2 percent in the United States, the absolute income gap between the two countries would widen for a further 41 years before starting to narrow, to finally disappear in 72 years."

The evaluative judgments drawn about the distributional changes associated with globalization may depend crucially on whether one thinks about inequality in

absolute terms or relative terms. There is no economic theory that tells us that inequality is relative, not absolute. Again, as with intercountry and international inequality, it is not that one concept is right and the other one wrong. Nor are they two ways of measuring the same thing. Instead, they are two different concepts. The revealed preferences for one concept over another reflect implicit value judgments about what constitutes a fair division of the gains from growth. Those judgments need to be brought into the open and critically scrutinized before one can take a well-considered position in this debate.

An examination of international inequality using absolute rather than relative measures of inequality reveals a steady increase over the long run, as well as in recent decades—this latter finding contrasts with relative international inequality trends. Atkinson and Brandolini (2004) find that absolute indexes of inequality, such as the Absolute Gini and the Kolm Index[22] (with various parameters of inequality aversion), have been increasing steadily since 1970 (figure 3.8).[23]

What happened to global inequality in the past 20 years or so has been the subject of fierce debate in the context of globalization and is perhaps the hardest question to answer. Some authors[24] claim that global inequality increased slightly, while others[25] argue that they have declined.

Examining global inequality requires knowledge of the distribution of inequality within each country. Household surveys that collect such data are a relatively new phenomenon, having become more common since the 1980s even in developing countries. So, if we want to know about the distribution of income for everyone in the world, we are confined to a much shorter time period. We have selected three waves, similar to those used by Milanovic (2005): 1986–1990, 1991–96, and 1997–current.

Global inequality (measured by the mean log deviation) did not change significantly over this period, although there is a slight decrease between 1993 and 2000 (figure 3.9). The mean log deviation for the world would have increased without China and India, consistent with the consensus in the literature that international inequality declined in this period thanks largely to these two countries. But if global inequality stayed roughly the same while international inequality declined, inequality within countries must have increased by approximately the same amount—a subject that we discuss below.

Most of the world's income inequality can be explained by the differences in country means—that is, by international (or between-country) inequality. Our estimates show that the share of global inequality, which can be attributed to inequality between countries, declined steadily from 78 percent around 1988 to 74 percent around 1993 and to 67 percent by around 2000. With global inequality staying roughly the same during this period, within-group inequality increased at a somewhat steady pace (figure 3.9). These results are consistent with the evidence (in chapter 2) of increasing inequality within countries in many parts of the world, including Bangladesh, China, the United Kingdom, and the United States.

The between-country share of global inequality is also consistent with Milanovic (2005), who puts this figure at about 71 percent in 1998. It is possible that the Milanovic figures overestimate between-country inequality because he assigns all households in a decile the same income instead of estimating a Lorenz curve (for percentiles). Our results use slightly improved data from Milanovic in three aspects. First, for many countries, we calculate our welfare measures using raw data at the household level, while Milanovic (and many others) use grouped data. Second, we incorporate more recent data for the current period, possibly providing an improvement in data quality, especially for Eastern European countries. Third, for the countries with grouped data, we estimate Lorenz curves instead of assigning everyone in the group with the same income.[26] That most of the global inequality in incomes is explained by between-country inequality seems to be a robust finding in the literature, in stark contrast with the picture in health and education.

Over a much longer period (1820–1992) Bourguignon and Morrisson (2002) estimate that global inequality has been steadily increasing, because of a rapid increase in international inequality until World War II, and then to smaller increases in both within-country and international inequality between 1970 and 1992 (figure 3.10).[27] They also argue that international

Figure 3.9 The inequality decline between countries was neutralized by increases within countries

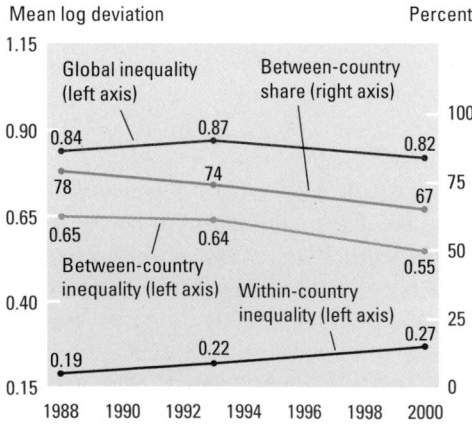

Source: Authors' calculations.

inequality was essentially negligible at the turn of the nineteenth century (accounting for roughly 12 percent of global inequality), but that it increased very rapidly until World War II, and then continued to increase, but at a much slower pace. Within country inequality, however, reached its peak around 1910 and declined dramatically between the two world wars (mainly because of equalizing forces in the now-developed countries), and started creeping back up only since the 1970s. The combined effect of these changes is an increase in the share of international inequality from roughly 10 percent in 1820 to more than 60 percent by 1992.

In summary, while the world got richer, income inequality—relative and absolute, international and global—increased tremendously over a long period of time (1820–1992). But the story is less clear-cut for a more recent time frame. In the post–World War II era, intercountry inequality (unweighted) has continued to increase while international inequality (weighted for population) declined. International inequality declined in the final decades of the twentieth century, because the inequality-reducing effects of income growth in China and South Asia more than offset the inequality-boosting effects of continued steady income growth in the now-developed countries and the declining incomes in Sub-Saharan Africa.

Pritchett (1997), examining the period between 1870 and 1990, argues that while there was convergence of incomes for today's developed countries (what Maddison 1995 calls the "advanced capitalist" countries), the growth rates between developed and developing economies show considerable divergence. He provides evidence that "the growth rates of developed countries are bunched in a narrow group, while those of less developed countries are all over with some in explosive growth and others in implosive decline."[28]

Further evidence of convergence among rich countries and divergence between rich and poor countries comes from Schultz (1998), who estimates that international inequality accounted for about two-thirds of total inequality (measured by log vari-

Figure 3.10 Inequality between countries became much more important over the long run

Mean log deviation

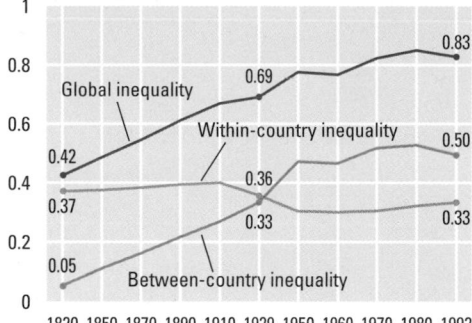

Source: Authors' manipulation of data from Bourguignon and Morrisson (2002).

ance) between 1960 and 1990; however, there also were large differences by region. Inequality between the countries of OECD (and the rest of Europe including Turkey) decreased by 50 percent during this period, at the end accounting for only one-third of total inequality. During the same period, international inequality in Sub-Saharan Africa nearly doubled, causing its share in total inequality to increase from 20 percent to 36 percent. In both Sub-Saharan Africa and Latin America and the Caribbean, overall inequality levels remain high, while high-income countries show signs of convergence.

One can also examine inequality trends by focusing on the mobility of countries rather than by taking an anonymous approach to inequality comparisons. Poor countries' mobility from the bottom has been limited in the past 25 years. With the exception of China, the six countries that occupied the bottom decile (population-weighted) in 1980—all in Sub-Saharan Africa—had no growth worth noting.[29]

While there is significant upward mobility between 1980 and 2002—the 97.08 percent entry in the first row of table 3.3 is China—there is also troubling stagnation and downward mobility. Note that approximately 8 percent of each of the second and third income ranges fell into the bottom range over these two decades. "It is clear that no Pareto improvement has taken place in the world between 1980 and 2002, which leaves room for different value judgments

Table 3.3 Mobility matrix in absolute country per capita incomes, 1980 to 2002

Income in 1980	Income in 2002				
	<710	711–1,100	1,101–2,890	2,891–10,000	10,001>
<710	1.28%	1.64%	0.00%	97.08%	0.00%
711–1,100	8.23%	3.89%	87.88%	0.00%	0.00%
1,101–2,890	8.09%	0.56%	59.08%	32.28%	0.00%
2,891–10,000	0.00%	0.00%	0.98%	90.84%	8.17%
10,001>	0.00%	0.00%	0.00%	3.99%	96.01%

Source: Bourguignon, Levin, and Rosenblatt (2004a).
Note: Incomes are per capita (constant PPP dollars).

Figure 3.11 Absolute poverty declined globally, but not in every region

Headcount ($1 per day) in 2001

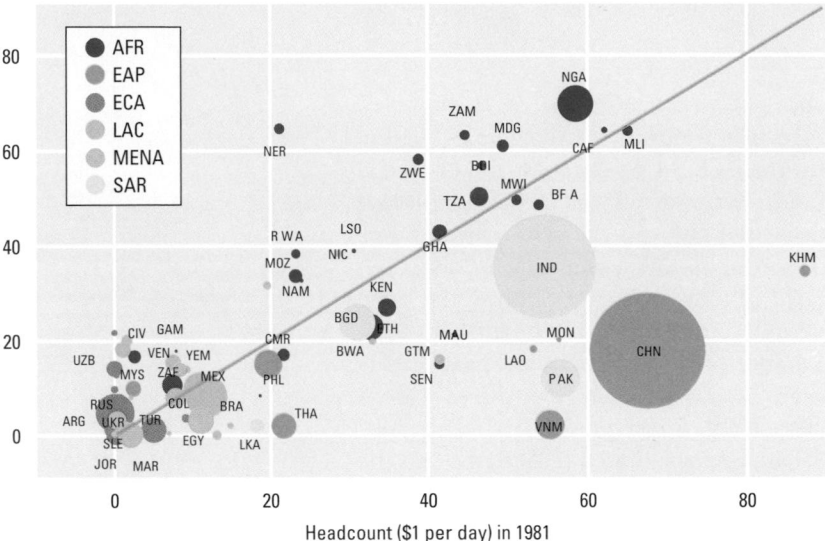

Headcount ($1 per day) in 1981

Source: PovcalNet (http://iresearch.worldbank.org/PovcalNet/jsp/index.jsp).

about the evolution of world welfare, inequality, and relative poverty."[30] Milanovic (2005) also point out the "downward mobility" of many countries in the past 40 years or so. Those who do not share the view that inequality between countries fell in the past 20 to 25 years—that is, those who take the "unweighted" view of the world—may have such mobility concerns in mind.

Absolute poverty rates have declined in the past 20 years or so, and a variety of studies have confirmed this trend (figure 3.11).[31] Overall, while there are roughly 400 million fewer people who live on less than a $1 a day in 2001 than there were in 1981, the number of poor people in Sub-Saharan Africa almost doubled, from approximately 160 million to 313 million.

While some populous countries, almost exclusively in Asia, such as Bangladesh, China, India, and Pakistan, made significant headway against extreme poverty, almost all increases in extreme poverty—especially in countries with high initial headcount rates—took place in Sub-Saharan Africa.[32] Among the larger countries with rising headcount rates are Nigeria, South Africa, and Tanzania.

If the poverty trends discussed here continue, the Millennium Development Goal of halving the proportion of people living on less than $1 a day will be met. But only East and South Asia will reach this goal. We cannot be satisfied if this were to happen. Other things equal, we would prefer to see the poverty rate falling at the same pace in all countries. Currently, hundreds of millions of people in numerous developing countries lack the opportunity to avoid hunger, poor health, and low access to vital services, such as education and clean water.[33]

Global inequalities in power

One of the main arguments in the concluding chapter of this report is that the rules and processes in global markets can be unfair to developing countries. A country's power in decision making in multilateral banks is usually correlated with its economic strength. Even when each country has equal representation in an international body, such as the United Nations system or the World Trade Organization (WTO), powerful forces can chisel away at developing-country interests (through separate bilateral agreements, for example). And the capacity of developing countries to make informed decisions can be limited.

> Poor countries lack the financial and human capital resources that would allow them to be equal participants in the international bodies in which decisions are taken that affect them and, beyond that, in setting the rules under which the international system operates.[34]

In the International Bank for Reconstruction and Development (IBRD)—the market-lending arm of the World Bank—a country's voting power depends on the percentage of IBRD shares it holds. The largest shareholders are the United States with 16.4

percent of the vote, Japan with 7.9 percent, Germany with 4.5 percent, France and the United Kingdom with 4.3 percent. Each has a representative on the Board of Directors. By contrast, all Sub-Saharan countries together have two representatives and 5.2 percent of the vote. China and India both have 2.8 percent of the vote.[35] Country influence in setting the agenda for the institutions is not limited to board membership. A 1998 study by Filmer and others (1998) shows that roughly two thirds of the senior management–level positions at the World Bank are occupied by citizens of Part I (mainly OECD) countries, although these countries account for less than one-fifth of the global population and a smaller share of the number of member countries.

At the WTO, each member country has one vote. Moreover, because decisions are by consensus, each country effectively has veto power. So the WTO is, at least on paper, perhaps the most democratic of international organizations. In practice, the ability of countries to influence the agenda and decisions depends crucially on their capacity to be present, to follow negotiations, to be informed, and to understand fully the impact of the complex issues at hand. A rough indicator of a country's capacity is the size of its representation in Geneva. A study by Blackhurst, Lyakurwa, and Oyejide (2000) found that only 8 of the 38 Sub-Saharan countries had close to five (the WTO average) resident delegates listed in the WTO directory. Worse, 19 of the 38 countries—half of the Sub-Saharan WTO membership—had no delegate resident in Geneva. Only Nigeria had a delegation that deals solely with the WTO.[36]

Even when country representation in the international arena is considered adequate, it is debatable whether the representatives of some countries are fully accountable to their citizens. There are considerable differences among countries in the extent to which their political and legal institutions provide citizens with fair, transparent, and inclusive environments to enhance and leverage their assets. While there are numerous problems with trying to measure such things, Kaufmann, Kraay, and Mastruzzi (2004), in the most comprehensive compar-

Figure 3.12 There is no one-to-one relationship between voice and income

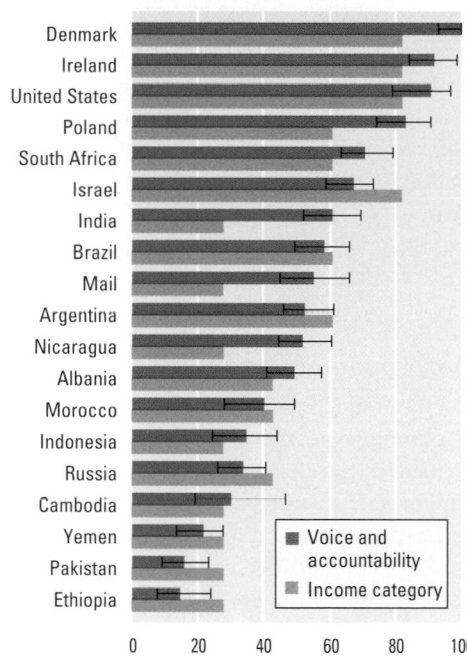

Source: Kaufmann, Kraay, and Mastruzzi (2004).
Note: "Voice and accountability" refers broadly to the extent to which citizens have freedom of expression, a free press, and open elections based on a statistical compilation of responses on the quality of governance given by a large number of enterprise, citizen, and expert survey respondents in industrial and developing countries, as reported by a number of survey institutes, think tanks, nongovernmental organizations, and international organizations. Countries' relative positions on these indicators are subject to margins of error that are clearly indicated. Consequently, precise country rankings should not be inferred from these data.

ative assessment to date, integrate data collected by 25 separate sources constructed by 18 (commercial and advocacy) organizations. The authors used the data to provide a common empirical basis to assess the relative differences among countries of the quality of their "governance."

Figure 3.12 summarizes information on "voice and accountability," which refers broadly to the extent to which citizens have freedom of expression, a free press, and open elections, using standardized measures for selected countries (the same ones as in figure 3.6). The upper bar for each country represents the country's percentile rank in the "voice and accountability" distribution with the intersecting black rule line representing the confidence interval. The lower bar is the average percentile score for the income category to which the country belongs.[37] The top of the "voice" rankings is filled with wealthy countries, such as Denmark, the United States, Ireland, and Israel. The voice ranking of such countries as South Africa, Poland, and especially Mali and India exceed their ranks in incomes. The opposite is true for China, Ethiopia, Pakistan, and the Russian Federation. Cambodia and the Republic of Yemen are both quite poor and rank low in freedom of expression. It is clear that there is no one-to-one relationship between citizens' voice and average income at the country level.

A glimpse of the future

Despite improvements over time, inequalities among countries in various dimensions remain unacceptably high. Each year 10.5 million child deaths are preventable in the sense that these children would not have died if they had been born in rich countries.[38] The mean educational attainment level for adults born in 1975–79 in Sub-Saharan Africa remains at 5.4 years, compared with 10.1 years in Latin America and Caribbean and 13.4 years in developed countries. Developing countries also face massive challenges in influencing the global rules and processes that determine outcomes, which matter greatly to the well-being of their citizens.

International inequalities in educational attainment have been steadily declining. This is also true in health—one's country of birth 50 years ago was much more pertinent to survival than it is today. In this sense, opportunities across countries are equalizing. But improvements in life expectancy at birth have reversed since the early 1990s, because of the devastating effects of HIV/AIDS and the difficult circumstances facing citizens of some transition economies. The world distribution of incomes, by contrast, was becoming secularly more unequal from the early nineteenth century until about the end of World War II. Since the war, international inequality between countries has decreased immensely, because of the fast growth in China and India in more recent times, and global inequality has leveled off. Because China and India are only two countries, intercountry inequality in incomes has continued to increase.

What explains the convergence in health and education and the lack of it in incomes? Deaton (2004) points out that, while gains in income were undoubtedly important for improving nutrition and funding better water and sanitation schemes, some countries made progress in reducing child mortality even in the absence of economic growth. These improvements came from the globalization of knowledge, facilitated by local political, economic, and education conditions. A possible explanation for the disconnect between the convergence in education and the divergence in incomes is that education is not translating into human capital and that the rise in per worker schooling explains only a small part of the growth in output per worker.[39]

We have seen that the story of income inequality in the world has been a story of falling international inequalities and rising within-country inequality. For global inequality, these two effects are offsetting, and the conclusion drawn depends on knowing which effect dominated. The decline in international inequality is largely due to fast income growth in China and South Asia.[40] But as China and South Asia catch up to the world average, their equalizing effect will diminish. And if they continue to develop at similar rates to that in the past two decades, the effect of their growth will increase international inequality.[41] Without the offsetting effect of declining international inequality, global inequality would also be on the rise again unless inequality within countries starts to decline and Sub-Saharan African economies begin to experience healthy growth. This suggests that the future of world income inequality will increasingly be a function of economic growth in Africa (and some other low-income countries under stress), especially if the population growth rates in Africa remain above the world average. That both population growth and economic growth in Africa have been stunted by the AIDS tragedy is doubly disturbing.

On whether today's poor countries with stagnant economies will take off, some researchers are optimistic. Lucas (2003) suggests that the countries that have not yet joined the industrial revolution (which he attributes to socialist planning, lawlessness, and corruption) will become the miracle economies of the future. He reckons that the growth rates in these catch-up countries may be quite high and that they will also go through a similar demographic transition experienced by today's developed countries. The world population will stop rising and world production growth will stabilize until all countries, economically, start resembling countries like the United States, thanks to free trade and the diffusion of technology.

Pritchett—who calls this idea "advantage to backwardness"[42]—remains more cautious. Conceding that such rapid gains in productivity are a possibility, he argues that "the cases in which backward countries, and especially the most backward of countries, actually gain significantly on the leader are historically rare."[43] He observes that there are also forces for "implosive" declines in these countries, suggesting that backwardness may also carry "severe disadvantages."

On health in Sub-Saharan Africa, the UN Population Division projects that life expectancy at birth in Africa will decline over the next 5 to 10 years and then start climbing again, reaching 65 years by about 2050.[44] These projections assume that HIV/AIDS prevalence rates in Africa will peak sometime before 2010 and then decline over the next decades. But the Joint United Nations Programme on HIV/AIDS estimated that 43 percent of pregnant females in 2000 were HIV positive in Botswana and 19 percent in South Africa.[45]

Thus, millions of babies are being infected at birth, which is mostly preventable with proper interventions. Life expectancy in Africa would not improve much, and certainly not soon, if these assumed improvements in HIV/AIDS prevalence rates do not materialize.

Because South Asia has almost caught up to the world average in life expectancy, Sub-Saharan Africa will be the only region significantly affecting health inequalities between countries, barring a major catastrophe elsewhere.[46] So, improvements in life expectancy in Sub-Saharan Africa are the key to future declines in international health inequalities. Chapter 2 documented within-country inequalities in health opportunities for children born to poor or rich parents, educated or uneducated mothers, in rural or urban areas, and so on. Steep gradients in health opportunities and outcomes exist along these dimensions in many countries. A confident assessment of past and future trends in health inequality awaits future research.

If the trends that brought about the catching up of many poor countries outside of Africa continue in health, education, and incomes, the biggest challenges will remain in Africa and some poor countries in other regions. Growth with equity needs to be revived in stagnating economies around the world, and the AIDS tragedy (along with the folly of preventable diseases) needs to be addressed urgently, especially in Sub-Saharan Africa. These remain the biggest global challenges in development today.

Popular participation and equitable transitions at the local level

Promoting equity through public action requires changes in the existing configurations of power and influence. Because established institutions privilege certain interests and marginalize others, making governance institutions more democratic and more equity-enhancing calls for reforms that increase the possibilities for effective participation by traditionally marginalized groups.

Local government is a critical domain for the exercise of democratic rights and for making effective public choices. But several factors have conspired against good governance, democracy, and equity at the local level in much of the developing world. The social and economic power of local elites has often translated into disproportionate influence over the political process, and top-down, insulated, and nontransparent decision-making structures have made it difficult for ordinary citizens to have voice.[1] Democratic deepening in the developing world often begins with the democratization of local government, and that is precisely what two participatory governance initiatives—in the Indian state of Kerala and in a variety of municipalities in Brazil—have tried to do.

In 1996 the state government of Kerala launched what is widely viewed to be the most ambitious initiative for democratic decentralization in India: the People's Campaign of Decentralized Planning. The government not only devolved significant resources and authority to Kerala's 1,214 panchayats (village councils) and municipalities, but it also promoted direct citizen participation by mandating village assemblies and citizen committees to plan and budget local development expenditures.

In Brazil, the city of Porto Alegre launched a participatory budgeting initiative in 1990 that has since been copied in at least 400 municipalities throughout the country. The process begins with neighborhood assemblies in which citizens deliberate and set budgeting priorities, and ends with a citywide budget formulated by delegates directly elected by neighborhood assemblies. The success in Porto Alegre has seen its steady diffusion, with at least 100 municipalities, including São Paulo, implementing variations of participatory budgeting in 1996–2000, and some estimated 250 municipalities in 2000–04.

These two initiatives have much in common. They were both conceived as direct and conscious efforts to break with the elite-dominated and clientelistic politics of local government by promoting redistributive policies through broad popular participation. Thus, they both shifted the political opportunity structure and involved action to strengthen the agency of subordinate groups.[2] Both have, in effect, complemented representative forms of democracy with participatory forms of democracy by opening institutions to the direct engagement of civil society. And both have strengthened public authority and public action by increasing both the depth and scope of democratic decision making.

Deepening democracy

The evidence shows that these initiatives have deepened democracy, expanding the range of social actors participating in the political arena. In Porto Alegre, an estimated 100,000 adults have participated at some point in the budgeting assemblies. Other cities that have adopted some form of the process have also experienced active participation, including municipalities without established civil societies. In Kerala, nearly one in four households attended village assemblies in the first two years of the campaign, and despite routinization of the process in subsequent years, these assemblies continue to draw large numbers. Hundreds of thousands of citizens have undergone training in planning and budgeting, and the committees that actually design and budget specific projects have been composed primarily of civil society actors.

A redesign of institutional incentives and new mobilizational efforts saw women account for 40 percent of the participants in village assemblies (a level otherwise unheard of in India) and the participation rate of dalits (scheduled castes) has exceeded their representation in the population.[3] Moreover, both these initiatives have created a new cadre of grassroots politicians who either did not exist before (delegates in Brazil) or who previously had no powers (the 14,000 elected panchayat councilors in Kerala). The local public sphere—the *sine qua non* of any vibrant democracy—has become more extensive, more inclusive, and more meaningful.

Extending democracy

These initiatives have been marked by the extension of democracy, specifically public decision making in arenas of authority previously dominated by private and state elites. Municipal budgets in Brazil have long been the preserve of oligarchic parties and narrow sectoral interests. Panchayats in Kerala have long been little more than passive recipients of top-down projects designed and delivered by state bureaucracies. In both cases, citizens now have a voice in determining how public resources are allocated. In the most successful participatory budgeting cases, the entire budget of the municipality is discussed and approved by delegates acting on priorities established by neighborhood assemblies, with citizens deliberating on capital and operational segments of the budget.

In some municipalities, direct participation has been extended to thematic areas, such as economic development, public transportation, education, social services, and urban planning. In Kerala, panchayats have been given authority for up to 35 percent of the development budget, a fivefold increase in their resources base. Panchayats have ranked, designed, and implemented hundreds of projects a year across all development sectors. These have included housing for the poor, small-scale irrigation, local roads and infrastructure, agricultural projects, support services in health and education, and a range of projects specifically targeted at women and dalits.

Enhancing equity

These initiatives have generally had equity-enhancing effects. In Porto Alegre, the best known and most documented case, there is clear evidence that expenditures on poorer areas of the city increased steadily with the introduction of participatory budgeting. In other large cities with participatory budgeting, such as Belém and Belo Horizonte, expenditures have also targeted the poor. A statistical analysis of all Brazilian municipalities in 1997–2000 revealed that participatory budgeting cities had significantly higher expenditures on sectors that affect the poor most directly.[4]

In Kerala, a large survey of key respondents found that "disadvantaged" groups were the prime beneficiaries of targeted schemes. Case studies show that panchayats have emphasized the need to bring all households up to a certain basic level of well-being, with a heavy emphasis on providing sanitation facilities, decent housing, and safe water to needy families.

In both cases, there is also strong evidence that the incidence of rent-seeking has fallen sharply.[5] The greater transparency of the budgeting process alone has raised the transaction costs of predation and patronage.

Empowering the most marginal groups

The Kerala and Porto Alegre cases illustrate the value of improving the accessibility, transparency, and accountability of local government. However, even when such initiatives have been undertaken, and where the economy is otherwise growing, the most marginalized social groups—widows, slum dwellers, sex workers, the very poor—may continue to be excluded. What can be done? The challenge is greater when the extent of commitment from above and mobilization from below is less than in these two cases.

As discussed in chapter 2, the most marginal groups are often stuck in more severe forms of an "inequality trap"—a situation characterized by dire material circumstances, rational expectations about limited mobility opportunities, and internalized beliefs regarding the legitimacy and immutability of their circumstances. Breaking out of such inequality traps and improving the terms by which the poor are "recognized" by others starts with building both a "capacity to aspire" and, equally important, a "capacity to engage."[6] This includes being able to envision and enact alternative futures, believing that it is desirable and possible to move out of poverty, and being able to more meaningfully participate in forums where decisions affecting their welfare are made.

Acquiring a "capacity to aspire" is largely a product of developing more broadly accessible and equitable mechanisms for interaction between the poor and elites, mechanisms that are reciprocally linked to attaining greater voice in associational interactions. It thrives in and through group organizing and public dialogue, and the opportunities these afford for practice, repetition, exploration, conjecture, and refutation.

An association of sex workers in a Calcutta slum, for example, gave its individual members a voice, a public presence, and a capacity to realize their interests and aspirations that would have been denied them otherwise.[7] Young, female, often illegal immigrants, contractually bound to work long hours for ruthless bosses, and facing sure rejection by their families if they managed to escape and return home, the sex workers had virtually no capacity to exercise their voices and realize their interests. Persistent efforts to organize the women into a union, however, eventually gave them the confidence and competence to bring about a change in condom use by clients.

In Indonesia, the Kecamatan Development Project (KDP), which operates in 28,000 villages across the country, seeks to improving the "terms of recognition" and political agency of marginalized groups.[8] The project allocates grant money at the subdistrict level, for which several groups of poor villagers (two of whom must be women) are invited to compete for funds on the basis of the presentation of a formal subproject proposal. KDP's procedures, institutions, and norms are largely decentralized, they focus on joint public problem solving, they invite broad public participation and scrutiny, and they occur in a more or less continuous and institutionalized way.[9]

Recent work assessing the impact of KDP on local decision making finds that KDP helps marginalized groups cultivate access to more constructive spaces and procedures for addressing project and non-project conflicts.[10] The beginning stage of such a transformation—in which unequal groups build the capacity to peacefully engage one another—is a humble but nontrivial outcome for a development project.

Why does equity matter?

PART II

IN THE FIRST PART OF THIS REPORT, WE SUMMARIZED some of the evidence on inequalities in several dimensions. In addition to affecting well-being directly, such dimensions as health, education, income, voice, and access to services shape the opportunities people face for future progress and achievement. We emphasized the interconnections between these various dimensions. Not only is there inequality in the distributions of income, health status, and educational attainment, but—even more important—these indicators tend to be correlated. The rich tend to be both healthier and better educated than others. The poorest of the poor tend to have the lowest attainment in years of schooling and some of the worst health indicators. These correlations generally also extend to public services, with the poor gaining access to infrastructure, electricity, water, sanitation, and garbage disposal much later than others, if at all.

Because education and wealth help a person gain influence in society, voice and political power are also generally thought to be correlated with economic well-being. The interaction between these mutually reinforcing economic, social, and political inequalities perpetuates them across generations. Chapter 2 discussed evidence indicating that a 10 percent difference in economic status between two families in one generation tends to imply, on average, a 4 percent to 7 percent difference in the next generation, depending on the country and measurement details. Opportunities clearly are not independent from social and family background, or from group identity.

Do such disparities matter? Are people concerned with the large observed differences in access to education and health, and in economic opportunities, or merely with the fact that some people have low absolute levels of income, years of schooling, and access to services? Should policymakers worry about the unequal opportunities that arise from discrimination, unequal access to justice or other unfair processes? Should an institution like the World Bank, whose primary objective is to assist its client countries in eradicating extreme poverty, care about inequalities—in opportunities, outcomes, and processes—at all?

Opinions on these questions are wide-ranging. Support for equal opportunities has long been a theme in domestic policy in the United States, for instance. Franklin D. Roosevelt once said that "We know that equality of individual ability has never existed and never will, but we do insist that equality of opportunity still must be sought."[1] Some participants in the consultations for this report were even offended that the question "Does inequality matter?" was asked at all, because they considered its answer to be "Obviously, yes." One participant felt that the very question indicated that "we are suffering [from] a terrible tolerance to horror."[2]

The next three chapters in this report address the following question: should good development policy be concerned with equity? Equity, as discussed in chapter 1, is understood here as the pursuit of equal opportunities and the avoidance of severe deprivation. Equity is *not* the same as equality in incomes, or in health status, or in any other specific outcome. It is the quest for a situation in which personal effort, preferences, and initiative—rather than family background, caste, race, or gender—account for the differences among people's economic achievements. A situation in which all institutions are color-blind and nonmarket institutions are equally responsive to the rich and the poor. In which personal and property rights are enforced equally for all. And in which all have access to the public services and the infrastructure to leverage their productivity and their chances of success in the markets.

The evidence we review here has been assembled in disciplines ranging from economics and history to sociology and anthropology. On balance, this evidence suggests that the pursuit of sustainable, long-term prosperity is inseparable from a broadening of economic opportunities and

political voice to most or all of society. One set of reasons for this arises from failures in capital, land, and labor markets. Those failures imply that productive opportunities are not necessarily seized by those with the highest potential returns on their talents or ideas, but instead by those with greater wealth, better connections, or larger land parcels. This would not happen if markets worked perfectly, as resources would flow to those with the most productive investment projects. But given that markets are not perfect, scope arises for efficient redistribution schemes.

Chapter 5 documents cases in which aggregate efficiency could be improved by redistributing wealth or power toward poorer or marginal groups. Sometimes, the evidence of inefficiency is seen in differences in marginal products of capital across firms. We know that smaller entrepreneurs pay interest rates much higher than the marginal product of capital accruing to other firms. We know that some farmers allocate effort between plots in a way that is not socially efficient, because they own one plot and sharecrop in another. We have experimental evidence suggesting that groups discriminated against perform below their own capacity, either because they internalize the stereotype or because they expect to be treated unfairly. Each of these pieces of carefully researched empirical evidence, and others discussed in chapter 5, provide reasons why more equitable economies would, in most cases, also be more efficient.[3]

Chapter 6 complements this picture by looking at historical evidence, suggesting that large inequalities in political rights and power give rise to exclusionary institutions that generally impair development processes. Greater political equality, by contrast, establishes limits on predation by the most powerful in each society. This tends to lead to institutions that level the playing field and provide opportunities for advancement and mobility to those from underprivileged backgrounds.

Such institutions seem to be associated with more sustained growth. One example comes from contrasting the exploitative labor practices of the Spanish *conquista-dores* in the mining centers of their American colonies from the sixteenth to the eighteenth century, with the greater freedom and opportunity afforded to early settlers in North America. Another example of inequitable treatment of citizens by the state, which was also enormously costly for efficiency, was the very high taxation of poor African farmers by state-owned or parastatal agricultural marketing boards in Ghana, Nigeria, and Zambia, which prevailed a few decades ago.

Equity and fairness matter not only because they are complementary to long-term prosperity. It is evident that many people—if not most—care about equity for its own sake. Some see equal opportunities and fair processes as matters of social justice and thus as an intrinsic part of the objective of development. In chapter 4, we briefly review arguments and evidence suggesting that most societies exhibit a pervasive and long-standing concern for equity.

Equity and well-being

People from many cultures seem to share a concern for equity that is reflected in religious and philosophical traditions, as well as in legal institutions, both national and international. Religions from Islam to Buddhism and secular philosophical traditions from Plato to Sen have shown both a concern for equity and an aversion to absolute deprivation. In modern legal institutions, equity remains a fundamental tenet of theory and practice.

That a concern with equity is so pervasive across cultures, religions, and philosophical traditions suggests that a fundamental preference for fairness is deeply rooted in human beings. We review experimental evidence showing that many people place a monetary value on "fairness" and are prepared to give up real money if they feel that a process they are involved in is unfair. Complementing this evidence are data from opinion surveys, and surveys on subjective well-being, suggesting that higher inequality in incomes is, on average, associated with lower aggregate levels of subjective well-being.

An empirical link between income inequality and poverty reduction reinforces the conceptual link between the aversion to inequality and the quest to avoid absolute deprivation. We highlight the obvious fact that, if inequality falls during a growth spell, poverty generally falls by more than if inequality had not changed. We also document the less obvious fact that higher-income inequality reduces the effectiveness of future economic growth in reducing absolute income poverty.

Ethical and philosophical approaches to equity

Perhaps the oldest manifestations of concern with equity and the avoidance of deprivation come from religion. Several major world religions endorse the notions of social justice and a duty toward the poor. Buddhists see a duty to care for the poor. Christians are to "love their neighbor as themselves." The Hebrew word for "charity" is the same as the one for "justice." One of Islam's five pillars of faith is *zakat,* providing for the poor and needy. The World Faiths Development Dialogue (1999) states that "all religions would see the extreme material poverty in the world today as a moral indictment to contemporary humanity and a breach of trust within the human family." And religious views on equity are not restricted to poverty. Despite varying interpretations, and a wealth of differences in perspective, a belief in the fundamental dignity of human beings is a theological tenet in most major religions. While there are important differences in how this belief manifests itself across faiths, and even among different groups within the main religions, some analysts see a growing emphasis on this principle of equality within various faiths.[1]

Equity is also a key theme in secular philosophical traditions. Western political and ethical philosophy, for instance, has long been concerned with distribution. In ancient Greece, Plato argued that "if a state is to avoid . . . civil disintegration . . . extreme poverty and wealth must not be allowed to rise in any section of the citizen-body, because both lead to disasters."[2] Roman law, while discriminating against slaves, as in all ancient empires, also laid the foundations for some of the principles of equality that underlie modern legal principles in many countries. Those principles applied only to Roman citizens who were free, but in modern nations they have become all-inclusive.

In the modern era, Western thinking about social justice was greatly influenced by utilitarianism—the idea, originally from

Bentham (1789), that the social goal should be to achieve "the greatest happiness for the greatest number." Although utilitarians were essentially unconcerned with the distribution of happiness, enjoining societies simply to maximize the sum of utilities across all individuals, the approach has earned the somewhat misbegotten reputation (at least among economists) of having egalitarian implications.[3]

Modern theories of distributive justice have largely moved beyond utilitarianism, in part because of its fundamental lack of concern with the distribution of welfare. Since the early 1970s, a number of influential thinkers, including John Rawls, Amartya Sen, Ronald Dworkin, and John Roemer, have made separate and important contributions to the way we think about equity. Although the theories of justice and social choice proposed by each of them are different in important respects, they share much in common.

All four reject final welfare (or utility) as the appropriate space in which to judge the fairness of a given allocation or system. All acknowledge the importance of individual responsibility in moving from resources to final outcomes, including welfare. All prefer to see some combination of the set of liberties and resources available to individuals as the right space to form a social judgment. All seem to appeal, at some stage, to the "veil of ignorance" argument, from Harsanyi (1955), that a fair allocation of resources should be one that all "prospective members of society" would agree on, before they knew which position they would occupy. They used this thought experiment to argue that justice implies equality in the allocation to all people of some fundamental concept, such as primary goods.

What Rawls, Sen, Dworkin, and Roemer disagree on is what exactly this concept should be. Rawls (1971) argued that social justice required that two basic principles should hold. The first "demands the most extensive liberty for each, consistent with similar liberty for others."[4] The second requires that opportunities—which he related to the concept of "primary goods"—should be open to all members of society. Under the Difference Principle, he proposes that the chosen allocation should be one that maximizes the oppor-

tunities of the least privileged group. (The Difference Principle is also known as Rawls's "maximin" principle).

Sen (1985) thought that different people might have different "conversion factors" from resources to actions and welfare. He argued that all goods, including Rawls' "primary goods," are inputs to a person's functionings—the set of actions a person performs and of states the person values or enjoys. For Sen, the concept to be equalized across people is the set of possible functionings from which a person might be able to choose (which he called a "capability set").

Dworkin (1981b) and Dworkin (1981a) argued that justice required that individuals should be compensated for aspects of their circumstances over which they had no control, or for which they could not be held responsible. He argued for a distribution of resources that compensated people for innate differences that they could not have helped, including differences in talent.

Roemer (1998) argued that equity demanded an "equal opportunity policy." He acknowledged that individuals bear some responsibility for their own welfare, but also that circumstances over which they have no control affect both how much effort they invest and the level of welfare they eventually attain. He argued that public action should therefore aim to equalize "advantages" among people from groups with different circumstances at every point along the distribution of efforts within the group.

Despite important (but subtle) differences, all four thinkers have contributed to shifting the focus of social justice from outcomes to opportunities. We also take a leaf from Nozick (1974), who is usually regarded as an anti-egalitarian. He argued that theories of justice generally placed an excessive emphasis on outcomes, such as welfare, utility, or even capabilities. Nozick reminded us of the (obvious) fact that outcomes are the result of processes and argued that the correct focus for a theory of justice should be on the fairness of processes. If a particular allocation departs from a fair initial state, and is arrived at through a fair process, it should be judged to be fair—even if it is unequal.

B O X   4 . 1   *A simple representation of different concepts of equity*

The figure below (adapted from figure 11-1 in Atkinson and Stiglitz 1980),* can help summarize what this report hopes to achieve—and what it does not. Suppose that a society consists of only two groups of people (1 and 2) and let the axes of the diagram depict the opportunity levels of each group. Opportunity sets are obviously multidimensional, but imagine for simplicity that the various dimensions can be meaningfully conflated onto an "opportunity index," O_1 for type 1s, and O_2 for type 2s. Now let the curved frontier AC represent the "opportunity possibility frontier" for this society.** It reflects the maximum opportunity indexes that types 1 and 2 can obtain, given the available resources and technology. The fact that it does not monotonically decline from A to C incorporates the fact that when type 1 individuals have very limited opportunities, type 2 people can also benefit from an expansion in type 1 opportunity sets, and vice versa. Over some ranges, improvements in the opportunity sets of the "poorest" types can be Pareto-improving—that is, can benefit everyone. Put another way, there is scope for efficient, growth-promoting redistribution.

Eventually, however, tradeoffs set in. Between points P and R, if society is on the opportunity possibility frontier, any improvement in type 1 sets must imply a reduction in type 2 sets, and vice-versa. Points B, R, and E are translations to this "opportunity space" of the welfare concepts associated with Bentham, Rawls, and full egalitarianism, respectively.

• If this society wished to maximize the sum of total opportunity indexes, it should aim for point B.

• If, instead, it wanted to maximize the opportunity set of the "poorest" group, it should aim for point R.

• If it insisted on absolute equality of opportunities, it must lie along the 45-degree ray through the origin, and would aim for point E.

What this report will not attempt to do is to advise countries on which of these criteria of social justice, or indeed any other, an individual society should aim for. Each of these three points can be defended by logical arguments, under different degrees of aversion to inequalities in opportunity.

What the report will try to do is as follows:

• Describe the inequalities in opportunity actually observed in society (at a point such as X).

• Investigate whether some of those disparities (which in this diagram greatly favor type 2) might actually be preventing the society from enjoying higher aggregate opportunities (and welfare, on another space).

• Suggest possible policy and institutional approaches that might help move from points such as X to whichever point society considers equitable, on the opportunity possibility frontier.

*Atkinson and Stiglitz (1980) refer, in turn, to a figure 1 in Buchanan (1976).
**In Atkinson and Stiglitz (1980), utilities are used instead of opportunities. While that distinction is fundamental in almost every respect, it is not for the point being made here, namely that different social justice criteria imply different optimal allocations.

An illustration of choices between the opportunities of two types of people

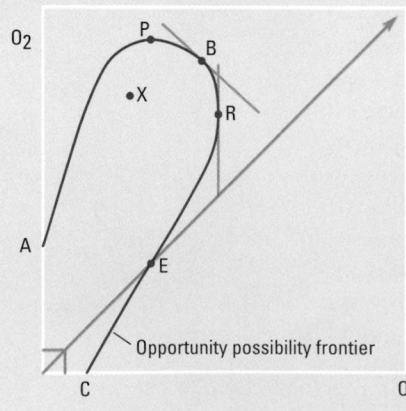

B: Maximize sum of total opportunity $(O_1 + O_2)$

R: Maximize opportunities for group 1 (O_1)

E: Absolute equality of opportunities between group 1 (O_1) and group 2 (O_1)

The concept of equity we adopt in this report draws on the contribution of these four thinkers by focusing on opportunities, rather than on welfare, utilities, or some other corresponding individual outcome. We do not dwell on the fine distinctions between Sen's capabilities and Roemer's opportunities. As in both frameworks, we acknowledge the central role of individual responsibility and effort in determining outcomes. We focus on eliminating disadvantage from circumstances that lie largely beyond the control of the individual but that powerfully shape both the outcomes and the actions in pursuit of those outcomes.

These different perspectives on what a social optimum should be can shed light on an important point for this report—one previously mentioned in chapter 1. It is not for us to advise countries on what exactly constitutes an equitable distribution in their societies. Instead, our role is to point out the inequities we can observe and to note that reducing them may be perfectly consistent with—perhaps even necessary for—greater efficiency and prosperity in the long run. Box 4.1 draws on a classic public economics discussion of these philosophical perspectives to illustrate this point.

Equity and legal institutions

The concerns with equity that feature in moral, religious, and ethical debates around the world are reflected in real-world institutions, through which people have sought to promote justice throughout history. Chief among them are legal institutions, where "equity" has a distinct—and specific—interpretation as a set of principles intended to guide and correct the application of the law. According to Kritzer (2002), how these principles merge with the written, codified law varies across legal traditions, but the overarching concept of "fairness" is a cross-cultural reality. And in practice, definitions often refer directly to shared values within a particular community[5] as well as to the belief that people should not suffer before the law as a result of having unequal bargaining power.[6]

In Western philosophy, Aristotle is regarded as the first author to distinguish between justice and equity.[7] He found that courts enact justice according to law—that is, by applying general rules that give an equitable solution in the majority of cases. In some cases, however, the results are inequitable. Equity then rectifies law in so far as the law is defective on account of its generality.[8] The Romans operationalized this concept of equity by distinguishing between *ius strictum* (strict law) and *ius aequum* (equity), with the latter used to interpret the law and to complement it. Equity prevailed in instances of conflict between the two.

In modern legal traditions, equity remains a fundamental tenet of legal theory and practice. In common law systems, equity was historically a separate branch of law administered by Chancery Courts.[9] The Judicature Act of 1873 in the United Kingdom "fused" the courts of law and equity, doing away with a bifurcated system of courts, while establishing the supremacy of equity in cases of conflict between equity and common law. Equitable principles, based on conscience and fairness, have continued to develop and be applied in common law jurisdictions around the world to mitigate harsh and unfair results produced by the application of formal legal rules in specific cases.[10]

In general, the use of equity as a source of law in the civil law traditions of the European continent is more limited than in the common law tradition. Civil legal codes, which have their origins in the Enlightenment era, aim at integrating equity into formal law—that is, by designing laws aimed at producing equitable results. Equity is seen as part of law and, therefore, should be achieved by applying the formal rules. Provisions in the codes that refer explicitly to equity, however, are used to correct inequitable results of the application of other formal provisions, in a way which is similar to common law systems.

Both the common law and the codified systems from the continental European tradition have spread to countries around the globe, and equity is now a global legal concept. The legal systems of Latin American countries, such as Argentina, Brazil, and Mexico, have approaches to equity similar to those in continental Europe, while Bangladesh, India, and Nigeria follow the common law tradition. Importantly, equity is not a purely Western concept—it can be found in legal systems around the world, including those that do not share European origins.[11] For example, the distinction between justice and equity is also found in Islamic law, in which the former is referred to as *adala,* the latter as *insaf,* and in Jewish law, with the distinction between *din* and *tsedek.*[12]

In today's more integrated world, legal understanding of equity has also influenced international law—serving as the basis for individualized justice, creating specific principles of fairness and reasonableness, or being identified with international equitable standards for sharing resources and redistributing wealth. Perhaps the foremost example of the development of international principles of equity is the international human rights regime. International human rights law is rooted in a commitment to protect the "equal and inalienable rights of all members of the human family," which itself is considered to be the "foundation of freedom, justice and peace in the world."[13]

The U.N. Charter laid the foundation for contemporary international human rights law. The preamble to the Charter states that the U.N. community "reaffirms faith in fundamental human rights, in the dignity and worth of the human person, in the equal rights of men and women and of nations large and small."[14] The Universal Declaration of Human Rights, adopted by the General Assembly of the United Nations on December 10, 1948, is viewed as the "source of inspiration and . . . the basis for the U.N. in making advances in standard setting as contained in the existing human rights instruments."[15] It has become a highly visible and widely recognized statement of moral, ethical, and political standards at the international level.[16]

The contemporary international human rights regime comprises a broad array of legal instruments,[17] many operating under the aegis of the United Nations. There also exist regional human rights regimes in Europe (European Convention on Human Rights and Fundamental Freedoms), the Americas (Inter-American Convention on Human Rights), and Africa (African Charter on Human and Peoples' Rights). In addition, the laws of some other international entities, such as the European Union, incorporate human rights norms (Treaty of Nice, Charter of Fundamental Rights of the European Union). Together, these different legal instruments are aimed at protecting people against a variety of harms, including potential harm by their governments, and at committing to the fundamental principles of equality and nondiscrimination.

People prefer fairness

Different cultures and religions around the world may differ in important respects, but they all share a concern with equity and fairness. This suggests something quite fundamental about the value human beings place on them. A fairly recent body of literature in economics sheds some light on these shared human preferences. It has amassed convincing evidence on individuals' preferences for fairness, based on controlled laboratory experiments. In these experiments, individuals interact through behavioral games and play with real money under tightly controlled conditions. Results from such experiments over the last 10 or so years reject the hypothesis in standard economic models that all individuals are exclusively concerned with their material self-interest. This new body of literature is large and rich, but its main findings can be summarized under three main points.

Figure 4.1 The distribution of observed offers in ultimatum games
Offers and rejections in high- and low-stakes ultimatum games

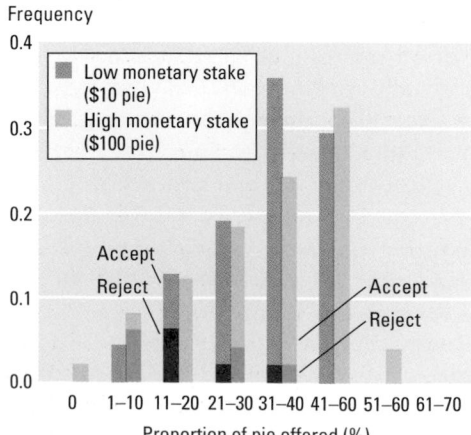

Source: Based on data from Hoffman, McCabe, and Smith (1996).

First, some people behave in ways clearly inconsistent with the rational self-interest hypothesis. According to Fehr and Fischbacher (2003), such people regularly display a willingness to engage in two specific forms of behavior: "*altruistic rewarding,* a propensity to reward others for cooperative, norm-abiding behavior, and *altruistic punishment,* a propensity to impose sanctions on others for norm violations" (785). These behaviors are observed in contexts in which it is possible to rule out individual motivation by a desire for reciprocity or a concern with reputation. While reciprocity and reputation are important additional determinants of cooperation in many settings, the experimental evidence suggests that they are not the only factors that influence cooperative behavior.

A classic example is the Ultimatum Game, in which a player (the Proposer) is asked to suggest a one-time division of a certain sum of money (say, $100) between himself or herself and another player. The second player (the Responder) has the power to simply accept or reject the offer. Acceptance leads to the implementation of the offer, whereas rejection leads to a zero payoff for both players. Monetary stakes are for keeps, and neither player knows the real identity of the other player. Both players are told that they will never play with each other again.

In such circumstances, standard game theory predicts a unique equilibrium: the Proposer should offer the smallest possible amount, and the Responder should accept (since a penny is higher than zero). But time and again, across hundreds of experiments in highly heterogeneous cultural circumstances and with amounts ranging from one hour's to one week's local wages, observed offers are substantially higher and, even so, rejections are often observed.[18] In many experiments, the modal (most frequent) offer is actually at 50 percent. Figure 4.1 depicts the actual distribution of observed offers in two sets of Ultimatum Games, one with lower monetary stakes (bar on the left) and one with higher (bar on the right).

Second, people are heterogeneous. A sizable fraction of people in most experiments (20 to 50 percent) engage in altruistic giving or altruistic punishment—expending real resources in a way that is unambiguously costly to them, without any hope of eliciting personal gain if the other person is rationally self-interested. But the behavior of others (a majority) is consistent with rational self-interest. This is brought out quite starkly in the Dictator Game, a variant of the Ultimatum Game in which the responder is purely passive. The second player is simply a Receiver, with no right to reject the offer. Positive offers in the Dictator Game are observed, but they are both rarer and smaller on average than under the Ultimatum Game, in which the Responder may—always at a cost—punish the Proposer. These results point to the importance of investigating more precisely the conditions under which people exhibit self-interested and other-regarding behavior.

Third, fair-minded people can behave selfishly, and self-interested people can behave fairly. Behaviors depend on the rules of the game. In games where competitive pressures are introduced, mimicking a competitive market, players tend to quickly converge toward actions consistent with self-interested behavior. An example is an Ultimatum Game with Multiple Proposers. If the Responder can choose among various offers from different Proposers, with all nonchosen Proposers receiving zero, observed behavior quickly tends to the Nash equilibrium. In the Nash equilibrium, all Proposers offer the full amount—or very close to it—despite this giving rise to a very unequal distribution, in which the Responder captures the entire surplus, and all Proposers get zero. In other settings, however—such as the Repeated Public Good Game with Punishment in Fehr and Gachter (2000)—even a small number of altruistic players can sustain a cooperative equilibrium.

These findings have been interpreted to suggest that a sizable fraction of human beings in most societies care not only about their own individual opportunities and outcomes but also about "fairness." There is also broad agreement that fairness consists of a concern for others, although some authors suggest that it is other people's intentions

toward us that attract reward or punishment, while others think it is their outcomes or opportunities.[19] These studies do not usually distinguish explicitly between outcomes or opportunities. But it is possible to speculate that the aversion to very unequal payoff distributions in the Ultimatum Game arises from the arbitrary and unequal nature of the endowments (or power) implicit in the initial allocation of the roles of Proposer and Responder.

The experiments also show that people's views of fairness are complex and do not depend entirely on outcomes. Some players are prepared to punish noncooperators until they receive less than other people, because of what they perceive to be the unfairness of their actions in the process of the game. This is consistent with our emphasis that observed distributions of certain outcomes—such as incomes—are the product of complex processes, and that the primary interest for those concerned with equity is *not* the outcome, but the fairness of the processes they participate in over their lifetimes. An income distribution in which some people are much richer than others because, given similar chances, they have worked much harder, may be regarded as fair. But the same income distribution may be regarded as unfair if it was generated by the richer group having access to much better schools or jobs, solely because of the wealth or connections of their parents.

A separate but related point is made by the social identity literature in social psychology (see Haslam 2001) and epidemiology (see Marmot 2004), which suggests that individual behavior and performance are heavily conditioned by group identity (for example, caste, gender, occupation); by whether those groups are seen as subordinate to others (for example, doctors and patients, the status accorded minority ethnic communities); and by whether the boundaries among groups are regarded as permeable (for example, the rules shaping whether and how employees get promotions, immigrants become citizens, and so on). Civil servants with low status and few upward mobility prospects suffer from higher mortality.[20] Employees of low-status firms undergoing a merger more readily

---

BOX 4.2   *Capuchin monkeys don't like inequity either . . .*

Research is under way on the roots of human altruism and the aversion to inequity, whether cultural or genetic. But there is some evidence that aversion to unfairness is not just human. In a recent article in *Nature,* "Monkeys Reject Unequal Pay," Brosnan and De Waal (2003) report the results of exchange experiments with brown capuchin monkeys (*Cebus apella*). The animals were given a token that they could immediately redeem for food by returning it to the experimenter. They were placed in adjoining compartments with visual and vocal contact.

In the baseline treatment (the equality test), both specimens received a quarter of a cucumber slice for each token exchanged.

In one treatment of interest (the "inequality test"), the first monkey received a grape, while the second was given the usual slice of cucumber. That capuchin monkeys prefer grapes to cucumber slices had apparently been amply established by previous research. The results were striking. Monkeys failed to exchange their tokens for food around 5 percent of the time under

the equality test, but this rate rose to more than 50 percent under the inequality test.

The refusal rate rose even further (to more than 80 percent) under an alternative treatment, known as "effort control." In this treatment, the first monkey received a grape with no effort—with no need to pick up a token and exchange it for food. Although few monkeys were used, these differences were all statistically significant.

In both treatments, refusal rates increased over time, as the experiment was repeated (never more than once a day) many times. Interestingly, only female monkeys completed these tests, as earlier experiments suggested that male capuchins are much less sensitive to the distribution of rewards.

The authors concluded that "tolerant species with well-developed food sharing and cooperation, such as capuchins [. . .] may hold emotionally charged expectations about reward distribution and social exchange that lead them to dislike inequity" (Brosnan and De Waal 2003, 299).

Source: Brosnan and De Waal (2003).

---

accept the new organizational structure because it benefits them individually, while members of the higher-status firm are more likely to resist change and act collectively in terms of their premerger identity.[21]

The experimental and subjective well-being literature in economics and social psychology remind us that there is something deep and fundamental about our taste for fairness and equity. Such "human altruism," argue Fehr and Fischbacher (2003) in *Nature,* may be what accounts for the much greater complexity of cooperative patterns in human societies compared with those of other animals (box 4.2). Equity, it seems, matters intrinsically and fundamentally for human beings.

Whatever the exact form of the true motives of individuals, the main implication for this report from this large body of experimental evidence is that a good proportion of people in most societies appear to dislike unfair outcomes and behaviors, so much so that they are prepared to pay to punish those responsible for them. If people are prepared to pay real money to reduce inequalities that appear unfair to them in a

laboratory, it is plausible that large inequalities in real life also reduce their well-being (particularly if the inequalities are not seen to reflect only differences in effort or merit). This provides support for the statistical association that the subjective well-being literature finds between income inequality and self-reported happiness—a subject we now turn to.

Income inequality and subjective well-being

To what extent do the concerns with equity shown in tightly controlled lab experiments also manifest themselves in the attitudes, feelings, and opinions of "regular people?" A recent study of labor strife in the United States suggests that worker perceptions of whether they have been treated fairly or unfairly can affect their efforts, and thus product quality, in important ways (box 4.3).

Other studies investigate the associations between the narrower concept of income inequality and measures of subjective well-being. One recent study of European nations and the United States relies on individual answers to the following question: "Taken all together, how would you say things are these days—would you say that you are very happy, pretty happy, or not too happy?"[22] Based on the variation in answers to this question, across European countries and U.S. states, and on objective income-inequality measures, Alesina, Di Tella, and MacCulloch (2004) find that "individuals have a lower tendency to report themselves happy when inequality is high, even after controlling for individual income, a large set of personal characteristics, and year and country [. . .] dummies" (2009).[23]

One reason that inequality might make people less happy, even when controlling for absolute income levels, is that it violates their sense of fairness. It may be that (at least some) people feel that a very unequal income distribution reflects unfair processes and unequal distributions of opportunity. A 2001 study of Latin American countries by Latinobarometro, a reputable Chile-based opinion survey company, asked respondents the following question: "Do you think that the income distribution in your country is very fair, fair, unfair, or very unfair?" On

BOX 4.3 *Worker perceptions of unfairness, product quality, and consumer safety*

Do people change their behavior because they feel they are being treated unfairly, when they are outside laboratories? And if so, is this likely to have any serious consequence? A study of industrial relations in Illinois, United States, suggests that the answer to both questions is yes.

Since the 1940s, Firestone tire plants had adhered to the industrywide bargain with labor unions. But when negotiations for a new contract began in 1994, Bridgestone/Firestone proposed deviating from the industrywide bargain in a way that worsened the terms for labor at a time when company profits were increasing. The company proposed moving from an 8- to a 12-hour shift that would rotate between days and nights. It also proposed cutting pay for new hires by 30 percent. The union at the plant in Decatur, Illinois, called a strike and, shortly after the strike, the company hired replacement workers.

Labor strife at the Decatur plant closely coincided with lower product quality and defective tires. In August 2000, Firestone announced the recall of 14 million ATX and AT tires, most of them on the Ford Explorer. The U.S. government reported that Firestone tires under investigation

were related to 271 deaths and more than 800 injuries. The most common source of failure of the recalled tires was tread separation, a sudden detachment of the rubber tread from the steel belts that caused the tire to blow out.

Krueger and Mas (2004) compare the number of claims of defective tires in the Decatur plant with those from the two other North American plants where Firestone ATX tires were produced: Joliette, Quebec, and Wilson, North Carolina. Neither of these two plants experienced labor strife in the relevant period. Tires produced during the labor dispute (1994–96) at Decatur had a much higher failure rate than those produced at Joliette or Wilson, although before and after the dispute period the rate of claims was similar for tires manufactured in Decatur and in the other plants. The pattern suggests that changes in technology cannot explain the rise in complaints against Decatur tires, because no such rise occurred in Joliette or Wilson.

Nor does it appear that the lack of experience of replacement workers is to blame. There was a spike in claims in the first half of 1994, around the

time concessions were demanded and the old contract expired, which occurred before replacement workers were hired. Through early 1995, when many replacement workers were making tires, there were no excess claims in the Decatur plant. It was not until the end of 1995, when many returning strikers were working side by side with replacement workers, that the excess number of claims became high. On the basis of this and a much broader analysis, it appears likely that the chemistry between the recalled strikers and the replacement workers, or the cumulative impact of labor strife in general, created the conditions that led to the production of many defective tires.

The authors of the study "recommend that the reader exercise caution in extending our results to other settings; our paper provides a detailed case study of only one firm in one unique period of its history" (Krueger and Mas 2004, 257). At least in that instance, it appears that perceptions of unfair treatment influenced worker attitudes—and product quality and the safety of consumers.

Source: Krueger and Mas (2004).

average, 89 percent of respondents regarded the distribution in their countries to be either unfair or very unfair. In 17 of the 18 countries surveyed, fewer than 20 percent of respondents answered fair or very fair.[24]

Such results may be particularly strong in Latin America, which is one of most unequal regions in the world, but they are not exclusive to that region. A recent analysis of several OECD countries (which are less unequal than most developing countries) was based on data from the International Social Survey Program. To construct a proxy measure of cross-national attitudes toward income inequality, Osberg and Smeeding (2004) ask what a number of different professions[25] "should earn" and what they "do earn." They find that citizens of most high-income countries[26] appear on average to have similar attitudes toward inequality, generally thinking that less well-paid professions should be paid more and that better-paid professions should be paid less.

Osberg and Smeeding (2004) findings reinforce the view that the normative preferences people have over distributions are

based not exclusively on actual incomes, but also on processes, and that some differences in outcomes may be considered fair (for example, because of differences in effort), while others are not (for example, because of differences in opportunities). People are clearly aware that income differentials can provide incentives for work and investment, including in education, if they are coupled with opportunities for reward to those actions. This comes across very clearly from the answers to one question in the latest wave of the World Value Survey, which split respondents around the world more or less evenly into those who felt that income inequality was too high and those who felt it was too low.

Income inequality and incentives: What do people say?

The World Value Survey is a multicountry survey of individuals designed and sponsored by the Inter-university Consortium for Political and Social Research, based at the University of Michigan. The survey aims to "enable a cross-national comparison of values and norms on a wide variety

Figure 4.2 Views on inequality from the World Values Survey

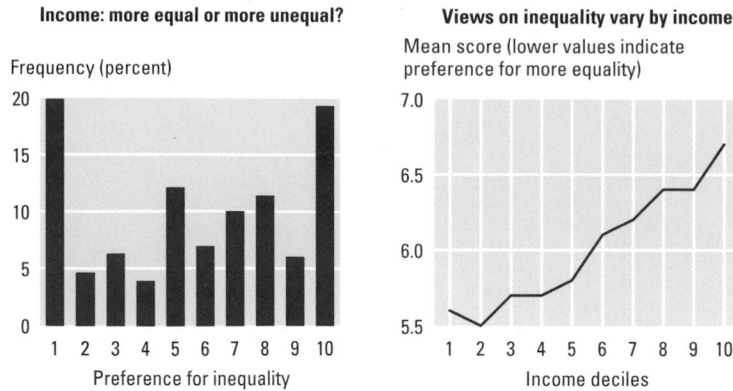

Income: more equal or more unequal?

Frequency (percent)

Views on inequality vary by income

Mean score (lower values indicate
preference for more equality)

Preference for inequality

Income deciles

Source: Inglehart and others (2004).
Note: Author's calculations are based on data for the years 1999–2000. Preference for inequality ranges from agreement with 1, "Income should be more equal," to agreement with 10, "We need larger income differences as incentives for individual effort."

of topics." Four main waves have been fielded since the early 1980s. In the latest wave, Inglehart and others 2004) asked representative samples of people in 69 countries to place their views on a scale from 1 to 10, where 1 implied agreement with the statement that "Incomes should be made more equal," and 10 implied agreement with the statement that "We need larger income differences as incentives for individual effort."

Figure 4.2a suggests considerable polarization on views about inequality. The median answer is 6, suggesting no strong agreement with the two polar statements. Yet almost 20 percent of all respondents were in strong agreement with each of the two extreme views, represented by scores of 1 and 10. Figure 4.2b shows a positive correlation between the score (which is negatively correlated with inequality aversion) and a respondent's own income. This is consistent with the evidence on the importance of relative incomes for welfare: if you are richer, you are less inclined to favor a reduction in income inequalities than if you are poorer.

The World Values Survey results caution against any preconceived notion that income inequality is viewed everywhere as inherently undesirable. When asked about income differences explicitly "as incentives for individual effort," (many) people seem quite happy to have them and, indeed, to

want more of them (although this tendency was less pronounced in countries with either very low or very high levels of inequality).

The balance of the survey evidence suggests that, although inequality in incomes seems to be associated with lower aggregate levels of subjective well-being, there is considerable heterogeneity in opinions about whether it should be reduced or not. Poorer people, and people in countries at very high or very low inequality levels, seem likelier to favor a reduction in inequality. People recognize that some inequality is important to generate incentives for investment and effort; however, when asked about relative pay scales across professions, they would on average prefer smaller differentials. While in Latin America, for instance, a majority judges the income distribution to be unfair, there is no worldwide agreement that income disparities should be reduced everywhere. This is generally consistent with a view that what matters for ethical judgment is not income, but fair processes and opportunities.

Income inequality and poverty reduction

To the philosophical and legal arguments for equity, and to the survey-based and experimental evidence that fairness matters intrinsically to people, we add a final argument: high levels of inequality make it more difficult to reduce poverty. First, we highlight the fact that if inequality falls during a growth spell, poverty generally falls by more than it would have if growth had been distribution-neutral. Second, we document the finding that the effectiveness of future economic growth in reducing absolute income poverty declines with initial income inequality.

If inequality falls, poverty falls more during spells of growth

By raising the incomes and consumption of people across the distribution of income, economic growth is the main driver of poverty reduction in the developing world. The negative association between the average annual rate of change in poverty and the average annual rate of growth in mean incomes is immediately clear from figure 4.3, suggesting that countries experiencing higher rates of economic growth can be expected to reduce poverty much faster than those that grow more slowly.[27] The slope of the simple regression line, −2.4, is the average total elasticity of poverty with respect to economic growth. It implies that, without controlling for any characteristics of the country, 1 percentage point growth in a country's mean income can be expected to reduce the incidence of poverty in that country by about 2.4 percentage points.

This powerful association between economic growth and poverty reduction is one of the central stylized facts of development economics. Its qualitative nature has long been understood, and it has recently been quantified by Ravallion and Chen (1997), Dollar and Kraay (2002), and others. Indeed, the growth-poverty relationship is probably more powerful than surprising: it merely reflects the fact that, on average, the growth in the incomes of the poor is similar to the growth of mean incomes (figure 4.4). Put differently: aggregate economic growth is, on average, distribution-neutral.[28]

There is, however, considerable variation around those averages. About half the total variation in poverty reduction is accounted for by economic growth (see the explanatory power of the underlying regression for figure 4.3).[29] The other half must reflect changes in the underlying distribution of relative incomes. This happens because the incidence of economic growth (its distributional pattern) can vary dramatically across countries. Two countries with similar rates of growth in mean incomes can have very different growth profiles across the population. As one would expect, reductions in inequality at a given growth rate add a "redistribution component" to the "growth component," leading to faster overall poverty reduction.

The contribution of inequality reduction alongside growth is illustrated by a comparison of the growth incidence curves (GIC) for Tunisia (1980–2000) and Senegal (1994–2001) (figure 4.5). In both countries, the average annual growth rate in the

Figure 4.3 Growth is the key to poverty reduction . . .

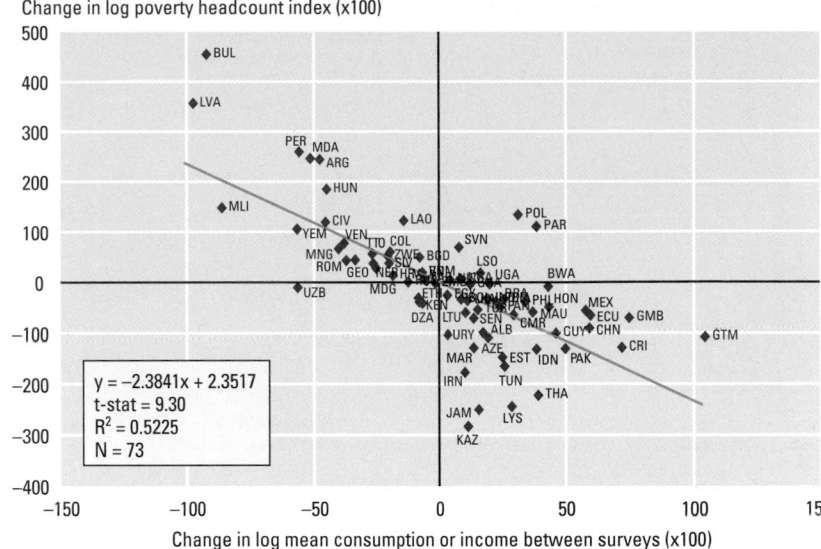

Source: Authors' calculations.

Figure 4.4 . . . and, on average, growth is distribution-neutral

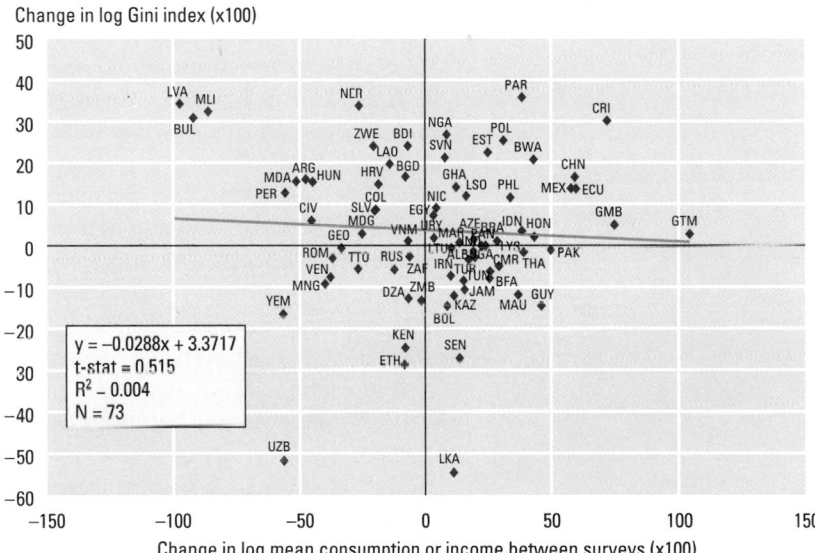

Source: Authors' calculations.

mean incomes from the household survey was close to 2.5 percent. In Tunisia, where the distribution of this growth was relatively more beneficial to the poor, the headcount index of poverty fell by 67 percent (from 30 percent to 10 percent). This corresponds to an annual rate of decline in poverty of 5.4 percent. In Senegal, where growth was less pronounced for the bottom half than for the upper half of the distribu-

Figure 4.5 The national growth incidence curves for Tunisia 1980–1995 and Senegal 1994–2001

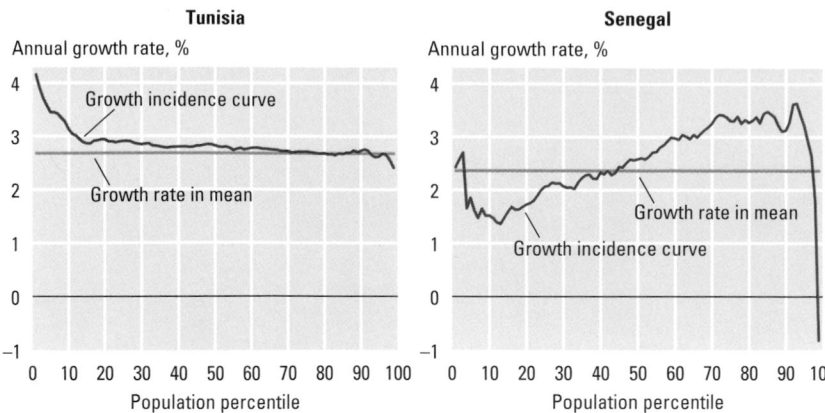

Sources: Ayadi and others (2004) for Tunisia and Azam and others (2005) for Senegal. These are two of 14 country case studies from the World Bank's "Operationalizing Pro-Poor Growth" Study.

tion, poverty fell by only 15 percent (from 68 percent to 57 percent), corresponding to an annual rate of poverty reduction of 2.3 percent. Although some of this difference is due to the fact that the actual growth rate was marginally higher in Tunisia (2.7 percent versus 2.3 percent in Senegal), much of it is clearly due to the different patterns in the incidence of growth, which is evident in figure 4.5.

This contribution of declines in inequality to poverty reduction holds more generally. According to Datt and Ravallion (1992), a decomposition of changes in poverty into growth and inequality components has been widely applied. Redistribution components are usually smaller than growth components and, because inequality often rises, they often have the "wrong" sign. But when inequality falls, this helps reduce poverty.

A second and separate point is that the power of growth to reduce poverty declines with higher initial income inequality. A reduction in inequality today therefore also tends to have a *future* impact on the effectiveness of (even distribution-neutral) growth in reducing poverty. This occurs because the shape of most income distributions means that the growth elasticity of poverty reduction tends to be smaller in more unequal countries. Put another way, because the initial distributions of income are different, the rate of poverty

reduction in two countries with the same distribution-neutral growth rate may well be different.

Perhaps the most flexible way to capture the variation in growth elasticity with inequality across the sample of countries available for these exercises is simply to compute the total and the partial growth elasticity of poverty reduction for each single country (in a single spell per country) and to plot it against the initial Gini coefficient (figure 4.6).[30] A positive relationship is apparent for both partial and total elasticity concepts, for all four poverty line/poverty measure combinations.[31] The absolute value of the growth elasticity of poverty reduction falls as countries become more unequal, both for the total and for the partial concepts. The slope of the line fitted through panel (a) suggests that a 10 percentage point increase in the Gini coefficient is, on average, associated with a decline of 1.4 in the (absolute value) of the elasticity. Given that the average elasticity is 2.53, this is not a small effect.

The fact that very unequal countries (with a Gini coefficient near 0.6) have a total elasticity near zero in this sample should not be overemphasized. It is caused, in part, by increases in inequality in some of these countries during the recorded growth spells. This is evident from the fact that the partial elasticity (which controls for changes in distribution) does not reach zero for the same sample. Growth still contributes to poverty reduction, even in high-inequality countries. The robust finding relates to the sign of the slope of the line, not its exact intercepts: higher initial inequality means that growth reduces poverty by a lesser amount.

It has been argued that this is a mechanical result in that, given a fixed functional form for the income distribution, greater inequality results in slower poverty reduction even if each individual's income grows at the same rate. Indeed, as indicated here, distributional change is on average uncorrelated with mean growth rates so that, on average, the poor see their incomes grow at the same rate as other people's. That does not, however, follow from any law of nature.

Figure 4.6 Greater inequality reduces the power of growth to reduce poverty

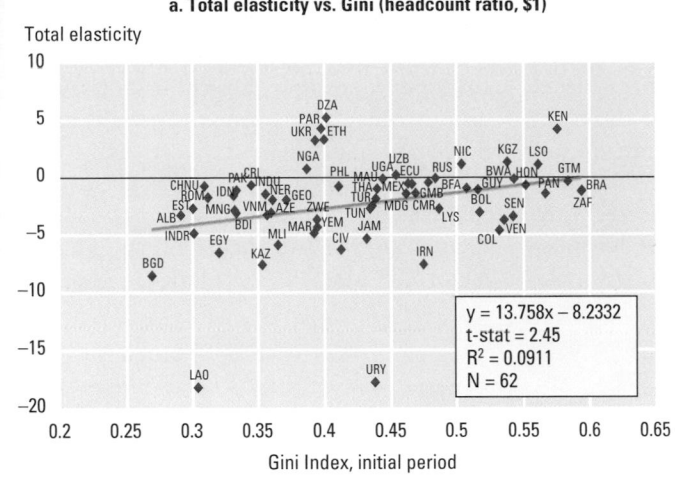

a. Total elasticity vs. Gini (headcount ratio, $1)

y = 13.758x − 8.2332
t-stat = 2.45
R² = 0.0911
N = 62

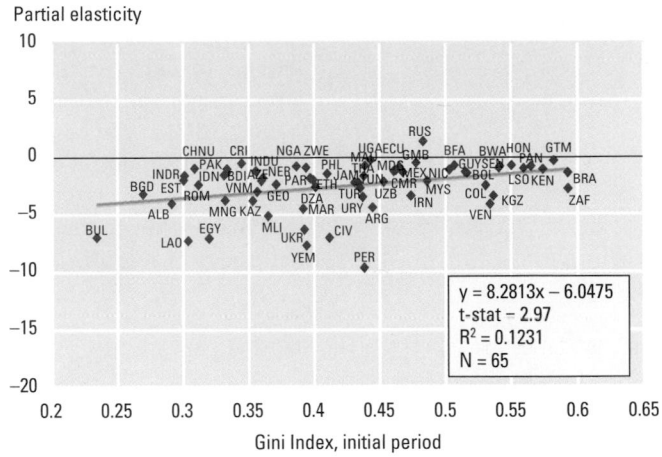

b. Partial elasticity vs. Gini (headcount ratio, $1)

y = 8.2813x − 6.0475
t-stat = 2.97
R² = 0.1231
N = 65

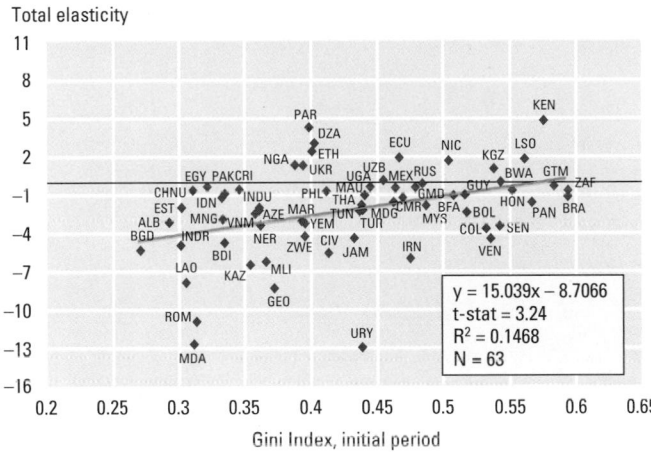

c. Total elasticity vs. Gini (squared poverty gap, $2)

y = 15.039x − 8.7066
t-stat = 3.24
R² = 0.1468
N = 63

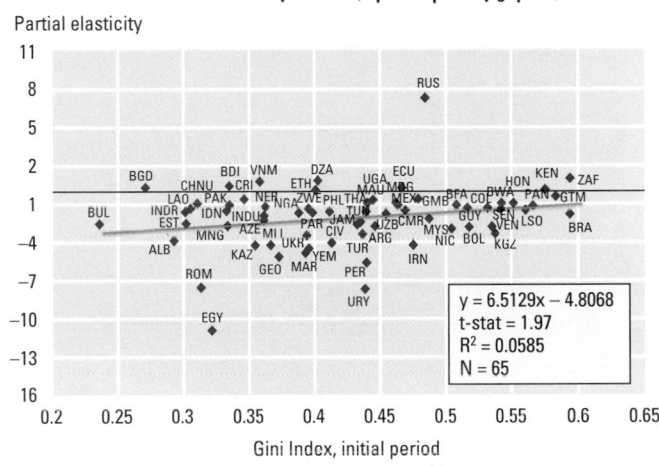

d. Partial elasticity vs. Gini (squared poverty gap, $2)

y = 6.5129x − 4.8068
t-stat = 1.97
R² = 0.0585
N = 65

Source: Authors' calculations.
Note: The figure shows the scatter plots of country-level elasticities against initial-year Gini coefficients. Panel (a) shows the total elasticity for the headcount measure of poverty incidence, with a $1 per day poverty line. Panel (b) shows the partial elasticity for the same measure and the same line. Panels (c) and (d) also show the total and partial elasticities respectively, but now for the squared poverty gap index FGT(2) and with respect to a $2 per day line.[32]

Income distributions in individual countries can and do change during spells of growth (see figure 4.5).[33] There is no mechanical rule that states that the incomes of the poor must grow at the same rate as the rest of the population.[34] If on average they do and if, given the shape of the empirical income distributions, the poverty elasticities are lower in countries with higher initial inequality, this is an empirical fact.

The balance of the evidence does not, therefore, allow much room for doubt that growth elasticities of poverty reduction are stronger in more equal societies. Inequality reduces the effectiveness of economic growth in reducing poverty. This means that, if all else remains the same, a reduction in income inequality today has a double dividend: it is likely to contribute to a contemporaneous reduction in poverty, and it is likely to make future growth reduce poverty faster.

Evidently, the caveat "if all else remains the same" is of crucial importance. The distribution of incomes is a reflection of the general equilibrium of an economy, based on the social, political, and institutional structures that condition its behavior.

Simple-minded attempts to change the way incomes are distributed, without taking into account the effects of policies on the incentives of all agents in the economy, are bound to fail. We return to the issue of appropriate policy design in part III of this report. All that can be said about the results here is that, if policies exist that can lead to a less unequal distribution of resources without major costs to the (static and dynamic) efficiency of resource allocation, such poli-cies are likely to lead to faster poverty reduction in the future, for any amount of growth that the economy generates.

It turns out, however, that some inequali-ties—not necessarily those of incomes—are also detrimental to economic growth itself. Such inequalities in power, assets, and access to markets and services are most likely to be the ones on which policy can productively focus. The next two chapters turn to a dis-cussion of these "inefficient inequalities."

Inequality and investment

In a world in which markets worked perfectly, investment decisions would have little to do with the income, wealth, or social status of the decision maker. They would be determined by the returns an investment promises and by the market price of capital, adjusted for the extra risk it entails. If people had good investment opportunities, it really would not matter whether they had the money—they could always borrow what they needed, and if the risk bothered them, they could always sell shares in their business and buy safer assets with the money from the sale.

However, for various reasons—mainly economic but also political—markets are not perfect. If borrowers can willfully default on their loans, lenders prefer to make loans to borrowers who can provide collateral assets. Private returns for politically connected firms can be higher than for those without such connections, and so these firms may attract more capital, even though social returns may not be any greater.[1] Members of groups subject to discrimination may rationally invest less in their human capital than they would in the absence of such explicit or subtle stereotypes.

After we give up the idea that markets work anywhere close to perfectly, the scope for a direct link between investment and the distribution of wealth or power widens substantially, in many instances leading to underinvestment by those who have good growth opportunities.[2] Correcting the market failures directly is often not feasible, and in these cases certain redistributions of wealth, power, and resources can serve as second-best alternatives.[3] In other words, interventions to enhance equity can improve efficiency.

One of the great advances in development economics in the past 15 years is the accretion of a substantial body of evidence on documenting how well (or badly) asset and financial markets work in developing countries. The fact that these markets rarely measure up to their ideal creates the possibility that wealth and social status, defined as one's position in society both in ascriptive identity and in connections, will have an important influence on investment decisions. It seems natural to start with this evidence.

Markets, wealth, status, and investment behavior
The market for credit

In a perfect credit market, there is a single interest rate and everyone can borrow or lend as much as they want at that rate. That individuals can borrow as much as they want at the current rate explains the presumption of a separation between the wealth or status of the investors and the amount they invest. Whether they are rich or poor, well-connected or just off the streets, an extra dollar of investment will be profitable for them only if the return they get from it is more than the interest rate. If the interest rate is higher, they would be better off lending that money if it was their own, or borrowing less if it were someone else's. So, two people with the same return on investment would end up investing the same amount.[4]

How close are real markets to this ideal market? Chambhar is a market town in Sindh (Pakistan), on the east bank of the Indus. In 1980–81 farmers from the area around Chambhar got most of their credit from about 60 professional moneylenders. Based on detailed data from 14 of these lenders and 60 of their clients, Aleem (1990) calculated the average borrowing interest rate charged as 78.5 percent. But if these farmers wanted to lend their money, the banking system would pay them only about 10 percent. It is possible, however, that they may not have been depositing in the banks. An alternative measure of the deposit rate that is relevant for these farmers is the opportunity cost of capital to the moneylenders, 32.5 percent. In either case, it suggests a gap of at least 45 percentage points between the borrowing and lending rates.

The borrowing rate also varied enormously across borrowers. The standard deviation of the interest rate was 38.1 percent, compared with an average lending rate of 78.5 percent. In other words, an interest rate of 2 percent and an interest rate of 150 percent are both within two standard deviations of the mean. One possibility is that these differences in interest rates reflect differences in the default rate: perhaps the expected repayment was the same for everybody, because those who paid higher rates were more likely to default. Also the expected repayment could have been equal to the actual interest rate paid to the depositors, if the default rate was high enough. But default was rare: for individual lenders, the median default rate was between 1.5 percent and 2 percent, with a maximum of 10 percent.

The same pattern—high and variable borrowing rates, much lower deposit rates, and low default rates—shows up in the "Summary Report on Informal Credit Markets in India."[5] This report summarizes results from case studies commissioned by the Asian Development Bank and carried out under the National Institute of Public Finance and Policy.

For the urban sector, the data are based on various case surveys of specific classes of informal lenders. For the broad class of nonbank financial intermediaries called finance corporations, the maximum deposit rate for loans of less than one year is 12 percent. These corporations offer advances for one year or less at rates that vary from 48 percent per year to the utterly astronomical 5 percent per day. The rates on loans of more than one year varied between 24 percent and 48 percent. Default, once again, is only a small part of the story: default costs explain only 4 percent of total interest costs. For hire-purchase companies in Delhi, the deposit rate was 14 percent and the lending rate was at least 28 percent and could be as high as 41 percent. Default costs were 3 percent of total interest costs.

For the rural sector, interest rates are high, but they are also variable (figure 5.1). This finding is based on surveys of six villages in Kerala and Tamil Nadu, carried out by the Centre for Development Studies, Trivandrum. The rich (with Rs 100,000 or more in assets) get most of the credit (nearly 60 percent) and pay a relatively low rate (33 percent), while those with assets between Rs 20,000 and Rs 30,000 pay rates of 104 percent and get only 8 percent of the credit. The average interest rate charged by professional moneylenders (who provide 45.6 percent of the credit) is about 52 percent.

While the average deposit rate is not reported, the maximum from all the case studies is 24 percent, and in four of them it is no more than 14 percent. In the category of professional moneylenders, about half the loans were at 60 percent or more, but another 40 percent or so had rates below 36 percent. Default rates were higher than in the urban sector, but they still cannot explain more than 23 percent of the interest costs.

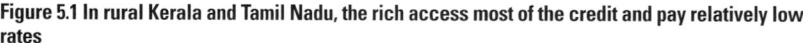

Figure 5.1 In rural Kerala and Tamil Nadu, the rich access most of the credit and pay relatively low rates

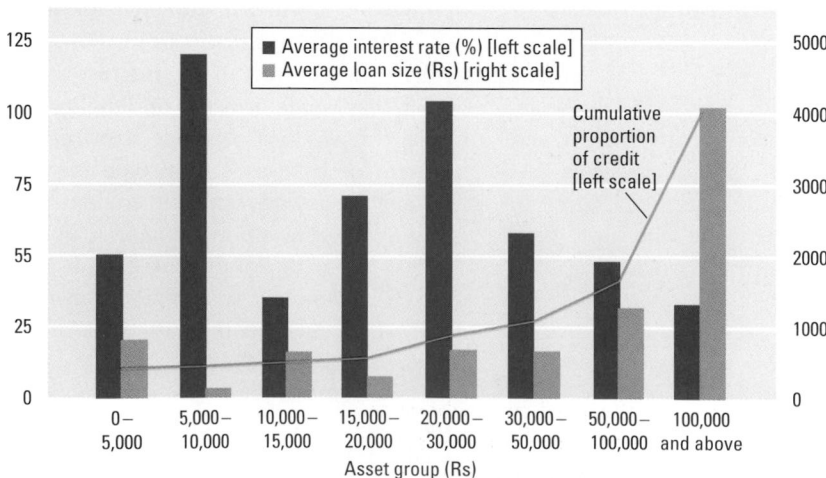

Source: Dasgupta, Nayar, and Associates (1989)

The fact that credit access depends on social status is also shown by Fafchamps' (2000) study of informal trade credit in Kenya and Zimbabwe. It reports an average monthly interest rate of just over 2.5 percent (corresponding to an annualized rate of 34 percent), but it also notes that the rate for the dominant trading group (Indians in Kenya, whites in Zimbabwe) is 2.5 percent a month, while the blacks pay 5 percent a month in both countries.[6] Chapter 9 also provides evidence that in many countries "insiders" effectively lobby to limit access to financial institutions and that lending is skewed toward the rich, consistent with the evidence in figure 5.1.

None of these facts is surprising. Contract enforcement in developing countries is often difficult, and it is not easy to get courts to punish recalcitrant borrowers.[7] As a result, lenders often spend a lot to make sure that their loans get repaid: it is plausible that these are the resources that drive a wedge between the borrowing rate and the lending rate. Indeed, Aleem (1990) shows that the resources spent by lenders to monitor borrowers explain the nearly 50 percentage point gap between the lending and borrowing rates in his data. It is easy to imagine that borrowers who are easier to monitor will enjoy better rates, which would explain why lending rates vary so much.

These imperfections in credit markets have immediate implications for the relationship between wealth and investment. First, with the rate of interest on deposits much lower than that on loans, the opportunity cost of capital for those who just want to invest their own money is much lower than the opportunity cost for those who have to borrow. This means that the wealthy will end up investing much more than the indigent, even if they face exactly the same returns on their investment. Second, the lower interest rates charged to rich people reinforce this conclusion, because the rich then face a lower opportunity cost when they too are borrowing. Third, in some cases, those who are unable to provide collateral will have no access to credit at any interest rate.

We would thus expect the poor to underinvest, certainly relative to the rich, but also relative to what would happen if markets functioned properly. The capital released because they underinvest is absorbed by the non-poor, who may actually end up overinvesting relative to how they would invest in perfect markets. This is the reason: because the poor cannot borrow, the non-poor cannot lend as much as they would like to (this is why deposit rates in developing countries are often very low). And because the non-poor cannot lend, it makes sense for them to keep investing in their own firms, even when the returns are low.

Because the poor underinvest, and because the opportunity cost of capital to the non-poor is thus lower than it would otherwise be, the composition of the investors also changes. In particular, firms that would not be viable if markets functioned perfectly (for example, because the interest rate would be too high) can survive and even expand because markets are the way they are. In other words, the "wrong" firms end up investing.

The market for insurance

The ideal insurance market is one in which people bear no avoidable risks. In a setting in which a single village constitutes a separate insurance market closed to the rest of the world (so that only people in the village can insure other people in the village, in some kind of mutual insurance arrangement), individual consumption should respond only to aggregate (village-level) income fluctuations and not to fluctuations in the income of specific individuals. Put in blunter terms, as long as aggregate consumption is unchanged, individual income fluctuations should not translate into fluctuations in individual consumption. When insurance markets work well, risk considerations should not have a significant impact on the choices people make, irrespective of their wealth, given that what an individual does has little impact on aggregate uncertainty.

While a perfect insurance market is more complex than a perfect credit market, and thus harder to detect, there have been attempts to test the prediction about the irrelevance of fluctuations in one's own income. The Côte d'Ivoire Living Standards Measurement Surveys from 1985 to 1987 provide panel data on the income and consumption of nearly 800 households, with each household tracked for two consecutive years (1985 and 1986 or 1986 and 1987). In table 5.1, the relationship between changes in consumption and changes in incomes is reported separately for the three main regions and separately for 1985–86 and 1986–87. The first row of the first block for each year reports the basic correlation between income and consumption: a fall in income always hurts consumption, although the coefficient varies between a low of 0.15 (a $1 reduction in income means that consumption goes down by $0.15) to a high of 0.46. The next row does the same thing, but now there is a village dummy intended to pick up any village-level changes in consumption. Remarkably, the coefficients on own income, which under perfect insurance should have fallen to zero after controlling for village-level changes, barely budge.[8]

Not all the evidence is quite so pessimistic. Townsend (1994) used detailed household-level data from four villages, which were intensively studied by the International Crop Research Institute in the Semi-Arid Tropics (ICRISAT) in India, to see whether the full insurance hypothesis is consistent with the data. He found that while the data did reject the exact prediction, it did not miss by very much. In other words, his evidence suggested that villagers do insure each other to a considerable extent: movements in individual consumption in his data seem largely uncorrelated with movements in income.

Later work by Townsend, based on data he collected in Thailand, turned out to be less encouraging.[9] Some villages seemed to be much more effective than others in providing insurance to their residents. Townsend describes in detail how insurance arrangements differ across villages. While in one village there is a web of well-functioning, risk-sharing institutions, the situations in other villages are different. In one village, the institutions exist but are dysfunctional; in another, they are nonexistent; in a third, close to the roads, there seems to be no risk-sharing whatsoever, even within families.[10]

As for credit, the failure of insurance could have something to do with informational asymmetries. It is not easy to insure someone against a shock that he alone observes, because he has every incentive to always claim that things had gone badly. But as Duflo and Udry (2004) demonstrate, spouses in Côte d'Ivoire do not seem to be willing to insure each other fully against rainfall shocks that affect them differentially. Because rainfall obviously is observable, at least part of the problem has to be elsewhere. One possibility is limited commitment. People may be happy to claim what was promised to them when it is their turn to be paid, and then default when the time comes for them to pay. This may be particularly easy in a setting in which the social relations between the sets of people who are insuring each other are not particularly close, perhaps explaining why Townsend found no insurance in the village closest to the road.

Lack of insurance should have an effect on the pattern of investment. That many insurable risks are uninsured means that one cannot invest without personally bearing a significant part of the concomitant risk. Indeed, big corporations able to sell

Table 5.1 The effect of income shocks on consumption, Côte d'Ivoire

	West Forest		East Forest		Savannah		All Rural	
			OLS 1985–6					
No dummies	0.290	(6.2)	0.153	(3.2)	0.368	(5.8)	0.259	(8.8)
Village dummies	0.265	(5.7)	0.155	(3.5)	0.373	(5.7)	0.223	(7.7)
			OLS 1986–7					
No dummies	0.458	(8.8)	0.162	(5.3)	0.168	(4.0)	0.239	(10.4)
Village dummies	0.424	(8.1)	0.173	(5.6)	0.164	(3.8)	0.235	(10.1)

Source: Adapted from Deaton (1997), table 6.5, 381.
Note: Absolute value of t-statistics are shown in brackets. The first row of each panel shows the coefficient on income change of a regression of consumption changes on income changes. The second row reports the same result when village dummies are included in the regression. OLS = Ordinary Least Squares.

their equity in organized equity markets may be the only players who can really hope to diversify away a large part of the risk of a particular project. Given this fact and the reasonable assumption that the poor are more risk-averse than the rich, we are likely to be in a perverse situation in which the poor may also find it hardest to reduce their exposure to risk. Thus, they are likely to shy away from riskier and higher-return investments, reinforcing the prediction that the poor invest too little.

The market for land

In a perfect land market, individuals can buy or lease as much land as they want for as long as they want at a price that depends only on the quality of the land (and the length of the lease). The lease should be at a fixed rent, so that the lessor is the residual claimant on the produce of the land. That land can be freely bought and sold ensures that there is no particular advantage or disadvantage to owning land compared with any other asset of similar value. That the lessor is a residual claimant means that the land is put to optimal use. Not so, however, in practice.

Many developing (and some developed) countries have regulations about who can buy land and how much or how little they can buy. Binswanger, Deininger, and Feder (1995) argue that almost every developing country today has gone through a phase when it had regulations intended to concentrate landownership. By contrast, Besley and Burgess (2000) provide a list of regulations from different states in India, each of which is an attempt to limit the concentration of ownership in land.

Governments also directly limit transactions in land, with the ostensible aim of preventing the accumulation of land in the hands of a few people. In Ethiopia in the late 1990s, Deininger and others (2003) note that selling and mortgaging land were against the law. While rentals were officially allowed (after being disallowed for two decades), local leaders and governments were free to restrict even these rental transactions in land. For example, the Oromia region allowed farmers to rent only 50 percent of their holding and stipu-

lates maximum contract terms of 3 years for traditional technologies and 15 years for modern technologies.

It is often unclear who has the right to sell a particular plot of land, when no single person or family has a clear, undisputed, legal title to the land. This ambiguity reflects encroachments and land grabs in the evolution of land rights, as well as the importance of custom in governing land relations, especially in Africa. The recent popularity of land titling as a social intervention is a direct consequence.

Where lease contracts exist, they are not always of the fixed-rent type, at least when the land is used for cultivation. Many countries, including the United States, have a long tradition of an alternative contractual form: sharecropping. Under sharecropping, the farmer gets only a fraction of the produce, but he does not need to pay a fixed rent. As Alfred Marshall pointed out more than one hundred years ago, this weakens incentives and reduces the productivity of the land, but the near universality of sharecropping suggests that it is a response to a real need. There is some disagreement among economists about the exact nature of that need.[11] It is plausible, however, that the need is related to the fact that farmers are often poor, and making them pay the full rent when their crop does poorly is difficult and probably not desirable.

Leaseholds in developing countries tend to be short-lived. The norm is either a year or a season. Longer leases are not unknown, but they are rare. This might reflect the fact that custom, rather than law, secures most of these leases: perhaps it is too much to rely on custom to enforce leases of arbitrary length.

The imperfect salability of land can, of course, hurt anyone who owns it. But the rural poor probably have more of their wealth in land than most people, so making land nonsalable might be particularly harsh on them.

What tends to discourage investment in the land is the lack of an explicit title, or the insecurity of tenure more generally (caused, for example, by the short duration of leases and the possibility that the landlord might threaten to take the land away at the end of the lease). It clearly helps if land is owned by the person contemplating the investment. That most who work in agriculture tend to be too poor to buy out the land they are cultivating is thus a potential source of underinvestment.

The market for human capital

One thing makes the market for human capital different from all the other asset markets: many decisions about investing in human capital are made by parents (or other family members) for their children. In other words, those making the decisions are different from those who receive the human capital. It is not hard to imagine why this separation might introduce important distortions to the functioning of this market. Gary Becker's classic formulation avoids this issue by assuming that the family can borrow against the child's future income, turning the problem into a conventional investment decision. Under that assumption, the amount invested will not depend on the family's means.

In practice, however, although human capital is an asset, it cannot be legally pledged or mortgaged, for the simple reason that pledging your human capital would be tantamount to selling yourself into slavery.[12] This obviously constrains people's ability to borrow money to finance investments in their education.

When parents cannot borrow against their children's future income—true most of the time in most developing countries—they may still hope that those children will take care of them in their old age. The hope might be that the children do grow up to reap the benefits of their parent's investment and that they will pay their parents back. But children know that they have no legal obligation to do so. If they do repay their parents, it is because they love their parents or because society expects them to do so.

Investments in human capital may thus be driven as much by parents' sense of what is the right thing to do, as by any calculation of costs and benefits. Once we accept this, it becomes clear that children's human capital may not be very different from any other consumption good—so richer families will tend to invest more in their children's health and education. And human capital decisions may be more a product of culture and tradition than of the cold calculation of benefits. Benefits are relevant, but the responsiveness to them may not be as large as one might have expected.

In the market for human capital, the reward should be based entirely on the human capital supplied, not on other attributes of the person supplying the skills. Discrimination based on gender, caste, religion, or race obviously violates this, but so does a system of job allocation based on contacts. Until very recently, job discrimination based on gender was the norm all over the world, and the number of countries where such discrimination is still either legally or socially accepted is dwindling but significant. Even where such discrimination is explicitly frowned on, there is some evidence of continuing discrimination. The same is true of race, caste, and religion. Most discrimination—unless legally mandated through affirmative action in favor of a historically disadvantaged group, such as low castes in India and African Americans in the United States—flies in the face of explicit laws against it.

One reason discrimination is so hard to eliminate comes from its sheer insidiousness. Beliefs about differences are embedded in everyday attitudes and practices in a way that neither the discriminator nor the discriminated against may be conscious of, even though these beliefs transform how they both behave. This is what underlies the power of the stereotype. In a telling example, Stone, Perry, and Darley (1997) asked all participants in a recent experiment (American Caucasians, hereafter referred to as whites) to listen to the same running account of an athlete's basketball performance on the radio. Half the participants were led to believe that the target player was white, half that he was African American. The results indicated that information was less likely to be absorbed if it was discordant with the prevailing U.S. stereotypes that whites are more academically talented than African Americans, and that African Americans are more athletically gifted. The white target player was perceived as exhibiting less natural athletic ability but more "court smarts." The African-American target player was perceived as exhibiting fewer court smarts but more natural athletic ability.

Such biases have also been documented in real-world settings. A recent study of the effect of stereotyping on judgment finds that prison inmates with more Afrocentric features receive harsher sentences than those with less Afrocentric features, controlling for race and criminal history.[13]

Bertrand and Mullanaithan (2003) show evidence from a field experiment proving beyond reasonable doubt that there is a high degree of African-American discrimination in the United States. They sent the same resumes to a large number of companies under either a stereotypically white name or a stereotypical African-American name, and found a 50 percent higher callback rate when the name was white. The data say that having a white name is worth as much as eight additional years of job experience. Moreover, the discrimination tended to be greater when the resume corresponded to someone who was better educated, suggesting that investment in human capital among African Americans probably is significantly underrewarded.

A very different form of discrimination comes from the allocation of jobs based on contacts. Munshi (2003) presents persuasive evidence that contacts are very important in the allocation of jobs for migrant labor in the United States. The employment prospects for Mexican migrants there, it turns out, are much better when they are from areas where there was an earlier outflow of migrants. Quite remarkably, it helps if migrants are from an area where there was a drought several years ago, which pushed out a cohort of migrants to the United States. These migrants then help the later generations of migrants from that area to find jobs. This is the clincher: it does not help to be from an area where there was a recent drought.

The perception of discrimination, conscious or not, can affect investments in human capital. Those who expect to be discriminated against in a particular labor market—rightly or wrongly, consciously or otherwise—will tend to invest less in acquiring the type of human capital that the market rewards. This could, perversely, gen-

erate self-reinforcing behavior. If members of the discriminated group invest less in their own education, or in searching for employment, others might use this underinvestment to confirm their prejudice against that group.

Stereotypes can be self-fulfilling not only because they influence perceptions of the target of the stereotype, but also because they influence the behavior of the individuals who are stereotyped. Stone and others (1999) asked college undergraduate volunteers to play a miniature golf course. Performance was measured by how many strokes were needed to put the ball in the hole: fewer strokes meant better performance. The variable that the experimenters manipulated was the description of the task. In one treatment, the task was described as a "standardized test of natural athletic ability," in the other as a "standardized test of sports intelligence." When the task was described as a test of natural athletic ability, the African-American participants performed better than the whites: they averaged 23.1 strokes to complete the 10-hole golf course, compared with 27.8 for the whites. But when the task was described as a test of sports intelligence, the race gap was reversed: African Americans averaged 27.2 strokes, whites 23.3.

One way to interpret this behavior is that social ideas—stereotypes about the talents of different social groups—impose bounds from within. Under the rational, self-interest hypothesis, individuals change their behavior only when their preferences or external constraints change. But the behavior of real individuals depends as well on belief systems that society impresses on them. Negative stereotypes create anxiety that may interfere with performance: that is why the psychologist Claude Steele termed this kind of behavior "stereotype threat."[14] The beliefs underlying the stereotypes, if deeply internalized, can affect early decisions about prospective careers, and attitudes toward society, by changing what Appadurai (2004) calls a person's "capacity to aspire." The reader may recall the example (from chapter 2) of the Batwa girl who wanted to be a cleaner upon completing school. Positive stereotypes, by contrast, can boost self-confidence and lead individuals to expend greater effort.

Stereotypes influence behavior twice—through their impact on individuals' self-confidence, and through their impact on the way individuals expect to be treated. To examine the effect of stereotypes on the ability of individuals to respond to economic incentives, Hoff and Pandey (2004) undertook experiments with low- and high-caste children in rural north India. The caste system in India can be described as a highly stratified social hierarchy in which groups of individuals are invested with different social status and social meaning.

In the first experiment, groups composed of three low-caste ("untouchable") and three high-caste junior high school students were asked to solve mazes and were paid based on the number of mazes they solved. In one condition, no personal information about the participants was announced. In a second condition, caste was announced with each participant's name and village. In a third condition, participants were segregated by caste and then each participant's name, village, and caste were announced in the six-person group.

When caste was not announced, there was no caste gap in performance (figure 5.2). But increasing the salience of caste led to a significant decline in the average per-

formance of the low caste, regardless of whether the payment scheme was piece rate (that is, participants were paid 1 rupee per maze solved) or tournament (that is, the participant who solved the most mazes was paid 6 rupees per maze solved, while the other participants received nothing). When caste was announced, the low-caste children solved 25 percent fewer mazes on average in the piece-rate treatments, compared with the performance of subjects when caste was not announced. When caste was announced and groups were composed of six children drawn from only the low caste (a pattern of segregation that for the low caste implicitly evokes their traditional outcast status), the decline in low-caste performance was even greater. While we cannot be sure from these data what the children were thinking, some combination of loss of self-confidence and expectation of prejudicial treatment likely explains the result.

The expectation by the low-caste subjects of prejudicial treatment may be rational given the discrimination in their villages. But the discrimination itself may not be fully rational. Cognitive limitations may prevent others from judging stigmatized individuals fairly. That people are bounded in their ability to process information creates broad scope for belief systems—in which some social groups are viewed as innately inferior to others—to influence economic behavior. If such beliefs persist, it will generally be rational for those discriminated against to underinvest (with respect to others) in the accumulation of skills for which the return is likely to be lower for them. This rational calculation is additional to any reduction in their "capacity to aspire," arising from the internalization of those beliefs.

The evidence on underinvestment

Highly imperfect markets suggest considerable scope for underinvestment.

Industry and trade

Direct estimates of marginal products show that there are many unexploited investment opportunities. For small Mexican firms

Figure 5.2 Children's performance differs when their caste is made public

Average number of mazes solved, by caste, in five experimental treatments

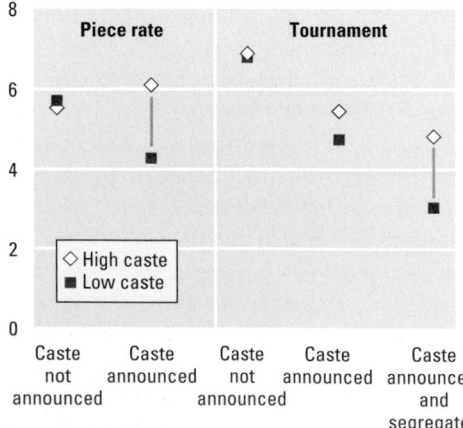

Source: Hoff and Pandey (2004).
Note: A vertical line in the figure indicates that the caste gaps are statistically significant.

with less than $200 invested, the rate of return reaches 15 percent per month, well above the informal interest rates available in pawn shops or through microcredit programs (on the order of 3 percent a month) (figure 5.3).[15] Estimated rates of return decline with investment, but the rates remain high—7 percent to 10 percent a month for firms with investments between $200 and $500, and 5 percent for firms with investments between $500 and $1,000. All these firms are thus too small and could reap large gains from increased investment.

Trade credit is an important form of credit everywhere, perhaps especially where the formal institutions of the credit market are underdeveloped. Fisman (2001a) looked at the relation between access to trade credit and capacity utilization for 545 firms in Côte d'Ivoire, Kenya, Tanzania, Zambia, and Zimbabwe. He finds that firms that receive trade credit from three main suppliers (on average, about one of the three suppliers provides trade credit) have 10 percent better capacity utilization than firms that receive no trade credit. The relation is much stronger in industries in which it is important to carry large inventories.

Such studies present serious methodological issues, however. The basic problem comes from the fact that investment levels are likely to be correlated with omitted variables. For example, in a world without credit constraints, investment will be positively correlated with the expected returns to investment, generating a positive "ability bias."[16] McKenzie and Woodruff (2003) attempt to control for managerial ability by including the firm owner's wage in previous employment. This goes only part of the way, however, if individuals choose to enter self-employment precisely because their expected productivity in self-employment is much higher than their productivity in an employed job. Conversely, if capital is allocated to firms to avoid their failure, there could be a negative ability bias.

Banerjee and Duflo (2004a) take advantage of a change in the definition of the "priority sector" in India to circumvent these difficulties. All banks in India are required to lend at least 40 percent of their net credit to the "priority sector," which

Figure 5.3 Returns to capital vary with firm size: evidence from small Mexican firms

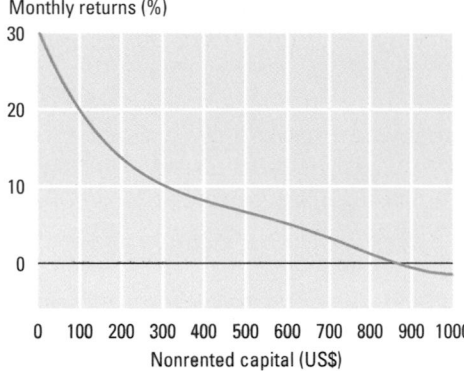

Monthly returns (%)

Nonrented capital (US$)

Source: McKenzie and Woodruff (2003).

includes small industry. In January 1998, the limit on total investment in plants and machinery for a firm to be eligible for inclusion in the small industry category was raised from Rs 6.5 million to Rs 30 million. The researchers first show that, after the reforms, newly eligible firms (those with investment between Rs 6.5 million and Rs 30 million) received, on average, larger increments in their working capital limit than smaller firms. They then show that the sales and profits increased faster for these firms during the same period. Putting these two facts together, researchers can estimate the impact of the increased access to working capital on the growth in profits. Allowing for the possibility that the firms in the priority sector were paying less than the true cost of capital for the extra money from the bank, they estimate that the returns to capital in these firms must be at least 94 percent.

A different kind of evidence for underinvestment comes from the fact that many people pay the high interest rates reported earlier. Given that this money typically goes into financing trade and industry, the presumption is that the people borrowing at these rates of often 50 percent or more must have a marginal product of capital that is even higher. But the average marginal product in developing countries seems to be nowhere near 50 percent. One way to get at the average of the marginal products is to look at the incremental capital-output ratio (ICOR) for the country as a whole.[17] For

Figure 5.4 Inefficient allocation of resources; the example of the Gounders vs. the outsiders

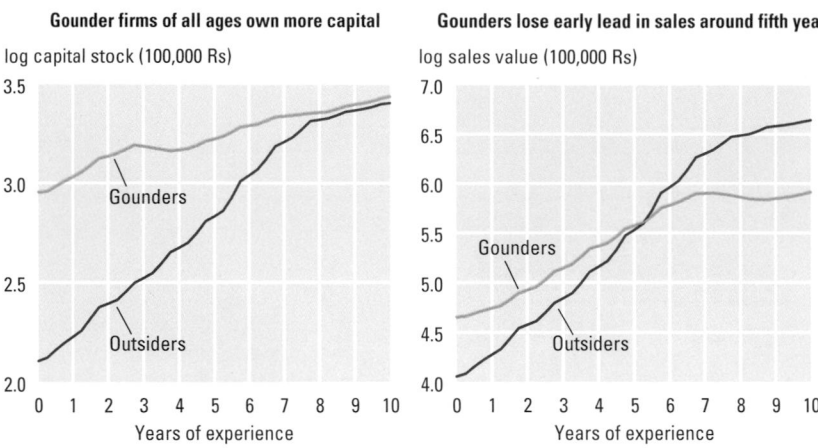

Gounder firms of all ages own more capital

log capital stock (100,000 Rs)

Gounders lose early lead in sales around fifth year

log sales value (100,000 Rs)

Source: Banerjee and Munshi (2004).

Figure 5.5 Average returns for switching to pineapples as an intercrop can exceed 1,200 percent

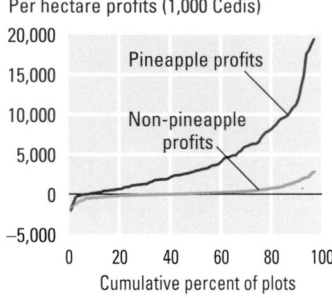

Per hectare profits (1,000 Cedis)

Source: Goldstein and Udry (1999).

the late 1990s the International Monetary Fund (IMF) estimates the ICOR to be more than 4.5 for India and 3.7 for Uganda. The implied upper bound on the average marginal product is 22 percent for India and 27 percent in Uganda.

That many firms in India have a marginal product of 50 percent or more, while the average marginal product is only 22 percent or so, is strong *prima facie* evidence for the misallocation of capital. The firms with the marginal product of 50 percent and more are clearly too small, while other firms (the ones who bring the average down to 22 percent) must, in some sense, be too large.

A specific example of this kind of misallocation of capital comes from a study of the knitted garment industry in the southern Indian town of Tirupur.[18] Two groups of people operate in Tirupur: Gounders and outsiders. The Gounders, who issue from a small, wealthy, agricultural community from the area around Tirupur, moved into the readymade garment industry because there were not many investment opportunities in agriculture. Outsiders from various regions and communities started joining the city in the 1990s.

The Gounders, unsurprisingly, have much stronger ties in the local community, and thus better access to local finance. But they may be expected to have less natural ability for garment manufacturing than the outsiders, who came to Tirupur precisely because of its reputation as a center for garment export. The Gounders own about

twice as much capital as the outsiders on average. Gounder firms of all ages own more capital, although there is a strong tendency toward convergence as the firms age (figure 5.4a). The Gounders, despite owning more capital, lose their early lead in sales by about the fifth year, and end up selling less (figure 5.4b). In other words, outsiders invest less and produce more. They are clearly more able than the Gounders,[19] but because they are less cash-rich and do not have the right connections, they end up working with less capital.

Agriculture

There is also direct evidence of high rates of returns on productive investment in agriculture. In the forest-savannah in Southern Ghana, cocoa cultivation, receding for many years because of the swollen shoot disease, has been replaced by a cassava-maize intercrop. Recently, pineapple cultivation for export to Europe offered a new opportunity for farmers in this area. In 1997 and 1998 more than 200 households cultivating 1,070 plots in four clusters in this area were surveyed every six weeks for about two years. Pineapple production dominates the traditional intercrop (figure 5.5),[20] and the average returns associated with switching from the traditional maize and cassava intercrops to pineapple is estimated to be in excess of 1,200 percent! Yet only 190 out of 1,070 plots were used for pineapple. When the authors asked farmers why they were not farming pineapple, the virtually unanimous response was, "I don't have the money,"[21] although some heterogeneity in ability between those who have switched to pineapple and those who have not, cannot be entirely ruled out.

Evidence from experimental farms suggests that, in Africa, the rate of returns to using chemical fertilizer (for maize) would also be high. But the evidence may not be realistic if the ideal conditions of an experimental farm cannot be reproduced on actual farms. Foster and Rosenzweig (1995) show, for example, that the returns to switching to high-yielding varieties were actually low in the early years of the green revolution in India, and the returns were even negative for farmers without an education. This, despite the fact that these varieties had been selected precisely for having high yields, in proper conditions. But they required complementary inputs in the correct quantities and timing. If farmers were not able or did not know how to supply them, the rates of returns were actually low.

Chemical fertilizer, however, is not a new technology, and the proper way to use it is well understood. To estimate the rates of returns to using fertilizer on farms in Kenya, Duflo, Kremer, and Robinson (2004), in collaboration with a small nongovernmental organization (NGO), set up small randomized trials on people's farms. Each farmer in the trial delimited two small plots. On one randomly selected plot, a field officer from the NGO helped the farmer apply fertilizer. Other than that, the farmers continued to farm as usual. The rates of return from using a small amount of fertilizer varied from 169 percent to 500 percent, depending on the year, although marginal returns declined quickly with the quantity of fertilizer used on a plot of a given size.

Evidence for a different type of underinvestment in agriculture is the negative size-productivity relationship, the idea that the smallest farms tend to be the most productive (table 5.2). The gap in the productivity of small and large farms within a country can be enormous: a factor of 5.6 in Brazil and a factor of 2.75 in Pakistan.[22] It is smaller in Malaysia (1.5), but a large farm in Malaysia is not very large. This is strong *prima facie* evidence that markets are somehow not allocating the right amount of land to those who currently farm the smaller plots.

The problem with this kind of evidence is that it ignores the many reasons why the bigger farm may be inherently less productive, for example, lower soil quality. Even so, similar (but somewhat less dramatic) results show up even after controlling for differences in land quality. The profit-wealth ratio in Indian ICRISAT villages is the highest for the smallest farms, and when risk is comparatively low, the gap is more than 3:1 (figure 5.6). Because wealth includes the value of the land, the measure implicitly takes into account differences in the quality of the land. It does so as long as land prices are a

Table 5.2 Farm size productivity differences, selected countries

Farm size	Northeast Brazil	Punjab, Pakistan	Muda, Malaysia
Small farm (hectares)	563 (10.0–49.9)	274 (5.1–10.1)	148 (0.7–1.0)
Largest farm (hectares)	100 (500+)	100 (20+)	100 (5.7–11.3)

Source: Berry and Cline (1979).
Note: 100 = land productivity in the largest farm size.

Figure 5.6 Profit-wealth ratios are highest for the smallest farms

Profit/wealth ratio

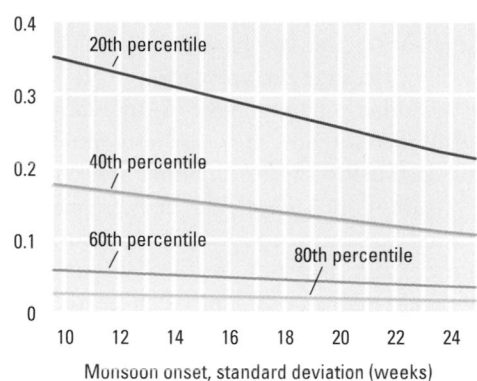

Monsoon onset, standard deviation (weeks)

Source: Rosenzweig and Binswansger (1993).
Note: The standard deviation of the date of monsoon onset is a measure of underlying risk. The onset date of the monsoon was the single most powerful of eight rainfall characteristics to explain gross farm output. The data come from the Indian ICRISAT villages.

reasonable measure of land quality, which, however, is not entirely clear. There are also residual doubts about whether the returns are well measured—it is possible that the land of the smaller farms is degrading faster, but the degradation is not being counted while calculating the returns.

For these same firms, when risk goes up, the average return goes down. In part this may be inevitable, but it may also reflect the fact that the lack of insurance encourages people to avoid risky (but remunerative) choices.[23] This is consistent with the fact that profitability falls faster for the poorer farmers (less able to self-insure) as the risk goes up. Specifically, a one-standard-deviation increase in the coefficient of variation of rainfall leads to a 35 percent reduction in the profit of poor farmers, a 15 percent reduction in the profit of median farmers, and no reduction in the profit of rich farmers. The study also finds that input choices are affected by variability in rainfall, and in particular, poor farmers make less efficient input choices in a risky environment.

In related work, Morduch (1993) specifically investigated how the anticipation of a credit constraint affects the decision to invest in high-yielding variety seeds. Using a methodology inspired by Zeldes (1989), he splits the sample into two groups—one group of landholders expected to have the ability to smooth their consumption, and one group that owns little land, expected to be constrained. He finds that the more constrained group devotes a considerably smaller fraction of land to high-yielding variety seeds for rice and castor.

Another consequence of the lack of insurance is that it may lead households to use productive assets as buffer stocks and consumption smoothing devices, which would be a cause for inefficient investment. Rosenzweig and Wolpin (1993) argue that bullocks (an essential productive asset in agriculture) serve this purpose in rural India. They show, using ICRISAT data covering three villages in semiarid areas in India, that bullocks, which constitute a large part of households' liquid wealth (50 percent for the poorest farmers), are bought and sold quite frequently (86 percent of households had either bought or sold a bullock in the previous year). Moreover, they buy when they are flush with money and sell when they are broke.

Since people are not simultaneously selling and buying land, they are not selling these animals because they no longer need them for production. Indeed, from the view point of production, most of these farmers should own two bullocks and never sell them. If they are selling, the reason is that they need the money for consumption. The data suggest that, for poor or midsize farmers, there is considerable underinvestment in bullocks, presumably because of the borrowing constraints and the inability to borrow and accumulate financial assets to smooth consumption: almost half the households in any given year hold no bullocks (most of the others own exactly two).[24]

There is also compelling evidence that sharecroppers lack incentives. Binswanger

and Rosenzweig (1986) and Shaban (1987) both show that productivity is 30 percent lower in sharecropped plots, controlling for farmers' fixed effects (that is, comparing the productivity of owner-cultivated and farmed land for farmers who cultivate both their own land and that of others) and for land characteristics. Shaban (1987) shows that all the inputs are lower on sharecropped land, including short-term investments (fertilizer and seeds). He also finds systematic differences in land quality (owner-cultivated land has a higher price per hectare), which could in part reflect long-term investment.

On the impact of security of property, Do and Iyer (2003) find that a land reform that gave farmers the right to sell, transfer, or inherit their land-use rights also increased agricultural investment, particularly the planting of multiyear crops (such as coffee). Laffont and Matoussi (1995) use data from Tunisia to show that a shift from sharecropping to owner cultivation raised output by 33 percent, and moving from a short-term tenancy contract to a longer-term contract increased output by 27.5 percent.[25]

Security of property rights is often linked to the local power structure. The connection between inequalities in power and underinvestment is nicely exemplified by the Goldstein and Udry (2002) study of investment in land in a setting where land is allocated by custom (rural Ghana). They show that individuals are less likely to leave their land fallow (an investment in long-run productivity of the land) if they do not hold a position of power within either the hierarchy of the village or the hierarchy of the lineage. The problem is that the land gets taken away from them when it is lying fallow. Because women rarely hold these positions, women's land is not left fallow enough and is much less productive than men's.

Human capital

According to the report of the Commission on Macroeconomics and Health (2001), returns to investing in health are on the order of 500 percent. But these numbers, arrived at through cross-country growth regressions, are not as easy to interpret as what would actually happen if someone were to invest an extra dollar in health. That said, there clearly are examples of specific health interventions that have enormous private and social returns. There is substantial experimental evidence that supplementation in iron and vitamin A increases productivity at relatively low cost.

- Basta, Soekirman, and Scrimshaw (1979) study iron supplementation among rubber tree tappers in Indonesia. Baseline health measures indicated that 45 percent of the study population was anemic. The intervention combined an iron supplement and an incentive (given to both treatment and control groups) to take the pill on time. Work productivity among those who got the treatment increased by 20 percent (or $132 a year), at a cost per worker-year of $0.50. Even taking into account the cost of the incentive ($11 a year), the intervention suggests extremely high rates of returns.

- Thomas and others (2005) obtain lower but still high estimates in a larger experiment, also in Indonesia. They found that iron supplementation experiments in Indonesia reduced anemia, increased the probability of participating in the labor market, and increased earnings of self-employed workers. They estimate that, for self-employed males, the benefits of iron supplementation amount to $40 per year, at a cost of $6 per year.[26]

- The cost-benefit analysis of a deworming program[27] in Kenya reports estimates of a similar order of magnitude. Taking into account externalities (because of the contagious nature of worms), the program led to an average increase in schooling of 0.14 years. Using a reasonable figure for the returns to a year of education, this additional schooling will lead to a benefit of $30 over the life of the child, at a cost of $0.49 per child per year. Not all interventions have the same rates of return, however. A study of Chinese cotton mill workers[28] led to a significant increase in fitness, but no corresponding increase in productivity.

Measured returns to private investment in education tend not to be quite so high. Banerjee and Duflo (2004b) survey cross-country evidence, and conclude that—

> Using the preferred data, the Mincerian rates of returns seem to vary little across countries: the mean rate of returns is 8.96, with a standard deviation of 2.2. The maximum rate of returns to education (Pakistan) is 15.4 percent, and the minimum is 2.7 percent (Italy).[29]

But most of the educational benefits of deworming mentioned above would be captured by a child whose parents are willing to spend $0.50 on the deworming medicine. This clearly offers a return much higher than the measured Mincerian returns at affordable absolute cost, although they are not strictly comparable. Deworming does not require the child to spend more years in school, but it does help the child get more out of the years he or she is already spending in school. However, when the deworming medicine was offered free to the children, the take-up was only 57 percent. In this sense, it is clear that at least some causes of underinvestment have to be found in the way the family makes decisions, rather than in the lack of resources.

The fact that a lack of connections alters the nature of human capital investment is nicely demonstrated in a recent paper by Munshi and Rosenzweig (forthcoming). They show that, in India, trade liberalization increased returns to knowing the English language in families with connections in the blue-collar sector compared with families with no connections. However, there is a much bigger gap between girls and boys in the increase in enrollment in English-medium schools. This is attributed to the fact that girls never really expected to get these blue-collar jobs, while for their brothers, it depended on whether they had the right contacts.

Inequalities and investment

Four important points follow from this body of evidence: first, markets in developing countries are highly imperfect, and those who do not have enough wealth or social status tend to underinvest. The resources underused because of this underinvestment end up being used for some less productive purpose, reducing overall productivity. In the example from the knitted garment industry in Tirupur, the Gounders were overinvesting in their own relatively unproductive firms, while the much more productive firms of the outsiders were starved of capital. The land owned by Ghanaian women was getting degraded, because they did not have the social status needed to hold on to the land during the fallowing period. This, once again, is a pure loss for society. The fact that other people who do have status and can fallow their land as needed is not, in any way, compensating for the loss of productivity on the lands of the powerless. This creates a strong presumption that certain specific types of redistribution, by empowering certain people or increasing their access to resources or contacts, can promote efficiency and equity.

Second, this hypothesis would imply a bias in favor of those kinds of redistribution that target the specific lack of access to resources or influence causing the inefficiency. In some situations this will mean redistributing assets, but it also might mean redistributing access to capital, perhaps by promoting microcredit, strengthening women's land rights or access to jobs and welfare programs, designing affirmative action programs to break down stereotyping, and improving access to justice systems.

Third, because investments build wealth and wealth makes it easier to invest in a world where markets do not function very well, a little help can go a long way. Starting the right business might be the biggest challenge: once started, the business might propel itself forward without any further help.

Fourth, it is not clear that the beneficiaries from this kind of efficiency-promoting redistribution have to be the poorest of the poor. Because the ideal is to promote productive investments, the target should be those most likely to make these investments. Whether the poorest are the right people from this point of view is an empirical question, and one for which the answer

might depend on the set of economic opportunities available.

The microcredit community, in particular, has long debated this last issue in trying to decide whether microcredit is best instrument for helping the poorest of the poor. This clearly turns partly on whether the poorest are the ones who have the projects with the highest returns, which could be the case if the poor and the less poor have the same kinds of production functions, and if there are diminishing returns to scale. If, instead, the most productive technology in this area had a fixed cost of production but (say) diminishing returns otherwise, giving the poorest access to more capital may not be very productive: even with all the capital they can get, they may not be able to cover the fixed cost. It may be more effective to help people who are slightly richer, because with some help they may actually be able to start a business.

How good or bad is the assumption of decreasing returns in the production function of an individual firm? As mentioned above, McKenzie and Woodruff (2003) estimate a production function for small Mexican firms, suggesting strong diminishing returns. Mesnard and Ravallion (2004) find weak diminishing returns using Tunisian data. But estimating a production function that exhibits local increasing returns is inherently difficult. A firm is likely to grow (or shrink) quickly when it is in the region of increasing returns. So we will observe few firms in this region, and be likely to reject too often the assumption of local increasing returns. Certainly the natural interpretation of the results in Banerjee and Duflo (2004a), showing close to 100 percent returns in medium firms in India, is that there are increasing returns over some range.

A corollary of this discussion is that the redistribution that maximizes productivity growth is not necessarily the one that has the strongest immediate effect on poverty. Nor is it the one that does most to reduce inequality. Indeed, except under very special circumstances, this discussion tells us nothing about the relation between some global measure of inequality and the efficiency of resource use or investment. Consider the case, discussed above, in which the production function has a fixed cost but also diminishing returns. If all firms are equal and the maximum they can each invest is less than the fixed cost, no one will be able to start a firm. Increasing inequality will raise the productivity of capital by making it possible for some firms to pay the fixed cost. Because there are also diminishing returns, however, there will be a point at which any further increase in overall inequality would be counterproductive.

More generally, the effect of inequality will depend on the shape of the production function, and the size of the investment potential of the average person relative to the fixed cost. Obviously, the issue gets even more complicated if different firms have different production functions and if productivity is correlated with the owner's wealth (as it might be if the owner's education is an important input into production and richer people tend to be more educated).

Several authors have tried to look for a systematic relation in cross-country data between inequality and growth (presumably what investment is meant to achieve). A lengthy body of literature[30] estimated a long-run equation, with growth between 1990 and 1960, for example, regressed on income in 1960, a set of control variables, and inequality in 1960. Estimating these equations tended to generate negative coefficients for inequality. But there are obvious concerns about whether such a relation could be driven entirely by omitted variables. To address this problem, Li and Zou (1998), Forbes (2000), and others used the time series dimension of the Deininger and Squire data set to look (effectively) at the effect of short-run changes in inequality on changes in growth.[31] The results change rather dramatically: the coefficient of inequality in this specification is positive and significant.

A recent review paper by Voitchovsky (2004) concludes that both these effects are quite robust. Most studies that look at the cross-sectional relationship between inequality and subsequent growth over a relatively long period in cross-country data, and especially those that use measures of asset inequality, find a negative relationship, often significant.[32] By contrast, most studies that look at the relationship between changes in

inequality and changes in growth, including several studies that do the analysis at the sub-national level within the same country, find a positive effect.

Both Banerjee and Duflo (2003) and Voitchovsky (2004) conclude that there is no reason to give one of these sets of results priority over the other. Indeed, both could be right. For example, in the short run, policies that allow large cuts in real wages might encourage investment, but in the long run, the consequent increase in poverty might make it harder for the population to maintain its human capital. Or both could be wrong. Most important among the many reasons for both the cross-sectional and the time series evidence to be misleading are the following: the possibility of a nonlinear relationship between inequality and growth, problems with comparability of cross-country data, and the difficult question of identifying the direction of causality when both variables are likely to influence one another.

This lack of clear-cut results is perhaps disappointing, but it is worth emphasizing that our focus here has been on redressing specific inequalities in productive opportunities rather than some overall measure of inequality. Despite the great attention devoted to the question of a systematic relationship between overall inequality and growth at the country level, the body of evidence remains unconvincing. But there clearly are situations in which there is a strong presumption that reducing a specific inequality would promote better investment.

One such example comes from *Operation Barga*, a tenancy reform in the Indian state of West Bengal in the late 1970s and 1980s. It has been known, at least since the work of the great Victorian economist Alfred Marshall, that sharecropping provides poor incentives and discourages effort. In such an environment, a government intervention that forces the landlords to give their sharecroppers a higher share of the output than the market would give them should increase effort and productivity. This is exactly what happened in West Bengal, India, when a Left Front government came to power in 1977. The tenant's share of output was set at a minimum of 75 percent as long as the tenant provided all inputs. In addition, the tenant was guaranteed a large measure of security of tenure, which may have encouraged him or her to undertake more long-term investments on the land. Survey evidence shows a substantial increase in both the security of tenure and the share of output going to the sharecropper. The fact that the implementation of this reform was bureaucratically driven, and proceeded at different speeds in different areas, suggests the possibility of using variation in the implementation of the reform to evaluate its impact. The evidence suggests that there was a 62 percent increase in the productivity of the land.[33]

A different program, also promoting equity and efficiency, had to do with redressing the effects of intrafamily inequality. A long line of research claims that income and expenditures are often controlled by the male members of the family and that this leads to underinvestment, especially in the health and education of girls. One fallout of dismantling the apartheid regime in South Africa was the expansion of the South African social pension program to the black population. Pension entitlements would accrue to elderly males and females, and many older women living alone were entitled to receive the benefit. In many cases, children of very poor parents were sent to live with grandparents who began to receive these pensions. Duflo (2003) compared the impact of these new transfers on the nutrition of children living with their grandparents, separately for households in which the pension was given to the grandmother and those in which it was assigned to a grandfather.

For children born before the expansion, in 1990 and 1991, height-for-age was slightly lower in families in which the grandmother would eventually get the pension. For children born after the expansion, in 1992 and 1993, the children are significantly taller (except for the newborns) in those families. There is no difference between noneligible families and families in which pension money goes to the grandfather. (Boys are essentially unaffected.) The estimates suggest that receipt of the pension (which was about twice the per capita income among blacks) was enough to help girls bridge half the gap in height-for-age between South African and American children.

These examples show that it is possible to enhance both equity and efficiency simultaneously. Judicious redistribution—of income to grandmothers, of power to poor women farmers, of credit to entrepreneurs in small firms—can increase the productivity of resources, such as land, human capital, and physical capital. If markets fail, resources do not always flow to where their return is greatest, particularly if that happens to be in projects run by people with limited wealth or influence. Careful microeconomic case study evidence, some of which was summarized in this chapter, suggests that certain forms of redistribution can reduce waste and contribute to a better use of resources, while also reducing inequality of opportunity. In fact, it enhances efficiency precisely because it reduces inequality of opportunity.

This is not to say that one cannot easily imagine certain types of redistribution that hurt efficiency. But given the near universality of market failures and underinvestment in poor countries, it should be possible, with a combination of good research and careful thinking, to identify opportunities for redirecting resources to poorer people who are in a position to make good use of them.

In making the case for improvements in equity that are also efficiency-enhancing, this chapter used mainly microeconomic evidence on markets, wealth, and agency of individuals. The next chapter uses a different set of historical, macroeconomic, and institutional evidence to argue that complex historical processes, combined with inequalities in influence and power, may lead to bad political and economic institutions, which severely impair the development of poor countries.

Equity and development in the Spanish transition to democracy

In the last half century, Spain has gone from authoritarianism and underdevelopment to democracy and wealth. Spain's history illustrates how the distribution of political agency and economic assets greatly influences the policy choices available to a society. The fundamentals of economic and political structure influence and constrain the choices. But the process is not deterministic: political agency and policies can shift the underlying fundamentals (as happened in Spain in the 1960s and 1970s) and open the space for new choices.

Before the civil war: social and economic polarization

Until the second half of the twentieth century, Spanish contemporary history was a tale of political and economic failure. After a period of territorial expansion and European hegemony in the early modern ages, Spain lapsed into economic decline and cultural stagnation in the following centuries. During most of the nineteenth century, its industrial takeoff was blocked by political instability, inefficient legal institutions, substantial inequalities, and a poorly educated population. In 1929, per capita income was $3,000 (in 1990 dollars)—two-fifths that of Britain and less than two-thirds that of France.

Spain was polarized by entrenched social and economic inequalities. In a country still eminently agrarian, the distribution of land was very unequal. About 1 percent of the holdings occupied 50 percent of the land. Educational attainment remained low, strictly linked to circumstances of birth. Social mobility was almost nonexistent. Except for Catalonia and the Basque country, which industrialized in the nineteenth century, Spain lacked a large middle class.

Against this backdrop of relative stagnation and high inequality, democratic institutions were introduced in 1931—only the second time in Spanish history. They did not last long. The brief democratic period (1931–36) was characterized by huge political instability and social agitation. The first Republican government pushed ahead with a strong reformist program: separation of church and state; a single system of state schools and a goal to universalize education; a process of land reform; a law to decentralize political power to Catalonia; and stepped up efforts to reform the army.

These reforms elicited a strong reaction from the right, which came to power in 1933 and quickly moved to halt them. Two and a half years later, in the spring of 1936, new elections were held, with a victory for the left. The threat of more radical policies prompted a military uprising, supported by the landed classes, much of the bourgeoisie, and the church. Spain became engulfed in a three-year civil war. The social polarization locked Spain into a zero-sum gain over the distribution of wealth. There was little political space for compromise or reformist solutions. The "haves" opposed all attempts at even minimalist reform. The "have-nots" wanted radical change, not gradual reform.

The Franco regime: from autarky to growth

With the defeat of the Republican government by the Nationalist army in 1939, Generalissimo Francisco Franco established an authoritarian regime that lasted until his death in 1975. The destruction caused by the civil war depressed the Spanish economy. Per capita income fell to its 1900 level and did not reach its 1918 level until 1950. The proportion of the active population in industry declined to 22 percent in 1940 (the level in 1920) and the share of employed in agriculture rose above 50 percent. Growth averaged only 1.2 percent a year in the 1940s.

Spain's economic recovery was hampered, above all, by the autarkic and statist policies of the Franco regime. Inspired by the corporatist ideologies of Italian Fascism and German Nazism, Franco's regime generalized a system of price controls and rationing and regulated foreign trade through quantitative controls. This interventionist strategy extended to the labor and housing market. To quell one of the main forces that opposed the military insurrection, Franco outlawed any independent labor unions. Instead, workers and employers had to affiliate in a national trade union organization. This repressive stance was "compensated" by strict labor legislation that made it hard for employers to dismiss workers or to hire them through temporary contracts. Emphasis on permanent jobs and cheap housing was seen as a substitute for the lack of direct social policies, an attempt by the regime to win legitimacy.

In the late 1950s, Spain eventually moved to break with this interventionist system. An acute political crisis—associated with a wave of strikes, an economic recession, and severe balance-of-payment crisis—led the government to adopt a stabilization plan in March 1959. In addition to fiscal and monetary restraint, the plan included wide-ranging measures to liberalize the economy. It was an outright success. From 1960 to the outbreak of the first oil crisis, output expanded at an average annual rate of more than 7 percent with very little interyear volatility. Per capita income almost tripled from about $3,000 (in 1990 dollars) to $8,500 in 15 years. Productivity growth averaged 6 percent.

The transformation of the Spanish economy led to significant structural changes in Spanish society. The combination of economic growth, industrial expansion and internal migration produced a substantial decline in the levels of interregional inequality (from a standard deviation in per capita income of 0.37 in 1955 to 0.27 in 1973). Interhousehold inequality also declined considerably: the Gini coefficient for wages and salaries of employees (agrarian and industrial) declined from 0.29 in 1964 to 0.23 in 1973; the Gini coefficient for household income fell from 0.39 in 1964 to 0.36 in 1974. The income share of the three central deciles went up from about 51 percent to 59 percent in that decade.

Still, significant social and economic inequities remained. Although the illiteracy rate had fallen to 10 percent by 1970, only 6 percent of the population had completed secondary studies. Wages remained dampened by repressive labor institutions. Taxation and public spending were low, and redistributive social programs nonexistent.

Transitioning to democracy and building the welfare state

Following Franco's death in 1975, King Juan Carlos became the Spanish head of state. He immediately launched a process of political change. Employing the legal mechanisms put in place by the very technocratic generation that had reformed the economy in the early 1960s, as well as pointing to wide popular support for democracy, he secured the consent of the old Francoist *Cortes* to establish a truly democratic parliament elected through direct, competitive elections.

The political reform was ratified with overwhelming popular support in a referendum in December 1976. Although conducted in a climate of uncertainty, particularly over the reaction of the army and the extent to which terrorist violence or labor mobilization could disrupt the negotiations, democratic elections were held in June 1977. After protracted negotiations, a new constitution was approved in 1978 with the support of all parliamentary groups. To reinforce the political pact in parliament, the government also struck a wide economic and social deal with employers and trade unions that same year.

Spain's democratization was rooted in the new economic and social conditions of the 1960s and 1970s. Rapid industrialization and urbanization deflated past conflicts around the distribution of land. The expansion of literacy and the increase in productivity and incomes generated a large middle class. Sustained growth defused social conflict with the credible promise of higher incomes and more social mobility. In short, Spain had overcome the zero-sum game it had been locked in for the past century and a half.

Economic growth resulted in a different economic structure and better distributional outcomes, supporting a swift and successful transition to democracy. In turn, the transition to democracy changed the role and size of the public sector.

Democratization reinforced social demands for progressive and redistributive policies—especially for public infrastructure, and education, health, and social programs. In 1979 more than 70 percent of Spaniards agreed with the statement that "the distribution of wealth in this country is totally unjust." In 10 years, social expenditure almost doubled to reach 80 percent of the European average. Public expenditure in education steadily increased from 2 percent of GDP in 1975 to 4.5 percent in 1995. By 2001 almost 50 percent of the population had completed secondary education—10 times more than in the mid-1970s. An ambitious public investment program tripled the public highway network, revamped and expanded metropolitan transportation, and modernized the railroad system.

Spain's transition to democracy and the resulting expansion of its welfare state shows how a mutually reinforcing package of policy and institutional choices leading to greater equity helped underpin the development and modernization of the Spanish economy and its integration into the European Union. It illustrates how political and economic structures shape the possibilities for policy choice, a theme of chapter 6. But it also illustrates that specific policy choices matter—across social sectors, infrastructure, the workings of markets, and international integration—and that there can be important complementarities for both equity and dynamic growth, notably between greater social provisioning and greater reliance on markets. This takes us to the issue of practical policy design, the central theme of part III of this report.

Sources: Synthesized from Boix (2005), with references to Gunther, Montero, and Botella (2004); North and Thomas (1973); and Revenga (1991).

Equity, institutions, and the development process

Product, land, labor, and capital markets are crucial for the allocation of resources and development. Market institutions, however, exist and function in the context of a whole set of nonmarket and political institutions. The nature of these other institutions—and the way they function—are influenced by inequalities in the political and social realm.

The most obvious of these other institutions are those that define and enforce property rights and contracts. People will not invest if property rights are not well defined and enforced, or if they believe that the contracts they write will not be honored or that courts of law will not be fair. The state must also provide a whole set of other inputs apart from social order and fair contract enforcement. These include various types of public services and regulations. Lying behind well-functioning markets are legal systems, judges, policemen, and, ultimately, social groups and politicians.

This chapter considers the circumstances and processes for creating institutions that promote prosperity. These circumstances are closely related to the concerns of this report. In essence, societies that create institutions to generate sustained prosperity are equitable in important ways. Because talent and ideas are widely distributed in the population, it is crucial that the property of all people is secure and that there is equality before the law for all, not just for some. Predetermined circumstances should not constrain anyone's innovation or investment opportunities. This implies that a good institutional environment will not block entry into new lines of business and that the political system will provide access to services and public goods for all. Institutions must be equitable.

To take an extreme example, institutions were severely inequitable in slave societies, such as Haiti or Barbados in the eighteenth century. Even though property rights in land and people were well defined and even well enforced (although subject to potential slave rebellions), most people had no property rights and were thus subject to expropriation by others, particularly their masters. For 95 percent of society, there were no incentives to engage in socially desirable activities. A similar, although somewhat less extreme, example of inequitable institutions is South Africa under apartheid. Institutions there were good for the whites but left 80 percent of the population without incentives or opportunities to engage in economically productive activities.

The distribution of power and institutional quality: circles vicious and virtuous

How do societies develop equitable nonmarket institutions? First, there must be sufficient political equality—equality in access to the political system and in the distribution of political power, political rights, and influence.

Poor institutions will emerge and persist in societies when power is concentrated in the hands of a narrow group or an elite. Such an elite may grant property rights to itself, but the property rights of most citizens will be unstable. There may be equality before the law for a particular elite group, but not for the majority of people. Government policies may favor such an elite, granting them rents and monopolies, but most people will be excluded from entering profitable lines of business. The education system may invest heavily in the children of such elites, but most will be excluded.

Many things determine the distribution of political power in society—the constitution, the nature of checks and balances, and the ability of different groups to solve collective action problems. But economic inequality often underpins political inequality. In a society with large inequalities of assets and incomes, the rich will tend to have more influence and an advantage in adapting and distorting institutions to their benefit.

Because the distribution of power, through its impact on institutions, helps to determine the distribution of income, the possibility of vicious and virtuous circles is clear. A society with greater equality of control over assets and incomes will tend to have a more equal distribution of political power. It will therefore tend to have institutions that generate equality of opportunity for the broad mass of citizens. This will tend to spread rewards and incomes widely, thereby reinforcing the initial distribution of incomes. In contrast, a society with greater inequality of assets and incomes will tend to have a less egalitarian distribution of power and worse institutions, which tend to reproduce the initial conditions.

The evidence in this chapter suggests that the first type of society will tend to be more prosperous. We argue that societies prosperous today are so because they have developed more egalitarian distributions of political power, while poor societies often suffer from unbalanced distributions. We also consider how some societies made the transition from one equilibrium to the other.

Because institutions have distributional effects, conflict arises naturally. One set of institutions will benefit some people, while another will benefit different people. Thus, there will be incentives for people to control power to create or keep the institutions that benefit them and to avoid or weaken the institutions that disadvantage them. If the groups in conflict are defined along ascriptive lines, such as ethnicity, then this may induce a more severe form of conflict than when groups are defined along other lines, or when there are cross-cutting cleavages. More polarized conflict seems to be an independent force leading to bad institutions that can help to explain the relatively weak performance in some societies (discussed below in a comparison between Guyana and Mauritius).

Political equality also matters for the quality of public policy. The basic role of the state is to provide public services. But politicians have the correct incentives to provide public services only when they have to appeal to the broad mass of citizens to attain power. If they can win power with a small number of key supporters, or with few votes, they will tend to be clientelistic and more inclined to buy votes or make individual exchanges of patronage for support without providing the goods and services critical to raising the mass of people out of poverty.

Some simple patterns in the cross-country data show that more egalitarian distributions of political power and income are associated with sustained and enduring prosperity. Figure 6.1 indicated that more secure property rights are associated with higher incomes. Crucially, however, better institutions and secure property rights are associated with greater political equality.

Although there is no perfect way of measuring political equality, protection against expropriation risk is highly correlated with measures of democracy and measures of "constraints on the executive" from the Polity IV database. This second variable is designed to capture the extent to

Figure 6.1 Countries with more secure property rights have higher average incomes

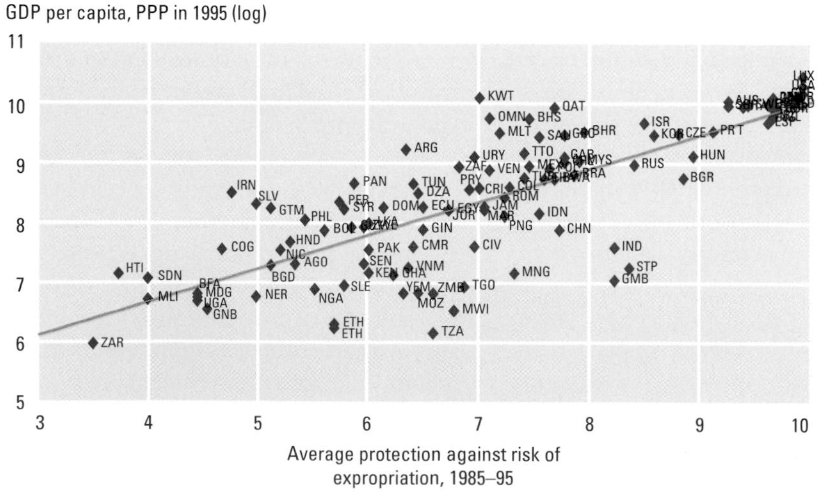

GDP per capita, PPP in 1995 (log)

Average protection against risk of
expropriation, 1985–95

Sources: Political Risk Services, International Country Risk Guide (ICRG) and World Bank database.
Note: The figure shows the relationship between GDP per capita in 1995 and a measure of the security of property rights, "protection against expropriation risk," averaged over the period 1985 to 1995. The data on institutions come from Political Risk Services, a private company that assesses the risk that investments will be expropriated in different countries. These data, first used by Knack and Keefer (1995) and subsequently by Hall and Jones (1999) and Acemoglu, Johnson, and Robinson (2001, 2002a, 2004), are imperfect as a measure of the relevant institutions because they pertain to investments by foreigners only. Even so, they seem in practice to capture how stable property rights are in general. The findings are robust to using other available measures of related institutions.

which those who control political power are constrained or checked by others. The types of checks and balances and separation of powers written into the U.S. Constitution are classic examples of such constraints. There is a negative correlation between constraints on the executive and the Gini coefficient of income distribution.

The simple correlations suggest complementarities between a relatively egalitarian distribution of political power, good institutions, and prosperity, and a relatively egalitarian distribution of economic resources. The correlations are consistent with many different causal stories, but recent research suggests that one can tell a causal story about this data along exactly the lines we are suggesting, which the rest of this chapter discusses. The different evolutions of banking systems in Mexico and the United States in the nineteenth century provide a good example of the sort of historic argument we rely on (box 6.1).

Institutions and political inequality matter for development: historical evidence

Figure 6.1 showed the relationship between security of property and prosperity for the whole world, but to interpret this causally we need to find a source of variation in institutions. Doing this is not easy, but Acemoglu, Johnson, and Robinson (2001) provide a partial answer. They show that the same basic pattern holds for a smaller sample of countries—those colonized by Europeans after 1492. Indeed, colonization of much of the world by Europeans provides something of a large natural experiment.

Beginning in the early fifteenth century and massively intensifying after 1492, Europeans conquered many other nations. Colonization transformed the institutions in many diverse lands conquered or controlled by Europeans. Most important, Europeans created very different sets of institutions in different parts of their global empire, as exemplified most sharply by the contrast between the institutions in the northeast of America and those in the plantation societies of the Caribbean. This experience persuasively establishes the central role of institu-

---

BOX 6.1   *Banking in the nineteenth century, Mexico and the United States*

Much recent work on growth and development has focused on financial and capital markets. A central issue is to understand why financial systems differ. For example, studies of the development of banking in the United States in the nineteenth century demonstrate a rapid expansion of financial intermediation, which most scholars see as a crucial facilitator of the economy's rapid growth and industrialization. Haber (2001) investigated the development of banks in the nineteenth century in Mexico and the United States. He shows that "Mexico had a series of segmented monopolies that were awarded to a group of insiders" (24). In 1910 "the United States had roughly 25,000 banks and a highly competitive market structure; Mexico had 42 banks, two of which controlled 60 percent of total banking assets, and virtually none of which actually competed with another bank."

Why this huge difference? The relevant technology was certainly widely available, and it is difficult to see why the various types of moral hazard or adverse selection connected with financial intermediation should have limited the expansion of banks in Mexico but not the United States. Indeed, Haber shows when the U.S. Constitution was put into effect in 1789, the structure of U.S. banking looked remarkably like that arising later in Mexico. State governments, stripped of revenues by the Constitution, started banks as a way to generate tax revenues and restricted entry to generate rents. Yet this system did not last because states began competing among themselves for investment and migrants. As Haber (2001) puts it,

The pressure to hold population and business in the state was reinforced by a second, related, factor: the broadening of the suffrage. By the 1840s, most states had dropped all property and literacy requirements, and by 1850 virtually all states …

had done so. The broadening of the suffrage, however, served to undermine the political coalitions that supported restrictions on the number of bank charters. That is, it created a second source of political competition—competition within states over who would hold office and the policies they would enact (10).

The situation was very different in Mexico. After 50 years of endemic political instability, the country became unified under the highly centralized 40-year dictatorship of Porfirio Díaz until the revolution in 1910.

In Haber's argument, political institutions in the United States allocated political power to people who wanted access to credit and loans. As a result, they forced state governments to allow free competitive entry into banking. In Mexico, political institutions were very different. There were no competing federal states, and suffrage was highly restrictive. As a result, the central government granted monopoly rights to banks, which restricted credit to maximize profits. The granting of monopolies turned out to be a rational way for the government to raise revenue and redistribute rents to political supporters (North 1981).

Haber (2001) documents that market regulation was not aimed at solving market failures, and it is precisely during this period that the huge economic gap between the United States and Mexico opened (on which see Coatsworth 1993, Engerman and Sokoloff 1997). Haber and Maurer 2004 examined in detail how the structure of banking influenced the Mexican textile industry between 1880 and 1913. They show that only firms with personal contacts with banks were able to get loans and that such firms were less efficient. Even though economic efficiency was hurt by regulations, those with political power were able to sustain them.

---

tions in development. It also provides fairly clear-cut evidence to support our conjectures about the joint evolution of prosperity and political and economic equality.

Colonial origins of contemporary institutions

Acemoglu, Johnson, and Robinson, building on the research of Engerman and Sokoloff (1997), explain that Europeans created good institutions in some colonies, particularly the United States, Canada, and Australasia (what

Crosby (1986) calls the neo-Europes), and bad ones in others (particularly in Latin America and Sub-Saharan Africa). These institutions had a strong tendency to persist and thus, today, generate the results seen in figure 6.1.

Why did different institutions develop in different European colonies? The simplest answer is that Europeans shaped the institutions in various colonies to benefit themselves. And because conditions and endowments differed among colonies, Europeans consciously created different institutions. There are several important empirical regularities connecting initial conditions to current outcomes. Of particular importance are initial population density, the disease environ-

ment, and the factor endowments that influenced economic organization.[1] There is a strong inverse relationship between population density in 1500 and current protection against expropriation risk for former European colonies (figure 6.2). And colonies with disease environments that were worse for European settlers also have worse institutions today (figure 6.3).

Other aspects of factor endowments are more difficult to measure directly, but Engerman and Sokoloff (1997) point out that where the climate and soils were suitable for crops such as sugarcane—which could be grown on large plantations with slave labor, such as northeastern Brazil—much worse institutions and more skewed distributions of political power evolved than in climates where wheat or other nonplantation crops could be grown.

Why did Europeans introduce better institutions in previously relatively unsettled and healthy areas than in previously densely settled and unhealthy areas? How did factor endowments influence institutions? Europeans were more likely to introduce or maintain bad institutions where there were a lot of resources and rents to extract—gold, silver, and, most important, people to provide the labor. In places with a large indigenous population, Europeans could exploit the population through taxes, tributes, or employment as forced labor in mines or plantations. And where plantation crops could be profitably grown, slave-based societies emerged. These types of colonization were incompatible with institutions providing economic or civil rights or equality of opportunity to the majority of the population. So, a more developed civilization with a denser population structure, and particular climatic and agricultural conditions, made it more profitable for the Europeans to introduce bad institutions.

In contrast, in places with little to extract, where plantation agriculture was not profitable, and in sparsely settled places where the Europeans became the majority of the population, it was in their interests to introduce much better institutions. In addition, the disease environments differed markedly among the colonies, with obvious consequences for the attractiveness of European

Figure 6.2 Low population density in 1500 is associated with a lower risk of expropriation today

Average protection against risk of expropriation, 1985–95

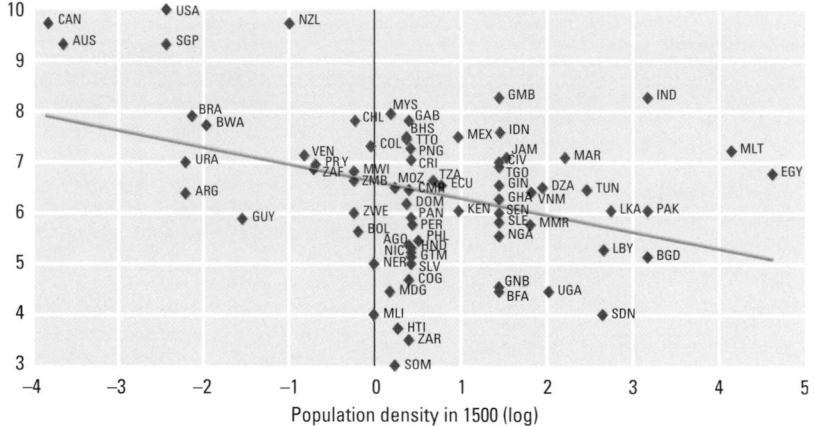

Population density in 1500 (log)

Source: Political Risk Services, International Country Risk Guide (ICRG) and Acemoglu, Johnson, and Robinson (2002).

Figure 6.3 Worse environments for European settlers are associated with worse institutions today

Average protection against risk of expropriation, 1985–95

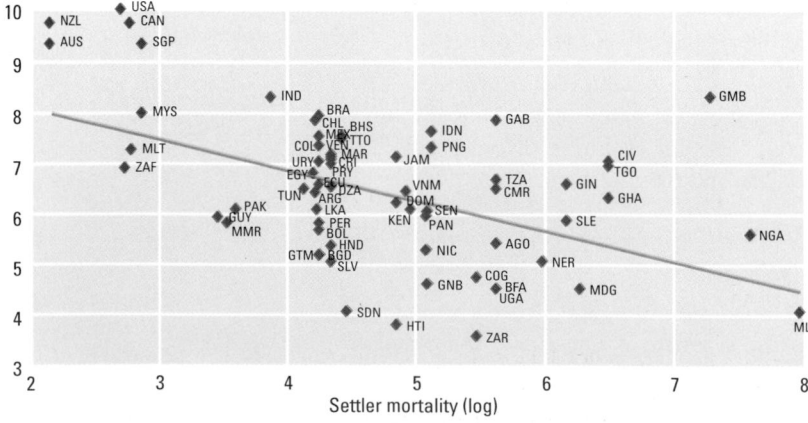

Settler mortality (log)

Source: Political Risk Services, International Country Risk Guide (ICRG) and Acemoglu, Johnson, and Robinson (2002).

settlement. When Europeans settled, they established institutions under which they themselves had to live.

This research suggests that most of the gap in per capita income between rich and poor countries today is due to differences in institutions. More precisely, if one takes two typical countries—in the sense that they both lie on the regression line—with high and low expropriation risk, such as Nigeria and Chile, almost the entire difference in income per capita between them can be explained by the differences in the historically shaped measure of the security of property rights.[2] The research also presented regression evidence showing that once the effect of institutions on GDP per capita is properly controlled for, geographic variables—such as latitude, whether or not a country is landlocked, the current disease environment—have no explanatory power for current prosperity.

Different types of societies thus developed in different colonies with radically different implications for subsequent development. Crucially, the societies that emerged in the neo-Europes had distributions of economic resources and political power that were much broader. And they placed constraints on the exercise of political power and the ability of elites to adopt policies favorable to themselves but deleterious for society (figure 6.4).

Development and inequality in the Americas: A case study in colonial origins

The colonization of Latin America began with the discovery of the "Indies" by Columbus in 1492, the assault on Mexico by Cortés after 1519, and the conquest of Peru by Pizzaro after 1532. From the beginning, the Spanish were interested in the extraction of gold and silver, and later in taking tribute and raising taxes. The colonial societies that emerged were authoritarian, based on the political power of a small Spanish elite who created a set of institutions to extract wealth from the indigenous population.

After Pizzaro conquered Peru, he imposed institutions to extract rents from the newly conquered Indians. The main such institutions were the *encomienda* (which gave Span-

Figure 6.4 A worse environment for settlers is associated with fewer constraints on the executive at independence

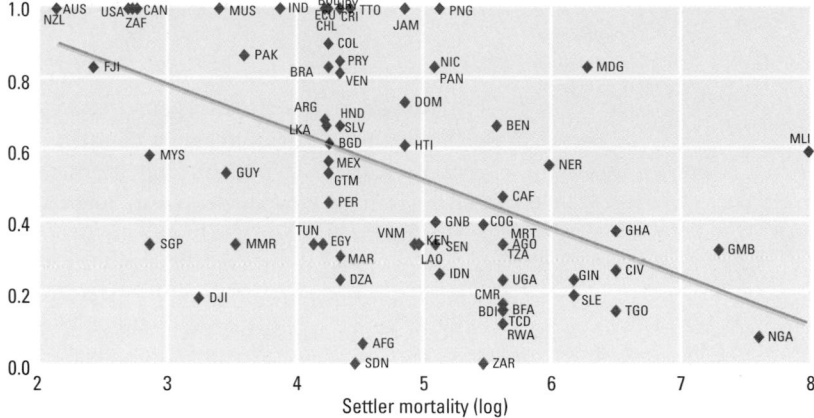

Constraint on the executive at independence

Source: Acemoglu, Johnson, and Robinson (2002a). The analysis indicates that that the same factors that gave rise to good institutions gave rise to a more egalitarian distribution of power. Without some measure of voice, it is impossible for a person's property rights to be guaranteed or for them to have real access to the legal system to make sure that contracts are honored. A more egalitarian distribution of political power is also associated with a more egalitarian distribution of economic resources. To get a better understanding of the mechanisms, we need to look further into historical analysis.

ish conquistadors the right to Amerindian labor),[3] the *mita* (a system of forced labor used in the mines), and the *repartimiento* (the forced sale of goods to Indians, typically at highly inflated prices). Pizzaro created 480 *encomenderos*, under whose care the entire Indian population was placed. In other colonies the situation was similar. For instance, in the territory of modern Colombia, there were about 900 *encomenderos*.[4]

The *encomienda* did not last for long in all parts of the empire because the Spanish Crown attempted to curtail it by the end of the sixteenth century. But the *mita* (from the Quechua word *mit'a*, meaning "turn") became a central institution until independence, and forced labor lasted far beyond this in most of Latin America (until 1945 in Guatemala). The effects of the *encomienda* also persisted because the concentration of political power that it was associated with led to the emergence of large landed estates.[5] The feasibility and attraction of this type of economic system was determined by the higher population densities of indigenous people in many parts of the Spanish empire and the extent to which such societies had already developed into "complex societies."[6]

Other institutions were designed to reinforce this system. For instance, indigenous people were not allowed to give testimony in some cases, and in others the testimony of 10 indigenous people was equal to that of 1 Spaniard.[7] Although indigenous people did use the legal system to challenge aspects of colonial rule, they could not alter the main parameters of the system. In addition, the Spanish Crown created a complex web of mercantilistic policies and monopolies from salt to gunpowder, from tobacco to alcohol and playing cards, to raise revenues for the state.

Spanish colonies that had small populations of Amerindians, such as Costa Rica, Argentina, or Uruguay, seem to have followed different paths of institutional development. The sharp contrasts along many institutional dimensions between Costa Rica and Guatemala (where population density was greater) have been much studied. Although the formal political institutions of the Spanish empire were the same everywhere, the way they functioned depended on the local conditions.[8]

The institutions that emerged in the main Spanish colonies greatly benefited the Spanish crown and the Spanish settler elite, but they did not promote prosperity in Latin America. Most of the population had no property rights, nor incentives to enter socially desirable occupations or to invest. Europeans developed coercive regimes monopolizing military and political power and respecting few constraints on their power (unless imposed by the mother country in Europe).[9]

In North America, the initial attempts at colonization were also based on economic motives. British colonies were founded by such entities as the Virginia Company and the Providence Island Company with the aim of profits. The model was not so different from that of the Spanish or Portuguese (a system that other British colonizing entities, such as the East India Company, used to great effect). Yet these companies made no money. Indeed, both the Virginia Company and the Providence Island Company went bankrupt. Because of the absence of a large indigenous population and complex societies, a colonial model involving the exploitation of indigenous labor and tribute systems was simply not feasible in these places.

Historical accounts show that initial conditions had a large impact on the institutions that the settlers built. Because there was low population density and no way to extract resources from indigenous peoples, early commercial developments had to import British labor. And, relative to much of the colonial world, the disease environment was benign, stimulating settlement. Indeed, the Pilgrim fathers decided to migrate to the United States rather than Guyana because of the high mortality rates in Guyana.[10] But these same conditions made it impossible to profitably exploit labor, whose bargaining power forced elites to extend political rights and create equal access to land and the law. These forces were reinforced by the fact that plantation agriculture and slavery were not profitable, at least in the northern United States and Canada.

These colonies ultimately provided access to land to a broad cross-section of society and the legal system became fairly impartial, ensuring secure property rights for smallholders and potential investors. The new institutions made investment possible through financial development and secure contracting and business relationships. Underpinning these institutions were fairly representative political institutions and a fairly egalitarian distribution of resources. As in Latin America, there was a synergy between economic and political institutions, but this time it was virtuous, not vicious. Institutions giving and protecting property rights for the mass of people and institutions of democratic politics complemented each other, ensuring an environment conducive to investment and economic progress.

Representative political institutions in Virginia were a direct result of the authorities realizing that, because of the different conditions, the colonization strategy that worked in Peru would not work in the United States. Virginia had many competing and fragmented tribes, not a large central tribal empire. It had no gold or silver, and the Indians, not used to paying tribute or engaging in forced labor, would not work. So, the settlers of Jamestown starved.[11] In response to these early failures, the Virginia Company tried various incentive schemes,

---

BOX 6.2 *Growth with poor institutions does not last*

The elite had good investment opportunities in Argentina in the golden age from the 1870s to the 1920s, in Czarist Russia in the decades leading up to World War I, in Colombia in the half century after 1900, and in the Côte d'Ivoire for the first two decades after independence (Widner 1993). Such situations are rarely sustainable, for three reasons. First, the possibilities for sustained growth are, by definition, limited because institutions exclude the majority of the population from effectively investing. Second, in the rare situations in which elites manage to create arrangements so that they can benefit directly from growth without the need to create good institutions more generally, such arrangements tend to be fragile, vulnerable to shocks or crises. Third, bad institutions create power struggles that undermine growth, because they generate large rents for those who control power.

Consider the growth of Argentina in the half century before 1930. After its independence from Spain in 1816, Argentina plunged into 50 years of civil wars and conflicts over control of the country, mainly clashes between those in control of Buenos Aires and the littoral and those in the interior. These conflicts abated after the 1853 constitution and the presidency of Bartolomé Mitre with a compromise between the Pampas and the interior. Pampean mercantile and agrarian interests would be allowed to cre-

ate institutions to take advantage of the huge economic opportunities emerging on world markets, but the structure of the political rules, such as their overrepresentation in national political institutions, guaranteed the interior provinces a large slice of the benefits (Samuels and Snyder 2001).

Although the majority was excluded from the political system, the economy boomed with the property rights of the Pampean elite guaranteed. But the huge rents created by this system began to cause conflict. In the 1890s, the Radical Party emerged under Hipólito Yrigoyen, and after a series of revolts it was incorporated into the political system by the democratizing impact of the Sáenz Peña Law in 1912.

Although Yrigoyen was elected president in 1916, the traditional interests were confident that they could keep control of the polity and the economy. They were mistaken. Significant changes in the social structure had occurred, with rapid immigration from Europe, induced by economic success, and the associated urbanization. The vote share of the Conservatives declined rapidly and the prospect of a Radical Party majority was a key factor behind the coup of 1930. Smith (1978) notes "this situation contrasts sharply with that in Sweden and Great Britain ... where traditional elites continued to dominate systems after the extension of

suffrage" (21). From this point onward political conflicts intensified, with a stream of coups and redemocratizations that lasted until 1983. Though among the richest countries in the world in the 1920s, Argentina gradually slid back to being a developing country.

Argentina shows that, even with poor institutions for political inclusion and conflict management, growth is possible if elites have good investment opportunities and can manage to forge compromises. But the booms eventually unravel. Even when elites, such as the agriculturalists of the Argentine Pampas, face very good investment opportunities, growth cannot be sustained forever by agricultural export booms. Moreover, the rents created by bad institutions create conflict without fundamental balances of power in society. This meant that democracy in Argentina after 1912 was unstable. The unchecked power of President Yrigoyen in the 1920s induced a coup in 1930, as did that of Perón in the 1940s and in 1955 and again in 1976 after his return from exile. Although temporary political solutions can sometimes ease conflict for a while, as they did in Argentina after 1853, in the absence of broader institutional inclusion, conflict ultimately reemerges, undermining the incentives to investment.

---

including a highly punitive, almost penal, effort to make money. Such efforts quickly collapsed, however, and by 1619 the Company had created an unusually representative set of institutions for that era: a general assembly with adult male suffrage.

The early history of the United States shows a possible path to good institutions. Early attempts to create an oligarchic society with close control of labor quickly collapsed. What emerged instead was a relatively egalitarian society, with representative institutions giving even the poorest colonists access to the law and some political representation. This laid the basis for economic and social institutions that underpinned the takeoff of the United States in the nineteenth century and its divergence from the fortunes of much of Latin America. Some countries with weak and unequal institutions have experienced periods of rapid growth, but these have proved to be unsustainable over the long term (box 6.2).

Institutions and political inequality matter for development: contemporary evidence

Our review of comparative history supports two conclusions. First, institutions, especially those that underpin property rights for all and broad-based investment, have a causative influence on long-run development processes. And second, greater political equality can lay the basis for better economic institutions. By greater political equality, we mean, in particular, checks on the predatory behavior of political and economic elites, and the political need for the state to be responsive to middle and poorer population groups. The basis for greater political equalities is often associated with underlying economic structures, although causation can run both ways.

How does this perspective relate to the variety of contemporary development experiences? It is consistent with the perspective that institutions and governance are central to a wide variety of development performance, from growth to service delivery.[12] While debate continues, an important thrust of this research has been to support the view that causation runs, at least in part, from better institutions to higher incomes, rather than the other way.[13] What is additional to this (ongoing) debate is the second part of the argument—that the nature and management of inequalities in power shapes the formation of institutions. Some cross-country analysis is suggestive: Rodrik (1999a) argues that the capacity of societies to manage adverse shocks—itself a crucial determinant of growth—depends on the depth of latent social conflict and the strength of conflict management mechanisms.

To illustrate the argument, we continue to draw on comparative development experiences. We first look at East Asia, and then look at agricultural pricing polices in Africa. We then examine in greater depth the comparative experience of Mauritius and Guyana, countries that started with similar initial conditions, but then followed radically different development paths. This is also related to different experiences in managing polarization, which can be contributory factors for violent social conflict.

Shared growth in East Asia: the Republic of Korea, Taiwan (China), and Indonesia

Elites may be forced by threats of social disorder to promote the prosperity of most citizens. Indeed, societies that have a political necessity to appeal to or appease middle and lower groups (initially the peasantry) can grow substantially in the short run. Long-run prosperity, however, requires institutionalized, rather than contingent checks and balances on elite power and capacities to adjust to changing circumstances. The response of elites to social disturbances sometimes leads to solutions that permanently change the political equilibrium in a beneficial way, as may have happened with the agrarian reforms in the Republic of Korea and Taiwan, China, in the late 1940s and early 1950s. More often, however, the transitory ability of citizens to act collectively dissipates without elites having to propose anything more than a transitory solution, as may have been the case in Indonesia under the New Order.

The rapid economic development of the Republic of Korea after the mid-1960s was not due to a set of institutions put in place through a domestic balance of political power. Instead, as in Indonesia under the New Order regime, a precarious geopolitical situation, particularly after the rundown of U.S. aid in the early 1960s, induced the Park regime to create a pro-growth environment.[14] This at least led to a contingent commitment to good institutions, as it did under an authoritarian regime in Taiwan, China, where a fairly egalitarian distribution of assets and incomes, perhaps eased the transition in the 1990s toward democracy, a greater equality of political influence, and good institutions. As in much of East Asia, there was a political necessity to deliver income growth and services to the peasantry.

In Indonesia, Suharto's New Order government also recognized that economic growth was necessary to keep the regime in power and that, to achieve this, good economic policies had to be in place. This induced Suharto to delegate macroeconomic policy to technocrats and to respond to the oil booms wisely. It also led him to intervene to attempt to control corruption and excesses that would put in jeopardy the underpinnings of the regime.[15]

Yet this constraint, real though it was, at least in the 1960s and 1970s, is only part of the story about Indonesian growth. Suharto managed to create a system that, while not introducing good institutions, induced investments and growth from which the regime could benefit. One of the secrets behind this appears to have been the role of Sino-Indonesian businessmen, the *cukong* entrepreneurs. Many firms and businesses were controlled by Indonesians of Chinese origin who were very marginal politically. Suharto granted such businessmen monopoly rights and placed members of the military and his supporters on their boards of directors.[16] Rock (2003) argues, "There is little doubt that the . . . distortions in New Order microeconomic policies thwarted competition, rewarded cronies, and encouraged substantial investment in uneconomic projects" (10). Yet they also generated wealth, economic growth, and rents for the regime. It was precisely the political marginality of the *cukong* entrepreneurs that made them an attractive business partner for the regime.

The economic success of Indonesia after 1966 elevated it into the class of an Asian "miracle economy."[17] The East Asia financial crisis in 1997, however, exposed and exacerbated Indonesia's institutional weaknesses, plummeting the country into an economic and political crisis from which it is only now beginning to recover, doing so on the basis of a new foundation of decentralization and democracy, which have progressively institutionalized greater relationships of accountability between citizens and state. (See focus 4 on Indonesia for a further discussion of the relationship between social and political context and policy choices.)

Agricultural pricing policies in Africa

Another important example illustrating the connections between institutions, the distribution of political power and growth comes from the seminal studies of price regulation prices in agricultural markets in Africa by Robert Bates.[18] Bates (1981) demonstrated that poor agricultural performance in Ghana, Nigeria, and Zambia was due to government-controlled marketing boards systematically paying farmers prices much below world levels. The marketing board surpluses were given to the government as a form of taxation. As a result of this pernicious taxation, reaching up to 70 percent of the value of the crop in Ghana in the 1970s, investment in agriculture collapsed, as did the output of cocoa and other crops. In poor countries with a comparative advantage in agriculture, this meant negative rates of economic growth.

Why were resources extracted in this way? Although part of the motivation was to promote industrialization, the main one was to generate resources that could be either expropriated or redistributed to maintain power. As Bates (1981) put it,

> governments face a dilemma: urban unrest, which they cannot successfully eradicate

through co-optation or repression, poses a serious challenge to their interests ... Their response has been to try to appease urban interests not by offering higher money wages but by advocating policies aimed at reducing the cost of living, and in particular the cost of food. Agricultural policy thus becomes a byproduct of political relations between governments and urban constituents (33).

In contrast to the situation in Ghana, Nigeria, and Zambia, Bates (1981), Bates (1989) showed that agricultural policy in Kenya over this period was much more profarmer. The difference was due to who controlled the marketing board. In Kenya, farmers were not smallholders, as they were in Ghana, Nigeria, and Zambia, and concentrated landownership made it much easier to act collectively. Moreover, farming was important in the Kikuyu areas, an ethnic group closely related to the ruling political party, the Kenya African National Union (KANU), under Jomo Kenyatta.[19] Farmers in Kenya therefore formed a powerful lobby and were able to guarantee themselves high prices. Even though the government of Kenya engaged in land reform after independence, Bates (1981) argued that—

> 80 percent of the former white highlands were left intact and ... the government took elaborate measures to preserve the integrity of the large-scale farms ... [which] readily combine in defense of their interests. One of the most important collective efforts is the Kenya National Farmer's Union (KNFU) ... The organization ... is dominated by the large-scale farmers ... [but] it can be argued that the KNFU helps to create a framework of public policies that provides an economic environment favorable to all farmers (93–4).

Bates concluded that in Kenya "large farmers ... have secured public policies that are highly favorable by comparison to those in other nations" (95).

Bates demonstrated why economic policies were better in Kenya than Ghana in the 1960s and 1970s, but this advantage did not survive the coming to power of Daniel arap Moi in Kenya.[20] The change in the ethnic basis of the regime, from Kikuyu to Kalenjin, undermined the coalition that had supported good agricultural policies, because the export farmers were not only large, but

Figure 6.5 Constraints on the executive are greater in Mauritius than in Guyana

Constraint on the executive

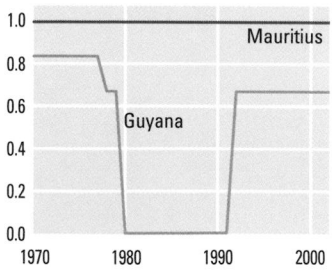

Source: Polity IV data set, downloaded from Inter-University Consortium for Political and Social Research. Variable described in Gurr (1997).

Figure 6.6 GDP per capita is rising in Mauritius, not in Guyana

GDP per capita (log)

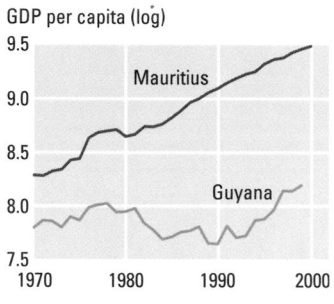

Source: World Bank (2005g).

also predominantly Kikuyu. As a result, economic performance declined precipitously in the 1980s and 1990s. The balance of power that sustained good policies in the 1970s did not endure.

The contrasting experience of Mauritius and Guyana

Mauritius and Guyana, in the 1960s, were both poor societies dominated by the production and export of sugarcane. They had similar histories, factor endowments, social and political cleavages, and institutions. If anything, Guyana, although slightly poorer, had better prospects, because of its proximity to the large U.S. market. Yet Mauritius has become one of the most dynamic and successful (and equal) developing countries, industrializing and maintaining competitive democratic politics. Guyana slumped into dictatorship and poverty.

The divergence between Mauritius and Guyana since independence is a fascinating example of economic and political divergence in apparently similar societies (figures 6.5 and 6.6).

What can explain this? Both countries have similar histories. Mauritius was taken from the French and Guyana from the Dutch during the Napoleonic wars.[21] In the nineteenth century both developed sugarcane economies and, after the abolition of slavery in the British Empire in 1834, imported large numbers of indentured laborers from India. Both have a similar population structure, with Indo-Guyanese and Indo-Mauritians forming the majority of the population with significant minorities of people of African, European, and Chinese descent.

After World War II, both colonies were moved by the British toward independence with early elections for democratic legislative assemblies dominated by pro-independence political parties led by Seewoosagur Ramgoolam in Mauritius and Cheddi Jagan in Guyana. Both groups used extensive socialist rhetoric and proposed land reforms and fairly radical policies. Many of the political struggles with British administrators over postindependence institutions, such as the form of the electoral system, were fought over similar issues. As independence arrived however, political forces re-formed into a situa-

tion in which parties led by Indo-Mauritians and Indo-Guyanese faced a coalition of parties supported by the non-Indian population, led by Gaetan Duval in Mauritius and Forbes Burnham in Guyana. Yet, at independence, politics and economics diverged.

The Mauritian Labour Party won power initially and quickly abandoned its radical policies—by the early 1970s, investment in the export processing zone had begun. The political hegemony of the Labour Party was quickly contested by a strong socialist party, the MMM (Mouvement Militant Mauricien) led by Paul Berenger and Dev Virahsawmy. In response, the Labour Party entered a coalition with Duval and his PMSD (Parti Mauricien Social Democrate) and the previous opposition groups. The Labour Party drew back from repressing the new political forces, allowed the MMM to contest the 1976 election, and instead adopted social policies, such as the provision of universal secondary education, to improve its popularity. It also quickly dropped populist macroeconomic policies and, in the late 1970s, implemented a serious stabilization program under the IMF. The final test of Mauritian institutions was the election of an MMM government for the first time in 1982. Once in power, the MMM abandoned its more radical policies, and when the broad political consensus for good institutions became clear, the export processing zone boomed.

The contrast with Guyana is stark. The first election on the eve of independence was won by Burnham and his People's National Party in a coalition against Jagan's People's Progressive Party. Burnham maintained power by increasingly fraudulent means, finally changing the constitution in 1980 to make himself executive president. He assassinated opponents, most famously the radical economist and political activist Walter Rodney in 1980. The economic policies of Burnham's regime were a disaster. He expropriated the sugar plantations, creating highly inefficient state industries, and he aggressively promoted his party members through patronage, particularly in the civil service. The implied or actual threat to property and person led to a huge diaspora of Indo-Guyanese from the country, including most of the professional and middle-class people. Only in the

1990s did a democratized Guyana begin to slowly recover from this legacy. But the ethnic divide endures, and the country continues to suffer from weak governance, a lack of political transparency, and ethnic tensions that hamper economic and social development.

What can explain such divergent outcomes in such apparently similar circumstances? In Guyana, there were fewer constraints on the use of power, and political conflict was more polarized, defined solely along ethnic lines. And although both countries started independence as democracies, what the majority could do (or wanted to do) to the minority was limited in Mauritius, but not in Guyana.

In Mauritius, the British colonial state faced a powerful and homogeneous French planter class that did not leave the island after Mauritius was annexed to Britain in 1812. In the 1870s, when Britain was reducing the autonomy of colonial administrations, it was forced to create a legislative assembly. Although this was initially dominated by the planters, by the turn of the twentieth century the first Indo-Mauritians were elected. This was a clear sign that the greater political autonomy of the island was allowing for a more open society with greater upward mobility of former indentured laborers. The power of the colonial state was checked, evident in the fact that Mauritian independence leaders were able in the 1960s to negotiate postindependence institutions closer to the ones they wanted.

This juxtaposition of different local interests and the weakening of the legacy of the colonial state gave rise to a more balanced distribution of political power in Mauritius. And from this situation more fluid interests emerged. Though ethnic identities were certainly important in politics, so were different cleavages, as is clear from the development of the MMM into a powerful political force and the coalition of Ramgoolam and Duval in the 1970s. Politics became much less polarized than they might have been.

In Guyana, there was no indigenous planter class to check the power of the colonial state. After the departure of the Dutch, the plantations came to be owned by absentee British companies. The authoritarian tendencies of the colonial state were reinforced by British military intervention, promoted in 1953 by the United States, to remove Jagan from power because of his socialist tendencies. Guyanese politicians, unlike those in Mauritius, had far less ability to get what they wanted from the colonial state. This meant that there were fewer indigenous checks on the exercise of power, and unfettered use of political power was the norm. The best example here is the electoral system. Britain imposed a proportional representation system on Guyana because it was afraid that the overrepresentation of large parties inherent in majoritarian systems would allow Jagan to win an absolute majority in the 1961 election (the People's Progressive Party won 42.6 percent of the vote in the 1961 election). This system facilitated Burnham's rise to power.

Although the British tried to do the same thing in Mauritius, political elites there held out and forced a compromise: a system with relatively large electoral districts with the three politicians who got the most votes being elected and with the eight best "losers" from the entire country being elected to parliament. This system maintained elements of the majoritarian institutions that Mauritian leaders believed were essential to maintaining the country's governability. Politics in Guyana became completely defined along ethnic lines. This occurred because the previous evolution of the economy, and the dominant power of colonial interests, left little room for the varied interests that emerged in Mauritius. While Guyana has not suffered outright social conflict, high levels of polarization and weak conflict management institutions can be contributory factors to civil wars (box 6.3).

Implications

In Mauritius, property rights are secure and the country has experienced open democratic politics. There has been intensive investment in education and free access into profitable investment opportunities, illustrated most clearly by the export processing zone. In Guyana, the opposite was true in the 1970s and 1980s. The puzzle is why institutions have been so good in one case and so

---

BOX 6.3 *Polarization, conflict, and growth*

Researchers have long recognized that deep social divisions make it harder to implement policies that benefit all. Getting a more precise measure of the nature and extent of such divisions, however, has proved problematic. For much of the 1990s, scholars used a measure known as "ethno-linguistic fractionalization"—first compiled by Russian social scientists in the 1960s—to show that economic growth was slower, controlling for other factors, in societies where there was a low probability that two citizens drawn randomly from a population group were of the same ethnic group. Africa's "growth tragedy" was, in part, blamed on its high level of "fractionalization" (Easterly and Levine 1997).

More recent work has sought to refine measures of social diversity by focusing instead on polarization, or the extent to which a small number of influential groups dominate a society, thereby providing a more theoretically informed basis for explaining the relationship between diver-

sity and conflict, and through this channel, economic growth (Esteban and Ray 1994). By this measure, a country with three groups that comprise, respectively, 49 percent, 49 percent and 2 percent of the population will be more polarized than a counterpart country where those same groups comprise 33 percent, 33 percent, and 34 percent of the population. The polarization measure is a far more robust predictor of civil conflict than either measures of the inequality of individual incomes or fragmentation. This statistical association is illustrated by the fact that, by this measure, 9 of the 10 most polarized societies in the world have experienced major civil conflict in the past few decades, including Eritrea, Guatemala, Nigeria, Sierra Leone, and Bosnia and Herzegovina (García-Montalvo and Reynal-Querol forthcoming). This is only one influence on conflict, of course, and other work has emphasized the role of resource dependence and state capacities (see World Bank 2003h).

---

bad in the other, given such apparently similar histories and circumstances.

But the two cases make sense in more detail. The colonial history of Mauritius diverged from Guyana's in significant ways that allowed the development of a stronger domestic political society. Mauritius resisted the colonial state more effectively and, ultimately, generated a more egalitarian distribution of political power and a less polarized structure of political conflict. In Guyana, however, there was no powerful domestic interest group that had a vested interest in opposing the colonial state or that was able to block the state from expropriating land and other assets after independence. The use of power was unconstrained, and politics were highly polarized along ethnic lines.

Indonesia shows that growth is possible even with underlying bad institutions when elites can credibly make a contingent commitment to improve institutions and when they manage to forge mechanisms that indirectly benefit from encouraging the investment opportunities of others. The acceleration of growth after 1966, and particularly the pro-poor aspect of growth, was clearly driven by the threat of communism and

rural social disorder. The spillover from the conflicts of 1965 and 1966 was a redistribution of power toward the rural sector, with sustained, inclusive growth necessary for the political survival of the regime.

Yet the redistribution of power in Indonesia was not institutionalized, unlike what occurred in the Republic of Korea, for example. Moreover, it did not force the New Order Regime to improve institutions outside the rural and education sectors, although the connection between promoting economic development and social order may well have helped the government to sustain its relationship with the *cukong* entrepreneurs. As the constraints on economic policies of the New Order Regime relaxed in the 1990s, it appears to have been more difficult to avoid a massive and debilitating upsurge in corruption and rent-seeking. Moreover, the collusive agreement that the state forged with the Sino-Indonesian entrepreneurs appears to have been very fragile. It rested on shared expectations about the longevity of the relationship, expectations that clearly deteriorated with Suharto's failing health and could not survive the financial crisis in 1997.[22]

Transitions to more equitable institutions

So far we have examined cases illustrating the mechanisms that create good institutions and sustain prosperity. They involve institutions that allow for greater equality of opportunity, and behind such a set of institutions lies a relative balance of economic resources and political power. Such institutions have emerged in some societies but not others. Although systems of institutions often tend to reinforce one another and persist for long periods, they also change. Countries with unequal distributions of resources and political power become more egalitarian and democratic, and previously powerless people gain power and influence. Although institutions are sometimes created by colonialism or military conquest, they can often evolve through good decisions, virtuous paths, and the intrinsic dynamics of the development process, as in Mauritius. It is also possible that even transitory conditional solutions lead to permanent change, because growth unleashes transformations that induce beneficial changes in institutions. This message from modernization theory[23] is precisely what may have happened in the Republic of Korea.

The biggest challenge is to understand processes of change and to distill from them lessons about how poorer societies can undergo beneficial institutional transitions. This does not appear to have happened in Argentina (box 6.2) or Guyana, but it did happen in Britain in the seventeenth, eighteenth, and nineteenth centuries and in Finland, Sweden, Spain, and the Republic of Korea in the twentieth century. It also happened in Mauritius. Here we briefly review three such transitions: early modern Britain, Finland and Sweden in the early twentieth century, and China in the last 20 years. The transitions and policy choices in Spain are discussed in focus 3 on Spain.

Early modern Britain

Around 1500 most European countries were highly hierarchical feudal societies ruled by absolute monarchs whose powers were endowed by God. The most prosperous places, such as the Italian city states of Venice, Genoa and Florence, had escaped feudalism and were ruled by republican governments strongly representing mercantile interests. The Netherlands also escaped intense feudalism and was relatively prosperous, but it was part of the autocratic Habsburg Empire. Nevertheless, the differences in income between the most and the least prosperous places were relatively small. After 1500, this picture began to change rapidly. First the Netherlands and then Britain became much more prosperous than the rest of Europe, and the Mediterranean world went into decline.

As North and Thomas (1973) argued, the most plausible explanation for these changes is the emergence of constitutional government in the Netherlands and Britain: diverging prosperity within the early modern period was tied to the evolution of political institutions.[24] Institutions improved because of a change in the distribution of resources and political power. Indeed, there was a virtuous circle of changes in institutions, the broader distribution of resources and power, and subsequent changes in institutions. These changes included the collapse of feudalism and serfdom and the move to a free labor market, the changes in land distribution, the commercialization of agriculture and the development of interoceanic commerce.[25]

Yet, even after 1688, the political system was at root oligarchic. Further changes were needed in the distribution of power toward greater political equality to sustain Britain's development path and eventually deliver a more egalitarian society. Even though Britain was a constitutional regime, it was a very limited democracy in 1800. Before the first reform act of 1832 set in motion political liberalizations that culminated in full democracy in 1918, fewer than 10 percent of adult males could vote. The reason for these changes seems to have been the effect of early industrialization and urbanization on the ability of the disenfranchised to contest the power of political elites.[26] British democratization in the nineteenth century was the outcome of a series of strategic concessions by political elites to avoid social disorder.[27]

While the political system of the eighteenth century was consistent with individual initiative, invention, and the start of the industrial revolution in Britain, sustained long-run growth called for broad investment, particularly in human capital. Such institutions had to wait for mass democracy to begin to arrive after 1867.[28] However, the longer history of the Poor Laws provide an example of how provisioning for adverse risks was also supportive of greater dynamism (box 6.4)—a theme we return to in chapter 7.

The types of political reforms in nineteenth-century Britain led to economic institutions that clearly influenced the distribution of income, most obviously the promotion of education after 1867. But the same period also saw extensive labor market reforms that strengthened the bargaining power of labor and led to the rise of the Labor Party. After 1906, the Liberal government of Herbert Asquith also began to introduce the basics of a welfare state, further extended by the Labor government after 1945. As Britain began to adopt institutions that promoted prosperity,

---

BOX 6.4 *Aiding equitable growth in early modern Britain: the role of the Poor Laws*

Far from being a consequence of successful economic growth, recent historical research on seventeenth- and eighteenth-century Britain has found that widespread but unique institutions of social security were in existence for several centuries before the industrial revolution. Indeed, scholars increasingly argue that a previously under-estimated influence on Britain's industrial revolution, in fact, lies in its prior agricultural revolution. The principal comparator here is with the immensely advanced Dutch rural and trading economy of the sixteenth and seventeenth centuries. Many of the most important technical innovations in British agriculture during this period, such as land drainage engineering, new crop types, and rotations, were directly borrowed from the Dutch. Yet it was the British agricultural and service economy that was increasingly out-pacing the Dutch as the seventeenth and eighteenth centuries progressed. Why?

Attention has recently been given to one major institutional difference between the two countries—the nationwide system of social security created in England by the Poor Laws, which gradually evolved during the course of the sixteenth century, culminating in the famous Elizabethan statutes of 1598 and 1601. This was a Christian human-ist response, imbued with a new optimism about what government could and should be able to achieve in the face of perceptions of increased poverty amid plenty in a time of population growth. The Poor Law was mandated by the central state but—most important for its practical effectiveness—its implementation was entirely locally devolved: it was funded by a local tax on property in every parish, administered by local officials but also rigorously enforced by local magistrates. It went side by side with a relatively efficient nationwide population registration system, the Church of England's

parish registers, which was instituted in 1538. This placed the English population on an entirely different basis, in terms of social security, from that of the rest of Europe.

The comprehensive social security system provided by the Poor Laws had a number of highly significant economic consequences. In combination with laws (dating from the thir-teenth century) granting complete alienability of land, it encouraged labor mobility and reduced the attachment to land holding as the only form of security for peasants. Individ-uals had a relative certainty of being provided for, wherever they moved to work in the econ-omy, no matter what their property-owner-ship status. Landlords and farmers could reap the economic gains to be had from increased farm sizes, from enclosure, and from laying off workers or changing their labor contracts to more efficient weekly or day labor, without provoking the same degree of peasant protest as occurred on the continent. But equally, employers in England had a strong incentive only to do this if it made economic sense because, through the Poor Law, they would also have to reckon with their liability to pay for the families of the laid-off workers.

What the Poor Law created in England was a public system of acknowledgment of collective responsibility for the basic subsis-tence of all, including for a strikingly non-moralistic approach to the support of single mothers and their illegitimate children. The comparative evidence suggests a relative lack of correspondence in England—alone in all of Europe—between fluctuations in the price of food and the death rate, and England—but not Ireland—was the first nation in the world to cease to experience famine-related mortality.

Sources: Szreter (2005) drawing on Slack (1990), Wrigley (1998), Solar (1997), Solar (1995), King (1997), King (2000), Lees (1998).

---

it was still a highly unequal society, and inequality almost certainly increased until the early or mid-nineteenth century (figure 6.7). Although precise measures of inequality dif-fer depending on the sources, inequality appears to have risen until the early and per-haps mid-nineteenth century.[29] After about 1870, there is wide consensus that inequality fell substantially for the next century.

The fall in inequality after 1870 is closely correlated with the Second Reform Act of 1867, which was the first reform that really expanded voting rights to working people. When democracy enfranchises the relatively poor, they usually can use democracy to tilt economic institutions and the distribution of income in society in their favor.[30]

Twentieth-century Finland and Sweden[31]

Finland and Sweden are popularly identi-fied as prosperous countries with generous welfare states that, in some measure, are products of a small and ethnically homoge-nous population. But, a closer reading of their economic histories shows that their contemporary "virtuous circles"—with growth and equity mutually reinforcing—are the outcome of a long and difficult political struggle to establish institutions and enact policies that provide broad eco-nomic opportunities and respond to the inherently wrenching social transitions of positive (economic growth, structural change) and negative shocks (macroeco-nomic crises, civil war).

Finland was part of Sweden in the Middle Ages, but following a war between Russia and Sweden in 1808–09, it became part of the Russian empire. It experienced one of the last European famines in 1867–68, an event that ushered in major demographic and eco-nomic changes as entire regions were devas-tated. The Russian revolution of 1917 led to a collapse of imperial authority in Finland, and the country soon declared its independence. But this immediately gave birth to a bloody civil war between "white guards" (bourgeois nationalists) and "red guards" (socialists loyal to Russia). More than 30,000 troops alone lost their lives.

In the aftermath, however, many progres-sive reforms laid the foundation for the mod-ern Finnish economy and society. Land reform—a major cause of the civil war—was enacted almost immediately. A law passed in 1918 allowed sharecroppers to buy their land, and amendments in 1922 facilitated the sub-sidized expansion of small farms. Progressive income and wealth taxation were in place by 1920, soon followed by expansions of women's rights (although universal suffrage in parliamentary elections had been in place since 1906) and commitments by the central government (not just local municipalities) to primary education.

From the late 1940s until the early 1990s the economy expanded steadily, with per capita incomes catching up with Great Britain in the 1980s and Sweden in the 1990s (from roughly half a century earlier). This success was a product of Asian-style "governed markets": collaboration between the state and private sector was harnessed to rapidly industrialize an economy that, as late as the 1950s, generated 40 percent of its output from agriculture.[32] A crucial counterpart to Finland's activist industrial policy (based on high rates of capital accumulation and public saving, low interest rates on credit, and major investments in manufacturing infrastructure), however, was the construction of a welfare state to cushion citizens of all ages against the unsettling social changes wrought by such a rapid economic transformation.

Strong and credible political leadership was central to making this possible. In the aftermath of World War II, President Urho Kekkoken famously asked his nation, "Do we have the patience to prosper?" Thereafter, he set about negotiating the arrangements ("social corporatism") among industrialists, trade unions, and citizen groups that would enable all to act as complements. The Finnish model has its problems (high unemployment), but it shows how state, market, and society can jointly generate the institutions, policies, and spaces needed to generate equitable development outcomes.

Sweden is perhaps most closely associated with the welfare state today. Less well known is the timing and sequencing of events putting it in place. Importantly, the Swedish welfare state was the product of, not a precursor to, the country's transition to modern economic growth. Indeed, it was designed in response to the very problems (old-age security, unemployment) generated by such growth. But to make such growth possible, and to have in place sociopolitical conditions that would enable the articulation of and sustained support for something like the welfare state (when such a system existed only in rather embryonic forms elsewhere in the capitalist world), it was vital that a prior set of equi-

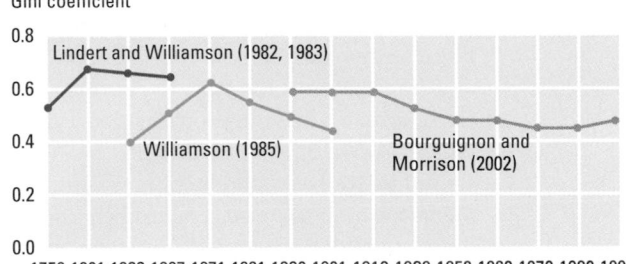

Figure 6.7 Inequality in Britain began to fall around 1870

Gini coefficient

Sources: Lindert and Williamson (1982), Lindert and Williamson (1983), Williamson (1985), and Bourguignon and Morrisson (2002).

table institutional arrangements be in place.

In Sweden, these prior arrangements were unusually favorable to upward mobility by subordinate groups: a long history of peasant autonomy, a correspondingly weak aristocracy, and an emerging nation-state able to secure support from farmers while also repudiating aristocratic claims on its powers. Sweden was also the first country to have a central bank (in 1668) and among the first to grant basic property rights. As such, "inclusion of the peasantry in the transformation of the agrarian economy and institutional arrangements that sustained egalitarianism were to become fundamental elements in the rise of the Swedish industrial market economy."[33] This was an economy increasingly grounded in broad political rights and social opportunities.

But history is not destiny. Equitable development is as much a function of key choices and decisions at pivotal historic junctures. The Middle Ages, the industrial revolution, and the tumultuous twentieth century unleashed sweeping forces on Swedish society. Some were leveling (rising agricultural productivity), others wrenching (mass unemployment). Each attempt to respond to these forces established the political contours for subsequent attempts. Drawing on and extending the equitable institutional foundations during these pivotal historic junctures have been the unifying elements of Sweden's development strategy. Its achievements to date have been remarkable, even as twenty-first-century realities present distinctive challenges to its welfare state.

The main implications of the Finnish and Swedish cases for today's developing countries are that economic growth and sociopolitical equity can be powerfully reinforcing, and can be underpinned by institutional transitions. These cases should not be seen as blueprints for others to follow. Instead, they should be read as examples of how commitments to equity in a given context help lay the foundations for short- and long-term prosperity by consolidating virtuous circles linking institutions and incentives.

China in the late twentieth century

Economic development in China since 1978 has been nothing short of spectacular. With the quadrupling of GDP per capita over the last 25 years, China has transformed itself from a poor centrally planned economy to a lower-middle-income emerging market economy. As a result, the number of people living in poverty (under $1 per day) fell from 634 million in 1981 to 212 million in 2001.[34]

From the perspective of this chapter, what is interesting is that the world's largest country has undergone profound economic transformation without substantially changing the political institutional structure, that remains dominated by the Chinese Communist Party. Yet institutional improvement did take place in China along with economic reform. And the large increase in nonstate investment and free entry into profitable economic opportunities suggest that property rights are secure, despite the absence of a Western-style judicial system.

While the particular institutional form is different from other cases reviewed here, the experience in China is broadly consistent with the thesis of this chapter. The earlier discussion of equitable transitions in Britain and Scandinavian countries illustrated the argument that a successful economic system depends on the political system to assign and enforce property rights and contracts, and to protect the market from political encroachment. China's recent history suggests that the starting point for reforms does not necessarily have to be in political institutions. Changes in economic institutions and in economic relations among levels of government can also establish credible commitment to a reform path and act as a check on the discretionary use of power by the central government. China's experience also demonstrates that what is important for equitable development are credible checks on the arbitrary use of power, assurance of property rights and fair treatment for a broad segment of society. The particular form that institutions take to deliver these functions can vary, especially during periods of transition.

The key to China's equitable development was the combination of initial conditions and the economic reforms launched in 1978 that unleashed entrepreneurial initiative and legitimized the profit motive. China's economic policies following the 1949 revolution proved seriously flawed: they stifled incentives for investment and innovation. But the social policies of the Mao Tse-Tung period leveled the distribution of assets in important and durable ways. As a result, both land and human capital were equitably distributed on the eve of reforms. With the adoption of the rural household responsibility system, peasants became the immediate beneficiaries of reform. This helped to reinforce equity, while unleashing entrepreneurial initiative and boosting productivity.

The economic reforms launched in 1978 aimed at decentralizing economic decisions—to individual farm households, enterprise managers, local governments—so as to generate incentives for investment and innovation. Importantly, the form these policies took and the transitional institutions that were created were designed to preserve the political support for reforms, by compensating potential losers.

The aftermath of the cultural revolution, and the recognition that China's economy had fallen behind—not least in relation to the East Asian Tigers—led to a growing consensus on the need for and urgency of change, and paved the way for the economic reforms initiated under Deng Xiaoping's leadership. These reforms were inspired by the widespread recognition of the failure of central planning as an instrument for economic organization, and reflected the need to deliver on economic growth for the legitimacy of the new leadership. The political need for growth implied a new focus on liberating markets and incentives. The sequencing of reforms and the transitional institutional arrangements that accompanied the economic decentralization, on the other hand, reflected the premium the leadership placed on social and political stability.

The impetus for economic decentralization on the one hand, and the need for an integrated national market on the other, helped to shape a dynamic relationship between the central government and local governments that held them mutually accountable and limited discretion on both sides. Over time, the result of these policies was to create a stake in new economic institutions for all the main actors, including the local governments which served as a credible check on the powers of the central government in the economic domain. The reforms also fueled the emergence of strong economic centers, such as Guangdong province and the Shanghai municipality. These centers now wield considerable influence and bargaining power relative to the central government and can serve as important countervailing forces.

How did economic decentralization reinforce private incentives? According to Walder and Oi (1999), "For almost 20 years, reform in China has proceeded through the gradual reassignment of specific property rights from higher government agencies to lower government agencies, or from government agencies to enterprises, managers, families, or individuals" (7). All of these reforms enhanced the power of economic agents to make decisions over economic activities in their respective domains, and boosted productivity through better incentives. Farmers retained their earnings and therefore worked harder and invested more. Township and village governments had rights to the profits made by township and village enterprises (TVEs) and therefore adopted policies that promoted business. But because they had no revenue authority, they did not have the ability to bail out poorly performing TVEs, which made for hard budget constraints and higher efficiency.

Higher levels of local governments (country and province) acquired control over local enterprises and therefore also had a stake in their performance. They were allowed to retain more local revenues through fiscal contracting and to have extrabudgetary funds, which generated incentives that focused on collection to provide local public goods that attracted local investments. These changes provided for significant autonomy from the central government and considerable independent authority over their economies.

> The modern Chinese system includes a division of authority between the central and local governments. The latter have primary control over economic matters within their jurisdictions. Critically, there is an important degree of political durability built into the system.[35]

China's reforms are also replete with innovative mechanisms for protecting potential losers during transitional periods. This often involved designing reforms that sustained sources of income for incumbents, by keeping important elements of pre-existing pricing and payment mechanisms, while providing incentives at the margin. "The transitional institutions [were] not created solely for increasing the size of [the] pie, [but also] to reflect the distributional concerns of how the enlarged pie is divided and the political concerns of how the interests of those in power are served."[36]

Dual pricing at the start of reforms is a prime example. The system obliged farmers and enterprises to sell specified quantities to the state at "plan" prices, while allowing them to obtain market prices for any above-quota production. This maintained the planning system for those who benefited from it, while creating incentives for efficient production. Equally important, it allowed time for market institutions to emerge, avoiding the institutional vacuum that plagued many transition economies when state institutions were dismantled. Fiscal contracting guaranteed the central government a certain level of revenues,[37] but it generated incentives for local governments to collect more because the marginal retention rate was much higher. Similarly, labor contracting allowed state workers to retain the guarantee of lifetime employment while introducing greater flexibility in labor policies for new contractual workers. These arrangements made reforms a win-win game, ensuring social stability and the support of those in power.

But there is a danger in such a strategy of incrementalism: getting stuck in incomplete reforms if local governments and incumbents acquire too much power and are able to block further progress. The prevalence of interprovincial barriers to trade in the 1990s, with each province vying to boost profits for the enterprises it owned, is an example. But there are some checks and balances in the system that help maintain the direction and momentum of reforms. These include competition among local governments, hard budget constraints for local governments, the central government's insistence on enforcing a unitary market, and a growing economy that reduces the economic influence of incumbents.

The struggle for the right balance between economic centralization and decentralization is constantly evident in many of China's domains of intergovernmental relations. The 1994 tax reforms recentralized fiscal revenues, in part to ensure greater regional equity in spending, and the central government continues to apply strict controls on deficit financing by local governments. Constraints on labor mobility have eased considerably over time, helping to create a more unified labor market, despite concerns by some provincial governments that this might aggravate problems of unemployment for established urban residents.

There are also some more recent and more permanent institutional changes that reconfirm the government's commitment to market-oriented reform. These include mechanisms that strengthen accountability at the local level and empower local populations. Local elections are the most important of these mechanisms but others include, for example, recent regulations to eliminate nuisance taxes on the rural population. China has also successfully used the external commitment device of WTO accession to signal its resolve to move ahead with market reforms and impose discipline on incumbents. For example, it is no longer possible for every province to have its own inefficient automobile factory erected behind trade barriers designed to provide local employment and local taxes. More broadly, China's desire to carve for itself an important place in the global order and to be recognized as a responsible global power places constraints on the shape of its future policies.

Qian (2003) notes the following:

> There is apparently a larger room than we thought for institutional innovation to simultaneously address both the economic and political concerns, that is, to make a reform efficiency improving and interest compatible for those in power (305).

But there are many challenges ahead, some of which will not be amenable to win-win solutions and therefore are likely to be politically and socially more costly. Continued reforms in the state enterprise and financial sectors, managing rural-urban migration, and addressing increasing regional disparities (see focus 6 on regional inequality) are some of these challenges. Macroeconomic policy and structural reforms will need to be underpinned by further institutional improvement to ensure broader participation and accountability so that the interests and desire of the people are better reflected in decision making, and to further strengthen the government's capacity to lead market-oriented reform while maintaining economic and social equity.

Conclusion

A few simple principles go a long way toward unifying different development experiences in the historic and the contemporary worlds. There is little disagreement among scholars that basic institutions, such as security of property rights and equality before the law, are keys to prosperity. These institutions lie behind the capital, financial, land, and labor markets that we saw in action in chapter 5. Because talent and ideas are widely distributed in the population, a prosperous modern society requires the mass of people to have incentives—and a state that can and will provide key complementary inputs and public goods. It therefore requires an underlying set of institutions that generate the equality of opportunity for individuals and assure the accountability of politicians to all.

Why do some societies have such institutions and not others? A relatively egalitarian distribution of political power underpins the institutions that promote prosperity. Institutions clearly have distributional effects, and bad institutions often arise because they benefit some group or elite. Good institutions arise when checks are placed on the power of elites and when the balance of political power becomes more equal in society. Often, equality of political power is supported by economic equality, and this connection gives rise to the possibility of both virtuous and vicious circles.

Growth certainly can occur in societies in which these conditions do not apply. But the preponderance of evidence suggests that such growth is unsustainable. This perspective is consistent with historical narratives, basic patterns in cross-country data, and more careful causal empirical work on the sources of prosperity.

The crucial question for the promotion of development is this: how can poor societies improve their institutions and move onto a dynamic path toward a virtuous circle of equity and prosperity? The organization of society is highly persistent, but we have seen many cases of transitions to better institutions. Sometimes, as in early modern Britain, economic changes lead to changes in the distribution of power, which promotes a more equitable society and better institutions. Contemporary China follows a similar pattern albeit with a different configuration of institutions. In other times, as in the Republic of Korea and Indonesia, regimes are forced, by external or internal threats, to change the trajectory of their society in ways that become institutionalized. In still other times, such as Mauritius and Botswana, leaders make good decisions that lead to reinforcing paths of better institutions and development.

Growth, equity, and poverty reduction in an East Asian giant

Indonesia presents an illuminating example of the long-term interactions of the three basic themes of this report on equity and development:

- The importance of market-driven processes in determining the distribution of opportunities and incomes.

- The role of political processes, and the engagement of the poor in these processes, in determining the policy framework for market and asset accumulation.

- The overriding dominance of institutions in determining the long-run conditions of governance for markets and politics to operate.

These complex interactions require long periods of developmental evolution to observe and identify.

Indonesia has substantial variance across all three of these themes. There is enough independence in the variance for each factor to sort out, if only roughly, what is driving what. In chapter 6, the political dimension of the economic performance of the Suharto regime was discussed. Here, we discuss the connections with policy choices.

Because Indonesia has been so important to the development profession, it has been studied for a long time. The Dutch exploited the Netherlands East Indies from the seventeenth century to early in the twentieth century. Then, under political pressure at home, the Dutch experimented with an "Ethical Policy" for the colony, and the poor benefited significantly. During the Great Depression, World War II, and the fight for Independence, the Indonesian economy deteriorated rapidly, and the poor suffered disproportionately. Java was the original home of the "dual economy" analyzed by Boeke (1946) and formalized by Lewis (1954). After declaring independence in 1945, President Sukarno eventually put "politics in command" in 1959 and produced a ruinous inflation that brought much of the population to near starvation in the mid-1960s. It was with just cause that Gunnar Myrdal pronounced in *Asian Drama*, 1967, that "no economist holds out any hope for Indonesia."

Indonesia's rapid, pro-poor growth for the 30 years after the fall of Sukarno astonished the development profession and, along with other countries in East and Southeast Asia, Indonesia became the object of intense analysis.[1] In Indonesia, the weak starting conditions significantly influenced how the economic planners approached the task of linking growth to the poor. They designed a three-tiered strategy for pro-poor growth, which connected sound macroeconomic policy to market activities that were facilitated by progressively lower transaction costs. Those policies were linked to household decisions about labor supply, agricultural production, and investment in the nontradable economy.

The extent to which the poor benefited from growth depended on the array of assets they controlled: their labor, human capital, social capital, and other forms of capital, including access to credit.[2] Appropriate government policies also influence those dimensions, especially in health and education. The "road to pro-poor growth" started from desperately poor economic conditions, weak institutions, and a decade of political instability. It seemed that everything needed to be done at once. The key was to focus on restarting and then sustaining rapid economic growth, empowering poor households to enter the market economy, and reducing the costs and risks of doing so by investments to lower transaction costs.

The strategy worked for three decades: between 1967 and 1996, income per capita increased by 5 percent a year. The incomes of the bottom quintile of the income distribution, all individuals below the national poverty line until the 1990s and all still subsisting on less than $2 a day, grew at the same rate (or possibly slightly faster). The distribution of household expenditures had been remarkably stable, with the overall Gini coefficient staying within a narrow range between 0.31 and 0.36.[3] Rural inequality had actually declined significantly since the 1970s, when access to land allowed substantial benefits to be reaped from the green revolution. By the mid-1980s, the labor market had become the primary determinant of income in rural areas.

But when the Asian financial crisis hit in 1997 and President Suharto was forced to resign in the face of widespread rioting in 1998, the country was entirely unprepared in political or institutional terms to cope with the rapid changes needed in corporate and public governance. The crisis sharply lowered inequality, as urban real estate and financial markets collapsed. But the dramatic reduction in GDP—over 13 percent in 1998 alone—caused poverty rates to triple. Only after 2002 did poverty rates return to the previous lows observed in 1996. By 2004 they still had not returned to the trend rate of decline disrupted in 1998.

Explaining these trends in per capita incomes and their distribution requires an understanding of how markets, politics, and institutions jointly shaped the rapid, pro-poor growth strategy, its subsequent collapse, and current efforts to revive it. Any such explanation is bound to be controversial, and there is no formal model behind the story about to be told.[4] But the story is plausible and anchored in the historical record.

The story begins with two concerns of the emerging Suharto government in the late 1960s. The first was the misery and discontent of the rural masses, who had supported Sukarno's communist leanings and populist rhetoric. After a decade of active discrimination against their livelihoods, rural households were near starvation and thus an obvious source of opposition unless the new government could incorporate them in its development plans. Second, the hyperinflation of the mid-1960s, the total disintegration of the market economy, and the political chaos meant the entire population was ready for a more stable life. A strategy that promised stability and rural recovery would win wide support (as it would throughout densely settled East and Southeast Asia).

This is the message that Suharto delivered to his technocrats. This economic team had engaged Suharto and other senior military officials in economic training exercises at the Military College. The technocrats were handed the macroeconomic portfolio and told to deliver on what became known in Indonesia as the development trilogy—growth, equity, and stability. To many in the political and military arena, stability meant repressive measures to stifle dissent, but to the technocrats it meant restraining inflation (which they did in spectacular fashion in just three years) and stabilizing the rice economy, which was still a quarter of GDP and providing half the average Indonesian's daily calories. The institutions built to provide this stability, in both macro terms and in the food economy, became essential to the Suharto regime's success.[5]

Thirty years of rapid economic growth, with equally rapid rates of poverty reduction, was politically popular (the elasticity of reduction of the headcount poverty index with respect to growth in per capita incomes was about 1.3 during the Suharto era). Every five years, the polling results for parliament were gleaned for signs of disappointment with the development program. Despite the heavy hand of Golkar, the president's party, real information was flowing from villages up to the center through these elections.

Almost despite the intentions of the Suharto regime, political institutions were taking root (people expected to vote) and these institutions provided feedback to the policy approach of the government. There were other feedback mechanisms as well, and the ones that threatened stability were taken very seriously. After the 1974 riots in Jakarta in reaction to the visibly widening income distribution, especially in urban areas, the government responded brutally by putting down the riots and imprisoning the student leaders. Then it mounted a serious effort to make the economy more equitable. The result, also stimulated by the world food crisis in 1973–4, was a major shift in priorities toward rural development and a specific push toward increasing domestic rice production. Behind this push were the objectives of stabilization and equity. To lose control of the rice economy was to lose control of what mattered to Indonesian society.

The restructuring of Indonesia's development approach after 1974, especially the pre-emptive devaluation of the rupiah in 1978, signaled the government's determination to include the poor in the development process. The stability of the Gini coefficient seen from the late 1960s to 2004 should not be taken as the result of market-driven forces in the face of given technology, but as a conscious government effort, led from the macroeconomic arena by the technocrats, to stimulate pro-poor growth.[6] This effort succeeded in spectacular fashion until the mid-1990s, when cronyism and the growing influence of Suharto's children on economic decision making caused the approach to unravel.

Part of the problem of post-Suharto governments has been their need to distance themselves from this record of repression and cronyism, despite three decades of pro-poor growth. This tension brought the failure of political and institutional development during the Suharto era to the fore. Questions about causality remain, particularly whether rapid, pro-poor growth can be implemented by authoritarian regimes. Indonesia's record, along with that of most of East and Southeast Asia, indicates that they can. But is such growth sustainable? And which is more important for managing long-run, pro-poor growth: good economics or good institutions?

In Indonesia, there was no "chicken or egg" problem. Something had to be done at once in view of widespread destitution and political chaos, and the sequencing was clear. Rapid, pro-poor economic growth was imposed by an authoritarian regime concerned about its survival. But this same regime also imposed on itself commitment mechanisms to make the growth process market friendly to rural households and to Chinese capitalists—that is, both ends of the economic system. Inflation was brought under control by a law requiring the national budget be balanced quarter by quarter—a law Suharto basically imposed on himself, but then touted to all constituents as a rule the government had to live under. To build confidence among the Chinese business community, the government opened the capital account in 1970 when it unified the exchange rate. The flow of foreign exchange to and from Singapore and Hong Kong was a sensitive barometer of the investment climate.

Thus the two constraints on the presidency, which Suharto felt personally and used as motivation for his bureaucracy and government (not the same thing in Indonesia), were the need for rural areas to participate in growth, and the need to keep the investment climate highly favorable for Suharto's business partners. The response to both constraints was an economic package—low inflation, food price stability, an open economy, and massive investments in rural infrastructure—that generated rapid pro-poor growth. But another part of the investment climate, a part only for those favored business partners, involved special licenses, trade protection, and lucrative access to domestic markets. This part unraveled the "open economy" part of the growth package.

The Suharto legacy, despite the deep commitment to pro-poor growth, did not build the groundwork for a political and institutional framework that would ultimately support it. A deep tension developed between the institutional framework to keep the open economy functioning efficiently and the political controls to keep the cronies' businesses profitable. Without political feedback about these very same political controls, the regime was blindsided by the ferocity of the opposition to its management of the Asian financial crisis. The depth of the crisis, both economic and political, reflected the vacuum of institutions in place to cope with an alternative political system.

The climb out of the chaos of 1998 mirrors that from the 1965 era, but this time without order imposed from above. The eagerness and skill with which the Indonesian population has participated in the democratic process suggests that social and political order will now be far more sustainable. The challenge now is to translate the same democratic process into rapid and sustainable pro-poor economic growth.

Leveling the economic and political playing fields

PART III

WHAT CAN BE DONE TO INCREASE EQUITY IN THE WORLD? Can this be done in ways that also spur long-term prosperity? We read in part I that there are large inequalities of opportunity between people within countries and—even more—between people in different countries. These inequalities are perpetuated through interlocking economic, political, and sociocultural mechanisms, creating inequality traps. Individuals from different groups and countries face a highly uneven playing field, both in their capacities to acquire endowments and aspire to a better life, and in their opportunities to reap returns from those endowments through market and nonmarket processes. Because differences between countries often exceed within-country differences, it is of particular importance that national policies support, or are at least consistent with, the narrowing of international differences, notably through the growth process.

We argued in part II that many inequalities not only violate people's concern for fairness, but actually have costs for the development process. The effects on development depend on specific forms of inequality and their interactions with market imperfections and institutions. Unequal opportunities are associated with inefficiencies and wasted economic potential. Pronounced inequalities in the distribution of power are often associated with weak economic institutions, undermining the investment and innovation that is central to long-run growth. Greater equity is thus not only intrinsically desirable but also is complementary to long-run growth and prosperity. For poorer and excluded groups, a focus on equity can bring a double benefit—a bigger pie and a greater share.

But the scope for such a complementary relationship between equity and aggregate development is often not exploited. When examining this, we suggest there are two kinds of pathology in policy design. First, there is the pathology associated with oligarchic dominance—institutions and policies that further the interest of elites but not those of the whole society. This may take the form of extreme predation and high-level corruption, as in Mobutu's Zaire or Haiti under the Duvaliers. Or it may take the form of enmeshed alliances between economic and political elites that favor rent-seeking, as in the Philippines under Marcos, in much of Latin America in past decades, and in more subtle forms in many countries of the world.

Second, there is a more complex pathology of policies pursued with the intent, or in the name, of equity that have high efficiency costs or perverse effects. Communist economic policy was disastrous for efficiency, even while many communist societies did much in social provisioning. Directed credit—in India, for example—was intended for the poor (and reached some of the poor), but proved a high-cost strategy. Populist macropolicy is always bad for growth, and almost always bad for equity sooner or later—witness Argentina during much of the second half of the twentieth century. Perverse or growth-sapping effects of policies under this pathology can be caused by adverse consequences for incentives, unaffordable fiscal burdens, or the capture of the benefits, often by middle groups, which "hoard opportunities" at a cost for other groups and the overall growth process.

What can be done? At a fundamental level, the analysis underscores the centrality of shifting to a state that is more accountable, has checks on predatory behavior of political and economic elites, is responsive to all citizens—especially from middle and poorer groups—and has effective conflict management mechanisms. In part II, we sketched cases of transitions in this direction from history and contemporary experiences, and at the local level. The emphasis in the development community on issues of governance and empowerment is entirely consistent with this perspective.

While such overall shifts are central to development, the World Bank has neither the mandate nor the comparative advantage to discuss specifics of the design of political institutions (even though action to support empowerment of the poor is now emphasized in the design of specific policies—see Narayan 2002). In part III, we focus on a set of areas that do lie squarely in the arena of development analysis and practice—in policies affecting the sectors, markets, and in the global arena. This recognizes the influence of the political and sociocultural context, but focuses rather on what an equity prism, based on the analysis of parts I and II, has to say about the policy design to break inequality traps and support aggregate growth The lesson from part II is that this implies paying attention to *specific* inequalities and their interactions with markets, social structure, and power. This involves both issues of technical design and mechanisms that provide the political underpinnings for change, notably through broader accountability, coalitions for change, or compensation of losers. And while an overarching message is of the potential complementarity between greater equity and long-run prosperity, there will often be tradeoffs in specific areas and context. One cross-cutting area concerns the need to raise taxes to finance desirable public spending. The design of tax instruments is of great importance to minimize adverse efficiency effects, while also promoting equity where feasible.

We organize the discussion of domestic action into three areas. First is building and protecting people's human capacities—from the start of people's lives and through adulthood and old age. Here we focus on equalizing from the bottom up—equalizing up the opportunities of the least advantaged in terms of skills, health, and risk management. There are certainly issues of equity among more advantaged groups, but we give priority to the disadvantaged (in part for reasons of space). As seen in part II, there are major market imperfections in human capital formation and insurance that affect poor or lower-status groups most, yet political action has also often been biased against these groups.

Second is ensuring equitable access to justice and complementary assets. A fair and accessible justice system is crucial for constraining the power of the political and economic elite, avoiding discrimination, and protecting property rights and personal safety for all—with important implications for the willingness to invest and innovate. Inequitable access to land and infrastructure—by wealth, location, or social group—is typical of developing societies and often enmeshed with political structures. Policy design can help shifts to more equitable and often more efficient patterns (chapter 8).

Third is the domain of markets—financial, labor, and product—that have a powerful influence on the returns to people's endowments. As chapters 5 and 6 argued, markets are typically far from ideal, working in noncompetitive and discriminatory ways, whether because of intrinsic market imperfections, or because power structures have shaped them to serve the purposes of those in power. In these areas, and notably in the case of finance, a primary concern is equalizing down, by reducing protecting privileges of incumbents. Closely related is the conduct of macroeconomic policy (chapter 9).

In the global arena, concern remains with individuals—and the enormous, unjustified differences in opportunity that people face through the morally irrelevant fact of country of birth. The global playing field between nation-states is uneven—and has uneven effects on different groups within countries. There is substantial scope for making the playing field more even. But as in the domestic arena, policy design involves both technical questions (such as the details of migration arrangements and the application and design of patent legislation) and the political underpinnings of rules and institutions for global governance. We examine the potential for change both in the key global markets— for labor, products, ideas, and capital—and in the potential scope for designing aid in ways that support (rather than undercut) domestic development, and through more effective and equitable management of the global commons (chapter 10).

The epilogue links the report's perspective on equity to the thinking and agreements that have evolved in the development community in the past decade—captured, for example, in the Millennium Declaration (2000) and the Monterrey Consensus (2002)—as well as the World Bank's own strategic pillars of an enabling investment climate and promoting empowerment. We argue that an approach to development that is deeply informed by equity is fundamental to the full integration of these frameworks into an effective development strategy.

Human capacities

Expanding people's capabilities to lead fuller lives, the aim of all development, means investing in their education and health and in their ability to manage risks. But as chapters 5 and 6 discussed, failures in markets and governments conspire to generate large inequalities in people's opportunities to build their capabilities. Children from poorer families start out life with greater disadvantages than their wealthier peers, attend lower-quality schools, have less access to health services, and are not as protected from economic downturns and family crises. By the time they are adults, they are far less equipped to be productive members of society. Economic, political, and sociocultural inequalities fuel such differences in life chances, perpetuating them across generations.

Public action can level the playing field and broaden opportunities by addressing inequalities in access to quality education, health care, and risk management. Well-designed policies will result in more equitably distributed opportunities to acquire endowments and boost overall productivity. As potentially talented and productive individuals gain access to the services from which they may have been excluded for reasons that have nothing to do with their potential, societies make gains through greater efficiency and greater social cohesion in the long run.

Still, there are challenges. Programs require resources, administrative capacity, and political support. This means paying attention to the design of tax systems, tailoring program intervention to context, and above all building constituencies for change. We focus on leveling the playing field mainly through augmenting the capacities of those with the fewest opportunities, but we recognize that it may be necessary to attack the undue influence of the powerful and the wealthy to be able to shape public policies to benefit the rest of society. As we have seen, successful transitions are far more likely where the power of the excluded to influence public action has been enhanced.

There are strong complementarities among the different investments in people. Better nourished children have higher cognitive abilities. Well-educated parents, especially mothers, invest more in their children's education and health. More educated individuals are likely to be more resilient to shocks. Instruments to smooth consumption will spur people to take on not only higher risk but also potentially higher return activities and prevent them from disinvesting in themselves (lowering food intake, forgoing treatment) or in their children (pulling them out of school) in times of shocks. And people with more human capital and better risk management capabilities can reduce the variability and increase the level of their incomes.

The policies we consider in this chapter are particularly important in arresting the intergenerational transmission of inequalities. We begin with a review of the rationale and potential for early childhood development programs. We next consider broader education and health policies for expanding access to quality education and care, and finally discuss transfer policies that help manage risks and provide for efficient and equity-enhancing redistribution.

Early childhood development: a better start in life

By the time poorer children in many countries reach school age, they are at a significant disadvantage in cognitive and social ability. The Ecuadorian study cited in chapter 2 documented substantial differences at six years of age, related to socioeconomic status and parental education. Differences in childhood cognitive abilities are indeed apparent as early as 22 months of age. One study in the United States shows that by age three the gaps in learning, measured by vocabulary, are already large among children from different social groups (figure 7.1).[1] Cognitive learning is affected by a child's socioeconomic status through health (malnutrition, iron and micronutrient deficiency, parasite infections) and the quality of the home environment, including care-giving and cognitive stimulation.[2] Scientific evidence on brain development supports this. Recent research findings revamp earlier thinking that assumed that the structure of the brain was genetically determined at birth and point to the determining influence of early experiences—from conception to age six, and particularly the first three years—on the architecture of the brain and capacities in adulthood.[3]

As a child ages, environmental effects appear to accumulate. Poor cognitive and social abilities are associated with weaker future academic performance and lower adult economic and social outcomes, including poor health, antisocial behavior, and violence.[4] These underachieving adults influence the cognitive abilities of the next generation of children, creating an intergenerational cycle of poverty and unequal opportunities.[5] Studies using internationally comparable student achievement tests confirm that socioeconomic background is the overwhelming determinant of learning outcomes, with schools accounting for no more than 20 percent of the variation in test performance.[6]

Benefits of early interventions

Early interventions can substantially enhance a child's life chances and loosen the intergenerational grip of poverty and inequality. In recent years, interest has expanded in early childhood development (ECD) in low- and middle-income developing countries, paralleling greater attention in developed countries.

Early childhood development programs comprise a range of interventions that include providing nutritional supplements to

children, regularly monitoring their growth, stimulating the development of their cognitive and social skills through more frequent and structured interactions with a caring adult, and improving the parenting skills of caretakers. The evidence suggests that these programs can be highly effective in addressing problems experienced later in schooling and adulthood.

A recent study in the United States shows that investments in the early years of life, before children reach the formal school system, give greater returns than later investments (figure 7.2).[7] Well-designed longitudinal studies—mainly from developed countries—indicate that programs typically register improvements for children in health, cognitive ability, academic performance, and tenure within the school system and, later in life, higher incomes, higher incidence of home ownership, lower propensity to be on welfare, and lower rates of incarceration and arrest.[8] This suggests a strong productivity case for investing in early childhood development; the arguments for public subsidies to disadvantaged families are compelling on both productivity and equity grounds. As Heckman argues,

> early interventions in children from disadvantaged environments raise no efficiency-equity trade-offs; they raise the productivity of individuals, the workforce and society at large, and reduce lifetime inequality by helping to eliminate the factor of accident of birth.[9]

Studies of ECD programs in developing countries also document strong benefits

Figure 7.2 Early childhood interventions are good investments

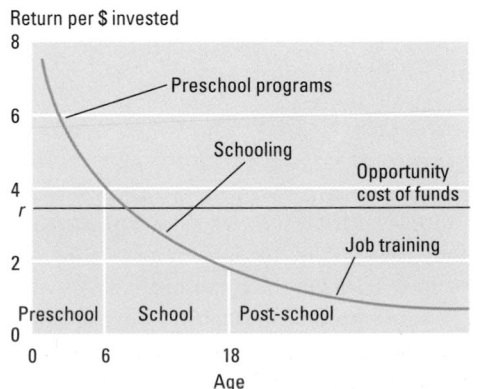

Source: Carneiro and Heckman (2003).

Figure 7.1 Children from better-off households have a big edge in cognitive abilities by age three

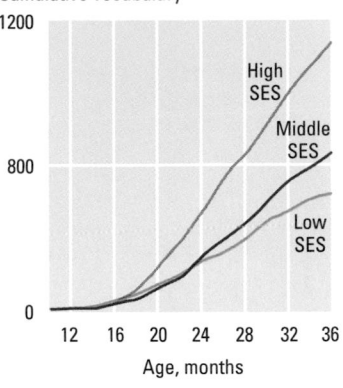

Source: Hart and Risley (1995).
Note: SES refers to socioeconomic status.

Figure 7.3 Catching up through early intervention

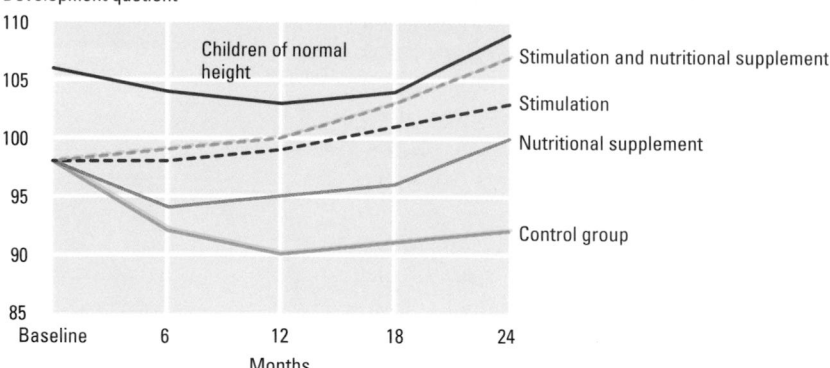

Source: Grantham-McGregor and others (1991).

Note: The Development Quotient is an index composed of ratings in four behavioral and cognitive development indicators: locomotor (large-muscle activities, running, and jumping), hand-eye coordination, hearing and speech, and performance (shape recognition, block construction, and block patterns). "Months" refers to time after entry into the program, generally at around 9 months old.

B O X 7 . 1 *ECD programs are an essential ingredient for the attainment of education for all*

There is sufficient evidence from studies throughout the world to make a case for placing early childhood education among the key interventions to achieve the education Millennium Development Goals (MDGs).

Higher school enrollment. Colombia's ECD program PROMESA reports significantly higher enrollment rates in primary school for children participating in the program, compared with children not participating. ECD programs in India (Haryana) and Guatemala resulted in a significant decline in enrollment age for girls.

Less grade repetition. In Colombia's PROMESA program, the Alagoas and Fortaleza PROAPE study of Northeast Brazil and the Argentina ECD study, children who participated in the programs repeated fewer grades and progressed better through school than did nonparticipants in similar circumstances.

Fewer dropouts. In India's Integrated Child Development Services program in Dalmau, attendance of children ages six to eight in primary school increased by 16 percent for children who had participated in the program; dropout rates did not change

significantly for children from the higher caste, but fell a dramatic 46 percent for the lower caste and an astonishing 80 percent for the middle-caste students. In Colombia the third-grade enrollment rates for children who participated in the PROMESA program increased by 100 percent, reflecting their lower dropout and repetition rates. In addition, 60 percent of the children who participated in the ECD program attained the fourth grade, compared with only 30 percent of the comparison group.

Higher intelligence. ECD programs encourage young children to explore and facilitate the social interaction that promotes cognitive development. Children who participated in Jamaica's First Home-Visiting Program, Colombia's Cali Project, Peru's Programa No Formal de Educación Inicial (PRONOEI), and the Turkish Early Enrichment Project in low-income areas of Istanbul averaged higher scores on intellectual aptitude tests than did nonparticipants. Evidence from other studies, however, suggests that these effects dissipate over time.

Sources: Chaturvedi and others (1987), Myers (1995), Young (2002).

---

ing school by 5.6 percentage points and led to higher completed schooling attainment and higher adult cognitive achievement test scores.

Evidence is also mounting that interventions in early childhood particularly benefit poor and disadvantaged children and families.[10] In Jamaica, nutritional supplementation and stimulation administered to undernourished children between the ages of 9 to 24 months—who are most likely to come from disadvantaged families—improved their mental development.[11] Malnourished children who received a milk supplement developed more than those who did not (figure 7.3). Children who benefited from stimulation did even better, while the benefits of supplements and stimulation were additive and allowed disadvantaged children exposed to them to almost catch up with the development trajectory of "normal" children over a period of 18 months. The results suggest that ECD programs may be one of the most cost-effective avenues for reaching the Millennium Development Goals for universal education and an important contributor to the attainment of gender parity in primary completion (box 7.1). They also help mothers participate in the labor force—poor women who had access to free child care in the *favelas* of Rio de Janeiro increased their income by as much as 20 percent—and improve the academic performance of older children, as documented for a community nursery program in rural Colombia.[12]

Designing ECD programs

Interventions to improve young children's capacity to develop and learn can focus on improving parents' teaching and child care skills, delivering services directly to children, or improving child care services in a community. Programs may be established in homes, day-care centers, or communities. The evidence suggests that three design features are important for the full realization of benefits from ECD programs: starting early, having strong parental involvement, and focusing on child health (especially nutrition) and cognitive and social stimulation. The focus on health leads to a virtuous cycle, because improved health also helps increase cognitive and

for all children, with cost-benefit analyses showing returns of $2–5 for every $1 invested. For example, preliminary results for experimental nutritional interventions at 6 to 24 months of age in rural Guatemala show that consuming a nutritional supplement increased the probability of attend-

social abilities.[13] Overly formal programs can be too expensive for poor families, culturally irrelevant, and insensitive to families' needs.[14] They thus run the risk of being abandoned even when they demonstrate high returns.

What then are the impediments to the widespread implementation of ECD programs given that they are such good investments? Political economy constraints arise from the difficulty of making a case for spending resources on a program with the promise of (uncertain) benefits to come only years in the future. Such a case is often made by the immediate beneficiaries (parents of school-age children) or intermediate beneficiaries (teachers), who organize themselves into powerful political forces. But the institutional setup for ECD program delivery—with funds in many instances channeled to myriad small NGOs, community centers, or home-based caregivers—and the absence of strong central responsibility inhibit organized political pressure. The same institutional setup generates problems of integration with other government programs and of coordination across several government departments.[15]

Thinking about the politics and the design of ECD from the start is thus important. Getting information to parents, community leaders, and policymakers about the objectives and efficacy of ECD services can build public awareness and strengthen demand. Monitoring systems build support by providing timely feedback on a range of intermediate outputs to policymakers and program managers, while proper evaluations provide more convincing evidence of impact and broader lessons from interventions. Integrating ECD programs into the broader development frameworks and involving parents, families, and community members enhance the sustainability of programs.[16]

There are two possible approaches to scaling up ECD interventions. The first is to expand publicly funded preschool programs to all children by making it a statutory right, as in several European countries. This would have significant funding implications, but the benefit is potentially widespread support from middle-class and poor families with children.

The second approach would target disadvantaged families. This may be more cost-effective in view of the evidence presented earlier on larger gains from interventions for disadvantaged children. To bolster participation, the program could be supplemented by a cash-transfer scheme, with transfers conditioned on various desirable behaviors, including changes in the homecare environment, as well as regular health center visits for growth monitoring, immunizations, and nutrition interventions.[17] This would concentrate even more resources on the poor, but the political economy implications are less clear. While targeted programs have a smaller constituency and thus would not benefit from a broad coalition of support, a national program, with transparent criteria for eligibility and good monitoring of "conditionality," could mobilize support not only from the direct beneficiaries but also from other stakeholders in society.

It is possible to combine a universal preschool approach with a conditional cash transfer (CCT) program. This would yield the highest benefits in the participation of the poor and the productivity gains for all, but it would also be more costly. The approach adopted in any country setting will have to emerge from considerations of costs, benefits, and fiscal capacity—and reflect the political economy.

Basic education: expanding opportunities to learn

Prominent in the Millennium Development Goals, education is a great equalizer of opportunities between rich and poor and between men and women. But the equalizing promise of education can be realized only if children from different backgrounds have equal opportunities to benefit from quality education. In the previous section, we argued that children's ability to benefit from school is strongly influenced by the cognitive and social skills they acquire in their early years. Evidence suggests that the gains from early interventions can dissipate if disadvantaged children go on to low-quality primary schools.[18]

Chapter 2 documented the large inequalities in educational attainment within countries by income, region, gender, and ethnicity.

Chapter 5 presented the economic reasons why credit-constrained households underinvest in education, making the efficiency case for subsidizing education for the poor. There are other reasons for parents to choose a level of education for their children that may be lower than what is optimal for the child and for society. Educational attainment has various societal benefits that are not fully captured by the individual. For example, it is generally associated with enhanced democracy and lower crime, while girls' schooling in particular has been shown to reduce fertility, empower women, and thereby contribute to the welfare of children in the family. In addition, education has intrinsic value, enabling people to lead fuller lives as informed and active participants in society.

The case for moving to equalizing access to education is therefore strong on both equity and efficiency grounds, especially for basic education. Beyond basic education, there is an important efficiency rationale for ensuring that the most talented and productive people in society have access to higher education. In today's globalized world, with competition largely on the basis of skills and ideas, countries need to cultivate latent talent, wherever it may reside. Motivated and talented children from poorer households deserve the opportunity to excel as much as their wealthier peers. While we acknowledge the important equity dimension of policies for tertiary education, the discussion here is devoted primarily to policies that expand access to and quality of basic education.

We argue that there is a case for public action to enhance equity in learning so that outcomes reflect not merely circumstances of luck—parental endowments, sociocultural environment, birth place, one dedicated teacher—but genuine differences in preferences, effort, and talent consistent with the notion of equal opportunities. This requires expanding affordable access and upgrading quality, with a particular focus on excluded groups, through various interventions that increase both the demand for schooling and the capacity and incentives of the school system to respond.

There are clear complementarities in this approach: quality improvements help only if children are in school, but they also influence the probability of their attendance. Even uneducated parents will pull their children out of school if they perceive low quality.[19] There may be tradeoffs, however, if resources devoted to upgrading quality benefit primarily the privileged who are already in school at the expense of reaching excluded groups or areas—or if the rapid expansion of access reduces the quality of instruction. While the long-run objective for school systems around the world is clear, priorities will vary by country, region, or group.

Expanding access, particularly for excluded groups

Expanding access for all. More than 100 million children of primary school age are out of school, either because they never entered the system or because they dropped out before finishing.[20] As a result, some 52 countries risk not reaching the goal of universal primary completion.[21] In most countries, improving opportunities in education means ensuring affordable access, especially for poor rural children and disadvantaged groups.

Higher public spending on the supply of schools is one way to expand access. Analysis of the determinants of school enrollment in various countries suggests that proximity to schools is a major factor.[22] A careful evaluation of Indonesia's school construction program in the 1970s, the largest such program on record, finds evidence of significant increases in both education and earnings.[23] The program yields large positive returns, but it takes more than 30 years to do so because upfront construction costs are high (more than 2 percent of Indonesia's GDP in 1973), while the benefits are spread over a generation's lifetime.

But for every success story there are many others in which higher spending has not translated into better access to infrastructure, inputs, and instruction for children. In many cases, the resources are not used effectively—too much is spent on teacher salaries or reducing class size and not enough is spent on instructional materials.

Incidence studies suggest that the poor stand to benefit more from expansion when mean levels of access to services are already reasonably high, now the case for primary schooling, even in many low-income countries. But spending alone is clearly not enough to get the children in school (and even less effective in ensuring that they learn). In many countries, the main problem is not facilities but children dropping out or not attending available schools.[24] Recent efforts to boost access thus focus on demand-side interventions: reducing the cost of schooling or providing incentives, even paying for attendance.

In many countries, parents have to pay a lot, either for school fees or for other inputs, such as uniforms and textbooks. Eliminating these costs can boost participation. Free uniforms and textbooks provided by an NGO program in Kenya (along with better classrooms) reduced dropout rates considerably: after five years, students in the program completed about 15 percent more schooling. In addition many students from nearby schools transferred to program schools to take advantage of the benefits. The result was a 50 percent increase in class size—an increase that does not appear to have deterred parents nor has it led to a measurable negative impact on test scores. This is at least suggestive that a reallocation of the education budget—larger class size with the savings used to pay for the inputs under the program—could raise school participation at no cost to quality.[25]

Eliminating user fees for basic schools has also been shown to boost student enrollment, but quality may be compromised if reliable alternative sources of financing are not available to schools (box 7.2). In both Tanzania and Uganda, eliminating school fees became an important political issue when the population could voice its discontent, helped by the democratic process, an active civil society, and (in Tanzania) the Poverty Reduction Strategy Paper process.

In some cases, there may be a need to go beyond removing the direct financial costs of schooling to induce poor parents to enroll their children. This could be accomplished by providing CCTs and free meals. CCT programs make payments to poor families, typically mothers, on the condition that children attend school regularly. The programs can be seen as compensating for the oppor-

---

BOX 7.2 *School fees—an instrument of exclusion or accountability?*

There are two schools of thought about school fees. Some claim that school fees deter poor families from sending their kids to school. Even nominally small amounts can be a large share of poor households' income, and these come on top of the forgone benefits of children contributing to family business or household chores. Schooling costs often figure in parents' responses about constraint to enrollment, and eliminating school fees appears to have spurred a large increase in enrollments in a number of countries, including Kenya, Tanzania, Uganda, and Vietnam. Others see user fees as an important accountability tool, a mechanism for empowering parents to demand quality services from the schools, and point to studies that show even poor households' willingness to pay for good quality services.

Sympathetic to the arguments in favor of greater accountability, we argue for eliminating user fees when the fiscal impact of forgone revenues can be managed without large efficiency costs or harmful spending cuts. The desirable voice and accountability aspects of school fees can be harnessed equally or better through contributing labor for school improvements or working on parent-teacher advisory committees. Such in-kind fees are cheaper to the parent and engage the parent more fully in school decision making.

---

tunity cost of schooling for poor families and represent one approach to addressing failures in credit markets and the imperfect agency of parents. Many of the cash-for-school-attendance programs are large, representing significant commitments of public resources. The biggest are Oportunidades (previously PROGRESA) in Mexico, the Bolsa Escola in Brazil, and the Food for Education Program in Bangladesh.[26]

The budgets allocated to these programs are between just under 1 percent of total government current expenditure in Brazil and more than 5 percent in Bangladesh. These significant, but not prohibitive, sums could be generated from savings on other expenditures, such as regressive subsidies for public services, including tertiary education. A question remains about how cost-effective the programs are in expanding education: the answer depends on how successful they are in reaching households that would not have participated in the school system without the transfers.

A careful evaluation of PROGRESA found an average increase in enrollment of 3.4 percent for all students in grades one through eight, with the largest increase (14.8 percent) for girls who had completed grade six.[27] Morley and Coady (2003) estimate an internal rate of return (taking into account the cost of grants) for the program of 8 percent a year and report that the transfers are 10 times more cost-effective than building schools. But De Janvry and Sadoulet (2004) find that most program benefits are received by those who would have gone to school anyway. They suggest calibrating transfers to increase program efficiency—for example, through larger transfers to the eldest child, to children with an indigenous father, or to children, especially girls, living in villages without a secondary school.

Reaching excluded groups. Schools with adequate supplies and well-trained and motivated teachers, who are accountable for the learning they produce, are good for everyone. But additional support may be necessary to improve access for excluded groups, such as disabled children, girls, and indigenous groups.

Including disabled children is possible at relatively modest costs. In Uruguay, grants of up to $3,000 are awarded for schools that put forward proposals for reaching disabled children. In the two years since the fund was set up, 6 percent of all schools in Uruguay have been awarded grants to cover expenses to adapt school materials, equipment, and infrastructure and to train teachers in appropriate pedagogical approaches.

Improving gender equity in access to schooling often requires making special provisions for girls, especially older girls.[28] Specific grants for girls have been effective in Bangladesh and Mexico. Private latrines for girls are essential. Other structural improvements including boundary walls, flexible or double sessions when sharing a facility with boys, and perhaps even gender-specific schools may allay parents' concerns about girls' privacy and safety. It is important for schools to undermine, not underscore, stereotypes and unequal treatment of women—and to be wary of giving boys more resources, leadership, and attention. Female teachers are good role models for boys and girls, and even young women can be effective teachers with training, support, and a programmed curriculum. Governments might consider setting national goals for hiring women and being flexible with age and education requirements for female teachers (while still providing adequate in-service training).[29]

To expand access for ethnic groups, teachers or teacher aides from the target ethnic group are particularly helpful in their ability to connect with the students as powerful role models. Bilingual schools have also been effective. In Mali, bilingual programs were associated with large declines in dropout and repetition, and rural students outscored urban children. In Mexico, geographic targeting under PROGRESA (now Oportunidades) led to the relatively high participation of indigenous people (but not those in the most remote areas without schools).[30] An innovative approach to encourage the attendance of Roma children in Vidin, Bulgaria, appears to have paid off (box 7.3).

Upgrading quality

Better quality for all. Expanding access to basic education is necessary but not enough; the quality of education matters for opportunities. But even children in middle-

---

BOX 7.3 *Desegregating Roma schools in Bulgaria: the Vidin model*

In Vidin, the Open Society Institute and the Roma NGO known by the initials DROM have been collaborating to integrate Roma students into the mainstream school system. Vidin is a town of 85,000 in northwest Bulgaria, and 6 percent of its population was identified as Roma in the 1992 census. In the 2000–01 school year, 460 Roma students, or half the school-age students, were enrolled in the mainstream school system. Students are bused from the settlement to school and back. And Roma monitors interact with parents and the school to encourage attendance. Low-income students also receive shoes and school lunches, with lunches given on the bus to reduce the stigma of receiving it at school.

While preparing the program, DROM went door-to-door in the Roma settlement and sought the support of the schools, the mayor, and the media. The project eventually gained the support of all the stakeholders except the mayor, who nevertheless agreed not to block it. DROM invited the six mainstream schools in Vidin to present the program, philosophy, and teachers on television. Roma parents then selected a school for their children. This marked the first time that their views had been solicited by the authorities.

At the end of the first semester, attendance was 100 percent, and first-term final-grade averages were identical to those of non-Roma pupils. Parents and teachers were satisfied, especially with the absence of reported incidents of anti-Roma prejudice. Education authorities were encouraged to scale up in other cities. In addition, 35 Roma parents of the bused children returned to school in adult education programs, and three teenagers who had dropped out in the third grade asked to join the program, prompting teachers to work extra hours with them. On the negative side, 24 pupils received failing grades in one or more subjects, and three left the program.

The success is attributable to three major factors. First, parents feel that their children are protected from prejudice because they are bused and monitored throughout the day by adult Roma. Second, Roma monitors in the schools assure that the children are not mistreated, encourage parental engagement and student participation in extracurricular activities, and help the teachers ease cultural differences. Third, the children are happy to be in schools where real learning takes place.

Source: Ringold, Orenstein, and Wilkens (2005).

income countries do a lot worse than the average OECD kid on international tests of learning achievement, suggesting that much of the learning in schools does not prepare children to be productive adults, let alone for the rigors of competition they will face in the global labor market.[31] The quality deficit is undoubtedly greater for children from poorer families, because the better-off children can go to better public schools or leave the public system and opt for private schooling.

Based on the results of a standardized international achievement test—the Third International Mathematics and Science Study (TIMSS)—Pritchett (2004a) estimates that the overwhelming majority of children ages 15 to 19 lacks education (not completing grade nine or performing poorly in the TIMSS) in five middle-income countries with data (figure 7.4).[32] But the enrollment problem remains large only in Morocco. Indonesia and Turkey have difficulty retaining kids in secondary school; in Colombia, Morocco, and the Philippines, three of four children who have completed grade nine have failed to learn enough.

How can countries improve basic learning outcomes for all? We know broadly from a large number of studies that have tried to account for the "production" of schooling outcomes that higher public spending does not always translate into better student learning.[33] A recent study analyzing the determinants of student performance on the TIMSS—using data for more than 260,000 students from 6,000 schools in 39 countries—finds that education spending (spending per student, class size, student-teacher ratio) at either the school or country level has no positive impact on student performance. Among factors at the school level, the only ones that have a significant impact on student performance are instructional material and teachers with an adequate formal education.[34]

These results are confirmed by several careful microlevel studies. Since 1996, a group of researchers working with a Dutch NGO, International Chirstelijk Steunfonds Africa, has been involved in the design and evaluation of a series of randomized experiments to improve learning outcomes in the Busia district in rural Kenya. The results

Figure 7.4 Boosting enrollments is not enough to overcome the learning gap

As a fraction of cohort

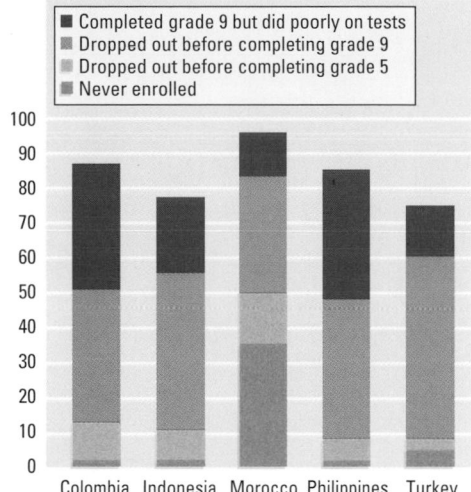

a. Based on TIMSS-R scores for eighth graders on mathematics in 1999. To calculate the fraction of students with scores below 400—one standard deviation (100 points) below the OECD median of 500)—Pritchett uses the country mean and standard deviation and assumes a normal distribution. This assumes that scores are roughly constant over time so the 1999 test represents the cohort ages 15–19 in the survey year, and that eighth- and ninth-grade competencies would be roughly similar.

indicate that increased availability of textbooks helps improve test scores, but only among the better-performing students, and that performance-based prizes for teachers increased test scores initially, but the gains dissipated later. What did work in raising test scores were merit scholarships for 13- to 15-year-old girls—with positive effects also on learning for boys, who were ineligible, and girls with low pretest scores, who were unlikely to win the scholarships. The scholarships were the most cost-effective of all the interventions tested, achieving the same learning results at less than 20 percent of the cost of textbook provision.[35]

The results underscore the importance of combining additional spending (of the right kind) with interventions that strengthen incentives to teach and to learn. As the teacher incentive program shows, project design—in this case, the behavior rewarded—matters.[36]

Better quality for the most disadvantaged. Many of the programs just discussed focus on improving performance at the school

---

BOX 7.4 *Remedying education: the Balsakhi program in India*

The Balsakhi program is a large remedial education program now implemented in 20 Indian cities by an NGO—Pratham—in collaboration with the government. Pratham hires young women from the community to teach basic literacy and numeracy skills to children who reach the third or fourth grade without having mastered them. Students are pulled out of regular classes for two hours of the school day for the remedial education. The program is inexpensive: $5 per child per year. Easily replicable, it has been scaled up rapidly since its inception in Mumbai in 1994, now reaching tens of thousands of students in the 20 cities.

A recent two-year randomized evaluation in Mumbai and Vadodara finds that the

program has highly significant positive results on student learning. On average, the program increased learning by 0.15 standard deviations in the first year and 0.25 in the second year. The gains were largest for children at the bottom of the distribution, with those in the bottom third gaining 0.20 deviations in the first year, and 0.32 in the second year (0.51 for math alone). The results were similar in the two grade levels and in the two cities. At the margin, extending this program would be 12 to 16 times more effective than hiring new teachers.

Source: Banerjee and others (2004).

---

level. What about improving learning outcomes for disadvantaged or poorly performing students? The merit scholarship program for 13- to 15-year-old girls in rural Kenya mentioned earlier is one such example. The Balsakhi program in India—a large remedial education program—represents another highly successful and cost-effective approach to giving poorly performing students a leg up (box 7.4). Because children with the lowest ability registered the largest gains in test scores, the program had an equalizing effect on student achievement.

Many countries group students together by similar abilities on efficiency grounds. However, recent findings in 18 to 26 countries show that such tracking increases education inequality, possibly by reinforcing the effects of family background, but it does not contribute to higher mean levels of performance.[37]

Another option to improve learning outcomes for disadvantaged children is to provide school vouchers. There is significant controversy around the equity and efficiency impacts of generalized voucher schemes (box 7.5). Targeted means-tested voucher programs may be more promising.[38] Results from one such scheme in Colombia are encouraging. The PACES program provided more than 125,000 students from poor neighborhoods with vouchers that covered

about half the cost of private secondary schools; vouchers could be renewed as long as students maintained satisfactory academic performance. An evaluation of this randomized natural experiment (vouchers were awarded by lottery) found lower repetition rates and higher test results among voucher winners.[39] But targeted voucher schemes may be politically difficult to implement—and the Colombia program was discontinued.

Strengthening accountability

Dismal learning outcomes in many countries are due to the combination of inadequate resources and the low responsiveness and accountability of school systems. Efforts to improve school performance will therefore need to focus on strengthening accountability processes: achieving societal consensus on expanding education, dealing with capture by vested interests, and tackling the weak incentives for service providers to raise the quality of learning.

Achieving societal consensus on expanding education helps tackle the pathology of elite capture, whereby the wealthy oppose increased spending in public education. Historically, expansion of voice in a country has led to wider access and quality improvements in basic education, notably in Europe and North America.[43] Democratic transitions have spurred recent expansions in basic education also in Brazil, Guatemala, and Uganda.[44] But these are long-term processes, and it is essential to make progress now toward meeting the urgent needs of millions of children around the world.

Some progress can be made by countering the stranglehold of interest groups on equity-enhancing reforms, such as when teachers unions block reforms that would strengthen the link between performance and accountability.[45] Significant payoffs can come from systemic reforms that strengthen accountability from clients directly to frontline providers.[46] The most crucial steps in any such reform are to increase the schools' accountability for performance and to ensure the availability of relevant information to monitor their performance. Accountability for performance also requires autonomy to manage results. This means delegating responsibility and

---

BOX 7.5   *School vouchers: efficient and equitable?*

School voucher programs increase the power of parents to choose schools for their children. Parents are given a voucher by the government, which (at least in theory) can be applied to the school of their choice, public or private. The expectation is that competition among schools and the availability of public resources to access private schools would improve the overall efficiency of the school system and student achievement. But research into the impacts of vouchers has not produced definitive or generalizable results—in large part because of methodological challenges and the differences in the specific design and institutional context of various reforms. Design can vary according to the size of the voucher, the pool of eligible students, whether schools can charge more than the value of the voucher, and regulations governing school choice (such as whether or not religious schools are eligible). Institutional management, bureaucratic control, governance of public schools, and oversight of eligible private schools also vary and influence the results of programs.[40]

Chile has more than 20 years of experience with large voucher programs. Yet detailed analysis on the effects of competition on school quality in Chile has not led to a consensus on impact. In the United States, one study found that competition improved achievement in the city of Milwaukee, while another found no impact. Similar variance is found in the related literature on the impact of school choice.[41] Competition between schools and school choice imply that weak public schools will lose students and could be forced to close. Successful schools would have to be enlarged, or new—and presumably more effective—schools would have to be built. Such institutional change presents significant political, technical, and administrative hurdles. The hurdles are particularly acute under a universal voucher program that enables large student migration.

Solid evidence on productivity differences between public and private schools is also lacking. Again consider Chile, whose voucher program generated a large number of new secular private schools that operated alongside more established Catholic schools. An analysis of Chilean fourth-grade achievement data showed that Catholic schools had higher achievement than public schools in math and Spanish, while secular private schools had lower achievement. Another study found that unrestricted nationwide school choice in Chile resulted in middle-class flight into private schools, but without achievement gains.[42]

Evidence on peer effects that could influence student achievement is equally inconclusive. It is not clear whether peer effects are linear, meaning that gains for students who move to a higher-quality peer group are offset by losses for either their new or old classmates—or nonlinear, meaning, for instance, that positive peer effects can disproportionately benefit students with low socioeconomic status.

While impacts on efficiency are ambiguous, there are reasons to be cautious about the equity effects of universal voucher programs. They could lead to increased racial and socioeconomic stratification of schools as parents seek to improve the quality of their children's peers (such as middle-class flight in Chile). Such stratification could occur if all parents were given vouchers but low-income families were in a less favorable position to exercise choice because of lack of information, prohibitive transportation costs, or extra fees. Disadvantaged students would simply be more concentrated in low-quality schools. Echoing similar concerns, a recent study concludes that, in the United States, "a large-scale universal voucher program would not generate substantial gains in overall student achievement and ... it could well be detrimental to many disadvantaged students" (Ladd 2002, 4).

There are ways to make voucher programs more beneficial for disadvantaged students, but these may reduce political support for such programs. For instance, vouchers and school choice can be limited to low-income families. Program design can also be enhanced by providing transportation to school, requiring that schools do not charge extra tuition or fees on top of the voucher, and requiring oversubscribed schools to select students randomly. Irrespective of design specifics, a voucher program needs to be embedded in a larger strategy of education reform that improves the overall institutional incentive environment for schools and gives underperforming schools the instruments and resources to improve.

---

power for decision making to the lowest feasible level consistent with incentives.[47]

Once the responsibilities of the school system are well defined, the resources and decision-making powers of providers are consistent with their responsibilities, and information is available to track performance, various mechanisms become available to pressure schools to deliver better performance. School autonomy, community control, nongovernment providers, voucher programs, and public sector reforms can strengthen the ability of citizens, communities, and public organizations to hold schools accountable for delivering results.[48] El Salvador's experience with rebuilding much of its education system following the destructive civil war of the 1980s is a good example of what can be accomplished through partnership with local communities. As a result of greater parental involvement, Educo schools had rapid enrollment increases without giving up quality, reduced absenteeism among teachers and students, and increased math and language scores.

Toward better health for all

The large inequalities in health care use and health outcomes in many developing countries do not just reflect different preferences or needs—they arise from constraints on the ability of individuals to achieve good health (chapter 2). Income is one important constraint, especially given incomplete financial markets. Low-income people around the world have worse health and use fewer health services (chapter 2). Ethnicity, race, and location also influence outcomes. Infant mortality rates among blacks in South Africa are 5.5 times higher than those among whites; life expectancy among the rural Chinese is almost 6 years lower than among urban dwellers, while the life expectancy gap between China's richest and poorest provinces (Beijing and Guizhou) is 10 years.[49]

These stark differences in outcomes and use reflect large group-based inequalities in access to information, facilities with reasonable standards of care and financial protection from health risk. A lack of knowledge about hygiene, nutrition, available services, and treatment options, particularly among the uneducated, lowers demand for health services. Within the household, some family members have less voice (women and children) and this can affect the level of resources used in their interest. Health clinics, especially in poor and remote areas, are often inaccessible, have high rates of absenteeism and low quality and responsiveness to clients. Finally, illness is certainly a burden on poor people, but catastrophic health shocks can also have disastrous consequences for the not so poor, mainly through loss of income but also through high out-of-pocket payments for health care.

These large group disparities in health outcomes are inequitable, because they imply vastly different opportunities to lead productive lives. And because they often arise from failures in markets and agency, reducing these disparities would have large payoffs in efficiency and productivity. We focus here on ways to level the playing field for attaining good health by boosting people's knowledge about basic health practices and services, expanding their access to affordable care, and enhancing the accountability of providers.

Expanding knowledge

Underinvestments in health by patients may reflect a lack of knowledge and agency and incentive issues within the household, as well as a lack of these resources. Lack of knowledge can keep people from seeking care when they need it, even when price is not an issue. As chapter 5 showed, when deworming medicine was offered free to children in Kenya, the take-up rate was only 57 percent. Similarly, in Bolivia, many poor babies are not delivered by a trained attendant even though mothers are eligible for free care. In India, 60 percent of children have not been fully immunized, although immunization is free; mothers cited ignorance of the benefits of vaccination and not knowing the clinic locations as the major reasons for why their children had not been immunized.

Lack of knowledge can also lead people to pay for inappropriate care. Unqualified or unethical providers can overprescribe treatments for patients who do not know what is in their best interest. For instance, instead of effective and inexpensive oral rehydration therapy, a poor child in Indonesia gets more than four (often useless) drugs per diarrhea attack.[50]

Education is a natural way to address the lack of patient knowledge. Elo and Preston (1996) estimate that one year of extra education nationally reduces mortality rates by about 8 percent—half directly and half through the effects of additional earnings. Female education is particularly powerful. Better-educated mothers are associated with better child-health practices, including hand washing, proper disposal of feces, antenatal care, delivery assistance by trained personnel, immunization, and well-baby clinics.

Community health agents also provide cost-effective instruction in disease prevention and healthy behavior. By employing these nonspecialized personnel, many countries have increased knowledge among the general public at low cost, as with Brazil's Family Health Program and Ethiopia's "mother coordinators," supporting home-based malaria treatment (box 7.6). Com-

---

BOX 7.6 *Working with mothers to treat malaria*

Malaria kills nearly 1 million children in Africa each year. Empowering mothers to take actions to treat their children in the home can be highly effective in reducing mortality. The Tigray region of Ethiopia trained "mother coordinators," who were selected from among the community to educate other mothers on the symptoms of fever and malaria. Mothers were provided chloroquine and information on how to administer the drug at a cost of $0.08 per child treatment dose. By educating mothers, Tigray provided rapid and effective treatment without forcing the child to relocate, which reduced under-five mortality by 40 percent and alleviated the burden of severe malaria cases on hospitals.

Source: World Bank (2004k).

munity health workers have also helped increase coverage of poor populations cost-effectively.

Public information campaigns can improve health knowledge by working through existing health clinics or by directly targeting the community. It is also possible to collaborate with the private sector in marketing socially valuable products, such as insecticide-treated mosquito nets, water purification methods, foods rich in vitamin A, and soap—as with the Central American Hand-Washing Initiative in Costa Rica, El Salvador, and Guatemala.[51] Media campaigns can also be effective. For instance, frequent broadcasts of AIDS messages in Thailand, Uganda, and Brazil were a key element in the campaign to reduce the spread of the disease. The Thai media campaign is credited with reducing the incidence of AIDS to a point at which the country is now able to consider a fiscally viable treatment program for AIDS patients.[52]

But neither information nor free services may be enough to boost use among the less empowered or those without voice. Maternal and child health is often viewed as meriting additional intervention. Through conditional transfers, Mexico's PROGRESA (now Oportunidades) program was designed to encourage women to attend pre- and postnatal clinical visits and bring their children for immunization and growth monitoring. The program saw an 8 percent increase in clinic visits by pregnant women in their first trimester, which led to a 25 percent drop in the incidence of illness in newborns and a 16 percent increase in the annual growth rate of children between one and three. An important design feature of the program is transferring funds to women. Although the program puts more demands on mothers' time, participants felt that the benefits were worth it. Women also reported feeling more self-confident and having more control over household resources and their time and travel. Similar schemes are delivering maternal and child care services in Brazil, Colombia, and Nicaragua.[53]

Expanding access

Access to quality health facilities remains a problem in many areas, often imposing a greater burden on rural dwellers through additional travel time and hospice costs. City dwellers are within easier reach of health centers. In Burundi, 98 percent of the urban population was within one hour of a health center, but only 65 percent of the rural population was. Even within rural areas, there is large variation. Only half of the poorest rural Nigerians were within an hour of a clinic, but 84 percent of the richest were.

Even when health facilities are accessible, they vary hugely in quality. Some have medicines and drugs in stock, are run by well-trained and motivated staff, and are well maintained. But many are not. They are often dilapidated, rarely have medicines in stock, and are run by poorly trained and rude medical staff, who frequently fail to come to work. It is often precisely the people who are materially disadvantaged who also have to struggle with poor quality and

---

BOX 7.7 *Poor people and ethnic minorities receive lower-quality care*

New studies from India, Indonesia, Mexico, and Tanzania demonstrate that the poor systematically receive lower-quality care from private and public providers.[54] The situation is often worse for ethnic minorities. Evidence from Mexico suggests that, even in poor rural villages, there is a difference in the quality of care between wealthy and poor and between indigenous and nonindigenous groups. Among the poorest fifth of the population in Mexico, indigenous women receive prenatal care from doctors who rank only in the twenty-fifth percentile in quality, while equally poor nonindigenous women receive care ranking in the fortieth percentile. The wealthiest fifth fare much better, but even among the wealthy, the indigenous receive worse care than the nonindigenous, suggesting that discriminatory practices or cultural barriers may be at play (see figure below).

Indigenous Mexicans receive lower-quality care, regardless of income

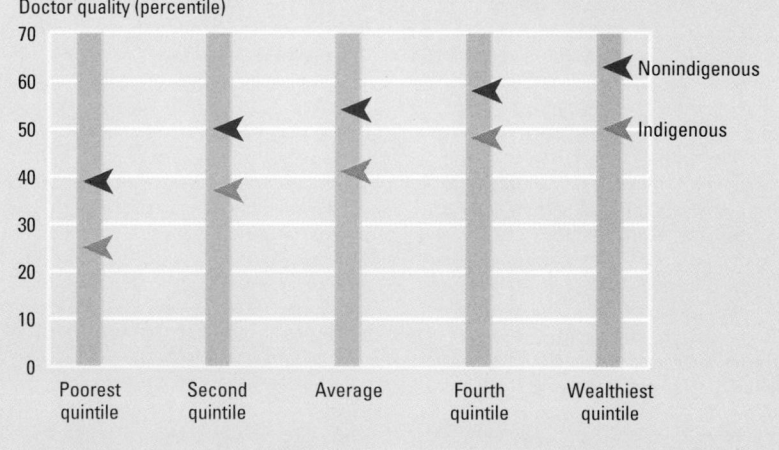

Source: Barber, Bertozzi, and Gertler (2005).

inaccessible health facilities. Ethnic minorities often fare even worse in terms of the quality of health care received (box 7.7).

An important obstacle to the provision of equitable health services everywhere is the difficulty of enticing urban-educated doctors to work in poor areas. Chile, Mexico, and Thailand have used financial and other incentives to encourage qualified staff to work in rural areas.[55] In Indonesia, doctors had to complete compulsory service in health centers before they could obtain a lucrative civil service post. Compulsory service was for five years, with shorter periods allowed for work in remote provinces. This system increased the number of doctors in health centers by an average of 97 percent from 1985 to 1994, with gains of more than 200 percent for the most remote provinces.[56]

Expanding rural health infrastructure and providing incentives to doctors to work in poor areas may not be affordable for many poor countries. But there are other approaches to reducing the indirect costs (for transport and time spent in transit) and the medical isolation of poor communities. Roving extension clinics visit sparsely populated areas in Afghanistan, Somalia, and Tunisia to provide care locally and offer transportation to better-equipped facilities when required. Bangladesh, Cuba, Gambia, India, and Madagascar have trained community health workers to scale up service delivery for a wide range of services, including malaria prevention, immunizations, family planning, treatment of TB patients, home visits, and neonatal care. The results have often yielded a substantial increase in coverage and measurable improvements in outcomes at much lower unit costs. Through a village health worker program that monitored infants' weight and health for the first month of life, rural infant mortality in Maharasthra, India, was cut in half from 75.5 to 38.8 per 1,000 live births between 1995 and 1998.[57]

Other outreach programs focus on maternal health and safe delivery. By making professional midwives and supervisory nurse-midwives widely available in rural areas, Malaysia and Sri Lanka dramatically reduced maternal mortality rates (box 7.8). In Bolivia, expectant mothers with high obstetric risk are transported to larger clinics a few days before their due date; in Sri Lanka, they are picked up by radio-dispatched four-wheel-drive vehicles.

Financing affordable care

For consumers, health care finance systems have two goals: affordable access to a basic package, and financial protection in the event of catastrophic illness costs. The classic case for government intervention (public subsidies) is when the full benefit of a "treatment" accrues not just to the individual but also spills over to the community more broadly. Interventions to avoid the spread of malaria fall into this category. A bed-net distribution program—involving the Red Cross and national ministries of health—increased use among the poorest quintile from 3 percent to nearly 60 percent in a northern district of Ghana and from 18

BOX 7.8 *Better maternal health in Malaysia and Sri Lanka*

Despite huge improvements in health, survival, and fertility around the world in recent decades, global maternal mortality has not declined significantly. Two exceptions are Sri Lanka and Malaysia. In Sri Lanka the maternal mortality ratio—the number of maternal deaths per 100,000 live births—dropped from 2,136 in 1930 to 24 in 1996. In Malaysia it dropped from 1,085 in 1933 to just 19 in 1997. What can account for this impressive decline? Improving access for rural and disadvantaged communities was an important part of the strategy in both countries.

Sri Lanka and Malaysia made competent, professional midwives and supervisory nurse-midwives widely available in rural areas. Midwives assisted deliveries in homes and small rural hospitals and performed initial treatment in the event of complications. They were given a steady supply of appropriate drugs and equipment and supported by improved communication, transportation, and back-up services. Besides reducing financial and geographic barriers, they also helped overcome cultural obstacles and allegiances to traditional practices. Because midwives were available locally and were well respected, they developed links with communities and partnerships with traditional birth attendants.

Malaysia and Sri Lanka pursued other complementary strategies. Transportation (in Malaysia) and transportation subsidies (in Sri Lanka) were provided for emergency visits to the hospital. In Malaysia, health programs were part of integrated rural development efforts that included investment in clinics, rural roads, and rural schools. Similarly, in Sri Lanka, the government invested in free primary and secondary education, free health care, and food subsidies for all districts. The concept was that basic health care acts in synergy with education and other types of infrastructure. For example, better roads make it easier to get to rural health facilities and facilitate transportation of obstetric emergencies. By addressing the multidimensionality of equity, these countries made significant health gains.

Dramatic improvements in maternal mortality are thus possible. Just as important, the experiences of Malaysia and Sri Lanka show that these can be attained with only modest expenditures. Since the 1950s, public expenditures on health services have hovered between 1.4 and 1.8 percent of GDP in Malaysia and averaged 1.8 percent in Sri Lanka, with spending on maternal and child health (MCH) services amounting to less than 0.4 percent of GDP in both countries. Countries with similar income levels have significantly higher health expenditures and similar, if not higher, maternal mortality ratios.

Source: Pathmanathan and others (2003).

percent to 82 percent in five rural Zambian districts.[58] Immunizations, vector control, and interventions for tuberculosis, HIV/AIDS, and other communicable diseases are similarly deserving.

But the case for government intervention goes beyond these well-accepted public health reasons: inequality in access to financial protection from health risk based on wealth, ethnicity, and location provides another important rationale. Out-of-pocket payments are the dominant form of health care finance in lower-income countries. But liquidity constraints and imperfect credit markets often make out-of-pocket payments more difficult for the poor, reducing their use rates, and health and productivity.

In Vietnam in 1998, before the establishment of health insurance, 30 percent of poor households' nonfood budget went to medical costs, while only 15 percent of spending for the richest fifth of the population was health related. In Cambodia, a single hospital stay absorbed 88 percent of an average household's nonfood consumption in 1997 and, for the poorest among them, the cost was higher than the entire nonfood budget. In the transition economies of Europe and Central Asia, with the collapse of prepayment in the 1990s, out-of-pocket spending skyrocketed, accounting for as much as 80 percent of health resources in Georgia and Azerbaijan. In Armenia, 91 percent of patients reported having to make some payment for service received.[59] While health care use has plummeted in the region, the collapse of prepayment especially hurts poor people.

The regressive nature of out-of-pocket payments is well understood, but there are no easy answers, especially in low-income countries. Given the small formal sector and limited administrative capacity, these low-income countries have limited capacity to mobilize resources to pay for essential health services and to establish large enough risk pools. So, developing countries face a difficult tradeoff between providing a basic package of health services and extending financial protection.[60] Some evidence suggests that the poor are better able to cover low-cost, high-frequency health shocks than low-frequency, high-cost events.[61] If so, poor people may be better served by having protection against these low-risk, high-cost events through some type of pooling mechanism. It is no easy task, however, to cover catastrophic health risks in ways that reach the poor.

Reducing out-of-pocket costs involves a combination of pooling health risks and prepayment—through contributory insurance schemes, national health services that are funded out of general revenues, or a mix of the two. In all instances, reaching the poor requires some means of subsidizing their health care costs, so fiscal room and political commitment are crucial. In very low-income countries, community insurance schemes, sometimes supplemented through NGO or donor funding, can provide some protection to some people, but generally these services do not reach the poorest.

Contributory schemes—private or social—operate best where the share of the formal labor market is high and administrative capacity is strong. And because premiums and copayments can be unaffordably high, purely contributory schemes generally bypass the poor. Private insurance is a significant part of health finance systems in Brazil, Chile, Namibia, South Africa, the United States, Uruguay, and Zimbabwe. But in all seven countries, private insurance is used by formal sector workers, leaving the ministries of health to provide public funds for programs for the poor and underserved.[62]

Social insurance is characterized by compulsory coverage financed by employment taxes. Benefits are often limited to contributors, and providers are often from the public sector even when private providers are eligible. Social insurance has the appeal of generating a large risk-sharing pool and can, in principle, reach the poor through cross-subsidization. But, when the formal sector is small this potential is limited, because of the difficulties of enrolling a large enough share of the population. This can turn the system into a ticket to privileged access to health services for some, while leaving the bulk of the population underserved. For example, in Mexico, social security health spending per person is five times higher than what the Ministry of Health spends per person.[63] And, the payroll tax required for social insurance introduces labor market distortions, especially in settings characterized by dual labor markets.

The challenges from both an equity and efficiency perspective are enormous, but a handful of mainly middle-income countries have made important attempts to make social insurance systems work. Colombia, for example, has a cross-subsidization scheme for the poor, topped up by general revenues. The scheme has delivered considerable benefits: higher coverage among the poor (48 percent, up from 9 percent, in 10 years); lower out-of-pocket costs for ambulatory care; large increases in physician-assisted delivery (by 66 percent) and prenatal care among rural women (by 48 percent); and lower child mortality rates (from 44 per

1,000 births to 15) among the insured. But there are questions about the program's sustainability in the face of mounting fiscal cost—reflecting the difficulty of systemic reforms that threaten the privileges of established interests, in this case, public hospitals and the prereform social security institution.[64]

Ministries of health in many developing countries operate essentially as national health services, with nationally owned health sector inputs and funding from general tax revenues. The systems they manage are often inefficient and inequitable, reflecting severe resource and institutional capacity constraints but also a bias in favor of the wealthy and influential. Services are meant to cover everyone, but high out-of-pocket payments keep many poor people from participating. Countries have tried various approaches to improve equity in access to health care provided by the national health system, such as eliminating user fees for all, waiving fees, or giving vouchers to poor people.

In 2001, Uganda abolished user fees for all. The result was a significant increase in health care use, lower probability of sickness, and better anthropometric measures, particularly for the poor.[65] But the elimination of user fees, if effective, can reduce the resources for the health sector, and thus its quality, unless budgetary funding is topped up to make up for the shortfall. Uganda appears to have avoided a fall in quality, thanks to a large increase in the health budget that more than compensated for the loss in revenues from eliminating user charges.

Introduced in 2002, Thailand's "30 baht" or universal coverage scheme aims to guarantee health care to every Thai citizen. It combines previously existing schemes targeted to the poor and uninsured, and allocates budgetary resources to providers on a capitation basis, with only a small copayment per visit (30 baht). The Ministry of Public Health remains a strategic manager and central financier, but the district offices make the decisions on choice of providers. The scheme has markedly increased use and coverage, with roughly three-quarters of the country benefiting from the scheme and 95 percent of the population insured overall, all at a limited additional budgetary cost (box 7.9).

BOX 7.9   *Mobilizing support for universal coverage in Thailand*

With the introduction of the universal coverage scheme in 2002, almost the entire Thai population now has health coverage (box figure 1). This was possible largely because the democratic transition of 1997 ushered in a period of increased voice and openness and raised the political profile of poor people's concerns. Technical preparation—with design details that had been under consideration and subject to experimentation for some time—also helped to garner support for the reform, while prior investments in health care infrastructure, establishing a health center in nearly every rural subdistrict, provided assurance of implementation success.

Thailand's increasing coverage

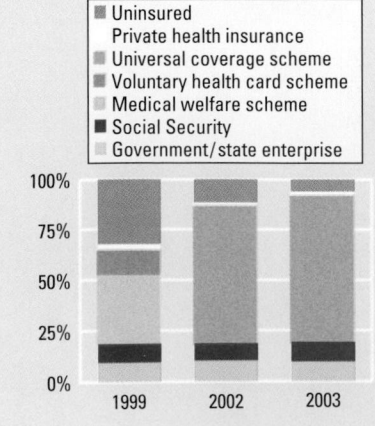

Years of corruption and political inequity in the early 1990s, together with the intervening period of military rule fueling social discontent, prepared the ground for democratic reforms and a liberal constitution in 1997. Two provisions of the new constitution were important for the ensuing health sector reforms: the principle of equity in health care access; and the scope for civil society to propose national legislation affecting citizen rights and the role of the state, if the measure had 50,000 signatures. In March 2000, nearly at the same time that a feasibility study for the scheme was completed, a network of 11 NGOs submitted to parliament a draft bill calling for universal health care coverage. Between 1999 and 2001, the press also captured the general public's interest and kept the issue on the political agenda by highlighting the shortcomings of the current health system.

This political foment attracted the attention of the opposition Thai Rak Thai (TRT) party. TRT adopted the policy because it was broadly supported, administratively and technically feasible, and consistent with the party's ideology. TRT effectively turned the 1997 financial crisis into an opportunity by highlighting the health issues precipitated by the crisis. Following its landslide victory in 2001, TRT introduced its own universal coverage legislation, which passed in November 2002.

Source: Pitayarangsarit (2004).

But there is broad agreement that existing capitation rates are too low and that the system is underfunded. This provides limited incentives for private providers to participate and could lead to a financial squeeze on public providers with adverse impacts on quality.[66] Higher use has also put a strain on human resources, with increased workloads (and low pay) accelerating the number of physicians leaving the public system. Clearly supply-side measures need to be considered in tandem with health finance reforms to expand access. Still, the achievements have been considerable, and the scheme has broad popular support. Thailand implemented the reform in large part thanks to the popular support that democratic reforms made possible; previous investments in sound design and health infrastructure also helped.

Other countries reduce costs for the poor through targeted programs funded from general revenues. Armenia's targeted fee-waiver system curbed plummeting use among the poor. But in many instances, simple legislation of free or reduced-price services can be counterproductive without good funding and targeting. Targeted payments, through government vouchers and civil society partnerships with hospitals, can help. Vouchers issued to poor patients, as by the MCH poverty alleviation fund in Yunnan Province in China, give providers a greater assurance of payment. In Cambodia, a promising partnership has emerged between government hospitals, Médecins Sans Frontières (MSF) and a small local NGO, covering the hospital fees of those considered indigent by the local NGO's social workers. Because the hospital is fully compensated, poor patients receive the same care as those who can pay.[67]

Vietnam has introduced health cards for the poor. More than 11 million of 14.3 million eligible people benefited from Vietnam's program in its first year of implementation in 2002. The program has already significantly increased the flow of government health funding to the poor and to predominantly poor areas of the country. The funding per beneficiary, however, is considered inadequate and the cost-sharing arrangements are likely to impose too large a burden on populations in poorer or ethnic minority regions.[68]

Many developing countries have a mixed system, with ministries of health, private insurance, social insurance, and targeted schemes coexisting to serve different segments of the population. These multitrack systems tend to fragment, increasing administrative costs, limiting pool sizes, and undermining both equity and efficiency objectives. Chile's two-track universal coverage system has caused severe segmentation, with the healthy and wealthy in the private scheme, leaving the public scheme overburdened with the poor and ill. Chile is trying to overcome this by creating a "virtual pool," mandating a common basic benefits package, instituting catastrophic insurance, allowing portability of benefits between schemes, and initiating minimum quality and maximum wait-time standards.

Community-based health insurance (CBHI) schemes have developed in some poor communities outside the reach of national health systems. Communities pool health risks through voluntary contributions to a local fund used when any member incurs a health shock. The schemes are reported to reduce out-of-pocket spending and increase use by their members, but they generally do not reach the poorest and socially excluded groups or offer members enough protection from financial risk. Many are limited by their small risk pools, exposing them to low-frequency but high-cost catastrophic events that can outstrip the community fund. Some communities address large health risks by increasing the maximum benefit, as in Cameroon. But they do so by limiting the number of family's claims to one a year and by requiring high premiums (which prohibit the poor from participating).[69]

Insurance alone is not enough for equitable use. Inadequate knowledge of the scheme's benefits and processes and even the paperwork for submitting claims to community insurance schemes can be a deterrent. Hospitals often require payment on or before discharge, but insurance claims are not settled until later, requiring patients to pay up front. India's Self-Employed Women's

Association (SEWA) has been seeking to remedy similar difficulties encountered in its large and well-established CBHI scheme. SEWA is testing door-to-door visits for member education, reimbursement assurance with selected hospitals, and reimbursement to members while still in hospital.[70]

Enhancing provider incentives

Addressing knowledge, access and affordability constraints are important, but they may not be enough to raise health use and outcomes. Hours of operation, waiting time, staff disposition, competence and integrity, and the cultural appropriateness of services are all important. Complaints of unprofessional treatment, abuse, and corruption abound worldwide. Public medical staff who take authorized or unauthorized leave from public clinics undermine the credibility of the public health sector, drive up costs for poor families, and induce the poor to use private providers, including traditional healers. In Bangladesh, such absenteeism rates amount to 40 percent for physicians in larger clinics and 74 percent in smaller subcenters with a single physician. More generally, poor service delivery has to do with weak management and incentives within the public health system—ineffective technical and structural backup, lack of professional career structures, and inadequate financial incentives all contribute. But the weak demand for service provider accountability and quality is also a problem.[71]

If they are organized, poor citizens and communities can have more voice and greater power to influence health providers. Governments can help support organization by communities and enhance provider accountability. It helps to have well-defined objectives for health service delivery with transparent metrics for monitoring progress. This allows for community oversight of health workers and facilities, and when coupled with sufficient management autonomy for providers to reach the established objectives, can lead to improved provider incentives and accountability.

There is also a need for governments to engage with nonpublic health care providers: in many countries, NGO and private providers make up a large part of the health network. NGOs are particularly helpful in serving remote areas and hard-to-reach populations: the Bangladesh Rural Advancement Committee (BRAC) trains community workers to seek out the extremely poor in need of urgent medical care. In Jordan, half or more of outpatient visits are to private providers.[72] Many private providers offer excellent services. But some do not—and misdiagnose, misprescribe, or overprescribe treatment. In Mexico, even wealthy women receive worse care from private providers than from public providers (Barber, Bertossi, and Gertler 2005). Without unduly discouraging beneficial private enterprise in health, governments need to ensure accreditation and appropriate regulation for nonpublic providers.

Social protection: managing risk and providing social assistance

Social protection policies typically have been thought of as a form of redistribution. This certainly is important. But more recent theoretical and empirical work also highlights a crucial opportunity-enhancing role for social protection.[73] As chapter 5 showed, pervasive financial market failures in developing countries lead to widespread uninsured risks and credit constraints. Unequal capacity to manage risk means unequal opportunities to engage in risky but high-return activities. Families may deal with crises in ways that narrow future opportunities, such as distress sales and forgoing health care, schooling, or food intake. By helping poor people manage risks, social protection programs expand their opportunities and enhance overall efficiency.

Even purely redistributive programs can have important opportunity-enhancing impacts. Take the example of social pension schemes in Brazil and South Africa. These schemes are pure transfers targeted to the elderly, geared strictly to avoiding destitution, but they have important welfare impacts beyond that. They improve the recipients' access to credit, thanks to the regularity of pension payments, and lead to higher investments in the household's physical capital and in the human capital of its children and elderly.[74]

But social protection systems do more than help individual households avoid destitution and expand their opportunities—they can also help societies embark on reforms that would have insurmountable equity and political costs without them. Reforms desirable for their beneficial impacts on efficiency and the government's fiscal position—such as increasing utility prices, eliminating general food subsidies, introducing a defined contribution pension system, liberalizing trade—may not be politically feasible unless policies are in place to compensate losers. Importantly, permanent social protection can help reduce the need for special compensatory programs for each and every reform[75]—all the more important because such programs are difficult to start and stop and are not always very efficient.

All of this confirms that there is a dynamic efficiency rationale for social protection. But there are also important efficiency arguments against transfer policies. Design issues are of particular concern, because poorly designed programs can have large negative consequences on efficiency. Taxes or contributions have distortionary costs, especially when they are not directly linked to benefits (see focus 5 for a discussion of tax policies), while transfers can dampen work incentives, reduce private savings, and weaken informal insurance mechanisms. Europe's experience in the second half of the 1900s suggests that well-designed social (and tax) policies can indeed be consistent with strong growth thanks to careful attention to productivity impacts.[76]

Program choices vary by country

Social protection generally encompasses two classes of interventions:

- Contributory schemes (social insurance) in which the primary focus is on managing risks through smoothing an individual's income over time and in the face of difficulties These programs often pool risks across large numbers of individuals and include old-age and disability pensions and health and unemployment insurance.

- General tax funded transfers (social assistance) in which the focus is on redistribution from the better off to the

Figure 7.5 Almost all countries spend more on social insurance than on social assistance (percent of GDP)

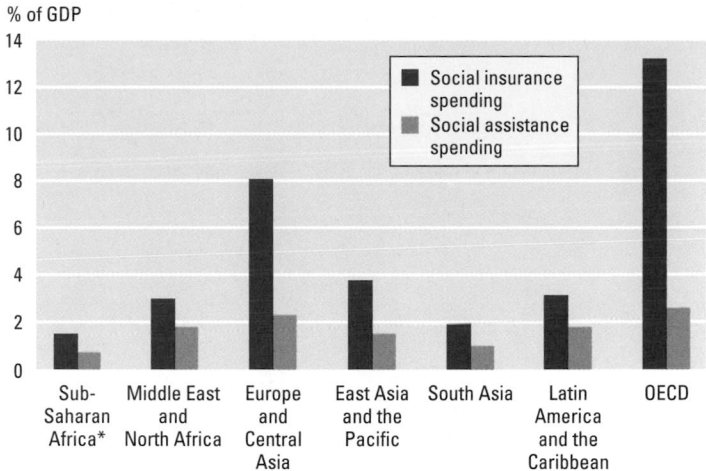

Source: Data on 74 countries taken from World Bank Public Expenditure reviews or other similar work. OECD data are from the OECD Social Expenditure database.
Note:* The average for Africa is based on data for only two countries. OECD excludes those OECD members (such as Poland and Mexico) that are already accounted for in the regional averages.

poor. These include a variety of cash or in-kind programs targeted at the poor.

These are complemented by labor market regulations (for example, on hiring and firing of workers) that are discussed in chapter 9. There is large variation in the share of GDP spent on social protection, with more-developed regions devoting considerable sums (figure 7.5). Almost all countries spend more on social insurance than social assistance programs.

There is no consensus on the appropriate balance of interventions—even in countries that have sufficient resources and capacity to implement any combination desired. Some observers argue for the universality of social insurance programs over the targeted nature of social assistance programs that are based on political economy considerations. They argue that targeted programs are exclusionary, by definition, and divisive as a result.[77] But a significant group of OECD countries (notably New Zealand, Australia, the United States, and the United Kingdom) have opted for systems with heavier components of targeted transfers and less generous or less universal programs.[78]

Many developing countries face constraints on the choice of systems because of limited fiscal and administrative capacity. Many poor and even middle-income coun-

Table 7.1 Examples of social protection programs

Group served	Social insurance	Safety net	Complementary Labor Market Regulation
Working poor or unemployed	Unemployment insurance	Transfers Public works programs General subsidies to food, utilities, or housing	Minimum wage laws Job security regulations Severance pay
Nonworking young	Universal child allowances Maternity benefits	Means-tested child allowances Transfers linked to MCH programs School feeding Conditional cash transfers	Child labor laws
Nonworking elderly	Contributory pensions	Transfers Social pensions	Retirement age
Special groups	Disability insurance for disabled	Transfers	Affirmative action for minorities

tries lack the administrative sophistication and levels of urbanization and formal employment needed to administer a social insurance scheme, and high social security taxes have segmented the labor market and encouraged informality.

What then are the options for the many developing countries that are far from able to achieve universal social insurance systems? There is a large range of social assistance programs, each different in groups served, administrative requirements, complementary benefits, incentive effects, and political factors (table 7.1). A judicious blending of these programs can usually result in a social protection system that covers the appropriate groups with feasible instruments. The mix of programs selected and their specific characteristics will depend on context—that is, the risks faced, the level of urbanization, the age structure, the size of the formal sector, the administrative capacity, and the complementary social policies and sociocultural or political factors.

Next, we discuss programs for four key groups:

- The working poor
- The nonworking young
- The nonworking elderly
- Special vulnerable groups

In many cases, the second two groups are part of households that could benefit from programs that target the working poor. So the more comprehensive the programs for the first group, the less the need for programs for the latter two, and the smaller and more focused they might be.

Programs for the working poor

Most people, especially poor people, rely on labor earnings for their livelihoods, many in the informal sector, through subsistence farming, or as agricultural laborers for others. Labor market risk can be reduced significantly by improving the functioning of labor markets and by pursuing sound macroeconomic policies (chapter 9). But even a well-functioning labor market will not fully eliminate the risk of unemployment. Moreover, in years with bad crops or low prices, earnings may not be enough to stave off poverty.

A range of instruments can help address the risk of inadequate incomes—for example, unemployment insurance, needs-based social assistance, or public works. Even food, utility, and housing price subsidies are geared in part to solving the problems of inadequate labor incomes, although with notably poor targeting and sometimes large distortionary costs.

Unemployment insurance, the obvious instrument for mitigating the risk of job loss in the formal sector, will not work well in countries with large informal sectors. Even so, schemes may be able to cover a useful share of workers and take some burden off programs more tailored to those in the informal sector (chapter 9). For example, in 1998 in response to the East Asian financial crisis, Korea expanded its young unemployment insurance program to smaller firms as well as to temporary and daily workers.[79]

Needs-based cash transfers, the classic social assistance instrument, are common in high-income countries. Such programs are potentially very efficient. Nontransfer costs can be low, usually 5 to 10 percent of total program costs. The programs need not impose significant forgone earnings on participants. And they give cash and, thus full consumer sovereignty, to the recipient.

But these programs face two challenges. First, they require a targeting mechanism. The classic mechanism in high-income countries has been a verified means test. Because income in these settings is mostly formal, it is possible and not too costly to collect accurate information on income and assets. Eastern Europe also has successful experience with means-tested programs, although verifying incomes and assets is more difficult and less accurate there than in high-income countries. Latin America's proxy means tests (relying on easily observable indicators of income) have been shown to be fairly accurate and low cost. Low-income countries with large shares of income from the informal sector experience greater difficulties in setting up targeting mechanism. Although the evidence is less clear-cut, community-based systems have been shown to work well in some countries around the world, especially in fairly homogenous rural communities (Albania, Bangladesh, Ethiopia, Indonesia, Uganda, and Uzbekistan) where elite capture is not a major concern. So the targeting issue could be surmounted.[80]

The second challenge is perhaps bigger—both for technical design and political support. Needs-based transfers inherently present a disincentive to work for those of working age because entry into the program (or the benefit level) depends on income. Traditional mechanisms to partly mitigate the work disincentives include keeping benefits substantially lower than minimum wage, as in Bulgaria or Romania, or lower than the earning of low-skilled agricultural laborers, as in Kyrgyz Republic, or using a sliding withdrawal of benefits as incomes rise, as in much of the industrial world, or an earned-income tax credit as in the United Kingdom and United States.[81]

A newer wave of efforts takes a more active approach to encouraging independence or "graduation" from the need for assistance than under the traditional mechanisms just mentioned. Chile's Puente program uses extensive social work to diagnose each household's barriers to independence and to pre-pare customized contracts with the household to address the most important of these barriers over a period of two years. Bangladesh's program of income generation for the development of vulnerable groups (IGVGD run by BRAC) gives in-kind assistance to destitute rural women for a period of 18 months. During this time, they are required to save some money and participate in business training. At the end of the cycle, women have the opportunity of "graduating" into the regular microfinance program. A few programs, as in Romania and Bulgaria, add a public service requirement (thus blurring the line between the means-tested social assistance and public works programs).[82] So, whether through traditional or more innovative mechanisms, the disincentive problem can also be mitigated.

Public works programs that support the working or unemployed poor have been used in many countries (box 7.10). By offering employment for low wages, these programs self-select the able-bodied poor, avoiding both the means-testing and work disincentives. In good programs, the work is in high-return activities that create assets and services. The self-targeting aspect is useful because informality is widespread in developing countries and incomes are hard to assess. It is doubly useful as part of a countercyclical measure in fighting poverty during periods of crisis—workers leave the program when their regular source of livelihood picks up again after the crisis. Public works programs for infrastructure are especially welcome in low-income countries, postconflict settings, and sometimes post–natural disaster settings.

Public works programs have some disadvantages too. The administrative capacity to select and run the programs is significant. Indeed the often-cited good programs are a minority of all the public works programs implemented around the world. Many have failed, often over the inability to line up and deliver useful public works, to provide sufficient nonlabor inputs, or to set the wage right.

Even when programs are well run, the net benefits transferred to participants are often a small share of total program costs. First, management, materials, equipment, and skilled labor requirements can run up to 40 to 60 percent of program costs. Second,

BOX 7.10 *Public works programs: key issues*

Public works programs have been demonstrated to work in some middle-income countries (Chile, Argentina, and South Africa) and low-income countries (Senegal, Kenya, India, and Bangladesh)—and not to work in many others. This international experience offers several lessons in the design and implementation of public works programs.

Wage rate. The key to self-targeting is setting the wage rate low enough—no higher than the market wage for unskilled manual labor in agriculture or the informal sector during a normal year. While determining the precise level of the wage rate may not be easy, it is better to start with a wage rate that is too low—if there is no demand at the offered wage rate, it can be raised. Setting a low wage rate level does more than ensure that the workfare scheme will be well self-targeted. It also maintains the incentive to take up regular work when it becomes available, and it helps ensure that the program can reach as many of those in need as possible.

Conditions of eligibility. Rationing should be avoided; ideally the only requirement should be the willingness to work at the offered wage. If rationing is unavoidable (for example, if the demand for employment at the wage set exceeds the available budget), explicit secondary criteria should be used—the program may target poor areas, work may be offered only in seasons of greatest need, the length of employment of any individual may be limited, or such addi-

tional options as community-based selection of the neediest or a lottery may be implemented. Least desirable is rationing with entry determined by foremen or political figures. Women's participation can be enhanced through nondiscriminatory wages, the provision of onsite child care, and adequately private latrines.

Employment guarantee. A workfare program that guarantees employment can reduce the longer-term risk the poor face. While highly desirable, guarantees have not been a feature of most public workfare schemes. One exception is the Employment Guarantee Scheme in Maharasthra, India, which guarantees unskilled manual work within the district within 15 days of registering for employment with the scheme. While this does not necessarily mean locally accessible employment, the scheme comes closest to offering a guarantee of any kind. India recently announced its intention to extend the guarantee by providing 100 days of employment on rural public works projects at a minimum wage. The scheme is not far enough into implementation to draw lessons. Murgai and Ravallion (2005) simulate some possible outcomes for a range of design parameters: the targeting could be good and impacts of poverty large, but the costs could also be substantial—1 to 2 percent of GDP for the 100-day scheme.

Labor intensity. The labor intensity—that is, the share of the wage bill in total costs—should be higher than normal for similar projects in the

same setting. There is a tradeoff between immediate income gains through employment of the poor, and gains to the poor from the quality and durability of the assets created. In a crisis situation, in which current transfers to the poor have high weight, a high labor intensity is desirable. Illustrative average labor intensities range from 0.5 to 0.65 percent in low-income countries and are somewhat lower (0.4) in middle-income countries, although labor intensity often varies significantly by subprojects.

Administration and implementation. Administering and implementing an effective scheme is hard—requiring the selection and management of a plethora of small projects over a wide geographic area and many administrative entities. Ideally, public works schemes require a menu of works well-integrated into the local planning process yet elastic in size and timing. This can be difficult in low-capacity settings because of the forward planning and interagency coordination needed. In high-capacity settings, fitting many small labor-intensive projects into the sophisticated and often capital-intensive infrastructure plans of large- and middle-income cities can be difficult. Moreover, ensuring that the workfare program is poverty focused is not easy because of conflicting pressures from alternative target groups, such as the skilled unemployed.

Sources: Subbarao (2003) and Murgai and Ravallion (2005).

workers have to forgo some income to participate: in the absence of the program, they usually would have been able to pick up some part-time work or engage in low-return self-employment activities. In Argentina's *Trabajar,* forgone earnings were half of gross earnings; in Maharashtra's Employment Guarantee scheme, 53 percent; and in Bolivia's ESF, 60 percent.[83] Theoretically, forgone earnings can be minimized by allowing flexible working hours or part-time work, but this can complicate the supervision of the public works and the workers.

Programs for the nonworking young

Earlier, we focused on interventions geared to overcoming the disadvantaged family circumstances of young children through a variety of services that improve their cognitive and social skills and prepare them for learning in school. Here we focus on ways of augmenting the family's income to alleviate poverty among children and improve their chances in life.

Programs aimed at children can be universal or means-tested, free-standing or linked to the use of health and education services. In both Eastern and Western Europe, the traditional approach to income support for children is through child allowances, independent from but complemented by extensive public education and health care. Most Western European programs are universal, although a few are means-tested (Italy and Spain). A higher fraction of Eastern European programs and those in other middle-income countries are means-tested (Bulgaria, Belarus, the Czech Republic, the Kyrgyz Republic, Poland, Romania, the Russian Federation, Serbia and Montenegro, the Slovak Republic, Argentina, Chile). In Africa, Latin America, and Asia, there is a long and extensive history of school feeding programs and maternal and child health programs that distribute food (or occasionally food stamps). Many of these programs rely on existing service delivery mechanisms to make their administration feasible or cheaper.

A new wave of CCT recognizes that imperfect markets can lead to underinvestment in human capital (chapter 5) and explicitly seeks to enhance the opportunity-generating potential of income support through links to the use of services. CCT programs are now being implemented in about two dozen countries, mainly in Latin America—but they are being discussed by many other countries and in all regions. These programs transfer income in cash or in kind to poor households with children. They grant benefits only if children comply with standards for attendance in school or participation in a health care program. In the CCT programs with good data, the targeting outcomes have been quite good at generally reasonable administrative costs. All five programs reviewed by Morley and Coady (2003) distribute far more than a proportional share to the bottom quintiles (table 7.2). On average, the share of program benefits going to the bottom 40 percent of the population is an impressive 81 percent. The evidence on poverty impact is more limited, but PROGRESA (now Oportunidades) had a powerful effect: program communities experienced declines of 17.4 percent in the incidence of poverty compared with the control group.[84]

The conditioning of benefits on use of health and education services serves the dual objectives of avoiding severe deprivation and enhancing opportunities for human development. But there is a tension between these goals. A simulation of the results that might be expected from the federal Bolsa Escola program in Brazil shows only a small reduction (1 percentage point) in the poverty index because of the (simulated) loss of labor income of children who drop out of the labor force to attend school. Mexico's PROGRESA (now Oportunidades) had impressive poverty impacts but increased primary enrollment rates by only about 1 percentage point because they were already above 90 percent. Cambodia's program, which focuses on grades seven through nine, may well help with the transition to secondary school, but it misses some of the poorest households because so many have dropped out by then.[85]

Table 7.2 Targeting performance of conditional transfer schemes[a]

Quintile	PRAF (Honduras)	RPS (Nicaragua)	PROGRESA (now Oportunidades) (Mexico)	SUF (Chile)	FFE (Bangladesh)
1	43	55	40	67	—
2	80	81	62	89	48
3	94	94	81	97	—
4	98	99	93	100	—
5	100	100	100	100	100

Source: Morley and Coady (2003), table 5-3.
Note: PRAF = Programa de Asignación Familiar; RPS = Red de Protección Social; SUF = Subsido Unitario Familiar; FFE = Food For Education; — = not available.
a. Cumulative share (percent) of benefit captured, by income quintile.

In settings with low access to health and education services, this tension means that conditional transfer programs may not be appropriate vehicles for social assistance. The conditions would keep the program from serving the poorest. The opposite may be true as well: when the use of services is already satisfactory, it may not be worth using administrative resources to verify compliance with service use conditions.

Programs for the nonworking elderly

Most countries have public pensions programs for the elderly. Two arguments provide a rationale for governments to mandate a pension system to provide for old-age security: imperfect financial markets limit the scope for redistribution over one's life, and human "failures" to see far enough into the future may lead to undersaving for old age. The need for old-age security will grow. The population of 60 year olds, about 10 percent of the world population today, is projected to reach about 21 percent by 2050. Within this group, the fraction of people over the age of 80, about 12 percent today, is expected to reach 19 percent by 2050.[86]

Contributory pension programs have not solved the problem of old-age security. Coverage is low—only 20 percent of the global workforce. Even in pension systems with extensive coverage, the lifetime poor cannot contribute enough to have a pension at old age that would keep them out of poverty. Elderly women who have not worked outside the home are particularly vulnerable. Moreover, in some countries, such as in Kenya, Uganda, Sri Lanka, and Zambia, poorly governed schemes gave lower-income workers returns less than bank deposits and the alternatives of investing in land, tools, or a vehicle.[87]

Options for assisting the elderly poor include the following: broadening pension systems to include more people, adding a redistributive element as part of an existing contributory pension scheme, or covering them through a separate "social pension" financed by general revenue. A fourth option is a general needs-based social assistance program.

Broadening the coverage of contributory pensions has been attempted, generally with little success. In the Republic of Korea, mandating the expansion of coverage to farmers, fishermen, and self-employed was met with massive protests; in the end, the government had to subsidize in full or in part the contributions of almost two-thirds of the target population. Adding a redistributive element is common, but as pension reforms strengthen the link between contributions and benefits for efficiency reasons, that redistributive element is becoming smaller.

Social pensions provide transfers to the elderly without requiring prior contributions or withdrawing from the labor force.[88] They can be universal, as in Botswana, Mauritius, Namibia, or Bolivia. Or they can be means-tested, as in South Africa, Senegal, India, Bangladesh, a number of Latin American countries, Australia, Italy, and New Zealand. Many of them complement contributory systems that cover higher-income groups. When the transfers are means-tested, the programs are really a special case of needs-based cash transfers limited to the elderly. The targeting challenges discussed earlier and the potential solutions are similar. Labor disincentives are lessened, however, because societies expect lower work efforts from the elderly.[89]

Evidence from various countries implementing large social pension schemes indicates that the costs are 1 to 2 percent of GDP, not negligible for low-income developing countries. Schwartz (2003) simulates the costs in six African countries of providing social pensions, limiting the benefit to 40 percent of GDP per capita and eligibility to those age 75 and above. The costs would range from 0.2 percent of GDP in Kenya to 0.7 percent of GDP in Ghana, still not insub-stantial. Kakwani and Subbarao (2005) simulate various options for 15 African countries, and conclude that the best—taking into account poverty impact, fiscal cost, and incentive effects—is to keep the benefit low (about one-third of the poverty threshold), the eligible age limit at 65 or older, and to target only the elderly poor, thus sacrificing the administrative simplicity and political advantage of universalism. There is enough variation across countries to warrant country-specific efforts to determine benefit and eligibility levels and targeting methods rather than relying on rules of thumb.

How should we think about the balance between social pensions for the elderly and other programs, such as those targeting families with children? Are the elderly poor more deserving than other poor? Brazil spends 1 percent of GDP to transfer $70 a month to 5.3 million elderly poor and only 0.15 percent of GDP to transfer $6 to $19 per month to 5 million families to support school attendance through the Bolsa Escola program.[90] When considering whether this the right balance, one can argue generally that young families with children, who have their entire lives ahead of them, should have higher priority. Indeed some argue for shifting public spending away from pensions and toward families with children in Brazil and others suggest that a focus on unemployment may be more appropriate to reduce poverty in South Africa.[91]

There may be important political economy reasons why programs for the elderly garner such political support. There is direct evidence from attitude surveys, across societies and age groups, that concerns about old age poverty are strong and widely shared— perhaps because most people expect to be old one day (but not necessarily unemployed, or a single parent, or disabled) and also because old age is more easily verifiable and less subject to moral hazard, for example, when compared with unemployment insurance.[92]

Programs for special vulnerable groups

Some groups are vulnerable regardless of age—the disabled, HIV infected, ethnic minorities, certain castes, internally displaced households, refugees, and orphans (box 7.11).[93] One of the key issues in providing transfers for these groups is whether to set up specific programs or to include them in a more general program. There is no universal answer to this, and a complex set of issues must be diagnosed in each case. One is targeting. Not all orphans, widows, or disabled are poor, so universal programs will include some non-poor. A second issue relates to the special needs of the groups. Will income support alone be sufficient, and if not (as is usually the case) does it make sense to link the income support to other programs for the group? For example, when large groups of internally displaced people or refugees emerge suddenly, their needs for housing, food, and health care may strain local availability. In such cases in-kind provision to the group is usually the first response. Only after the groups become long-standing or somewhat smaller does the question of whether to switch to a needs-based cash assistance or workfare program arise. Special programs for groups viewed positively or as deserving, such as veterans or the disabled, may have adequate political support, but if the group is excluded, as ethnic minorities or the HIV positive are in many cases, such programs may not garner sufficient support.

While standard transfers may protect these groups, a broader set of policies can help expand their opportunities and facilitate their integration into society. Some countries have used affirmative action (see chapter 8). Others have used regulations and awareness campaigns that sanction harmful local practices to help prevent discrimination. Policy responses include creating a framework to hear advocacy groups and mainstreaming such concerns into government practice, often building on informal or private arrangements, such as those of faith-based organizations.

Summary

Equity in the acquisition of human capacities—through early childhood development, formal education, health services, and social protection—is at the core of a strategy to equalize the opportunities for people to lead productive, fulfilling lives. Broad provisioning of these services is also good for development and poverty reduc-

---

BOX 7.11 *Africa's orphans and public action*

Conflict and the HIV/AIDS pandemic are generating a major humanitarian crisis for families in Sub-Saharan Africa. There are as many as 43 million orphaned children in the region today, 10 percent of whom have lost both parents. Orphans make up more than 15 percent of all children in 11 countries, and the numbers are rising .

The death of an earning family member is most likely to drive a family into penury because of the costs of funeral, the loss of regular income, and the risk of losing one's property. Erosion of human capital is another major risk: microstudies and analysis of household surveys suggest that, relative to other children in the household, fostered children are underenrolled in schools, work longer hours doing household chores, and have lower immunization coverage—and the disadvantage is stronger for fostered girls than for fostered boys. Psychological risks are also high because the death of a parent often leaves the child in a state of trauma, lacking nurturance and guidance, and impeding socialization.

The main coping strategy in Africa is fostering by the extended family. When possible, interventions should first try to strengthen grassroots responses to orphan care, and turn to supplementary interventions only when the extended family is no longer sufficient or capable. When no other living arrangement is possible, experience and research show that orphanages must be the "last resort." Recognizing the scope for exploitation of vulnerable children under all arrangements, appropriate checks and balances must be in place, including oversight by NGOs or community-based organizations.

When access to basic education and health services is generally low, waiving school fees and uniform obligations would help increase enrollment rates of all children including orphans, as in Uganda. When average access to services is high, but the difference in access between the poor and the non-poor, and between orphans and non-orphan children, is large, cash transfers conditional on children attending school seem appropriate. Innovative programs along these lines are just beginning (as in Swaziland).

Sources: Subbarao and Coury (2004); USAID, UNAIDS, and UNICEF (2004).

---

tion through impacts on innovation, productivity, and social cohesion. But there are big challenges to equitable provisioning—getting the relevant issues on the policy agenda, fighting political capture of institutions so that they do not only serve the powerful and the influential, and managing efficiency-equity tradeoffs, especially in the short term. There are also good prospects for incremental change through advocacy to point out long-run benefits even when there are short-run costs, through sound program and tax design to minimize efficiency costs and build accountability structures, and through political coalitions that can thwart elite holdups.

The power of greater equity in human capacities to unhinge inequality traps is tremendous—through directly contributing to leveling the economic, political, and sociocultural playing fields. But achieving greater equity in human capacity is not enough to break the inequality trap. It needs to be complemented with fairness in the returns to those capacities and in the access to complementary assets, topics discussed in the next chapter.

Justice, land, and infrastructure

It takes more than building human capacities to broaden people's opportunities. People also need complementary assets, access to the marketplace, and security of person and property. This chapter starts with a description of justice systems, showing how critical they are in ensuring a level playing field and fair returns. It then turns to policies for expanding access to the complementary assets of land and infrastructure. Promoting fairness in markets is addressed in chapter 9.

Building equitable justice systems

Society's rules, and the institutions that establish, maintain, and transform them, govern market and nonmarket interactions. They determine people's endowments, their rights and obligations, and their ability to generate fair returns. Reflecting and producing the distribution of power among groups, good institutions (so necessary for prosperity) emerge only when the distribution of political power and enforceable rights is equitable.

Legal institutions play a key role in the distribution of power and rights. They also underpin the forms and functions of other institutions that deliver public services and regulate market practices. Justice systems can provide a vehicle to mediate conflict, resolve disputes, and sustain social order. But inequitable justice systems may perpetuate inequality traps by maintaining or reproducing elite interests and discriminatory practices. Equitable justice systems are thus crucial to sustained equitable development.

Building more equitable justice systems runs into three main challenges—often interrelated and reinforcing. First, legal institutions may be open to capture by elite interests or may discriminate against certain groups. Second, these institutions are often inaccessible, because they are incompatible with local norms and customs and they are physically or economically inaccessible, or because people lack the knowledge or capacity to navigate the system. Third, elite capture and the inaccessibility of the legal system may mean that policies relating to crime and personal security are inequitable and perpetuate crime-related inequality traps.

Combating elite capture and discrimination

Political and economic elite interests often coincide at the expense of a disempowered majority. When power is in the hands of a narrow elite, the rights of most citizens are unstable. A century of banking in Mexico, outlined in chapter 6, illustrates how deals between the political and economic elite led to the establishment of banking monopolies and laws that maintained a system of rent-sharing between banks and governments.[1] Another striking example of elite capture comes from the transition economies and the rise of oligarchs who manipulated politicians and shaped institutions to get rich.[2] Legal systems that cater to narrow interests also tend to discriminate against other groups through inequitable laws and practices.

Ensuring equality before the law and securing both personal and property rights for a broad section of the community give individuals the incentive and the opportunity to take part in economic and political life. This requires an independent and accountable judiciary and laws and practices that protect citizen's rights in a nondiscriminatory way.

Enhancing judicial independence and accountability. In many countries, a rule of law system—administered by multiple arms of government—constrains political power.[3] In this system, an independent judiciary acts as a safeguard against abuses of state and nonstate power. Because judges are also open to elite capture and corruption, accountability mechanisms are a key aspect of legitimate judicial independence.[4]

In many developing countries, shifts toward an accountable and independent judiciary require a change in culture and institutional practice. Ethiopia established an independent judiciary for the first time in 1995.[5] In Vietnam "telephone justice" was common, with party elites habitually contacting judges to direct decisions.[6] Changing ingrained institutional practices in both countries has been a slow process. Poor conditions of judicial service in many countries can increase corruption.[7] For example, low remuneration for magistrates in Kenya made them open to alternative funding for their services; Kenya removed almost one-third of judicial staff for corruption in 2004.[8]

Promoting judicial independence without establishing accountability mechanisms can further entrench elite interests. Institutional safeguards, transparency, and the existence of a civic constituency are key to both accountability mechanisms and judicial independence. Institutional safeguards include providing for security of tenure and improving conditions of service for judges; rigorous and transparent appointment and disciplinary processes; transparent mechanisms of case allocation and case management; transparent and open hearings; appeal rights and the publication of judicial decisions; and public information about the courts.[9] Many countries have enshrined judicial independence in the constitution or state laws.[10] Bolivia has established open competitions for judgeships and ethical standards for judges. Courts in the Philippines have a performance management system for judicial and nonjudicial personnel.

Public information campaigns can enhance the independence and accountability of the courts, increasing public confidence in and commitment to the system, and enhancing people's capacity to demand better governance and hold those in positions of power

accountable. In Colombia public information centers in major courts disseminate information and help people use the court. In Venezuela information is provided to the public through an Internet-based judicial portal for the Supreme Tribunal.[11]

Strengthening the relationship among civil society, the media, and the courts has also improved public awareness and scrutiny of the judicial system. Bad judges have resigned because of high-pressure media campaigns, such as the recent media scrutiny in the Philippines.[12] The media can also disseminate information, such as the "My Rights" television show in Armenia (box 8.1). Similar shows have been developed in other parts of Eastern Europe. In Georgia, an NGO disseminating information about the courts increased public satisfaction with the courts.

The existence of an independent and accountable judiciary is not enough to protect citizens against abuses of state power. Adequate laws and institutional mechanisms are also needed. In Thailand, for example, separate administrative courts were established for the first time in 2001 to protect citizens against arbitrary uses of state power. The courts aim to ensure that state authorities act in accordance with state laws and regulations. They also aim to enhance citizen participation in public policy formulation and oversight. In the first three years, the courts processed almost

---

BOX 8.1 *Increasing legal literacy and public awareness: "My Rights" on Armenian public television*

Many people in Armenia have no understanding of the legal system or the rights afforded them under the law. And distrust of the courts is widespread. In a recent public awareness campaign, the government funded a television show to provide citizens with examples, advice, and information on their legal rights.

"My Rights" uses mock trials to depict real-life disputes in Armenian courts. The television judge is a deputy minister of justice, and the parties are often those in the real dispute. The topics—such as rental and property disputes, customs issues, and family law matters—are timely and of broad interest. A live studio audience of judges, lawyers, legal officials, and others discusses the trials on air.

The show airs once a week on Armenia's state television channel. After only five or six shows, "My Rights" became the number one show in Armenia. There have been numerous reports of viewers requesting legal documents and decisions from notaries, judges, and other legal officials based on what they learned from the show. And when the power went out in one village a few minutes before "My Rights" was going on the air, the people in the town marched on the mayor's office and accused the local officials of intentionally cutting the power so that people could not watch the show!

Source: Decker and others (2005).

17,000 cases, most concerning corruption or other unlawful acts by public officials. Many of the cases made front-page news in Thailand because of their social impact.

Combating discriminatory norms and practices. Laws that reinforce exclusionary practices in norm-based institutions perpetuate unequal power relations. Some laws may discriminate against particular groups, such as laws affecting indigenous people or the laws in apartheid South Africa. The absence of laws can also reinforce unequal power relations as for domestic violence, often relegated to the nonlegal private realm.

In many countries, antidiscrimination and equal opportunity laws have reduced discriminatory practices. Historical disadvan-

tage may mean, however, that legal equality is not enough. Some countries have passed laws that discriminate in favor of certain groups, creating affirmative action programs on the basis of race, ethnicity, and gender or for people with disabilities. An assessment of two of the most widely implemented affirmative action programs, in India and the United States, suggests mixed impacts (box 8.2).

The mere existence of "equitable laws" for affirmative action does not guarantee their equitable implementation or enforcement. For example, in Peru and Honduras, gender discrimination in judicial decisions and treatment by police and judges discourage women from using the system to resolve disputes.[13] Such disadvantaged groups are more likely to experience the law-and-order side of the law than the protection of their rights (as discussed below under crime and personal security).

Making justice accessible

People's legal rights remain theoretical if the institutions charged with enforcing them are inaccessible. Accessibility depends on how compatible laws are with the norms and understandings that shape people's lives. Legal institutions need to be physically and economically accessible and people need to have the knowledge and capacity to claim their rights.

Addressing the compatibility of state and customary justice systems. Forms of customary or nonstate law operate in a majority of countries.[14] Yet they are often neglected in justice sector reform policies. Engaging with customary systems is an important part of equitable reform strategies for two main reasons. First, customary law is often a fundamental part of a community's identity and belief system; thus, a lack of recognition can be intrinsically discriminatory and serve to exclude communities from the wider state system. Second, a failure to engage with customary systems may leave inequitable and inefficient practices at the local level unchecked.

Where state and nonstate systems have developed in tandem, they often complement each other and reinforce socially accepted codes and rules. But in communi-

---

BOX 8.2 *Affirmative action in India and the United States*

The affirmative action program in India is based primarily on caste and gender and that in the United States primarily on race. Before independence in India, the British government introduced affirmative action to address discrimination against "untouchable" castes (now known as Dalits) and "tribals" (now known as Adivasis). After independence in 1947 the policy of reserving 22.5 percent of seats in education institutions, government jobs and electoral seats was written into the constitution. Since 1991, a further 27 percent quota has been introduced for other low castes (called Other Backward Castes), but with no constitutional guarantee. And since 1993, 33 percent of the seats in local governments have been reserved for women, Dalits, and Adivasis (Deshpande 2005).

In the United States, slavery was pervasive for more than two centuries, and not until 1866 were blacks granted citizenship rights. The system that replaced slavery was only marginally better, with several features similar to the Indian caste system: segregation, denial of education, restrictions to low-paid, menial jobs, social and economic discrimination, negative stereotyping, and violence. The Civil Rights Act of 1964 and subsequent legislation, Supreme Court rulings, and executive orders in the 1970s introduced affirmative action into the political, judicial, administrative, and economic spheres of American society. Starting with the label "equal opportunity," selection procedures incorporate compensatory correction to ensure adequate representation of

minorities in education and employment (Deshpande 2005).

The programs in both countries have become centerpieces of political battles over race and caste. Critics argue that they tend to benefit the upper echelon of minority groups, and they are difficult to end. In India, the programs are said to apply to subcastes that have not traditionally faced discrimination (Sowell 2004). They may also reinforce negative stereotypes by placing minorities in positions they are not qualified for (Coate and Loury 1993). Despite these weaknesses, India's program has provided formal sector employment and higher education for many Dalit and Adivasi families, freeing them from subservient roles. With the reservations in local government, elected women leaders make decisions in line with women's needs (Chattopadhyay and Duflo 2004). Low-caste representatives in state assemblies increase the allocation of quota-based jobs to low-caste constituents (Pande 2003). And Dalit representatives in village government improve the targeting of benefits to Dalits (Besley and others 2004).

In the United States, disparities between blacks and whites continue to be significant on all economic indicators, and there is evidence of discriminatory gaps in earnings. But affirmative action in jobs has increased black employment and enrollment in higher education (Holzer and Neumark 2000, Bowen and Bok 1998). But the U.S. program's quasi-voluntary element means that litigation can dilute the program, and black representation in government bodies continues to be very low.

ties where the state systems lack legitimacy and political reach, customary systems often act independently from the state legal system, which may be rejected, ignored, or not understood. Real difficulties arise when local customary systems are at odds with the rights and responsibilities articulated in state law.

In many developing countries, customary systems are the dominant form of regulation and dispute resolution. In Sierra Leone, about 85 percent of the population fell under customary law as of 2003.[15] Customary tenure, discussed below, affects 90 percent of land transactions in Mozambique and Ghana.[16] Customary justice depends on local traditions, as well as the political history of a country or region. Ethiopia officially recognizes more than 100 distinct "nations or peoples" and more than 75 languages.

Customary systems can be incompatible with economic, social, and civil rights. Many forms of customary law are seen to discriminate against marginal groups. In much of Sub-Saharan Africa, for example, customary systems systematically deny women's rights to land, assets, or opportunities.[17] Customary practices are also seen as archaic and rigid—not amenable to modernization, efficient market relations, or broader development goals. They are often seen as overly localized and complex, making more generalized reform initiatives difficult. They can lack legitimacy at the local level. For example, many systems in Sub-Saharan Africa have been substantially distorted by colonial rule, which often used local chiefs to maintain control and established more authoritarian and ethnic-based structures than previously existed.[18]

However, it is wrong to presume that all customary law discriminates against marginalized groups—or that western law does not. For example, in the AmaHlubi community of KwaZulu Natal Province in South Africa, women and men are considered equal, with both entitled to own property.[19] Furthermore, there are often good reasons for people to choose to use customary systems. The state systems may lack legitimacy or be seen as mechanisms of control used by oppressive regimes. Or the state systems may

lack capacity, be inaccessible, or dramatically increase transaction costs.[20] In rural Tanzania, a perception that state institutions can not supply law and order has led to the emergence of "new" forms of organized village defense groups called *sungusungu.* While technically illegal, the *sungusungu* are often informally supported by the state, given their success in reducing crime.[21]

Ignoring or trying to stamp out customary practices can also have serious negative implications. Top-down reform can undermine informal institutions without providing viable alternatives, and the vacuum can lead to power grabbing, lawlessness, or even violent conflict. When neither formal nor informal mechanisms are functioning, human rights abuses and serious conflict are more likely. For example, a study in rural Columbia found the incidence of vigilantism, "mob justice," or lynching to be five and a half times greater in communities in which informal mechanisms are no longer functioning effectively and the state presence remains limited.[22]

A failure to engage with customary systems may mean that discriminatory practices go unchallenged. While state law officially protects women's rights in many countries, local norms and power structures continue to make it almost impossible for women to claim these rights.

Considered attention to customary systems in broader institutional reform is fairly new. But many governments, such as South Africa, have begun working toward integrating customary institutions into wider state frameworks (box 8.3).[23] Many countries have attempted to integrate customary land systems into formal land law systems (box 8.7). Local NGOs and community groups have also helped empower marginal groups to challenge discriminatory norms at the local level.

Establishing adequate and open legal institutions. Even when formal systems do exist, they often lack adequate infrastructure or are so institutionally weak that citizens cannot claim their rights. Formal institutions may exist only in large cities, and even then excessive delays, unfair procedures, or unreasonable costs may leave

---

BOX 8.3 *State frameworks and customary institutions in South Africa*

The coexistence of various official state laws in South Africa began as early as the 1830s when chiefs in Cape Colony were granted authority to enforce indigenous law (subject to review by a colonial official).[24] At the end of the apartheid era there were approximately 800 officially recognized traditional communities and traditional leaders, 12,000 headmen, and 12 kings.

Since 1994, South Africa has worked toward bringing traditional systems into the state framework. Traditional institutions and laws are all officially recognized in the 1996 constitution. After a long political process, the national Traditional Leadership and Governance Framework Act was promulgated in 2004, setting out the roles and responsibilities of different levels of traditional leaders and institutions, and their relationships to the different levels of government.

Many celebrated the constitutional and administrative recognition of customary law, but there clearly are difficulties. Customary practices have been criticized as incompatible with rights in the constitution and the new South African Bill of Rights.[25] Of 800 traditional leaders recognized by the state in South Africa, only one is female. In an attempt to deal with this, the state issued a regulation in early 2005 that female participation must be at 30 percent by the end of the year, but there is no consensus on how this might be achieved. Recognizing the difficult task of effectively integrating the different systems, the South African model aims at "progressive alignment" with the constitution.

Source: Adapted from Chirayath and others (2005).

BOX 8.4 *The impact of legal aid in Ecuador*

As in much of the rest of the world, Ecuador's poor face numerous barriers in using the legal system. Women considering claims against their former spouses may face an added obstacle: physical violence.

As part of a larger judicial reform effort, three local NGOs—Centro Ecuatoriano para la Promoción y Acción de la Mujer, Corporación Mujer a Mujer, and Fundación María Guare—provide legal information and representation as well as psychological counseling and referrals to shelters. A survey in 2002 revealed that women's use of legal aid clinics reduced the probability of severe physical violence after separation by 17 percent. Legal aid clients also

attained better legal and economic results than nonclients, raising their chances of obtaining a child-support award by 20 percent and their chances of receiving a child-support payment by 10 percent.

Receiving assistance from the legal aid clinics also had intergenerational impacts. Child-support payments increased the probability of the child attending school (by 4.8 percent) as did the lower incidence of violence. Anecdotal evidence also suggests that the payments, a small but important source of family income, were used to pay for food.

Source: World Bank (2003g).

---

them inaccessible to much of the community.[26] Institutions can also be inaccessible if people do not know their rights and cannot navigate the systems charged with protecting them.

A large array of information campaigns has informed citizens about their rights (discussed above). But even if people know their rights, they may have limited capacity to navigate the system. Access to legal services is often restricted or costly. In Honduras, legal fees to obtain a monthly alimony of 100 lempiras (US$5.30) in a

child-support case could amount to as much as 2,000 lempiras (US$106.00), or almost two years of alimony. Adding to the costs are requirements that parties be represented by lawyers. For example, most Latin American countries do not permit self-representation, effectively denying access based on economic status. Legal aid can increase people's access to basic legal services and the courts (box 8.4). So can community mediation centers, lay judges, and mobile courts. The mobile courts introduced in remote areas of Brazil in 1999 have been replicated in the Philippines and Mexico. In Guatemala, 24 mediation centers have been created, employing mediators fluent in Spanish and local Mayan languages.[27]

In some situations, social movements provide the support for people to use the courts and claim their formal rights, as with the landless peasant movements in Brazil and Mexico. In Argentina, too, unemployed factory workers have occupied closed factory sites and pursued their rights through the courts and the legislative process. In other cases, civil society organizations have assisted groups in claiming their rights—as in the "right to health" cases discussed in chapter 10.

Civil unrest and conflict may further weaken legal institutions. In Sierra Leone, a decade of civil war left the justice system in shambles: courthouses were destroyed, and judges, lawyers, and police officers were killed or forced to flee. During the conflict in Liberia, more than three-quarters of the population left their homes.[28] In Bosnia, 2.3 million people—more than half the country's population—fled their homes during and immediately after the war. To prevent the return of minorities, many property records were destroyed or tampered with.

Reestablishing legitimate legal institutions is crucial to restoring such people's personal and property rights and enhancing confidence in newly established governance structures. In postwar Bosnia, the Dayton Agreement established the Commission for Real Property Claims of Displaced Persons and Refugees, which collected claims for 318,780 properties. As of June 2003, it had issued about 290,000 final decisions on property titles.[29]

Improving crime and personal security policies—breaking crime-related inequality traps

The cycle of inequality, crime, victimization, and discrimination exemplifies the processes by which inequality traps, outlined in chapter 2, are perpetuated. Marginal groups are not only more likely to move into criminal behavior, they are also more likely to be victims of crime. Furthermore, discriminatory practices in the justice sector mean that marginal groups are more likely to experience the law-and-order side of the legal system— black men in the United States are incarcerated on drug charges at a rate 13.4 times that of white men, bearing little relation to differences in offenses[30]—and are less likely to have access to institutions charged with protecting them. At the same time, given their role in shaping these processes, legal institutions are also places for change—that is, vehicles for challenging inequality traps.

Breaking the cycle of inequality, crime, and violence. Traditional approaches to reducing crime and violence based on increasing mechanisms of control and harsher sanctions have failed to reduce crime. By contrast, promoting protective strategies and minimizing the risk of crime have more success at lower cost.[31]

To target the many risk factors of increased crime, crime prevention programs often require support from the judicial services, social services, health, education, media, police, local government, civil society organizations, and the private sector (box 8.5). Local governments and police services often coordinate such programs.[32]

Many more effective interventions target children and adolescents, who are seen as particularly at risk of falling into criminal behavior.[33] Preventative interventions include family support and parenting skills programs, early childhood development programs, special needs programs, after-school care, antibullying programs, life skills and cultural programs, and community participation programs.[34]

School-based interventions have targeted youth crime and have kept young people in schools in many countries.[35] *Tilsa Thuto* is a school crime prevention program imple-

***

BOX 8.5 *Bogota, Colombia: civic culture program*

Unlike most Colombian cities, Bogota—a city previously considered unsafe and violent—has seen a huge reduction in crime since the early 1990s and a substantial increase in citizen perception of safety.

The city's administration targeted civic culture and education, urban planning and safety, and the regeneration of public spaces. Individual and community behavior were changed by establishing a citizen disarmament program; restricting alcohol consumption and use of fireworks; increasing the number of social service centers; enhancing awareness through media campaigns and educational programs; preventing domestic violence and child abuse; strengthening the capacity of the police and the judiciary to deal with crime, violence, and victimization;

enhancing neighborhood watch programs; and revitalizing urban public spaces. Employment and educational programs were introduced to support populations most at risk.

No longer one of the most dangerous cities in the western hemisphere, Bogota has seen remarkable results. The homicide rate fell from 80 per 100,000 inhabitants in 1993 to 22 in 2004, with homicides related to intoxication falling dramatically. By 2001, 6,500 weapons had been turned in and gun confiscations fell from 6,000 in 1995 to 1,600 in 2003. Arrests for homicide, assault, and car theft rose by 500 percent between 1994 and 2003 (with no increase in police personnel).

Sources: Llorente and Rivas (2005), World Bank (2003a).

***

mented in 42 schools in Soweto, South Africa, in 2000, in areas known for high levels of crime, unemployment, and poverty.[36] The program—established in partnership with the department of education, community organizations, and local police—creates safer schools through the active participation of students, teachers, parents, school administrators, and the local community in different training modules. Both teacher and student attendance at school increased by some 70 percent, acts of violence and aggression fell by 67 percent, and the pass rate increased by an average of 78 percent.

Alternative ways of dealing with young offenders have also been effective in breaking the cycle of crime. Interventions include diversion programs, restorative justice, alternative sentencing, and reintegration projects. Diversion programs aim to move young offenders into welfare-based programs, as with attempts in Africa to keep street children out of prison. Restorative justice programs, such as community conferencing, mediate between offenders and those affected by the crime, helping to reintegrate young offenders into their communities. Noncustodial sentencing, such as community service orders, is used in different parts of Africa today to promote the reintegration and rehabilitation of offenders.[37]

Increasing personal safety. Appropriate and accessible police and support services for all are crucial. Violence against women, a huge problem in many parts of the world, is exacerbated by underreporting, inadequate support systems for victims, discriminatory practices within justice sector institutions, and the lack of adequate sanctions for perpetrators. Many governments have attempted to address the problem by introducing more severe sentences for perpetrators, establishing remedial programs for offenders, and running gender-sensitive training programs for police and the judiciary.

More recently, some countries, including Argentina, Brazil, Colombia, Peru, and Uruguay, have set up women's police stations. Other countries have set up police cells for women in regular police stations. These services have shown mixed results.[38] Women's police stations have increased reporting of abuse and the likelihood that women will receive medical and social services. But critics argue that services encourage regular police to abdicate responsibility for crimes against women and that women officers have not necessarily demonstrated better attitudes toward victims of violence. Where stations are working fairly well, their efforts are often undermined by other parts of the justice system, as prosecution rates remain unchanged.

The notion that the physical environment can increase personal safety has been an integral part of many recent crime prevention strategies,[39] and it has been applied to city-planning, public transport systems, parks and recreational spaces, low-income housing, and downtown areas where people feel most vulnerable to violence and crime.[40]

Toward greater equity in access to land

Land is a key asset for poor people. Owning it provides a means of livelihood to many, facilitates access to credit markets, has an insurance value, determines influence in local politics, permits participation in social networks, and influences intrahousehold dynamics. That is why inequality in the ownership of land has such far-reaching consequences for the distribution of well-being and the organization of society for generations to come. Yet landownership in many countries is highly unequal, substantially more so than income or consumption.

Building on chapters 5 and 6, we argue here that there are strong equity and efficiency reasons for addressing inequalities in land distribution—both rural and urban—and then discuss the experience with land reform and options for broadening access to land: providing security of tenure, improving the functioning of land markets, and implementing cost-effective land redistribution.

Equity and efficiency reasons to address inequalities in land distribution

Inequalities in landownership in dozens of countries can be traced to interventions over the past 500 years to establish and support large farms at the expense of indigenous peoples and the local peasantry. This historical discrimination against certain groups—or more generally a lack of legitimacy for the prevailing pattern of landownership—offers a rationale for equity-enhancing reforms. Additional motivation comes from the fact that the landless are among the poorest in developing countries.[41]

Access to land can give the poor more voice in the political arena and can lead to higher investments in children's education, arresting the intergenerational transmission of poverty. Galasso and Ravallion (2005), in their study of the Food for Education program in Bangladesh, find that villages with more unequal distribution of land were worse at targeting the poor. This is consistent with the view that land inequality is associated with less power for the poor in village decision making. Land inequality has also been found to impair the ability of communities to engage in socially optimal collective action, resulting in the underprovisioning of public goods. It also contributes to social tensions that can lead to considerable upheaval, as in Southern Africa.[42]

Inequalities in landownership can weigh particularly heavily on women. Land rights (and control of other assets) often reside with the head of household, which has implications for intrafamily bargaining power and control of resources. Women with secure land rights (including inheritance on the death of a husband) are more likely to engage in independent economic activity, a result that has positive economic and equity implications for the household. Inheritance rights that disadvantage women are of particular concern in Africa, where they are often based on customary institutions that conflict with constitutional norms and international conventions on women's rights. In fact, insecure inheritance rights pose an additional burden on widows who lose their husbands, often through HIV/AIDS.[43]

There are strong efficiency reasons to address inequalities in land distribution. Pervasive imperfections in land and financial markets in developing countries reduce investment in land and keep countries from efficient land allocations (chapter 5). These effects—together with lower human capital investment, reduced social cohesion, and distorted political power—are consistent with a positive association between more unequal land distribution and lower GDP growth (figure 8.1).[44]

Experience with land reform

The discussion here implies that redistributing land could enhance equity and efficiency. This is likely to be true, but there are significant hurdles in practice. For instance, the specter of land redistribution can also worsen efficiency, because farmers are reluctant to invest in land that they might lose. Or political imperatives can override sound program design. Successful land reforms—such as in Japan, the Republic of Korea, and Taiwan, China—are rare and often associated with exceptional events, such as war or political upheaval. Indeed, the history of land reforms is littered with partial successes and failures.

In India, abolishing the land rights of rent-collecting intermediaries[45] has been highly successful, whereas the implementation of landownership ceilings and laws to protect tenants was, with few exceptions, half-hearted. The absence of political leadership has been identified as the "prime reason for the poor implementation of land reforms in India."[46] Still, where tenant protection was implemented seriously—primarily in West Bengal—it helped improve productivity.[47] But restrictions on subleasing land by beneficiaries (or their children) tend to reduce the scope for productivity-enhancing land trans-

Figure 8.1 Unequal initial land distributions go together with slower economic growth

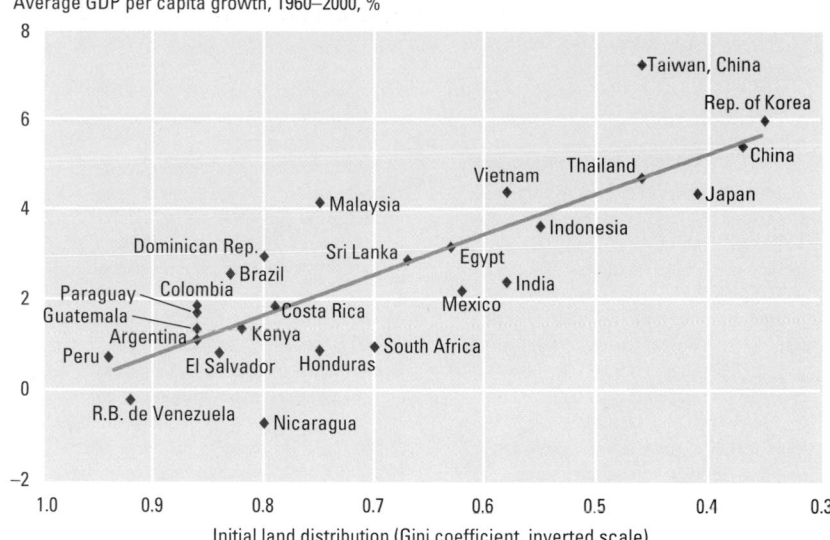

Average GDP per capita growth, 1960–2000, %

Source: World Bank (2003i).

Note: Land distribution is measured using the Gini coefficient.

fers. And the fact that both tenants and landlords have rights to the same plot of land severely undermines investment incentives.[48]

In Latin America, where the potential for land reform should have been highest given the high inequality of landownership, reforms have generally been "incomplete." Beneficiaries have often lacked the tools to become competitive and, as a result, the impact on poverty has been disappointing.[49] In Kenya and Zimbabwe, postindependence reforms were quite effective but short lived for political reasons.[50] In South Africa, the government's land redistribution program in the late 1990s fell way short of its targets but recently gathered steam (box 8.6). Clearly, both the politics of land reform and its implementation are complex.

Why the rather disappointing results from attempts at land reform? First, given that the motivation for land reform is often to address political grievances, efficiency and poverty reduction tend to be secondary. Guided by short-term political objectives, bureaucrats often targeted high-productivity areas rather than high-potential areas, resulting in costly land acquisition and limited scope for sustained productivity impacts. Central administration of the programs also often meant that a large portion of land reform budgets was spent on the

---

BOX 8.6 *Land reform in South Africa: picking up steam*

To redress apartheid-era asset inequality, South Africa embarked on land reform in 1994 with a program that rested on redistribution, restitution, and tenure. Targets for redistribution were ambitious: the government aimed to transfer 24 million hectares of agricultural land (30 percent of the total) to about 3 million people between 1994 and 1999. Under the program, self-selected groups use grants to purchase land from willing sellers and to invest in the land's development. But by February 2005, only about 3.5 million hectares had been redistributed to 168,000 households. Restitution proceeded at a snail's pace—only 41 of 79,000 claims were settled between 1995 and 1999. And progress on tenure in the former "homelands" was equally slow.

After this sluggish start, some key changes accelerated the restitution and redistribution programs. The Restitution Act was amended to allow for negotiated settlements, speeding the process considerably; previously all claims had to be settled in court. By March 2005, more than 58,000 claims were settled, and all claims are scheduled to be resolved by March 2008.

The redistribution program was improved in 2001, making it more flexible and decentralized. The grants for land purchase and farm development now follow a sliding scale, depending on the contribution by the beneficiaries, and can be obtained by individuals as well as groups. Approval authority is now delegated from the minister to the provincial directors of land affairs. As a result, redistribution has significantly increased. For the first time since 1994, land delivery is now constrained only by the budget for it.

But some big challenges remain. Pressure is growing from civil society on government to meet the revised target of redistributing 30 percent of agricultural land by 2014. Restitution settlements can be complex when rural claims target highly productive, capital-intensive farms and the claimants refuse, as is their right, to accept financial compensation, instead of the physical restoration of the claimed land. The agricultural impact of the redistribution scheme has been stunted by an inappropriate emphasis on collective farming and a lack of beneficiary power in decision making. The land market continues to be biased against family farming through costly restrictions on subdividing agricultural land and a regressive land tax dating from 1939. A new land tax based on the value of unimproved agricultural land could provide incentives for large farms to sell unused or underused parcels. New legislation that transfers communal lands from state to community ownership is now in place, but it still needs to be implemented.

Sources: World Bank (2003i), van den Brink, de Klerk, and Binswanger (1996).

---

wages and salaries of civil servants rather than used to benefit the poor. The prospect of gaining access to valuable real estate, instead of having to put in sweat equity to develop a piece of land, undermined the self-targeting properties of reform programs, often politicizing beneficiary selection.

Second, the relationship between farm size and productivity depends on the type of crop, quality of land, degree of mechanization, and such associated factors as marketing and credit. For most crops, under normal availability of mechanical services, production is neutral to farm size. But when management requirements are substantial (labor-intensive crops, erratic weather conditions, frequent pest incidence) family farms—as opposed to larger, wage-labor farms—can be more efficient because of advantages in supervising labor. By contrast, large farms often have better access to input and output markets, financing, and technical

assistance. Such advantages can be countered if small farmers coordinate their efforts through cooperatives.[51] If policymakers do not properly account for all these conditions in land reform schemes, efficiency can suffer.

Third, many traditional land reform efforts failed to provide beneficiaries with secure long-term rights backed by a well-functioning and equitable legal system. Affordable channels to adjudicate land access and ownership claims must be open to everyone. Without such channels, disadvantaged groups cannot take full advantage of tenure security, land market, and distributive reforms. Even with full property rights, underdeveloped credit and insurance markets limit the use of land for collateral.

Fourth, the full productivity benefits of land reform cannot be realized without complementary inputs and training; putting land in the hands of inexperienced farmers without the needed support often led to high rates of desertion.[52] More generally, a broader rural development strategy is required to complement land reform because rural households get their livelihoods from several different sources. This has implications for the design of land reform (for example, determining viable farm size) and highlights the importance of investments that can facilitate off-farm employment, such as education.

Broadening access by improving the security of tenure

The benefits of secure tenure for rural households are well known: higher productivity, greater access to credit, higher propensity to invest in physical assets (figure 8.2) and the education of children, and time and effort saved in securing land rights.[53] Further benefits arise from removing the discretionary power of bureaucrats to decide on the allocation of land (improved local governance was mentioned as a benefit of property rights reforms introduced after 1992 in Mexico).[54]

These benefits are observed also in urban contexts. Capitalizing on a natural experiment that allocated land titles to some squatters but not others in a poor suburban area of Buenos Aires, Galiani and Schargrodsky (2004) found significant effects of titling on housing investment, household size, and school achievement. The quality of houses in titled parcels was higher. Titled households had fewer members (even though their houses were larger), and they seemed to invest more in their children's education. In India, unclear land titles combined with unreliable courts were found to limit the supply of land and discourage investments. Southern states tend to have higher tenure security, which increases the share of modern retailers. Evidence from a massive urban squatter titling program in Peru suggests that titling resulted in more work done outside the home and substitution of adult for child labor.[55]

Formal land titling is one way to provide for secure tenure, but titling takes time and can be expensive. Thailand, the first country with a national program, completed the program this year, 20 years after its inception. One solution is to allow alternatives to conventional private land titles, especially in urban areas.[56] In Trinidad and Tobago, a 1998 law authorized three incremental levels of statutory security, each requiring additional documentation and commitment from the settler and the government. In one year, an estimated 80 percent of informal settlers on state land had applied for the lowest level.[57] Because many of these instruments do not require prior physical planning, infrastructure servicing, and surveying of settlements, they can offer widespread coverage at lower costs. The limitations on transfer associated with many of these instruments also check the tendency of some informal dwellers to capitalize land subsidies immediately through land sales.

Several countries have taken steps to require joint titling of land in the names of husband and wife, bolstering women's effective right to land, particularly during their husbands' absences. Vietnam has targets for the joint titling of land as part of the Vietnam Development Goals, incorporated in its Poverty Reduction Strategy. Attention to women's land rights is particularly important when women are the main cultivators, when out-migration is high, when control of productive activities is differentiated by gender, or when high levels of adult

Figure 8.2 Title to land increases investment and access to credit

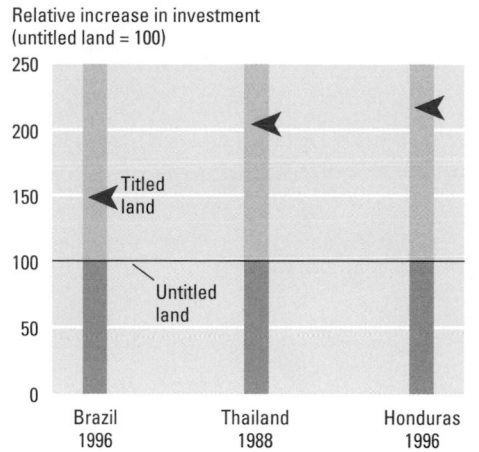

Source: Feder (2002).

mortality and unclear regulation could undermine a woman's livelihoods in case of her husband's death.[58]

Despite potentially large benefits from titling, there are challenges in urban and rural contexts. In urban areas, access to credit may not increase if banks are unwilling to accept titled shanties in marginal areas as collateral. And where squatters' land is valuable, titling programs can be subverted by powerful interests who use the opportunity to relocate squatters to marginal areas—for example, in Phnom Penh, Cambodia. This does not reflect a problem with titling per se, but suggests that when the urban poor lack voice and governance is weak, titling programs can backfire.[59] One way to protect squatters from predatory urban developers would be to grant them group land rights as a first step toward individual titles.[60]

Some studies indicate that formal land titles in several African countries did not bring the expected benefits in higher incomes and investment. This may reflect weaknesses in the institutions responsible for registration and recordkeeping and for the adjudication of rights and resolution of conflicts. In some cases, it appears that indigenous tenure was already sufficiently secure.[61] It may thus be more appropriate and more cost-effective to strengthen the security of tenure through institutions that combine legality with social legitimacy. This

BOX 8.7 *Clarifying how customary rights fit with formal systems*

Customary land tenure is created, maintained, and protected by norm-based customary systems at the local level. Rights to land, whether communal or individual, are generally based on family lineage or membership in a particular cultural grouping. Exchanges through sales or rentals are limited to members of the community. Customary systems are dominant in most African countries and in indigenous areas of many Latin American and Asian countries. Having evolved over long periods in response to local conditions, they are often quite flexible. Problems arise when transfers to outsiders become widespread or internal land dispute resolution mechanisms become inadequate.

There have been many efforts to make the transition from collective or customary systems to more individual landholdings. But the transition, if not properly managed, can end in disaster, such as in Kenya. Because the elimination of lineage rights and the legalization of land sales were not accepted by rural populations, conflicts over land, sometimes violent, ensued between those claiming land under customary norms and those seeking to enforce the new rules.

Botswana has had more success. Since 1970, the authorities have gradually strengthened individual rights, starting with the right to exclude other people's animals and to fence arable lands. Common law residential leases for commercially valuable land have been introduced, as have laws allowing the allocation of land to all adult citizens, whether male or female, married or single (Adams 2000 and Toulmin and Quan 2000 in World Bank 2003i). South Africa is just starting down the road to communal land reform, having recently passed legislation that will transfer state-owned land to communities and create democratic, transparent, and secure property rights regimes in these areas.

Mexico made a hybrid transition from collective land—known as the *ejido* sector—toward more individual landholdings. *Ejidos* are rural communities modeled after a mixture of soviet-style collectives and precolonial indigenous social structures. Reforms in 1992 strengthened the self-governance of *ejidos,* allowing them to choose a property rights regime. Each *ejido* could choose whether land would be held under communal or individual ownership and issue property rights certificates accordingly. By 2001 the program had issued property certificates to more than 3 million households and given secure land rights to more than 1 million households that previously had no formal recognition of occupancy rights (World Bank 2001d).

Clarifying how customary rights—in rural and urban areas—relate to the formal system of property rights protected through modern law is important for millions of people. It is also important for expanding the scope for outside investment, particularly in urban areas. Experience with managing the intersection between the two systems suggests the importance of effective dispute resolution mechanisms and a transparent and well-defined trajectory for transition, with the extension of secure landownership rights to an entire group as an effective and low-cost first step (World Bank 2003i).

approach is particularly pertinent where customary tenure practices predominate. Recognizing customary rights and institutions in the law helps protect large populations that are governed by them and builds a bridge to the formal system (box 8.7). Clearly, the complexities of engaging with customary justice systems outlined earlier in the chapter need to be considered—and when formalizing customary rights, care should be taken not to simply codify existing inequities, particularly for women.

Broadening access by improving the functioning of land markets. Land markets, both in sales and rentals, can in theory do much to equalize land access. In practice, however, land sales/purchases are generally not an avenue to expand access by the poor and may actually reduce it. High transaction costs, undeveloped credit markets, and high prices for land, reflecting its collateral value and any government subsidies to crops, lead to thin sales markets that keep poor farmers out altogether. This suggests that land sales markets will not contribute to greater equity in landholdings, especially in settings characterized by long-standing discrimination against specific groups, unless the government relieves the savings constraints of the poor through subsidies (as we will see in the next section).[62]

Distress sales of land by the poor can occur in risky environments where small landowners do not have access to insurance. Thus, they are unable to smooth consumption through mechanisms other than land sales, such as safety nets.[63] In a comparison of land transactions in Indian and Bangladeshi villages during 1960–80, Cain (1981) found that poor farmers who had access to safety net programs used the land market to augment their landholdings and undertook productivity-enhancing investment. Distress sales to obtain food and medicine predominated when safety nets were absent.

While government interventions to impose restrictions on the transferability of land can undermine investment incentives and depress off-farm activity, they can play a role, especially during periods of transition. In many Commonwealth of Independent States (CIS) countries the unrestricted transferability of land led to a concentration of landholdings in the hands of a small number of farm bosses, as poorer rural households were enticed to sell their land in conditions of uncertainty and incomplete markets and information.[64] Initially limiting the transferability of land to lease transactions rather than outright sales would have been better.

A gradual transition may be preferable in cases in which an equitable distribution of land has been the primary instrument of social protection, as in China and Vietnam. Governments in both countries rightly perceive the tensions in active land sales markets, which could lead to efficiency-enhancing consolidation but also run the risk of increasing the number of landless poor. In China, the government is considering moving on several fronts, including developing safety nets and rural finance and eliminating residency-based restrictions (*hukou*) on labor mobility.

While land sales markets have ambiguous impacts on equity, the equity case for broadening access to land rentals appears more clear-cut. When farmers do not have access to credit that would enable them to purchase land outright, rental markets are an important avenue for enhancing productivity and equity by facilitating low-cost transfers of land to more productive producers (chapter 5). Rental markets also enable landholders with low agricultural skills (or no desire to farm) to seek employment in the nonfarm sector while still earning a return on their land.[65] Evidence from Sudan suggests that land rental markets do transfer land to smaller producers. And in Colombia, rental markets have been more effective than government-sponsored land reforms in bringing land to productive and poor producers.[66]

If land rental markets have so much potential to improve equity and efficiency, why is there such a large variation in the incidence of rentals across countries? One reason is a lack of tenure security—or trust that the security will last. Without it, landlords are unwilling to rent out their land for fear that they will not be able to reclaim it. Other reasons include current or past government interventions to restrict tenancy, the availability of reliable conflict resolution mechanisms, and imperfections in information.[67] While concern about exploitation in sharecropping arrangements may be justified,[68] tenant protection and rent ceilings can backfire. Such restrictions on land rentals often push transactions into informality or lock poor farmers into less efficient and less equitable wage-labor arrangements. Estimates indicate that new tenancy legislation in India was associated with the eviction of more than 100 million tenants, causing the rural poor to lose access to about 30 percent of the total operated area.[69] Interventions to enhance the bargaining power of the poor—including better access to financial

markets, off-farm employment opportunities, and equitable contract enforcement mechanisms—are likely to be preferable.

Well-functioning rental markets can be a rung in the ownership ladder, but they probably are not in circumstances of extreme inequality in landownership and power. In these instances, options for directly redistributive policies need to be exploited.

Options for cost-effective land redistribution to broaden access

Improving tenure security and promoting land rental markets are good for both equity and efficiency. Analysis and experience indicate that land redistribution is not nearly as straightforward. It can be costly in program resources and reduced productivity, and it can be an instrument of political patronage. Substantial personnel and financial resources are necessary to assess and purchase (or expropriate) land, select beneficiaries, and supply training and credit.

When does land redistribution make sense? In some countries, redistribution could be a necessary political step to address historical inequities and stave off violence. In others, it could simply be a tool to shift underused land to more productive uses while enhancing equity. In countries where state landownership is high, land redistribution could involve limited budgetary costs if bundled into a one-time transfer of state land to private ownership. Conversely, in countries with strong traditions of tenure security, just the threat of redistribution could undermine investment.

The feasibility of land redistribution also depends on the instrument. Expropriation is likely to be the most disruptive. Divesting state lands and recuperating illegal settlements may be two cost-effective alternatives. For example, the mayor of Brasilia (Brazil) identified lands with uncertain titles and negotiated the surrender of part of those lands. In exchange, official titles were granted to the remaining areas. Expropriating with compensation and assisting land purchases and rentals—for example, through community-driven land reform—are also feasible alternatives. Subsidizing land purchases can be costly, however, because land is often overpriced relative to its income generation potential from productive use (reflecting its speculative, insurance, and status value). Also, subsidies are difficult to justify if the current pattern of landownership is not considered legitimate.[70]

Market- or community-driven land reforms are a potential option. The reforms tend to be decentralized and transparent, allowing community members to obtain resources for land access. They can be flexible, allowing for land rental or purchase according to the willing-buyer-willing-seller principle. Community-driven land reforms often give beneficiaries full property rights and involve coordination between local government and NGOs to provide access to training, technology, and credit. A community-driven approach has been tried in several countries, including Brazil, Columbia, Guatemala, Honduras, India, Malawi, and South Africa. But the programs are relatively new, so rigorous impact evaluations are not yet available.

A land tax, possibly combined with an output tax, can be an important complement. It can generate revenues to purchase land to redistribute or encourage redistribution by disproportionately taxing large landholders or owners of unused or underused land, both rural and urban (box 8.8).

Regardless of the instrument, common lessons can be drawn from previous attempts at land redistribution.

- *Complementary investments—training and credit.* Evidence from Latin America[71] and Africa indicates that simply redistributing land does little. Beneficiaries must be provided with a package of assistance to ensure self-sufficiency and maximize productivity. The right package will vary by country but could include training and credit. Technical assistance, such as help elaborating farm plans and crop budgets or instruction on new technologies, can be a success factor for subsistence farmers and those who lack commercial farming expertise. Credit can allow beneficiaries to make productivity-enhancing investments, for example in irrigation, fencing, tools, or draft animals.

- *Beneficiary selection and targeting.* When beneficiary selection is politicized, redistributed land will not always go to the most needy and capable farmers. The solution is to have transparent rules that allow communities to understand exactly how and why each beneficiary was chosen. Self-targeting—where potential beneficiaries seek out land for sale at low cost and then apply for grants and/or loans—can also be effective.

- *Tenure security.* Those who gain access to redistributed land should be given clear ownership rights. In some instances, it may be enough to have less than full ownership (such as a certificate of control or long-term lease) to reduce uncertainty, encourage investment, and promote the benefits discussed above.

Providing infrastructure equitably

Infrastructure in most developing countries is characterized by low and unequal provision—about 2 people of every 10 in the developing world were without access to safe water in 2000, 5 of 10 lived without adequate sanitation, and 9 of 10 lived without their wastewater being treated[72]—with many families suffering from inadequate access especially in rural areas.

Economic opportunities are strongly shaped by access to infrastructure. Much infrastructure is traditionally government provided and so is driven by the political process. Financing constraints and technical design challenges are very real but perhaps easier to overcome. When more equal voice

---

BOX 8.8 *Land and output tax combinations*

Taxes on land can be an effective, nondistortionary tool for collecting local revenue and facilitating land redistribution. They can also encourage productive land usage by taxing underused land at higher rates. This can be attractive when large unproductive plots of land (often held for speculative reasons) create artificially high land prices and limit land access for poor farmers. But administering a tax on land requires data on the size, value, ownership status, productive capacity, and output of each plot. Because it is hard for the government to measure the actual degree of land use, especially for large landholders, there is a strong incentive for tax evasion.

One way to limit evasion by large landholders is to use a mix of land taxes and a value-added tax (VAT). A VAT can have much lower rates of evasion and facilitate accurate reporting of cultivation levels. Knowledge of true cultivation levels would then limit the scope for overreporting the degree of land use to evade higher tax rates for underused land. In the absence of insurance markets, a mix of VAT and land taxes can also reduce the risk facing smallholders because tax burdens would be correlated with output fluctuations.

Sources: Assunção and Moreira (2001), World Bank (2003i).

or the political interests of the governing regime make for more broadly accountable policies, infrastructure is provided in ways that are supportive of the economic interests of poorer groups—for example, in East Asia's intensification of irrigation and transport (see focus 4 on Indonesia). In more unequal societies, those without influence receive less and lower-quality access to public services—this often means the poor. This inequitable access also applies to remote regions and excluded groups, and sometimes it has a gender dimension. Even worse, some infrastructure services (utilities especially) often become instruments of patronage and riddled with problems of inefficient provision and corrupt practices.

As in the case for land, more equal access to infrastructure would be good for equity and will often be good for growth. This requires addressing difficult financing issues, constraints that limit the poor's ability to access infrastructure, and major accountability issues through institutional designs that support more equitable response to needs.

More equitable access to infrastructure is good for growth and equity

There is solid evidence that infrastructure investments broaden opportunities for people and communities by integrating them into regional and national systems of production and commerce, and by improving their access to public services. Location strongly influences household market participation in Vietnam. And households with the same characteristics and endowments yield different returns in different geographic settings in parts of rural China.[73] Leipziger and others (2003), based on a sample of 73 countries, find that a 10 percent improvement in a country's infrastructure index is associated with a 5 percent reduction in child mortality, a 3.5 percent reduction in infant mortality, and a 7.8 percent reduction in maternal mortality, controlling for incomes and the availability of health services. Microevidence from rural India lends support to these cross-country findings: the prevalence and duration of diarrhea among children under five are significantly lower for families with piped water.[74]

Investments in basic water and energy infrastructure can improve gender equity. Around the world, the burden of gathering and transporting fuelwood and water traditionally falls on women and girls. In Ghana, Tanzania, and Zambia women account for two-thirds of all household time devoted to water and fuel collection, while children—mostly girls—account for between 5 and 28 percent of time spent on these activities. In rural Morocco, having wells or piped water increases the probability that both girls and boys will enroll in school, with larger impacts for girls, who are responsible for collecting water. Studies in Pakistan show that poor access to firewood and water in rural areas means that women work longer hours and have less time for income-generating activities, with impacts on the intrahousehold balance of power. Women and children are also more subject to health risks from indoor air pollution, given the disproportionate amount of time spent inside the home. Electricity in the home can reduce the need to burn polluting fuels for light and cooking. And improvements in electricity and gas distribution can eliminate time spent collecting traditional fuels.[75]

Improving rural transport infrastructure can reduce transactions costs, expand access to markets, and improve rural incomes. It is estimated that nearly two-thirds of African farmers are effectively insulated from national and world markets because of poor market access.[76] In contrast, substantial investments in Indonesian roads over the last three decades have allowed poor households to successfully enter the market economy.[77] And many of the roads were built as labor intensive public works, making jobs available to unskilled labor. Similarly, investments in rural infrastructure (roads, bridges, culverts, and marketplaces) in Bangladesh have deepened the vibrancy of the rural economy for both agriculture and non-agriculture. Investing in rural roads is an example of how expanding access to infrastructure can benefit equity and efficiency in the long run, especially in areas with large numbers of poor people and agroclimatic potential.[78]

BOX 8.9 *Lagging infrastructure in Africa*

Infrastructure development in Africa is abysmal, lagging behind the rest of the world in terms of quantity, quality, cost, and equality of access. Only 16 percent of roads are paved, the average waiting time for a telephone connection is three and half years, transport costs are the highest of any region, and fewer than one in five Africans has access to electricity. What can explain this tremendous underdevelopment?

- *Difficult geography and complex history.* Distance from major markets, the Sahara Desert, a shortage of natural ports, and vast tracts of landlocked areas all increase transport costs. Infrastructure development during colonial times focused on building transportation from resource sites to a port. And the postcolonial division of Africa into many small states drives up transport and energy costs, with cumbersome border crossings, little regional cooperation on water and power projects, and incompatible rail systems, among other factors.

- *Financing constraints.* Lack of investment has led to a deterioration in infrastructure, especially road transport. For instance, in nine East African countries, maintenance spending could cover only 20 percent of current networks. Lack of disposable income means low demand for infrastructure, and small and scattered populations make economies of scale difficult and require higher investments. Widespread subsidies that go to the relatively wealthy (the poor generally do not have connections to networked utilities) undermine governments' ability to expand access.

- *Bad policies and poor accountability.* Licensing, competition barriers, and corruption also impede affordable infrastructure provision.

Despite the difficult geographic and structural factors, there are opportunities to improve Africa's infrastructure. One necessary step is to boost investment, especially in rehabilitation and maintenance. Higher public investment will be needed. Private participation can help finance some investments and increase efficiency, but it is unlikely to solve Africa's infrastructure problem. A sound institutional and policy environment is required to attract fresh investment and use it effectively.

Macroeconomic stability, freedom to repatriate capital, competitive taxes, contract enforcement, low corruption, and adherence to transparent rules are all important to private investors, especially given the long payback periods of many infrastructure investments. In contexts in which policies are sensible but foreign private investment is hard to attract, foreign aid can provide both financing for public provision and guarantees to help foster private participation. Prudent oversight, regulation, and contract design can also ensure that public and private financing are equitably and efficiently used.

Increasing cross-border and regional cooperation is one way to make African infrastructure more affordable. Streamlined border crossings and improved road and rail links would reduce transport costs. Trade in power and water resources could significantly cut costs as well. For example, it is estimated that South Africa could save $80 million a year in operating costs by exchanging electricity with its neighbors (Masters, Sparrow, and Bowen 1999). Seeking innovative ways to broaden access is also needed. Mozambique has tested a promising approach: the government set up utility companies using diesel generators in rural areas and then sold them to private investors below cost for continuing commercial operation. Grants from government, NGOs, or donors for community-driven infrastructure projects are another possibility. Regardless of the approach, community and user involvement in infrastructure construction, maintenance, and management is one of the most effective ways to expand access in rural areas.

Source: World Bank (2000a).

Is privatization the answer?

What accounts for the failure of infrastructure services to serve poor people, especially in Africa (box 8.9)? Beyond the important role played by historical and geographic contexts, there are major financing constraints and governance challenges. In most developing countries, the public sector is fiscally strapped—public investment in infrastructure in Latin America dropped from 3 percent of GDP in 1980 to less than 1 percent in 2001[79]—and public spending requires taxes, which can exert a drag on efficiency and can mean forgone investments in other areas. Local financial markets are generally not sufficiently developed to intermediate private savings into long-term, risky infrastructure investments (and, in any case, private savings are often not large). Foreign private capital is interested generally in large markets and even then only when risks (including policy and exchange rate risks) are acceptable. State-owned infrastructure companies in many countries—especially when political inequalities are large—are often inefficient and become instruments of patronage.

The 1990s were characterized by a massive policy redirection toward private participation in infrastructure—reflecting the disappointment with ineffective state-operated utilities, the promise of private funding, and the greater flexibility offered by technological change and regulatory innovation.[80] But the privatization wave bypassed many developing countries—Sub-Saharan Africa received only 3 percent of total private infrastructure investment in developing countries between 1995 and 2000[81]—and even where private capital became the dominant source of investment (as in Latin America in the mid-1990s when private investment was 2.5 percent of GDP), the results for equity were mixed. There were many cases of privatization in which access for the poor improved, especially when competition reduced political capture, but evidence suggests that private operators also focused on wealthier segments of the population (box 8.10).

BOX 8.10 *The distributional impact of infrastructure privatization in Latin America: a mixed bag*

Private participation in infrastructure increased dramatically in Latin America during the late 1990s. It went from $21 billion in 1995 to a peak of $80 billion in 1998, dropping back to $20 billion by 2002 (World Bank 2004f). The distributional impact of private investment depends on how efficiency gains are allocated between public and private interests. In the best cases, privatization can solve patronage problems and lead to greater efficiency and equity. In worse cases, efficiency gains can be shared between government and private operators, or go primarily to the private sector and lead to the consolidation of private monopoly power (as in Mexican telecommunications). The outcome depends on the market and accountability structure, including the effectiveness of regulation. Evidence from Latin America shows that privatizations fall into each of these categories, yielding mixed results for affordable access by the poor.

Research from Argentina, Bolivia, Mexico, and Nicaragua shows that utility privatization increased access and enhanced service quality for poor consumers in some cases (McKenzie and Mookherjee 2003). In Chile, access to power services increased greatly for low-income groups during the first 10 years of private operation (Estache, Gómez-Lobo, and Leipziger 2001). In Colombia, private utilities have connected more of the poorest consumers than their public counterparts (World Bank (2001a). Other research shows that child mortality caused by waterborne diseases fell by 5 to 9 percent in the 30 Argentine locales where water services were privatized, with the strongest benefit—a more than 25 percent decline in mortality—occurring in the poorest neighborhoods (Galiani, Gertler, and Schargrodsky 2002).

Despite the increases in access, there are two reasons why privatization may have had adverse effects on the poor through higher tariffs and connection costs. First, privatization can reduce the scope for cross-regional subsidies. One study (Campos and others 2003) showed that the fiscal cost of utilities increased a few years after privatization. This was the result of "cream-skimming," as observed in Argentina. In some of the provinces of Argentina, the water concessions were for the large cities only, leaving the responsibility for the small cities and rural areas to the governments. Because the big cities were cross-subsidizing the other regions under public provision, privatization reduced this source of funding and increased the net fiscal costs once the transaction payoffs from privatization had disappeared.

Second, connection costs and tariffs were adjusted to cost-recovery levels following privatization, leading in many instances to higher prices. In the early 1990s, public utilities in developing countries subsidized an average of 20 percent of gas and 70 percent of water costs (World Bank 1994). So when subsidies were cut, services often became too expensive for poor consumers. For the water concession in Buenos Aires, the initial connection charge was set so high that many users could not afford it (Estache, Foster, and Wodon 2001), which was an issue at the center of one of the first major adjustments to the contract (Ugaz and Price 2003). The telecommunications sector in Argentina also saw price increases following privatization, largely to rebalance local and long distance charges. But price increases are not the norm—competition can drive them down. In

Chile, the liberalization of the telecommunications market in 1994 reduced call prices by more than 50 percent. In Argentina, thanks to the entry of 21 new operators in the generation sector, residential electricity customers enjoyed a 40 percent drop in tariffs in the five years after privatization (1992–97) (World Bank 2002b). Ultimately, price changes depend on initial conditions, quality improvements, and regulatory and institutional frameworks that determine profits.

Episodes of privatization can be opportunities to strengthen accountability. They can generate public discussion about the current state of service delivery, the options for reform, the terms of the contract, and the tradeoffs under consideration. Such occasions can be powerful in overcoming collective action problems and mobilizing consumers to express their interests. But there is also the danger that, in the absence of the voice of consumers, the process of privatization may be captured by narrow interests with political connections and better information. Indeed, that might be one reason why the public perception of privatization in Latin America is so negative.[82] There is evidence that privatization has been associated with increased power for conglomerates and their foreign partners—and with higher profits in noncompetitive sectors. Accusations of corruption during the privatization process, concentrated gains by a few actors (whether made legally or illegally) contrasted with worker layoffs, and unrealistic customer expectations regarding service levels (driven by politicians overselling the promise of privatization) are also probably to blame for privatization's negative public image (De Ferranti and others 2004).

In the end, experience suggests that privatization alone is not the answer. Whether infrastructure services are provided by private operators or public utilities seems less important for equity and efficiency than specific measures to improve access for the poor, the structure of incentives facing providers, and provider accountability to the general public.

Expanding access and making services affordable

Whether expanding general access benefits the poor depends on initial levels of coverage. In many African countries, overall access rates improved over the last decade, but the bottom 40 percent of the population registered no gains at all (figure 8.3). This is not

surprising. Given the low initial coverage in many of these countries, the expansion favored wealthier households. This does not mean, however, that expanding access when overall levels of service provision are low is bad for equity. On the contrary—better to expand access in this case than to focus on upgrading quality, which would benefit only the few who already have access.

To expand access to the poor, policymakers can set service obligations or create incentives for providers. One way is to specify universal service obligations, which is common in the telecommunications sector.[83] While this is a worthy social objective, it may not be practical in the short run when starting from low access rates. That is why service obligations should include details on

Figure 8.3 Poor families did not benefit from an expansion of access in Africa

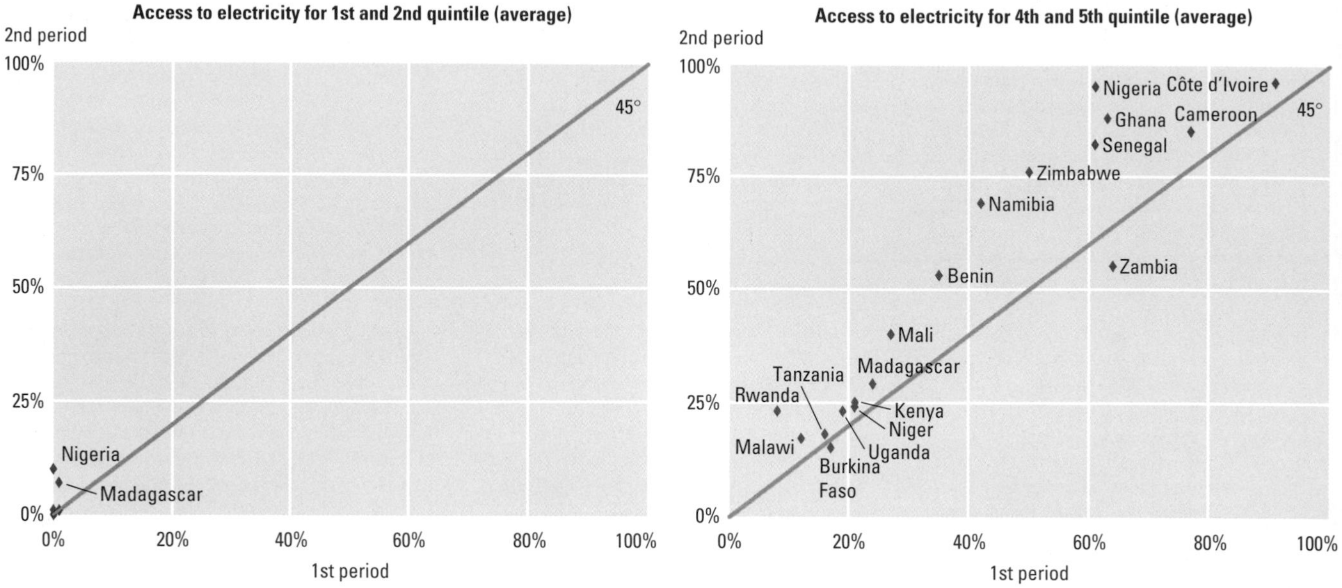

Access to electricity for 1st and 2nd quintile (average)

Access to electricity for 4th and 5th quintile (average)

Source: Diallo and Wodon (2005).
Note: First and last observation dates vary for each country. The first observation is in the early to mid-1990s and the last in the late 1990s or early 2000s. The average time between observations is seven years.

time frames and ways to finance the obligation when customers are unable to pay. Defining connection targets is another way to promote access. Targets are easy to monitor and can be enforced by financial penalties. Of course, connection targets can be met only if customers are able and willing to take up the service—and this depends on their ability to overcome impediments, including title requirements and income and liquidity constraints (given the lumpiness of connection charges).

In many countries, new connections are subsidized to meet access objectives and keep providers solvent. New connections can be subsidized from charges to existing users, particularly if the group of existing users is much larger and wealthier than potential new users. The water and sanitation concessionaire in Buenos Aires adopted this type of cross-subsidy after renegotiating an initial contract that charged onerous connection fees to the poor. Government financing for connection subsidies is also an option, as is offering credit to consumers for connection purchases. In Colombia, the law requires that connection charges for poor customers be spread over at least three years.[84]

A complement to connection subsidies are consumption subsidies, either through means-tested transfers financed out of general tax revenues or through lifeline tariffs. Subsidized lifeline tariffs require a transfer from those with high levels of consumption to those with low levels.[85] When considering lifeline subsidies, care must be taken to set a threshold that is high enough to garner political support, yet low enough that the poor are the primary beneficiaries. For instance, evidence from Honduras suggests that their electricity subsidy is too high—83.5 percent of residential customers benefit from the subsidy (those consuming under 300 kWh monthly). Means-tested vouchers for purchasing services are another subsidy option. They are similar to means-tested tariff subsidies with added flexibility for the user to select a service provider.[86]

Given the liquidity constraints of the poor and the possible seasonality of use and income, introducing flexibility in payment is likely to help expand access. Increasing the frequency of billing is one such option. Prepayment devices, which facilitate budgeting for low-income households, are another. On the downside, prepayment could lead to frequent "self-disconnection."

Utilities could also allow customers to choose from a menu of tariffs with different combinations of fixed (standing) and variable charges. Allowing lower fixed charges in exchange for slightly higher variable ones could benefit smaller consumers.[87]

Enabling consumers to make certain quality-price tradeoffs by encouraging lower-quality services is also likely to be beneficial. This can be done by allowing lower standards of formal provisioning in certain poor areas or by encouraging a vibrant network of informal providers that can either operate independently or through subcontracting arrangements with the formal provider.

Water service provides an example. A study using data from 47 countries shows that informal providers such as point-source vendors (kiosks) and mobile distributors (such as tanker trucks and carters) systematically charge more than networked providers, both public and private.[88] Micro-economic evidence supports this. In Niger, for example, wealthier households are more likely to use networked rather than informal providers and pay less per unit consumed (figure 8.4). But informal providers can offer a valuable service, because many poor users cannot afford connection charges or monthly lump-sum bills or live in areas inaccessible to utilities for legal or technical reasons. Recognizing that private connections for all households may not be a feasible goal in the near term, governments and utilities can work with informal providers. For instance, kiosk services could be improved by subsidizing kiosk connections, increasing competition among kiosks, and introducing performance measures and quality standards.[89] In Senegal, one study argues for directing subsidies away from private connections toward water provided at standposts or by other informal providers (box 8.11).

High tariffs for the consumer reflect the pricing decisions of the utilities concerned and the taxation decisions of local and central governments. Avoiding exclusivity in contracts and liberalizing entry, including through the participation of independent private providers or communities in non-network services, can help reduce costs.

Figure 8.4 Poorer households have lower-quality water and pay more in Niger

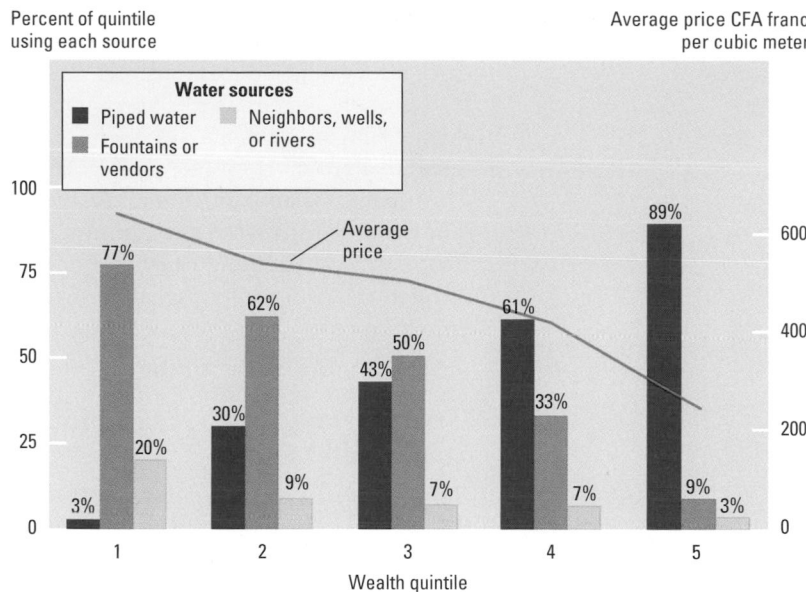

Source: Bardasi and Wodon (2004).

BOX 8.11 *The pro-poor agenda for urban water in Senegal*

In 1995, the government of Senegal launched sweeping reforms in the urban water sector. The bankrupt public sector utility was dissolved. A new state asset-holding company was created to manage the sector. And a private operator was contracted to run the system based on an international competitive bidding process. The reform had positive outcomes for the poor, thanks to strong government commitment, connection subsidies in low-income neighborhoods, and well-designed operator incentives. But tariff inequities and poor targeting of subsidies remain.

Subsidies targeted at the poor take three forms: consumption subsidies, connection subsidies, and construction of standposts in areas lacking private connections. In Senegal, consumption subsidies are delivered through an increasing block tariff with a low "social tariff" for household consumption under 10 m³ per month. The problem with consumption subsidies is that many poor families do not

have a connection at all or share a connection with several other families, which bumps them into a higher consumption block.

Connection subsidies have benefited the poor, but those who could benefit most are likely to be ineligible because they lack title to their land and an established house. The construction of public standposts has expanded access but does not necessarily provide the lowest-cost water. Tariffs on water sold to licensed standpost vendors are considerably higher than the subsidized social tariff and vendors also charge an overhead fee. Analysis of one NGO-run standpost showed that users were paying 350 percent more than the social tariff rate. Given these shortcomings, it would make more sense to direct consumption subsidies away from private connections and into water provided at standposts or by other informal providers who serve the poorest.

Source: Brocklehurst and Janssens (2004).

Moreover, many governments view utilities and telecommunications as cash cows, imposing indirect consumption taxes that tend to be regressive where connectivity to the formal system is high. In Argentina, utilities generate about 1 percent of tax revenue; in addition to the income tax, there is a 21 percent VAT plus municipal and provincial taxes. So indirect taxes can be as high as 55 percent in some municipalities. Reducing such taxes would reduce tariffs.[90]

Naturally, benefits can be lower and costs higher for investments in poor, remote areas that are short on economic potential. This analysis is not blind to those considerations, but also it recognizes the argument that there can be long-run benefits from greater inclusion of groups that are marginalized because of location or poverty (see focus 6 on regional inequality).

Strengthening governance, voice, and accountability

Infrastructure provision suffers from severe problems of corruption and lack of accountability. Because infrastructure investments are typically large and lumpy, and often exhibit increasing returns to scale or network externalities, they are less amenable to competition in financing and provision and generate significant scope for corruption and patronage. Politicians bribe public utility officials and pursue political goals by transferring resources to politically influential groups, rather than encouraging utilities to expand service and cut costs.

One possible solution is to subject utilities to performance pressures and reduce politicians' willingness or ability to use them for political purposes.[91] The prudent use of regulation is another way to strengthen accountability and reduce political capture and corruption. Regulators have a key role in ensuring that the public interest is being served. This includes safeguarding the value of public assets, upholding the sectoral norms relating to health and safety, providing information about the performance of the service provider, and enforcing compliance with contractual obligations.

If effective, regulation will have an important impact on efficiency and equity. Evidence comes from a study of the energy, telecommunications, and water sectors in Argentina that separated the benefits of privatization from those of effective regulation. The study found that effective regulation yielded operational gains more than one-third higher than the gains from privatization alone and equivalent to 0.35 percent of GDP, or 16 percent of the average expenditure on utility services. Gains for the lowest quintiles were proportionately higher. Another study of 1,000 concessions in Latin America found that even a moderately well-functioning regulator can temper opportunistic renegotiation of contracts. It concluded that the probability of renegotiation goes from 17 percent in a setting in which a regulatory body exists to 60 percent in settings it does not.[92]

Positive impacts of regulation are conditioned on the ability to insulate regulators somewhat from pressures coming from politicians and providers. Measures to strengthen the independence of the regulator are paramount, and this may require a separate agency with reliable and ring-fenced funding and staffing. When assets are decentralized, the regulatory agency can be at the level of the central or regional government. In short, regulators should be subject to substantive and procedural requirements that ensure integrity, independence, transparency, and accountability (box 8.12).

In situations in which local provision is more susceptible to capture by local elites, the central government can influence local outcomes by using fiscal incentives to nudge local governments toward broader access and by reducing costs for the poor through contingent intergovernmental transfers. This

---

BOX 8.12 *Addressing accountability and transparency in telecommunications in Brazil and Peru*

Brazil's National Telecommunications Regulatory Agency has a Web site that provides information on service price comparisons, laws, and operator compliance. Its Advisory Council (with civil society representatives) assesses the agency's annual reports and publishes the findings in the official gazette and on the Web. And an ombudsperson evaluates the agency's performance every two years. In 2000, it became the world's first telecommunications regulator to receive ISO-9001 certification, an international standard for meeting customers' technical needs.

Peru has made similar progress in improving regulation by increasing transparency. The Supervisory Authority for Private Investment in Telecommunications sets prices, ensures a competitive market, and monitors compliance with concession contracts and quality standards. The agency sets norms through a transparent process. Regulatory proposals must be supported by assessments of welfare benefits and best practices, published in the official gazette, and undergo a 30-day consultation period. Some proposals also are subject to public hearings. In addition, the agency has multiple dispute resolution mechanisms. Independent committees, supported by experts, resolve disputes among service providers and an internal tribunal handles consumer complaints not satisfactorily managed by phone companies.

Source: World Bank (2004l).

requires setting performance targets, eliciting competition among local governments, and benchmarking to monitor performance. It also requires sufficient policy autonomy at the local level to meet the specified targets.

Monitoring the performance of providers requires reliable information and performance benchmarks. This is more easily done when there is a management contract or a concession agreement with clear service obligations or when there are performance contracts with similar features for public utilities. Community involvement can help monitor compliance. A national regulator can benchmark local government performance when infrastructure assets and policy decisions are decentralized and provide useful information for intergovernmental fiscal transfers.

Summary

Justice systems can do much to level the playing field in the political, economic, and sociocultural domains, especially when societies press for equitable laws and for transparency and accountability in their implementation. Legal institutions can uphold the political rights of citizens and curb the capture of the state by the elite. They can equalize economic opportunities by protecting property rights for all and ensuring nondiscrimination in the market. They can force change in the social domain by challenging inequitable practices. But justice systems and legal institutions, embedded as they are in the political and socioeconomic structure of societies, can be hijacked by special interests.

Broadening access to land can enhance people's opportunities to engage in productive activities. The distribution of land rights, especially ownership rights, is skewed in many countries, and challenging this pattern is difficult. Past land reform efforts show the need for a broader menu of policies that go beyond redistribution through expropriation and include improvements to tenure security and the functioning of rental markets. There is also scope for redistribution through channels other than expropriation.

More equitable access to infrastructure also has equity and efficiency benefits. Broadening access to infrastructure brings people closer to markets and services and to the power and water they need for productive activities and daily existence, expanding their economic opportunities. Expanding affordable access for poor people and poor areas requires tackling difficult financing issues, designing subsidies effectively, working with informal providers, as well as making providers more accountable and strengthening the voice of beneficiaries. The challenges of expanding access to justice, land, and infrastructure and rooting out corruption and elite capture remain significant for many developing countries.

Raising revenues for equitable policies

The publicly-provided, equity-enhancing programs outlined in this report, from early childhood development interventions to water supply, have to be financed. The resources to fund them must generally be raised through taxation. In fact, a key ingredient for a well-functioning public sector is a societal understanding that the quality of public services depends on everyone paying their share of the tax burden. Where this perception fails, the social compact breaks down, and tax avoidance and evasion become widespread. This leads to a vicious circle of free-riding and tax rate increases, with adverse consequences for the public finances, the quality of service delivery, and social cohesion.

It follows that the same institutions that influence the quality and breadth of service delivery also affect the overall tax effort. Revenues, like spending, increase with a country's level of income, but the quality of institutions—notably voice and accountability—also matters, even when controlling for income[1] (see figure S5.1). Voice and accountability can strengthen the tax effort, as the services provided become a reflection of the desires of the broader electorate rather than of a privileged few. Lindert (2004) argues that the expansion of voice in twentieth-century Europe was the driving force behind fashioning the social compact that delivered high and equitable growth alongside extensive public provi-

sion of services during 1950–80. In Chile and the Republic of Korea, too, the emergence of representative institutions (and higher incomes and administrative capacity) led to higher taxation and spending.

For similar reasons, high inequality in the distribution of political power and wealth may be prejudicial to the tax effort. The low tax revenues in most of Central America may reflect the low solidarity of the elite with middle- and lower-income groups: the small, wealthiest segment of the population is unwilling to pay more in taxes to provide public services, because the elite can procure many private substitutes for publicly-provided services, ranging from public safety to education and roads.[2]

Resource rents can relieve the fiscal constraint on spending and in principle provide resources for equitable provision, though they raise a host of governance challenges. The ability of resource-rich states to rely on "unearned" revenues can undermine the accountability embedded in the social compact underpinning sound public finance.[3] If not properly addressed, the result may be wasted natural resources, corrupt state institutions, and poorer prospects for long-run growth and equity. A few recent efforts to harness resource rents for broad-based development in countries with poor institutions aim to introduce greater transparency and accountability (see box on next page).

Foreign aid can also weaken the social

compact, in much the same way as resource revenues, by making governments less beholden to civic interests.[4] Some evidence suggests that higher levels of aid are associated with lower revenue collection, especially among poorly governed countries.[5] Donors should thus consider ways of supporting accountable institutions in recipient countries—both for spending and taxation (see chapter 10 for discussion of aid).

While institutional transparency and accountability and linking good public services to the taxes that fund them are probably the first-order determinants of successful revenue-raising, technical aspects of public finance are important to reduce efficiency costs. Lindert (2004) argues that among industrial countries, high social benefit/high tax societies—most notably Scandinavia—have paid particular attention to tax design to reduce adverse incentive effects for labor effort and capital investment to sustain growth. Tax design is an immense area. From the perspective of equity, the primary contribution of taxation is in providing the resources to fund equity-enhancing spending. For this, the principal criteria are minimizing efficiency costs, administrative feasibility, and political supportability. For specific tax instruments, there can also be potential for positive direct effects on equity. Here we suggest seven basic principles for mobilizing tax revenues in ways that minimize efficiency costs, while not undermining equity.[6]

1. *Tax bases should be as broad as possible.* A broad-based consumption tax, for example, will still discourage labor supply on the margin, but choices between tradable and nontradable goods and services will not be distorted, if all are taxed at the same rate. A few items (such as gasoline, tobacco products, and alcohol) may be chosen for higher tax rates, because of their negative spillover effects or because the demand for these products is relatively unresponsive to taxation. As a result, at any given tax rate, efficiency costs will be relatively low and revenues relatively high. Income tax bases should also be broad, treating all incomes, from every source, as uniformly as possible.

2. *Tax rates should be as low as possible* (as long as they raise sufficient revenue to finance the appropriate expenditures of government). Of course, the broader the

Fiscal effort increases with income and the quality of institutions

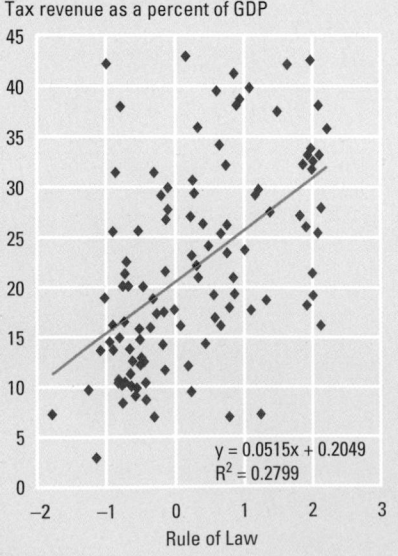

Tax revenue as a percent of GDP

$y = 0.0515x + 0.2049$
$R^2 = 0.2799$

Rule of Law

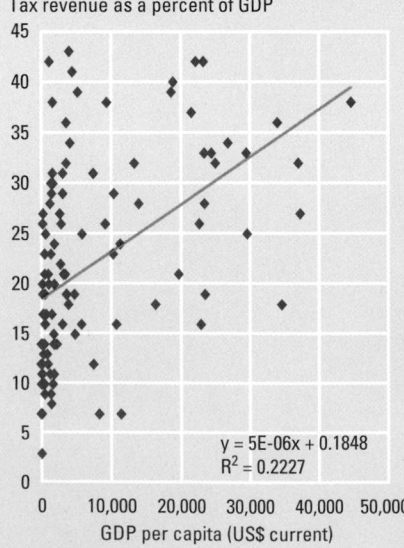

Tax revenue as a percent of GDP

$y = 5E{-}06x + 0.1848$
$R^2 = 0.2227$

GDP per capita (US$ current)

Source: Authors' calculations based on Kaufmann, Kraay, and Mastruzzi (2005).

base, the lower the rate needed to generate a given revenue level. Lower rates lower the efficiency costs. The general rule is that the distorting effect of taxes increases proportionally to the square of the tax rate, so halving the tax rate implies a fourfold increase in efficiency. From an efficiency perspective, it is better to impose a single rate on a broad base of taxpayers, rather than dividing that base into segments and imposing different rates on each one. This needs to be balanced against the distributional argument for graduated rate schedules.

3. *Keep indirect taxes from being regressive.* With a few key exemptions, value-added taxes (VAT) can be made less regressive. Bird and Miller (1989) show in Jamaica that exempting just five specific items from VAT halves the burden on the poorest 40 percent of the population. Reducing regressive excise taxes (as well as import duties), on food or kerosene is also desirable. To make up for lost revenue from any of these measures, there are often good reasons for higher taxes on private transport. Export taxes are generally best avoided, both on efficiency and on equity grounds.

4. *Raise personal income tax collections.* Collection from personal income taxes is low in developing countries. But in the light of the second point, higher revenues should be sought first by closing loopholes and enforcing greater compliance, and only later through higher marginal rates. Income taxes need to apply to persons and to corporations. To keep tax avoidance in check, the top marginal rate of the personal income tax should be fairly close to the rate of the corporate income tax, which means that the rate is not likely to be all that high.

5. *Use property taxes more.* Property taxes account for only a small share of taxes in developing countries. Their coverage is typically not comprehensive, and assessments and collection rates are low. Although nominal rates are also low, governments usually find rate increases in this very visible tax difficult to sell politically. Simply raising the tax rate usually would burden only the few actually paying taxes. Higher nominal rates are likely to be acceptable only with better tax administration, such as more comprehensive coverage, better and more frequently evaluated assessments, and enforced penalties for late payment.[7]

6. *Consider inheritance taxes.* Because heirs have not earned the wealth, taxing gifts, estates, and inheritances are consistent with this report's notion that predetermined circumstances should not affect a person's life chances.[8] The efficiency arguments and the evidence are mixed: parents may work more or less to avoid inheritance taxes, and so may save more or less. Although inheritance taxes may be difficult to collect and are likely to represent only a modest reduction in wealth concentration, they may help prevent "extreme concentrations of wealth from being passed from generation to generation."[9] In addition, a design that restricts transfers of control rights on corporations can be good for both equity and efficiency.[10]

7. *Avoid implicit taxes.* In many instances, the most important taxes affecting the poor are not formal ones levied through the tax code, but implicit taxes, including bribes[11] and inflation. Other implicit taxes to be avoided include many instances of "regulation as taxation" such as quasi-taxes imposed through controls on trade, prices, credit, foreign exchange, or capital markets.[12]

Managing resource rents transparently and equitably

High overall standards of transparency and accountability are essential if the revenues from extractive industries are to be used well. However, as a second best solution in weak institutions of accountability, many countries, developed and developing, do not pool the revenues from extractive industries with other resources in a unified planning and budget process. Instead, they are channeled to a dedicated fund, with special arrangements to earmark the revenues for specific purposes; define reporting and disclosure requirements; and establish oversight bodies to ensure that the arrangements are properly implemented.

One common objective of such revenue management arrangements is to save part of the revenue stream. The savings may be used for short-term budgetary stabilization, so that expenditures are protected from fluctuations in prices and output. They may also be used to build up financial assets, which can generate revenues over an extended period, in some cases constituting a perpetual fund, so that future generations can benefit from the revenues generated from the depletion of resources. Azerbaijan, Chad, and Kazakhstan have legislated savings to deflect pressures to spend revenues quickly and unproductively.

Revenue management arrangements can also serve distributional objectives. In Chad, the Oil Revenue Management Law assigns a share of revenues to a "future generation fund" and specifies allocations for poverty reduction. Such earmarked allocations may be anathema to financial managers, but they communicate and underline the government's commitment to prudent and redistributive spending. Nigeria's experience in the Niger Delta during the 1980s and 1990s highlights the resentment and political instability that can result when local communities see no demonstrable benefits from the extractive industries in their midst. The democratic government has responded by creating a Niger Delta Development Commission to fund local development, with statutory contributions from the federal government and the oil companies.

High standards of transparency and accountability are essential if the revenues from extractive industries are to be used for development purposes. To reduce the risk of diversion of revenues, the Extractive Industries Transparency Initiative (EITI), championed by the United Kingdom, calls on governments and extractive industries to report and reconcile payments and revenues. Some companies have taken the initiative of publishing payments to government in some of the countries in which they operate—for example, Shell in Nigeria and British Petroleum in Azerbaijan. The "Publish What You Pay" coalition advocates more systematic disclosure of companies' annual reports and for home-country legislation to make such declarations mandatory. Equally important are improvements in government reporting arrangements to ensure transparency in the application of revenues generated by large projects, such as the Chad-Cameroon pipeline and the Nam Theun 2 hydropower project in the Lao People's Democratic Republic.

Revenue management arrangements are likely to be more successful when they are the product of a broad consultative process and the rationale is widely understood. Timor-Leste has facilitated broad civil society involvement in the design of the revenue management arrangements for its offshore oil and gas industry. Draft legislation on the industry's commercial and tax regime and legislation on a proposed petroleum fund, have been published and subjected to numerous public consultations.

Markets and the macroeconomy

Achieving more equal access to markets is fundamental to greater equity within societies as well as to moving countries onto dynamic growth paths, thus enhancing global equity. And both equity and growth are best served by prudent macropolicy (allowing for its countercyclical role). This chapter is organized around the three markets for capital, labor, and goods (land was covered in chapter 8) and the macroeconomy, exploring in each domain the potential and options for leveling the economic playing field and strengthening voice and accountability.

How markets relate to equity

Issues of design of market-related reforms and macroeconomic policy are often allocated to ministries of finance, macro- and trade economists, financial specialists, and the like. By contrast, policies for equity, including those for managing the consequences of market conditions and macro-conditions, are typically considered the domain of the providers of schools, health centers, rural roads, safety nets, and justice systems. This division of labor is profoundly incorrect. The first set of policy domains is as important for equity as the second.

The main issue is access. The playing field is typically far from level in the workings of markets. Barriers are intrinsically inequitable when they privilege insiders' access to capital, good jobs, and favored product markets. But they are also bad for the innovation and investment that lie at the heart of modern economic growth. That is why leveling the playing field has the potential to be both more equitable and more efficient. It is also why broadening access typically requires more economic competition and more political accountability.

There are two broad categories of pathology that make the playing field uneven (see table 9.1). The first pathology arises when the influence of powerful political and economic elites is bad for equity and typically bad for growth—whether this takes the form of outright predation by political elites or excessive influence of economic elites in the shaping of policies and institutions, as under "oligarchic capitalism." As we read in chapter 6, Mexico's financial system through much of the country's history provides an example of elite capture—a protected, relational, incumbent-oriented financial system.

The second pathology arises when policy efforts to control or manage markets are directed, at least notionally, to improve equity, but with high costs for efficiency, and are often captured by middle groups (or indeed elites) in ways that harm the poor. This had its extreme manifestation in communist economic policy, but it is also prevalent in societies in which markets play a large role. Another example is when protection for formal sector workers, while bringing valued benefits to some, slows processes of restructuring and job creation for other workers. Both pathologies, but especially the first, reflect Adam Smith's concern that the influential may shape markets to serve the interests of incumbents. As he said, "People of the same trade seldom meet together, even for merriment and diversion, but the conversation ends in a conspiracy against the public, or in some contrivance to raise prices."[1]

The main purpose of this chapter is not to diagnose from where such pathologies came but to explore possibilities for change that are feasible within the prevailing political, sociocultural, and economic context. Casual observation suggests that change is

Table 9.1 Two pathologies in the interaction between equity and growth

Domain	Policy capture by powerful elites	Ill-designed attempts at equity with large inefficiencies
Financial markets	Protected, relational, incumbent-oriented financial system in Mexico for much of its history	Directed subsidized credit in India and elsewhere, with dismal repayment largely from better-off farmers
Labor markets	Repressive labor market conditions in the predemocratic Republic of Korea	Excessive protection of formal sector insiders in the middle of the distribution—India, South Africa
Product markets	Clove and timber monopolies in Indonesia	Protection for inefficient agricultural food production (Philippines) and industry (Morocco) before trade liberalization
Macroeconomic management	Regressive resolution of macroeconomic crises in Latin America and Indonesia	Populist macroeconomic policies (Peru under García) that fuel future (regressive) crises

possible. The Mexican financial system has been reformed after the 1995 Tequila Crisis. Moroccan industry was (partially) disprotected. And many countries no longer pursue populist macropolicy, especially after they experienced its ill effects.

Reducing barriers to market access will often bring initial benefits, or redistributions, not to the poorest but to middle groups. There may even be temporary rises in inequalities in parts of the income distribution, for example when there are increases in returns to skills. This is desirable for efficiency and consistent with equity if institutions allow households and individuals to respond to the new incentives, and there are safety nets to manage those who are hurt. It is undesirable, however, if it creates new possibilities for middle groups to "hoard opportunities" at the cost of future growth and gains for the poor.[2]

Design choices will depend on the market and local context, including the political context, but two cross-cutting issues are worth highlighting. First, there is often an apparent paradox: when systems are shaped to favor those with influence and connection, economic liberalization should be good for equity; however, that is not always the case. Liberalization can also be captured by the powerful, perpetuating inequitable and inefficient economic structures—and risking political and social backlash to market-oriented reforms. This is why liberalization needs to be designed in ways that promote genuine competition and effective accountability structures, whether in the form of regulation, transparency, or other forms of societal control, and sequenced properly.

Second, while greater equity can be complementary to long-run prosperity, the second pathology vividly shows the potential for inefficient choices in the name of equity. Tradeoffs between equity and efficiency exist. And even when there are aggregate gains, protected incumbents will be losers, at least in the short to medium term (in economists' jargon, changes will often not be Pareto-improving). Whether societies choose to compensate losers is a matter of social welfare (especially if they are poor) and political economy (especially if they are not poor).

We now turn to the three markets for capital, labor, and goods and the macroeconomy, exploring in each domain the potential and options for broadening access and strengthening accountability. Box 9.1 illustrates some of the interactions among equity, inequality, and growth in China.

Achieving equity and efficiency in financial markets

The performance of enterprises drives economic growth. An innovative and dynamic enterprise sector requires low barriers to entry, effective guarantees for property rights, and access to finance. We focus on the latter here. Unequal access to finance is associated with reduced productive opportunities and reflects unequal influence. Financial market liberalization can increase access, but it can also be captured. Sound technical design and strengthened accountability can help expand access while reducing both the risk of capture and disincentives to broader lending, thus enhancing opportunities.

BOX 9.1 *Markets and development: policy, equity, and social welfare in China*

China looms large in any attempt to interpret development, especially the role of equity in development processes. Hasn't it moved from a highly equitable form of communism to extensive use of domestic and international markets? And didn't this lead to both rising income inequality and the most extraordinary pace and scale of reduction in poverty and expansion in social welfare in history? This looks, at first glance, like a brute fact refutation of a central message of this report: that equity can lay the basis for prosperous development.

An account along these lines misreads change in China in important ways: many of the changes were equity-enhancing in the sense of leading to expansion of opportunities of the bulk of the population (chapter 6 discussed the institutional underpinnings of these changes). Consider some of the major shifts in Chinese policy that the literature interprets as having driven growth and income poverty: the institutional shift to the household responsibility system allowing peasants to produce for themselves (1979 and early 1980s), the expansion of township and village enterprises (TVEs) and the massive indirect effects of opening to international trade (whole period), the opening to inward foreign direct investment (especially in the 1990s), and the huge internal migration flows. All these led to major expansions in opportunity (and were major sources of growth) for large segments of the population. Rural reform quickly expanded opportunities for most peasants. TVEs were broadly dispersed. While the effects of international opening were concentrated initially in coastal areas, they have broadened in scope, both through the indirect effects of migration and the relocation of industries inland.

By contrast, where investment has been linked to connections and corruption, it is clearly inequitable, in the sense of lacking fair process and equality of opportunity to all potential investors. In the long term, introducing fairer and more transparent process will be important to sustained growth.

There were periods in which policy-related shifts (such as selective opening, the pricing of foodgrains, tighter controls on internal migration, and access to urban jobs) were associated with biases either against inner provinces of China or against rural areas. These were factors behind the rise in inequality in outcomes and stagnating income poverty between the late 1980s and early 1990s. This was probably inequitable in terms of rising inequality of opportunity. For these cases there may have been some tradeoff, but few observers argue that such policy-induced biases were essential to Chinese growth, in contrast to the overall institutional change and opening.

Moreover, even using the much narrower lens of income inequality, the periods when inequality fell (notably the early 1980s and the mid-1990s) actually had the highest growth rates, not the lowest. And the provinces where rural inequality rose the least had the highest growth rates.

There are rising concerns in China over the adverse consequences for development of growing inequality, including in some areas of social provisioning (in health, for example), and concentrations of wealth through connections. But there is no evidence that these brought benefits in income growth, the issue of concern here, and most observers (and the Chinese government) would see this as an area in which policy could be improved.

Sources: Ravallion and Chen (2004), World Bank (1997b).

Unequal access to finance is associated with unequal productive opportunities and reflects unequal influence

As discussed in chapter 5, the access to financial services and their cost are unequally distributed, especially in developing countries. Many firms and households complain that the right financial services are not provided, that procedures for opening an account or getting a loan are too cumbersome and costly (with high rejection rates), and that financial institutions demand collateral, which (poorer) borrowers typically lack.

Financial institutions respond that they cannot provide services profitably for technical and economic reasons. Poorer groups have small savings, and seek small loans and insurance (life, health, crop), which are hard to provide. Smaller clients borrow frequently and repay in small installments, making serving their needs very costly. And the underserved are new and not experienced in business, making them poor credit risks. But such reasons form only part of the story. The microcredit movement and large banks, such as Bank Rakyat Indonesia and ICICI Bank in India, show that it is possible to provide financial services profitably to poorer customers and small firms. Access is also unequal in areas of finance in which enforcement is not as much of a concern—such as deposit-taking.

Inequalities in access are also, in part, a product of unequal influence. Incumbents who benefit from restricted patterns of finance may lobby to limit access to finance, or erect other barriers to protect the rents of established firms. Barriers to entrepreneurial activity are indeed generally more onerous in poorer, more corrupt, and more unequal countries.[3] Weak property rights are part of the problem. But weak property rights can be the outcome of political economy forces— economic elites have an interest in the selective protection of property rights, because they stand to gain more when security of contracts and property depends on their position, connections, and wealth.[4]

We are primarily concerned here with the first pathology mentioned earlier, namely the influence of economic elites on the shaping of financial systems. In many countries, a small number of wealthy families or groups exert extensive control over the corporate sector, notably through control pyramids in which cross-shareholdings lead to dominant control rights in extensive parts of the corporate sector, often substantially in excess of the share of capital owned. These wealthy families are typically linked to political elites through economic deals, family connections, and shared social and

Table 9.2 Financial policy and institutions are often captured by the few: case study evidence

Country	Evidence
Brazil	Public financial institutions in Brazil appear to have served larger firms more than private banks have (Kumar 2005).
Chile	Following liberalization in the late 1970s, many privatizations of state-owned banks went to groups of insiders (Larrain 1989).
Czech Republic	Mass privatization in the Czech Republic delayed the establishment of a securities and exchange commission, facilitating tunneling (stealing assets by channeling to another firm owned by insiders) (Cull, Matesova, and Shirley 2002).
Indonesia	Market attributes large financial value for political connections, suggesting politics rather than economics determined access or rents (Fisman 2001b).
France, pre-1985	Banks, protected and dependent on government support, lend to less productive firms (Bertrand, Schoar, and Thesmar 2004).
Korea, Rep. of	The opening up of new segments of financial services provision was dominated by insiders. Increasing openness primarily expanded and strengthened the politically most connected firms (Haggard, Lim, and Kim 2003, Siegel 2003).
Malaysia	The imposition of capital controls in September 1998 primarily benefited firms with ties to Prime Minister Mahathir (Johnson and Mitton 2003).
Mexico late 1800s	There was capture of the financial sector in Mexico in the late 1800s blocking entry in emerging industries (Haber, Noel, and Razo 2003).
Mexico early 1990s	Lending to connected interests in the early 1990s was prevalent (20 percent of commercial loans) and took place on better terms than arms' length lending (annual interest rates were 4 percentage points lower). Related loans were 33 percent more likely to default and had lower recovery rates (30 percent less) than unrelated ones (La Porta, López-de-Silanes, and Zamarripa 2002).
Pakistan	Insider activities have significant economic costs. Politically connected firms borrowed twice as much from government banks and had 50 percent higher default rates between 1996 and 2002, with economywide costs of rent-seeking estimated to be 0.3 percent to 1.9 percent of GDP per year. Brokers trading on their own behalf earned annual rates of return 50–90 percentage points higher than those earned by outside investors. Hence, price manipulation by intermediaries helps keep equity markets marginal with few outsiders investing and little capital raised (Khwaja and Mian 2004, 2004b).
Russian Federation	Russia's free-for-all banking entry, combined with its choice of a universal banking system, gave great discretion to insiders to conduct asset stripping through the loan-for-shares scheme. The weak political accountability could not stop the capture of state resources or protected rents (Perotti 2002, Black, Kraakman, and Tassarova 2000).
Thailand	Connected lending was large before the 1997 crisis and firms with connections to banks and politicians had greater access to long-term debt (Wiwattanakantang, Kali, and Charumilind forthcoming).
United States, early 1800s	New bank licenses went largely to insiders in New York state (Haber 2004).
Ghana, Kenya, Tanzania, Zambia, and Zimbabwe	Firms that have an owner of Asian or European descent have a 0.34 higher probability of obtaining credit from suppliers (Fisman 2003).

cultural capital. Examples include the Mexican banking system, until the reforms of the second half of the 1990s, and the concentrated wealth and close connections between economic and political elites in East Asia (figure 2.8).[5]

Concentrated corporate control and wealth should be a concern if it leads to biases in access toward the influential and, even more, if it is associated with reduced innovation and dynamism. Reduced innovation can occur through direct restrictions on opportunity and the indirect effects of weaker property rights. Cross-country evidence suggests that there is a relationship. Countries with more self-made billionaires tend to grow faster, whereas those with more hereditary billionaires grow more slowly, suggesting costs of dynastic family control over economies. Societies with greater family control over the corporate sector also grow more slowly.[6]

More compelling evidence on the links between unequal power and financial sector distortions comes from case study material, from the historical experience of now-developed societies, and from contemporary developing countries.[7] Table 9.2 provides a selective list of results from recent studies of developing and transition countries. These case studies illustrate that unequal wealth and influence and low political accountability can be bad for entry and bad for the broad protection of property rights—and so can hurt the efficiency, growth, and the health of the financial system.

Such adverse long-term effects can be magnified through crises, further dampening growth and reducing equity. Connected lending lowers asset quality and makes financial systems more vulnerable. And well-connected interests do disproportionately well in crises, through looting or securing greater protection and bailouts, as discussed in the section on macroeconomic management.[8]

The liberalization paradox: Rapid and premature liberalization can also be captured

A seemingly obvious implication of the pathology sketched above is that a more open and liberalized financial system should be good for access, innovation, and growth. Yet overly rapid liberalization can bring new perils. Table 9.2 includes examples of liberalization and privatization of financial systems leading to highly concentrated benefits. Rapid privatizations of state-owned banks often meant that banks went to powerful insiders or corporate groups, as in Chile in the 1970s, Mexico in the 1980s, and the Russian Federation in the 1990s.[9] In Chile and Mexico, the largest banks were sold to a small number of wealthy families in dubious auctions, with foreigners stopped from bidding. The buyers were allowed to fund the purchases with loans from the banks themselves, leading to extremely poor incentives for solvency. In both countries, the owners used the banks to grant themselves large loans, aimed in part at accumulating control over other firms. In Mexico, this was associated with a major consumer credit boom.

In the Republic of Korea, *chaebols* (family-run conglomerates) came to dominate nonbank financial institutions. This caused serious conflicts of interest and "produced numerous incidents of illegal and unfair activities, where funds from affiliated financial institutions were exploited for the benefit of *chaebol's* ailing subsidiaries."[10] And in the particularly dramatic case of Russia, the free-for-all liberalization was a source of both rapid concentration of assets and increased financial vulnerabilities (box 9.2).

Rapid or premature liberalization in a context of low political accountability can increase financial fragility, and the risk of opportunistic default.[11] Reckless lending strategies in Chile and Mexico created extreme vulnerability for the financial system, which collapsed when there were shocks to interest and exchange rates. A greater percentage of large loans defaulted and subsequent losses on large loans were larger than losses on smaller loans; losses were particularly large on loans to parties connected with the owners, who escaped significant sanctions. In both countries, the banking system had to be bailed out at enormous public cost, while much of the lent capital probably disappeared in capital flight, as in Russia. These cases suggest that rash liberalization with limited scrutiny can result in concentrated control of the banking system, with owners putting up limited amounts of their own capital, and weak or corrupt supervision and public guarantees to depositors. In all these cases the rise in low-quality liabilities (and the associated moral hazard) became a major factor in the subsequent financial crises.

In countries with greater accountability, financial liberalizations went a different way. In France, before the 1985 financial reforms, government subsidies and limits on competition led banks to support less productive firms and provide poor-quality loans. After 1985, the loan allocations improved and employment increased.[12] Although the reforms exposed some problematic lending patterns, there was no

---

BOX 9.2 *Too much and too little regulation: Russia before and after the transition*

Within a couple of years of liberalization, the number of banks in Russia had risen from four to around 3,000. One could argue that this was prime evidence that no elite was blocking entry. But such rapid entry in a regulatory power vacuum precluded any chance of regulatory oversight. It compromised the public perception of what a bank is and how it operates, undermining the very foundation required for the development of the domestic banking sector. In practice, many of these "banks" were not banks but private fund management entities used to channel capital flight. Those raising deposits from the general public lent the cash to insiders, gambled it irresponsibly, or simply shipped it abroad, leaving the banks as empty shells full of liabilities.

Banks could get away with such behavior not just because rapid entry overwhelmed the (rather unprepared) regulators, but also because the banking lobby further promoted laws that granted banks an extraordinary freedom to operate and dispose of other people's money. Russia endorsed the "universal bank" model, for example, hardly a structure suited to a legal and regulatory vacuum (although there is debate as to whether this was a key factor in itself). Bank lobbyists also ensured that banks were exonerated from the new commercial bankruptcy code (the bankruptcy code established before the 1998 crisis vaguely stated that banks would be subject to a specific bankruptcy legislation, which was not even tabled before 1998).

The universal banking structure and lack of bankruptcy system contributed to the severity of the financial crisis of August 1998, resulting in massive losses to depositors, foreign investors, and cost to the state budget (as many liabilities were transferred to the state-owned Sberbank).

Source: Claessens and Perotti (2005).

financial crisis or capture by the few. The system was less concentrated to begin with, and the reform process received more public scrutiny.

Premature or ill-designed liberalization can also lead to reform backlash, if the benefits are perceived to be concentrated in a few powerful groups while the losses are broadly socialized. There is less specific evidence on this for the financial system, but it forms part of a broader pattern of reaction against liberalizing processes. Witness the dramatic fall in support for privatization in Latin America between the mid-1990s and early 2000s (as documented by the Latinobarómetro surveys). Such a backlash is likely to be particularly sharp when associated with gains for particular groups—"economically dominant minorities" in the interpretation of a series of case studies by Chua (2004)—that can heighten the sense of horizontal inequities for other groups. It can undercut support for the very reforms that are critical for equity and growth. This is why policy designs need to consider both technical and political economy concerns.

Increasing access to financial services: Technical design, accountability, and competition

If both financial systems and financial liberalizations are often captured, what does this imply for the design of reform? The answer is complex and to some degree specific to the initial financial and legal institutions and political context of a country. But we can outline some general principles. Options to expand access entail moving financial institutions closer to the country's "access possibilities frontier." This will not necessarily imply finance for all: for all the success of microcredit for the poor, the major beneficiaries of greater access will be small and medium entrepreneurs from the middle class. But this is good for the broad-based growth that will benefit all groups. This involves both issues of technical design and developing the political and social accountabilities that will support and sustain change.

Technical design issues. For financial institutions, expanding the client base has much to do with scale, which is often too small. Recent experiences like those of ICICI bank in India show that the high transaction costs for small volumes and the large cost of expanding reach can be overcome. One option is the innovative use of existing networks. Postal systems, with their broad coverage, can be used to deliver new services by many private financial services providers. Many technological solutions now exist for small-scale banking, from mobile banking to broadening the range of delivery points—through kiosks, small branches, and joint ventures with nonbanks. Simpler banking products, like the "Mzansi" account in South Africa, and prepaid cards for small transactions can lower costs. Handheld computers have been used for quick approval of microfinance loans. Reverse factoring (lending on the basis of receivables from a creditworthy institution) using an Internet platform has allowed Nacional Financiera (NAFIN) in Mexico to extend trade finance. There has also been much innovation in the market for international remittances, which many banks have entered.

Some of these innovations need regulatory changes—for example, customer identification, anti-money-laundering rules and other rules can hinder access to a bank account, as when individuals do not have a fixed address or formal job. Better regulatory approaches for consumers can involve adopting "truth in lending" requirements for small borrowers and educating people on the risks of (new) financial services. However, a general lesson is to be wary of regulation in weak environments: all too often regulation ostensibly designed to protect savers and borrowers is ineffective in protection but still hinders access.

Are there shortcuts to enhancing access, especially when overall institutional improvements will take time? Too often there is emphasis on the more complicated and sophisticated aspects of financial systems, while, some of the basics—broadening access to financial services, including deposit-taking institutions—can be more important from an equity viewpoint. Information sharing can help improve competition in banking systems and can be encouraged more quickly in some segments, including allowing nonbank financial institutions access to existing networks (such as payments systems). There can also be some scope for specific government interventions. But government interventions to broaden access through directed credit have typically been unsuccessful, causing inefficient distortions with few access benefits—the second type of pathology discussed in this chapter. Many governments, especially in the 1960s and 1970s, used various forms of subsidized directed credit, typically through state banks, to try to channel finance to poor farmers and small enterprises. Directed credit undermines institutional development because banks have no reason to develop credit analysis skills, as plentiful examples of defunct development banks show. By one account, default rates ranged from 40 to 95 percent throughout the developing world.[13]

Moreover, subsidies for housing, lending for small and medium enterprises, and agricultural finance are often captured by the well connected. Some schemes do reach the poor: India's social banking program did so, but at a high cost.[14] Such schemes then become, at best, an inefficient means of support for the poor, fostering unsustainable models of financial sector development. For example, India's Integrated Rural Development Program provided loans to socially excluded groups (certain castes and tribes, and women) with high levels of subsidy (25 to 50 percent of the loan volume to such weak sectors). By 2000, loan recovery was only 31 percent, and there was little evidence of repeat borrowing.

Microfinance clearly has a role in expanding access. It is best viewed as a complement, not a substitute, for more equitable financial reform and core financial system development. In most countries, microcredit and similar microfinance institutions reach less than 2 percent of the population. Only in a few countries is access really extensive—Bangladesh, Indonesia, and Sri Lanka stand out with coverage ratios in the order of 8 percent or more.[15] Subsidies are often used to encourage the setup of microfinance institutions, but they need to be designed carefully because they can increase final costs, by encouraging the formation of institutions that are too small and that are forced to raise prices to recover fixed costs. Co-sharing costs and risks with the private sector is a key market test. Start-up subsidies and other support can foster exploration of alternative business models, phasing out support over time. Maintaining a segmented system makes sense until the microfinance sector matures, with stronger microfinance institutions coming into the core financial system as they evolve.

Accountability and competition. Technical design is important, but the core of a reliable reform is building political and regulatory accountability. Public scrutiny has a key role, given the risks of capturing reform process and institutions. Potential actors to help oversee the process include associations of small firms, consumer groups, NGOs, media, and labor unions. But given the technical and complex nature of financial sector functioning, societal accountability is likely to be most effective if groups with an interest in a more open financial system are empowered, engaging independent nongovernmental technical bodies with the capacity to analyze financial sector conditions. The shadow regulatory commissions established in almost all regions, and such research centers as the recently formed Center for Financial Stability in Argentina, can be sources of education and avenues for interest groups to express their voice. It will remain important to design these mechanisms with care to avoid the creation of veto powers to reform (which can lead to counter-reform capture!)

It is possible to promote reforms that build more reliable and inclusive financial systems in a context of unequal influence. Formal regulatory structures can complement societal accountability. The development of the stock markets in Poland and the Czech Republic show what regulation and disclosure can do. At the transition from communism in 1989, these two countries were quite similar in economic structure and history. But the design of financial reforms was very different, driven primarily by differences in philosophy toward markets.[16]

The Czech Republic went for a radical voucher-based privatization of state-owned assets, convinced of the power of the market to organize itself: with property rights transferred to the private sector, it was expected that private actors would efficiently contract with one another. Poland pursued a more gradual approach, based on case-by-case privatization and a measured institutional development effort to build regulatory and supervisory capacity. Company and securities laws in the two countries reflected these differences in approach, with much greater requirements in Poland than in the Czech Republic for disclosure to the public, more protection of minority shareholders, and more power for the independent regulator.

The results were quite different. The stock market in the Czech Republic started bigger but was quickly dominated by corporate insiders, who captured "58 percent of the values of companies over and above their legitimate shareholding, compared with an insignificant 1 percent in the United States."[17] There was widespread "tunneling," a form of asset stripping by insiders through transfers to other institutions they controlled. The Polish stock market, by contrast, started more slowly, but then overtook the Czech market (figure 9.1) Public scandals led to the regulator effectively pursuing violations, using the greater legal protections, and laying the basis for more broad-based property rights, greater confidence, and openness. By the late 1990s, there were already several initial public offerings in the market.

Segmentation provides another example of the need for appropriate accountability mechanisms. Financial sector regulation in many countries, including developed ones, enforced segmentation for long periods—both on a geographic basis and by type of financial services, as among commercial banking, investment banking, and insurance. The Italian experience with dispersed local banking suggests that mutual and cooperative banks performed an important function in supporting local activities, which was much better than state-owned banks or banks dominated by politicians.[18] But regu-

latory capacity has been eroded by technological change. Given that segmentation often resulted in capture by local elites, the erosion of barriers has likely improved access as often as not. Yet there is room for smaller, locally managed intermediaries to promote access. Such locally focused intermediaries need explicit disclosure and accountability requirements to local users (as opposed to local politicians), which has been the tradition in cooperative or mutual banks, to limit the undue political influence of the few.

Opening the financial sector to competition from foreign financial institutions can also spur financial broadening. Foreign bank entry can help by improving efficiency and stability, reducing protected profits, and forcing (local) financial institutions to focus more on providing financial services to all. Financing obstacles are perceived to be much lower by borrowers in countries with high levels of foreign bank penetration, with evidence that even small enterprises benefit. But note that allowing the entry of foreign banks is not synonymous with capital account liberalization. Rapidly opening the capital account before adequate domestic regulatory and supervisory structures are in place can be dangerous, especially in a world of large, and often herdlike, international capital flows, coupled with politically connected lending of poor quality. This increased the vulnerability of Indonesia, the Republic of Korea, and Thailand in the East Asian crisis.

Finally there is the potential for external commitment. The relative success of Central European countries in strengthening accountability has been attributed to the constraint on abuse induced by the need to prepare for accession to the European Union. In Slovakia, after a decade of influence-peddling and slow reform in the financial sector, the pendulum swung toward reform only as the date of possible EU accession approached.[19]

Achieving equity and efficiency in labor markets

For most of the world's people, economic opportunities are primarily determined, or

Figure 9.1 Poland's stock market started slowly but then surpassed the Czech Republic's

US$ millions, end of year

Czech Rep.

Poland

1991 1992 1993 1994 1995 1996 1997 1998

Source: Glaeser, Johnson, and Shleifer (2001).

at least mediated, by the labor market—in formal and informal work. The wages and employment conditions in the labor market affect the quality of life of workers and their families, sometimes in ways that may seem harsh or unfair. The functioning of the labor market has a profound effect on equity—across workers, in patterns of access to work, and between workers and employers. Government intervention to achieve greater equity is frequent in labor markets, but often with costs in terms of efficiency—exemplifying the second pathology. While this is an area in which genuine trade-offs exist between protection of weaker workers (which is good for equity) and flexibility (which is good for growth), elite capture and gross inefficiencies can be addressed through better design and broader accountability.

Equity and efficiency reasons to intervene in the labor market

Labor markets are different from other markets. Unlike the markets for many commodities, labor markets generally are not competitive. They may be characterized by uneven market power (between employers and workers), by imperfect mobility of workers, by insufficient information, or by discrimination. These imperfections generate rents in the employment relationship, which both sides can try to capture. This can lead to unfair and inefficient outcomes when the bargaining position of the workers is weak. For example, employers may underpay workers who are not mobile, force workers to work in hazardous conditions, or discriminate against vulnerable groups. Private markets, left to themselves, also do a poor job of protecting workers against the risk of unemployment. In the absence of perfect access to financial markets, or complete insurance markets, workers may not be able to smooth consumption in response to labor income shocks. If they cannot gain access to financial markets, they may also be prevented from moving from bad jobs to good.

All governments, irrespective of income, intervene heavily in the labor market. Governments typically intervene to correct these

failures: to protect workers and endow them with rights and "voice" in the employment relationship, to empower unions to represent workers in negotiations with employers, to ensure compliance with labor laws and regulations, and to provide insurance against income shocks. Public intervention can improve market outcomes and lead to significant equity gains: more equal opportunities for workers, better working conditions, and less discrimination. It can also lead to large gains in efficiency: for example, by allowing full use of the labor of discriminated groups, by increasing labor mobility, or by better managing income risk.[20]

The problem is that poorly designed or inappropriate government intervention can also make things worse, with results that are bad for equity and efficiency. For example, excessive protection of formal sector insiders can lead to "rationing" jobs in the formal sector, pushing surplus labor into either informal employment (as in India)[21] or unemployment (as in South Africa).[22]

The problem is particularly acute in developing countries, because labor market regulations and standards typically apply only to formal sector workers, leaving the majority of the workforce uncovered.[23] Protecting workers through legislation and regulation that is enforced only in the formal sector, without other measures to improve working conditions in informal employment, can reinforce the segmentation between formal and informal employment in ways that are inherently unfair. In Colombia, workers are legally entitled to severance payments for dismissals deemed unjust, but these entitlements are not enforced in the informal sector, which employs more than half the workforce. Not only do Colombian informal sector workers not benefit from the legislation, but arguably they are harmed by it, because the resulting higher cost of labor in the formal sector limits formal employment opportunities for "outsiders" (mainly women and youth).[24]

In reality, the distinction between formal and informal employment is often blurred. Some authors argue that the informal economy functions partly as an unregulated entrepreneurial sector, often voluntarily entered even at the expense of lower income.[25] It is clear that the informal sector is heterogeneous, and includes both those who choose to work there and those who work there out of necessity. Those in the top strata—microentrepreneurs who hire others and many of the self-employed—do relatively well in average earnings. Those at the bottom—intermittent casual laborers and industrial outworkers—do not. Women tend to be underrepresented in the top strata and overrepresented in the bottom.[26] They also often earn less than men within each strata—although some of these differences may reflect voluntary choices for more flexible, part-time work. In a recent study, the International Labour Office (ILO) argued that the formal and informal sectors are part of a continuum of working conditions, earnings, and rights.[27] A significant share of formal sector employees had some of the (poor) working conditions associated with informality, while a fraction of informal sector workers enjoyed conditions more typically associated with formal sector jobs. The challenge for governments is to shift more jobs along this continuum toward better working conditions and higher wages, and to do so in ways that do not come at the expense of efficiency.

Indeed, poorly designed or inappropriate government intervention can also be inefficient and bad for long-term growth. Recent research on India, for example, suggests that starting from a common legal framework (the Industries Disputes Act of 1947), the states that amended the legislation in the direction of reinforcing security rights of workers and other prolabor measures had lower output and productivity growth in formal manufacturing than those that did not change it or that made labor regulations more flexible.[28] Relatively protective legislation may have reduced opportunities for workers—especially the majority without a formal sector job.

A look at some African labor markets illustrates the impact of government policies (figure 9.2). Many countries—including Ghana, Uganda, and Tanzania—have large self-employment sectors, which absorb increases in the labor supply and help keep unemployment low. South Africa stands in sharp contrast, with a small informal sector—absorbing only about 19 percent of the total workforce in 2002, much lower than the share of nonagricultural employment in other African countries—and high unemployment (42 percent in 2003).[29] Part of the story lies in much larger wage differences between formal and informal sector work in South Africa than in the other cases. But it also appears to be caused by the unusually small size of the informal sector (compared with Latin America, for example). Some suggest that the legacy of apartheid that inhibited the development of traditions of small-scale entrepreneurial activity, and labor regulations that are enforced for firms of all sizes (depending on the industry and region), may explain the lack of entrepreneurs and small firms in South Africa.

In Ethiopia, on the other hand, the majority of the urban unemployed are well educated and from middle-class households.[30] They also tend to be young, have never held paid work, and have a median duration of unemployment of nearly four years. Indeed, about half of young unemployed males are searching for public sector jobs, which pay on average a 125 percent premium over self-employed work.

Addressing links with unequal power

Government intervention in the labor market is often a reflection of the underlying distribution of political agency. Governments may (and often do) intervene in the labor market in pursuit of goals other than addressing market failure. They may intervene to buy off the support of certain groups (for example, urban formal sector workers) or to suppress social dissent under an authoritarian regime or to serve the interests of those with greater political influence. Oligarchic capitalist societies can be associated either with labor repression or with unionized and (relatively) advantaged formal sector workers who share in the rents.

Interventions aimed at shifting aggregate welfare toward politically powerful middle groups, often in the name of equity, at the expense of others (an illustration of our

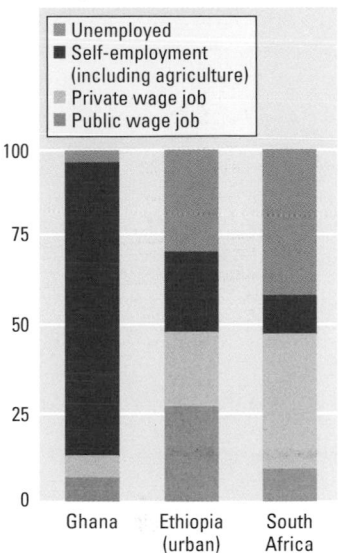

Figure 9.2 Patterns of employment and unemployment vary widely across African countries

Employment by sector for selected African countries
Percentage of total labor force

- Unemployed
- Self-employment (including agriculture)
- Private wage job
- Public wage job

Ghana | Ethiopia (urban) | South Africa

Source: Kingdon, Sandefur, and Teal (2005). *Note:* Ghanaian data are for 1998/99 and public wage employment includes government and state enterprise workers. South African data are for 2003 (Labor Force Survey). Ethiopian data are for urban areas in 1997 (Labour Force Survey) and because of definitional issues may not be fully comparable.

second pathology) are inherently bad for equity and usually bad for efficiency. Politically influential energy sector and teacher unions in Mexico, for example, have protected their employment and wage entitlements by blocking reforms that would lead to, respectively, energy sector reform and higher-quality and more equitable schooling. Public sector workers in France have used their political force, with the aid of massive strikes, to curtail attempts to bring their nonwage benefits and other entitlements in line with those of the private sector.

Stronger civil and political rights and broader mechanisms for voice can reduce the likelihood that the government's labor policy agenda will be hijacked by politically powerful groups. There is a strong association between democracy and the level of wages, both across countries and within societies that have experienced a political transition, such as the Republic of Korea, and Taiwan, China.[31] Stronger respect for civic rights in Latin America has also been associated with greater formalization of employment and a higher wage share.[32] In Spain, the transition to democracy in the mid-1970s led to demands for greater equity that were associated with the legalization of free trade unions,[33] the rapid

introduction of extensive social transfers (including pensions and unemployment insurance), and the implementation of progressive income taxation. The result was a shift from a regulated state, in which protection for workers came mainly through permanent jobs and controlled housing rentals, to a liberal economy with flexible markets, and more extensive public provisioning of services (see focus 3 on Spain).

Better design: Can labor market institutions be designed to be pro-growth and pro-equity?

The challenge for governments is to design interventions that balance equity and efficiency goals in ways that are within a country's institutional capacity. History suggests that this is a complex task, and there are real tradeoffs that need to be assessed. Different societies are likely to make different choices.

Scandinavia and the United States have very different sets of labor market institutions, yet they share a good track record of solid growth and high employment-to-population ratios (figure 9.3). The Nordic countries have mandated generous benefits and protection for workers, financed by a high tax effort. But they also have a highly coordinated and centralized approach to wage-setting and policymaking, which allowed all parties to internalize the consequences of their actions, with the union movement historically an advocate for openness and competition. The United States leaves the setting of wages and work conditions, including benefits, much more to discretion and employer-worker negotiation. This fits well within its tradition of decentralized bargaining, which gives freedom to individual firms to bargain with their workers in response to their varying economic and financial conditions. It leads to greater wage inequality and more workers without health and other forms of insurance. But it is consistent with lower taxes and high levels of flexibility.[34] The Nordic countries and the United States opted for different labor market models (in line with their history, legal tradition, and societal preferences), but all succeeded in delivering to their workforces a large pool

Figure 9.3 Different labor market institutional setups can yield equally good productivity growth paths: Scandinavia versus the United States

Labor productivity (GDP per hour worked, US$)

Source: Underlying series for OECD (2005).
Note: Measures used are GDP volumes, in U.S. dollars, at constant prices, constant purchasing power parity (PPPs) prices with a base year of 2000 and total hours worked for total employment.

of job opportunities, productivity growth, and rising incomes over the long term.

What doesn't work? There are also many ways of getting labor market institutions "wrong." And when countries get it wrong, one segment of the labor market (typically public and formal sector workers who represent the middle and high end of the usage distribution) benefits from extra protection at the expense of others. Outcomes are highly unequal, and the costs to efficiency and growth are usually severe. The experiences of India, South Africa, and Colombia cited earlier are vivid examples.

Governments also get it wrong if they intervene extensively in the labor market when product markets are not competitive. A typical example is the unionization of public sector workers. In Mexico, before the reforms of the 1990s, workers in public utilities and in the public oil sector secured high wages by capturing a share of the rents generated in these monopolistic sectors. But their gain came at a cost for employment and competitiveness in Mexico's private sector. Mexico's experience is not unique: it applied equally to state enterprise workers in Turkey until the 1990s and to public sector workers in India and many other countries.

Things can also go greatly wrong when governments mandate protection with no attention to incentives. In much of Europe, governments implemented generous unemployment benefits with little connection to workers' actual job search behavior. The result was an increase in the duration of unemployment and the emergence of long-term unemployment, with its destructive impact on human capital, loss of employability, weakened ties to economic and social life, and for many, high degrees of poverty and social exclusion.[35]

What works? The key to avoiding these pitfalls is achieving a balance between protection and flexibility. Design specifics matter a lot, as does the underlying structural context. Collective organization of workers is one of the main channels for securing better and more equitable working conditions. Free trade unions are the cornerstone of any effective system of industrial relations. Unions act as agents for labor, coordinating the demands of workers and organizing them into a single entity whose collective bargaining power matches that of the employer. Trade unions can help provide a positive work environment by reducing labor turnover and by promoting worker training and higher productivity. Unions have also been found to reduce inequality and wage discrimination in countries as diverse as Ghana, the Republic of Korea, Mexico, and Spain.[36] Unions also can have an important noneconomic role. They have been a force for progressive political and social change in many countries (Poland, the Republic of Korea, and South Africa).

But the involvement of unions in wage-setting can also have significant negative economic effects. Evidence from industrial societies suggests that union involvement reduces the employment of young and older workers ("outsiders") and benefits prime-age males and females.[37] Unions often act as monopolists, improving wages and work conditions for their members at the expense of consumers and nonunion labor. For example, recent studies of manufacturing wages in Africa show substantial union wage premiums (30 to 40 percent in some countries).[38]

Formal trade unions are most effective at improving conditions for workers without huge efficiency costs when product markets are competitive, so that unions cannot raise wages for their members by capturing rents at the expense of other parts of society; when collective bargaining arrangements and institutions have enough flexibility to accommodate different demand and supply conditions for different types of workers; and when unions operate in a context that allows them to internalize and absorb the cost of their actions. On the other hand, when unions are co-opted by political elites or by the state, their actions can have significant costs for efficiency.

An illustration of the potentially highly positive role of unions in improving working conditions while supporting productivity growth comes from a study of worker-firm relationships in high-value export crops in

---

BOX 9.3 *Organizing in the informal economy*

Developing countries have trade unions and large informal economies, two phenomena commonly thought to be incompatible. But recent work by Women in Informal Employment: Globalizing and Organizing (WIEGO) has uncovered a surprising amount of organizing in the informal economy. Formal trade unions that extend their coverage to informal workers and trade unions of informal workers are two organizational forms that have emerged. Organizing can also be done by cooperatives, savings-and-credit groups, producer groups, and neighborhood and trade associations.

Organizing in the informal economy differs from organizing in the formal economy along several dimensions. Collective bargaining can take many forms. Bargaining partners are not just employers but can also include municipal authorities, police, wholesalers, and other interest groups. Activities of informal workers' trade unions can also extend beyond collective bargaining and include a range of services, such as savings, credit, social security, and advocacy. Because members do not work in a standard workplace or for a single employer, membership in trade unions can take unusual forms.

- Registered as a trade union, the Self-Employed Women's Association (SEWA) in India is both an organization of poor self-employed women workers and a movement combining elements of the labor, cooperative, and women's movements. It offers a broad range of services to its nearly 700,000 members, including banking, health care, child care, insurance, legal aid, housing assistance, and capacity building (www.sewa.org).

- StreetNet International, launched in 2002 in South Africa, has 15 affiliates (unions, cooperatives, or associations) in Asia, Africa, and Latin America that organize street vendors, informal market vendors, and hawkers. As of early 2004, these affiliates represented 128,000 members (UNRISD Gender Policy Report).

- HomeNet Thailand is a network that helps organize informal home-based subcontracted and own-account workers (mainly women). It drew attention to the plight of these workers following the financial crisis in 1998.

Sources: United Nations Research Institute for Social Development (UNRISD) (2005); Women in Informal Employment Globalizing and Organizing (2005).

---

northeastern Brazil. Union activity among landless agricultural laborers in this case was an important factor behind improvements in work practices that led to higher quality (critical for export crops), higher productivity, and better working conditions for landless workers. To effect this change, however, the union had to shift from defending the interests of its traditional base of support (small farmers) to representing the interests of a larger group of landless laborers. Success was also facilitated by the fact that, on the employer side, the union was negotiating with large firms from southeastern Brazil. These southeastern firms had experience in collective bargaining, in contrast to the more traditional large farmers of the northeast, which were accustomed to more repressive and conflictive labor relations.[39]

Collective organization of workers can also secure greater bargaining power and thus better working conditions for informal economy workers. Studies of informal worker associations in India, South Africa, and Thailand suggest that organizing informal workers decreases the workers' invisibility to policymakers and legislators, helps them gain access to information, gives them voice and self-identity, and in some cases helps to provide them with a range of social protection services (box 9.3).

Providing income security is another area in which the structural context and design specifics, which pay attention to incentives and reward desirable behaviors, are critical to policy outcomes (box 9.4). This is also true of minimum wage policies for which the key to avoiding large efficiency costs is to get the level right and to allow for enough flexibility across types of workers to accommodate different demand and supply elasticities for their labor.[40]

Design specifics and the broader structural context are equally critical to the success of legislation on other work standards (health and safety) or protection for specific vulnerable groups (such as child laborers, ethnic minorities, or the disabled). There is an international consensus that core labor standards—freedom from forced and child labor, freedom from discrimination at work, freedom of association, and the right to collective bargaining—have such intrinsic value that they should always be pursued. But even for these core standards there are questions about how to achieve them most effectively and with minimum cost.[41]

An example of government intervention to protect workers from abuse comes from Cambodia's successful experience with implementing core labor standards in the garment industry. Starting in 1999 Cambodia could earn a higher quota for exports to the United States by demonstrating improvements in working conditions. A monitoring system—developed and implemented by the ILO, with support from the U.S. Department of Labor, the Government of Cambodia, and the Garment Manufacturers Association of Cambodia—has virtually eliminated the worst labor abuses, such as child labor and sexual harassment. A recent survey showed enforcement of core labor standards in the garment sector has boosted Cambodian exports to Europe and North America.[42] But

BOX 9.4 *Employment protection legislation*

Left to itself, the labor market does a poor job of protecting workers against a sharp loss in income associated with unemployment. As a result, most societies have developed ways to cope with the threat of job loss. Often this involves some combination of informal support mechanisms, private savings, and obligations on employers. When these mechanisms break down—as they do when the shocks are large, sudden, protracted, or affect an entire community—the government needs to step in. Government intervention typically involves one or several of the following instruments: job security regulations, mandated severance pay, unemployment insurance, or mandatory self-insurance mechanisms.

Job security legislation is typically aimed at protecting jobs and preventing job destruction. Most evidence suggests that it is quite effective at doing so. Across countries, more stringent employment protection legislation (EPL) appears strongly associated with more stable employment. But EPL reduces job destruction at a significant cost, as the expectation of high separation costs makes firms more reluctant to expand employment, and makes it less profitable to start new ventures or create new firms. So, employment protection also reduces job creation. For example, researchers found that strict new job-security laws enacted in the 1980s reduced employment in many industries in Zim-

babwe (Fallon and Lucas 1993). Overall, the net effect of job security legislation on employment is ambiguous (Bertola 1990; OECD 1999; Bertola, Blau, and Kahn 2001; Kugler 2004).

What is clear is that EPL changes the nature of unemployment. Lower job destruction reduces the *incidence* of unemployment. But lower job creation increases the *duration* of unemployment and can lead to the emergence of long-term unemployment.

Not surprisingly, EPL appears to have a different impact on different groups of workers. In both Colombia and Spain the reduction of dismissal costs and job security provisions was associated with moderate increases in the employment of young men and women (Kugler 2004; Kugler, Jimeno, and Hernanz 2003). For Chile, Montenegro and Pagés 2004 find that job security regulations reduce the employment rate of youth and the unskilled to the benefit of older and more skilled workers. A study across the countries of the Organisation for Economic Co-operation and Development arrives at a similar conclusion: consistent with the story that EPL protects "insiders," stricter EPL increases the employment of adult men and reduces that of young workers and women (OECD 1999).

Given the complex effects of EPL, how can governments best intervene to help protect workers against temporary drops in income

associated with unemployment? Some EPL may be efficient, reducing excessive volatility in turnover. But too strong EPL—as is typical of many formal sectors in the developing world—slows the pace of creative destruction central to innovation and growth, with disproportionate adverse effects on those without "good" jobs. Yet reducing EPL needs to be complemented by greater worker security that is not linked to specific jobs, both on social welfare and political economy grounds.

The design of the optimal solution depends on the institutional and administrative capacity of government and on the structural characteristics of the labor market (Blanchard 2004). Countries with significant administrative capacity and medium to high incomes can implement unemployment insurance systems with incentives for job search (declining benefits with duration and provision of benefits conditional on acceptance of acceptable job offer). Middle-income countries reluctant to implement a full-blown unemployment insurance system can support self-insurance mechanisms, such as mandatory savings accounts (but because of the limits to self-insurance, these are not as effective). Low-income countries can opt for public works schemes, which if effectively designed are self-targeting and can be implemented even when levels of informality are high (chapter 7).

---

whether the system will survive the end of the U.S. quota incentives remains to be seen (see chapter 10).

How to reform a "bad" set of labor market institutions

Reforming labor market institutions is technically and politically difficult. It is technically difficult because reforms need to be coordinated across a variety of labor market institutions, and often also with reforms outside the labor market. It is politically difficult because there usually are vested interests in maintaining the status quo. Moreover, the short-term costs of reform can be large and unevenly distributed. Take reforms to reduce employment protection: those currently protected see themselves as having much more to lose from reform than to gain from such a reduction. And if they are also politically influential—represented by unions and with political voice—their power to block

reforms may be an insurmountable barrier.

Several countries have implemented substantial labor market reforms more or less successfully: Ireland, the Republic of Korea, the Netherlands, New Zealand, and the Slovak Republic among OECD countries; Chile and Colombia among developing countries (see box 9.5 for Colombia and the Slovak Republic). China is in the midst of a large labor market transition, and the Balkans are struggling through dramatic labor market reforms.

Experience suggests that effective change involves a combination of factors: designing and implementing a consistent and comprehensive policy package; tackling vested interests; broadening societal accountability, including increasing the voice of poorer groups; and, in some cases, compensating losers. Macroeconomic and financial shocks can facilitate change, although not always a positive one. Reforming institutions in the

---

BOX 9.5 *Two cases of labor market reform: one comprehensive, one partial*

Comprehensive reform in the Slovak Republic

In 2000 unemployment in the Slovak Republic reached 19 percent of the labor force—the highest in the OECD at that time. The main factor was the substantial job reallocation generated by the transition to a market economy, compounded by low labor mobility because of skill and regional mismatches. But the impact of the transition shock on the labor market was worsened by an inadequate set of institutions: high rates of taxation of labor and overly generous unemployment benefit and social assistance systems, which discouraged job search and encouraged informality.

Reforming these institutions in the midst of high unemployment was extremely difficult, particularly for a reformist government with a small majority in parliament. But in early 2003, bolstered by its reelection, the reformist Slovak government undertook a comprehensive and ambitious reform of social and labor market policy. The government's multipronged strategy combined measures to reduce the taxation of labor, increase the incentives to work through reform of unemployment insurance and social assistance, invest in the skills of labor and employability, improve the matching of workers

and jobs through higher labor flexibility and mobility, and strengthen state administration in labor and social policy.

The new strategy represented a marked change in philosophy in labor and social policy in the Slovak Republic: from a system that mixed ingredients of insurance and redistribution toward one that separates social insurance from equity objectives; and from a tradition of entitlements based on subjective or "moral" norms to one that guarantees a certain living standard to all citizens irrespective of the reason they may have for being poor, but that rewards individual initiative and motivation.

The key ingredients in pushing the reform through were a reformist government with a strong popular mandate; strong leadership and technical competency from the Ministry of Labor and Social Affairs; accession into the European Union as a disciplining device; and widespread public perception, built on analysis and dissemination of this analysis, that institutional reforms were needed. Moreover, labor market reform was carried out not in isolation but as part of a broader policy package to make the Slovak economy more competitive in light of EU accession. This package included a substantial

overhaul of personal income taxes, as well as reform of the education system.

Partial labor market reform in Colombia

In 1990 Colombia introduced a labor market reform that substantially reduced the costs of dismissing workers. The reform reduced severance payments, widened the definition of "just" dismissals, extended the use of temporary contracts, and speeded up the process of mass dismissals. The joint effects of these reforms were to reduce the costs associated with firing workers in firms covered by the legislation. But the reforms did not affect informal sector firms, which did not comply with the legislation.

An analysis of the effects of the reforms suggests that they did increase the dynamism of the Colombian labor market by increasing exit rates into and out of unemployment (greater churning). There was an increase in worker turnover for formal sector worker, greatest among young workers, more educated workers, and workers employed in larger firms. The reforms may have also contributed to increasing compliance with labor legislation by reducing the costs of formality.

Source: Kugler (2004).

---

midst of widespread job loss and high unemployment (as in the Republic of Korea following the 1998 financial crisis) is particularly difficult, even though it may be easier at such times to achieve societal consensus for reform.

Designing a consistent and coherent policy package. One of the strongest lessons from country experience is that piecemeal reform does not work (tinkering at the margin usually has perverse distributional effects). Moreover, reforms need to cover a range of labor market policies and to be linked with reforms in social protection systems. Reform is more effective and more equitable when different labor market instruments are coordinated: measures to reduce insider power and increase flexibility by lowering the restrictions and costs of firing can be linked to setting up of unemployment insurance mechanisms and eliminating dual status contracts. Reforms in other markets and the public sector are often key to the success of labor market reform. The

depth and competitiveness of other markets (including product and financial markets) are critical.

Tackling vested interests. Reforms are often held hostage by politically more powerful groups. For example, policies to reduce employment protection, allow for subminimum wages, or streamline and improve public sector employment typically encounter sharp resistance from unions. Building broad societal consensus for reform is often the only way to tackle these vested interests. As a first step, this may require documenting the high costs of bad labor market policies through good data collection, analysis, and dissemination (as in the Slovak Republic).

Broadening social accountability. Building societal consensus in support of labor market reform may require specific measures to empower the groups of so-called outsiders or disenfranchised workers who bear the costs of nonreform. It helps to have political parties and societal organizations with broad bases of representation and support. When this is not the case, it may be necessary to look for ways to open up institutions and give greater voice in bargaining (at all levels) to representatives of disenfranchised groups. This is easier when there are democratic local governments and strong autonomous associations—independent private business associations, worker associations that represent the interests of specific groups, and so on. The independent private sector is also a natural ally when it comes to reforming public sector employment and wage practices.

Compensating losers. The short-term costs of reforms can be high for certain groups of workers: unemployment insurance and social assistance reform in the Slovak Republic disproportionately hurt Roma workers and those living in high unemployment regions. So it may be necessary to compensate the losers. It is best to do this in ways that address the obstacles that losers face in reentering the labor market (support for education or training) or that facilitate labor mobility and reward work incentives (transport vouchers for workers moving from social assistance to work). Such compensatory measures have been introduced as part of the Slovak Republic's labor market reform package.

Product markets and trade reform

Product markets are intimately related to equity, with two-way patterns of causation: product markets shape the distribution of economic opportunities, and inequalities in influence shape the functioning of product markets. Both the design of external trade policy and the workings of internal product markets reflect patterns of influence. Removing barriers and excessive regulation needs to be complemented by measures to expand skills, infrastructure, and safety nets to achieve genuine access and help losers.

Market broadening and deepening are central to the expansion of opportunity: directly for firms and the self-employed, indirectly for workers. How equitable this expansion of opportunity is depends on interactions among external trade opening, domestic markets, patterns of infrastructure, labor markets, safety nets, and other measures to improve the business climate. Product market and trade reforms have great potential to bring expansion in opportunity, but there can be costs in the short to medium term, and these can hit particular groups, from relatively powerful protected incumbents to middle and poorer groups. The costs are associated with how markets and investment processes work: labor is typically not fully mobile, new skills take time to acquire, and new investments are often lumpy and can take time, especially when firms face imperfect credit markets (see earlier section) and an uncertain investment environment.

The functioning of product markets is embedded in political and social structures. Elite capture ranges from the apparent and egregious—as in the granting of the Indonesian clove monopoly to a son of President Suharto (a monopoly since disbanded)—to the less transparent shaping of trade policy to protect the profits of the influential. It is also true that policies with (genuine or rhetorical) equitable purpose can lead to outcomes that are bad for growth and mixed for equity. This is evident in the characteristically high levels of protection for relatively labor-intensive manufacturing and for food production (such as maize in Mexico, rice in the Republic of Korea, and the infamous agricultural subsidies in the European Union, Japan, and the United States). While poorer groups sometimes gain, it is more common that middle and elite groups are the main beneficiaries, while food consumers lose out.

While policies that reduce the power of incumbents in product markets will typically be good for efficiency and equity, a version of the "liberalization paradox" discussed earlier may often apply. Groups and individuals with economic capacity and political influence are best positioned to take advantage of market opening. Under some conditions this can lead to market backlash. Chua (2004) documents cases of "market-dominant minorities" who benefit from free market reforms, including trade liberalization. Traditionally dominant ethnic minorities, such as the Chinese in Southeast Asia, the Lebanese in West

Africa, and whites in Latin America and South Africa, seem to be the primary beneficiaries of the marketization of their economies. Such outcomes can fuel deep-seated resentments and lead to violence. These political economy and reform backlash considerations are additional reasons for integrating attention to equity into the design of product market reforms and trade liberalization.

Trade liberalization

Trade liberalization changes relative prices in an economy, causing shifts in output, wages, and employment. Analyses of trade liberalization are primarily about outcomes, providing only indirect evidence on opportunities. They show that trade openness is positively associated with growth and, on average, there are no strong correlations with income distribution. Morley (2001), using data from Latin America, found slightly negative effects of trade liberalization on income distribution, while Behrman, Birdsall, and Székely (2003) found positive influences of trade liberalization on wage inequality. Another study using panel data for 41 countries found that trade openness is associated with increases in inequality, after controlling for a set of other structural and policy influences.[43]

These average effects mask a great deal of diversity in impacts across groups, especially over the short to medium term. The impact of trade-induced price changes depends not only on average pass-through but also on exactly which prices change and how producers and consumers respond.[44] For example, the effects of removing protection for agriculture will depend on whether agricultural prices subsequently rise or fall and whether the poor are net producers or consumers of disprotected products. Normally, it is assumed that trade liberalization in agriculture will benefit poor small-scale farmers and be good for equity. After all, "developing countries have traditionally taxed the agricultural sector while developed countries have protected it."[45] But the impacts must be analyzed case by case at the microlevel.

Cereal protection in Morocco offers an illustration. In a simulation analysis of removal of wheat tariffs, Ravallion (2004b) finds that, contrary to expectations, rural families would tend to lose while urban ones would gain. Although the results predict that there would be more gainers than losers among the rural poor, aggregate losses outweigh aggregate gains. Furthermore, expected effects would be enormously varied, with significant horizontal inequalities: households with the same incomes were predicted to experience widely differing outcomes, depending on their specific structure of production and consumption. Using a similar simulation analysis, China's accession to the World Trade Organization (WTO) was found to have a small aggregate poverty-reducing effect, but this masked considerable variation in impacts across households in rural versus urban areas and across different regions.[46]

While aggregate effects of trade reform on poverty and equity are not always clear—whether diverse impacts translate into inequalities in opportunities depends on how new activities open up, and whether labor can move into them—we do know that there will be winners and losers. Outcomes depend on the ability and willingness of governments to mitigate losses to particularly hard-hit sectors, possibly by redistributing some of the gains accruing to winners.

Domestic product markets and equity

Lack of competition among traders, remote geography, poor infrastructure, and high transport costs can all prevent the transmission of border price changes to intended reform beneficiaries. Addressing such problems can improve the impact of trade reforms on equity.

The case of public or private marketing agencies for export crops is a typical example. Small farmers in many countries traditionally have had no option but to sell to a marketing agency at prices substantially lower than the free on board (f.o.b.) export price. Legitimate transport and marketing costs account for some of the price difference, but monopsonistic profits often do as well. Marketing agencies can thus prevent trade-induced price changes from reaching farmers at all.[47] A 1998 study found that the Vietnamese rice marketing system was controlled by a small number of state enterprises. These enterprises limited the transmission of border price changes to farmers and pushed up transaction costs.[48] A more extreme example was when marketing boards became instruments for extraction of surplus from agricultural exporters, such as for cocoa farmers in the post-independence period in Ghana. Malawi has faced similar issues: cartels by companies buying tea, sugar, and tobacco have forced down the returns to farmers.[49]

Abolishing marketing boards does not guarantee efficient marketing, however, they may play a useful role when markets are thin, or a tradition of trading has not developed, as in the raw cashew export market in Mozambique. Although the state trading company was privatized in the late 1980s, there was insufficient competition among private marketers when raw cashew export restrictions were lifted in the early 1990s. Indeed, raw cashews had to move through three tiers of intermediaries with near monopsony power before reaching world markets. As a result, the trading margin from the farm to the factory was 50 percent and the expected liberalization price increases never reached farmers.[50]

Trade reforms in Mexico show how infrastructure and transportation costs can shape opportunities through their impact on price transmission. Mexico's trade liberalization in the 1980s and entry into North American Free Trade Agreement (NAFTA) in 1994 appear to have led to wage increases in states bordering the United States relative to the rest of the country.[51] A different study on Mexico found that tariff reductions translate into domestic price reductions less and less as distance from the main port of entry increases. This effect can be substantial (figure 9.4). Studies of Rwanda and Indonesia have also documented the isolation of remote households from border price changes.[52]

Even when trade liberalization is intended to be pro-poor, incomplete transmission of

Figure 9.4 It's better for household welfare to be close to economic opportunities

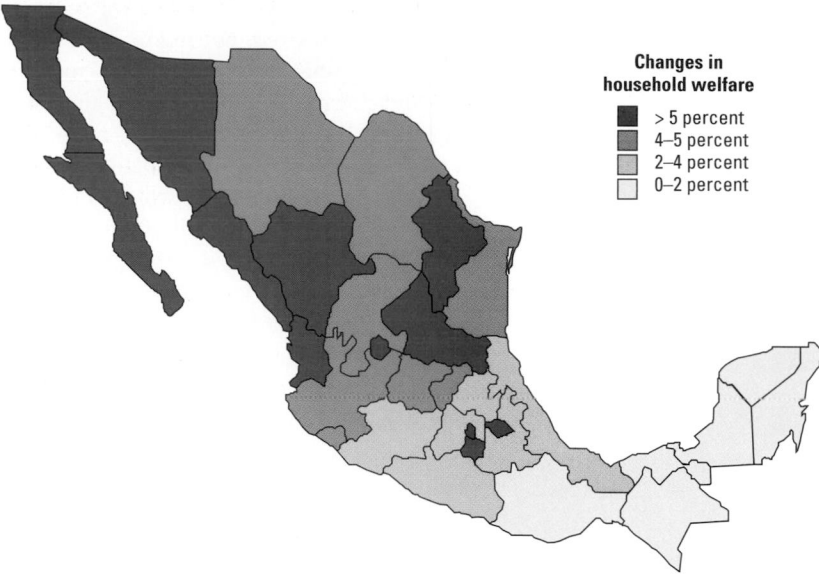

Changes in household welfare

- ■ > 5 percent
- ▨ 4–5 percent
- ▧ 2–4 percent
- □ 0–2 percent

Source: Nicita (2004).
Note: Welfare changes were calculated from the effects of trade liberalization–related price changes that affected both the purchasing power and incomes of households.

border price changes for both exports and imports means that benefits are not evenly distributed. In other words, ease of access to international markets matters. Unfortunately, those who could benefit most from favorable price changes—the poor in remote rural areas—are those least likely to be affected by them.

Many of the factors responsible for transmitting trade-related price changes are also important to the functioning of domestic product markets. For instance, competition among traders, infrastructure quality, and transportation costs all influence how profits are allocated across a product's life cycle or value chain. And the percentage of a good's final price that goes to the primary producer, intermediary producer, distributor, and retailer can vary tremendously.

The cashmere sector in Mongolia shows how product market reforms could be both equity- and efficiency-enhancing. If properly developed, cashmere could be a pillar of Mongolia's successful transition from a command to a market economy. It is the country's single largest employer and a principal source of livelihood for the poor. It provided jobs for more than 16 percent of the workforce and accounted for more than 6.3 percent of GDP during 1993–2002. But unsatisfactory public sector policies have meant that the industry has not lived up to its potential.

One significant bottleneck is in marketing and distribution. Mongolia's major cashmere market is in Ulaanbataar, 600–1,000 km from most regional production centers. Herders generally have to sell to traders at the farmgate or at informal provincial marketplaces at discounts of 10 to 45 percent from prices in Ulaanbataar. With little knowledge of market demand, individual herders can incur costs traveling to markets with no certainty of a sale. Policies that encourage regional market centers and herder cooperatives, as well as infrastructure improvements, could reduce marketing costs and increase herder's margins.[53]

Soybean farming in India offers another illustration of how product marketing channels can improve equity. Ninety percent of the soybean crop is sold by small farmers to traders, who act as purchasing agents for buyers at a local, government-mandated marketplace, called a *mandi*. Farmers have only general information about price trends and no choice but to accept prices offered to them by traders or the auction price on the day they bring their goods to the *mandi*. As a result, traders can exploit farmers and buyers using practices that create systemwide inefficiencies.

Under the e-Choupal Initiative, ITC, one of India's leading private companies, placed computers with Internet access in rural farming villages. Each computer—placed in a farmer's home and serving about 10 villages—becomes a social gathering place for the exchange of information and an e-commerce hub. Farmers can use the computers to check prices, learn about farming techniques, purchase inputs, and sell their soybean crops at the previous day's market price. Farmers then have to transport their crop to an ITC processing center, where it is electronically weighed and the farmer is immediately paid. Farmers selling to ITC through an e-Choupal receive, on average, 2.5 percent more for their crops, and ITC saves an additional 2.5 percent on procurement costs by cutting traders out of the loop. Farmers also benefit from accurate weighing,

prompt payment, and information about prices and price trends that allows them to optimize their sales decisions. The e-Choupal system continues to grow rapidly, reaching more than 3.1 million farmers by late 2004.[54] The initiative illustrates how improvements in technology and communications infrastructure can be good for both equity and efficiency in product markets.

In addition to better marketing channels and new technology, there are other ways to improve product market competition that can be good for equity. Measures that facilitate the entry of new firms often mean that small and medium enterprises benefit at the expense of large, politically connected incumbents. Product market competition can also drive consumer prices down and make goods more affordable for the poor. Of course, measures to improve competition benefit efficiency and growth as well, improving the welfare of the poor.

Licensing restrictions—even when designed in the name of equity—are one way to hamper competition. India reserves the production of more than 600 manufactured products, including apparel and textiles, to small companies. This licensing regime could cost the country jobs by preventing small producers from growing and competing with larger manufacturers in, for example, China. High regulatory, administrative, and fiscal burdens can also harm product markets by keeping firms in the informal sector. Informal firms face a number of constraints, including limited access to financing, which tend to leave them significantly less productive than their formal sector counterparts. For example, informal Turkish brake manufacturers achieve only 22 percent of U.S. productivity, while their formal sector competitors achieve 89 percent. Affordable access to titled land and reliable infrastructure (chapter 8) can also enhance firm and product market competitiveness.[55]

As discussed, improving transportation and logistical infrastructure can reduce the cost of moving goods. Better transportation links with other regions can also provide insurance against regional price fluctuations. For example, if there is a drought or food shortage in one area, efficient regional connections would allow consumers to import reasonably priced food from other parts of the country. Finally, better transport and logistics systems reduce inventory costs by making the timing of delivery more reliable, again benefiting producers and consumers.[56]

Interactions between product and labor markets

Changes in product markets, whether induced by internal developments or external trade-related changes, can have powerful influences on the opportunities facing workers. Standard trade theory predicts that countries should export products that use relatively abundant factors intensively. Labor-abundant countries that open up should see relative gains in unskilled wages, as indeed occurred among the East Asian tigers in the 1960s and 1970s.[57]

The Latin American experience stands in sharp contrast. Many countries, including Argentina, Chile, Colombia, Costa Rica, Mexico, and Uruguay, saw wider wage differentials with increasing trade openness during the late 1980s and 1990s. Some argue that this was due to the massive insertion of low-income Asian countries into global markets. Others interpret the evidence as supporting generalized skill-biased technical change, in which trade opening facilitated processes of restructuring, including the destruction of jobs in inefficient industries, and rising demand and relative wages for skilled workers.[58] Whatever the reason, the question is whether this was a source of rising inequality in opportunity. Over the short to medium term, this was almost certainly the case, because unskilled workers cannot increase skills quickly. Over the longer term, rising wage differentials provide incentives for investment in education, if education systems provide equal opportunities (chapter 7).

Effects of economic restructuring on workers also depend on the extent of labor mobility. One study from India shows that the effects of trade liberalization in the early 1990s on poverty varied by state, depending on the flexibility of labor laws. In states with less flexible laws, where liberalization did not produce any measurable effect on the allocation of labor across sectors, the adverse impact of trade opening on poverty was felt the most. In states with more flexible labor laws, movements of labor across sectors eased the shock of relative price changes.[59] While greater mobility is desirable, the design of measures that increase flexibility needs to be balanced with the levels of worker protection that are appropriate for the institutional setting (see the earlier discussion on labor markets).

Safety nets and opportunity

Safety nets complement product market deepening and are often an essential element of a strategy to ensure that market expansion leads to more equal opportunities. General questions of the design of safety nets were discussed in chapter 7; here we highlight the links with product market change. As discussed above, trade opening creates winners and losers. How this affects equity depends partly on how governments can offer support to the losers.

Rodrik (1998) finds that openness is associated with higher government spending. The argument is that open economies are more subject to external shocks and spend more on social insurance to mitigate external risk. In more advanced economies with the capacity to manage social welfare systems, exposure to external risk is strongly correlated with spending on social security and welfare. In less-developed economies, governments rely on a broader set of tools, such as public employment, to reduce risk.

The specific design of safety nets can expand opportunities to those who suffer adverse effects. For instance, trade adjustment assistance programs in the United States extended unemployment benefits, training, and relocation subsidies to displaced workers. While the United States was offering the programs in response to the NAFTA, the Mexican government established *Procampo*, a cash transfer program for grain farmers to ease the pain of NAFTA-induced competition from the United States. It was designed to provide consumption support to compensate for price declines and to allow farmers to diversify into other activities. While the size of the transfers was hurt by the 1995 Tequila Crisis, there is evidence of gains to farmers and of the use of proceeds for investment purposes.[60]

While the ideal policy mix may be one that combines reduced barriers and extensive safety nets, in practice, this is not always feasible. Many countries phase liberalization to seek to ensure that processes of job creation precede or accompany job destruction—this has been a central feature of the East Asian experience (see discussion of China in chapter 6). This carries risks of slowing restructuring and extending protection beyond periods justified by equity concerns because of capture by influential beneficiaries.

Credibility, political supportability, and the design of product market reform

While technocrats can design trade and other product market reforms that appear to be good for growth and equity, the expected gains will never materialize if there is not enough political support. Because of the nature of trade policy—a concentrated set of winners from trade barriers versus a diffuse set of winners from liberalization (consumers in general)—it is easy for vested interests to capture policy. Steel tariffs in the United States and agricultural subsidies in the United States, Japan, and Europe are obvious examples.

Even after trade liberalization laws have been passed, they are still not immune to capture. If economic actors do not believe that reforms are credible—that is, that politicians will recant at the behest of vested interests—the anticipated adjustments will never take place. Cashews in Mozambique again provide an apt example. In the early 1990s, the Mozambican government (working with the World Bank) implemented a new pricing regime that liberalized the export of raw cashews. But there was no credible political commitment to the new pricing regime, so neither cashew farmers nor cashew processors adjusted to the new price signals. Efficiency gains from the reallocation of resources never materialized.[61]

While this section has emphasized the heterogeneity of effects of product market changes, the policy message is not necessarily one of detailed fine-tuning of reforms. That

brings risks of greater capture. The ideal balance is a combination of gradual but committed liberalization with extensive engagement in the complementary measures that broaden opportunities for all: education, infrastructure, competition, and safety nets. Societal debate and information can ensure that governments remain accountable to all groups, not just those with access and connections. Of particular importance for external opening is the role of external commitments. Entry into international agreements, such as the WTO, the European Union, or NAFTA, can effectively lock politicians into trade reforms. When trade regulations are bound by international agreements, reform commitments are more credible and less susceptible to capture by domestic special interests (asymmetries in power among the international parties to such agreements remain, as we will read in chapter 10).

Macroeconomic management and equity

Macroeconomic instability is both a cause and consequence of inequity

Macroeconomic stability is a public good and might be expected to equally affect all. There is a well-established association between macroeconomic stability and long-term growth, and growth typically brings expansion in opportunities to everyone. But the fact that stability is a public good does not mean that the incidence of benefits is equal. As discussed in chapter 4, the distribution of income gains from economic growth is typically as unequal as the initial income distributions. Moreover, macroeconomic instability, whether in the form of volatility or high inflation, can have differential and potentially inequitable effects, because the pattern of power and wealth can influence the distribution of losses—and different groups have differential capacities to manage the consequent shocks.

As in many other areas, there are two-way patterns of causation between macroeconomic conditions and equity. Unequal patterns of power and associated institutional structures are at the center of causative influences from inequity to instability and in regressive effects of crises. By emphasizing these links, we are not arguing against the large body of literature on economic causes of crises. Depending on the type of crisis, this literature sees the causes as fiscal imbalances, herdlike movements of investors behind exchange rate crises, and interactions among external liabilities, exchange rates, and financial-corporate conditions, especially under "crony capitalism."[62] Some of the processes in this literature complement the diagnosis here; others are manifestations of underlying distributional and institutional conditions.

Figure 9.5 shows the bivariate correlation between macroeconomic volatility and a measure of "constraints on the executive" branch of government, which would be expected to be closely linked to restraints on elite power. Weaker constraints are associated with greater volatility (and a higher propensity for macroeconomic crises).

The correlation says nothing about causation. But there is evidence supporting the view that "weak and unequal" institutions have a causative influence on economic instability. A tradition of work interprets instability as a consequence of distributional struggles that are ineffectively managed by institutions.[63] As discussed in chapter 6, the seminal work by Bates (1981) on Ghana interprets exchange rate overvaluation and internal pricing policies as mechanisms for governments to severely tax cocoa farmers in the early postindependence period to provide resources to buy off urban groups. A combination of predatory governments and weak or absent balancing institutions created the preconditions for fights over rents and systematic political instability until the early 1980s. Analyses of hyperinflation, in settings as diverse as Bolivia and Israel, interpret macroeconomic instability as a consequence of failures to manage societal conflicts.[64]

Macroeconomic instability can interact with unequal influence in the fallout from crises

Crises, whatever the causes, are systematically bad for growth, more so in the presence of distributional struggles. Rodrik

Figure 9.5 Weaker institutions are associated with macroeconomic volatility and crises

Standard deviation of GDP growth

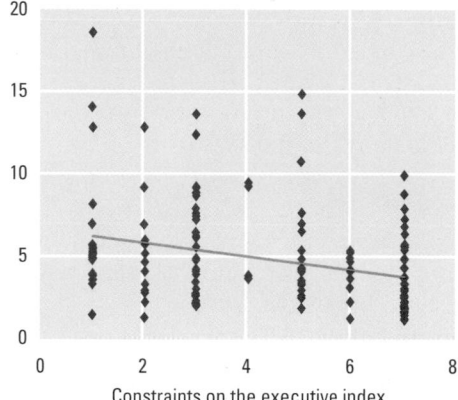

Constraints on the executive index

Source: Authors' calculations, using World Bank statistics and the Polity IV database for constraints on the executive index.
Note: A higher value for the constraints on the executive index denotes greater accountability.

(1999a) argues in a cross-country empirical analysis that the effects of external shocks in the 1970s were significantly worse for subsequent growth in societies in which latent distributional conflicts (proxied by income inequality or ethnolinguistic fragmentation) were more severe and conflict-management mechanisms (proxied by institutional strength and indicators of democracy) were weaker.

High inflation and macroeconomic crises can be particularly harmful to the poor, who are least equipped to manage adverse shocks. For the impacts on distributional outcomes, household survey evidence does not display systematic disequalizing or equalizing biases across countries: the Mexican 1994–95 crisis was slightly equalizing (although strongly poverty-increasing); the 2001 Argentine crisis was disequalizing. There is some evidence that high inflation is worse for poorer groups, for example, in the Philippines[65] and Brazil.[66]

Mechanisms for crisis resolution tend to be inequitable as a result of unequal influence. Many of the results are not fully reflected in household income and spending surveys. The reason is that the big action usually takes place elsewhere, notably in changes in capital income and fiscal positions that the surveys typically fail to capture.

Figure 9.6 Labor shares fall during crises and don't fully recover afterward

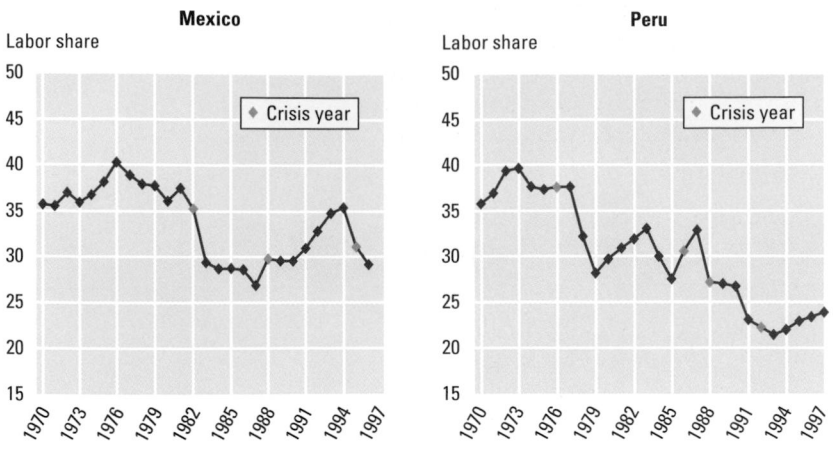

Source: Authors' calculations, based on national accounts.
Note: Crisis years are defined as years in which at least two out of three of the following occur: a 25 percent (or higher) nominal devaluation, negative growth, and 50 percent (or higher) rate of inflation.

Table 9.3 Fiscal costs of selected banking crises

Country and episode	Fiscal cost (percent of GDP)
Argentina, 1980–82	55.1
Brazil, 1994–96	13.2
Chile, 1981–83	41.2
Ecuador 1996–	13.0
México, 1994–	19.3
Venezuela, 1994–97	22.0
Korea, Rep. of, 1997–	26.5
Indonesia, 1997–	50.0
United States, 1981–91	3.2

Source: Honohan and Klingebiel (2000).
Note: Costs refer to both fiscal and quasi-fiscal outlays and the present value of the future stream of costs. Banking crises in Ecuador, Mexico, the Republic of Korea, and Indonesia were ongoing at the time of the study.

There is evidence that crises lead to reductions in measured labor share (strongly influenced by formal sector earnings and employment). Diwan (2001) finds that labor shares systematically fall during crises and don't fully recover afterward, a cross-country result illustrated for Mexico and Peru in figure 9.6.[67] The flip side of this pattern is that the shares of corporate and financial sector capital income rise relative to wages. There are also significant interactions with structural variables. In particular, closed trade, capital controls, and fiscal deficits are associated with higher labor shares in normal times, but with larger falls in labor shares when crises occur. Crises are mechanisms for the resolution of distributional conflicts that are not tackled during good economic times. Labor is relatively immobile and so typically bears a higher proportion of the cost. Pre-crisis labor shares may, in some cases, have been too high for competitiveness and stability, but the point is that crises are a high-cost form of conflict resolution. And the interaction between shocks and weak conflict resolution mechanisms is associated with weaker long-run growth.[68]

In addition to any effects through the distribution of labor and capital income, important mechanisms work through the financial sector and associated fiscal action.

Major crises lead to large financial losses, typically financed by both explicit and implicit fiscal outlays. Case study evidence indicates that these are highly regressive, through gainers and losers from capital flights, transfers from those outside to within the financial system, and the patterns of bailout among financial sector participants.

The fiscal costs of crises are large (table 9.3). For example, the post–Tequila Crisis Mexican bailout is estimated at $112 billion, with a large additional amount spent trying to prevent crises through liquidity support, sovereign bond swaps, and the financing of large investors who withdraw money from projects.[69] Halac and Schmukler (2003) use the $23 billion decline in the central bank's reserves between February and December 1994 as a proxy, calculating a total fiscal and quasi-fiscal cost of the crisis of $135 billion. This represents about one-quarter of Mexico's GDP in 2000 and some four times the $33 billion in capital receipts from privatization during the 1990s.

What is the pattern of gainers and losers? Some wealthy individuals undoubtedly lose their shirts. But there are strong tendencies for the poor to lose, sometimes to lose a lot. First, the wealthy with information and access to international banking systems get their money out first. And they may actually experience capital gains when domestic asset prices tumble and the exchange rate goes against the currency. In Argentina, the ratio of foreign assets to domestic GDP rose from about a quarter to more than 90 percent between 2001 and early 2002, because of a combination of capital flight and currency depreciation (figure 9.7).

Second, the recipients of fiscal bailouts are those within the financial system—depositors, creditors, and equity owners, who are systematically better off than those outside. (There are of course small middle-income depositors but, as noted below, it is possible to protect them without providing blanket protection for all.) Case study evidence finds biases toward wealthy and more influential individuals and groups within financial systems. Owners of large deposits enjoyed the greatest compensation (and sometimes capital gains) in crises in Argentina, Ecuador, and Uruguay, often through getting their money out of the country, while small depositors suffered capital losses. In addition, there is evidence that large borrowers with close connections to banks were especially favored in crises in Chile, Ecuador, and Mexico.[70]

Crisis costs are paid for by some combination of higher taxes and lower spending. Who pays depends on the marginal pattern of taxation and spending. As a first approximation on the tax side, many developing-country tax systems are roughly proportional (everyone pays the same proportion of their income, primarily through indirect taxation). On the spending side, work on Latin America and Asia in the 1990s finds that marginal spending was generally progressive, as the expansion of social and infrastructure programs "crowded in" poorer groups.[71] Thus, the forgone spending hurt poorer groups the most. The net effect is a regressive workout financed largely by regressive fiscal adjustment.

While case study evidence indicates a strong pattern of regressive consequences of

crises, this is contingent on initial structures, patterns of influence, and policy specifics. For example, the Russian crisis, while undoubtedly costly in social terms, may have led to a surprisingly positive shift to more equitable structures of resource management (box 9.6).

Policy directions need to take account of policy design and accountability structures

Macroeconomic instability is thus both product and cause of underlying inequalities and associated weak institutions. The costs are large to equity and growth. What can be done? As in other areas, it helps to answer this question in terms of the com-

Figure 9.7 In Argentina, the wealthy had a way out during the crisis

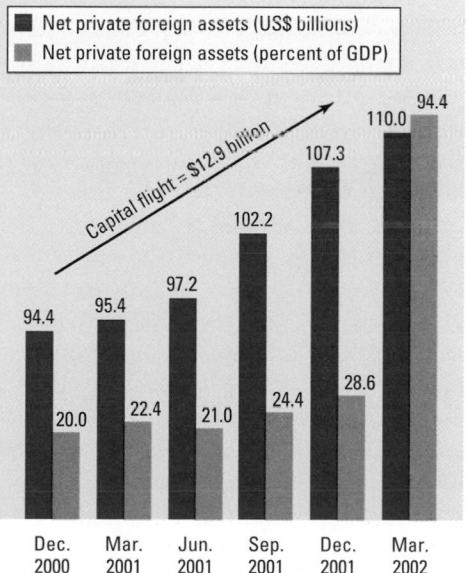

Source: Ministry of the Economy, Argentina.
Note: The sharp increase between December 2001 and March 2002 was because of the exchange rate devaluation.

BOX 9.6 *Did the Russian 1998 crisis have equitable consequences?*

The Russian crisis was at first glance typical of crises of the 1990s—driven by interactions between private capital movements and domestic institutional structures that encouraged moral hazard, and with large adverse effects for welfare. The social costs were severe, with a fall in GDP of 5 percent in 1998. Between 1996 and 1998 household per capita expenditures fell 25 percent, expenditure poverty rose from 22 to 33 percent and government transfers fell by 18 percent, albeit with better targeting (Lokshin and Ravallion 2000). There was also major capital flight, with many of the rich getting their assets out fast, leaving the rest of the society to share the costs. This fact alone is a sign of great inequity: the rich had more opportunity to protect their assets by shifting money out of the country. This (individually rational) behavior imposed costs on less wealthy groups.

But the transition appears to have had additional effects that were, at least to some degree, more equitable. Russia before the crisis was in a particularly inefficient and inequitable equilibrium, in which firms did not pay their energy or tax bills, and the energy sector didn't pay its taxes. Firms were not allowed to go under for fear of employment effects, but this was a highly ineffective safety net. Subsidies were estimated at 15 to 20 percent of GDP in the three years before the crisis, fueling corruption and delaying enterprise restructuring. There was extensive asset-stripping at the cost of the broader society.

The crisis triggered major changes in economic relationships. The strategy of "devalue and default" led to large relative price movements and cut Russia off from international capital markets. The cutoff, combined with the authorities' recognition of the unpopularity of hyperinflation, finally forced hard budget constraints on the system, which had powerful ripple effects in inducing the demise of the nonpayments system, making economic transactions more transparent and laying the basis for a recovery in taxes. Real exchange rate depreciation made many firms competitive again, and this fed through into employment. Furthermore, the big Moscow banks were allowed to fail (with total costs, largely incurred before the meltdown, a relatively low 2 percent of GDP). And the default meant that external holders of Russian paper took an immediate loss, effectively allowing a degree of international burden-sharing. While there were undoubtedly reputational costs, there may have been an advantage in taking this upfront, rather than after protracted negotiations. Overall, while a serious analysis of impacts on equality of opportunity is not feasible, the effective shift in regime from a system in which influence played a dominant role in resource allocation to one of hard budget constraints and greater transparency was probably good for efficiency and equity.

Source: Pinto and others (forthcoming).

plementary role of specific policy design and the deepening of accountability structures and societal mechanisms to manage conflict. The Israeli hyperinflation provides an illustration. Its resolution involved both a full set of financial and macroeconomic policies and an intensive process of societal interaction to manage underlying conflicts between organized labor, the corporate sector, and other interest groups.[72]

There is an extensive body of literature on design specifics. Thus, we conclude with some comments on the principles of macroeconomic management that emerge from a focus on equity. Some of the principles are fairly familiar, especially the need to build stronger regulatory and supervisory structures for the financial system and comprehensive insurance mechanisms while out of crisis. Once a crisis hits, it is particularly difficult to design and implement such measures and politically difficult to implement more equitable outcomes. By contrast ex ante insurance design—whether for depositors, bankruptcy, or unemployment—is more likely to be broad based and, if already in place, reduces the case for ex post deals tailored to the influential.

Less obvious is a heightened emphasis on fiscal prudence. In public debates, adopting a less stringent macroeconomic stance is often portrayed as a distributionally progressive approach, whether in good times or bad. While there will always be specific judgments about the distributional impacts of a range of fiscal and monetary policy options, the analysis here suggests that taking a "superprudent" position over the course of the cycle provides greater hope for supporting a more equal development pattern. On one level, this sharply reinforces the common prescription to break procyclical policy positions. Macroeconomic restraint in good times will facilitate automatic stabilizers and a sensible easing of policies to be applied in a disciplined fashion when adverse shocks occur. Thus, the priority is to build fiscal rules and institutions that help overcome the political pressures to deplete potential surpluses in good times, as well as informational asymmetry problems. These insi-

tutions should also improve the credibility of countercyclical fiscal policies during downturns.[73] This strategy would, in particular, provide the macroeconomic foundation for broad-based, self-expanding safety nets.

Finally, there is a case for different forms of accountability. Over the long term, the most effective approach is to move to new fiscal and social contracts built on deeper accountability structures—to a better political equilibrium.[74] There is then a need for an appropriate mix of stronger regulatory accountability shielded from short-run political pressures from all sides—more independent central banks and stronger financial sector supervision—and greater transparency and debate about the overall design of macropolicy and the incidence of workouts. There are important interactions with external actors and rules for crisis management that will be taken up in chapter 10.

In sum, we have explored policies that, by leveling the playing field in the markets for capital, labor, and goods and by managing the macroeconomy, can lead to greater equity and prosperity. Financial markets are typically biased toward incumbents, reflecting the historical political influence of the powerful. Yet rapid and ill-designed liberalizations can lead to further concentration of influence. Greater societal controls are needed as well as a more measured tackling of barriers—especially to small and medium firms—backed by regulatory structures and more information to reduce the power of connections.

Labor market outcomes may reflect the weak bargaining position of workers, but labor policies often lead to patterns of job protection that create economic rigidities and help those in good jobs, to the detriment of those in the informal economy. Support for unions and security for workers are important objectives, but designs need to be adapted to economic conditions in ways that reach poorer, informal workers and minimize impediments to economic restructuring.

Both the design of external trade policy and the workings of internal product markets reflect patterns of influence. Removing biases and ensuring access to all need to be complemented by measures to expand skills, infrastructure, and safety nets to achieve genuine access and to manage losses (especially horizontal inequities). Imprudent macroeconomic policy is typically inequitable: high inflation hurts those least capable of managing its consequences, and financial crises are particularly pernicious, because the powerful can benefit or be bailed out at the expense of the rest of society. Prudent macroeconomic management, backed by strong countercyclical policy and independence in policy design is an ally, not a foe, of greater equity. We now turn to policies that can help level the global playing field.

The role of public policy in addressing spatial inequalities

The persistence of regional disparities within countries is a major policy concern confronting many governments in rich and poor countries alike. Clarity on the causal factors of weak regional performance and careful consideration of potential tradeoffs are needed to guide policy choice over regional interventions.

The average income in Brazil's northeast is less than half the national average. Poverty rates are far higher than the national average in India's densely populated states of Bihar, Uttar Pradesh, and Orissa, and the regional income gap appears to be widening. In 1990, children in the northwest region of Nigeria were four times less likely to receive any immunizations and 50 percent more likely to die by age five than those near the capital in the southwest; by 1999 they were five times less likely to receive any immunizations and 85 percent more likely to die before age five. Chronic regional underperformance can give rise to many concerns and threaten national unity—lost economic potential, unfairness in regional opportunities, potential instability, loss of social cohesion, and adverse social consequences, including higher crime and disease.

The geographic and historical factors underlying interregional inequality are complex and overlapping. Weak resource endowments and distance from markets can constrain development in lagging regions. In many cases, economic differences are linked with long-standing, unequal relations of power between advantaged and lagging regions, and institutional weaknesses within the latter.[1] When actors in advantaged regions control the assets, decision-making and policy formation processes, and the terms of the policy debates on which lagging regions depend, regional "catch up" is much more difficult.[2]

When historically disadvantaged ethnic, racial, and social groups are concentrated in particular regions, group-based inequities become reflected in regional inequalities. This is the case in parts of Latin America, where indigenous groups are both poorer and concentrated in poorer regions,[3] and in Vietnam and in India where tribal groups (*adivasis*) are spatially concentrated.[4]

In the absence of redistributive fiscal transfers, recent reforms in many countries toward greater decentralization may aggravate regional disparities. The positive effects of decentralization may be lost in regions that have weaker fiscal capacity, such as in Argentina's experience with decentralizing reforms in education.[5] In poor regions where regional elites have particularly concentrated power, decentralization may also deepen both intra- and inter-regional inequalities.[6]

Trends in inter-regional inequality have varied considerably across countries. The United States has experienced convergence and lower interregional income disparities. Indonesia shows convergence of provincial incomes since the 1970s. Brazil has seen divergence over many decades, but recently has shown convergence. Evidence on India also suggests divergence. China's pattern of growth has reduced gaps in the 1970s and 1980s, which widened in the 1990s. And in Mexico a long-run trend of slow convergence in incomes shifted to one of slow divergence after an opening that started in the late 1980s.

Characteristics of lagging regions

The reasons for regions to lag varies, and we present a simple taxonomy.

Low poverty density, low market access. These regions are sparsely populated, remote, and face particular geographic challenges. Distance and poor resource endowment—often with weak social indicators, generally poor infrastructure, and weak regional voice—place these regions at the periphery of national economic activity and opportunity. Supporting development of these regions may be desirable on poverty grounds, but it is likely to be expensive.

Low poverty density, high market access. These regions typically have been booming at one point in history, and were well integrated with the national economy. But changing demand patterns or resource exhaustion became sources of decline, even though political influence may have persisted. For such "rustbelt" regions, there is a case for public support for movement of people and resources out of declining industries, backed by social safety nets for the affected workforce.

High poverty density, high or low market access. These regions are most often considered for targeted interventions: poverty is concentrated in them, population density is relatively high, and the lack of market integration is due to history rather than geography. Possible culprits include weak governance, poor institutional capacity and human capital, a history of sociocultural conflict and domination, a poor investment climate, and security problems. Such regions are often home to socially, racially, and ethnically disadvantaged groups. Where such groups are dispersed or patron-client relationships dominate, the challenge of fostering organization, agency, and political influence is especially great.[7]

Regional development policies and tradeoffs

Regional development policies involve interventions to facilitate inward investment, enhance income opportunities and well-being in lagging regions, help households move to opportunities elsewhere, and shift interregional power relations. Policies are context specific and involve tradeoffs. If lagging regional performance reflects geographic disadvantages or an absence of

Market access (population density, transport costs)

Poverty density (poor or disadvantaged people per square kilometer)		Low	High
	Low	• Chile's "zonas extremas" • Russian North (state-sponsored settlements) • Northern Canada	• N.E. China's "rustbelt" region • Developed country "coal towns" (France, U.K., U.S.)
	High	• Thailand's northeast • Mexico's southern states	• India's "Hindu Belt" poor and populous states • Italy's southern Mezzogiorno

agglomeration and scale economies, public interventions may be particularly expensive. But when public policy is designed to correct market failures (such as underdeveloped insurance or credit markets), address specific social or historical factors handicapping regional performance, or capture externalities intrinsic to national welfare (cultural, environmental, security), there may be few or no efficiency tradeoffs.

Fiscal incentives

A popular approach involves fiscal incentives to induce industry to locate and invest in lagging regions: tax advantages, insurance or risk-sharing arrangements, direct subsidies, or indirect subsidies through provision of low-cost public services. But evaluations of fiscal incentives generally indicate that they can be costly and ineffective. Brazil's efforts to develop the manufacturing center of Manaus in the north have been a success by some measures, but costs per job created are high.[8] Interregional "fiscal wars" can also occur as regions compete to attract businesses. If uncoordinated or unconstrained, these can have adverse consequences for local tax bases and public services in competing jurisdictions. Compared to the alternatives listed below, this tends to be a high-distortion strategy.

Public investment

Targeted public investment, particularly in core infrastructure, is another policy response aimed at reducing geographic disincentives to firm location, whether for existing or new firms. China has followed this strategy, first in the coastal special economic zones, and now in western regions (see box below).

Investment in regional infrastructure links may enhance productivity of existing firms and attract new firms. But, it also allows more efficient firms in richer regions to sell to lagging regions. This is one factor that has slowed development of the relatively poor Mezzogiorno region of southern Italy, despite large investments in national north-south infrastructure that has reduced transport costs.[9]

Facilitating labor mobility

Facilitating voluntary labor movement to higher opportunity areas is another strategy. In contrast to fiscal incentives and public investments that focus on bringing jobs to poor areas, this strategy focuses on bringing poor people to areas with more potential. Relocation assistance can include transport, housing, training, resettlement allowances, and portable safety nets. Examples included incentives in Russia for families to relocate from their northern settlements—developed at huge state expense for resource extraction and security purposes during the Cold War—and incentives to support movement of labor out of declining industries, such as the moribund coal sectors in Western Europe and the former Soviet Union since the 1960s. While the programs have helped ease the impact of unemployment, there are questions about cost effectiveness and long-term impact.

There is also a long history of efforts to direct settlement of remote regions or encourage migration to frontier lands. Early settlers to the Americas, including the west and midwestern regions of the United States, were beneficiaries of legal land grants to clear and use new land. More recent programs include Indonesia's transmigration program that shifted Javanese to sparsely populated outer islands in the 1970s and 1980s, or early Ethiopian resettlement programs to fertile areas in the south and southwest regions of the country. However, these and other resettlement programs have been criticized for their coercive or ethnic dimensions, raising questions about the adverse impact on indigenous population groups and settlers.

Enhancing agency

Where intergroup inequalities in agency underlie regional disadvantage, national and regional policies addressing discrimination, racism, and citizenship deficits can be important instruments for dealing with spatial inequality. Enhancing voice and participation of excluded groups is also important for national peace and cohesion. While ethnic discrimination and regional disadvantage do not necessarily lead to conflict, researchers and truth and reconciliation commissions alike have identified them as contributing factors.[10] In Aceh, Indonesia, oil rents have been transferred back to the region since 1976, yet regional conflict and demands for autonomy have increased rather than abated.[11] This suggests that transfers alone are not sufficient to address regionally concentrated grievances—they must be accompanied by meaningful political participation and dialogue.

Conclusion

The specific nature of the constraints to regional growth and investment performance in lagging regions needs to be identified and prioritized. Policies that provide fiscal incentives to investors are likely to fail if the main factors that adversely influence regional investment climate—quality of local institutions, skilled labor availability, proximity to key markets, functioning capital and land markets, security risks—still pose binding constraints.

Public investment in infrastructure that reduces transport costs for both people and goods has often proved an effective strategy for integration. And, as with other policies, well designed technical solutions are more likely to be implemented if those living in poorer regions are empowered.

Development of lagging regions in China

Unprecedented economic growth and poverty reduction in China have been accompanied by significant increases in regional disparities since the economic reform in the late 1970s. The socioeconomic costs of a sustained divergence in income between leading and lagging regions has become a major concern of the government.

In 1999, the government initiated the "Go West" strategy to develop the lagging western region. Through targeted public investments and fiscal subsidies, the central government spent some 1,000 billion yuan (US$120 billion) in the past five years, focusing on infrastructure, education, health, and the environment. A variety of investment incentives and low interest loans aimed to attract domestic and foreign firms to areas in which the western region has some comparative advantage, such as energy, agriculture, and agroprocessing.

The relative decline of the historically advantaged northeastern region has also attracted concern. China's northeast currently suffers from slow growth and high unemployment in declining industries, along with many severely distressed towns and cities. The government started the "Revitalize Northeast" strategy in 2003. This involves new initiatives, including strengthening the investment climate, developing greater flexibility in factor markets, using public funds to support rather than postpone adjustment, and mitigating social costs through improved and portable safety nets.

Achieving greater global equity

We read in chapter 2 that there are huge inequities in the world. Even better-off citizens in most of the developing world face worse opportunities than the poor in rich countries. The fact that country of birth is a key determinant of people's opportunities runs counter to our view of equity—that is, that people should enjoy the same opportunities regardless of their background, including where they are born.

Greater global equity is desirable for itself to all those who find equity intrinsically valuable. The international human rights regime testifies to the shared belief that all should have equal rights and be spared extreme deprivation. Some even argue that there is a powerful moral case for rich countries to take action, because of the huge disparities and (arguably) because they partly created and perpetuate global inequities.[1] Greater equity is also desirable because it would likely be beneficial to global prosperity in the long run. Greater equity in access to health and health remedies, especially for transmittable diseases, would reduce global health inequalities and be beneficial to poor and rich countries alike. Greater equity in access to and control over natural resources and the global commons may lead to more sustainable use. Some argue that greater equity could also lead to greater international stability: fragile and failed states pose a threat to local and global stability.[2]

What can be done to reduce the huge inequities we experience today? The debate about what causes global inequities and how to address them is highly contentious. Some see globalization—greater global integration—as a source of equalization, others a source of widening inequalities, with richer countries and corporations making rules that benefit themselves at the cost of the weak, poor, and voiceless. There is some truth on all sides of the debate. In terms of trends, we saw in chapter 2 that the picture is mixed: convergence in health and (probably) education for many, convergence in incomes for some, but divergence in incomes and health for others. In terms of causes, just as some of the major sources of convergence have been associated with globalization of markets and knowledge—the East Asian tigers, China, India making use of global markets, the spread of the green revolution and health-related technology—so unequal rules and unequal influence profoundly shape opportunity.

Domestic action is clearly central to reducing inequities. Developing countries hold the keys to their prosperity; global action cannot substitute for equitable and efficient domestic policies and institutions. But global conditions powerfully affect the scope for and impact of domestic policies. Global action—by governments, people, and organizations in developed countries and by international institutions—can determine whether the globalization process brings about greater equity, peace, and prosperity, or fuels tensions and conflicts that will lead to backlash and violence.

Current disparities are products of interactions between two factors: the endowments of different countries, and the rules shaping the options for deploying these endowments on domestic and global markets. Endowments are greatly unequal due to history and geography—although some of the history and aspects of geography are a product of unequal development patterns. Infrastructure underdevelopment in Africa, for example, is partly a legacy of colonial political and economic patterns. Institutional weaknesses of poorer societies—now part of their endowment—also reflect historical patterns, as discussed in chapter 6. Differences in endowments are often exacerbated by the inequitable functioning of markets. As in the domestic realm, market imperfections can be either a product of policy (as in barriers to labor mobility or agricultural protection) or of intrinsic market failures (as in weak protection of global commons and lack of incentives for knowledge creation).

Achieving greater global equity thus requires global policies that improve endowments and address market imperfections and more representative global insitutions. We first discuss the global markets for labor, goods, ideas, and capital—all functioning within the context of international law (box 10.1). For each market, we highlight existing inequities and their impact, discuss the processes that lead to such inequities, and explore some options for change. We next turn to rectifying past and present inequities in the use of natural resources. Then we look at whether aid—the traditional response to global inequity—can be used effectively to accelerate domestic efforts to build endowments. The current state of international relations may cause some to wonder whether any change is possible. So we close the chapter by examining factors that have facilitated transitions to more equitable policies and institutions in the past. We conclude that change may be difficult but not impossible.[3]

Making global markets work more equitably

Global markets have many faces: Filipino nurses, Sri Lankan domestic workers, Polish care providers, Indian engineers, Ugandan coffee growers, Bangladeshi women working in garment factories, Moroccan craftsmen, employers of migrants, and the consumers of developing-country products in Australia,

---

BOX 10.1 *International law, globalization, and equity*

Globalization takes place (mostly) in the context of international law, which governs relations among states, and other international legal subjects, such as international organizations. More equitable development, application, monitoring, and enforcement of international law is essential to make globalization more equitable.

The meaning of equity in international law. Equity considerations inform the development of international law, confirming that greater global equity is a shared value. The principle of equity has accompanied the development of international law over the centuries (chapter 4). Equity in international law encompasses notions of corrective justice and distributive justice—that the strict application of the law should be tempered by considerations of equity or fairness to achieve a just result, and that international law should promote a more even distribution of resources among states. Equitable principles have been applied to many areas of international law, from the sharing of scientific benefits, technology, and natural resources to laws governing the sea, international waterways, outer space, and carbon emissions. As highlighted in chapter 4, the most pertinent example of the application of principles of equity in international law is the international human rights regime. In today's international law, equity has not only an interstate dimension; it also has an intergenerational dimension, in the preservation of the environment and other global commons, as we will see below.

Rule-setting processes. International laws are formed through complex negotiating processes. The degree to which these processes are perceived to be equitable affects their adoption and implementation—so processes matter greatly. Generally, a state remains free to decide whether to become a party to a convention or covenant. And a state's satisfaction with the process leading to the adoption of a convention may facilitate signing and subsequent adoption. For example, the Universal Declaration of Human Rights, seen by many as the basis of subsequent human rights instruments, was adopted by the U.N. General Assembly, where all countries are represented and have one vote. While only a declaration, and not intended to bind states at the time it was adopted, the process leading to its adoption was perceived to be equitable. The body of standards set by the ILO is another example of rules set through an international process that is broadly consultative, encompassing not just governments but unions and private sector representatives. On the other hand, the rule-setting processes of the World Trade Organization (and its predecessor, the General Agreement on Tariffs and Trade) are perceived by some as inequitable, and this is partly responsible for the current stalemate.

Application and enforcement mechanisms. The processes that interpret, apply, and enforce international laws are crucial to realizing greater equity. In general, the ability of states to pursue and enforce rights under international law depends on appropriate adjudication processes or complaint mechanisms and their effectiveness. A number of international courts and other adjudicative bodies often have voluntary jurisdiction, but there is a trend toward judicialization and compulsory jurisdiction. For example, dispute settlement arrangements established under the 1982 U.N. Convention on the Law of the Sea and the 1994 World Trade Organization Dispute Settlement Understanding mark a significant move toward compulsory jurisdiction and binding decision making.

The ability of citizens and other nonstate actors to pursue their rights and seek redress under international law depends on whether their state has become a party to the instruments that allow the use of compliance mechanism. For example, for citizens to make a complaint against their state under the International Covenant of Civil and Political Rights, the state must have signed and ratified the First Optional Protocol, which allows a complaint to be heard by the Human Rights Committee established by the covenant. As the discussion indicates and in parallel to what happens on the domestic arena, rules often block access, even before expenses, knowledge, and capacity limit effective recourse.

the European countries, Japan, the United States, and the richer middle-income countries. Global markets create valuable economic opportunities for millions of people, who develop ideas, raise capital, and sell their products and their labor.

But unequal endowments and unfair processes mean that opportunities and rules are not the same for all. Inequities exist in the functioning of these markets. Unskilled workers from poor countries, who could earn higher returns in rich countries, face great hurdles in migrating. Developing-country producers face obstacles in selling agricultural products, manufactured items, and services in developed countries. Foreign investors often get better deals in debt crises.

In most cases, more equitable rules would bring benefits to both developed and developing countries, but the extent of benefits varies by market. Barriers are massively greater in the market for labor—the factor of production that the poor own in relative abundance—than in the markets for goods and capital, and factor price equalization clearly does not work through trade alone. So removing barriers to migration could have a significant impact on expanding

people's opportunities (of course, migration raises complex issues that are politically and socially difficult to tackle in sending and receiving countries).

Benefits also vary greatly depending on country context. The fast-growing developing countries, including China and India that are home to half the world's poorest people, stand to benefit significantly from more equitable global markets. Leveling the global playing field can help them sustain fast growth, while equitable domestic policies help ensure that this growth is shared. Countries with more limited endowments, such as many African countries, that are left behind in the global economy, stand to benefit less in the short to medium run from more equitable global markets.

Greater international labor mobility

Returns to capital, and to some extent skilled labor, tend to equalize across countries, but returns to unskilled labor, owned by poor people and in abundant supply in poor countries, generally do not converge. Wage differentials across countries for jobs requiring similar skills are large, and substantially larger than the wage gap between the United States and migrant-sending countries in the late nineteenth century (figure 10.1). Developed countries severely limit in-migration of unskilled and semi-skilled workers, which contributes to the lack of equalization in returns to unskilled labor.

Greater migration of unskilled labor would tend to equalize returns, with winners and losers, but with potentially beneficial effects on efficiency. History teaches us that migration has, at various times, alleviated human suffering and promoted cultural and technological exchanges. The mass migration from Europe to the Americas in the nineteenth and early twentieth centuries enabled 60 million people to escape poverty and persecution, creating some of today's wealthiest societies (although Native Americans faced enormous losses in the process).[4]

Economic analyses indicate that gains from expanding migration could be very significant. Hamilton and Whalley (1984) use a highly simplified economic model of the world to suggest that the benefits from reallocation of labor could be huge (on the

Figure 10.1 Wage differentials are substantially larger today than at the end of the nineteenth century
Ratios of purchasing power parity adjusted wages of the United States and its migration partners in 1870 and pairs of countries in the 1990s

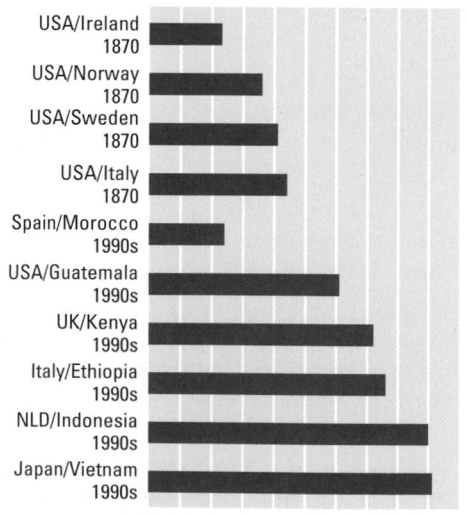

Ratio of wages in PPP

Source: Pritchett (2003).

order of doubling GDP). This, of course, depends on the specific assumptions used and ignores a host of adjustment issues, but it does serve to illustrate that the gains could be large and probably much larger than the gains from the, by comparison, already greatly liberalized trade in goods. Indeed, using an approach similar to that of analyses of trade impacts, Walmsley and Winters (2003) estimated that increasing temporary migration into industrial countries by 3 percent of host countries' current skilled and unskilled work force— equivalent to permitting an extra 8 million skilled and 8.4 million unskilled workers to be employed at any time, roughly a doubling of current net migration into high-income countries—would generate an estimated increase in world welfare of more than $150 billion a year. This increase would be shared fairly equally between developing- and developed-country citizens. Much of the gain would come from the migration of unskilled workers. Country studies confirm that migration could have a significant impact. Annabi and others (forthcoming) found that a 50 percent increase in the flow of remittances to Bangladesh would reduce the incidence of $1 per day income poverty by 0.8 percent in the short run and by 4 percent by 2020.[5]

Doesn't migration raise income inequality in sending countries? As a high-risk, high-return activity, migration is more likely to be undertaken first by members of wealthier, less credit-constrained, better-educated households. Successful migrants later provide information and assistance to potential migrants through social networks, thus lowering risks and costs and making it possible for members of households in lower parts of the income distribution to migrate.[6] In the first stages of the migration process, remittances sent to wealthier households can increase inequality, if they are higher than forgone income.[7] As migration expands, remittances begin to arrive to less well-off households and income distribution improves.[8] Remittances also have indirect effects through greater spending, risk diversification, and easing of credit constraints, which are generally inequality-reducing.[9] On balance, the evidence does not support the view that migration leads unequivocally to higher inequality in sending countries.

In receiving countries, migration relieves labor shortages in labor-intensive sectors, such as health care, hotels and restaurants, and construction. As developed-country populations age and their levels of education and training rise, these shortages are likely to become more severe. Demographic trends are another powerful force behind migration. Current population projections imply that the labor forces of Europe and Japan will decline over the next century, and that the ratio of people of working age to people of retirement age (the support ratio) will grow to levels that would make current pension and social transfer schemes unviable. Meanwhile, the population of the North Africa countries south of Europe is growing rapidly.

Despite its large benefits, migration is fiercely opposed in receiving countries. Migration involves complex issues of national and individual identity exacerbated by concerns over security. Cultural and social integration appears more difficult in some countries than it was earlier thought. Moreover, unskilled workers experience wage erosion and unemployment. For industrial workers, however, this is no different than if goods produced in countries with lower labor costs displace domestic production.

In sending countries, there are concerns about the human and social costs of migration, for instance, on how migration of nurses and doctors hinders progress toward the Millennium Development Goals (MDGs) and migration of women creates major deficits in child rearing, family support, and care for the elderly.[10] Licensing restrictions (as for doctors) often force skilled migrants to work in lower-skilled jobs in host countries—the "brain waste," and higher returns to education, do not appear to spur human capital accumulation or "brain gain."[11]

Going against the political tide—with the partial exceptions of some currents in the United States, Canada and Spain—we argue that greater migration would be good for both equity and efficiency. But what are the prospects for greater migration in the current political climate? Multilateral negotiations in the World Trade Organization (WTO) offer a framework to address migration under Mode IV of the General Agreement in Trade and Services (GATS), part of the treaty establishing the WTO.[12] But progress toward greater liberalization of temporary migration under GATS Mode IV is unlikely in the near future, given that contentious issues on agricultural and merchandise trade are dominating negotiations on the Doha Round.

In this context, progress is more likely to come from bilateral and regional negotiations. Receiving countries could bilaterally expand temporary migration (box 10.2 discusses some features of "development-friendly" temporary migration schemes). These countries could also extend greater protection to migrants. One way to do this could be to ratify the 1990 U.N. Convention on the Rights of All Migrant Workers and Their Families. If a significant number of host countries were to ratify the convention, none would risk being considered a haven for undocumented migrants, and fears about ratification leading to greater inflows might be allayed.[13] Facilitating remittance flows is another action with potentially high payoffs, and governments should work together with the private sector and NGOs to achieve this.[14]

Sending countries should take action to reduce the likelihood that their migrants become victims of exploitation, with a focus on combating trafficking of girls and women.[15] Two possible areas for action are to better regulate recruitment agencies to ensure greater respect for workers' rights and to enter agreements that regulate migrant flows and conditions with key destination countries, as the Philippines has done. Sending countries should also help migrants use remittances properly, invest back home, and reintegrate upon return.

It is unclear whether an international organization in which poor countries have an equal seat at the table could help make progress toward freer migration. Bhagwati (2003) argued that a new World Migration Organization—or even a stronger International Organization for Migration in the U.N. system—might help increase the developmental impact of migration by protecting migrants' rights, providing a forum to set rules on migration, and monitoring and enforcing compliance. But migrant-receiving developed countries resist proposals to give up even some control over immigration policies, which they view as part of the domestic policy agenda.

Freer and fairer trade

Inequities in the trade arena are well known: rich countries protect their markets with tariff and nontariff barriers on the goods that poor countries produce more advantageously (such as agricultural produce and textiles). They provide handsome subsidies to their farmers, subsidize their exports, and discourage value-added processing in developing countries. Reducing such protection and subsidies would have a beneficial impact on world trade, growth, and poverty reduction.

Potential benefits from liberalization. Several recent studies have estimated the potential impact of various trade liberalization measures, including those being considered during the Doha Round of negotiations under the WTO. Estimates vary, depending on the reforms considered (various packages of partial reforms up to full liberalization) and on whether dynamic productivity gains are taken into account. At the lower end of the range, Hertel and Winters (forthcoming) estimated that the measures being discussed in the Doha Round would have a modest impact on world prices, welfare gains, and poverty, with the number of people living below $2 a day declining by 9 million in 2015 over a baseline estimate of around 2 billion. According to this study, even full liberalization would not bring huge gains, as it would help lift 80 million people out of $2 a day poverty. At the higher end of the range, Cline (2004) estimated that full trade liberalization would lift up to 440 million people out of $2 a day poverty by 2015.

Whatever the size of the overall impact, researchers agree that it would be heterogeneous across countries and regions. In both partial and full reform scenarios, the gains would accrue mostly to large countries already significantly integrated in global markets, such as Brazil, China, India, and Indonesia. Parts of many Sub-Saharan countries and remote areas in Asia and elsewhere are simply not connected to global markets, and farmers eke out a living on subsistence agriculture, far from roads, markets, technology, and information. Many countries are unable to make full use of improved market access because of significant supply-side and institutional constraints. Detailed studies on Cambodia, Ethiopia, Madagascar, and Zambia showed that the potential impact of the trade reforms likely to be included in the Doha Round would be small for such countries. Some countries would even lose in the short run: Bangladesh and Mozambique, for instance, would experience a decline in incomes, as existing preferences are eroded and the prices of key food imports rise. Similarly, Bourguignon, Levin, and Rosenblatt (2004b) found that countries in the bottom two deciles of the international distribution of income would benefit more from a doubling of aid over current levels than from full trade reform. The estimated impact of trade liberalization varies greatly within countries as well (chapter 9).

Specific liberalization measures would also have differential impacts. Anderson and Martin (2004) found that the removal of OECD agricultural subsidies would hurt net food-importing least developed countries, such as those in the Middle East and North Africa, and countries that now enjoy special preferences, such as the Philippines, because of the consequent increase in prices.[16] But net food-producing countries, and farmers within them, would benefit. There is, indeed, some evidence that rising agricultural world prices were partly responsible for the fact that rural incomes in China grew more rapidly than urban incomes in 2004.

The phasing out of the Multi-Fiber Agreement, which set quotas on exports of textiles from developing countries, also has heterogeneous effects. Chinese textile exports have made significant gains in markets not protected by tariffs—for instance, their share of Australian and Japanese markets, where there were no quota restrictions, is 70 percent. Their share of the U.S. baby clothes segment, where quotas were removed in 2002, jumped from 11 to 55 percent in two years. Exports from Cambodia and Nepal are reported to have declined significantly. The impact of these shifts on global income inequality is not clear and it depends on the relative position of garment workers and of those benefiting from indirect effects in the global distribution. Changes in the existing tariff structure, whereby producers from the poorest countries have duty-free access to markets in the United States and Europe while others face a 16 percent tariff on average, would also have an unclear impact on inequality.[17] Conversely, renewed protectionism in developed countries is likely to have negative effects.

Currently, no global assistance program exists to compensate losers from trade liberalization. However, international assistance to help meet adjustment costs is an important focus, along with addressing supply-side constraints, of current efforts by a range of donors, recipients, and international organizations, including the World Bank, to increase aid for trade in the context of the WTO Doha round.

Setting trade rules. Where do the rules that govern trade come from, and what are the chances of changes? Trade rules, including the most egregiously inequitable, are part of complex multilateral, regional, and bilateral agreements. As mentioned in box 10.1, there are significant concerns about the fairness of WTO decision-making processes, and these processes are partly responsible for the current stalemate in negotiations.

But the reality of WTO negotiations is complex. In the WTO, each country has one vote, and the practice of decision making by consensus means that each country can veto decisions (although the practice of "single undertaking," or voting on all matters together, in practice weakens veto power). Countries choose to sign on to the WTO following not only extensive external negotiations but also domestic decision-making processes. So this is not a *prima facie* example of unfair rule-setting. In practice, however, poor countries find it difficult to follow negotiations, to understand the implications of proposals to them, and to develop alternative proposals—we saw in chapter 3 that even their capacity to be present in Geneva is limited.

So, in the end, the rules may at times be unfair not because the formal processes are unfair but because of the underlying power imbalance between rich countries with strong commercial interests and poor countries with weak capacity.[18] The balance is even tilted against taxpayers and consumers in rich countries, who often stand to lose from the protection of vested commercial interests. Consider, for example, cotton subsidies (see box 10.3) and international cartels.[19] Poor countries are in an even weaker position when negotiating bilaterally with stronger trading partners than they are when negotiating multilaterally. Paradoxically, in light of the intense antiglobalization protests, multilateral negotiations in the context of the WTO hold the greatest promise to reduce inequities that harm poor countries. Although even an ambitious Doha Round would bring limited benefits, it remains an important goal to pursue because failure would further undermine confidence in multilateral negotiations.

The WTO has another advantage: it provides for a mechanism to adjudicate disputes. This is important, as seen earlier, to ensure that international law is applied and enforced. The WTO dispute settlement mechanism provides a forum for poor countries to bring complaints and possibly win them. Unfortunately, winning a case does

---

BOX 10.3 *Cotton subsidies are huge—and tenacious*

The International Cotton Advisory Committee estimated that, in 2001/02, direct production assistance by the eight countries that provided subsidies (United States, China, the European Union, and to a much smaller extent Turkey, Egypt, Mexico, Brazil, Cote d'Ivoire, in that order) was around $5.8 billion. Direct assistance to U.S. cotton producers reached $3.3 billion, China's support totaled $1.2 billion (although some question this estimate), and the European Union's support was $979 million (for Greece and Spain) (International Cotton Advisory Committee 2003). The main impact of U.S. and European subsidies is to make cotton produced in the United States and Europe competitive and depress world prices. It is estimated that in 2001/02 prices would have been 71 percent higher without subsidies.

Subsidies benefit large rich farmers in the United States and not-so-rich but relatively well-off farmers in Europe, and harm poor, small farmers in Africa. Cotton is a crucial commodity for a number of poor African and Central Asian countries, contributing up to 40 percent of merchandise exports and 5 to 10 percent of GDP. Most growers are smallholders, so the impact of cotton prices on poverty is significant. A study on Benin found that a 40 percent reduction in farmgate cotton prices—equivalent to the price decline from December 2000 to May 2002—

implied an 8 percent reduction in rural per capita income in the short run and a 6 to 7 percent reduction in the long run, with the incidence of poverty among cotton growers rising in the short run from 37 percent to 59 percent (Minot and Daniels 2002).

Estimates of the impact of subsidy removal on cotton prices are in the range of 8 to 12 percent. Increases of this magnitude would not hurt consumers—the price of raw cotton is a small component of the price of textiles and garments. Full subsidy removal and the consequent rise in prices would help African countries, although the distribution of in-country benefits would depend on domestic reforms. A recent study of the impact of subsidy removal on three cotton-producing provinces of Zambia, for instance, indicates that the direct impact of the subsequent cotton price increase would be small: about 1 percent of income on average. Greater gains would require farmers switching from subsistence crops to cotton, which in turn requires complementary domestic reforms in extension services and robust growth of demand for cotton exports (Balat and Porto forthcoming).

Benefits to African countries would increase if they were to expand their clothing production and exports. The U.S. African Growth and Oppor-

tunity Act provides an opening, but under rather restrictive conditions: apparel from 14 African countries gets duty-free and quota-free access to U.S. markets, but only if made from U.S. fabric, yarn, and thread. So to take advantage of this provision, countries need to establish an effective input visa system to ensure compliance with rules of origin (Baffes 2004), which seems exceedingly complex.

Within the WTO, poor cotton-producing West African countries took the unusual step of issuing a joint statement calling for full subsidy removal and for cotton to be treated separately. But the July 2004 Framework Agreement of the Doha Development Agenda does not include separate treatment of cotton, stating only that cotton will receive "adequate priority" in agricultural negotiations. Subsidy removal is politically unlikely.

In the current climate, a second-best option would be to implement well-designed decoupled support, in which subsidies do not depend on production and thus do not encourage over-production and consequent "dumping," as is the case with the current schemes. Existing mechanisms would need to be reformed, because they still depend on acreage and thus create incentives for overproduction. Less overproduction may help lift prices a bit.

not automatically bring redress: the loser in the case may not necessarily change its action. The existing mechanisms to enforce decisions rely on voluntary compensation of the loser and, when this is not satisfactory, the possibility of retaliatory action (such as suspension of tariff and other concessions) on the part of the winner. Clearly, poor countries' retaliation against powerful trading partners is unlikely to provide much of an incentive for rich countries to comply with unfavorable rulings, because of their typically smaller volume of trade with a developed-country defendant. Even so, developing countries have in recent years brought forward, and won, an increasing number of cases.

The fair and ethical trade movements. Interestingly, some NGOs and civil society organizations in both developed and developing countries have acted directly to establish more equitable trade relations. One such example is "fair trade." Fair trade initiatives, led by consumer groups, NGOs, trade unions, and other civil society organizations, aim to control the supply chain from production to market to improve the well-being of developing-country producers by ensuring a stable price for their commodities, linking them more directly with markets in rich countries, and strengthening their organizations. The approach is working: sales of fair trade bananas, cocoa, coffee, brown sugar, tea, and a few other products have seen phenomenal growth in recent years and now represent a significant share of exports for some countries (for instance, 11 percent of Ecuadorian bananas and 20 percent of Ghanaian coffee are now sold through fair trade).

The few impact studies that exist show that fair trade initiatives have indeed made a difference to producers, not only through the premiums paid over world prices but also thanks to the services and assistance provided to farmers by producer cooperatives supported by fair trade organizations. When inequities arise from unequal access to markets and lack of information, credit, and risk-mitigation mechanisms, strengthening producer associations can lead to more equitable outcomes, even without paying a premium, in the context of existing trade rules.[20]

The reach of fair trade initiatives, while growing, remains small. In Switzerland, where consumer support is strong, fair trade bananas still represented only 25 percent of overall banana purchases and consumer spending on all fair trade products was a mere $10 per person in 2002 (Swiss agricultural subsidies amounted to roughly $750 per person in the same year). Fair trade coffee accounts for, at most, 3 percent of world sales, and only about 20 percent of the capacity of certified fair trade producers is absorbed by the fair trade circuit.[21]

Another example of organizations acting directly to establish more equitable trade relations is the growing number of initiatives for corporate social responsibility and ethical trade. Companies that join an ethical trade organization, such as the Ethical Trading Initiative in the United Kingdom or the Fair Labor Association in the United States, pledge to respect a code of conduct in return for favorable consideration by consumers and investors who care about equitable development.[22] Codes of conduct generally cover fair labor practices (usually those set out in ILO conventions), environmental standards, and monitoring mechanisms—and apply not just to a firm's direct production facilities but also to those of all its suppliers along the supply chain.

Are consumers in rich countries willing to pay a bit more to ensure that the goods they buy are produced in fair and safe conditions? Proponents of codes of conduct believe they are. Researchers found that almost 90 percent of Americans said they would pay at least an extra $1 on a $20 item if they could be sure it had not been produced by exploited workers.[23] Skeptics point to the fact that prices dominate the decisions of the major corporate buyers.

Codes of conduct inspired by ethical considerations might have a positive impact on equity, but are they applied? Impact studies conducted by the Ethical Trading Initiative found mixed evidence. Consumers may not be willing to pay higher prices in exchange for an uncertain (and often unmonitored) positive impact. Consumer pressure may thus not be enough (box 10.4). So, these initiatives, while important, are no

---

BOX 10.4 *Will improved working conditions in Cambodia's textile industry survive the end of the quota system?*

As mentioned in chapter 9, the 1999 bilateral trade agreement between Cambodia and the United States included a provision whereby Cambodia's clothing exports would increase each year if labor standards improved. The ILO was mandated to prepare a report twice a year based on factory visits and interviews with workers and unions and to make it widely available.

The provision helped bring about a gradual improvement in working conditions in clothing factories, but this progress is under threat with the end of the quota system. The government agreed to continue ILO inspections until 2008, but employers can no longer count on increases in exports to the United States if they uphold labor standards. Some are aware that labor standards compliance is their only real competitive advantage, but

there are reports of union leaders being fired, lack of adherence to minimum and overtime pay rules, and repressed demonstrations. Employers are allegedly using the threat of tough competition from China to cut salaries and benefits. But the employers are being watched—an independent union movement has grown in the industry and ILO monitoring is increasingly sophisticated. Monitors are now using hand-held computers to transmit findings from their factory visits, allowing timely reporting. If working conditions deteriorate, activists, researchers, unions, and, most important of all, consumers will know. Whether their pressure will be enough to ensure adherence to labor standards is an open question.

Sources: International Confederation of Free Trade Unions (2005), Washington Post (2004).

---

substitute for more equitable trade rules under the WTO and other arrangements.

Intellectual property rights and the global market for ideas

Protection of intellectual property rights (IPR) is another area in which market failure and power structures shape unequal processes and outcomes; the interests of a few powerful actors impose costs on the general public, particularly the poor. The requirement set forth in the Trade-Related Aspects of Intellectual Property Rights agreement (TRIPS)[24]—that all member countries offer 20-year patent protection—is perceived by many to be grossly inequitable. Because patent protection was adopted in OECD countries before the 1990s, the main result of this requirement is to strengthen patent protection in poor countries that become WTO members. Countries adopting patent protection today are doing so at levels of GDP between $500 and $8,000 per capita, while OECD countries did so when their GDP per capita was around $20,000 in 1995 prices.[25]

Patents stem from a legitimate desire to provide incentives for the generation of knowledge and cover the cost of developing new knowledge. A drug or other patented innovation cannot be copied while a patent is in force, so developers enjoy a monopoly

position and can charge higher prices. Extending patent protection to developing countries can thus increase total profits by allowing companies to earn them in poor countries—and changes the distribution of R&D financing, with a greater share borne by poorer countries. But protection of IPR must be balanced by the concern that it restricts access to new technologies. Patents restrict access to innovations by making them more expensive and more difficult to copy. There is great concern in developing countries on the availability of various innovations, including patented seeds and drugs. Antiretroviral drugs to fight AIDS are a case in point (box 10.5).

We look in more detail at pharmaceutical patents as an illustration of the broader issues. Chaudhuri, Goldberg, and Jia (2004) estimate that the gains to the Indian economy from not following international patent protection standards were around $450 million, of which $400 million were a gain to consumers and the rest profits of domestic producers. Profit losses to foreign producers were only around $53 million a year. This study illustrates the important point that the profits pharmaceutical companies could gain in poor countries are not very large. Lanjouw and Jack (2004) estimate that extending patent protection to developing countries to 20 years would be equivalent, for firm profits, to extending patents in developed countries by two weeks.

A solution exists that would lead to more equitable provision without undermining efficiency: wherever rich country markets already support the cost of research, poor countries could be allowed to produce or import cheaper generic substitutes, at no significant cost to either rich countries or the firms that carry out research (see focus 7 on drug access at the end of this chapter).

As with all international law, the existing IPR protection rules are the result of complex negotiations. TRIPS—which was basically written by industry lawyers[26]—is part of the agreement establishing the WTO, a multifaceted deal that included the Multi-Fiber Agreement and other provisions that developing countries deemed beneficial to them. Many bilateral free trade agreements (such as recent agreements between the

BOX 10.5 *Expanding access to antiretroviral drugs in South Africa*

In response to the rising AIDS crisis, the government of South Africa in 1997 amended the Medicines and Related Substances Control Act of 1965 in an attempt to ensure the supply of more affordable drugs to all South Africans. The amendment encouraged pharmacists to substitute costly patented drugs with cheaper generic equivalents, allowed for the importation of cheaper drugs available on the market elsewhere (parallel imports), and introduced a compulsory licensing system allowing competitors to produce patented drugs.

The Pharmaceutical Manufacturers Association and 39 drug companies challenged the government's legislation in the Pretoria High Court on several grounds, including that it violated South Africa's obligations under TRIPS. The Treatment Action Campaign (TAC) and a labor union, COSATU, supported the government defense in the case, asserting that the legislation was valid in that it constituted the government's positive duty to fulfill the right to health. Arguably as a result of public pressure and attention, the Pharmaceutical Manufacturers Association and the drug companies withdrew their case. An indirect result was to bring down the price of antiretroviral medicine

from about 4,000 rand a month to 1,000 rand a month.

Other legal cases (not involving TRIPS) helped expand access to antiretroviral drugs. In 2002, a group of complainants, including TAC, brought a case against GlaxoSmithKline and Boehringer Ingelheim at the South African Competition Commission. In its October 2004 ruling, the commission found that the two firms had engaged in excessive pricing of patented antiretrovirals and refused to allow generic production of the drugs in return for royalty payments, actions that the commission ruled were in violation of the South Africa Competition Act. To keep the case from moving to a higher tribunal, the firms came to a settlement agreement that included licensing generic production.

TAC also attempted to compel the national and provincial governments to provide antiretroviral drugs to all pregnant women to prevent the transmission of HIV from mothers to their children; the impact of the existing government policy was to make the drug Nevirapine unavailable in public health facilities other than the 10 or so pilot sites. The government appealed to the Constitutional Court after TAC secured a successful decision.

The Constitutional Court declared that the South African Constitution required the South African government to devise and implement within its available resources a comprehensive and coordinated program to realize progressively the rights of pregnant women and their newborn children to have access to health services to combat mother-to-child transmission of HIV. The Court found the state policy of restricting the availability of antiretroviral drugs and related services for preventing mother-to-child transmission of HIV to a few pilot test sites unreasonable, and ordered the government to rectify the situation by taking reasonable steps to facilitate the availability and use of antiretroviral drugs in all public health facilities.

In 1999, TAC had also been part of a successful constitutional challenge relating to discrimination of South African Airways cabin attendants with HIV. The judgment reinforced the right to equality for people with HIV. These legal challenges had important indirect impacts, setting groundbreaking precedents, increasing judicial awareness of human rights obligations, and heightening public awareness of rights.

Sources: Decker and others (2005), South Africa Competition Commission (2003).

United States and Chile, Jordan, Morocco, Singapore, Vietnam, and others) include even stronger IPR protection rules than TRIPS, such as granting patent extensions on pharmaceuticals and specific types of protection on clinical trial data submitted to obtain marketing approval. Signatories to these agreements agreed on these rules generally in exchange for preferential access to U.S. markets for their products.

But it is hard to argue that the parties to these various bilateral and multilateral agreements were on a level playing field. Poor countries are in a weaker bargaining position overall. For example, the preferential access they gain through bilateral trade agreements is eroded whenever the United States reduces remaining tariffs and quotas in bilateral or multilateral negotiations, while IPR protection does not weaken over time.[27] Moreover, the issues involved in IPR protection are complex and require skills and capacity that rich countries can better afford—often with input from pharmaceutical firms. Some capacity-building efforts for developing countries are under way, but

at least some of the agencies responsible (such as WIPO and developed-country patent offices) are perceived as biased. Inequitable as TRIPS may be, it still provides an internationally agreed standard subject to intense scrutiny and study, which does make it harder for rich countries to get more favorable deals in bilateral agreements.

An additional advantage of negotiating sessions under the WTO is that they provide focal events for mobilizing public opinion. An example of how positive results can be achieved within the WTO process is the Declaration on the TRIPS Agreement and Public Health adopted at Doha in 2001, which affirms the primacy of public health concerns over IPR protection. Three subsequent U.S. bilateral agreements include side letters on public health that affirm the signatories' understanding that IPR protection does not affect their ability to "protect public health by promoting medicines for all."[28] When negotiations are shifted away from the spotlight, as drug companies managed to do with drug licensing under the July 2004 Doha Development Agenda Framework Agreement, monitoring progress and campaigning become more difficult. So multilateral negotiations within the WTO, which are held under the spotlight, probably hold the most promise in terms of adopting more equitable rules.

Financial market liberalization

Capital flows to developing countries have grown tremendously in the 1990s, bringing both advantages and challenges. Short-term capital flows are at times accused of contributing to financial instability while not enhancing growth in countries with immature financial systems. Most countries that received high volumes of short-term capital inflows in the 1990s—Argentina, Brazil, Indonesia, Korea, Mexico, Russia, Thailand, and Turkey—have been hit by financial crises, triggered or deepened by the flight of foreign short-term capital.

Domestic factors play a key role in financial instability, but global rules also play a role. For instance, debt workout mechanisms follow informal processes; the IMF's proposal for a Sovereign Debt Workout Mechanism was not adopted. The result is that deals tend to benefit international lenders at the expense of domestic investors and taxpayers.[29]

In contrast to short-term capital flows, foreign direct investment (FDI) is generally regarded as having a positive impact on receiving countries, but it goes to only a few countries. In 2002, 84 percent of FDI to developing counties went to 12 mostly middle-income countries (including China and India), with the other 150-odd developing countries receiving almost nothing. Only 5.3 percent of FDI went to Sub-Saharan Africa.[30] Domestic factors play a key role also in determining the location of FDI, but again global rules contribute to inequitable outcomes. The Basel II Capital Accord, that sets capital adequacy standards for banks, may overestimate the risk of bank lending to developing countries (in part because it ignores the benefits of diversifying portfolios across countries), thus raising the cost and reducing access to external capital, in addition to increasing the procyclicality of loans and possibly contributing to increased volatility.[31] Emerging global standards—including those assessed under the Reports on the Observance of Standards and Codes (ROSC), international accounting standards, and the Core 25 Principles for Banking Supervision—are also costly for developing countries and may not be appropriate to their level of development.

Rules-setting in global financial markets. Some of the key rules governing global financial markets are developed by institutions to which developing countries do not belong. The Financial Stability Forum, established in 1999 to promote global financial stability, brings together senior representatives of central banks, supervisory authorities and treasury departments of nine OECD countries, international financial institutions, international regulatory and supervisory groupings, committees of central bank experts, and the European Central Bank. The only emerging market economies that are members are Hong Kong (China) and Singapore.

The Basel Committee on Banking Supervision, which developed the Basel II Capital Accord, comprises representatives of the central banks and banking supervision authorities of Belgium, Canada, France, Germany, Italy, Japan, Luxembourg, the Netherlands, Spain, Sweden, Switzerland, the United Kingdom, and the United States. Its main interlocutor in the development of the Accord was the Institute for International Finance, a Washington-based consultative group of major international banks. Neither the Financial Stability Forum nor the Basel Committee can legitimately represent the interests of developing countries.[32] Various other standards, often developed by semiprivate agencies (such as the International Accounting Standards Board), are based on practices in the United States and European Union. Greater participation and voice in rule-setting bodies would help ensure that outcomes are more favorable to developing countries.

Rectifying past and present inequities in the use of natural resources

The use of natural resources is another major arena in which market failures and unequal power conjure to create major inequities.

This is greatly skewed in favor of developed countries and impacts are grossly inequitable. Without major technological innovations several key resources, such as oil, could be exhausted before the world's poor get a chance to attain standards of living comparable to those of today's developed-country citizens. Moreover, global warming threatens to destroy the livelihoods of people living in low-lying coastal areas, small islands, and semiarid regions. Yet the people potentially affected by these changes (tomorrow's citizens and many of today's poor) have virtually no voice in setting rules.

The international community has taken some steps to manage natural resources in a more equitable way. Some international legal instruments, such as the Convention on the Law of the Sea of 1982, reflect the concept of distributive justice discussed earlier by taking an approach whereby the seabed and ocean floor, beyond national jurisdiction, are classified as global commons and subject to a system of equitable sharing of the economic benefits derived from activities in these areas.

Key steps toward redressing inequities in the use of global resources are the 1992 U.N. Framework Convention on Climate Change and the 1997 Kyoto Protocol. The protocol is structured to reflect the principle of "common but differentiated responsibilities" between developed and developing countries. It recognizes that industrial nations have emitted the majority of greenhouse gases in the atmosphere, causing the majority of the harm, and places greater demands on them. It sets binding quantified commitments for industrial countries to reduce their greenhouse gas emissions by 2008–12, with the understanding that the agreement would include emission reduction efforts by developing nations some time after 2012.

One important aspect of the Kyoto Protocol is the unique set of provisions that allow industrial nations to meet their commitments through actions not only within their borders but also outside. One of these provisions, the Clean Development Mechanism, helps address the perceived inequality of obligations and the costs of compliance.

It allows industrial countries to purchase emission reduction "credits" generated from activities that reduce greenhouse gas emissions in developing countries and to apply these credits against their obligations under the Protocol. It thus assists industrial countries in meeting their commitments under the Kyoto Protocol more cost effectively and promotes sustainable development in developing countries, through supporting greater investments in cleaner, more efficient technologies as well as forestry projects.

Fairness in processes is also an issue. In negotiating the Kyoto Protocol, as in most global treaty negotiations, industrial nations had greater power at the negotiating table. An imbalance of technical expertise, a lack of adequate public support for the issues, and problems forming coalitions because of diverse interests have attenuated the bargaining power for many developing countries.

The United States, the single largest emitter of greenhouse gases, has announced that it is not becoming a party to the Kyoto Protocol, significantly reducing the protocol's efficacy. With the protocol having come into effect in February 2005, the United States will be a mere observer at the Meetings of the Parties to the Kyoto Protocol, but because of the size of its emissions, the other parties will not want to ignore U.S. concerns.[33]

Equitable access to information is an important ingredient for more equitable use of global resources. The UN/ECE Convention on Access to Information, Public Participation in Decision-making and Access to Justice in Environmental Matters (Aarhus Convention) deals with public participation in environmental management and access to information on environmental issues. The Convention, adopted in 1998 and in force among 35 parties since 2001, grants citizens the right to impose obligations on public authorities and parties to international environmental conventions, including information disclosure, access to information, public participation in environmental decision making, and access to justice. A Convention Compliance Committee has been established, to which citizens and NGOs can bring allegations of noncompliance.

Providing development assistance to help build endowments

In shaping global inequities, rules and processes interact with unequal endowments. Even if all the reforms suggested in the previous sections were implemented, many poor countries would still not be able to participate in global markets because of their limited endowments of skills, capital, infrastructure, knowledge, and ideas. Action to build endowments is primarily domestic, through private and public investments in infrastructure and other areas. Can domestic action be supported by aid?

Better development assistance

From an equity perspective, the main roles of aid are to help countries build the endowments of those who are resource-poor, generally through no fault of their own, and avoid extreme deprivation (which justifies to some extent the use of aid to support current consumption). The focus on building endowments implies that both the level of aid and its effectiveness matter.

Enhancing aid effectiveness. If the goal is to equalize opportunities for the poor, aid effectiveness is crucial. Aid that sustains corruption or marginal projects, or is used to increase the resources at the disposal of the rich, does not help. Aid effectiveness hinges crucially on aid delivery modalities and on the fairness and transparency of domestic political processes. Birdsall (2004) cites seven "deadly sins": impatience with institution building, failure to exit, failure to evaluate, pretending that participation equals ownership, failure to collaborate, stingy and unreliable financing, and underfunding of regional and global programs—in addition to tying aid to the use of consultants and firms from the donor country and allocating it according to political priorities. Existing aid planning and delivery practices are rooted in political and incentive constraints that the donors face, so change is difficult and slow. But some current directions are promising: emphasizing results (including through tracking indicators of intermediate actions and final outcomes related to the MDGs), moving away from ex ante conditionality, and progressively shifting design and management from donors to countries. The United Kingdom's Commission for Africa (2005) recommended a major shift away from ex ante conditionality toward a new partnership in which African countries continue to work to improve governance and accountability, and donors deliver more, cheaper, more predictable aid. High levels of aid reduce the need for domestic tax efforts, which have historically helped strengthen overall accountability of governments and citizen demand for quality services, so particular attention should be paid to revenue collection.[34] The preparation of poverty reduction strategies is a key, if imperfect, instrument to shift to country-led processes with greater participation and monitoring of how public resources are spent.

Fragile states pose a special challenge. Stabilization and peacekeeping need to be complemented with efforts to build state institutions and legitimacy. The sequencing of interventions matters—there is some evidence that ring-fenced, long-term investment in human capital development and working with NGOs and the private sector can be useful first steps. Technical assistance appears more effective after reforms take off and can help lay the basis for capital investment and service delivery interventions.[35]

When domestic political processes are manifestly inequitable and corrupt, donors can try to support moves toward a more equitable revenue collection and allocation; decentralization to lower levels of government, which can challenge central control; and the strengthening of community-based organizations, the media, and domestic entrepreneurship, which can help create a middle class with a voice and a stake in better governance.

Improving the allocation of aid. The distribution of aid matters as well. A lively debate has taken place in recent years on aid allocation criteria. Burnside and Dollar (2000) and Collier and Dollar (2001, 2002) found that aid was more effective in reducing poverty if it was allocated to countries that followed good policies and had good institutions. They calculated that reallocating actual aid provided in 1996 across countries to maximize poverty reduction according to their formula would have led to directing aid to roughly 20 instead of the 60 countries considered, and lifted twice as many people out of poverty.[36]

Their findings have been questioned by Hansen and Tarp (2001) and others, who argued that their analysis does not take country conditions into account and is not robust to different specifications. If aid effectiveness varies across countries not because of policies but as the result of different country circumstances, such as climate, a different aid allocation rule would maximize the poverty impact of foreign aid.[37] Cogneau and Naudet (2004) suggested an alternative rule for aid allocation and showed that gains in poverty reduction similar to those found by Collier and Dollar could be obtained if aid was directed to countries that have greater structural disadvantages (geographic, historical, or economic, as discussed in chapter 3). The resulting allocation would spread the risk of poverty more evenly across the world's population, while reducing global poverty almost as much as the allocation proposed by Collier and Dollar.

In sum, an equity perspective suggests that an approach that does not take a country's circumstances into account is likely to ignore important information about need. But an approach that ignores aid effectiveness does not lead to expanded opportunities. To contribute toward an equalization of opportunities across the world's individuals, aid should be targeted where the probability is greatest that it effectively reaches those with the most limited opportunities—the poorest of the poor, in opportunity terms. That clearly depends on the poverty and deprivation levels in each country and on its government's ability and political commitment to deliver the aid where and how it is intended. But more research is needed to fully understand the causal mechanisms.

In practice, recent research showed that many donors indeed seem to rely on both good policies and poor initial conditions. A study of 40 donor agencies by Dollar and Levin (2004) found that aid was positively correlated with a measure of good policies and with per capita GDP, and the agencies that focused the most on good policies also directed their aid to poor countries. However, some fragile states ("aid orphans") receive less

aid than predicted by their policy and institutional strength, mostly because of disproportionately low flows from bilateral donors, while others ("aid darlings") received more.[38]

Increasing aid levels. Conditional on effectiveness and distribution, levels of aid do matter. Aid levels fell between 1990 and 2001 both as a share of rich countries' gross national income (GNI) and in nominal terms. Calls for more aid to help countries achieve the MDGs have resonated loudly in recent international gatherings. At the 2002 International Conference on Financing for Development in Monterrey, rich countries committed to increasing their aid flows significantly. Net aid flows indeed increased significantly in 2002–04 in nominal and real terms, reaching $78 billion.[39] Three major factors were behind these increases: continuing growth in bilateral grants (but with a large share going to technical cooperation, debt forgiveness, emergency and disaster relief, and administrative costs); the provision of reconstruction aid to Afghanistan and Iraq by the United States (in 2004, $0.9 billion to Afghanistan and $2.9 billion to Iraq); and the depreciation of the U.S. dollar. While there was a small increase in new development assistance to Sub-Saharan Africa in 2003, even after accounting for debt relief and emergency assistance, Highly Indebted Poor Countries (HIPC) received less in real terms in 2004 than the year before. On the positive side, the International Development Association, the soft-lending arm of the World Bank, recently received a replenishment for 2006–8, which is at least 25 percent higher than the previous one and represents the largest funding increase in two decades.

These recent increases notwithstanding, aid flows remain small not just in relation to need but also in comparison to domestic human development and safety net programs that aim to equalize opportunities and ensure against deprivation. Such programs generally account for more than 10 percent of GDP in donor countries. Official development assistance (ODA), by contrast, was only 0.25 percent of donor countries' GNI in 2003. Only Denmark, Luxembourg, the Netherlands, Norway, and Sweden meet the U.N. target of providing ODA equal to or greater than 0.7

Table 10.1 ODA as a share of GNI, 2002, 2003, and simulation for 2006

Country	Net ODA 2003 ($ millions)	Net ODA 2004 ($ millions)	ODA as % of GNI 2003	ODA as % of GNI 2004	ODA as % of GNI Simulation 2006
Austria	505	691	0.20	0.24	0.33
Belgium	1,853	1,452	0.60	0.41	0.64
Denmark	1,748	2,025	0.84	0.84	0.83
Finland	558	655	0.35	0.35	0.41
France	7,253	8,475	0.41	0.42	0.47
Germany	6,784	7,497	0.28	0.28	0.33
Greece	362	464	0.21	0.23	0.33
Ireland	504	586	0.39	0.39	0.61
Italy	2,433	2,484	0.17	0.15	0.33
Luxembourg	194	241	0.81	0.85	0.87
Netherlands	3,981	4,235	0.80	0.74	0.80
Portugal	320	1,028	0.22	0.63	0.33
Spain	1,961	2,547	0.23	0.26	0.33
Sweden	2,400	2,704	0.79	0.77	1.00
United Kingdom	6,282	7,836	0.34	0.36	0.42
EU members, total	**37,139**	**42,920**	**0.35**	**0.36**	**0.44**
Australia	1,219	1,465	0.25	0.25	0.26
Canada	2,031	2,537	0.24	0.26	0.27
Japan	8,880	8,859	0.20	0.19	0.22
New Zealand	165	210	0.23	0.23	0.26
Norway	2,042	2,200	0.92	0.87	1.00
Switzerland	1,299	1,379	0.39	0.37	0.38
United States	16,254	18,999	0.15	0.16	0.19
DAC members, total	**69,029**	**78,569**	**0.25**	**0.25**	**0.30**

Source: OECD-DAC (2004).
Note: DAC = Development Assistance Committee; EU = European Union; GNI = gross national income; ODA = official development assistance.

Figure 10.2 More subsidies than aid

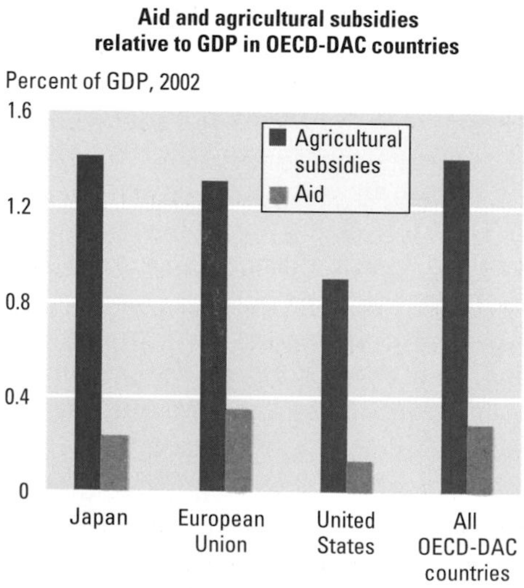

Aid and agricultural subsidies relative to GDP in OECD-DAC countries

Sources: OECD-DAC (2004) and OECD (2003).

percent of GNI. Many countries are not on track to meet their Monterrey commitments (table 10.1).

Aid also is low in comparison with other uses of public resources. Agricultural subsidies, for instance, were almost five times larger than aid in 2002. Japan, the European Union, and the United States had subsidies equal to 1.4, 1.3, and 0.9 percent of GDP and aid of 0.23, 0.35, and 0.13 percent respectively (figure 10.2). Rich countries should deliver on their Monterrey commitments; this alone would add around $18 billion to development assistance by 2006. To make further progress toward the 0.7 percent goal, countries could establish intermediate targets for 2010. But again, higher aid that is poorly spent, supports corrupt regimes, or undermines domestic accountability can hinder, rather than support, greater equity.

Additional debt relief. Aid should not be undermined by debt payments. Multilateral debt, the largest share of debt for the HIPC, is the result of loans received in the 1980s, and new loans, while generally on more concessional terms, continue to add to the debt burden. Supporters of debt relief argue that debt payments divert scarce resources from health and education and other pro-poor spending.

There has been progress in the last decade. In 1995, debt relief was not on the agenda of international organizations, partly because of financing issues and partly because of concerns about creating a moral hazard (if debts are forgiven, governments of borrowing countries may think they are really not expected to repay). Over the following five years, thanks to a strong grassroots mobilization in rich countries, effective research on the impact of debt and committed leadership in some rich countries and the World Bank, the HIPC Initiative was launched and then expanded. As of March 2005, 27 countries had received debt relief expected to amount to about $54 billion over time, up from $34.5 billion at the end of 2000. The ratio of debt service to exports for HIPC has declined roughly by half, to 15 percent. Poverty-reducing expenditures in the 27 countries that receive HIPC assistance are estimated to have increased from 6.4 percent of GDP in 1999 to 7.9 percent of GDP in 2003.

Even so, many countries continue to bear an unsustainable debt burden, and more needs to be done. The agreements reached in October 2004 to extend the HIPC Initiative and in June 2005 to grant 100 percent debt cancellation of the debt owed to the African Development Bank, IMF, and World Bank to 18 countries are important steps.[40] This and any further debt relief should truly be additional rather than substitute fresh aid. Further debt relief should also be accompanied by careful consideration of debt sustainability issues, including increasing grants for very low-income countries, to avoid the buildup of unsustainable debt in the future.

Innovative mechanisms to fund development assistance. Several innovative mechanisms to expand development assistance are under discussion, including the International Financing Facility (IFF), global taxes, and vol-untary contributions. The IFF would make future aid available for immediate use (front-load aid) and possibly reduce volatility. It is an option for some donors, such as France and the United Kingdom, given their accounting and legislative frameworks, but not for others, who would not be able to make long-term commitments or consider them off-budget. Even when feasible, the IFF would move aid off-budget in the short term, but it would expand financing for development only if it increased overall aid levels rather than simply shift future aid forward.

Proposals involving global tax instruments have also been advanced, including a "Tobin" tax on short-term capital movements; taxes related to pollution, such as a global carbon tax, an international aviation fuel tax, and a maritime pollution tax; taxes on arms sales; and surcharges on multinational profits and on value-added or income taxes. These proposals would need to be assessed on the basis of the revenues they could generate, their efficiency, collectability, feasibility, and not least their impact on equity.

Voluntary contributions from individuals, corporations, private foundations, and NGOs—another source of development assistance alongside public aid—are increasing. But effectiveness is an issue for private assistance too. As seen for the December 2004 Asian tsunami, private charity can be mobilized faster than public resources. But private contributions are influenced by press coverage more than actual need; contributors were much less generous for the Iranian earthquake that hit in February 2005, which was virtually ignored in the news. Moreover, lack of coordination, fragmentation, and infrastructure bottlenecks—such as bad roads and a lack of electricity and telecommunications, which cannot generally be alleviated through private charity—can hinder its effectiveness. Moreover, alignment with recipient country strategies needs to be ensured.

Transitions to greater equity

Equity-enhancing changes in global policies and institutions come about through action by governments and coalitions of governments—often within international fora, informed leadership and grassroots mobilization, analysis and policy research to inform alternatives, and networks that disseminate those alternatives. This section looks at some examples illustrating the change processes; it does not attempt to be comprehensive or to assess the weight of individual factors.

Examples include developed-country governments that take initiative unilaterally—such as the countries that have already reached the target of 0.7 percent of GNI for developing assistance or that cancelled a large portion of the debts owed to them by the poorest countries—as well as governments acting jointly to form coalitions for change. The latter are becoming more frequent in trade negotiations, in which a group of large developing countries (including Brazil, China, and India) is spearheading proposals for greater trade liberalization.

A way to spur equity-enhancing policy changes by developed countries is to accompany calls for change with tracking mechanisms. The eighth MDG relates to greater provision of aid and debt relief and more equitable trade policies. Progress toward this goal has been reviewed in September 2005 as part of the Millennium Summit+5.

Another exercise to monitor rich country policies, conducted by the Center for Global Development and *Foreign Policy* magazine, is the Commitment to Development Index. The index examines more indicators than the eighth MDG, including environment, security, investment, and technology (Center for Global Development 2004). While there are questions about the methodology, particularly on aggregating scores in various areas, the index exposes how some countries do better in some areas than in others—Norway, for instance, does well on aid but poorly on trade; Switzerland scores poorly on trade but does better on environment; the United States scores poorly on environment but has, with Canada, the most favorable migration policies—and how all countries have considerable opportunities to improve their policies.

Citizen mobilization. Citizen mobilization, combining both grassroots and middle-class interest groups across countries, has grown in recent years. In some cases, an international social movement, network, or alliance has emerged to try to influence the global agenda. An example is the launching of the Enhanced HIPC Initiative in 2000. The original HIPC Initiative benefited some countries, but progress was slow and there were several problems. By 1999 these were largely recognized, but an expanded initiative needed to garner support in creditor countries and in the World Bank and IMF governing committees, because it required additional funding. The Jubilee 2000 campaign, which combined awareness of the pernicious effects of excessive debt with a call to debt forgiveness inspired by the Christian Jubilee idea, mobilized hundreds of thousands of people in countries such as Germany, Italy, the United States, and United Kingdom. The governments of these countries took notice and finally agreed to various actions, expanding the HIPC Initiative and canceling bilateral debt. Other examples of pressure by civil society organizations leading to changes in rules are the campaigns to reform World Bank policies on indigenous peoples, resettlement, and other safeguards.

In a second set of cases, international rules already exist on paper, and social movements bring them into effect by making them visible and insisting that they be implemented. In many cases, this process happens at the country level, but it involves an interaction with global rule and policy changes. The ethical trade initiatives discussed earlier are citizen mobilizations to enforce global and local laws. Similarly, efforts by indigenous movements, NGOs, and other activists ensured that ILO Covenant 169 on indigenous peoples was recognized as having legal weight (in practice) in various countries. Experience shows that citizen mobilization is most effective when it builds broad-based coalitions for change across countries and groups.

But citizen mobilization also poses risks. Civil society movements may partly counter unequal formal channels, but they are highly imperfect mechanisms of aggregating voice, and their accountability is often unclear. In recent years, there have been instances of NGO campaigns that have led to perverse outcomes, such as donors withdrawing from infrastructure and resettlement projects only to see governments move ahead anyway without international monitoring of social and environmental consequences.

Analysis and research. Socioeconomic analysis and policy research also contribute to making particular domains of inequity objects of public debate and action. Global analysis of gender discrimination and missing girls and women (box 2.9) has fostered public action to redress gender inequities. Ex ante analysis and policy research are also vital ingredients for informing the design of policy proposals. A vast body of recent research, including serious impact evaluations, has focused on efficient and effective ways to achieve the MDGs. The more research is conducted by and with developing-country researchers, the more likely it is that its results will inform policymaking.

Some of these key elements have been missing in failed attempts at change. Analysis and policy research is carried out and technical solutions are proposed; the political will to implement them is missing, however, because political leaders do not think the issue is important or coalitions are not formed that ensure sufficient support. In other cases, grassroots mobilization is strong, but it lacks well-developed, implementable proposals for reform. Indeed, some NGO campaigns have led to perverse outcomes, as when international organizations have withdrawn support for projects under international criticism only to see governments proceed without international monitoring of social and environmental safeguards.

International organizations. International financial institutions can help bring about global equity-enhancing action through setting agendas and providing a focal point for international negotiations. Their dispute settlement and enforcement mechanisms help ensure that their policies are implemented. But the governance structures of the World Bank and IMF have not evolved in line with the increased size and role of emerging market, developing, and transition countries in the world economy. Moreover, small and low-income countries have a limited role in their decision-making processes. Developed-country governments have a majority of the votes on the boards of the IMF and World Bank, and two executive directors represent more than 40 African countries.

Several options to enhance voice in the IMF and World Bank have been explored, but limited progress has been made. In April 2005, the ministers of the intergovernmental Group of Twenty-Four urged that a new quota formula be developed (voting rights depend on quotas), which would give greater weight to measures of gross domestic product measured in purchasing power parity terms. They also suggested that, in order to strengthen the voice of small and low-income countries, basic votes should be increased to restore their original share of total voting power.[41] Making progress on enhancing the voice and participation of developing countries in the decision-making processes of the World Bank and IMF is of fundamental importance to increase the legitimacy of international financial institutions and enhance their effectiveness in fostering greater global equity. The 13th General Review of IMF Quotas provides an important opportunity to make progress on issues of quotas, voice, and participation.

Summary

In sum, global actions can play a key role in redressing inequitable rules and helping equalize endowments. The rules that govern markets for labor, goods, ideas, capital, and the use of natural resources need to become more equitable. Domestic action to build the endowments of the poor can be supported through aid, but not if aid is poorly spent, supports corrupt regimes, or undermines domestic accountability. Changes will require, above all, greater accountability at the global level, with greater representation of poor people's interests in rule-setting bodies.

Balancing access to medicines for the world's poor with incentives for pharmaceutical innovation

What's the best way to expand access to drugs in developing countries, while preserving incentives for pharmaceutical research? A possible solution entails recognizing that medicine markets are far from uniform and that both the nature of diseases and the income of countries matter for access and incentives.

Some diseases, such as malaria, mainly affect poor countries, but they have received little R&D investment, and few treatments are available. Much attention has been devoted in recent years to creating the right incentives and structuring financing to increase R&D investment in drugs for diseases that affect poor countries, for which commercial potential does not provide enough stimulus.[1] Policy initiatives include the following:

- Increasing research through public sector institutions—for example, programs coordinated by the U.S. National Institute of Allergy and Infectious Diseases, the World Health Organization's Special Programme for Research and Training in Tropical Diseases, and the nonprofit Drugs for Neglected Diseases Initiative founded by Medécins Sans Frontiéres.

- Establishing public-private partnerships, such as the Medicines for Malaria Venture and the Malaria Vaccine Initiative, the International AIDS Vaccine Initiative, and the Global Alliance for Tuberculosis Drug Development.

- Designing a purchase commitment for new vaccines ("AdvancedMarkets"). Sponsored by the Bill and Melinda Gates Foundation, the groundwork has been laid to create markets by having donors commit, in advance, to paying part of the cost at a guaranteed price for a new, as yet undiscovered, vaccine. This would give firms an incentive to invest in this area.[2] (A similar initiative has been proposed for agricultural research relevant to developing countries.[3])

- Developing an open-source approach to early-stage tropical diseases research. The idea is to harness the expertise and resources of academic scientists, students, public sector researchers, and others who may be happy to spend some of their time doing research on tropical diseases either for altruism or scientific curiosity (similar to what happens with open-source software). Leads that emerge could then feed into any of the other schemes for the next stages of development and clinical testing.[4]

Providing patent protection in poor countries for drugs primarily for their markets would not by itself provide sufficient incentives, because their purchasing power is very low. But, even a small increase in market-based research incentives could be a useful part of a larger strategy to address the treatment of diseases specific to the developing world.

Other diseases have global incidence and worldwide markets, and they are an important cause of death and disability among the poor. In the high-mortality regions of the world, cardiovascular disease is estimated to cause a greater share of the total disease burden than malaria and other tropical diseases combined.[5]

Although many people in poor countries suffer from global diseases, they are an insignificant part of the commercial market. Estimates suggest that currently almost half of the world's people live in countries that together represent less than 2 percent of global spending on drugs for cardiovascular disease.[6] Because of the great asymmetries in markets, many of the poor could be allowed generic access to important classes of drugs without damaging research incentives. The foreign filing license approach described below is a feasible way to attain this outcome.

Legally binding commitments not to enforce patent rights

The proposal considered here[7] would have inventors in developed countries make legally binding commitments to their own governments not to enforce patent rights in certain pharmaceutical markets. These markets would be defined as those together representing the bottom, say, 2 percent of global drug sales in each disease class (see figure below).

Along the horizontal axis of the figure are disease classes, listed with those concentrated in poor countries toward the left, and those with worldwide incidence toward the right. Along the vertical axis are countries ordered by per capita income. The white area shows the "generic region" that would be created by the policy. Within the generic region, firms would be able to manufacture and trade in generic products without any political or procedural complexity arising from the patent system. The generic region would be recalculated each year to accommodate changes in income and the evolution of markets.

Because diseases to the left are more concentrated in developing countries, the 2 percent of global markets cutoff is reached at lower levels of real GDP per capita. It may seem counterintuitive to propose differentiating in this way, but it is precisely for diseases that are concentrated in developing countries that some incentive for product development may need to come from sales in the developing world.

The proposed generic region

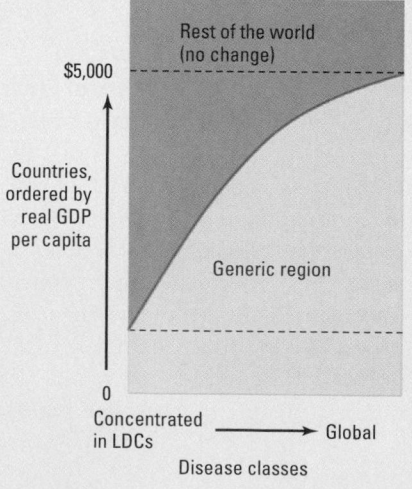

Source: Lanjouw (2004).

The poorest countries falling below the dashed line would be allowed generics on all pharmaceuticals. Countries higher up, such as India, would have a mixed situation. They would be in the TRIPS environment for diseases concentrated in the developing world, while in the generic region for more global diseases. For markets in the gray area above the curved line, the policy as no effect. Both the responsibilities and the flexibilities of TRIPS remain unchanged.

The size of the generic region depends on two parameters: the ceiling income level (here $5,000) and, more important, the global sales cutoff (here 2 percent).

The proposal would be implemented by having inventors in developed countries make a legally binding commitment to their own governments not to enforce patent rights in the generic region, as part of obtaining a license to make foreign patent filings (the foreign filing license). Firms would continue to obtain patents wherever they like, and no decisions related to the policy would be needed at the time of applying for a patent. Instead, decisions that relate to the policy—about where to enforce patent rights—would arise only after products have reached the market. To ensure compliance, the patent holder would lose the right to enforce the domestic patent on the same product if the holder were to break the commitment and begin an enforcement action in one of the proscribed markets.

Implementation would need to be coordinated across the developed countries that have pharmaceutical research activity, including, at least, Canada, Europe, Japan, and the United States. The policy would require legislation to amend the patent code in each country. In the United States and the United Kingdom this would include adding an inventor declaration to an existing foreign filing license process; other countries would need to put a foreign filing license provision into their codes.[8] The classification of countries and disease classes could be carried out by an international organization and reviewed annually.

Developing countries would not be required to take any action to implement this policy. They would continue to take steps to comply with TRIPS and any bilateral treaty obligations in accord with their current plans. The countries in the generic region could be treated as one country from the viewpoint of patents. Production could be based in any one country and drugs could be exported to all other countries in that group, without any costs associated with patents and compulsory licensing.

So, if any country in the generic region had the ability to produce a given drug, then all other countries in the region could take advantage of its production capacity. This would help get around the problem that most small countries do not have the capacity or market size to make domestic production of generic drugs a viable activity.

Firms have been willing to make a voluntarily commitment not to exercise patent rights in the poorest countries. The foreign filing license proposal discussed here would take that commitment and convert it into a reliable part of the global rules-based system.

Source: Lanjouw (2002, 2004).

Epilogue

This report has argued that equity has a central place in the interpretation of development experience and in the design of development policy—and that this place has been inadequately understood and undervalued in much current thinking. We do not propose, however, yet another new framework for development. Instead, recognizing the importance of equity (that is, equality of opportunity and the avoidance of absolute deprivation) implies the need to integrate and extend existing approaches. In this epilogue, we seek to place the analysis and messages of the report in the context of some of the major contemporary strands of thinking and action in development.

Four broad strands of thinking have been at the core of development discourse and practice over the last three decades or so: the central role of markets as resource allocation mechanisms, the importance of human development, the role of institutions, and a focus on empowerment.

The first strand emphasizes the superiority of markets over central planning as broad mechanisms to allocate resources and determine the evolution of economic activity. This has long been understood in economics, but there was a time when it was a minority view among development economists.[1] The situation had definitely changed by the 1980s, as first India and then China moved away from planning, and the importance of incentives in determining individual behavior (as consumers, producers, and regulators) became more widely understood. The rapid and sustained growth that followed in those two countries underlined the point. In the 1990s, the economic transition away from planning in the formerly communist states of Eastern Europe and Central Asia dispelled any serious view that

development was possible without markets and the private sector.

Although the resulting "Washington Consensus" is sometimes interpreted as anti-state, this is not the main message that survives after more measured consideration. Instead, just as events in the 1990s confirmed that markets were essential for development, they also showed that good governments are essential for well-functioning markets. Markets operate within a framework determined by institutions, and they work only as well as those institutions do. They work best, therefore, when a capable state maintains order within the rule of law, provides effective regulation, macroeconomic stability and other public goods, and corrects other market failures.

The second strand sees human development as central to the development process, through the expansion of the skills, health, and capacity of all people to engage in social and economic activities and to manage the risks they face. Although the World Development Report 1980 was on Human Development,[2] U.N. agencies—notably the UNDP in their series of Human Development Reports (United Nations 2003)—later took the lead in putting these concerns at the center of the development agenda. In this, they have been followed (rightly) by the whole development community.

For the World Bank, the 1990 World Development Report on Poverty[3] marked the beginning of a multiyear process of making poverty reduction the overarching objective of the institution, building on these first two strands of development thought. The 1990 Report argued that poverty reduction required a two-part strategy—employment creation through market-based growth; and expansion of human capital, especially through broad-based provisioning of social services.

During the 1990s, the third and fourth strands of thought rose to prominence. The third strand emphasized the role of "institutions" in development, building both on trends in academic thought and on development practice across many organizations. It reflected the acknowledgment that markets, however important, do not work in a vacuum. They need rules and the institutional enforcement of those rules. The emphasis on institutions took a variety of forms: a focus on the costs of corruption; a broader concern with governance; support for judicial reform; and a greater practical understanding of the need for well-designed, accountable, and effective public regulation of privatized monopolies.

The fourth strand sought the empowerment of the people for whom development was supposedly taking place. If the central goal of development is poverty reduction, the poor should have a great deal of voice over its directions. If development needs markets, and markets need institutions, it should clearly matter how those institutions are governed. If power helps determine the outcomes in market and government processes alike, the distribution of that power over the population must be important for development. In practical terms, the emphasis on empowerment has sought greater participation of the poor in projects affecting them, a greater preoccupation with the political economy of support for reforms, and explorations of the role of culture in development.

Several World Development Reports have sought to integrate the third and fourth strands of thought: the 1997 Report on the "State in a Changing World,"[4] the 2002 Report on "Building Institutions for Markets,"[5] and, emblematically, the millennial 2000/01 Report on "Attacking Poverty."[6] The 2001 Report argued that poverty reduction required an expansion in the opportunities of the poor (notably through market-oriented growth), the empowerment of the poor, and measures that provide security for the poor. At the World Bank, this synthesis was crystallized in a Strategic Framework for development, which consisted of two pillars:

building a good climate for investment and empowering the poor.[7]

The first pillar combined the strands of thinking on the primacy of markets and on the centrality of institutions. It argued that only by having governance institutions that were at once effective and accountable could markets generate the best possible results for investment and growth. This theme was explored in the 2005 Report, "A Better Investment Climate for Everyone."[8]

The second pillar was also a merger of sorts: in seeking the empowerment of poor people—who should be seen as the driving subjects, not as passive objects of development—it combined thinking on human development, institutions, and empowerment. The 2004 Report, "Making Services Work for Poor People," explored these themes in the delivery of basic services.[9]

Although the various elements of thinking and policy are complementary—and indeed have been considered elements of a "comprehensive" or "holistic" development process—the narratives associated with the different strands have often suffered, in practice, from two important limitations. One is a tendency to compartmentalize poverty. The second is to treat actions in the various realms as separate. There is a tendency to assign market-related and macro-policies to macroeconomic managers and trade ministries, as though the "investment climate" concerned only rich people or as though the poor stood to benefit only indirectly from the trickle-down effects of the investments by the rich today.

Conversely, it sometimes seems as though empowerment would have no impact on the quality of institutions, on the investment opportunities of the poor, or on the economy's growth process. According to this view, empowerment should be the preserve of well-meaning NGOs and social development folk, of little import for economic performance.

Such a separation of the two pillars—for the investment climate and for empowerment—is profoundly misguided. The analysis in this report suggests that the root causes of poverty are to be found in the combined deprivations of power and investment opportunities. Lack of incomes, lack of access to services, lack of assets—these deprivations go together with lack of voice, lack of power, lack of status. Public action *could* enhance the investment capabilities of those who have limited opportunities by investing in their human capital and in the infrastructure they use and by ensuring fairness and security in the markets in which they transact. And if public action fails to do that, it is because it somehow has been decided otherwise. In that case, the government will invest in expensive schools or universities, rather than in those used by the poor, for example. It will not enforce tax collection, rather than build rural roads. It will allow banks to retain a degree of market power and lend to the friends of the government, rather than allow for entry and promote competition that forces intermediaries to seek the greatest returns on capital. Observed policies that fail to address inefficient inequities are the result of political choices, implicitly or explicitly.

Such failures in public action, which arise from and perpetuate inequity, are also inimical to prosperity. Those who have no opportunities cannot contribute to the development of their countries. Their potential talents are wasted, and capital, land, and other resources are used in inferior ways. Unequal control over resources reinforces the unequal concentration of power, and this is reflected in worse governance institutions: public service delivery agencies are not pushed to become more accountable. If all the power brought to bear on regulators is that of the friends of the regulated, the quality of regulatory agencies is not likely to improve much. Police forces and judicial systems will not treat everyone the same way. And so on. These institutional failures only add to the negative effects of inequity on development.

Government policies are what they are—from Mali to Chile—because someone is making them. No group is power*less,* unless some other group is power*ful.* If an inequitable distribution of opportunities means that the investment climate for large groups is poor, this is intimately linked to the lack of power in those groups to affect the decision-making processes that could

lead to changes in that distribution over time. And if power is imbalanced, it is because wealth and economic opportunities are uneven. Inequality traps are vicious circles, with economic and political inequalities mutually reinforcing one another.

This report has argued that policy and institutional reforms can help break these inequality traps, and turn the vicious circles into a virtuous process of greater equality in economic opportunities reinforcing greater political equality, and vice versa. Reforms can do this in many ways, which are closely related to the four strands of thinking discussed above. Interventions that build greater human capacities for those with the most limited opportunities (generally the poor) will prepare them to be more economically productive and more politically effective. Processes that redistribute access to land, or to infrastructure services, or indeed to justice, can add both to empowerment and to the investment opportunities of the poor. And promoting fairness in markets is all about improvements in the quality of institutions that support and complement markets in ways that broaden access and ensure equitable rules.

This is consistent with the twin pillars of a better investment climate and greater empowerment for the poor. It makes it clear that—for most people in the developing world, and certainly for the poor—it is not possible to have one without the other. A good investment climate is about real economic opportunities. Equity is about leveling the playing field so that opportunities are available on the basis of talent and efforts, rather than on the basis of gender, race, family background, or other predetermined circumstances. A level economic playing field is not sustainable without a level political playing field, and vice versa. If we want a better investment climate for everyone, we want empowerment. The combination of both implies equity.

These issues apply with equal force at the global level. The extraordinary inequalities in opportunity faced by individuals born in different countries reflect different political and economic histories across nations. While domestic policy is undoubtedly fundamental, global interactions help shape the context for national economic and social advance. The Monterrey Consensus explicitly emphasizes the need for a compact between rich and poor societies if the Millennium Development Goals are to be achieved. It recognizes the role of action by rich countries, especially in the areas of aid and trade. For aid, this is reflected in the quest to change the donor-recipient relationship from one of giving to one of partnership, with developing countries clearly in the lead in designing their policies and institutions.

This report underlines the importance of that compact and a more equal international partnership. But it also highlights inequalities in the processes forming the rules of the game in the international playing field. Inequalities in economic and political power in the global arena influence the design of rules in ways that often restrict, rather than expand, the opportunities of poorer countries—and, even more, of poorer groups within these countries. Just as in the domestic context, therefore, equity and efficiency in the international arena are more likely to be attained by reforms that enhance the power and broaden the economic access of the countries where the world's poor live.

Bibliographical Note

This Report draws on a wide range of World Bank documents and on numerous outside sources. Background papers were prepared by Martin Andersson, Armando Barrientos, Carles Boix, Leila Chirayath, Stijn Claessens, Klaus Decker, Ashwini Deshpande, Leopoldo Fergusson, José Fernández-Albertos, Christer Gunnarsson, Emmanuel Gymi-Boadi, Karla Hoff, Markus Jäntti, José Antonio Lucero, Marco Manacorda, Siobhan McInerney-Lankford, Joy Moncrieffe, Enrico Perotti, Vibha Pinglé, Pablo Querubi, Martin Ravallion, Michael Ross, Juho Saari, Rachel Sabates-Wheeler, Carolina Sánchez-Páramo, Norbert Schady, Andrew Shepherd, Milena Stefanova, and Juhana Vartiainen. Background papers for the Report are available either on the World Wide Web http://www.worldbank.org/wdr2006, under Background Papers or through the World Development Report office. The views expressed in these papers are not necessarily those of the World Bank or of this Report.

Many people inside and outside the World Bank gave comments to the team. Valuable comments and contributions were provided by Nisha Agrawal, Asad Alam, Sabina Alkire, Sudhir Anand, Cristian Baeza, Gianpaolo Baiocchi, Catherine Baker, Judy L. Baker, Giorgio Barba Navaretti, Catherine Barber, Jacques Baudouy, Gordon Betcherman, Lisa Bhansali, Vinay K. Bhargava, Amar Bhattacharya, Nancy Birdsall, Andrea Brandolini, John Bruce, Barbara Bruns, Donald Bundy, Luis Felipe López Calva, Shubham Chaudhuri, Martha Chen, Shaohua Chen, Aimee Christensen, Denis Cogneau, Giovanni Andrea Cornia, Anis Dani, Roberto Dañino, Jishnu Das, Klaus Decker, Arjan de Haan, Klaus Deininger, Asli Demirguc-Kunt, Kemal Dervis, Jean-Jacques Dethier, Shanta Devarajan, Peter A. Dewees, Charles Di Leva, Mala Escobar, Antonio Estache, Joan Maria Estebán, Shahrokh Fardoust, Massimo Florio, David Freestone, Adrian Fozzard, Teresa Genta Fons, Vivien Foster, M. Louise Fox, Sebastián Galiani, Alan Gelb, Alec Gershberg, Elena Glinskaya, Delfin Go, Carol Graham, Maurizio Guadagni, Susana Cordeiro Guerra, Isabel Guerrero, David Gwatkin, Jeff Hammer, Patrick Heller, Amy Jill Heyman, Bert Hofman, Patrick Honohan, R. Mukami Kariuki, Christine Kessides, Homi Kharas, Elizabeth King, Larry Kohler, Jacob Kolster, Somik Lall, Ruben Lamdany, Danny M. Leipziger, Victoria Levin, Sandy Lieberman, Peter Lindert, Amy Luinstra, Xubei Luo, Bill Maloney, Katherine Marshall, Siobhan McInerney-Lankford, Stephen Mink, Pradeep Mitra, Ed Mountfield, Chris Murray, Edmundo Murrugarra, Mamta Murthi, Ijaz Nabi, Mustapha K. Nabli, Julia Nielson, Pedro Olinto, Robert O'Sullivan, Çağlar Özden, John Page, Sheila Page, Guillermo Perry, Lant Pritchett, Agnes Quisumbing, Maurizio Ragazzi, Robin Michael Rajack, Raghuram G. Rajan, Dena Reingold, Kaspar Richter, Maria Estela Rivero-Fuentes, Peter Roberts, John Roemer, Fabio Sánchez, Milena Sánchez de Boado, Stefano Scarpetta, George Schieber, Maurice Schiff, Jesica Seacor, Binayak Sen, Shekhar Shah, Tony Shorrocks, Ricardo Silveira, Nistha Sinha, Milena Stefanova, Nicholas Stern, Kalanidhi Subbarao, Mark Sundberg, Rosa Alonso i Terme, Vinod Thomas, Peter Timmer, Bernice K. Van Bronkhorst, Rogier J.E. van den Brink, Rudolf Van Puymbroeck, Tara Vishwanath, Adam Wagstaff, L. Alan Winters, Ruslan Yemtsov, Nobuo Yoshida, Mary Eming Young, Hassan Zaman, and Heng-Fu Zou.

Other valuable assistance was provided by Jean-Pierre S. Djomalieu, Gytis Kanchas, Polly Means, Nacer Mohamed Megherbi, and Kavita Watsa. Christopher Neal and Stephen Commins assisted the team with consultations and dissemination.

Despite efforts to compile a comprehensive list, some who contributed may have been inadvertently omitted. The team apologizes for any oversights and reiterates its gratitude to all who contributed to this Report.

Background Papers

Andersson, Martin, and Christer Gunnarsson. "Egalitarianism in the Process of Modern Economic Growth: The Case of Sweden."

Barrientos, Armando. "Cash Transfers for Older People Reduce Poverty and Inequality."

Boix, Carles. "Spain: Development, Democracy and Equity."

Chirayath, Leila, Caroline Sage, and Michael Woolcock. "Customary Law and Policy Reform: Engaging with the Plurality of Justice Systems."

Claessens, Stijn, and Enrico Perotti. "The Links Between Finance and Inequality: Channels and Evidence."

de Haan, Arjan. "Disparities Within India's Poorest Regions: Why Do The Same Institutions Work Differently In Different Places?"

Decker, Klaus, Siobhan McInerney-Lankford, and Caroline Sage. "Human Rights and Equitable Development: 'Ideals', Issues and Implications."

Decker, Klaus, Caroline Sage, and Milena Stefanova. "Law or Justice: Building Equitable Legal Institutions."

Deshpande, Ashwini. "Affirmative Action in India and the United States."

Hoff, Karla. "What Can Economists Explain by Taking into Account People's Perceptions of Fairness? Punishing Cheats, Bargaining Impasse, and Self-Perpetuating Inequalities."

Jäntti, Markus, Juho Saari, and Juhana Vartiainen. "Country Case Study: Finland-Combining Growth with Equity."

Lucero, José Antonio. "Indigenous Political Voice and the Struggle for Recognition in Ecuador and Bolivia."

Moncrieffe, Joy. "Beyond Categories: Power, Recognition, and the Conditions for Equity."

Pinglé, Vibha. "Faith, Equity, and Development."

Rao, Vijayendra. "Symbolic Public Goods and the Coordination of Collective Action: A Comparison of Local Development in India and Indonesia."

Ravallion, Martin. "Why Should Poor People Care about Inequality?"

Ross, Michael. "Mineral Wealth and Equitable Development."

Sabates-Wheeler, Rachel. "Asset Inequality and Agricultural Growth: How Are Patterns of Asset Inequality Established and Reproduced?"

Shepherd, Andrew and Emmanuel Gyimah-Boadi, with Sulley Gariba, Sophie Plagerson, and Abdul Wahab Musa. "Bridging the North-south Divide in Ghana."

Endnotes

Overview

1. The infant mortality rates are computed separately at the province level only, and do not take into account racial, gender, or other social differences. The life expectancy statistics are for race and gender groups, and do not take regional or income differences into account. The real differences between typical individuals with the listed characteristics are therefore likely to be understated. In addition, Nthabiseng's life expectancy could be much lower if she were to become infected with HIV/AIDS, as are many young South African women. Data come from Day and Hedberg (2004). Predicted years of schooling rely on disaggregated information—by province, sex, race, rural-urban location, consumption expenditure quintile, and mother's education—from the Labor Force Survey and the Income and Expenditure Survey for 2000, which were carried out by the South Africa Statistics Office.

2. Predicted monthly consumption expenditures in 2000 for persons with those characteristics were Rand 119 ($45 adjusted for purchasing power parity) for Nthabiseng and Rand 3,662 ($1,370) for Pieter. The average white male with a highly educated mother, who lives in Cape Town and is in the top 20 percent of the distribution, happens to be in the ninety-ninth percentile of the overall income distribution. Data come from the Labor Force Survey and the Income and Expenditure Survey for 2000.

3. There are also income, consumption, and other differences: Sven can expect to earn $833 a month compared with the South African mean of $207 (Nthabiseng will have $44 a month). If Sven had been even luckier, and had been born at the same rank in Sweden's income distribution as Pieter occupied in South Africa, his expected monthly earnings would climb to $2,203. Sven will be able to visit any country on a whim, whereas Nthabiseng and Pieter can expect to spend hours waiting for a visa, which they may or may not obtain.

4. In some cases, such as China's decollectivization of agriculture in the late 1970s, a reform may lead to more efficiency, broader opportunities, and yet greater (intrarural) income inequality. China's experience—and the decompression of wages in a number of transition economies in Europe and Central Asia—is a good illustration of a more general point: because equity refers to fair processes and equal opportunities, it cannot be inferred from income distributions alone. Greater fairness will generally lead to lower income inequality, but not always. And not all policies that reduce inequality increase equity.

5. Mazumder (2005).

6. Other interactions between unequal opportunities and social conditions are also of societal concern, including links between inequality and crime, and between inequality and health. We review them briefly in the report, but focus on the channels of more direct significance to equity.

7. There may be many sound economic reasons for these risk-adjusted interest rates to vary, including fixed administrative loan costs, greater informational asymmetries, and the like. The point is that this affects poorer groups more, in ways unrelated to their investment opportunities, thus leading to both greater inefficiency and the perpetuation of inequalities.

8. These averages are based on actual episodes and refer to the total growth elasticity of poverty reduction, inclusive of any changes in inequality. "Low" and "high" inequality refers to a Gini coefficient of 0.3 and 0.6 respectively. The partial elasticity of poverty to growth, assuming no change in the Lorenz curve, shows a similar decline, but not to zero (see chapter 4).

9. While equity-enhancing redistribution will usually be from richer groups to poorer groups, it could happen that "good" redistributions will be to groups that are not poor, especially those in the middle. This will depend on the nature of the market failure. For example, the initial beneficiaries of a less-captured financial system may be small and medium entrepreneurs. Benefits to the poor will occur when enhanced access to financial services among middle-class entrepreneurs translates into faster growth and job creation.

Chapter 1

1. This formulation draws loosely on Roemer (1998), but it is also related to the works of Dworkin (1981b), Dworkin (1981a), and Sen (1985).

2. See Rawls (1971).

3. See Acemoglu and Robinson (2000), Bourguignon and Verdier (2000), and Ferreira (2001).

4. This theme is one that recurs across many disciplines—in sociology and anthropology see Bourdieu (1986), Bourdieu (1990), and Tilly (1998), in economics see Engerman and Sokoloff (2001), Bénabou (2000), and Piketty (1995).

5. See Acemoglu and Robinson (2000) for various perspectives on the interconnections among cultural, social, and economic inequality, and Stewart (2001) for a general discussion of group-based inequalities.

6. Appadurai (2004).

7. See Bourdieu (1990) on symbolic violence for more on this.

8. Steele (1999).

9. Appadurai (2004).

10. See Rao and Walton (2004) for more on such "inequalities of agency."

11. See also Birdsall, Graham, and Sabbot (1998) and Thorbecke (2005).

12. "Too much" and "too little" are used here with respect to the social optimum. The choices are usually privately rational.

13. The role of high inequality of political power and wealth as a barrier to economic development in the modern era is a rapidly growing area of research. Striking results are reported in Sokoloff and Khan (1990), Engerman and Sokoloff (1997, 2002), Acemoglu, Johnson, and Robinson (2001, 2002), and Banerjee and others (2001). Overviews of the broad set of research questions are Engerman and Sokoloff (2002), Hoff (2003), and Acemoglu, Johnson, and Robinson (2004).

14. This is so if the distribution of talents and informational asymmetries between employers and employees are similar between men and women. Notice that the efficiency gain does not satisfy the Pareto criterion. Some individual men might lose out. The efficiency criterion here is first-order dominance, under the anonymity axiom.

15. Of course, the intrinsic valuation of equity may be reflected in the appropriate distributional weights underpinning these benefits.

16. This has been a recurrent theme in development economics and at the World Bank. For an influential early treatment, see Chenery and others (1994).

17. World Bank (1990).

18. World Bank (2001h).

Focus 1 on Palanpur

1. The study was launched out of the Agricultural Economics Research Centre of the University of Delhi and Oxford University, and then continued from the London School of Economics.

2. Drèze, Lanjouw, and Sharma (1998), 51.

3. Drèze, Lanjouw, and Sharma (1998), 211.

Chapter 2

1. Filmer (2004).

2. See, for instance, Wilkinson (1992) and Wilkinson (2000).

3. High rank, on the other hand, can be protective of health, including enhancing one's resistance to infectious disease.

4. Fujii (2005).

5. Interestingly, for each of the three population groupings, the relative gap in infant mortality between groups rose in approximately half of the countries and fell in the other half.

6. Chaudhury and others (2005).

7. Araujo, Ferreira, and Schady (2004) use a new data set, constructed from individual record data in household surveys for 124 countries. Qualitatively similar results were also obtained by Castello and Domenech (2002) and Thomas, Wang, and Fan (2002), both of which rely on the Barro and Lee (2001) international education data set.

8. See, for example, Kanbur (2000).

9. See Kanbur (2000), Elbers and others (2005).

10. Wan, Lu, and Chen (2004).

11. These correlations hold whether or not between-group inequality is measured on the basis of the conventional or alternative methodology. They also hold after controlling for outliers (although South Africa is a particularly influential observation in the regression of inequality on social group differences). The results also hold when all the between-group shares are combined into a single-count indicator that reflects whether a particular country has a higher-than-median value of the between-group share for a particular population breakdown.

12. Bourguignon and Morrisson (1998).

13. Li, Squire, and Zou (1998).

14. The consumption module in India's National Sample Survey was slightly modified between the 1993/4 round and the 1999/0, compromising both poverty and inequality comparisons over time. Deaton and Kozel (2004) provide a clear overview of the issues and their implications.

15. Deaton and Drèze (2002), Sen and Himanshu (2004) and Banerjee and Piketty (2003) all document increases in inequality, but by varying amounts. These estimates are all predicated on certain assumptions given the fundamental problems of data comparability referred to above.

16. Khan and Sen (2001).

17. Narayan and Yoshida (2004).

18. Nepal National Planning Commission (1995–6).

19. For a sociological perspective on the inheritance of inequality, see Erikson and Goldthrope (2002).

20. Solon (1999).

21. Mazumder (2005).

22. Hertz (2001) for South Africa; Dunn (2003) for Brazil.

23. Solon (2002).

24. World Bank (2001h).

25. Jha, Rao, and Woolcock (forthcoming).

26. Appadurai (2004).

27. See, for example, Fernández-Kelly (1995) on life in the U.S. inner city.

28. Appadurai (2004).

29. This term comes from Nussbaum (2000) and her work on gender discrimination and development, although the core idea has a long intellectual history in social science.

30. It is also important to note that the *appearance* of "internalizing disadvantage" (for example, working slowly, being tardy) can actually be a covert strategy used by marginalized groups to subvert systems over which they otherwise have little influence. See Scott (1986).

31. If income inequality, a static measure, is a good proxy for social mobility, a dynamic concept, then these theories find support in the large literature on income inequality and crime. See, for example, Demombynes and Özler (2005) for a discussion of the subject at the country level, and Fajnzylber, Lederman, and Loayza (2000), among others, on the cross-country level relationship between income inequality and crime.

32. See Narayan (2002) for a categorization of approaches and case studies.

33. See Petesch, Smulovitz, and Walton (2005).

34. Gibson and Woolcock (2005); for methodological details on the broader research project of which this study is a part (and the evidence base on which the assertions made here rest), see Barron, Smith, and Woolcock (2004).

35. See also Rao (2005) on the related idea of such spaces as "symbolic public goods."

36. Maynard (1966); Casagrande and Piper (1969).

37. Oster (2005) has recently argued that hepatitis B affects offspring ratios and has suggested that geographic patterns of hepatitis B prevalence can explain about 45 percent of the missing women. The magnitude of the hepatitis B effect is currently still the subject of controversy (see e.g., Klasen 2005).

38. Das Gupta and others (2003).

39. Lloyd (forthcoming), with original data from The Center for Reproductive Law and Policy.

40. Lloyd (2005)(forthcoming).

41. Agarwal (1994); Deere and León (2003).

42. Mason and Carlsson (forthcoming).

43. Rahman and Rao (2004).

44. Kabeer (1999).

45. Kabeer (1997).

46. This disparity is less apparent in enrollments in primary school, which has become more equitable over the last decade.

47. Browning and Chiappori (1998).

48. See Strauss, Mwabu, and Beegle (2000) for an excellent survey of economic models of intrahousehold allocation.

49. Thomas (1990).

50. Lundberg, Pollak, and Wales (1997).

51. Quisumbing and Maluccio (2003).

52. Heise, Ellsberg, and Gottemoeller (1999).

53. Kabeer (1997).

54. Rahman and Rao (2004).

55. Munshi and Rosenzweig (forthcoming).

56. Quisumbing, Estudillo, and Otsuka (2004).

57. Das Gupta and others (2004).

Chapter 3

1. Deaton (2004), 31. The large differences in mortality do not just exist between rich and poor countries, or between different groups of citizens in poor countries only. In 2002, the median age at death in Australia for indigenous people was roughly 20 years less than that for nonindigenous males, which was approximately 76 years (Australian Bureau of Statistics 2003).

2. Botswana, which has one of the highest HIV/AIDS infection rates in the world, has seen its life expectancy drop from its peak of 60 years in the mid-1980s to 39 years in 2000.

3. Bourguignon, Levin, and Rosenblatt (2004a), 3.

4. See the following quotes that nicely demonstrate the debate on globalization and the inequality of incomes: "Globalization raises incomes and the poor participate fully," *The Economist*, May 27, 2000, 94. "There is plenty of evidence that current patterns of growth and globalization are widening income disparities." Policy Director of Oxfam, letter to *The Economist*, June 20, 2000, 6.

5. Doing this in practice requires household survey data and various adjustments and assumptions—all far from simple—which is why so many people discuss international or intercountry inequality using National Accounts data instead of global inequality.

6. Pritchett (1997).

7. It is important to note that all the evidence presented here refer to *intercountry* or *international* inequality in life expectancy at birth, and not to *global* inequalities, because we do not use any evidence on within-country differences in life expectancy.

8. Goesling and Firebaugh (2004).

9. Note that the declines in life expectancy for the mainly Sub-Saharan African countries do not seem to be a direct result of changes in infant mortality, which in many cases continued to decline. However, as Cornia and Menchini (2005) argue, the rate of decline in infant mortality also slowed down significantly in the last decade, which cannot be explained solely by the changes in Europe and Central Asia and Sub-Saharan Africa.

10. Deaton (2004).

11. Pritchett (forthcoming). The richest quintile is defined based on an asset index created by Filmer and Pritchett (1999).

12. One example of such decomposition is Pradhan, Sahn, and Younger (2003), who claim that less than one-third of the world inequality in child health is attributable to differences between countries.

13. Gwatkin (2002). Again, the richest decile here is defined based on the asset index by Filmer and Pritchett (1999).

14. Preston (1980) as cited in Deaton (2004).

15. Also note that all of the countries that are significantly below the curve, that is, those with much lower life expectancy at birth than their GDP per capita would predict, such as South Africa, are in Sub-Saharan Africa.

16. See Deaton (2004). In fact, Cornia and Menchini (2005) cite the rise in parents literacy and female education as the main reason behind the remarkable declines in infant mortality rates in Latin America and the Caribbean and Middle East and North Africa in the 1980s.

17. The increase in inequality between countries in life expectancy at birth in the 1990s is also confirmed by Goesling and Firebaugh (2004).

18. A recent paper by Brainerd and Cuttler (2004) cites increased alcohol use and psychosocial stress brought on by an unpredictable future as the two main contributors to the decline in life expectancy in Russia and other countries of the former Soviet Union.

19. This figure in Morocco compares with roughly three-quarters of the same cohort in Indonesia and Turkey, and about 85 percent in Colombia and Philippines.

20. While making these comparisons between countries, the reader should bear in mind the discussion on the comparability of these data from box 2.5 and not interpret these differences literally.

21. The urban and rural figures for China (and India) have not been corrected for cost-of-living differences. Given that rural-urban price differentials have been increasing over time and are significant today (Chen and Ravallion 2004), the figures here exaggerate the differences in living standards between the rural and urban Chinese.

22. Kolm (1976) proposed the following class of absolute measures of inequality:

$$K = \frac{1}{\kappa} \ln \left[\frac{1}{n} \sum_{i=1}^{n} e^{\kappa(\mu - y_i)} \right],$$

where $\kappa > 0$ is a parameter that captures inequality aversion.

23. Atkinson and Brandolini (2004) discuss changes in international as well as global inequality. We use only their results on international inequality to make our point on the trend differences when one switches from a relative concept of inequality to an absolute one.

24. Such as Milanovic (2005).

25. See Firebaugh and Goesling (2004), Sala-i-Martin (2002).

26. Our analysis shows that we can estimate GE(0), that is, mean log deviation, from grouped data, especially if the number of groups is larger than 10, without any significant bias using our smoothing techniques.

27. The difficulties in assembling a database to calculate global inequality over such a long time period are detailed in Bourguignon and Morrisson (2002), 729–30.

28. Pritchett (1997), 14.

29. Bourguignon, Levin, and Rosenblatt (2004a).

30. Ravallion (2004a) as cited in Bourguignon, Levin, and Rosenblatt (2004a).

31. See, for example, Chen and Ravallion (2004).

32. Vietnam and Thailand practically eliminated $1 a day poverty during this period.

33. The projections for meeting some of the other Millennium Development Goals do not give one cause for greater optimism. East Asia and Europe and Central Asia are close to the target on primary education, while others are falling behind. A handful of countries are on track to attain the child mortality goal, mainly in Latin America and the Caribbean. Only 21 percent of the developing world's population is expected to achieve the maternal mortality goal. Halving the proportion of people without access to safe water and sanitation will require providing about 1.5 billion people with access to safe water and 2 billion with basic sanitation facilities between 2000 and 2015. At current rates of service expansion, only about one-fifth of countries are on track. See http://www.un.org/millenniumgoals/ for more details on the 8 goals, 18 targets, and nearly 50 indicators that comprise the Millennium Development Goals.

34. Deaton (2004). The rules of the game at the global level, and especially the process of setting those rules, will be discussed in great detail in chapter 10.

35. Voting shares in the soft-lending arm of the World Bank, the International Development Association, are similar: Part I countries hold 61 percent of the vote and Part II countries 39 percent. Developing countries are somewhat better represented in regional development banks, but developed countries hold large voting shares there too.

36. In all other cases, the delegates in charge of economic matters may be covering, in addition to the WTO, also UNCTAD, ITU, ILO and WIPO.

37. Each country belongs to one of the following four categories based on its GDP per capita in 2002: low income, lower-middle income, higher-middle income, and high income.

38. López (2000) as cited in Deaton (2004).

39. Pritchett (2001) and Pritchett (2004b).

40. Firebaugh and Goesling (2004).

41. Sala-i-Martin (2002).

42. Pritchett attributes this phrase to Gerschenkron (1962).

43. Pritchett (1997), 15.

44. As cited in Goesling and Firebaugh (2004).

45. As cited in Sala-i-Martin (2002).

46. Goesling and Firebaugh (2004).

Focus 2 on empowerment

1. Evans (2004).

2. See Petesch, Smulovitz, and Walton (2005) for the interactions between opportunity structure and the agency of subordinate groups.

3. Chaudhuri and Heller (2003).

4. Baiocchi, Chaudhuri, and Heller (2005).

5. Chaudhuri, Harilal, and Heller (2004).

6. The concepts of "terms of recognition" and "capacity to aspire" come from Appadurai (2004); "capacity to engage" is from Gibson and Woolcock (2005).

7. Rao and Walton (2004).

8. On the origins, structure and goals of KDP, see Guggenheim (forthcoming).

9. Gibson and Woolcock (2005).

10. Barron, Diprose, and Woolcock (2005).

Part II

1. In his second inaugural address, Roosevelt also suggested that avoiding deprivation in outcomes was a legitimate policy aim. As he put it, "The test of our progress is not whether we add more to the abundance of those who have much; it is whether we provide enough for those who have too little" (Washington, DC, January 20, 1937). There tends to be less agreement on the importance of inequality in specific outcome spaces. Writing about income inequality, Feldstein (1998) argues that increases in inequality caused by larger incomes at the very top warrant no policy attention, and represent "pure Pareto improvements," to which only "spiteful egalitarians" would object.

2. Michel Ferry, online consultation message, dated October 26, 2004, 10:56 a.m.

3. As chapter 1 also indicated, this is *not* equivalent to saying that implementing redistributions is free of tradeoffs, particularly in the short run, or that terrible inefficiencies cannot arise if redistributions are implemented in ways that pay no heed to incentives. We return to these difficult policy issues in chapters 7, 8, and 9.

Chapter 4

1. See Pinglé (2005).

2. Plato, *The Laws,* 745, quoted in Cowell (1995), 21.

3. The reason for this reputation is the combination of a utilitarian objective with a set of (rather restrictive) assumptions about individual utilities: (i) individual preferences can be represented by a utility function; (ii) cardinal utility levels are meaningful indicators of the individual's well-being; (iii) utilities can be compared across different people; (iv) the utility functions are increasing but concave (that is, increase at a declining rate) in incomes; and (v) all individuals have identical utility functions. If they all hold, then, for a fixed level of aggregate income, the greatest sum of utilities is achieved by an equal division of incomes across all individuals.

4. Sen (2000), 69.

5. For example, within German Courts, the standard of what is equitable is based on "the opinion of all those people who think in equitable and just terms"(Palandt 2004, article 242).

6. For example, within common law jurisdictions, key principles that guide the application of equity include the principles of "unconscionability," "undue influence," "duress," and "unjust enrichment." A transaction has been deemed unconscionable where "one party to a transaction is at a special disadvantage in dealing with the other party because illness, ignorance, inexperience, impaired faculties, financial need, or other circumstances affect his ability to conserve his own interests, and the other party unconscientiously takes advantage of the opportunity thus placed in his hands" (High Court of Australia, *Blomley v. Ryan* 1956, 99 CLR 362 at p. 415, per Kitto J.).

7. Aristotle, *The Nicomachean Ethics,* book 5, chapter 10, 350 BC.

8. Kritzer (2002), p. 495. For a more detailed discussion of the philosophical evolution of the concept, see Alland and Rials (2003).

9. The Chancellory Courts have their origin in the residual discretionary power of the King, generally exercised by the Chancellor,

to correct or overturn cases in which justice could not be obtained by a common law court.

10. In the common law tradition, equitable jurisdiction is also associated with a number of well-established principles, sometimes called the "maxims of equity." Examples of these include: *He who seeks equity must do equity*—that is, a claimant who seeks equitable relief must be prepared to act fairly toward the defendant (future conduct); *He who comes to equity must come with clean hands*—similar to the previous principle, but related to the claimant's past conduct; *Equity looks at intent rather than form*—equity is more concerned with substance than form.

11. Cadiet (2004), 425.

12. See Arnaud (1993) and Draï (1991).

13. Preamble to the Universal Declaration of Human Rights (1948).

14. Note also Article 1(3)—purposes of Charter—"promoting and encouraging respect for human rights and for fundamental freedoms for all without distinction as to race, sex, language or religion" Article 2(1)—"sovereign equality of all members"—indicates balance between the principles of sovereignty and noninterference and of respect for human rights; Article 55—"universal respect for, and observance of human rights." Other references to human rights include Articles 13(b)(1), 62(2), and 68.

15. Vienna Declaration and Programme of Action Vienna Declaration (UNGA) (A/CONF. 157/23), July 12, 1993. This was issued by the U.N. World Conference on Human Rights, Vienna, Austria, June 14–25, 1993.

16. Rights identified in the UDHR include the right "without any discrimination to equal protection before the law" (Article 7), the right to "take part in the government of his country, directly or through freely chosen representatives" (Article 21), and the right to education (Article 26).

17. There exist several different characterizations of the "core human rights treaties." One is the "International Bill of Rights," which comprises the Universal Declaration on Human Rights, the International Covenant on Civil and Political Rights, and the International Covenant on Economic, Social and Cultural Rights. Another conceptualization is that there are six major human rights treaties: the ICCPR (1966), the ICESCR (1966), the Convention on the Elimination of All Forms of Racial Discrimination (ICERD) (1964), the Convention on the Elimination of All Forms of Discrimination Against Women (CEDAW) (1989), the Convention Against Torture (CAT) (1984) and the Convention on the Rights of the Child (CRC) (1989). None of these characterizations should be taken as exhaustive or exclusive; there are several other extremely important human rights treaties beyond these, both within the U.N. system and outside it in regional systems. The OHCHR lists "seven core international human rights instruments": the six above, plus the International Convention on the Protection of the Rights of Migrant Workers and the Members of their Families (1990). In addition to this, mention should also be made of the Genocide Convention (1948).

18. Henrich and others (2004) report on Ultimatum Games played in 15 small-scale societies around the world. In an Indonesian experiment, Cameron (1999) found that high offers persisted in games played with (locally) very high monetary stakes.

19. See, for instance, Fehr and Schmidt (1999) on a theory of "inequity aversion," and Rabin (1993) on a model of behavior that takes other people's intentions directly into account.

20. Ibid.

21. Terry, Carey, and Callan (2001).

22. This is the question in the United States General Social Survey, which was fielded every year between 1972 and 1997. A similar question is included in the Euro-Barometer surveys, which are also used in the study.

23. Subjective well-being—or "happiness"—surveys have also been used to test the relative income hypothesis in a number of different settings. Following on original work by Easterlin (1974), which suggested that, despite sustained economic growth, people in some rich countries were not growing any happier, a number of recent studies have found that reported well-being rises with personal income, but declines with the income of other people in a person's reference group. This is usually interpreted to mean that well-being is driven at least in part by relative incomes, rather than purely by their absolute levels. See Graham and Felton (2005) for Latin America, Ravallion and Lokshin (2002) for the Russian Federation, and Luttmer (2004) for the United States. The relative income literature is of tangential interest for this report, because it provides additional backing for the idea that one's position in society in relation to others matters, both for individual behavior and for welfare.

24. See De Ferranti and others (2004) for an earlier discussion of this data.

25. The professions included skilled factory worker, doctor in private practice, chairman of a large national company, lawyer, shop assistant, federal cabinet minister, judge of the nation's highest court, owner/manager of a large factory, and unskilled worker. Respondents were also asked about their own income.

26. Countries in the ISSP sample include the following: Austria, Australia, Canada, France, Germany, Italy, Israel, Japan, the Netherlands, New Zealand, Norway, Portugal, Spain, Sweden, Switzerland, the United Kingdom, and the United States.

27. This figure is an update, based on more recent data, of an original figure that appeared in Ravallion and Chen (1997).

28. See, once again, Ravallion and Chen (1997) and Bourguignon (2003).

29. Using a slightly different dataset, and a decomposition technique that also accounts for the differential sensitivity of different poverty measures to changes in mean incomes, Kraay (forthcoming) finds that the growth share in this variance is closer to 70 percent. In a sample of long spells only, that share rises to 94 percent.

30. Whereas the total growth elasticity of poverty reduction simply relates total change in poverty to the growth in mean incomes, without controlling for changes in the relative distribution and is therefore given by

$$\varepsilon_\mu^T = \frac{\Delta P}{P} \frac{\mu}{\Delta\mu},$$

the partial growth elasticity of poverty reduction controls for changes in inequality. That means that it is calculated for a given Lorenz curve:

$$\varepsilon_\mu^P = \frac{\Delta P}{P} \frac{\mu}{\Delta\mu}\bigg|_{Lt} = \frac{P\left(L_t, \frac{\mu_{t+1}}{z}\right) - P\left(L_t, \frac{\mu_t}{z}\right)}{P\left(L_t, \frac{\mu_t}{z}\right)} \frac{\mu}{\Delta\mu}.$$

This definition, like the decomposition on which it is based, is path-dependent, and the elasticity would be somewhat different if it was calculated on the basis of the final-period Lorenz curve, rather than the initial one. In this report, we always use the initial period relative distribution when computing partial growth elasticities. No regression method is used, so no functional form of any kind is imposed on the relationship.

31. This finding is qualitatively consistent with alternative estimates of the relationship between partial and total growth elasticities, on the one hand, and income inequality, on the other. See Bourguignon (2003) and Ravallion (2005).

32. The other four combinations of poverty lines and measures were also computed, and the upward-sloping pattern is qualitatively robust.

33. See also Bourguignon, Ferreira, and Lustig (2004) for a detailed discussion of seven country studies.

34. In fact, World Bank (2005b) finds that, on average, the poorest 20 percent of the population in each of 14 countries in their study grow 0.7 percent for each 1 percentage point growth in mean incomes.

Chapter 5

1. See, for example, Fisman (2001a).

2. Even in a hypothetical world with perfectly functioning markets, there may still be an indirect influence, coming from the effect of wealth or income on savings decisions. It has been suggested that the poor are less inclined to save than the rich, and as a result, aggregate savings as a proportion of aggregate income may go up if the rich gain at the expense of the poor. This could affect investment decisions through the effect of the supply of savings on the price of capital. Inequality, in this Kaldorian view of the world (after Nicholas Kaldor, the Cambridge economist), would enhance growth, although it might yet be a Pyrrhic victory. Kaldor worried about the inevitability of crises under capitalism, and he saw faster growth accompanied by burgeoning inequality as a recipe for ongoing crises.

3. Note that such redistributions from wealthier to poorer people do not necessarily have to be to the poorest people in society, but rather to those with good growth opportunities.

4. Unless there are two different investment opportunities that have the exact same payoff, net of interest.

5. Dasgupta, Nayar, and Associates (1989).

6. See also Gill and Singh (1977) and Swaminathan (1991).

7. See Djankov and others (2003).

8. See Deaton (1997) for more details.

9. See Townsend (1995).

10. Fafchamps and Lund (2003) find that, in the Philippines, households are much better insured against some shocks than against others. In particular, they seem to be poorly insured against health risk, a finding corroborated by Gertler and Gruber (2002) in Indonesia.

11. See Banerjee (2000) for a discussion of the alternative views.

12. Although, there are instances of government scholarships for tertiary education in many countries that require beneficiaries to provide a specified number of years of service in government after graduation.

13. Blair, Judd, and Chapleau (2004). See also Loury (2002) for a wide-ranging study.

14. See the survey in Steele and Aronson (1995).

15. From McKenzie and Woodruff (2003), figure 1.

16. Olley and Pakes (1996).

17. The ICOR measures the increase in output predicted by a one-unit increase in capital stock. It is calculated by extrapolating from the past experience of the country and assumes that the next unit of capital will be used exactly as efficiently (or inefficiently) as the previous one. The inverse of the ICOR therefore gives an upper bound for the average marginal product for the economy—it is an upper bound because the calculation of the ICOR does not control for the effect of the increases in the other factors of production, which also contributes to the increase in output. The implicit assumption that the other factors of production are growing is probably reasonable for most developing countries, except perhaps in Africa.

18. Banerjee and Munshi (2004); Banerjee, Duflo, and Munshi (2003).

19. This is not because capital and talent happen to be substitutes. In these data, as is generally assumed, capital and ability appear to be complements.

20. From Goldstein and Udry (1999), figure 4.

21. From Goldstein and Udry (1999), 38.

22. Based on Berry and Cline (1979).

23. Some of the effects of lack of insurance may be quite subtle. Banerjee and Newman (1991) argue, for example, that the availability of insurance in one location (the village) and its unavailability in another (the city) may lead to inefficient migration decisions, because some individuals with high potential in the city may prefer to stay in the village to remain insured.

24. The fact that there is underinvestment on average, and not only a set of people with too many bullocks and a set of people with too few, is probably due to the fact that bullocks are a lumpy investment, and owning more than two is inefficient for production (there is no small adjustment possible at the margin).

25. Another piece of relevant evidence comes from the effects of titling nonagricultural land. Field (2003) shows evidence from a land-titling program in the slums of urban Peru that suggests that the lack of a clear title to the land where you have built your home reduces the ability of the household members to work outside. Field hypothesizes that this is because someone needs to be home to defend the untitled property from expropriation by others. But she does not find any evidence that land titling improves access to credit.

26. This number takes into account the fact that only 20 percent of the Indonesian population is iron deficient. The private returns of iron supplementation for someone who knew they were iron deficient—which they can find out using a simple finger prick—would be $200.

27. Kremer (1993).

28. Li and others (1994).

29. Banerjee and Duflo (2004b), 11.

30. See Bénabou (1996) for a survey.

31. Forbes (2000) also corrects for the bias introduced by introducing a lagged variable in a fixed-effect specification by using the Generalized Method of Moments (GMM) estimator developed by Arellano and Bond (1991).

32. Barro (2000) estimates a cross-sectional relationship between inequality and short-term growth and finds a negative relation in poor countries but a positive relation in rich ones.

33. Banerjee, Gertler, and Ghatak (2002).

Chapter 6

1. Engerman and Sokoloff (1997).

2. Acemoglu, Johnson, and Robinson (2001), 1387.

3. Klarén (2000), 44–48.

4. See Hemming (1970), 264 on Pizarro and Melo (1996), 222 on Colombia.

5. Bakewell (1984), Cole (1985), Lockhart (1969) and Mörner (1973).

6. Lockhart and Schwartz (1983), 34.

7. Parry (1948).

8. Cardoso (1991), Mahoney (2001), and Lang (1975), 28.

9. An analogous story applies to the parts of the region suitable for plantation agriculture, especially sugar. Colonists in the Caribbean, present-day Brazil, and the southern United States took advantage of the international market in slaves and developed distinct but also highly coercive regimes.

10. See Crosby (1986), 143–44.

11. See Craven (1932) and Morgan (1975).

12. See Acemoglu, Johnson, and Robinson (2002), Acemoglu, Johnson, and Robinson (2004), and Rodrik, Subramanian, and Trebbi (2002).

13. In addition to arguments noted above, see the econometric analysis arguing that governance causes growth, but not the other way, in Kaufmann and Kraay (2002).

14. Haggard (1990) and Kang (2002).

15. Liddle (1991) and MacIntyre (2001b), 259.

16. Geertz (1963), Elson (2001), 194–201, 280–81; Rock (2003), 14.

17. World Bank (1993).

18. Bates (1981).

19. Bates (1981), 122.

20. Bates (1989).

21. Bowman (1991).

22. Fisman (2001b), MacIntyre (2001a), Stern (2003).

23. Lipset (1959).

24. This conjecture is substantiated by the standard account of the evolution of institutions in Britain, culminating in the Glorious Revolution of 1688 (North and Thomas 1973, North and Weingast 1989, and O'Brien 1993).

25. See Brenner (1976), Tawney (1941), Moore (1966), and Acemoglu, Johnson, and Robinson (2002b).

26. See Thompson (1963), Tilly (1995), and Tarrow (1998).

27. Acemoglu and Robinson (2000), Acemoglu and Robinson (2005).

28. Lindert (2003), Lindert (2004).

29. Other data on real wages and real rental rates on land supports this claim; see O'Rourke and Williamson (2002).

30. Li, Squire, and Zou (1998), Rodrik (1999b).

31. This section is based on Andersson and Gunnarsson (2005) and Jäntti and others (2005).

32. Wade (1990).

33. Andersson and Gunnarsson (2005), 4.

34. Chen and Ravallion (2004).

35. Montinola, Qian, and Weingast (1995), 51–52.

36. Qian (2003), 305.

37. In China revenues were collected at the local level and shared up with higher levels of government

Focus 4 on Indonesia

1. World Bank (1993).

2. Using data from van der Eng (1993a, 1993b, 2002), it is possible to construct an index of pro-poor growth from 1880 to 1990 (Timmer 2005). Using this index, the rates of pro-poor growth for each historical era were as follows: 1880–1905 = 0.05 percent per year; 1905–1925 = 4.57 percent per year; 1925–1950 = –2.57 percent per year; 1950–1965 = 2.37 percent per year; and 1965–1990 = 6.56 percent per year.

3. All Indonesian distributional data are subject to the usual caveats about the difficulty of obtaining adequate responses from both the very poor and the very rich. In particular, SUSENAS does not capture the extremely uneven accumulation of wealth or the conspicuous consumption of the ultra rich.

4. There is a "standard" economic model behind this story, in which the capital of individuals—formal and informal skills, land, location, and even accumulated savings—is deployed to earn incomes, with the possibilities determined by technology, transactions costs, and market prices. See Alatas and Bourguignon (2004).

5. Temple (2001). These institutions, for better and worse, lived well beyond the Suharto era.

6. Timmer (2005).

Chapter 7

1. The study finds that it is the quality of parent-child interactions, especially talking to the child, that matters the most (Hart and Risley 1995).

2. Pollitt, Watkins, and Husaini (1997), Grantham-McGregor and Ani (2001), Stoltzfus, Kvalsvig, and Chwaya (2001), Black (2003), Dickson and others (2000), Smith, Brooks-Gunn, and Klebanov (1997).

3. Shore (1997).

4. Rutter, Giller, and Hagell (2000), Karr-Morse and Wiley (1977).

5. Paxson and Schady (2005).

6. Pritchett (2004a).

7. Carneiro and Heckman (2003).

8. Three of the best-documented studies for the United States are on the Chicago Child-Parent Centers, a half-day program on a large scale in the Chicago public schools; the Abecedarian program, a full-day year-round education program in Chapel Hill, North Carolina, with followup to age 21; and the High/Scope Perry Preschool, a half-day program on a small scale in the Ypsilanti, Michigan, public schools with follow up to age 40. The last two are small randomized experiments. Studies on the Chicago program use statistical techniques to control for selection bias and other factors that might confound interpretation of results.

9. Slide 5 of presentation on Heckman and Masterov (2004), at http://www.ced.org/docs/presentation_heckman1.pdf.

10. Young (2002). In the United States, Currie (2000) notes that, while all the children in the North Carolina Abecedarian project were at risk of mental retardation, positive effects were twice as large for the most disadvantaged children among them. Currie and

Thomas (1999) find that gains in test scores associated with Head Start were greater for Hispanic children than for non-Hispanic whites.

11. Grantham-McGregor and others (1991).

12. Deutsch (1998), Attanasio and Vera-Hernandez (2004).

13. Paxson and Schady (2005).

14. Scott-McDonald (2004).

15. Doryan, Gautman, and Foege (2002).

16. Kirpal (2002).

17. Many conditional cash transfers in Latin America already have some of these features.

18. Currie and Thomas (1995) find that gains in vocabulary and reading test scores faded out among black Head Start children while they were still in elementary grades but not among whites even though initial gains in test scores were the same for both groups. Currie and Thomas (2000) attribute this to their finding that black children who attended Head Start go on to attend lower-quality schools than other black children but that the same is not true for whites.

19. King, Orazem, and Paterno (1999).

20. UNESCO (2005).

21. Thirty-two more countries have too little data to assess (Bruns, Mingat, and Rakotomalala 2003 and FTI Secretariat 2004).

22. See Wodon (2005) for Niger and Senegal—in Senegal, when the school is located less than 15 minutes away from home, the probability of enrollment for boys goes up by 30 percentage points as compared with having the school more than one hour away. Burney and Irfan (1995) found negligible impacts of proximity.

23. The study finds that children age two to four, in 1974, had an additional 0.12 to 0.19 years of education and 1.5 to 2.7 percent higher wages for each new school built per 1,000 children (Duflo 2001). Other studies that find positive impacts of expanding school infrastructure include Birdsall (1985) in urban Brazil, DeTray (1988) and Lillard and Willis (1994) in Malaysia, Lavy (1996) in Ghana, and Case and Deaton (1999) in South Africa.

24. Pritchett (2004a).

25. Kremer, Moulin, and Namunyu (2002).

26. In Brazil in 2001, the Bolsa Escola program was spending almost $700 million a year and reaching 8.6 million school children, one-third of all primary school children in Brazil. In Bangladesh, the Food for Education budget in 2000 was $77 million, benefiting 2.2 million children, 13 percent of total school enrollment (Morley and Coady 2003). In Mexico, according to government figures, by 2004, Opportunidades was spending approximately $2.3 billion annually, or about 1.5 percent of total expenditter, and reaching 5 million households—almost 20 percent of all families in Mexico.

27. Morley and Coady (2003) and Schultz (2004).

28. There are some countries in which gender disparities require attention to boys even for primary schooling (Mongolia) and quite a few for higher levels of attainment (Brazil, Philippines).

29. Herz and Sperling (2004).

30. World Bank (2004d).

31. Pritchett (2004a).

32. A score of more than one standard deviation below the OECD mean is considered poor performance.

33. See Hanushek (1986) and Hanushek (1996).

34. Wößmann (2000).

35. See Glewwe, Kremer, and Moulin (2002), Glewwe, Ilias, and Kremer (2003), Glewwe and others (2004), Kremer, Miguel, and Thornton (2004), Miguel and Kremer (2004).

36. It is also important to take account of household behavior in response to changes in school inputs. Das, Dercon, Habrayimana, and Krishnan (2004) find that household spending and (nonsalary) cash grants to schools are close substitutes with no impact on learning from anticipated increases in school funds. Unanticipated funds have significant learning impacts.

37. Hanushek and Wößman (2005).

38. Ladd (2002).

39. The analysis is not able to separate the effects of private schools from the effects of the incentives for greater effort generated by the voucher policy. The distinction is important because effort can be encouraged also by awarding scholarships to students attending public schools, as we saw with the Balshaki program. See Angrist and others (2002).

40. Chubb and Moe (1990).

41. See McEwan (2000) on Chile. Hoxby (2002) finds improvements from school choice from charter schools in Michigan and Arizona; Holmes, DeSimone, and Rupp (2003) find that competition from school choice in North Carolina improved test scores significantly. Cullen, Jacob, and Levitt (2000) and Cullen, Jacob, and Levitt (2003) found no impact from school choice in Chicago. See also Witte (2000). Hoxby (2000) finds significant productivity gains for a representative sample across the United States, while Rothstein (2005) uses the same data to find far more modest results.

42. McEwan and Carnoy (2000) and Hsieh and Urquiola (2003).

43. Lindert (2004).

44. In Brazil, a 1997 reform set a minimum floor on education spending in all regions, which led to an increase in primary school enrollments from 55 to 85 percent in only six years (World Bank 2005f).

45. See Grindle (2004) and Fiszbein (2005) for examples in Latin America.

46. World Bank (2003j).

47. Wößmann (2004) argues for giving decision-making authority to those with the most relevant information and the lowest prospects for personal gain. He finds that student performance improves with central control over the curriculum, budget, and exams; delegation of process and personnel decisions to the school; greater say for teachers in the selection of appropriate teaching methods; regular scrutiny of students' education performance; and parental interest in education content. Competition from private education institutions and the presence of teacher unions, on the other hand, have adverse effects.

48. See World Bank (2003j) and Pritchett (2004a).

49. World Bank (2003j) for South Africa; Duan (2005).

50. World Bank (2004k).

51. World Bank (2004k).

52. Thailand's Ministry of Public Health and World Bank (2005).

53. Rawlings (2004).

54. See Barber, Bertozzi, and Gertler (2005) for Mexico; Das and Hammer (2004) and Das and Hammer (2005) for India; Barber, Gertler, and Harimurti (2005) for Indonesia; and Leonard and Masatu (2005) for Tanzania.

55. World Bank (2003j).

56. Gertler and Barber (2004).

57. World Bank (2005f).

58. World Bank (2004h).

59. See World Bank (2001c) for Vietnam, World Bank (2005f) for Cambodia, and Lewis (2002) on ECA countries.

60. Schieber (2005).

61. Gertler and Gruber (2002) find that while Indonesian families were able to self-insure reasonably well the costs of minor illness (up to 70 percent of the income loss associated with these), they were able to insure only 38 percent of the income loss associated with illness that severely limits physical functioning.

62. Sekhri and Savedoff (2005).

63. Savedoff (2004).

64. Escobar (2005); Escobar and Panopoulou (2002); Castaneda (2003).

65. Uganda's use rates had dipped with the introduction of fees in the 1990s, and although Uganda's poor were formally exempt, they often paid as much as other users. Deininger and Mpuga (2004) estimate that the revenues lost to the health system from the elimination of user fees in 2001 were smaller than the value of benefits from the reduction in foregone earnings, thanks to a healthier population.

66. Thailand's Ministry of Public Health and World Bank (2005).

67. See Chaudhury, Hammer, and Murrugarra (2003) for Armenia, World Bank (2005f) for China, and Meesen and Van Damme (2004) for Cambodia.

68. Socialist Republic of Vietnam and World Bank (2005).

69. Preker and Carrin (2004), Atim (1999).

70. Ranson and others (2005).

71. World Bank (2004k), World Bank (2003j), Banerjee, Deaton, and Duflo (2004), Chaudhury and Hammer (2004) on Bangladesh.

72. World Bank (1997a).

73. The equity- and opportunity-enhancing role of social protection is the conceptual underpinning of the Bank's social protection sector strategy (World Bank 2001e, Holzmann and Jorgensen 2001). Other sources are World Bank (2003f), Devereux (2001), and Ravallion (2003).

74. Improved access to credit is reported for South Africa (Ardington and Lund 1995) and Brazil (Schwarzer and Querino 2002), where the electronic banking card issued by the program is often used as proof of creditworthiness. A significant share of rural pension beneficiaries in Brazil report using part of the pension to purchase seeds and agricultural tools (Delgado and Cardoso Jr. 2000); others report investing in improvements in their housing. Children and older people in beneficiary households had better health in South Africa (Case 2001) and enrollment rates of school-age children were higher among pension beneficiary households in both South Africa (Duflo 2003) and Brazil (de Carvalho Filho 2000).

75. Kanbur (2005).

76. Lindert (2004).

77. Esping-Andersen (1990) argues, for example, that the success of the welfare system in continental Europe is based on its universality.

78. Alesina and Glaeser (2004) suggest that the different choices depend on political and institutional factors, including the form of democracy, the degree of ethnic homogeneity, and societal beliefs about the causes of poverty.

79. This scheme covered about 10 percent of the unemployed labor force, so it was usefully supplemented by workfare (World Bank 2000b).

80. Coady, Grosh, and Hoddinott (2004).

81. See World Bank (2002a), World Bank (2003d), and World Bank (2003e).

82. Social workers assess 52 separate factors grouped in 7 dimensions (identification, health, education, family dynamics, housing, work, and income). See Chile's Ministry of Planning (2004); on Bangladesh, see Hashemi (2000).

83. On Argentina, see Jalan and Ravallion (1999); on the Maharashtra scheme, Ravallion (1991); on Bolivia, Newman, Jorgensen, and Pradhan (1992).

84. The analysis showed a decline in poverty of 11 percent in the PROGRESA communities and an increase in poverty in the control group.

85. See Bourguignon, Ferreira, and Leite (2004) on Brazil's Bolsa Escola; see Rawlings (2004) and Morley and Coady (2003) on Mexico's PROGRESA; and see World Bank (2005d) on Cambodia's lower secondary school program.

86. United Nations (2002).

87. See Holzmann and Hinz (2005) and World Bank (2001b).

88. Except for the implicit constraint imposed by a means-tested scheme (Barrientos 2005).

89. Case and Deaton (1998).

90. Barrientos (2005), Rawlings (2004), De Ferranti and others (2004).

91. See James (2000) for the general argument, van der Berg and Brendenkamp (2002) on South Africa, and Paes de Barros and de Carvalho (2004) on Brazil.

92. Lund (1999) and Atkinson (1995).

93. Hoogeveen and others (2004).

Chapter 8

1. See Haber (2001).

2. Hellman, Jones, and Kaufmann (2003).

3. The separation of powers between the executive, legislative, and judicial arms of government aims to combat the dangers of investing state power in one person or group, with each branch holding the others accountable through differing "checks and balances." This system also arguably maintains competition within political institutions. See Haber (2001).

4. Asian Development Bank (2003), 24–25; Garapon (2003), Russel and O'Brien (2001).

5. The *Constitution of the Federal Democratic Republic of Ethiopia* (1995).

6. Tien Dung (2003), 8.

7. See Buscaglia and Dakolias (1999).

8. Ringera and others (2003).

9. See Langseth and Stolpe (2001), Dakolias and Thatchuk (2000).

10. For East Asia, see Asian Development Bank (2003).

11. See www.tsj.gov.ve for an explanation of the judicial portal.

12. The important distinction here is between campaigns that impede judicial independence (targeting unpopular decisions) and those that serve as a check on judicial misbehavior (exposing judicial corruption). See Asian Development Bank (2003), 8–9.

13. See World Bank (2004g), World Bank (2004c), and Hammergreen (2004).

14. It is important to note that a vast array of practices, systems, and traditions have been defined as informal, traditional, or customary law, all existing within vastly differing contexts. The use of "informal" is used in contrast to "formal" state systems and is not meant to imply that such institutions are procedurally informal.

15. World Bank (2004j), 12.

16. Augustinus (2003).

17. See Centre for Housing Rights and Evictions (2004).

18. Mamdani (1996).

19. Fortman (1998).

20. See Buscaglia (1997) and Mattei (1998). See also Kranton and Swamy (1999) and Pistor and Wellons (1999).

21. The *sungusungu* have avoided cooption by the state, and their lack of knowledge of the law and people's rights can lead to abuse. See Mwaikusa (1995), 166–78, and Bukurura (1994).

22. Buscaglia (1997).

23. See Bush (1979) discussion on different African nations' attempts at dynamic integrations.

24. Interestingly, a hundred years later, the 1927 Black Administration Act, which recognized a dual system of official law, formed the basis for separating whites and Africans under apartheid. See Van Niekerk (2001).

25. See Bennett (1999) for a discussion of this issue.

26. More than two-thirds of the European Court of Human Rights' case load between 1999 and 2003 was about violations of the right to a fair trial, in particular, the excessive length of court proceedings.

27. Between 2002 and 2004, 14,992 mediation cases were handled. See Malik (2005).

28. Feierstein and Moreira (2005).

29. Das (2004).

30. See Human Rights Watch (2000).

31. See Greenwood and others (1998), Gottfredson (1998), Tremblay and Craig (1995), Waller, Welsh, and Sansfaçon (1999), Waller and Sansfaçon (2000), World Bank (2003a).

32. World Bank (2003a), Council for Scientific and Industrial Research (2000).

33. Graham and Bowling (1995), Shaw (2001).

34. Sloth-Nielsen and Gallinetti (2004), Bottoms (1990), Shaw (2001).

35. See Harber (1999), Shaw (2004).

36. For further details see the project Web site at http://www.bac.co.za/Web%20Content/Projects/Tiisa%20Thuto/Intro%20Template%20for%20Tiisa%20Thuto.htm.

37. Penal Reform International assisted in establishing community service orders as alternative sentencing in Zimbabwe, Kenya, Malawi, Uganda, Zambia, Burkina Faso, Congo, the Central African Republic, and Mozambique.

38. Morrison, Ellsberg, and Bott (2004).

39. Council for Scientific and Industrial Research (2000).

40. Mtani (2002).

41. See Binswanger, Deininger, and Feder (1995). In India, employment in agricultural wage labor (as opposed to self-employed cultivation) is strongly correlated with poverty (Kijima and Lanjouw 2004). Similarly, in Thailand, controlling for other factors, tenancy increases the risk of poverty by nearly 30 percent compared with being a landowner (World Bank 2001f).

42. Cardenas (2003), Conning and Robinson (2002).

43. Deininger (forthcoming).

44. Deininger and Olinto (2000) go further and suggest that asset inequality is a causal determinant of growth performance.

45. Intermediaries were essentially tax collectors who received land rights (in different forms, depending on the state) to "intermediate" the flow of resources between cultivators and the colonial administration.

46. Appu (1997), 196.

47. Banerjee, Gertler, and Ghatak (2002). In West Bengal, efforts in the late 1970s and 1980s to register sharecroppers and codify their rights were backed by the ruling left parties (Appu 1997).

48. Building on spontaneous transactions in which either the tenant or landlord buys out the other party's interest, the government is considering ways to facilitate such buyouts in a more systematic and equitable fashion, thereby allowing one party to obtain full ownership rights to the land (Nielsen and Hanstad 2004).

49. De Janvry and Sadoulet (2002).

50. Scott (1976), Gunning and others (2000), Deininger, Hoogeveen, and Kinsey (2004), and Kinsey and Binswansger (1993).

51. De Ferranti and others (2004).

52. See De Janvry and Sadoulet (1989), Jonakin (1996), Alston, Libecap, and Mueller (1999).

53. See, for instance, Feder (1988) and Jacoby, Li, and Rozelle (2002). Some studies report a doubling of investment and large gains in land values (30–80 percent) with more secure tenure (World Bank 2003i). To the extent that highly visible investments, such as trees or fences, may be a means to establish landownership rights, causality might run the other way (Brasselle, Gaspart, and Platteau 2002). A recent study from Ethiopia demonstrates that tenure insecurity indeed encourages investment in trees that have little impact on productivity, while higher levels of tenure security are unambiguously associated with productivity-enhancing investments (Deininger and others 2003).

54. De Ferranti and others (2004).

55. See Palmade (2005) on India. See Field (2003) on Peru.

56. Payne (2002), Durand-Lasserve (2003).

57. The three levels are as follows: (1) the right to somewhere to live (either on the occupied plot or an alternative should relocation be necessary); (2) a 30-year lease transferable in the event of death; and (3) a 199-year lease effectively conferring ownership rights upon survey and payment for the land.

58. World Bank (2003i).

59. Land regulation can also work against the urban poor. When formal land development parameters (such as minimum plot sizes, setbacks, and infrastructure servicing standards) are not benchmarked against affordability levels for the majority of the urban population, the poor are excluded from access to formal landownership. Bertaud and Malpezzi (2001), Payne and Majale (2004).

60. Gravois (2005)

61. Brasselle, Gaspart, and Platteau (2002).

62. World Bank (2003i)

63. Historically, distress sales have played a major role in the accumulation of land by large manorial estates in China (Shih 1992) and in early Japan (Takeoshi 1967) and by large landlord estates in Punjab (Hamid 1983). The abolition of communal tenure and the associated loss of mechanisms for diversifying risk are among the factors underlying the emergence of large estates in Central America (Brockett 1984).

64. World Bank (2003i).

65. World Bank (2003i).

66. For Sudan, see Kevane (1996); for Colombia, Deininger, Castagnini, and González (2004).

67. World Bank (2003i).

68. Long-term fixed rental contracts are the most efficient from an economic perspective because they are compatible with incentives for effort and investment but various imperfections in markets make these rare (chapter 5).

69. In most states, lack of political support for the legislation allowed landlords to subvert the intent of the laws. West Bengal is an exception—a tenant registration campaign had strong political support and succeeded in protecting tenants (Appu 1997).

70. De Janvry and Sadoulet (2002).

71. De Ferranti and others (2005).

72. World Bank (2003j).

73. See Van de Walle and Cratty (2004) on Vietnam. See Jalan and Ravallion (2002) on China.

74. See Jalan and Ravallion (2003). The findings also indicate that the health gains largely bypass children in poor families with poorly educated mothers.

75. See Malmberg Calvo (1994) on African countries; Ilahi and Grimard (2000) and Ilahi and Jafarey (1999) on Pakistan; World Bank (2001g) on electricity and gas; and Khandker, Lavy, and Filmer (1994) on Morocco.

76. Some 60 percent of the rural population in Africa lives in areas of good agricultural potential, but with poor market access, while only 23 percent live in areas of good agricultural potential and good market access. The remainder have both poor market access and poor agricultural potential (Byerlee and Kelley 2004).

77. Between 1970 and 1998, roads (in km) increased by 8.3 percent per year (World Bank 2005c).

78. World Bank (2005c).

79. De Ferranti and others (2004).

80. Economies from large production and delivery have diminished in some activities, especially telecommunications and power generation. And regulatory innovation made unbundling possible. Unbundling promoted competition by separating activities in which economies of scale are important (for example, electricity transmission and distribution) from activities in which it is less so (electricity generation). See World Bank (1994) and World Bank (2004l).

81. World Bank (2004f) and chapter 10.

82. According to the Latinobarómetro, the proportion of respondents who said they thought privatization had benefited their country dropped steadily from 46 percent in 1998 to 21 percent in 2003 (Lagos 2005).

83. Estache, Foster, and Wodon (2001).

84. Estache, Foster, and Wodon (2001).

85. Lifeline tariffs mean that rates increase after surpassing a certain consumption threshold (the level deemed necessary to meet basic household needs).

86. Wodon, Ajwad, and Siaens (2005) and Estache, Foster, and Wodon (2001).

87. Estache, Foster, and Wodon (2001).

88. Kariuki and Schwartz (2005).

89. Gulyani, Talukdar, and Kariuki (2005).

90. Estache (2003).

91. Irwin and Yamamoto (2004).

92. See Chisari, Estache, and Romero (1999) and Guasch (2003).

Focus 5 on taxation

1. Bird, Martínez-Vazquez, and Torgler (2004).

2. Bird, Martínez-Vazquez, and Torgler (2004).

3. Moore (2001); Davis, Ossowski, and Fedelino (2003).

4. Moore (2001).

5. Gupta and others (2003).

6. De Ferranti and others (2004).

7. Bird and Slack (2002).

8. Rudnik and Gordon (1996).

9. Boskin (1977).

10. Rajan and Zingales (2003).

11. Prud'Homme (1990).

12. Bird (1991).

Chapter 9

1. Smith (1776), 128.

2. See Tilly (1998) on opportunity hoarding by middle groups.

3. World Bank (2004b), Perotti and Volpin (2004).

4. See De Soto (2000), Glaeser, Sheinkman, and Shleifer (2003), and Haber, Noel, and Razo (2003).

5. See Morck, Wolfenzon, and Yeung (2004) and Claessens, Djankov, and Lang (2000).

6. Morck, Stangeland, and Yeung (2000), Morck and Yeung (2004).

7. On developed countries, see Rajan and Zingales (2003).

8. Halac and Schmukler (2003) and Perotti and Feijen (2005).

9. See Velasco (1988), Valdés-Prieto (1992), Haber and Kantor (2004), Claessens and Pohl (1994), and Perotti (2002). Also see box 9.2 on Russia.

10. Haggard, Lim, and Kim (2003), 87. See also Siegel (2003) for a discussion of the importance of political connectedness in the Republic of Korea.

11. Feijen and Perotti (2005); Claessens and Perotti (2005).

12. Bertrand, Schoar, and Thesmar (2004).

13. Braverman and Guasch (1986).

14. See discussion in Armendáriz de Aghion and Morduch (2005), Pulley (1989), and Meyer and Nagarajan (2000) for the poor repayment performance, and Burgess and Pande (2004) for positive impacts on the poor of social banking.

15. Honohan (2004).

16. The discussion of the Czech and Polish stock markets builds on Glaeser, Johnson, and Shleifer (2001).

17. Rajan and Zingales (2003), 159.

18. Guiso, Sapienza, and Zingales (2004).

19. Roland and Verdier (2000) and Claessens and Perotti (2005).

20. See, for example, Diamond (1981), Blanchard (2004), Bertola (2003), Agell (2002), among others.

21. For discussions of India's labor market regulation and its adverse effects, see Stern (2002), Hasan, Mitra, and Ramaswamy (2003), and Besley and Burgess (2004). For example, industrial sector legislation requires employers with more than 100 workers to seek prior approval of the government before dismissing workers. This has earned the country a 90 out of 100 on the World Bank's Doing Business in 2005 "difficulty in firing index" (World Bank (2005e).

22. See Kingdon, Sandefur, and Teal (2005). Strict enforcement of labor market regulations in South Africa—even for small firms—can also contribute to unemployment by inhibiting the development of informal sector firms.

23. In 1997–98, 83 percent of nonagricultural employment in India was informal (ILO 2002).

24. Kugler (2004).

25. Maloney (1999), Maloney and Nuñez Mendez (2004).

26. Chen, Vanek, and Carr (2004).

27. ILO (2002).

28. Besley and Burgess (2004).

29. The unemployment figure relies on the broad definition of the labor force (employed + searching and nonsearching unemployed). Using the strict labor force measure (employed + searching unemployed), the unemployment rate was 32 percent in 2003. Data is from the 2003 Labor Force Survey cited by Kingdon, Sandefur, and Teal (2005). "The ratio of non-agricultural informal sector employment to unemployment is 0.7 in South Africa but 4.7 in Sub-Saharan Africa, 7.0 in Latin America and 11.9 in Asia." (Kingdon, Sandefur, and Teal 2005).

30. Estimates suggest high levels of unemployment (20 to 30 percent for urban males), but there are measurement problems that bias the estimates upward.

31. Rodrik (1999b).

32. Galli and Kucera (2004).

33. The unions then played a critical role pushing the social and economic agenda toward more welfare-oriented policies (Fishman 1990, Boix 1998, and Boix 2005).

34. Some might argue that the Scandinavian systems are not easily replicable, on the grounds that they rely on extraordinary levels of trust and social capital. In other words, the political conditions necessary to obtain Scandinavian-type social democracy and "solidaristic bargaining" might be difficult to achieve in developing countries, despite their potential economic benefits. See Moene and Wallerstein (2002). But this was not always the case; high levels of trust emerged from widespread conflict in the mid-1930s.

35. Nickell (1997).

36. Boeri (2002); Blunch and Verner (2004); Bover, Bentolila, and Arellano (2002); Chaykowsky and Slotsve (2002); Panagides and Patrinos (1994).

37. Bertola, Blau, and Kahn (2001).

38. Kingdon, Sandefur, and Teal (2005).

39. Damiani (2003).

40. See Neumark, Cunningham, and Siga (forthcoming) for a discussion of how Brazil's minimum wage does not seem to have lifted family incomes at the lower points of the income distribution. In Colombia, Arango and Pachón (2004) find that "the minimum wage ends up being regressive, improving the living conditions of families in the middle and the upper part of the income distribution with net losses for those at the bottom."

41. See the ILO Web site (www.ilo.org) for a description of labor standards. As an example of the range of policy choices for the specific case of child labor, see ILO (2003) and Burra (1995).

42. See World Bank (2004a). Almost 80 percent of Cambodia's overseas buyers rated labor standards as one of their top priorities in sourcing decisions. They also stated that standards have had positive effects on accident rates, workplace productivity, product quality, turnover, and absenteeism.

43. López (2004).

44. There are two ways to measure outcomes: ex ante simulation using CGE (Computable General Equilibrium) analysis and ex post econometric analysis relying on household survey data. In the absence of such analysis, it is hard to predict the impact of trade reform on poverty or equity. A number of studies related to the themes of this section can be found in Hertel and Winters (2005).

45. Schiff and Valdés (1998), 30.

46. The CGE analysis generates price and wage changes that include the direct price effect of trade policy changes and "second-round" indirect effects on factor returns and nontraded goods prices. Certain dynamic gains from greater trade openness are not captured. For instance, trade could bring new technologies and innovations that boost long-term productivity (Ravallion 2004b).

47. Winters, McCulloch, and McKay (2004); Mundlak and Larson (1992); Lloyd and others (1999); McKay, Morrissey, and Vaillant (1997).

48. Minot and Goletti (1998).

49. See Bates (1981) and chapter 6 for Ghana, and CUTS (Consumer Unity and Trust Society) (2003) for Malawi.

50. McMillan, Rodrik, and Horn Welsh (2002).

51. See Hanson (2003). Other research attributes some of the benefits of trade reform in border states to higher levels of human and industrial capital and better communications and transportation infrastructure (Chiquiar 2005).

52. See Nicita (2004) on Mexico and Goetz (1992); International Fund for Agricultural Development (2001); Minot (1998); and Thomas and others (1999) on Indonesia.

53. Arulpragasam and others (2004), World Bank (2003c).

54. Annamalai and Rao (2003), India Today (2004).

55. Palmade (2005).

56. Carruthers, Bajpai, and Hummels (2004).

57. Wood (1997).

58. See Wood (1997), Sánchez-Páramo and Schady (2003), and De Ferranti and others (2004).

59. Topalova (2004).

60. World Bank (2004i), Cord and Wodon (2001).

61. McMillan, Rodrik, and Horn Welsh (2002).

62. For a brief survey of the different generations of models of crises, see Krugman (1999). For selected references see Aghion, Bacchetta, and Banerjee (2001), Chang and Velasco (2001), Krugman (1979), Obstfeld (1996), and Velasco (1996).

63. Acemoglu and others (2003).

64. On Bolivia, see Morales and Sachs (1998); on Israel, see Bruno (1993).

65. Blejer and Guerrero (1990).

66. Ferreira and Litchfield (2001).

67. See also Diwan (2002).

68. Rodrik (1999a).

69. Honohan and Klingebiel (2000).

70. Halac and Schmukler (2003).

71. See De Ferranti and others (2004), Lanjouw and Ravallion (2005).

72. Bruno (1993).

73. Perry (2003).

74. Robinson (2003); see focus 5 on taxation for discussion of social-fiscal contracts.

Focus 6 on regional inequality

1. Massey (2001).

2. Shepherd and others (2005); Massey (2001).

3. Psacharopoulos and Patrinos (1994); Hall and Patrinos (2005); Vakis (2003).

4. de Haan (2005).

5. Galiani and Schargrodsky (2002).

6. Manor (1999).

7. Fox (1990).

8. Ferreira (2004).

9. Funck and Pizzati (2003).

10. Shepherd and others (2005); Willanakuy (2004).

11. Ross (2005).

Chapter 10

1. Pogge (2004).

2. Chauvet and Collier (2004) estimated that the cost, to a country and its neighbors, of a country descending into the status of low-income country under stress (LICUS), as defined by the World Bank, is in present value terms approximately $80 billion, and that this cost was mostly borne by neighbors.

3. These conclusions are consistent with the findings of the World Commission on the Social Dimensions of Globalization (2004).

4. Goldin and others (forthcoming).

5. That is, 4 percent not 4 percentage points.

6. Stark and Bloom (1985); Cox, Eser, and Jimenez (1998).

7. The assumption that income after migration is higher than income forgone does not always hold. Adams finds that income levels would have been higher without migration in three Egyptian villages and would have been the same in four rural districts in Pakistan (Adams 1989, 1992). Barham and Boucher (1998) find essentially similar results for three neighborhoods in Nicaragua. On the potential impact on income inequality, Mendola (2004) finds that remittances from members of households with large land holdings in rural Bangladesh are correlated with adoption of new agricultural technologies, thus leading to higher productivity for already better-off households and a possible increase in inequality.

8. McKenzie and Rapoport (2004).

9. A number of studies by the World Bank Research Program on International Migration and by others document the positive impact of remittances. See Taylor (1992), Taylor and Wyatt (1996), and Yang (2004) for examples of easing of credit constraints. Adams (2005) finds that Guatemalan households receiving remit-tances spend significantly more on housing, which has positive indirect effects on wages, business, and employment opportunities. Yang (2004) finds that Filipino households receiving higher remittances, because of positive exchange rate shocks, had greater child schooling, reduced child labor, more hours worked in self-employment, and greater entry into relatively capital-intensive enterprises.

10. Ehrenreich and Hochschild (2003).

11. On the phenomenon of brain waste, see Mattoo, Neagu, and Ozden (2005); on brain drain, see Faini (2003) and Schiff (2005).

12. Mode IV is one of four interrelated modes of supply of services across borders considered in the GATS.

13. As of May 2004, only 25 countries, mostly migrant-sending, had ratified the convention.

14. An interesting example of innovative partnerships to facilitate remittance flows is the New Alliance Task Force launched by the Federal Deposit Insurance Corporation (FDIC) and Mexican Consulate of Chicago, which aims to improve access to the U.S. banking system, provide financial education, and develop products with remittance features.

15. Smuggling and trafficking are a multibillion dollar industry increasingly run by criminal networks. The United Nations International Organization for Migration (2000) estimated that up to 2 million women and children are trafficked globally every year.

16. One option to address these losses is to lock development assistance to poor countries hurt by specific measures into the WTO agreements on these measures; see Ricupero (2005).

17. The current tariff structure could change through both bilateral and multilateral negotiations. For instance, if the Central American Free Trade Agreement is approved by the U.S. Congress, most textiles from countries such as Honduras and El Salvador would benefit from tariff-free entry into the United States, now the case for some items under existing unilateral preferences.

18. See for example Birdsall (2002).

19. Price-fixing by international cartels brings significant losses to developed- and developing-country consumers alike. Analysis of six high-profile cartels uncovered in the 1990s (vitamins, citric acid, bromine, seamless steel tubes, graphite electrodes, lysine) indicated that the estimated price increases ranged from 10 percent for stainless steel tubes to 45 percent for graphite electrodes, and that cumulative overcharges to developing countries over the life of the six cartels ranged from $3 billion to $7 billion, depending on the calculation method. See Connor (2001), OECD (2000), and World Bank (2003b).

20. Ronchi (2001) and Ronchi (2002).

21. Lewin, Giovannucci, and Varangis (2004).

22. For more information, see www.ethicaltrade.org and www.fairlabor.org.

23. Fung, O'Rourke, and Sabel (2001).

24. "Trade-Related Aspects of Intellectual Property Rights," Annex 1C of the Agreement Establishing the World Trade Organization.

25. Lanjouw and Jack (2004).

26. Sell (2003).

27. Fink and Reichenmuller (2005).

28. These are the agreements between the United States and Morocco (2004), Bahrain (2004), and the Dominican Republic–CAFTA (signed but not yet approved by the U.S. Congress).

29. Claessens and Underhill (2004).

30. World Bank (2005g) and UNCTAD (2004).

31. See Claessens, Underhill, and Zhang (2003) and Bhattacharya and Griffith-Jones (2004).

32. We discuss representation on the World Bank and IMF Boards below.

33. O'Sullivan and Christensen (2005).

34. Moore (2004).

35. McGillivray (2005).

36. Updating the results for 2001 led to similar results (Levin 2005).

37. The findings of Burnside and Dollar (2000) and Collier and Dollar (2001), Collier and Dollar (2002) are not robust to changes in functional form, the specification of the interaction terms, and sample selection; see Hansen and Tarp (2001), Easterly, Levine, and Roodman (2004), and Dalgaard, Hansen, and Tarp (2004). These studies also point to the importance of climate, among other factors.

38. Levin and Dollar (2005).

39. These figures include official development assistance (ODA) provided by countries that are members of the Development Assistance Committee (DAC) of the Organisation for Economic Co-operation and Development (OECD). Non-DAC countries also provide ODA; the largest non-DAC donors are Saudi Arabia (providing $2.4 billion in 2003 out of a total of $3.4 billion), the Republic of Korea ($366 million), the United Arab Emirates ($188 million), and Kuwait ($133 million).

40. Eighteen countries qualify immediately, and as many as another 20 could qualify over time. See the G-8 Finance Ministers' Conclusions on Development, London, June 10–11, 2005 (G-8 Finance Ministers, 2005) at http://www.hm-treasury.gov.uk/otherhmtsites/g7/news/conclusions_on_development_110605.cfm. The G8 Finance Ministers' agreement was confirmed at the July 2005 G8 Gleneagles Summit.

41. See the G-24 Communique, available at http://web.worldbank.org/WBSITE/EXTERNAL/DEVCOMMEXT/0,,menuPK:60001663~pagePK:64001141~piPK:64034162~theSitePK:277473,00.html.

Focus 7 on drug access

1. See Lanjouw and MacLeod (2005) and World Health Organization (2004).

2. See Kremer and Glennester (2004) and Barder (2004).

3. See Masters (2005).

4. See an interesting article by Maurer, Sali, and Rai (2004) on how an open-source approach could work.

5. World Health Organization (2004).

6. Based on data from IMS HEALTH Global Services at http://www.ims-global.com.

7. This proposal is detailed in Lanjouw (2002).

8. For legal details see Lanjouw (2002).

Epilogue

1. This is evident from the very title of Bauer (1971).

2. World Bank (1980).

3. World Bank (1990).

4. World Bank (1997c).

5. World Bank (2002b).

6. World Bank (2001h).

7. See Stern, Dethier, and Rogers (2005) for a detailed treatment of this synthesis.

8. World Bank (2005h).

9. World Bank (2003j).

References

The word "Processed" describes informally reproduced works that may not be commonly available through libraries.

Acemoglu, Daron, Simon Johnson, and James Robinson. 2001. "The Colonial Origins of Comparative Development: An Empirical Investigation." *American Economic Review* 91(5):1369–401.

————. 2002a. "Reversal of Fortune: Geography and Institutions in the Making of the Modern World Income Distribution." *Quarterly Journal of Economics* 117(4):1231–94.

————. 2002b. "The Rise of Europe: Atlantic Trade, Institutional Change, and Economic Growth." Cambridge, MA: National Bureau of Economic Research Working Paper Series 9378.

————. 2004. "Institutions as a Fundamental Cause of Long-run Growth." *In* Philippe Aghion and Steven Durlauf, (ed.), *Handbook of Economic Growth.* Amsterdam: North Holland.

Acemoglu, Daron, Simon Johnson, James Robinson, and Yunyong Thaicharoen. 2003. "Institutional Causes, Macroeconomics Symptoms: Volatility, Crises and Growth." *Journal of Monetary Economics* 50(1):49–131.

Acemoglu, Daron, and James Robinson. 2000. "Why Did the West Extend the Franchise? Growth, Inequality and Democracy in Historical Perspective." *Quarterly Journal of Economics* 115(4):1167–99.

————. 2005. *Economic Origins of Dictatorship and Democracy.* Cambridge, U.K.: Cambridge University Press.

Adams, Martin. 2000. *Breaking Ground: Development Aid for Land Reform.* London: Overseas Development Institute.

Adams, Richard. 1989. "Workers' Remittances and Inequalities in Rural Egypt." *Economic Development and Cultural Change* 38(1):45–71.

————. 1992. "The Impact of Migration and Remittances on Inequality in Rural Pakistan." *Pakistan Development Review* 31(4):1189–203.

Adams, Richard H. Jr. 2005. "Remittances, Household Expenditures and Investment in Guatemala." Washington, DC: World Bank Policy Research Working Paper Series 3532. Available on line at http://econ.worldbank.org/resource.php?type=5.

Agarwal, Bina. 1994. *A Field of One's Own: Gender and Land Rights in South Asia.* Cambridge, UK: Cambridge University Press.

Agell, Jonas. 2002. "On the Determinants of Labor Market Institutions: Rent Seeking vs. Social Insurance." *German Economic Review* 3(2):107–35.

Aghion, Philippe, Philippe Bacchetta, and Abhijit Banerjee. 2001. "A Corporate Balance Sheet Approach to Currency Crises." London: Centre for Economic Policy Research 3092.

Alatas, Vivi, and François Bourguignon. 2004. "The Evolution of Income Distribution during Indonesia's Fast Growth, 1980–96." *In* François Bourguignon, Francisco Ferreira, and Nora Lustig, (ed.), *The Microeconomics of Income Distribution Dynamics: In East Asia and Latin America.* New York: Oxford University Press for the World Bank.

Aleem, Irfan. 1990. "Imperfect Information, Screening, and the Costs of Informal Lending: A Study of Rural Credit Market in Pakistan." *World Bank Economic Review* 4(3):329–49.

Alesina, Alberto, Rafael Di Tella, and Robert MacCulloch. 2004. "Inequality and Happiness: Are Europeans and Americans Different?" *Journal of Public Economics* 88(n9-10):2009–42.

Alesina, Alberto, and Edward Glaeser. 2004. *Fighting Poverty in the US and Europe: A World of Difference.* Oxford: Oxford University Press.

Alland, Denis, and Stéphanie Rials. 2003. *Dictionnaire de la Culture Juridique.* Paris: Presses Universitaires de France.

Alston, Lee J., Gary D. Libecap, and Bernardo Mueller. 1999. "A Model of Rural Conflict: Violence and Land Reform Policy in Brazil." *Environment and Development Economics* 4(2):135–60.

Andersson, Kim, and Will Martin. 2004. "Agricultural Trade Reform and the Doha Development Agenda." Paper presented at the International Trade Brown Bag Lunch Seminar. December 15. Washington, DC.

Andersson, Martin, and Christer Gunnarsson. 2005. "Egalitarianism in the Process of Modern Economic Growth: The Case of Sweden." Background paper for the WDR 2006.

Angrist, Joshua D., Eric Bettinger, Eric Bloom, Elizabeth M. King, and Michael Kremer. 2002. "Vouchers for Private Schooling in Colombia: Evidence from a Randomized Natural Experiment." *American Economic Review* 92(5):1535–58.

Annabi, Nabil, Bazlul Khandkher, Selim Raiham, John Cockburn, and Bernard Decaluwe. Forthcoming. "The Impact of Trade Reforms on Bangladesh." *In* Thomas W. Hertel and L. Alan Winters (ed.) *Putting Development Back into the Doha Agenda: Poverty Impacts of a WTO Agreement.* Washington, DC: World Bank.

Annamalai, Kuttayan, and Sachin Rao. 2003. *What Works: ITC's E-Choupal and Profitable Rural Transformation.* University of Michigan: World Resource Institute Digital Dividend. Available on line at http://povertyprofit.wri.org/.

Appadurai, Arjun. 2004. "The Capacity to Aspire: Culture and the Terms of Recognition." *In* Vijayendra Rao and Michael Walton, (ed.), *Culture and Public Action.* Stanford, CA: Stanford University Press.

Appu, P. S. 1997. *Land Reforms in India: A Survey of Policy, Legislation and Implementation.* New Delhi: Vikas Publishing House.

Arango, Carlos A., and Angelica Pachón. 2004. "Minimum Wages in Colombia: Holding the Middle with a Bite on the Poor." Colombia: Banco de la República (The Colombian Central Bank) 280. Available on line at http://www.banrep.gov.co/docum/ftp/borra280.pdf.

Araujo, Caridad, Francisco Ferreira, and Norbert Schady. 2004. "Is the World Becoming More Unequal? Changes in the World Distribution of Schooling." World Bank. Washington, DC. Processed.

Ardington, E., and F. Lund. 1995. "Pensions and Development: Social Security as Complementary to Programmes of Reconstruction and Development." *Development Southern Africa* 12(4):557–77.

Arellano, Manuel, and Stephen Bond. 1991. "Some Tests of Specification for Panel Data: Monte Carlo Evidence and an Application to Employment Equations." *Review of Economic Studies* 58(2):277–97.

Armendáriz de Aghion, Beatriz, and Jonathan Morduch. 2005. *The Economics of Microfinance.* Cambridge, MA: MIT Press.

Arnaud, André-Jean, eds. 1993. *Dictionnaire Encyclopédique de Théory et de Sociologie du Droit (2nd edition).* Paris: Librairie Générale de Droit et de Jurisprudence.

Arulpragasam, Jehan, Francesco Goletti, Tamar Manuelyan Atinc, and Vera Songwe. 2004. "Trade in Sectors Important to the Poor: Rice in Cambodia and Vietnam and Cashmere in Mongolia." *In* Kathie Krumm and Homi Kharas, (ed.), *East Asia Integrates.* Washington, DC: Oxford University Press for the World Bank.

Asian Development Bank. 2003. *Judicial Independence Overview and Country-Level Summaries.* Manila, Philippines: Asian Development Bank. Available on line at http://www.adb.org/Documents/Events/2003/RETA5987/Final_Overview_Report.pdf.

Assunção, Juliano Junqueira, and Humberto Moreira. 2001. "Towards a Truthful Land Taxation Mechanism in Brazil." Paper presented at the LACEA. October 18. Montevideo, Uruguay.

Atim, C. 1999. "Social Movements and Health Insurance: A Critical Evaluation of Voluntary, Non-profit Insurance Schemes with Case Studies from Ghana and Cameroon." *Social Science and Medicine* 48(7):881–896.

Atkinson, A. B. 1995. *Incomes and the Welfare State: Essays on Britain and Europe.* Cambridge: Cambridge University Press.

Atkinson, Anthony B. 2003. "Income Inequality in OECD Countries: Data and Explanations." Munich: CESifo Working Paper Series 881.

Atkinson, Anthony B., and Andrea Brandolini. 2001. "Promise and Pitfalls in the Use of 'Secondary' Data-sets: Income Inequality in OECD Countries as a Case Study." *Journal of Economic Literature* 39(3):771–99.

————. 2004. "Global World Inequality: Absolute, Relative or Intermediate?" Paper presented at the 28th General Conference of the International Association for Research on Income and Wealth. August 22. Cork, Ireland.

Atkinson, Anthony B., A. Maynard, and Christopher Trinder. 1983. *Parents and Children: Incomes in Two Generations.* London: Heinemann.

Atkinson, Anthony B., and Joseph E. Stiglitz. 1980. *Lectures on Public Economics.* London: McGraw-Hill International Editions.

Attanasio, Orazio P., and A. Marcos Vera-Hernandez. 2004. "Medium and Long Run Effects of Nutrition and Child Care: Evaluation of a Community Nursery Programme in Rural Colombia." London: Institute for Fiscal Studies Working Paper EWP04/06. Available on line at http://www.ifs.org.uk/publications.php?publication_id=3146.

Augustinus, Clarisa. 2003. "Comparative Analysis of Land Administration Systems: African Review with Special Reference to Mozambique, Uganda, Namibia, Ghana, South Africa." World Bank. Washington, DC. Processed.

Australian Bureau of Statistics. 2003. *Deaths in Australia 2002.* Canberra: Australian Bureau of Statistics.

Ayadi, Mohamed, Ghazi Boulila, Mohamed Lahouel, and Philippe Montigny. 2004. *Pro-Poor Growth in Tunisia.* Paris: International Development and Strategies. Available on line at http://www.kfw-entwicklungsbank.de/EN/Fachinformationen/Pro-PoorGr77/oppgtunisia.pdf.

Azam, Jean-Paul, Magueye Dia, Clarence Tsimpo, and Quentin Wodon. 2005. "Has Growth in Senegal after the 1994 Devaluation Been Pro-Poor?" World Bank. Washington, DC. Processed.

Baffes, John. 2004. "Cotton: Market Setting, Trade Policies and Issues." Washington, DC: World Bank Policy Research Working Paper Series 3218.

Baiocchi, Gianpolo, Shubham Chaudhuri, and Patrick Heller. 2005. "Evaluating Empowerment: Participatory Budgeting in Brazil." World Bank. Washington, DC. Available on line at http://siteresources.worldbank.org/INTEMPOWERMENT/Resources/Brazilpres.pdf. Processed.

Bakewell, Peter J. 1984. *Miners of the Red Mountain.* Albuquerque: University of New Mexico Press.

Balat, Jorge, and Guido Porto. Forthcoming. "The WTO Doha Round, Cotton Sector Dynamics and Poverty Trends in Zambia." *In* Thomas W. Hertel and L. Alan Winters (ed.) *Putting Development Back into the Doha Agenda: Poverty Impacts of a WTO Agreement.* Washington, DC: World Bank.

Banerjee, Abhijit. 2000. "Land Reforms: Prospects and Incentives." *In* Boris Pleskovic and Joseph E. Stiglitz, (ed.), *Annual World Bank Conference on Development Economics, 1999.* Washington, DC: World Bank.

Banerjee, Abhijit, Shawn Cole, Esther Duflo, and Leigh Linden. 2004. "Remedying Education: Evidence from Two Randomized Experiments in India." Massachusetts Institute of Technology. Cambridge, MA. Available on line at http://econ-www.mit.edu/faculty/download_pdf.php?id=677. Processed.

Banerjee, Abhijit, Angus Deaton, and Esther Duflo. 2004. "Health Care Delivery in Rural Rajasthan." Cambridge, MA: Poverty Action Lab Papers 7.

Banerjee, Abhijit, and Esther Duflo. 2003. "Inequality and Growth: What Can the Data Say?" *Journal of Economic Growth* 8(3):267–99.

————. 2004a. "Do Firms Want to Borrow More? Testing Credit Constraints using a Direct Lending Program." London: CEPR Working Paper Series 4681.

————. 2004b. "Growth Theory Through the Lens of Development Economics." Cambridge, MA: MIT Department of Economic Working Papers 05-01.

Banerjee, Abhijit, Esther Duflo, and Kaivan Munshi. 2003. "The Miss(allocation) of Capital." *Journal of the European Economic Association* 1(2-3):484–94.

Banerjee, Abhijit, Paul Gertler, and Maitreesh Ghatak. 2002. "Empowerment and Efficiency: Tenancy Reform in West Bengal." *Journal of Political Economy* 110(2):239–80.

Banerjee, Abhijit, Dilip Mookherjee, Kaivan Munshi, and Debraj Ray. 2001. "Inequality, Control Rights, and Rent Seeking: Sugar Cooperatives in Maharashtra." *Journal of Political Economy* 109(1):138–90.

Banerjee, Abhijit, and Kaivan Munshi. 2004. "How Efficiently is Capital Allocated? Evidence from the Knitted Garment Industry in Tirupur." *Review of Economic Studies* 71(1):19–42.

Banerjee, Abhijit, and Andrew Newman. 1991. "Risk-Bearing and the Theory of Income Distribution." *Review of Economic Studies* 58(2):211–35.

Banerjee, Abhijit, and Thomas Piketty. 2003. "Top Indian Incomes: 1956–2000." Cambridge, MA: MIT Department of Economics Working Paper 03-32.

Barber, Catherine. 2003. "Making Migration 'Development-Friendly'." Kennedy School of Government Master's thesis. Harvard University.

Barber, Sarah, Stefan Bertozzi, and Paul Gertler. 2005. "Variations in Prenatal Care Quality in Mexico Mirror Health Inequalities." World Bank. Washington, DC. Processed.

Barber, Sarah, Paul J. Gertler, and Pandu Harimurti. 2005. "Promoting High Quality Care in Indonesia: Roles for Public and Private Ambulatory Care Providers." World Bank. Washington, DC. Processed.

Bardasi, Elena, and Quentin Wodon. 2004. "Comparing Subsidies for Access or Consumption in Basic Infrastructure: A Simple Approach." World Bank. Washington, DC. Processed.

Barder, Owen. 2004. "Making Markets for Vaccines: A Practical Plan." Washington, DC: Center for Global Development Brief 1. Available on line at http://www.cgdev.org/Publications/ ?PubID=173.

Barham, Bradford, and Stephen Boucher. 1998. "Migration, Remittances and Inequality: Estimating the Net Effect of Migration on Income Distribution." *Journal of Development Economics* 55(2):307–31.

Barrientos, Armando. 2005. "Cash Transfers for Older People Reduce Poverty and Inequality." Background paper for the WDR 2006.

Barro, Robert J. 2000. "Inequality and Growth in a Panel of Countries." *Journal of Economic Growth* 5(1):5–32.

Barro, Robert J., and Jong-Wha Lee. 2001. "International Data on Educational Attainment: Updates and Implications." *Oxford Economic Papers* 53(3):541–63.

Barron, Patrick, Rachel Diprose, and Michael Woolcock. 2005. "Local Conflict and Community Development in Indonesia: Assessing the Impact of the Kecamatan Development Program." World Bank Jakarta Regional Office. Jakarta. Processed.

Barron, Patrick, Claire Q. Smith, and Michael Woolcock. 2004. "Understanding Local Level Conflict in Developing Countries: Theory, Evidence and Implications for Indonesia." Washington, DC: World Bank, Social Development Papers, Conflict Prevention & Reconstruction 19.

Basta, S., D. Soekirman, and N. Scrimshaw. 1979. "Iron Deficiency Anemia and the Productivity of Adult Males in Indonesia." *American Journal of Clinical Nutrition* 32(4):916–25.

Bates, Robert H. 1981. *Markets and States in Tropical Africa: The Political Basis of Agricultural Policies.* Berkeley, CA: University of California Press.

————. 1989. *Beyond the Miracle of the Market.* Cambridge, NY: Cambridge University Press.

Bauer, Peter. 1971. *Dissent on Development: Studies and Debates in Development Economics.* London: Weidenfeld and Nicolson.

Behrman, Jere, Nancy Birdsall, and Miquel Székely. 2003. "Economic Policy and Wage Differentials in Latin America." Washington, DC: Center for Global Development Working Paper 29. Available on line at http://www.cgdev.org/Publications/ ?PubID=29.

Bénabou, Roland. 1996. "Inequality and Growth." *In* Ben Bernanke and Julio J. Rotemberg, (ed.), *National Bureau of Economic Research Macroeconomics Annual 1996.* Cambridge, MA: MIT Press.

————. 2000. "Unequal Societies: Income Distribution and the Social Contract." *American Economic Review* 90(1):96–129.

Bennett, T. W. 1999. *Human Rights and African Customary Law under the South African Constitution.* Cape Town: Juta and Co.

Bentham [1781], Jeremy. 2000. *The Principles of Morals and Legislation.* Kitchener, Ontario Canada: Batoche Books.

Berry, R. Albert, and William Cline. 1979. *Agrarian Structure and Productivity in Developing Countries: A Study Prepared for the International Labour Office within the Framework of the World Employment Program.* Baltimore: Johns Hopkins University Press.

Bertaud, Alain, and Stephen Malpezzi. 2001. "Measuring the Costs and Benefits of Urban Land Use Regulation: A Simple Model with an Application to Malaysia." *Journal of Housing Economics* 10(3):393–418.

Bertola, Giuseppe. 1990. "Job Security, Employment and Wages." *European Economic Review* 34(4):851–86.

————. 2003. "Distribution, Efficiency, and Labor Market Regulation in Theory." Paper presented at the Séptima Conferencia Anual del Banco Central de Chile: Mercado Laboral e Instituciones. November 6. Santiago de Chile.

Bertola, Giuseppe, Francine D. Blau, and Lawrence M. Kahn. 2001. "Comparative Analysis of Labor Market Outcomes: Lessons for the US from International Long-run Evidence." Cambridge, MA: National Bureau of Economic Research Working Paper Series 8526.

Bertrand, Marianne, and Sendhil Mullanaithan. 2003. "Are Emily and Greg more Employable than Lakisha and Jamal?: A Field Experiment on Labor Market Discrimination." Cambridge, MA: National Bureau of Economic Research Working Paper Series 9873.

Bertrand, Marianne, Antoinette S. Schoar, and David Thesmar. 2004. "Banking Deregulation and Industry Structure: Evidence from the French Banking Reforms of 1985." London: CEPR Discussion Papers 4488.

Besley, Timothy, and Robin Burgess. 2000. "Land Reform, Poverty Reduction, and Growth: Evidence from India." *Quarterly Journal of Economics* 115(2):389–430.

—————. 2004. "Can Labor Regulation Hinder Economic Performance? Evidence from India." *Quarterly Journal of Economics* 119(1):91–134.

Besley, Timothy, Rohini Pande, Lupin Rahman, and Vijayendra Rao. 2004. "The Politics of Public Good Provision: Evidence From Indian Local Governments." *Journal of the European Economic Association* 2(2-3):416–26.

Bhagwati, Jagdish. 2003. "Borders Beyond Control." *Foreign Affairs* 82(1):98–104.

Bhattacharya, Amar, and Stephany Griffith-Jones. 2004. "The Search for a Stable and Equitable Global Financial System." *In* Jan Joost Teunissen and Age Akkerman, (ed.), *Diversity in Development: Reconsidering the Washington Consensus.* Washington, DC: Fondad.

Binswanger, Hans, Klaus Deininger, and Gershon Feder. 1995. "Power Distortions, Revolt and Reform in Agricultural Land Relations." *In* Jere Behrman and T. N. Srinivasan, (ed.), *Handbook of Development Economics, vol. 3B.* Amsterdam: North Holland.

Binswanger, Hans, and Mark Rosenzweig. 1986. "Behavioural and Material Determinants of Production Relations in Agriculture." *Journal of Development Studies* 22(3):503–39.

Bird, Richard M. 1991. *More Taxing than Taxes? The Tax-like Effects of Non-tax Policies in LDC's.* San Francisco: ICS Press.

Bird, Richard M., Jorge Martínez-Vazquez, and Benno Torgler. 2004. "Societal Institutions and Tax Effort in Developing Countries." Toronto: University of Toronto, International Tax Program Paper 04011.

Bird, Richard M., and Barbara Diane Miller. 1989. "The Incidence of Indirect Taxes on Low-income Households in Jamaica." *Economic Development and Cultural Change* 37(2):393–409.

Bird, Richard M., and Enid Slack. 2002. "Land and Property Taxation: A Review." Paper presented at the Workshop on Land Issues in Latin American and the Caribbean. May 19. Pachuca, México.

Birdsall, Nancy. 1985. "Public Inputs and Child Schooling in Brazil." *Journal of Development Economics* 18(1):67–86.

—————. 2002. "Asymmetric Globalization. Global Markets Require Good Global Politics." Washington, DC: Center for Global Development Working Paper 12.

—————. 2004. "Seven Deadly Sins: Reflections on Donor Failings." Washington, DC: Center for Global Development Working Paper Series 50.

Birdsall, Nancy, Carol Graham, and Richard Sabot. 1998. *Beyond Tradeoffs: Market Reforms and Equitable Growth in Latin America.* Washington, DC: Brookings Instittution Press.

Black, Bernard, Reinier Kraakman, and Anna Tassarova. 2000. "Russian Privatization and Corporate Governance: What Went Wrong?" *Stanford Law Review* 52(6):1731–808.

Black, Maureen M. 2003. "Micronutrient Deficiencies and Cognitive Functioning." *Journal of Nutrition* 133(11 Suppl 2):3927S–3931S.

Blackhurst, Richard, Bill Lyakurwa, and Ademola Oyejide. 2000. "Options for Improving Africa's Participation in the WTO." *World Economy* 23(4):491–510.

Blair, Irene V., Charles M. Judd, and Kristine M. Chapleau. 2004. "The Influence of Afrocentric Facial Features in Criminal Sentencing." *Pscyhological Science* 15(10):674–79.

Blanchard, Olivier. 2004. "Reforming Labor Market Institutions: Unemployed Insurance and Employment Protection." Cambridge, MA: MIT Department of Economics Working Paper Series 04-38.

Blejer, Mario, and Isabel Guerrero. 1990. "The Impact of Macroeconomic Policies on Income Distribution: An Empirical Study of the Philippines." *Review of Economics and Statistics* 72(3):414–23.

Bloch, Francis, and Vijayendra Rao. 2002. "Terror as a Bargaining Instrument: A Case-study of Dowry Violence in Rural India." *American Economic Review* 92(4):1029–43.

Blunch, Niels-Hugo, and Dorte Verner. 2004. "Asymmetries in the Union Wage Premium in Ghana." *World Bank Economic Review* 18(2):237–52.

Boeke, Julius Herman. 1946. *The Evolution of the Netherlands Indies Economy.* New York: Netherlands and Netherlands Indies Council, Institute of Pacific Relations.

Boeri, Tito. 2002. "Increasing the Size of the European Labor Force: The Relevant Trade-offs." *Economic Survey of Europe* 2:99–108.

Boix, Carles. 1998. *Political Parties, Growth and Equality: Conservative and Social Democratic Economic Strategies in the World Economy.* Cambridge, UK: Cambridge University Press.

—————. 2005. "Spain: Development, Democracy and Equity." Background paper for the WDR 2006.

Boskin, Michael J. 1977. "An Economist's Perspective on Estate Taxation." *In* Edward C. Halbach Jr., (ed.), *Death, Taxes and Family Property.* St. Paul, MN: West Publishing Co.

Bottoms, A. E. 1990. "Crime Prevention Facing the 1990s." *Policy and Society* 1(1):3–22.

Bourdieu, Pierre. 1986. "The Forms of Capital." *In* John G. Richardson, (ed.), *Handbook of Theory and Research for the Sociology of Education.* Westport, CT: Greenwood Press.

—————. 1990. *The Logic of Practice.* Stanford, CA: Stanford University Press.

Bourguignon, François. 2003. "The Growth Elasticity of Poverty Reduction: Explaining Heterogeneity across Countries and Time-periods." *In* T. Eichler and S. Turnovsky, (ed.), *Growth and Inequality.* Cambridge, MA: MIT Press.

Bourguignon, François, Francisco Ferreira, and Phillippe G. Leite. 2004. "Conditional Cash Transfers, Schooling, and Child Labor: Microsimulating Brazil's Bolsa Escola Program," *World Bank Economic Review* 17(2):229–54.

Bourguignon, François, Francisco Ferreira, and Nora Lustig. 2004. *The Microeconomics of Income Distribution Dynamics in East Asia and Latin America.* New York: Oxford University Press for the World Bank.

Bourguignon, François, Francisco Ferreira, and Marta Menendez. 2005. "Inequality of Opportunity in Brazil?" World Bank. Washington, DC. Processed.

Bourguignon, François, Victoria Levin, and David Rosenblatt. 2004a. "Declining Economic Inequality and Economic Divergence: Reviewing the Evidence through Different Lenses." *Economie Internationale* 100(4).

————. 2004b. "Global Redistribution: The Role of Aid, Market Access, and Remittances." World Bank. Washington, DC. Processed.

Bourguignon, François, and Christian Morrison. 1990. "Income Distribution, Development and Foreign Trade: A Cross-sectional Analysis21`." *European Economic Review* 34(6):1113–32.

Bourguignon, François, and Christian Morrisson. 1993. "External Trade and Income Distribution." *Journal of Development Economics* 41(1):207–9.

————. 1998. "Inequality and Development: The Role of Dualism." *Journal of Development Economics* 57(2):233–57.

————. 2002. "Inequality among World Citizens: 1820–1992." *American Economic Review* 92(4):727–44.

Bourguignon, François, and Thierry Verdier. 2000. "Oligarchy, Democracy, Inequality and Growth." *Journal of Development Economics* 62(2):285–313.

Bover, Olimpia, Samuel Bentolila, and Manuel Arellano. 2002. "The Distribution of Earnings in Spain During the 1980s: The Effect of Skill, Unemployment and Union Power." Madrid: Banco De Espana, Servicio de Estudios, Documento de Trabajo 015. Available on line at http://www.bde.es/informes/be/docs/dt0015e.pdf.

Bowen, William G., and Derek Bok. 1998. *The Shape of the River: Long Term Consequences of Considering Race in College and University Admissions.* Princeton, NJ: Princeton University Press.

Bowman, Larry W. 1991. *Mauritius: Democracy and Development in the Indian Ocean.* Boulder, CO: Westview Press.

Brainerd, Elizabeth, and David M. Cuttler. 2004. "Autopsy on an Empire: Understanding Mortality in Russia and the Former Soviet Union." Cambridge, MA: National Bureau of Economic Research Working Paper Series 10868.

Brasselle, Anne-Sophie, Frederic Gaspart, and Jean-Philippe Platteau. 2002. "Land Tenure Security and Investment Incentives: Puzzling Evidence from Burkina Faso." *Journal of Development Economics* 67(2):373–418.

Braverman, Avishay, and J. Luis Guasch. 1986. "Rural Credit Markets and Institutions in Developing Countries: Lessons for Policy Analysis from Practice and Modern Theory." *World Development* 14(10/11):1253–67.

Brenner, Robert. 1976. "Agrarian Class Structure and Economic Development in Preindustrial Europe." *Past and Present* 70(1976):30–75.

Brockett, C. D. 1984. "Malnutrition, Public Policy, and Agrarian Change in Guatemala." *Journal of Interamerican Studies and World Affairs* 26(4):477–97.

Brocklehurst, Clarissa, and Jan G. Janssens. 2004. "Innovative Contracts, Sound Relationships: Urban Water Sector Reform in Senegal." Washington, DC: World Bank Water Supply and Sanitation Sector Board Discussion Paper 1.

Brosnan, Sarah F., and Frans B. M. De Waal. 2003. "Monkeys Reject Unequal Pay." *Nature* 425(6955):297–99.

Browning, Martin, and Pierre-Andre Chiappori. 1998. "Efficient Intra-household Allocation: A General Characterization and Empirical Tests." *Econometrica* 66(6):1241–78.

Bruno, Michael. 1993. *Crisis, Stabilization, and Economic Reform: Therapy by Consensus.* New York: Clarendon Press.

Bruno, Michael, Martin Ravallion, and Lyn Squire. 1998. "Equity and Growth in Developing Countries: Old and New Perspectives on the Policy Issues." *In* Vito Tanzi and Ke-young Chu, (ed.), *Income Distribution and High-quality Growth.* Cambridge, MA: MIT Press.

Bruns, Barbara, Alain Mingat, and Ramahatra Rakotomalala. 2003. *Achieving Universal Primary Education by 2015: A Chance for Every Child.* Washington, DC: World Bank.

Buchanan, James M. 1976. "A Hobbesian Interpretation of the Rawlsian Difference Principle." *Kyklos* 29(1):5–25.

Bukurura, Sufian Hemed. 1994. " The Maintenance of Order in Rural Tanzania: The Case of the Sungusungu." *Journal of Legal Pluralism* 34:1–29.

Burgess, Robin, and Rohini Pande. 2004. "Do Rural Banks Matter? Evidence from the Indian Social Banking Experiment." London: Center for Economic Policy Research Discussion Papers 4211.

Burney, Nadeem A., and Mohammad Irfan. 1995. "Determinants of Child School Enrollment: Evidence from LDCs Using Choice-theoretic Approach." *International Journal of Social Economics* 22(1):24–40.

Burnside, Craig, and David Dollar. 2000. "Aid, Policies and Growth." *American Economic Review* 90(4):847–68.

Burra, Nera. 1995. *Born to Work: Child Labour in India.* New York: Oxford University Press.

Buscaglia, Edgardo. 1997. "Introduction." *In* Edgardo Buscaglia, Louise Cord, and W. Ratliff, (ed.), *Law and Economics of Development.* Greenwich, CT: JAI Press Inc.

Buscaglia, Edgardo, and Maria Dakolias. 1999. *An Analysis of the Causes of Corruption in the Judiciary.* Washington, DC: World Bank, Legal and Judicial Reform Unit.

Bush, Robert A. 1979. "Access to Justice and Societal Pluralism." *In* Mauro Cappelletti and Bryant Garth, (ed.), *Access to Justice, Vol. 3.* Milan: Guiffre Editore.

Byerlee, D., and T. Kelley. 2004. "Surviving on the Margin: Agricultural Research and Development Strategies for Poverty Reduction in Marginal Areas." World Bank, Agriculture and Rural Development. Washington, DC. Processed.

Cadiet, Loïc. 2004. *Dictionnaire de la Justice.* Paris: Presses Universitaires de France.

Cain, Mead. 1981. "Risk and Insurance: Perspective on Fertility and Agrarian Change in India and Bangladesh." *Population and Development Review* 7(3):435–74.

Cameron, Lisa. 1999. "Raising the Stakes in the Ultimatum Game: Experimental Evidence from Indonesia." *Economic Inquiry* 37(1):47–59.

Campos, Javier, Antonio Estache, Noelia Martin, and Lourdes Trujillo. 2003. "Macroeconomic Effects of Private Sector Participation in Infrastructure." *In* William Easterly and Luis Servén, (ed.), *The Limits of Stabilization.* Washington, DC: World Bank and Stanford Social Sciences, an imprint of Stanford University Press.

Cardenas, Juan-Camillo. 2003. "Real Wealth and Experimental Cooperation: Experiments in the Field Lab." *Journal of Development Economics* 70(2):263–89.

Cardoso, Ciro F. S. 1991. "The Liberal Era, 1870-1930." *In* Leslie Bethell, (ed.), *Central America Since Independence.* Cambridge, UK: Cambridge University Press.

Carneiro, Pedro, and James Heckman. 2003. "Human Capital Policy." Cambridge, MA: National Bureau of Economic Research Working Paper Series 9495.

Carruthers, Robin, Jitendra N. Bajpai, and David Hummels. 2004. "Trade and Logistics: An East Asia Perspective." *In* Kathie Krumm and Homi Kharas, (ed.), *East Asia Integrates: A Trade Policy Agenda for Shared Growth.* Washington, DC: Oxford University Press for the World Bank.

Casagrande, Joseph B., and Arthur R. Piper. 1969. "La Transformación Estructural de una Parroquia Rural en las Tierras Altas del Ecuador." *América Indígena* 29:1029–64.

Case, Anne. 2001. "Does Money Protect Health Status? Evidence from South African Pensions." Cambridge, MA: National Bureau of Economic Research Working Paper Series 8495.

Case, Anne, and Angus Deaton. 1998. "Large Cash Transfers to the Elderly in South Africa." *Economic Journal* 108(450):1330–61.

———. 1999. "School Quality and Educational Outcomes in South Africa." *Quarterly Journal of Economics* 114(3):1047–84.

Castaneda, Tarsicio. 2003. "Targeting Social Spending to the Poor with Proxy-Means Testing: Columbia's SISBEN System." World Bank. Washington, DC. Processed.

Castello, Amparo, and Rafael Domenech. 2002. "Human Capital Inequality and Economic Growth: Some New Evidence." *Economic Journal* 112(478):C187–C200.

Center for Global Development. 2004. *Ranking the Rich: The 2004 CGD/FP Commitment to Development Index.* Washington, DC: Center for Global Development. Available on line at http://www.cgdev.org/rankingtherich/home.html.

Centre for Housing Rights and Evictions. 2004. *Bringing Equality Home: Promoting and Protecting the Inheritance Rights of Women.* Geneva: Centre for Housing Rights and Evictions. Available on line at http://www.cohre.org/downloads/womens-inheritance-rights-africa.pdf.

Chang, Roberto, and Andrés Velasco. 2001. "A Model of Financial Crises in Emerging Markets." *Quarterly Journal of Economics* 116(2):489–517.

Chattopadhyay, Raghabendra, and Esther Duflo. 2004. "Women as Policy Makers: Evidence from a Randomized Policy Experiment in India." *Econometrica* 72(5):1409–43.

Chaturvedi, S., B. C. Srivastava, J. V. Singh, and M. Prasad. 1987. "Impact of Six Years Exposure to ICDS Scheme on Psycho-social Development." *Indian Pediatrics* 24:153–64.

Chaudhuri, Shubham, Pinelopi K. Goldberg, and Panle Jia. 2004. "Estimating the Effects of Global Patent Protection in Pharmaceuticals: A Case Study of Quinolones in India." World Bank. Washington, DC. Available on line at http://www.econ.yale.edu/~pg87/TRIPS.pdf. Processed.

Chaudhuri, Shubham, K. N. Harilal, and Patrick Heller. 2004. *Does Decentralization Make a Difference? A Study of the Peoples Campaign for Decentralized Planning in the Indian State of Kerala.* New Delhi: Ford Foundation.

Chaudhuri, Shubham, and Patrick Heller. 2003. "The Plasticity of Participation: Evidence from a Participatory Governance Experiment." New York: Columbia University ISERP Working Paper 03-01.

Chaudhury, Nazmul, and Jeffery Hammer. 2004. "Ghost Doctors: Absenteeism in Rural Bangladeshi Health Clinics." *World Bank Economic Review* 18(3):423–41.

Chaudhury, Nazmul, Jeffery Hammer, K. Muralidharan, and F. H. Rogers. 2005. "Missing in Action: Teacher and Health Worker Absence in Developing Countries." World Bank. Washington, DC. Processed.

Chaudhury, Nazmul, Jeffery Hammer, and Edmundo Murrugarra. 2003. "The Effects of a Fee-Waiver Program on Health Care Utilization among the Poor: Evidence from Armenia." Washington, DC: World Bank Policy Research Working Paper Series 2952.

Chauvet, Lisa, and Paul Collier. 2004. "Development Effectiveness in Fragile States: Spillovers and Turnarounds." Oxford University, Centre for the Study of African Economies. Oxford, UK. Available on line at http://www.oecd.org/dataoecd/32/59/34255628.pdf. Processed.

Chaykowsky, Richard P., and Richard A. Slotsve. 2002. "Earnings Inequality and Unions in Canada." *British Journal of Industrial Relations* 40(3):493–519.

Chen, Martha, Joann Vanek, and Marilyn Carr. 2004. *Mainstreaming Informal Employment and Gender in Poverty Reduction.* London: Commonwealth Secretariat.

Chen, Shaohua, and Martin Ravallion. 2004. "How Have The World's Poorest Fared since the Early 1980's?" *World Bank Research Observer* 19(2):141–69.

Chenery, Hollis, Clive Bell, J. Duloy, and Richard Jolly. 1974. *Redistribution with Growth.* Oxford: Oxford University Press.

Chile's Ministry of Planning. 2004. *Sistema de Proteccion Social: Chile Solidario.* Santiago de Chile: Ministry of Planning, Government of Chile.

Chiquiar, Daniel. 2005. "Why Mexico's Regional Income Convergence Broke Down." *Journal of Development Economics* 77(1):257–75.

Chirayath, Leila, Caroline Sage, and Michael Woolcock. 2005. "Customary Law and Policy Reform: Engaging with the Plurality of Justice Systems." Background paper for the WDR 2006.

Chisari, Omar, Antonio Estache, and Carlos Romero. 1999. "Winners and Losers from the Privatization and Regulation Utilities: Lessons from a General Equilibrium Model of Argentina." *World Bank Economic Review* 13(2):357–78.

Chua, Amy. 2004. *World on Fire: How Exporting Free Market Democracy Breeds Ethnic Hatred and Global Instability.* New York: Anchor Books.

Chubb, John E., and Terry M. Moe. 1990. *Politics, Markets, and America's Schools.* Washington, DC: The Brookings Institution.

Claessens, Stijn, Simeon Djankov, and Larry H. P. Lang. 2000. "The Separation of Ownership and Control in East Asian Corporations." *Journal of Financial Economics* 58(1-2):81–112.

Claessens, Stijn, and Enrico Perotti. 2005. "The Links Between Finance and Inequality: Channels and Evidence." Background paper for the WDR 2006.

Claessens, Stijn, and Gerhard Pohl. 1994. "Banks, Capital Markets, and Corporate Governance: Lessons from Russia for Eastern Europe." Washington, DC: World Bank Policy Research Working Paper Series 1326.

Claessens, Stijn, and Geoffrey R. D. Underhill. 2004. "The Need for Institutional Changes in the Global Financial System: An Analytical Framework." Paper presented at the Developing Countries, Global Finance, and the Role of the IMF: Towards a New Relationship? November 12. The Hague.

Claessens, Stijn, Geoffrey R. D. Underhill, and Xiaoke Zhang. 2003. "Basle II Capital Requirements and Developing Countries: A Political Economy Perspective." Paper presented at the Quantifying the Impact of Rich Countries' Policies on Poor Countries. October 23. Washington, DC.

Cline, William R. 2004. *Trade Policy and Global Poverty.* Washington, DC: Institute for International Economics.

Coady, David, Margaret Grosh, and John Hoddinott. 2004. *Targeting Transfers in Developing Countries: Review of Lessons and Experience.* Washington, DC: World Bank.

Coate, Stephen, and Glenn Loury. 1993. "Antidiscrimination Enforcement and the Problem of Patronization." *American Economic Review* 83(2):92–8.

Coatsworth, John H. 1993. "Notes on the Comparative Economic History of Latin America and the United States." *In* W. L. Bernecker and H. W Tobler, (ed.), *Development and Underdevelopment in America: Contrasts of Economic Growth in North and Latin America in Historical Perspective.* Berlin: de Gruyter.

Cogneau, Denis. 2005. "Equality of Opportunity and Other Equity Principles in the Context of Developing Countries." Paris, France: Développement, Institutions & Analyses de Long terme (DIAL) Working Paper DT/2005/01.

Cogneau, Denis, and Jean-David Naudet. 2004. "Who Deserves Aid? Equality of Opportunity, International Aid, and Poverty Reduction." Paper presented at the Equity and Development Workshop. September 6. Berlin.

Cole, Jeffrey A. 1985. *The Potosi Mita, 1573-1700: Compulsory Indian Labor in the Andes.* Palo Alto, CA: Stanford University Press.

Collier, Paul, and David Dollar. 2001. "Can the World Cut Poverty in Half? How Policy Reform and Effective Aid Can Meet International Development Goals." *World Development* 29(11):1787–802.

———. 2002. "Aid Allocation and Poverty Reduction." *European Economic Review* 46(8):1475–500.

Commission on Macroeconomics and Health. 2001. *Macroeconomics and Health: Investing in Health for Economic Development.* Geneva: World Health Organization.

Conning, Jonathan H., and James A. Robinson. 2002. "Land Reform and the Political Organization of Agriculture." London: CEPR Working Paper 3204.

Connor, John M. 2001. *Global Price-Fixing: Our Customers Are the Enemy.* Boston, MA: Kluwer Academic Publishing.

Cord, Louise, and Quentin Wodon. 2001. *Do Mexico's Agricultural Programs Alleviate Poverty: Evidence from the Ejido Sector.* Washington, DC: World Bank.

Cornia, Andrea Giovanni, and Leonardo Menchini. 2005. "The Pace and Distribution of Health Improvements during the Last 40 Years: Some Preliminary Results." Paper presented at the Forum on Human Development. January 17. Paris.

Council for Scientific and Industrial Research. 2000. *Making South Africa Safe: A Manual for Community Based Crime Prevention.* Pretoria: Deparment of Safety and Security, South African Police Service.

Cowell, Frank A. 1995. *Measuring Inequality (second edition).* Wheatsheaf: Prentice Hall.

Cox, Donald, Zekeriya Eser, and Emmanuel Jimenez. 1998. "Motives for Private Transfers Over the Life Cycle: An Analytical Framework and Evidence for Peru." *Journal of Development Economics* 55(1):57–80.

Craven, Wesley F. 1932. *Dissolution of the Virginia Company.* New York: Oxford University Press.

Crosby, Alfred. 1986. *Ecological Imperialism: The Biological Expansion of Europe 900-1900.* Cambridge, UK: Cambridge University Press.

Cull, Robert, Jana Matesova, and Mary Shirley. 2002. "Ownership and the Temptation to Loot: Evidence from Privatized Firms in the Czech Republic." *Journal of Comparative Economics* 30(1):1–24.

Cullen, Julie Berry, Brian A. Jacob, and Steven Levitt. 2000. "The Impact of School Choice on Student Outcomes: An Analysis of the Chicago Public Schools." Cambridge, MA: National Bureau of Economic Research Working Paper Series 7888.

———. 2003. "The Effect of School Choice on Student Outcomes: Evidence from Randomized Lotteries." Cambridge, MA: National Bureau of Economic Research Working Paper Series 10113.

Currie, Janet. 2000. "Early Childhood Intervention Programs: What do we Know?" Chicago: JCPR Working Paper 169.

Currie, Janet, and Duncan Thomas. 1995. "Does Head Start Make a Difference?" *American Economic Review* 85(3):341–64.

———. 1999. "Does Head Start Help Hispanic Children?" *International Journal of Social Economics* 74(2):235–62.

———. 2000. "School Quality and the Longer-Term Effects of Head Start." *Journal of Human Resources* 35(4):755–74.

CUTS (Consumer Unity and Trust Society). 2003. *Spine Chilling Experiences of Anti-Competitive Practices in Malawi.* India: CUTS.

Dakolias, Maria, and Kim Thatchuk. 2000. "The Problem of Eradicating Corruption from the Judiciary." *In* Marco Fabri and Philip M. Langbroek, (ed.), *The Challenge of Change for Judicial Systems.* Amsterdam: IOS Press.

Dalgaard, Carl-Johan., Henrik Hansen, and Finn Tarp. 2004. "On the Empirics of Foreign Aid and Growth." *Economic Journal* 114(496):F191–F216.

Damiani, Octavio. 2003. "Effects on Employment, Wages and Labor Standards of Nontraditional Export Crops in Northeast Brazil." *Latin American Research Review* 38(1):83–112.

Das Gupta, Monica, Sunhwa Lee, Patricia Uberoi, Danning Wang, Lihong Wang, and Xiaodan Zhang. 2004. "State Policies and Women's Agency in China, The Republic of Korea, and India, 1950–2000: Lessons from Contrasting Experiences." *In* Vijayendra Rao and Michael Walton, (ed.), *Culture and Public Action.* Stanford: Stanford University Press.

Das Gupta, Monica, Jian Zhenghua, Li Bohua, Xie Zhenming, Woojin Chung, and Bae Hwa-Ok. 2003. "Why is Son Preference so Persistent in East and South Asia? A Cross-country Study of India, China and the Republic of Korea." *Journal of Development Studies* 40(2):153–87.

Das, Hans. 2004. "Restoring Property Rights in the Aftermath of War." *International and Comparative Law Quarterly* 53(2):429–44.

Das, Jishnu, and Jeffery Hammer. 2005. "Poverty and the Access to Quality Health-Care: Evidence from Delhi." World Bank. Washington, DC. Processed.

Das, Jishnu, and Jeffrey Hammer. 2-28-2004. "Strained Mercy; Quality of Medical Care in Delhi." *Economic and Political Weekly.*

Dasgupta, A., C. P. S. Nayar, and Associates. 1989. *Urban Informal Credit Markets in India.* New Delhi: National Institute of Public Finance and Policy.

Datt, Gaurav, and Martin Ravallion. 1992. "Growth and Redistribution Components of Changes in Poverty Measures: A Decomposition with Applications to Brazil and India in the 1980s." *Journal of Development Economics* 38(2):275–95.

Davies, James B., and Anthony F. Shorrocks. 2005. "Wealth Holdings in Developing and Transition Countries." Paper presented at the Luxembourg Wealth Study Conference. January 27. Luxembourg.

Davis, Jeffrey, Rolando Ossowski, and Annalisa Fedelino, eds. 2003. *Fiscal Policy Formulation and Implementation in Oil-Producing Countries.* Washington, DC: International Monetary Fund.

Day, Candy, and Calle Hedberg. 2004. "Health Indicators." *South African Health Review* 2003(4):349–420.

de Carvalho Filho, Irineue Evangelista. 2000. "Household Income as a Determinant of Child Labour and School Enrollment in Brazil: Evidence from a Social Security Reform." Boston University. Boston. Processed.

De Ferranti, David, Guillermo Perry, William Foster, Daniel Lederman, and Alberto Valdés. 2005. *Beyond the City: The Rural Contribution to Development.* Washington, DC: World Bank.

De Ferranti, David, Guillermo E. Perry, Francisco H. G. Ferreira, and Michael Walton. 2004. *Inequality in Latin America: Breaking with History?* Washington, DC: World Bank.

de Haan, Arjan. 2005. "Disparities Within India's Poorest Regions: Why Do The Same Institutions Work Differently In Different Places?" Background paper for the WDR 2006.

De Janvry, Alain, and Elisabeth Sadoulet. 1989. "A Study in Resistance to Institutional Change: The Lost Game of Latin American Land Reform." *World Development* 17(9):1397–407.

———. 2002. "Land Reforms in Latin America: Ten Lessons toward a Contemporary Agenda." Paper presented at the World Bank's Latin American Land Policy Workshop. June 14. Pachuca, Mexico.

———. 2004. "Conditional Cash Transfer Programs: Are they Really Magic Bullets?" University of California. Berkeley, CA. Available on line at http://are.berkeley.edu/~sadoulet/papers/ARE-CCTPrograms.pdf. Processed.

De Soto, Hernando. 2000. *The Mystery of Capital: Why Capitalism Triumphs in the West and Fails Everywhere Else.* New York: Basic Books.

Dearden, Lorraine, Stephen Machin, and Howard Reed. 1997. "Intergenerational Mobility in Britain." *Economic Journal* 107(440):47–66.

Deaton, Angus. 1997. *The Analysis of Household Surveys.* Washington, DC: World Bank.

———. 2003. "Health, Inequality and Economic Development." *Journal of Economic Literature* 41(1):113–58.

———. 2004. "Health in an Age of Globalization." Paper presented at the Brookings Trade Forum. May 13. Brookings Institution, Washington, DC.

Deaton, Angus, and Jean Drèze. 2002. "Poverty and Inequality in India: A Reexamination." *Economic and Political Weekly* September 7:3729–48.

Deaton, Angus, and Valerie Kozel. 2004. *Data and Dogma: The Great Indian Poverty Debate.* New Delhi: McMillan.

Decker, Klaus, Siobhan McInerney-Lankford, and Caroline Sage. 2005. "Human Rights and Equitable Development: 'Ideals', Iissues and Implications." Background paper for the WDR 2006.

Decker, Klaus, Caroline Sage, and Milena Stefanova. 2005. "Law or Justice: Building Equitable Legal Institutions." Background paper for the WDR 2006.

Deere, Carmen Diana, and Magdalena León. 2003. "The Gender Asset Gap: Land in Latin America." *World Development* 31(6):925–47.

Deininger, Klaus. Forthcoming. "Land Policy Reforms." *In* Aline Coudouel and Stefano Paternostro (ed.) *The Distributional Impact of Reforms: A Practitioners' Guide, Volume I, Trade, Monetary and Exchange Rate Policy, Utility Provision, Agricultural Markets, Land, and Education.* Washington, DC: World Bank.

Deininger, Klaus, Raffaella Castagnini, and María A. González. 2004. "Comparing Land Reform and Land Markets in Colombia: Impacts on Equity and Efficiency." Washington, DC: World Bank Policy Research Working Paper Series 3258.

Deininger, Klaus, J. Hoogeveen, and B. Kinsey. 2004. "Economic Benefits and Costs of Land Redistribution in Zimbabwe in the early 1980s." *World Development* 32(10):1697–709.

Deininger, Klaus, Songquing Jin, Berhanu Adenew, Samuel Gebre-Selassie, and Berhanu Nega. 2003. "Tenure Security and Land-Related Investment: Evidence from Ethiopia." Washington, DC: World Bank Policy Research Working Paper Series 2991.

Deininger, Klaus, and Paul Mpuga. 2004. "Economic and Welfare Effects of the Abolition of Health User Fees: Evidence from Uganda." Washington, DC: World Bank Policy Research Working Paper Series 3276.

Deininger, Klaus, and Pedro Olinto. 2000. "Asset Distribution, Inequality and Growth." World Bank: World Bank Policy Research Working Paper Series 2375.

Deininger, Klaus, and Lyn Squire. 1996. "A New Data Set Measuring Income Inequality." *World Bank Economic Review* 10(3):565–91.

————. 1998. "New Ways of Looking at Old Issues: Inequality and Growth." *Journal of Development Economics* 57(2):259–87.

Delgado, Guilherme, and José Celso Cardoso Jr., eds. 2000. *A Universalização de Direitos Sociais no Brasil: A Previdência Rural nos Anos 90.* Brasília: IPEA.

Demombynes, Gabriel, and Berk Özler. 2005. "Crime and Local Inequality in South Africa." *Journal of Development Economics* 76(2):265–92.

Deshpande, Ashwini. 2005. "Affirmative Action in India and the United States." Background paper for the WDR 2006.

DeTray, Dennis. 1988. "Government Policy, Household Behavior and the Distribution of Schooling: A Case Study in Malaysia." *In* T. P. Schultz, (ed.), *Research in Population Economics, Vol. 6.* Greenwich, CT: JAI Press.

Deutsch, Ruthanne. 1998. "Does Child Care Pay? Labor Force Participation and Earnings Effects of Access to Child Care in the Favelas of Rio." Washington, DC: Inter-American Development Bank, Office of the Chief Economist Working Paper Series 384.

Devereux, Stephen. 2001. "Livelihood Insecurity and Social Protection: A Re-emerging Issue in Rural Development." *Development Policy Review* 19(4):507–19.

Diallo, Amadou Bassirou, and Quentin Wodon. 2005. "A Note on Access to Network-based Infrastructure Services in Africa: Benefit and Marginal Benefit Incidence Analysis." World Bank. Washington, DC. Processed.

Diamond, Peter A. 1981. "Mobility Costs, Frictional Unemployment, and Efficiency." *Journal of Political Economy* 89(4):798–812.

Dickson, Rumona, Shally Awasthi, Paula Williamson, Colin Demellweek, and Paul Garner. 2000. "Effects of Treatment for Intestinal Helminth Infection on Growth and Cognitive Performance in Children: Systematic Review of Randomized Trials." *British Medical Journal* 320(7251):1697–701.

Diwan, Ishac. 2001. "Debt as Sweat: Labor, Financial Crisis, and the Globalization of Capital." World Bank. Washington, DC. Available on line at http://info.worldbank.org/etools/docs/voddocs/150/332/diwan.pdf. Processed.

————. 2002. "The Labor Share during Financial Crisis: New Results." World Bank. Washington, DC. Processed.

Djankov, Simeon, Rafael La Porta, Florencio López-de-Silanes, and Andrei Shleifer. 2003. "Courts." *Quarterly Journal of Economics* 118(2):453–517.

Do, Toan, and Laksmi Iyer. 2003. "Land Rights and Economic Development: Evidence from Vietnam." Washington, DC: World Bank Policy Research Working Paper Series 3120.

Dollar, David, and Aart Kraay. 2002. "Growth is Good for the Poor." *Journal of Economic Growth* 7(3):195–225.

————. 2004. "Trade, Growth and Poverty." *Economic Journal* 114(493):F22–F49.

Dollar, David, and Victoria Levin. 2004. "The Increasing Selectivity of Foreign Aid." Washington DC: World Bank Policy Research Working Paper Series 3299.

Doryan, Eduardo A., Kul C. Gautman, and William H. Foege. 2002. "The Political Challenge: Commitment and Cooperation." *In* Mary Eming Young, (ed.), *From Early Childhood Development to Human Development: Investing in our Children's Future.* Washington, DC: World Bank.

Draï, Raphaël. 1991. *Le Mythe de la Loi du Talion.* Paris: Alinea.

Drèze, Jean, Peter Lanjouw, and Naresh Sharma. 1998. "Economic Development in Palanpur, 1957–93." *In* Peter Lanjouw and Nicholas Stern, (ed.), *Economic Development in Palanpur over Five Decades.* New York: Clarendon Press.

Duan, Chengrong. 2005. "China: Gender Inequality Status Report." Renmin University. Beijing. Processed.

Duflo, Esther. 2001. "Schooling and Labor Market Consequences of School Construction in Indonesia: Evidence from an Unusual Policy Experiment." *American Economic Review* 91(4):795–813.

————. 2003. "Grandmothers and Granddaughters: Old-age Pensions and Intrahousehold Allocation in South Africa." *World Bank Economic Review* 17(1):1–25.

Duflo, Esther, Michael Kremer, and Jonathan Robinson. 2004. "Understanding Technology Adoption: Fertilizer in Western Kenya, Preliminary Results from Field Experiments." Paper presented at the LSE Conference 'Behavioral Economics, Public Economics and Development Economics. May 28. London.

Duflo, Esther, and Christopher Udry. 2004. "Intrahousehold Resource Allocation in Côte d'Ivoire: Social Norms, Separate Accounts and Consumption Choices." Cambridge, MA: National Bureau of Economic Research Working Paper Series 10498.

Dunn, Christopher. 2003. "Assortative Matching and Intergenerational Mobility in Family Earnings: Evidence from Brazil." University of Michigan. Ann Harbor, MI. Processed.

Durand-Lasserve, A. 2003. "Land Issues and Security of Tenure. Background Report for the UN Millennium Project Task Force on Improving the Lives of Slum Dwellers." National Centre for Scientific Research. France. Processed.

Dworkin, Ronald. 1981a. "What is Equality? Part 2: Equality of Resources." *Philosophy and Public Affairs* 10(3):283–345.

————. 1981b. "What is Equality? Part 1: Equality of Welfare." *Philosophy and Public Affairs* 10(3):185–246.

Easterlin, Richard. 1974. "Does Economic Growth Improve the Human Lot?: Some Empirical Evidence." *In* David A. Paul and Melvin W. Reder, (ed.), *Nations and Households in Economic Growth: Essays in Honor of Moses Abramowitz.* New York: Academic Press.

Easterly, William, and Ross Levine. 1997. "Africa's Growth Tragedy: Policies and Ethnic Divisions." *Quarterly Journal of Economics* 112(4):1203–50.

Easterly, William, Ross Levine, and David Roodman. 2004. "Aid, Policies, and Growth: Comment." *American Economic Review* 94(3):774–80.

Ehrenreich, Barbara, and Arlie Russell Hochschild, eds. 2003. *Global Woman. Nannies, Maids, and Sex Workers in the New Economy.* New York: Metropolitan Books.

Elbers, Chris, Peter Lanjouw, Joan Mistiaen, Berk Özler, and K. Simler. 2004. "On the Unequal Inequality of Poor Communities." *World Bank Economic Review* 18(3):401–21.

Elbers, Chris, Peter Lanjouw, Johan Mistiaen, and Berk Özler. 2005. "Reinterpreting Sub-group Inequality Decompositions." World Bank.

Washington, DC. Available on line at http://globetrotter.berkeley.edu/macarthur/inequality/papers/OzlerReinterpretingDecomp.pdf. Processed.

Elo, Irma, and Samuel H. Preston. 1996. "Educational Differences in Mortality: United States." *Social Science and Medicine* 42(1):47–57.

Elson, Robert E. 2001. *Suharto: A Political Biography.* Cambridge, UK: Cambridge University Press.

Engerman, Stanley, and Kenneth Sokoloff. 1997. "Factor Endowments, Institutions, and Differential Paths of Growth Among New World Economies: A View from Economic Historians of the United States." *In* Stephen Haber, (ed.), *How Latin America Fell Behind.* Stanford, CA: Stanford University Press.

Engerman, Stanley L., and Kenneth Sokoloff. 2002. "Factor Endowments, Inequality, and Paths of Development among New World Economies." *Economia* 3(1):41–88.

Engerman, Stanley L., and Kenneth L. Sokoloff. 2001. "The Evolution of Suffrage Institutions in the New World." Cambridge, MA: National Bureau of Economic Research Working Paper Series 8512.

Erikson, Robert, and John Goldthrope. 2002. "Intergenerational Inequality: A Sociological Perspective." *Journal of Economic Perspectives* 16(3):31–44.

Escobal, Javier, and Máximo Torero. 2003. "Adverse Geography and Differences in Welfare in Peru." Helsinki: United Nations University, World Institute for Development Economics Research, Discussion Paper 2003/73.

Escobar, María-Luisa. 2005. "The Columbia Health Sector Reform and the Poor." World Bank. Washington, DC. Processed.

Escobar, María-Luisa, and Panagiota Panopoulou. 2002. "Chapter 6: Health." *In* Giugale, Lafourcade, and Luff, (ed.), *Columbia: The Economic Foundations for Peace.* Washington, DC: World Bank.

Esping-Andersen, Gosta. 1990. *The Three Worlds of Welfare Capitalism.* Cambridge, UK: Polity Press.

Estache, Antonio. 2003. "On Latin America's Infrastructure Privatization and its Distributional Effects." Paper presented at the Distributional Consequences of Privatization Conference. February 24. Washington, DC.

Estache, Antonio, Vivien Foster, and Quentin Wodon. 2001. *Accounting for Poverty in Infrastructure Reform: Learning from Latin America's Experience.* Washington, DC: World Bank.

Estache, Antonio, Andrés Gómez-Lobo, and Danny Leipziger. 2001. "Utilities Privatization and the Poor: Lessons and Evidence from Latin America." *World Development* 29(7):1179–98.

Esteban, Joan, and Debraj Ray. 1994. "On the Measurement of Polarization." *Econometrica* 62(4):819–51.

Evans, Peter. 2004. "Development as Institutional Change: The Pitfalls of Monocropping and Potentials of Deliberation." *Studies in Comparative International Development* 38(4):30–53.

Fafchamps, Marcel. 2000. "Ethnicity and Credit in African Manufacturing." *Journal of Development Economics* 61(1):205–35.

Fafchamps, Marcel, and Susan Lund. 2003. "Risk-sharing Networks in Rural Philippines." *Review of Economic Studies* 71(2):261–87.

Faini, Riccardo. 2003. "The Brain Drain: An Unmitigated Blessing?" Milan: Centro Studi Luca d'Agliano Development Studies 173. Available on line at http://ssrn.com/abstract=463021.

Fajnzylber, Pablo, Daniel Lederman, and Norman Loayza. 2000. "Crime and Victimization: An Economic Perspective." *Economía* 1(1):219–78.

Fallon, Peter R., and Robert E. B. Lucas. 1993. "Job Security Regulations and the Dynamic Demand for Industrial Labor in India and Zimbabwe." *Journal of Development Economics* 40(2):241–75.

Feder, Gershon. 1988. *Land Policies and Farm Productivity in Thailand.* Baltimore, MD: Johns Hopkins University.

————. 2002. "The Intricacies of Land Markets: Why the World Bank Succeeds in Economic Reforms through Land Registration and Tenure Security." Paper presented at the International Federation of Surveyors Conference. April 19. Washington, DC.

Fehr, Ernst, and Urs Fischbacher. 2003. "The Nature of Human Altruism." *Nature* 425(October):785–91.

Fehr, Ernst, and Simon Gachter. 2000. "Cooperation and Punishment in Public Goods Experiments." *American Economic Review* 90(4):980–94.

Fehr, Ernst, and Klaus M. Schmidt. 1999. "A Theory of Fairness, Competition and Cooperation." *Quarterly Journal of Economics* 114(3):817–68.

Feierstein, Mark, and John Moreira. 2005. *Liberians Have New Outlook On Their Future.* Washington, DC: Greenberg Quinland Rosner Research Inc. Available on line at http://www.greenbergresearch.com.

Feijen, Erik, and Enrico Perotti. 2005. "Lobbying for Strategic Default." University of Amsterdam. Amsterdam. Processed.

Feldstein, Martin. 1998. "Income Inequality and Poverty." Cambridge, MA: National Bureau of Economic Research Working Paper Series 6770.

Fernández-Kelly, Patricia. 1995. "Social and Cultural Capital in the Urban Ghetto: Implications for the Economic Sociology of Immigration." *In* Alejandro Portes, (ed.), *The Economic Sociology of Immigration: Essays in Network, Ethnicity, and Entrepreneurship.* New York: Rusell Sage Foundation.

Ferreira, Francisco H. G. 2001. "Education for the Masses? The Interaction between Wealth, Educational and Political Inequalities." *Economics of Transition* 9(2):533–52.

Ferreira, Francisco H. G., and Julie A. Litchfield. 2001. "Education or Inflation? The Micro and Macroeconomics of the Brazilian Income Distribution during 1981–95." *Cuadernos de Economía* 38(114):209–38.

Ferreira, Pedro Cavalcanti. 2004. *Regional Policy in Brazil: A Review.* Rio de Janeiro: Fundacao Getulio Vargas.

Field, Erica. 2003. "Entitled to Work: Urban Tenure Security and Labor Supply in Peru." Princeton, NJ: Princeton University, Princeton Law & Public Affairs Working Paper 02-1.

Fields, Gary S. 1989. "Changes in Poverty and Inequality in Developing Countries." *World Bank Research Observer* 4(2):167–85.

Fields, Gary S., and George H. Jakubson. 1994. "New Evidence on the Kuznets Curve." Cornell University. Ithaca, NY. Processed.

Filmer, Deon. 2004. "If you Build it, Will They Come? School Availability and School Enrollment in 21 Poor Countries." Washington, DC: World Bank Policy Research Working Paper Series 3340.

Filmer, Deon, Margaret Grosh, Elizabeth M. King, and Dominique Van de Walle. 1998. "Pay and Grade Differentials at the World Bank." Washington, DC: World Bank Policy Research Working Paper Series 1912.

Filmer, Deon, and Lant Pritchett. 1998. The Effect of Household Wealth on Educational Attainment. Policy Research Working Paper #1980, The World Bank.

Filmer, Deon, and Lant Pritchett. 1999. "The Effect of Household Wealth on Educational Attainment: Evidence from 35 Countries." *Population and Development Review* 25(1):85–120.

Fink, Carsten, and Patrick Reichenmuller. 2005. "Tightening TRIPs: The Intellectual Property Provisions of Recent US Freed Trade Agreements." Washington, DC: World Bank, Trade Note 20.

Firebaugh, Glenn, and Brian Goesling. 2004. "Accounting for the Recent Decline in Global Income Inequality." *The American Journal of Sociology* 110(2):283–312.

Fishman, Robert M. 1990. *Working Class Organization and the Return to Democracy in Spain.* Ithaca, NY: Cornell University Press.

Fisman, Raymond. 2001a. "Trade Credit and Productive Efficiency in Developing Countries." *World Development* 29(2):7311–21.

———. 2001b. "Estimating the Value of Political Connections." *American Economic Review* 91(4):1095–102.

———. 2003. "Ethnic Ties and the Provision of Credit: Relationship-Level Evidence from African Firms." *Advances in Economic Analysis and Policy* 3(1):1211–1211.

Fiszbein, Ariel. 2005. *Citizens, Politicians and Providers: The Latin American Experience with Service Delivery Reform.* Washington, DC: World Bank.

Fleshman, Michael. 2001. "AIDS Orphans: Facing Africa's Silent Crisis." *Africa Recovery* 15(3):1–1.

Forbes, Kristin J. 2000. "A Reassessment of the Relationship Between Inequality and Growth." *American Economic Review* 90(4):869–87.

Fortman, Louise. 1998. "Why Women's Property Rights Matter." Paper presented at the International Conference and Workshop on Land Tenure in the Developing World. Cape Town.

Foster, Andrew D., and Mark R. Rosenzweig. 1995. "Learning by Doing and Learning from Others: Human Capital and Technical Change in Agriculture." *Journal of Political Economy* 103(6):1176–209.

Fox, Jonathan, eds. 1990. *The Challenge of Rural Democratization: Perspectives from Latin America and the Philippines.* London: Frank Cass and Company.

FTI Secretariat. 2004. *Education for All (EFA)-Fast Track Initiative (FTI); Status Report.* Washington, DC: World Bank. Available on line at http://www1.worldbank.org/education/efafti/documents/Brasilia/status_report_dec6.pdf.

Fujii, Tomoki. 2005. "Micro-level Estimation of Child Malnutrition Indicators and its Application in Cambodia." Washington, DC: World Bank Policy Research Working Paper Series 3662.

Funck, Bernard, and Lodovico Pizzati, eds. 2003. *European Integration, Regional Policy, and Growth.* Washington, DC: World Bank.

Fung, Archon, Dara O'Rourke, and Charles Sabel. 2001. *Can we Put an End to Sweatshops? A New Democracy Forum on Raising Global Labor Standards.* Boston, MA: Beacon Press.

Galasso, Emanuela, and Martin Ravallion. 2005. "Decentralized Targeting of an Anti-poverty Program." *Journal of Public Economics* 89(4):705–27.

Galiani, Sebastián, Paul Gertler, and Ernesto Schargrodsky. 2002. "Water for Life: The Impact of the Privatization of Water Services on Child Mortality." Stanford, CA: Stanford University, Center for Research on Economic Development and Policy Reform Working Paper 154.

Galiani, Sebastián, and Ernesto Schargrodsky. 2002. "Evaluating the Impact of School Decentralization on Ecucational Quality." *Economía* 2(2):275–314.

———. 2004. "Effects of Land Titling." Paper presented at the World Bank Poverty and Applied Micro Seminar Series. October 6. Washington, DC.

Galli, Rossana, and David Kucera. 2004. "Labor Standards and Informal Employment in Latin America." *World Development* 32(5):809–828.

Garapon, Antoine, eds. 2003. *Les Juges Un Pouvoir Irresponsable?* Paris: Éditions Nicolas Philippe.

García-Montalvo, José, and Marta Reynal-Querol. Forthcoming. "Why Ethnic Fractionalization? Polarization, Conflict and Growth." *American Economic Review.*

Geertz, Clifford. 1963. *Peddlers and Princes; Social Change and Economic Modernization in Two Indonesian Towns.* Chicago: University of Chicago Press.

Gerschenkron, Alexander. 1962. *Economic Backwardness in Historical Perspective: A Books of Essays.* Cambridge: Belknap Press of Harvard University Press.

Gertler, Paul, and Sarah Barber. 2004. "The Returns to Investing in Quality Healthcare." Institute of Business and Economic Research, University of California. Berkeley, CA. Processed.

Gertler, Paul, and Jonathan Gruber. 2002. "Insuring Consumption against Illness." *American Economic Review* 92(1):51–76.

Gibson, Christopher, and Michael Woolcock. 2005. "Empowerment and Local Level Conflict Mediation in Indonesia: A Comparative Analysis of Concepts, Measures, and Project Efficacy." World Bank. Washington, DC. Processed.

Gill, A., and U. C. Singh. 1977. "Financial Sector Reforms, Rate of Interest and the Rural Credit Markets: The Role of Informal Lenders in Punjab." *Indian Journal of Applied Economics* 6(4):37–65.

Glaeser, Edward L., Simon Johnson, and Andrei Shleifer. 2001. "Coase versus the Coasians." *Quarterly Journal of Economics* 116(3):853–99.

Glaeser, Edward L., José Sheinkman, and Andrei Shleifer. 2003. "The Injustice of Inequality." *Journal of Monetary Economics* 50(1):199–222.

Glewwe, Paul, Nauman Ilias, and Michael Kremer. 2003. "Teacher Incentives." Cambridge, MA: National Bureau of Economic Research Working Paper Series 9671.

Glewwe, Paul, Michael Kremer, and Sylvie Moulin. 2002. "Textbooks and Test Scores: Evidence from a Prospective Evaluation in Kenya." Harvard University. Cambridge, MA. Available on line at http://post.economics.harvard.edu/faculty/kremer/webpapers/Textbooks_Test_Scores.pdf. Processed.

Glewwe, Paul, Michael Kremer, Sylvie Moulin, and Eric Zitzewitz. 2004. "Retrospective vs. Prospective Analyses of School Inputs:

The Case of Flip Charts in Kenya." *Journal of Development Economics* 74(1):251–68.

Goesling, Brian, and Glenn Firebaugh. 2004. "The Trend in International Health Inequality." *Population and Development Review* 30(1):131–46.

Goetz, Stephan J. 1992. "A Selectivity Model of Household Food Marketing Behavior in Sub-Saharan Africa." *American Journal of Agricultural Economics* 74(2):444–52.

Goldin, Ian, Kenneth A. Reinert, and Andrew Beath. Forthcoming. "Migration." *In* Ian Goldin and Kenneth A. Reinert (ed.) *Globalization and Poverty.* Washington, DC: World Bank.

Goldstein, Markus, and Christopher Udry. 1999. "Agricultural Innovation and Resource Management in Ghana." Yale University. New Haven, CT. Processed.

————. 2002. "Gender, Land Rights and Agriculture in Ghana." Yale University. New Haven, CT. Processed.

Gottfredson, Denise. 1998. "School-based Crime Prevention." *In* Lawrence W. Sherman, Denise Gottfredson, Doris MacKenzie, John Eck, Peter Reuter, and Shawn Bushway, (ed.), *Preventing Crime. What Works. What Doesn't. What's Promising.* Washington, DC: U.S. Department of Justice.

Graham, Carol, and Andrew Felton. 2005. "Does Inequality Matter to Individual Welfare?: An Initial Exploration based on Happiness Surveys from Latin America." Washington, DC: Brooking Institution, CSED Working Paper 138. Available on line at http://www.brookings.edu/es/dynamics/papers/csed_wp38.pdf.

Graham, Jean, and Benjamin Bowling. 1995. "Young People and Crime." London: Home Office Research Study 145.

Grantham-McGregor, S, and C. Ani. 2001. "A Review of Studies on the Effect of Iron Deficiency on Cognitive Development in Children." *Journal of Nutrition* 131(2S-2):649S–668S.

Grantham-McGregor, S., C. Powell, S. P. Walker, and J. H. Himes. 1991. "Nutritional Suplementation, Pshychosocial Stimulation, and Mental Development of Stunted Children: The Jamaican Study." *The Lancet* 338(8758):1–5.

Gravois, John. 1-28-2005. "The De Soto Delusion." *Slate.*

Greenwood, Peter W., Karyn T. Model, C. Peter Rydell, and James Chiesa. 1998. *Diverting Children from a Life of Crime: Measuring Cost and Benefits.* Santa Monica, CA: Rand Corporation.

Grindle, Merilee S. 2004. *Despite The Odds: Contentious Politics of Education Reform.* Princeton, NJ: Princeton University Press.

Guasch, J. Luis. 2003. *Concessions of Infrastructure Services: Incidence and Determinants of Renegotiation: An Empirical Evaluation and Guidelines for Optimal Concession Design.* Washington, DC: World Bank Institute.

Guggenheim, Scott. Forthcoming. "Crises and Contradictions: Understanding the Origins of a Community Development Project in Indonesia." *In* Anthony Bebbington, Scott Guggenheim, Elizabeth Olson, and Michael Woolcock (ed.) *The Search for Empowerment: Social Capital as Idea and Practice at the World Bank.* Bloomfield, CT: Kumarian Press.

Guiso, Luigi, Paola Sapienza, and Luigi Zingales. 2004. "Does Local Financial Development Matter?" *Quarterly Journal of Economics* 119(3):929–69.

Gulyani, Sumila, Debabrata Talukdar, and R. Mukami Kariuki. 2005. "Water for the Urban Poor: Water Markets, Household Demand, and Service Preferences in Kenya." Washington, DC: World Bank Water Supply and Sanitation Sector Board Discussion Paper Series 5.

Gunning, Jan Willem, John Hoddinott, Bill Kinsey, and Trudy Owens. 2000. "Revisiting Forever Gained: Income Dynamics in the Resettlement Areas of Zimbabwe, 1983–96." *Journal of Development Studies* 36(6):131–54.

Gunther, Richard, José Ramón Montero, and Joan Botella. 2004. *Democracy in Modern Spain.* New Haven, CT: Yale University Press.

Gupta, Sanjeev, Benedict Clements, Alexander Pivovarsky, and Erwin R. Tiongson. 2003. "Foreign Aid and Revenue Response: Does the Composition of Aid Matter?" Washington, DC: International Monetary Fund Working Paper Series WP/03/176.

Gurr, Ted Robert. 1997. "Polity II: Political Structures and Regime Change, 1800–1986." Ann Arbor, MI: ICSPR Study No. 9263. Available on line at http://webapp.icpsr.umich.edu/cocoon/ICPSR-STUDY/09263.xml.

Gwatkin, Davidson R. 2002. "The Poor Come Last: Socio-Economic Inequalities in Use of Maternal and Child Health Services in Developing Countries." Paper presented at the Presentation at the Meeting of the Fogarty International Center. July 24. National Institutes of Health, Bethesda, MD.

Gwatkin, Davidson R., Shea Rutstein, Kiersten Johnson, Eldaw Abdalla Suliman, and Adam Wagstaff. 2004. *Socio-economic differences in health, nutrition, and population, volumes I–III.* Washington, DC: World Bank.

Haber, Stephen. 2004. "Political Institutions and Economic Development: Evidence from the Banking Systems of the United States and Mexico." Paper presented at the Economics, Political Institutions, and Financial Markets II: Institutional Theory and Evidence from Europe, the United States, and Latin America Conference. February 5. Palo Alto, CA.

Haber, Stephen, and Shawn Kantor. 2004. "Getting Privatization Wrong: The Mexican Banking System, 1991–2003." Paper presented at the World Bank Conference on Bank Privatizacion in Low and Middle-Income Countries. November 23. Washington, DC.

Haber, Stephen, and Noel Maurer. 2004. "Related Lending and Economic Performance: Evidence from Mexico." Paper presented at the Sixty Fifth Annual Meeting of the American Finance Association. January 7. Philadelphia.

Haber, Stephen, Maurer Noel, and Armando Razo. 2003. *The Politics of Property Rights: Political Instability, Credible Commitments, and Economic Growth in Mexico: 1876–1929.* Cambridge, UK: Cambridge University Press.

Haber, Stephen H. 2001. "Political Institutions and Banking Systems: Lessons from the Economic Histories of Mexico and the United States, 1790–1914." Department of Political Science, Stanford University. Stanford, CA. Processed.

Haggard, Stephan. 1990. *Pathways from the Periphery: The Politics of Growth in the Newly Industrializing Countries.* Ithaca, NY: Cornell University Press.

Haggard, Stephan, Wonhyuk Lim, and Euysung Kim, eds. 2003. *Economic Crisis and Corporate Restructuring in Korea: Reforming the Chaebol.* New York: Cambridge University Press.

Halac, Marina, and Sergio L. Schmukler. 2003. "Distribution Effects of Crises: The Role of Financial Transfers." Washington, DC: World Bank Policy Research Working Paper Series 3173.

Hall, Gillette, and Harry Anthony Patrinos, eds. 2005. *Indigenous Peoples, Poverty and Human Development in Latin America: 1994–2004.* New York: Palgrave MacMillan.

Hall, Robert E., and Charles I. Jones. 1999. "Why Do Some Countries Produce so Much More Output per Worker than Others?" *Quarterly Journal of Economics* 114(1):83–116.

Hamid, N. 1983. "Growth of Small-scale Industry in Pakistan." *Pakistan Economic and Social Review* 21(1-2):37–76.

Hamilton, Bob, and John Whalley. 1984. "Efficiency and Distributional Implications of Global Restrictions on Labor Mobility." *Journal of Development Economics* 14(1-2):61–75.

Hammergreen, Linn. 2004. "Use and Users Study of the Justice System in Peru." World Bank. Washington, DC. Processed.

Hansen, Henrik, and Finn Tarp. 2001. "Aid and Growth Regressions." *Journal of Development Economics* 64(2):547–70.

Hanson, Gordon H. 2003. "What Has Happened to Wages in Mexico since NAFTA? Implications for Hemispheric Free Trade." Cambridge, MA: National Bureau of Economic Research Working Paper Series 9563.

Hanushek, Eric A. 1986. "The Economics of Schooling: Production and Efficiency in Public Schools." *Journal of Economic Literature* 24(3):1141–77.

———. 1996. "School Resources and Student Performance." *In* Gary Burtless, (ed.), *Does Money Matter? The Effects of School Resources on Student Achievement and Adult Success.* Washington, DC: Brookings Institution.

Hanushek, Eric A., and Ludger Wößman. 2005. "Does Educational Tracking Affect Performance and Inequality? Differences-in-Differences Evidence Across Countries." Cambridge, MA: National Bureau of Economic Research Working Paper Series 11124.

Harber, Clive. 1999. *Protecting Your School from Violence and Crime: An Evaluation of One-Year Programme.* KwaZulu-Natal, South Africa: Independent Project Trust.

Hargreaves, James R., and Judith R. Glynn. 2002. "Educational Attainment and HIV Infection in Developing Countries: A Systematic Review." *Tropical Medicine and International Health* 7(6):489–98.

Harsanyi, John C. 1955. "Cardinal Welfare, Individualistic Ethics, and Interpersonal Comparisons of Utility." *Journal of Political Economy* 63(4):309–21.

Hart, Betty, and Todd R. Risley. 1995. *Meaningful Differences in Everyday Experiences of Young American Children.* Baltimore, MD: Paul H. Brookes Publishing Co.

Hasan, Rana, Devashish Mitra, and K. V. Ramaswamy. 2003. "Trade Reforms, Labor Regulations and Labor-demand Elasticities: Empirical Evidence from India." Cambridge, MA: National Bureau of Economic Research Working Paper Series 9879.

Hashemi, Syed. 2000. "Linking Microfinance and Safety Net Programs to Include the Poorest: The Case of IGVGD in Bangladesh." Washington, DC: World Bank, Focus Notes 21.

Haslam, Alexander S. 2001. *Psychology in Organizations: The Social-identity Approach.* Thousand Oaks, CA: Sage Publications Ltd.

Heckman, James, and Dimitri V. Masterov. 2004. "The Productivity Argument for Investing in Young Children." Washington, DC: Committee for Economic Development Working Paper 5.

Heise, L., M. Ellsberg, and M. Gottemoeller. 1999. "Ending Violence Against Women." Baltimore, MD: Johns Hopkins University School of Public Health, Population Information Program Population Report Series L, number 11.

Hellman, Joel S., Geraint Jones, and Daniel Kaufmann. 2003. "Seize the State, Seize the Day: State Capture and Influence in Transition Economies." *Journal of Comparative Economics* 31(4):751–73.

Hemming, John. 1970. *The Conquest of the Incas.* London: Papermac.

Henrich, Joseph, Robert Boyd, Samuel Bowles, Colin Camerer, Ernst Fehr, and Herbert Gintis, eds. 2004. *Foundations of Human Society: Economic Experiments and Ethnographic Evidence from Fifteen Small-Scale Societies.* New York: Oxford University Press.

Hertel, Thomas W., and L. Alan Winters. Forthcoming. "Putting Development Back into the Doha Agenda: Poverty Impacts of a WTO Agreement." World Bank. Washington, DC. Processed.

Hertz, Thomas. 2001. "Education, Inequality and Economic Mobility in South Africa." PhD thesis. University of Massachussetts.

———. 2005. "Rags, Riches and Race: The Intergenerational Economic Mobility of Black and White Families in the U.S." *In* Sam Bowles, Herb Gintis, and Melissa Osborne Grove, (ed.), *Unequal Chances. Family Background and Economic Success.* Princeton, NJ: Princeton University Press.

Herz, Barbara, and Gene B. Sperling. 2004. *What Works in Girls' Education.* New York: Council on Foreign Relations.

Hoff, Karla. 2003. "Paths of Institutional Development: A View from Economic History." *World Bank Research Observer* 18(2):2205–26.

Hoff, Karla, and Priyanka Pandey. 2004. "Belief Systems and Durable Inequalities: An Experimental Investigation of Indian Caste." Washington, DC: World Bank Policy Research Working Paper Series 3351.

Hoffman, Elizabeth, Kevin A. McCabe, and Vernon L. Smith. 1996. "On Expectations and Monetary Stakes in Ultimatum Games." *International Journal of Game Theory* 25(3):289–301.

Holmes, George M., Jeff DeSimone, and Nicholas G. Rupp. 2003. "Does School Choice Increase School Quality?" Cambridge, MA: National Bureau of Economic Research Working Paper Series 9683.

Holzer, Harry, and David Neumark. 2000. "Assessing Affirmative Action." *Journal of Economic Literature* 38(3):483–568.

Holzmann, Robert, and Richard Hinz. 2005. *Old-Age Income Support in the Twenty-First Century: An International Perspective on Pension Systems and Reform.* Washington, DC: World Bank. Available on line at http://www1.worldbank.org/sp/incomesupport.asp.

Holzmann, Robert, and Steen Jorgensen. 2001. "Social Risk Management: A New Conceptual Framework for Social Protection and Beyond." Washington, DC: World Bank, Social Protection Discussion Paper 0006.

Honohan, Patrick. 2004. *Financial Sector Policy and the Poor: Selected Findings and Issues.* Washington, DC: World Bank.

Honohan, Patrick, and Daniela Klingebiel. 2000. "Controlling the Fiscal Costs of Banking Crises." Washington, DC: World Bank Policy Research Working Paper Series 2441.

Hoogeveen, Hans. 2003. "Census-Based Welfare Estimates for Small Populations: Poverty and Disability in Uganda." World Bank. Washington, DC. Processed.

Hoogeveen, Johannes, Emil Tesliuc, Renos Vakis, and Stefan Dercon. 2004. "A Guide to the Analysis of Risk, Vulnerability and Vulnerable Groups." World Bank. Washington, DC. Available on line at http://siteresources.worldbank.org/INTSRM/Publications/20316319/RVA.pdf. Processed.

Hoxby, Caroline M. 2000. "Does Competition Among Public Schools Benefit Students and Taxpayers?" *American Economic Review* 90(5):1209–38.

———. 2002. "School Choice and School Productivity (or Could School Choice be a Tide that Lifts All Boats?)." Cambridge, MA: National Bureau of Economic Research Working Paper Series 8873.

Hsieh, Chang-Tai, and Miguel Urquiola. 2003. "When Schools Compete, How Do They Compete? An Assessment of Chile's Nationwide School Voucher Program." Cambridge, MA: National Bureau of Economic Research Working Paper Series 10008.

Human Rights Watch. 2000. *United States Punishment and Prejudice: The Racial Disparities in the War on Drugs.* New York: Human Rights Watch. Available on line at http://www.hrw.org/reports/2000/usa/.

Ilahi, Nadeem, and Franque Grimard. 2000. "Public Infrastructure and Private Costs: Water Supply and Time Allocation of Women in Rural Pakistan." *Economic Development and Cultural Change* 49(1):45–75.

Ilahi, Nadeem, and Saqib Jafarey. 1999. "Guestworker Migration, Remittances, and the Extended Family: Evidence from Pakistan." *Journal of Development Economics* 58(2):485–512.

ILO. 2002. *Women and Men in the Informal Economy: A Statistical Picture.* Geneva: International Labour Organization. Available on line at http://www.ilo.org/public/english/employment/gems/download/women.pdf.

———. 2003. *Investing in Every Child—An Economic Study of the Costs and Benefits of Eliminating Child Labor.* Geneva: International Labour Organization. Available on line at http://www.ilo.org/public/english/standards/ipec/publ/download/2003_12_investingchild.pdf.

India Today. 12-13-2004. "Rural Markets: Call of the Countryside." *India Today.*

Inglehart, Ronald, Miguel Basáñez, Jaime Díez-Medrano, Loek Halman, and Ruud Luijkx, eds. 2004. *Human Beliefs and Values: A Cross-cultural Sourcebook based on the 1999–2002 Values Surveys.* Mexico, DF: Siglo Veinteiuno.

International Confederation of Free Trade Unions. 2005. *The Impact of the Ending of Quotas on the Textile Industry. Cambodia: Increasing Pressure on Trade Union Rights.* Brussels: International Confederation of Free Trade Unions. Available on line at http://www.icftu.org/displaydocument.asp?Index=991221551&Language=EN.

International Cotton Advisory Committee. 2003. *Production and Trade Policies Affecting the Cotton Industry. A Report by the Secretariat.* Washington, DC: International Cotton Advisory Committee. Available on line at http://www.icac.org/cotton_info/publications/statistics/stats_wtd/prod_trade_policies_03.pdf.

International Fund for Agricultural Development. 2001. *Rural Poverty Report 2001: The Challenge of Ending Rural Poverty.* Oxford: Oxford University Press. Available on line at http://www.ifad.org.

Irwin, Timothy, and Chiaki Yamamoto. 2004. "Improving the Governance of State-owned Electricity Utilities." Washington, DC: World Bank Energy and Mining Sector Board Discussion Paper 11.

Jacoby, Hanan G., Guo Li, and Scott Rozelle. 2002. "Hazards of Expropriation: Tenure Insecurity and Investment in Rural China." *American Economic Review* 92(5):1420–47.

Jalan, Jyostna, and Martin Ravallion. 1997. "Spatial Poverty Traps?" Washington, DC: World Bank Policy Research Working Paper Series 1862.

———. 2002. "Geographic Poverty Traps? A Micro Model of Consumption Growth in Rural China." *Journal of Applied Econometrics* 17(4):329–46.

———. 2003. "Does Piped Water Reduce Diarrhea for Children in Rural India?" *Journal of Econometrics* 112(1):153–73.

Jalan, Jyotsna, and Martin Ravallion. 1999. "Income Gains to the Poor from Workfare: Estimates for Argentina's Trabajar Program." Washington, DC: World Bank Policy Research Working Paper Series 2149.

James, Estelle. 2000. "Old-age Protection for the Uninsured: What are the Issues?" *In* Nora Lustig, (ed.), *Shielding the Poor: Social Protection in the Developing World.* Washington, DC: Brookings Institutiond and Inter-american Development Bank.

Jäntti, Markus, Juho Saari, and Juhana Vartiainen. 2005. "Country Case Study: Finland-Combining Growth with Equity." Background paper for the WDR 2006.

Jha, Saumitra, Vijayendra Rao, and Michael Woolcock. Forthcoming. "Governance in the Gullies: Democratic Responsiveness and Community Leadership in Delhi's Slums." *World Development.*

Johnson, Simon, and Todd Mitton. 2003. "Cronyism and Capital Controls: Evidence from Malaysia." *Journal of Financial Economics* 67(2):351–82.

Jonakin, Jon. 1996. "The Impact of Structural Adjustment and Property Rights Conflicts on Nicaraguan Agrarian Reform Beneficiaries." *World Development* 24(7):1179–91.

Kabeer, Naila. 1997. "Women, Wages and Intra-household Power Relations in Urban Bangladesh." *Development and Change* 28(2):261–302.

———. 1999. "Resources, Agency, Achievements: Reflections on the Measurement of Women's Empowerment." *Development and Change* 30(3):435–64.

Kakwani, Nanak, and Kalanidhi Subbarao. 2005. *Ageing and Poverty in Africa and the Role of Social Pensions.* Washington, DC: World Bank. Available on line at http://www-wds.worldbank.org/.

Kanbur, Rabi. 2000. "Income Distribution and Development." *In* Anthony B. Atkinson and François Bourguignon, (ed.), *Handbook of Income Distribution.* Amsterdam: North Holland.

Kanbur, Rabi, and Xiaobo Zhang. 2001. "Fifty Years of Regional Inequality in China: A Journey through Revolution, Reform and Openness." London: Centre for Economic Policy Research Discussion Paper 2887.

Kanbur, Ravi. 2005. "Pareto's Revenge." Cornell University. Ithaca, NY. Available on line at http://www.arts.cornell.edu/poverty/kanbur/ParRev.pdf. Processed.

Kang, David C. 2002. *Crony Capitalism: Corruption and Development in South Korea and the Philippines*. Cambridge, UK: Cambridge University Press.

Kariuki, Mukami, and Jordan Schwartz. 2005. "Small-Scale Private Service Providers of Water Supply and Electricity: A Review of Incidence, Structure, Pricing and Operating Characteristics." World Bank—Energy and Water Department, Bank Netherlands Water Partnership, Public-Private Infrastructure Advisory Facility. Washington, DC. Processed.

Karr-Morse, Robin, and Meredith S. Wiley. 1977. *Ghost from the Nursery: Tracing the Roots of Violence*. New York: Atlantic Monthly Press.

Kaufmann, Daniel, and Aart Kraay. 2002. "Growth without Governance." *Economia* 3(1):169–215.

Kaufmann, Daniel, Aart Kraay, and Massimo Mastruzzi. 2004. "Governance Matters III: Governance Indicators for 1996, 1998, 2000, and 2002." *World Bank Economic Review* 18(2):253–87.

———. 2005. "Governance Matters IV: Governance Indicators for 1996–2004." World Bank. Washington, DC. Available on line at http://www.worldbank.org/wbi/governance/pubs/govmatters4.html. Processed.

Kevane, Michael. 1996. "Agrarian Structure and Agricultural Practice: Typology and Application to Western Sudan." *American Journal of Agricultural Economics* 78(1):236–245.

Khan, Azizur Rahman, and Binayak Sen. 2001. "Inequality and Its Sources in Bangladesh: 1991/92 to 1995/96: An Analysis Based on Household Expenditure Surveys." *Bangladesh Development Studies* 27(1):1–50.

Khandker, Shahidur, Victor Lavy, and Deon Filmer. 1994. "Schooling and Cognitive Achievements of Children in Morocco: Can the Government Improve Outcomes?" Washington, DC: World Bank Discussion Paper 264.

Khwaja, Asim Ijaz, and Atif Mian. 2004. "Unchecked Intermediaries: Price Manipulation in an Emerging Stock Market." Boston: Bureau for Research in Economic Analysis of Development Working Paper 061. Available on line at http://www.cid.harvard.edu/bread/papers/working/061.pdf.

Kijima, Yoko, and Peter Lanjouw. 2004. "Agricultural Wages, Non-Farm Employment and Poverty in Rural India." World Bank. Washington, DC. Processed.

King, Elizabeth M., Peter F. Orazem, and Elizabeth M. Paterno. 1999. "Promotion with and without Learning: Effects on Students Dropouts." Washington, DC: World Bank Working Paper Series on Impact Evaluation of Education Reforms No. 18.

King, Steve. 1997. "Poor Relief and English Economic Development Reappraised." *Economic History Review* 50(2):360–68.

———. 2000. *Poverty and Welfare in England, 1700-1850: A Regional Perspective*. Manchester, UK: Manchester University Press.

Kingdon, Geeta, Justin Sandefur, and Francis Teal. 2005. "Patterns of Labor Demand in Sub-Saharan Africa: A Review paper." Centre for the Study of African Economies, Department of Economics, University of Oxford. Oxford, UK. Processed.

Kinsey, Bill H., and Hans P. Binswangser. 1993. "Characteristics and Performance of Resettlement Programs: A Review." *World Development* 21(9):1477–94.

Kirpal, Simone. 2002. "Communities Can Make a Difference: Five Cases Across Continents." *In* Mary Eming Young, (ed.), *From Early Childhood Development to Human Development: Investing in our Children's Future.* Washington, DC: World Bank.

Klarén, Peter Flindell. 2000. *Peru: Society and Nationhood in the Andes.* New York: Oxford University Press.

Klasen, Stephen. 2005. Comments on "Hepatitis B and the Case of the Missing Women" by Emily Oster. University of Göttingen. Processed.

Knack, Steven, and Philip Keefer. 1995. "Institutions and Economic Performance: Cross-Country Tests using Alternative Measures." *Economics and Politics* 7(3):207–27.

Kolm, Serge-Christophe. 1976. "Unequal Inequalities I." *Journal of Economic Theory* 12(3):416–42.

Korinek, Anton, Johan Mistiaen, and Martin Ravallion. Forthcoming. "Survey Non-response and the Distribution of Income." *Journal of Economic Inequality.*

Kraay, Aart. Forthcoming. "When is Growth Pro-Poor? Evidence from a Panel of Countries." *Journal of Development Economics.*

Kranton, Rachel E., and Anand V. Swamy. 1999. "The Hazards of Piecemeal Reform: British Civil Courts and the Credit Market in Colonial India." *Journal of Development Economics* 58(1):1–24.

Kremer, Michael. 1993. "The O-Ring Theory of Economic Development." *Quarterly Journal of Economics* 108(3):551–75.

Kremer, Michael, and Rachel Glennester. 2004. *Strong Medicine - Creating Incentives for Pharmaceutical Research on Neglected Diseases.* Princeton, NJ: Princeton University Press.

Kremer, Michael, Edward Miguel, and Rebecca Thornton. 2004. "Incentives to Learn." Cambridge, MA: National Bureau of Economic Research Working Paper Series 10971.

Kremer, Michael, Sylvie Moulin, and Robert Namunyu. 2002. "Unbalanced Decentralization." Harvard University. Cambridge, MA. Available on line at http://econ.bu.edu/dilipm/40-kremounam.pdf. Processed.

Kritzer, Herbert M. 2002. *Legal Systems of the World: A Political, Social and Cultural Encyclopedia.* Santa Barbara, CA: ABC-CLIO.

Krueger, Alan B., and Alexandre Mas. 2004. "Strikes, Scabs, and Tread Separations: Labor Strife and the Production of Defective Bridgestone/Firestone Tires." *Journal of Political Economy* 112(2):253–89.

Krugman, Paul. 1979. "A Model of Balance-of-Payments Crises." *Journal of Money, Credit, and Banking* 11(3):311–25.

———. 1999. "Balance Sheets, the Transfer Problem and Financial Crises." *In* P. Isard, A. Razin, A. K. Rose, and Kluwer Dordrecht, (ed.), *International Finance and Financial Crises, Essays in Honor of Robert P. Flood.* Netherlands and Washington, DC: Kluwer Academic Publishers and International Monetary Fund.

Kugler, Adriana. 2004. "The Effect of Job Security Regulations on Labor Market Flexibility: Evidence from the Colombian Labor Market Reform." Cambridge, MA: National Bureau of Economic Research Working Paper Series 10215.

Kugler, Adriana, Juan F. Jimeno, and Virginia Hernanz. 2003. "Employment Consequences of Restrictive Permanent Contracts." London: Centre for Economic Policy Research Discussion Paper 3724.

Kumar, Anjali. 2005. *Assessing Financial Access In Brazil.* Washington, DC: World Bank.

La Porta, Rafael, Florencio López-de-Silanes, and Guillermo Zamarripa. 2002. "Related Lending." Cambridge, MA: National Bureau of Economic Research Working Paper Series 8848.

Ladd, Hellen F. 2002. "School Vouchers: A Critical View." *Journal of Economic Perspectives* 16(4):3–24.

Laffont, Jean-Jacques, and Mohamed Salah Matoussi. 1995. "Moral Hazard, Financial Constraints and Sharecropping in El Oulja." *Review of Economic Studies* 62(3):381–99.

Lagos, Marta (2005). Personal communication with Marta Lagos, Director, Latinobarómetro.

Lang, James. 1975. *Conquest and Commerce: Spain and England in the Americas.* New York: Academic Press.

Langseth, Petter, and Oliver Stolpe. 2001. *Strengthening Judicial Corruption against Corruption.* Vienna: United Nations Office for Drug Control and Crime Prevention, Global Programme Against Corruption. Available on line at http://www.unodc.org/pdf/crime/gpacpublications/cicp10.pdf.

Lanjouw, Jean O. 2002. "A New Global Patent Regime for Diseases: U.S. and International Legal Issues." *Harvard Journal of Law and Technology* 16(1):85–124.

———. 2004. *Outline of the Foreign Filing License Approach.* Washington, DC: Center for Global Development.

Lanjouw, Jean O., and William Jack. 2004. "Trading Up: How Much Should Poor Countries Pay to Support Pharmaceutical Innovation?" *CGD Brief* 4(3):1–8.

Lanjouw, Jean O., and Margaret MacLeod. 2005. "Statistics Trends in Research on Tropical Diseases." Berkeley University. Berkeley, CA. Available on line at http://www.who.int/intellectualproperty/studies/Lanjouw_Statistical%20Trends.pdf. Processed.

Lanjouw, Peter, and Martin Ravallion. 2005. "Progresiveness of Social and Infrastructure Spending in India." World Bank. Washington, DC. Processed.

Larrain, Mauricio. 1989. "How the 1981–1983 Chilean Banking Crisis was Handled." Washington, DC: World Bank Working Paper 300.

Lavy, Victor. 1996. "School Supply Constraints and Children's Educational Outcomes in Rural Ghana." *Journal of Development Economics* 51(2):291–314.

Lees, Lynn Hollen. 1998. *The Solidarities of Strangers: The English Poor Laws and the People.* Cambridge, UK: Cambridge University Press.

Leipziger, Danny, Marianne Fay, Quentin Wodon, and Tito Yepes. 2003. "Achieving the Millennium Development Goals: The Role of Infrastructure." Washington, DC: World Bank Policy Research Working Paper Series 3163.

Leonard, Kenneth L., and Melkiory C. Masatu. 2005. "Variation in the Quality of Care Accessible to Rural Communities in Tanzania." University of Maryland. College Park, MD. Processed.

Levin, Victoria. 2005a. "Updating Aid Allocation Estimates." Background Note for the WDR Note 2006.

———. 2005b. "Updating the Poverty-efficient Aid Allocation to 2001." World Bank. Washington, DC. Processed.

Levin, Victoria, and David Dollar. 2005. "The Forgotten States: Aid Volumes and Volatility in Difficult Partnership Countries (1992–2002)." OECD, DAC Learning and Advisory Process on Difficult Partnerships. Paris. Available on line at http://www.oecd.org/dataoecd/32/44/34687926.pdf. Processed.

Lewin, Bryan, Daniele Giovannucci, and Panos Varangis. 2004. "Coffee Markets: New Paradigms in Global Supply and Demand." Washington, DC: World Bank, Agriculture and Rural Development Discussion Paper 3.

Lewis, Arthur. 1954. "Economic Development with Unlimited Supplies of Labor." *Manchester School of Economic and Social Studies* 22(2):139–91.

Lewis, M. 2002. "Informal Health Payments in Central and Eastern Europe and the Former Soviet Union: Issues, Trends and Policy Implications." *In* Elias Mossialos, Ana Dixon, Josep Figueras, and Joe Kutzin, (ed.), *Funding Health Care: Options for Europe.* Buckingham: Open University Press.

Lewis, Stephen. 2003. "Opening Address to the 13th International Conference on AIDS and STIs in Africa (ICASA)." Paper presented at the 13th International Conference on AIDS and STIs in Africa (ICASA). September 21. Nairobi.

Li, Hongyi, Lyn Squire, and Heng-fu Zou. 1998. "Explaining International and Intertemporal Variations in Income Inequality." *Economic Journal* 108(446):26–43.

Li, Hongyi, and Heng-fu Zou. 1998. "Income Inequality is not Harmful for Growth: Theory and Evidence." *Review of Development Economics* 2(3):318–34.

Li, R., X. Chen, H. Yan, P. Deurenberg, L. Garby, and J. G. Hautvast. 1994. "Functional Consequences of Iron Supplementation in Iron-deficient female Cotton Workers in Beijing China." *American Journal of Clinical Nutrition* 59(4):908–13.

Liddle, R. William. 1991. "The Relative Autonomy of the Third World Politician: Soeharto and Indonesian Economic Development in Comparative Perspective." *International Studies Quarterly* 35(4):403–27.

Lillard, Lee A., and Robert J. Willis. 1994. "Intergenerational Educational Mobility: Effects of Family and State in Malaysia." *Journal of Human Resources* 29(4):1126–66.

Lindert, Peter H. 2003. "Voice and Growth: Was Churchill Right?" *Journal of Economic History* 63(2):315–50.

———. 2004. *Growing Public: Social Spending and Economics Growth since the Eighteenth Century.* Cambridge, UK: Cambridge University Press.

Lindert, Peter H., and Jeffrey G. Williamson. 1982. "Revising England's Social Tables, 1688–1812." *Explorations in Economic History* 19(4):385–408.

———. 1983. "Reinterpreting Britain's Social Tables, 1688–1913." *Explorations in Economic History* 20(1):94–109.

Lipset, Seymour M. 1959. "Some Social Requisites of Democracy: Economic Development and Political Legitimacy." *American Political Science Review* 53(1):69–105.

Llorente, María, and Angela Rivas. 2005. "Reduction of Crime in Bogota: A Decade of Citizen's Security Policies." World Bank, Department of Finance, Private Secton and Infrastructure. Washington, DC. Processed.

Lloyd, Cynthia B., eds. 2005. *Growing up Global: The Changing Transitions to Adulthood in Developing Countries.* Washington, DC: The National Academies Press.

Lloyd, Tim, Wyn Morgan, Tony Rayner, and Charlotte Vaillant. 1999. "The Transmission of World Agricultural Prices in Côte d'Ivoire." *Journal of International Trade and Economic Development* 8(1):125–41.

Lockhart, James B. 1969. "Encomienda and Hacienda: The Evolution of the Great Estate in the Spanish Indies." *Hispanic American Historical Review* 49(3):411–29.

Lockhart, James B., and Stuart B. Schwartz. 1983. *Early Latin America: A History of Colonial Spanish and America and Brazil.* Cambridge, UK: Cambridge University Press.

Lokshin, Michael, and Martin Ravallion. 2000. "Welfare Impacts of the 1998 Financial Crisis in Russia and the Response of the Public Safety Net." *Economics of Transition* 8(2):269–95.

López, Alan D. 2000. "Reducing Chile's Mortality." *Bulletin of the World Health Organization* 78(10):1173–73.

López, J. Humberto. 2004. "Pro-growth, Pro-poor: Is there a Trade-off?" Washington, DC: World Bank Policy Research Working Paper Series 3378.

Loury, Glenn C. 2002. *The Anatomy of Racial Inequality.* Cambridge, MA: Harvard University Press.

Lucas, Robert. 2003. *The Industrial Revolution: Past and Future.* Minneapolis: Federal Reserve Bank of Minneapolis.

Lund, Frances. 1999. "Understanding South African Social Security through Recent Household Surveys: New Opportunities and Continuing Gaps." *Development Southern Africa* 16(1):55–67.

Lundberg, Mattias, and Lyn Squire. 2003. "The Simultaneous Evolution of Growth and Inequality." *Economic Journal* 113(487):326–44.

Lundberg, Shelley J., Robert A. Pollak, and Terence J. Wales. 1997. "Do Husbands and Wives Pool their Resources?" *Journal of Human Resources* 32(3):463–80.

Luttmer, Erzo F. P. 2004. "Neighbors as Negatives: Relative Earnings and Well-Being." Cambridge, MA: Faculty Research Working Paper Series 4-029.

MacIntyre, Andrew. 2001a. "Institutions and Investors: The Politics of the Economic Crisis in Southeast Asia." *International Organization* 55(1):81–122.

————. 2001b. "Rethinking the Politics of Agricultural Policy Making: The Importance of Institutions." *In* J. Edgard Campos, (ed.), *The Evolving Roles of State, Private, and Local Actors in Asian Rural Development.* Cambridge, UK: Oxford University Press.

Maddison, Angus. 1995. *Monitoring the World Economy:1820–1992.* Paris: Development Centre of the Organisation for Economic Co-operation and Development.

Mahoney, James. 2001. *The Legacies of Liberalism: Path Dependence and Political Regimes in Central America.* Baltimore, MD: Johns Hopkins University Press.

Malik, Waleed Haider. 2005. "Guatemala: The Role of Judicial Modernization in Post Conflict Reconciliation." Washington, DC: Social Development Notes, World Bank 99.

Malmberg Calvo, Christina. 1994. "Case Study on the Role of Women in Rural Transport: Access of Women to Domestic Facilities." World Bank and Economic Commission for Africa, Washington, DC: Sub-Saharan Africa Transport Policy Program Working Paper 11.

Maloney, William F. 1999. "Does Informality Imply Segmentation in Urban Labor Markets? Evidence from Sectoral Transitions in Mexico." *World Bank Economic Review* 13(2):275–302.

Maloncy, William F., and Jairo Nuñez Mendez. 2004. "Measuring the Impact of Minimum Wages, Evidence from Latin America." *In* James Heckman and Carmen Pagés, (ed.), *Law and Labor Markets.* Chicago: University of Chicago Press.

Mamdani, Mahmood. 1996. *Citizen and Subject: Contemporary Africa and the Legacy of Late Colonialism.* Princeton, NJ: Princeton University Press.

Manor, James. 1999. *The Political Economy of Democratic Decentralization.* Washington, DC: World Bank.

Marmot, Michael G. 2004. *The Status Syndrome: How Social Standing Affects our Health and Longevity.* New York: Times Books.

Mason, Karen O., and Helene M. Carlsson. Forthcoming. "The Development Impact of Gender Equality in Land Rights." *In* Philip Alston and Mary Robinson (ed.) *Human Rights and Development: Towards Mutual Reinforcement.* New York: Oxford University Press.

Massey, D. 2001. "The Progress in Human Geography Lecture, Geography on the Agenda." *Progress in Human Geography* 25(1):5–17.

Masters, Williams A. 2005. "Paying for Prosperity: How and Why to Invest in Agricultural R&D for Development in Africa." *Journal of International Affairs* 58(2):35–64.

Masters, Williams A., F. T. Sparrow, and Brian H. Bowen. 1999. *Modeling Electricity Trade in Southern Africa 1999–2000.* West Lafayette, Indiana: Purdue University. Available on line at https://engineering.purdue.edu/IE/Research/PEMRG/PPDG/SAPP/1999proposal.pdf.

Mattei, U. 1998. "Legal Pluralism, Legal Change and Economic Development." *In* Lyda Favali, E. Grande, and M. Guadagni, (ed.), *New Law for New States.* Torino, Italy: L'Harmattan Italia.

Mattoo, Aaditya, Ileana Cristina Neagu, and Caglar Ozden. 2005. "Brain Waste? Educated Immigrants in the U.S. Labor Market." Washington, DC: World Bank Policy Research Working Paper Series 3581.

Maurer, Stephen M., Andrej Sali, and Arti Rai. 2004. "Finding Cures for Tropical Disease: Is Open Source the Answer?" *Public Library of Science: Medicine* 1(3):33–7.

Maynard, E., eds. 1966. *The Indians of Colta. Essays on the Colta Lake Zone, Chimborazo (Ecuador).* Ithaca, NY: Cornell University.

Mazumder, Bhakshar. 2005. "The Apple Falls Even closer to the Tree than We Thought: New and Revised Estimates of the Intergenerational Inheritance of Earnings." *In* Samuel Bowles, Herbert Gintis, and Melissa Osborne Groves, (ed.), *Unequal Chances: Family*

Background and Economic Success. Princeton, NJ: Princeton University Press.

McEwan, Patrick J. 2000. "The Impact of Vouchers on School Efficiency: Empirical Evidence from Chile." Ph.D. thesis. Stanford University.

McEwan, Patrick J., and Martin Carnoy. 2000. "The Effectiveness and Efficiency of Private Schools in Chile's Voucher System." *Educational Evaluation and Policy Analysis* 22(3):213–39.

McGillivray, Mark. 2005. "Aid Allocation and Fragile States." Paper presented at the Senior Level Forum on Development Effectiveness in Fragile States. January 13. London.

McKay, Andrew, Oliver Morrissey, and Charlotte Vaillant. 1997. "Trade Liberalization and Agricultural Supply Response: A Study of Rural Asia." *European Journal of Development* 9(2):129–47.

McKenzie, David, and Dilip Mookherjee. 2003. "Distributive Impact of Privatization in Latin America: An Overview of Evidence from Four Countries." *Economia* 3(2):161–218.

McKenzie, David, and Hillel Rapoport. 2004. "Network Effects and the Dynamics of Migration and Inequality: Theory and Evidence from Mexico." Washington DC: BREAD Working Paper Series 63.

McKenzie, David, and Christopher Woodruff. 2003. "Do Entry Costs Provide an Empirical Basis for Poverty Traps? Evidence from Mexican Microenterprises." Cambridge, MA: Harvard University, Bureau for Research in Economic Analysis of Development (BREAD) Working Paper 20. Available on line at http://www.cid.harvard.edu/bread/papers/working/020.pdf.

McMillan, Margaret, Dani Rodrik, and Karen Horn Welch. 2002. "When Economic Reform Goes Wrong: Cashews in Mozambique." Cambridge, MA: National Bureau of Economic Research Working Paper Series 9117.

Meesen, Bruno, and Wim Van Damme. 2004. "Health Equity in Cambodia, A New Approach to Fee Exemptions." Paper presented at the Reaching the Poor with Effective Health, Nutrition, and Population Services: What Works, What Doesn't, and Why. February 18. Washington, DC.

Melo, Jorge Orlando. 1996. *Historia de Colombia: La Dominación Española.* Bogotá: Biblioteca Familiar.

Mendola, Mariapia. 2004. "Migration and Technological Change in Rural Households: Complements or Substitutes?" Milano, Italy: Centro Study Luca d'Agliano, Development Studies Working Paper 195.

Mesnard, Alice, and Martin Ravallion. 2004. "The Wealth Effects on New Business Startups in a Developing Economy." Institute of Fiscal Studies and World Bank. London, U.K. and Washington, DC. Available on line at http://www.cefims.ac.uk/pdfs/mesnard_paper.pdf. Processed.

Meyer, Richard, and Geetha Nagarajan. 2000. "Rural Financial Markets in Asia: Policies, Paradigms, and Performance." *In* Asian Development Bank, (ed.), *A Study of Rural Asia vol. 3.* Hong Kong, China: Oxford University Press for the Asian Development Bank.

Miguel, Edward, and Michael Kremer. 2004. "Worms: Identifying Impacts on Education and Health in the Presence of Treatment Externalities." *Econometrica* 72(1):159–217.

Milanovic, Branko. 2002. "Can We Discern the Effect of Globalization on Income Distribution? Evidence from Household Surveys." Washington, DC: World Bank Policy Research Report Working Paper Series 2876.

—————. 2005. *Worlds Apart: International and Global Inequality 1950-2000.* Princeton, NJ: Princeton University Press.

Minot, Nicholas W. 1998. "Distributional and Nutritional Impact of Devaluation in Rwanda." *Economic Development and Cultural Change* 46(2):379–402.

Minot, Nicholas W., and Lisa Daniels. 2002. "Impact of Global Cotton Markets on Rural Poverty in Benin." Washington, DC: International Food Policy Research Institute Discussion Paper 48.

Minot, Nicholas W., and Francesco Goletti. 1998. "Rice Market Liberalization and Poverty in Vietnam." Washington, DC: International Food Policy Research Institute Research Report 114.

Moene, Karl Ove, and Michael Wallerstein. 2002. "Social Democracy as a Development Strategy." University of Oslo, Department of Economics: Memorandum 35/2003.

Moncrieffe, Joy. 2005. "Beyond Categories: Power, Recognition, and the Conditions for Equity." Background paper for the WDR 2006.

Montenegro, Claudio E., and Carmen Pagés. 2004. "Who Benefits from Labor Market Regulations?" *In* James Heckman and Carmen Pagés, (ed.), *Law and Employment: Lessons from the Latin American and the Caribbean.* Chicago: University of Chicago Press. Reprinted in Jorge Enrique Restrepo and Andrea Tokman R. (ed.) *"Labor Markets and Institutions,"* (2005), Santiago de Chile: Banco Central de Chile.

Montinola, Gabriela, Yingyi Qian, and Barry Weingast. 1995. "Federalism Chinese-Style: The Political Basis for Economic Success in China." *World Politics* 48(1):50–81.

Moore, Barrington Jr. 1966. *The Social Origins of Dictatorship and Democracy: Lord and Peasant in the Making of the Modern World.* Boston, MA: Beacon Press.

Moore, Mick. 2001. "Political Underdevelopment: What Causes 'Bad Governance'?" *Public Management Review* 3(3):385–418.

—————. 2004. "Revenues, State Formation, and the Quality of Governance in Developing Countries." *International Political Science Review* 25(3):297–319.

Morales, Juan Antonio, and Jeffrey D. Sachs. 1998. "Bolivia's Economic Crisis." Cambridge, MA: National Bureau of Economic Research Working Paper Series 2620.

Morck, Randall, Daniel Wolfenzon, and Bernard Yeung. 2004. "Corporate Governance, Economic Entrenchment and Growth." Cambridge, MA: National Bureau of Economic Research Working Paper Series 10692.

Morck, Randall, and Bernard Yeung. 2004. "Special Issues Relating to Corporate Governance and Family Control." Washington, DC: World Bank Policy Research Working Paper Series 3406.

Morck, Randall K., David A. Stangeland, and Bernard Yeung. 2000. "Inherited Wealth, Corporate Control, and Economic Growth: The Canadian Disease?" *In* Randall Morck, (ed.), *Concentrated Corporate Ownership. National Bureau of Economic Research Conference Volume.* Chicago: University of Chicago Press.

Morduch, Jonathan. 1993. "Risk Production and Saving: Theory and Evidence from Indian Households." Cambridge, MA. Harvard University. Processed.

Morgan, Edmund S. 1975. *American Slavery, American Freedom: The Ordeal of Colonial Virginia.* New York: W. W. Norton & Co.

Morley, Samuel. 2001. *The Income Distribution Problem in Latin America and the Caribbean.* Santiago de Chile: Economic Commission for Latin American and the Caribbean.

Morley, Samuel, and David Coady. 2003. *From Social Assistance to Social Development: A Review of Targeted Education Subsidies in Developing Countries.* Washington, DC: International Food Policy Research Institute.

Mörner, Magnus. 1973. "The Spanish American Hacienda: A Survey of Recent Research and Debate." *Hispanic American Historical Review* 53(2):183–216.

Morrison, Andrew, Mary Ellsberg, and Sarah Bott. 2004. "Addressing Gender-Based Violence in the Latin American and Caribbean Region: A Critical Review of Interventions." Washington, DC: World Bank Policy Research Report Working Paper Series 3438.

Mtani, Anna. 2002. "Safety Audits and Beyond." Paper presented at the First International Seminar on Women's Safety. May 9. Montreal.

Mundlak, Yair, and Donald F. Larson. 1992. "On the Transmission of World Agricultural Prices." *World Bank Economic Review* 6(3):399–422.

Munshi, Kaivan. 2003. "Networks in the Modern Economy: Mexican Migrants in the U.S. Labor Markets." *Quarterly Journal of Economics* 118(2):549–97.

Munshi, Kaivan, and Mark Rosenzweig. Forthcoming. "Traditional Institutions Meet the Modern World: Caste, Gender and Schooling in a Globalizing Economy." *American Economic Review.*

Murgai, Rinku, and Martin Ravallion. 2005. "A Guaranteed Living Wage in Rural India: Who Would Gain and at What Cost?" World Bank, Washington, DC. Processed.

Mwaikusa, Jwani T. 1995. "Maintaining Law and Order in Tanzania: The Role of Sungusungu Defence Groups." *In* Joseph Semboja and Ole Therkildsen, (ed.), *Service Provision Under Stress in East Africa: The State, NGOs, and People's Organizations in Kenya, Tanzania, and Uganda.* Copenhagen: Center for Development Research.

Myers, Robert. 1995. *The Twelve Who Survive: Strengthening Programs of Early Childhood Development in the Third World.* Ypsilanti, MI: High Scope Press.

Narayan, A., and N. Yoshida. 2004. "Poverty in Sri Lanka: The Impact of Growth with Rising Inequality." Paper presented at the World Development Consultation Meeting. December 12. Delhi.

Narayan, Deepa, eds. 2002. *Empowerment and Poverty Reduction: A Sourcebook.* Washington, DC: World Bank.

Neumark, David, Wendy Cunningham, and Lucas Siga. Forthcoming. "The Effects of Minimum Wages in Brazil on the Distribution of Family Incomes: 1996–2001." *Journal of Development Economics.*

Newman, John, Steen Jorgensen, and Menno Pradhan. 1992. "How Did Workers Benefit?" *In* Steen Jorgensen, Margaret Grosh, and Mark Schacter, (ed.), *Bolivia's Answer to Poverty, Economic Crisis and Adjustment: The Emergency Social Fund.* Washington, DC: World Bank.

Nicita, Alessandro. 2004. "Who Benefited from Trade Liberalization in Mexico? Measuring the Effects on Household Welfare." Washington, DC: World Bank Policy Research Working Paper Series 3265.

Nickell, Stephen. 1997. "Unemployment and Labor Market Rigidities: Europe versus North America." *Journal of Economic Perspectives* 11(3):55–74.

Nielsen, Robin, and Tim Hanstad. 2004. "From Sharecroppers to Landowners: Paving the Way for West Bengal's Bargadars." Seattle, WA: Rural Development Institute, Reports on Foreign Aid 121. Available on line at http://www.rdiland.org/PDF/PDF_Reports/RDI_121.pdf.

North, Douglas C. 1981. *Structure and Change in Economic History.* New York: W. W. Norton & Co.

North, Douglas C., and Robert P. Thomas. 1973. *The Rise of the Western World: A New Economic History.* Cambridge, U.K.: Cambridge University Press.

North, Douglas C., and Barry R. Weingast. 1989. "Constitutions and Commitment: The Evolution of Institutions Governing Public Choice in Seventeenth-Century England." *Journal of Economic History* 49(4):803–32.

Nozick, Robert. 1974. *Anarchy, State And Utopia.* New York: Basic Books.

Nussbaum, Martha C. 2000. *Women and Human Development: The Capabilities Approach.* New York: Cambridge University Press.

O'Brien, Patrick K. 1993. "Political Preconditions for the Industrial Revolution." *In* Patrick O'Brien and Roland Quinault, (ed.), *The Industrial Revolution and British Society.* Cambridge, UK: Cambridge University Press.

O'Rourke, Kevin H., and Jeffrey G. Williamson. 2002. "From Malthus to Ohlin: Trade, Growth and Distribution Since 1500." Cambridge, MA: National Bureau of Economic Research Working Paper Series 8955.

O'Sullivan, Robert, and Amiee Christensen. 2005. "Equity and Inequity in the Context of Climate Change." Background note for the WDR 2006.

Obstfeld, Maurice. 1996. "Models of Currency Crises with Self-fulfilling Features." *European Economic Review* 40(3-5):1037–47.

OECD. 1999. *Employment Outlook.* Paris: Organisation for Economic Co-operation and Development.

————. 2000. *Hard Core Cartels.* Paris: Organisation for Economic Co-operation and Development. Available on line at http://www.oecd.org/dataoecd/36/24/2367816.pdf.

————. 2003. *Agricultural Policies in OECD Countries: Monitoring and Evaluation 2003.* Paris: Organisation for Economic Co-operation and Development. Available on line at www1.oecd.org/publications/e-book/5103081E.PDF.

————. 2005. "OECD Productivity Database (February 2005 version)". Paris, Organisation for Economic Co-operation and Development.

OECD-DAC. 2004. *Development Cooperation Report Statistical Annex 2004.* Paris: Organization for Economic Co-operation and Development. Available on line at http://www.oecd.org/document/9/0,2340,en_2649_33721_1893129_1_1_1_1,00.html.

Olley, G. Steven, and Ariel Pakes. 1996. "The Dynamics of Productivity in the Telecommunications Equipment Industry." *Econometrica* 64(6):1263–97.

Osberg, Lars, and Timothy Smeeding. 2004. "'Fair' Inequality?: An International Comparison of Attitudes to Pay Differentials." Dalhousie University. Dalhousie. Available on line at http://wwwcpr.maxwell.syr.edu/faculty/smeeding/selectedpapers/Economicaversion27October2004.pdf. Processed.

Oster, Emily. 2005. "Hepatitis B and the Case of the Missing Women." Cambridge, MA: Harvard University, CID Graduate Student and Postdoctoral Fellow Working Paper 7. Available on line at http://www.cid.harvard.edu/cidwp/graduate.html.

Paes de Barros, Ricardo, and Mirela de Carvalho. 2004. "Targeting as an Instrument for a more Effective Social Policy." Inter-American Development Bank. Washington, DC. Available on line at http://www.iadb.org/sds/doc/POV-SEFVI-Barros_Carvalho.pdf. Processed.

Palandt, Otto. 2004. *Bürgerliches Gesetzbuch.* Munich: C. H. Beck.

Palmade, Vincent. 2005. "Industry Level Analysis: The Way to Identify the Binding Constraints to Economic Growth." Washington, DC: World Bank Policy Research Working Paper Series 3551.

Panagides, Alexis, and Harry Anthony Patrinos. 1994. "Union-nonunion Wage Differentials in the Developing World: A Case Study of Mexico." Washington, DC: World Bank Policy Research Report Working Paper Series 1269.

Pande, Rohini. 2003. "Can Mandated Political Representation Increase Policy Influence for the Disadvantaged Minorities? Theory and Evidence from India." *American Economic Review* 93(4):1132–51.

Parry, John H. 1948. *The Audiencia of New Galicia in the Sixteenth Century: A Study in Spanish Colonial Government.* Cambridge, UK: Cambridge University Press.

Pathmanathan, Indra, Jerke Liljestrand, Jo M. Martins, Lalini C. Rajapaksa, Craig Lissner, Amalia de Silva, Swarna Selvajuru, and Prabha Joginder Singh. 2003. *Investing in Maternal Health: Learning from Malaysia and Sri Lanka.* Washington, DC: World Bank.

Paxson, Christina H., and Norbert Schady. 2004. "Child Health and Economic Crisis in Peru." Washington, DC: World Bank Policy Research Working Paper Series 3260.

————. 2005. "Cognitive Development among Young Children in Ecuador: The Roles of Wealth, Health and Parenting." Washington, DC: World Bank Policy Research Working Paper Series 3605.

Payne, Geoffrey, eds. 2002. *Land, Rights, and Innovation: Improving Tenure for the Urban Poor.* London, UK: ITDG Publishing.

Payne, Geoffrey, and Michael Majale. 2004. *The Urban Housing Manual: Making Regulatory Frameworks Work for the Poor.* London, U.K.: Earthscan Publications.

Perotti, Enrico. 2002. "Lessons from the Russian Meltdown: The Economics of Soft Legal Constraints." *International Finance* 5(3):359–99.

Perotti, Enrico, and Erik Feijen. 2005. "Lobbying for Exit: The Political Economy of Financial Fragility." University of Amsterdam. Amsterdam. Available on line at http://papers.ssrn.com/sol3/papers.cfm?abstract_id=686661. Processed.

Perotti, Enrico, and Paolo Volpin. 2004. "Lobbying on Entry." London, UK: Centre for Economic Policy Research Discussion Paper Series 4519.

Perry, Guillermo. 2003. "Can Fiscal Rules Reduce Macroeconomic Volatility in the Latin American and Caribbean Region?" Washington, DC: World Bank Policy Research Working Paper Series 3080.

Petesch, Patti, Catalina Smulovitz, and Michael Walton. 2005. "Evaluating Empowerment: A Framework with Cases from Latin America." *In* Deepa Narayan, (ed.), *Measuring Empowerment: Cross-disciplinary Perspectives.* Washington, DC: World Bank.

Piketty, Thomas. 1995. "Social Mobility and Redistributive Politics." *Quarterly Journal of Economics* 110(3):551–84.

Pinglé, Vibha. 2005. "Faith, Equity, and Development." Background paper for the WDR 2006.

Pinto, Brian, Evsey Gurvich, and Sergei Ulatov. Forthcoming. "Lessons from the Russia Crisis of 1998 and Recovery." *In* Joshua Aizenman and Brian Pinto (ed.) *Managing Volatility and Crisis: A Practitioner's Guide.* Washington, DC: World Bank.

Pistor, Katharina, and Phillip A. Wellons. 1999. *The Role of Law and Legal Institutions in Asian Economic Development: 1960-1995.* Hong Kong, China: Oxford University Press for the Asian Development Bank.

Pitayarangsarit, Siriwan. 2004. "Agenda Setting Process." *In* Viroj Tangcharoensathien and Pongpisut Jongudomsuk, (ed.), *From Policy to Implementation: Historical Events During 2001–2004 of Universal Coverage in Thailand.* Nonthaburi, Thailand: National Health Security Office.

Pogge, Thomas W. 2004. "Assisting the Global Poor." *In* Deen K. Chatterjee, (ed.), *The Ethics of Assistance: Morality and the Distant Needy.* Cambridge, UK: Cambridge University Press.

Pollitt, E., W. E. Watkins, and M. A. Husaini. 1997. "Three-Month Nutritional Supplementation in Indonesian Infants and Toddlers Benefits Memory Function 8 Years Later." *American Journal of Clinical Nutrition* 66(6):1357–363.

Pradhan, Menno, David E. Sahn, and Stephen D. Younger. 2003. "Decomposing World Health Inequality." *Journal of Health Economics* 22(2):271–93.

Preker, Alexander, and Guy Carrin, eds. 2004. *Health Financing for Poor People: Resource Mobilization and Risk Sharing.* Washington, DC: World Bank.

Preston, Samuel H. 1980. "Causes and Consequences of Mortality Declines in Less Developed Countries During the Twentieth Century." *In* Richard Easterlin, (ed.), *Population and Economic Change in Developing Countries.* Chicago: University of Chicago Press.

Pritchett, Lant. 1997. "Divergence: Big Time." *Journal of Economic Perspectives* 11(3):3–17.

————. 2001. "Where Has All the Education Gone?" *World Bank Economic Review* 15(3):367–91.

————. 2003. "The Future of Migration: Irresistible Forces Meet Immovable Ideas." Paper presented at the The Future of Globalization: Explorations in Ligth of the Recent Turbulence Conference. October 11. New Haven, CT.

————. 2004a. "Towards a New Consensus for Addressing the Global Challenge of the Lack of Education." Kennedy School of Government, Harvard University. Cambridge, MA. Available on line at http://www.copenhagenconsensus.com/Files/Filer/CC/Papers/ Education_230404.pdf. Processed.

————. 2004b. "Does Learning to Add Up Add Up? The Returns to Schooling in Aggregate Data." Cambridge, MA: Bureau for Research in Economic Analysis of Development (BREAD) Working Paper 053.

————. Forthcoming. "Who is *Not* Poor? Dreaming of a World Truly Free of Poverty." *World Bank Research Observer.*

Prud'Homme, Rémy. 1990. "Decentralization of Expenditures or Taxes: The Case of France." *In* Robert J. Bennett, (ed.), *Decentralization, Local Governments, and Markets.* Oxford, UK: Clarendon Press.

Psacharopoulos, George, and Harry Anthony Patrinos. 1994. *Indigenous People and Poverty in Latin America: An Empirical Analysis.* Washington, DC: World Bank.

Pulley, Robert V. 1989. "Making the Poor Creditworthy: A Case Study of the Integrated Rural Development Program in India." Washington, DC: World Bank Discussion Paper 58.

Qian, Yingyi. 2003. "How Reform Worked in China." *In* Dani Rodrik, (ed.), *In Search of Prosperity: Analytic Narratives of Economic Growth.* Princeton, NJ: Princeton University Press.

Quisumbing, Agnes R., Jona P. Estudillo, and Keijiro Otsuka. 2004. *Land and Schooling: Transferring Wealth Across Generations.* Baltimore, MD: Johns Hopkins University Press.

Quisumbing, Agnes R., and John A. Maluccio. 2003. "Resources at Marriage and Intrahousehold Allocation: Evidence from Bangladesh, Ethiopia, Indonesia, and South Africa." *Oxford Bulletin of Economics and Statistics* 65(3):283–327.

Rabin, Mathew. 1993. "Incorporating Fairness Into Game Theory and Economics." *American Economic Review* 83(5):1281–302.

Rahman, Lupin, and Vijayendra Rao. 2004. "The Determinants of Gender Equity in India: Examining Dyson and Moore's Thesis with New Data." *Population and Development Review* 30(2):239–68.

Rajan, Ragurham G., and Luigi Zingales. 2003. *Saving Capitalism from the Capitalists: Unleashing the Power of Financial Markets to create Wealth and Spread Opportunity.* New York: Crown Business.

Ranson, Kent, Tara Sinha, Mirai Chatterjee, Akash Adharya, Ami Bhavsar, Saul Morris, and Anne J. Mills. 2005. "Making Health Insurance Work for the Poor: Learning from SEWA's Community-based Health Insurance Scheme." Processed.

Rao, Vijayendra. 2005. "Symbolic Public Goods and the Coordination of Collective Action: A Comparison of Local Development in India and Indonesia." Background paper for the WDR 2006.

Rao, Vijayendra, and Michael Walton. 2004. *Culture and Public Action.* Stanford, CA: Stanford University Press.

Ravallion, Martin. 1991. "Reaching the Rural Poor through Public Employment: Arguments, Evidence and Lessons from South Asia." *World Bank Research Observer* 6(2):153–75.

————. 2001. "Growth, Inequality and Poverty: Looking Beyond Averages." *World Development* 29(11):1803–15.

————. 2003. "Targeted Transfers in Poor Countries: Revisiting the Trade-Offs and Policy Options." Washington, DC: World Bank Social Protection Discussion Paper Series 0314.

————. 2004a. "Competing Concepts of Inequality in the Globalization Debate." *In* Susan Margaret Collins and Carol Graham, (ed.), *Brookings Trade Forum 2004.* Washington, DC: Brookings Institution.

————. 2004b. "Looking Beyond Averages in the Trade and Poverty Debate." Washington, DC: World Bank Policy Research Working Paper Series 3461.

————. 2005. "Why Should Poor People Care about Inequality?" Background paper for the WDR 2006.

Ravallion, Martin, and Shaohua Chen. 1997. "What Can New Survey Data Tell us about Recent Changes in Distribution and Poverty?" *World Bank Economic Review* 11(2):357–82.

————. 2004. "China's (Uneven) Progress Against Poverty." Washington, DC: World Bank Policy Research Working Paper Series 3408.

Ravallion, Martin, and Michael Lokshin. 2002. "Self-rated Economic Welfare in Russia." *European Economic Review* 46(8):1453–73.

Ravallion, Martin, and Quentin Wodon. 1999. "Poor Areas, or only Poor People?" *Journal of Regional Science* 39(4):689–711.

Rawlings, Laura B. 2004. "A New Approach to Social Assistance: Latin America's Experience with Conditional Cash Transfer Programs." Washington, DC: World Bank, Social Protection Discussion Paper Series 0416.

Rawls, John. 1971. *A Theory of Justice.* Cambridge, MA: Harvard University Press.

Revenga, Ana. 1991. "La Liberalización Económica y la Distribución de la Renta: La Experiencia Española." *Moneda y Crédito* 193:179–224.

Ricupero, Rubens. 2005. "Why Should Small Developing Countries Engage in the Global Trading System? Three Points of View on a Hot Topic in the Doha Round: Overcoming Fear First." *Finance and Development* 42(1):10–11.

Ringera, A., J. W. Onyango-Otieno, W. Karanja, and M. W. Muigai. 2003. *An Anatomy of Corruption in the Kenyan Judiciary: The Report of the Integrity and Anti-Corruption Committee of the Judiciary.* Nairobi, Kenya: The Judiciary.

Ringold, Dena, Mitchell A. Orenstein, and Erika Wilkens. 2005. *Roma in an Expanding Europe: Breaking the Poverty Cycle.* Washington, DC: World Bank.

Robinson, James. 2003. "Politician-Proof Policy?" Washington, DC: World Bank, Working Paper 26945. Available on line at http://www.people.fas.harvard.edu/~jrobins/researchpapers/ unpublishedpapers/jr_WDR2004.pdf.

Rock, Michael T. 2003. "The Politics of Development Policy and Development Policy Reform in New Order Indonesia." Ann Arbor, MI: University of Michigan, William Davidson Institute Working Paper 632.

Rodrik, Dani. 1998. "Why Do More Open Economies Have Bigger Governments?" *Journal of Political Economy* 106(5):997–1032.

————. 1999a. "Where Did All the Growth Go? External Shocks, Social Conflict, and Growth Collapses." *Journal of Economic Growth* 4(4):385–412.

————. 1999b. "Democracies Pay Higher Wages." *Quarterly Journal of Economics* 114(3):707–38.

Rodrik, Dani, Arvind Subramanian, and Francesco Trebbi. 2002. "Institutions Rule: The Primacy of Institutions over Geography and Integration in Economic Development." Cambridge, MA: National Bureau of Economic Research Working Paper Series 9305.

Roemer, John E. 1998. *Equality of Opportunity.* Cambridge, MA: Harvard University Press.

Roland, Gérard, and Thierry Verdier. 2000. "Law Enforcement and Transition." London, UK: Centre for Economic Policy Research Discussion Paper Series 2501.

Ronchi, Loraine. 2001. "The Impact of Fair Trade on Producers and Their Organizations: A Case Study with Coocafe in Costa Rica." Brighton: University of Sussex, Poverty Research Unit Working Paper 11. Available on line at http://www.sussex.ac.uk/Units/PRU/wps/wp11.pdf.

————. 2002. *Monitoring Impact of Fair Trade Initiatives: A Case Study of Kuapa Kokoo and the Day Chocolate Company.* London: Twinsight. TWIN. Available on line at http://www.divinechocolate.com/ImpactAssessmentLeaflet.pdf.

Rosenzweig, Mark R., and Hans P. Binswanger. 1993. "Wealth, Weather Risk and the Composition and Profitability of Agricultural Investments." *Economic Journal* 103(416):56–78.

Rosenzweig, Mark R., and Kenneth I. Wolpin. 1993. "Credit Market Constraints, Consumption Smoothing, and the Accumulation of Durable Production Assets in Low-income Countries: Investments in Bullocks in India." *Journal of Political Economy* 101(2):223–44.

Ross, Michael. 2005. "Mineral Wealth and Equitable Development." Background paper for the WDR 2006.

Rothstein, Jesse. 2005. "Does Competition Among Public Schools Benefit Students and Taxpayers? A Comment on Hoxby (2000)." Cambridge, MA: National Bureau of Economic Research Working Paper Series 11215.

Rudnik, Rebecca S., and Richard K. Gordon. 1996. "Taxation of Wealth." *In* Victor Thuronyi, (ed.), *Tax Law Design and Drafting.* Washington, DC: International Monetary Fund.

Russel, Peter H., and David M. O'Brien, eds. 2001. *Judicial Independence in the Age of Democracy: Critical Perspectives from Around the World.* Charlottesville, VA: University of Virginia Press.

Rutter, Michael, Henri Giller, and Ann Hagell. 2000. *Antisocial Behavior by Young People.* Cambridge, UK: Cambridge University Press.

Sala-i-Martin, Xavier. 2002. "Unhealthy People are Poor People . . . And vice-versa." Paper presented at the European Conference on Health Economics of the International Health Economics Association. July 7. Paris.

Samuels, David, and Richard Snyder. 2001. "Devaluing the Vote in Latin America." *Journal of Democracy* 12(1):146–59.

Sánchez-Páramo, Carolina, and Norbert Schady. 2003. "Off and Running? Technology, Trade, and the Rising Demand for Skilled Workers in Latin America." Washington, DC: World Bank Policy Research Working Paper Series 3015.

Savedoff, William D. 2004. "Is there a Case for Social Insurance?" *Health Policy and Planning* 19(3):183–84.

Schady, Norbert. 2005. "Changes in the Global Distribution of Life Expectancy and Education." World Bank. Washington, DC. Processed.

Schieber, George. 2005. "Financing Health Systems in the 21st Century." World Bank. Washington, DC. Processed.

Schiff, Maurice. 2005. "Brain Gain: Claims About its Size and Impact on Welfare and Growth are (Greatly) Exaggerated." Bonn, Germany: IZA Discussion Paper 1599.

Schiff, Maurice, and Alberto Valdés. 1998. "Agriculture and the Macroeconomy." Washington, DC: World Bank Policy Research Working Paper Series 1967.

Schultz, Paul T. 1998. "Inequality in the Distribution of Personal Income in the World: How is it Changing and Why?" *Journal of Population Economics* 11(3):307–44.

————. 2004. "School Subsidies for the Poor: Evaluating the Mexican Progresa Poverty Program." *Journal of Development Economics* 74(1):199–250.

Schwartz, Anita. 2003. *Old Age Security and Social Pensions.* Washington, DC: World Bank.

Schwarzer, H., and A. C. Querino. 2002. "Non-contributory Pensions in Brazil: The Impact on Poverty Reduction." Geneva: ILO, Social Security Policy and Development Branch, ESS Paper 11.

Scott, James C. 1976. *The Moral Economy of the Peasant: Rebellion and Subsistence in Southeast Asia.* New Haven, CT: Yale University Press.

————. 1986. "Everyday Forms of Peasant Resistance." *In* James C. Scott and Benedict J. Tria Kerkvilet, (ed.), *Everyday Forms of Peasant Resistance in Southeast Asia.* London: Frank Cass. & Co.

Scott-McDonald, Kerida. 2004. "Elements of Quality in Home Visiting Programs: Three Jamaican Models." *In* Mary Eming Young, (ed.), *From Early Child Development to Human Development: Investing in our Chidren's Future.* Washington, DC: World Bank.

Sekhri, Neelam, and William Savedoff. 2005. "Private Health Insurance: Implications for Developing Countries." *Bulletin of the World Health Organization* 83(2):127–134.

Sell, Susan K. 2003. *Private Power, Public Law: The Globalization of Intellectual Property Rights.* Cambridge, UK: Cambridge University Press.

Sen, Abhijit, and Himanshu. 2004. "Poverty and Inequality in India: Getting Closer to the Truth." Centre for Economic Studies and Planning, Jawaharlal Nehru University. New Delhi. Available on line at http://www.networkideas.org/featart/may2004/Poverty_WC.pdf. Processed.

Sen, Amartya. 1985. *Commodities and Capabilities.* Amsterdam: North-Holland.

————. 2000. "Social Justice and the Distribution of Income." *In* Anthony B. Atkinson and François Bourguignon, (ed.), *Handbook of Income Distribution.* Amsterdam: North-Holland.

————. 2001. "10 Theses on Globalization." *Global Viewpoint,* July 12. Available on line at http://www.digitalnpq.org/global_services/global%20viewpoint/07-12-01.html.

————. 2004. "Disability and Justice." Disability and Inclusive Development Conference, keynote speech, World Bank. Washington, DC. Processed.

Shaban, Radwan. 1987. "Testing between Competing Models of Sharecropping." *Journal of Political Economy* 95(5):893–920.

Shaw, M. 2001. *Investing in Youth: International Approaches to Preventing Crime and Victimization.* Montreal: International Center for the Prevention of Crime.

Shaw, Margaret. 2004. *Police, Schools and Crime Prevention: A Preliminary Review of Current Practices.* Montreal: International Center for the Prevention of Crime. Available on line at http://www.crime-prevention-intl.org/publications/pub_110_1.pdf.

Shepherd, Andrew, Emmanuel Gyimah-Boadi, with Sulley Gariba, Sophie Plagerson, and Abdul Wahab Musa. 2005. "Bridging the North-south Divide in Ghana." Background paper for the WDR 2006.

Shih, James C. 1992. *Chinese Rural Society in Transition: A Case Study of the Lake Tai Area.* Berkeley, CA: University of California, Inst.of East Asian Studies.

Shore, Rima. 1997. *Rethinking the Brain: New Insights into Early Development.* New York: Family and Work Institute.

Shorrocks, A. F. 1980. "The Class of Additively Decomposable Inequality Measures." *Econometrica* 48(3):613–25.

Siegel, Jordan. 2003. "Is Political Connectedness a Paramount Investment after Liberalization? The Successful Leveraging of Contingent Social Capital and the Formation of Cross Border Strategic Alliances Involving Korean Firms and their Global Parners (1987–2000)." Cambridge, MA: Harvard NOM Working Paper No. 03-45 03-45.

Slack, Paul. 1990. *The English Poor Law, 1531–1782.* London: The Macmillan Press.

Sloth-Nielsen, Julia, and Jackie Gallinetti. 2004. *Child Justice in Africa: A Guide to Good Practice, Community Law Center.* Bellville, South Africa: University of the Western Cape Community Law Centre.

Smith [1776], Adam. 1937. *An Inquiry into the Nature and Causes of the Wealth of Nations.* New York: The Modern Library.

Smith, J. R., J. Brooks-Gunn, and P. K. Klebanov. 1997. "Consequences of Living in Poverty for Young Children's Cognitive and Verbal Ability and Early School Achievement." *In* J. Duncan and J. Brooks-Gunn, (ed.), *Consequences of Growing up Poor.* New York: Russell Sage Foundation.

Smith, Peter H. 1978. "The Breakdown of Democracy in Argentina: 1916-1930." *In* Juan J. Linz and Alfred Stepan, (ed.), *The Breakdown of Democratic Regimes: Latin America.* Baltimore, MD: Johns Hopkins University Press.

Socialist Republic of Vietnam, and World Bank. 2005. *Vietnam: Managing Public Expenditure for Poverty Reduction and Growth; Public Expenditure Review and Integrated Fiduciary Assessment 2004 (Vols. I and II).* Washington, DC: World Bank.

Sokoloff, Kenneth L., and B. Zorina Khan. 1990. "The Democratization of Invention During Early Industrialization: Evidence from the United States, 1790–1846." *Journal of Economic History* 50(2):363–78.

Solar, Peter. 1995. "Poor Relief and English Economic Development before the Industrial Revolution." *Economic History Review* 48(2):1–22.

———. 1997. "Poor Relief and English Economic Development: A Renewed Plea for Comparative History." *Economic History Review* 50(2):369–74.

Solon, Gary. 1999. "Intergenerational Mobility in the Labor Market." *In* Orley Ashenfelter and David Card, (ed.), *Handbook of Labor Economics.* Amsterdam: North-Holland.

———. 2002. "Cross-country Differences in Intergenerational Earnings Mobility." *Journal of Economic Perspectives* 16(3):59–66.

South Africa Competition Commission. 2003. *Competition Commission Media Release 33.* Johannesburg: South Africa Competition Commission. Available on line at http://www.compcom.co.za/resources/Media%20Releases/MediaReleases%202003/Jul/Med%20Rel%2034%200f16%20Dec%202003.asp.

Sowell, Thomas. 2004. *Affirmative Action Around the World: An Empirical Study.* New Haven: Yale University Press.

Stark, Oded, and David E. Bloom. 1985. "The New Economics of Labor Migration." *American Economic Review* 75(2):173–78.

Steele, Claude M. 1999. "Thin Ice: 'Stereotype Threat' and Black College Students." *Atlantic Monthly* 284(2):44–54.

Steele, Claude M., and J. Aronson. 1995. "Stereotype Threat and the Intellectual Test Performance of African Americans." *Journal of Personality and Social Psychology* 69(5):797–811.

Stern, Joseph J. 2003. "The Rise and Fall of the Indonesian Economy." Cambridge, MA: Harvard University, KSG Working Paper Series RWP03-030.

Stern, Nicholas. 2002. *A Strategy for Development.* Washington, DC: World Bank.

Stern, Nicholas, Jean-Jacques Dethier, and F. Halsey Rogers. 2005. *Growth and Empowerment: Making Development Happen.* Cambridge, MA: MIT Press.

Stewart, Frances. 2001. "Horizontal Inequalities: A Neglected Dimension of Development." Oxford, UK: Queen Elizabeth House, University of Oxford, Working Paper 1.

Stoltzfus, R. J., J. D. Kvalsvig, and H. M. Chwaya. 2001. "Effects of Iron Supplementation and Anthelmintic Treatment on Motor and Language Development of Preschool Children in Zanzibar: Double Blind, Placebo Controlled Study." *British Medical Journal* 323(7326):1–8.

Stone, Jeff, Christian I. Lynch, Mike Sjomeling, and John M. Darley. 1999. "Stereotype Threat Effects on Black and White Athletic Performance." *Journal of Personality and Social Psychology* 77(6):1213–27.

Stone, Jeff, Zachary W. Perry, and John M. Darley. 1997. "White Men Can't Jump: Evidence for the Perceptual Confirmation of Racial Stereotypes Following a Basketball Game." *Basic and Applied Social Psychology* 19(3):291–306.

Strauss, John, Germano Mwabu, and Katheleen Beegle. 2000. "Intrahousehold Allocations: A Review of Theories and Empirical Evidence." *Journal of African Economies* 9(0):83–143.

Subbarao, Kalanidhi. 2003. "Systemic Shocks and Social Protection: Role and Efectivenss of Public Works Programs." Washington, DC: World Bank, Social Protection Discussion Paper 0302.

Subbarao, Kalanidhi, and Diane Coury. 2004. *Reaching Out to Africa's Orphans: A Framework for Public Action.* Washington, DC: World Bank.

Sudjana, Brasukra G., and Satish Mishra. 2004. "Growth and Inequality in Indonedia Today: Implications for Future Development Policy." Jakarta: UNSFIR Discussion Paper Series 04/05.

Swaminathan, Madhura. 1991. "Segmentation, Collateral Undervaluation, and the Rate of Interest in Agrarian Credit Markets:

Some Evidence from Two Villages in South India." *Cambridge Journal of Economics* 15(2):161–78.

Szreter, Simon. 2005. "Public Health and Security in an Age of Globalizing Economic Growth: The Awkward Lessons of History." *In* Simon Szreter, (ed.), *Health and Wealth: Studies in Policy and History.* Rochester, NY: University of Rochester Press.

Takeoshi, Yosoburo. 1967. *The Economic Aspects of the History of the Civilization of Japan.* London: Taylor & Francis.

Tarrow, Sidney. 1998. *Power in Movement: Social Movement and Contentious Politics.* New York: Cambridge University Press.

Tawney, R. H. 1941. "The Rise of Gentry: 1558–1640." *Economic History Review* 11(1):1–38.

Taylor, J. Edward. 1992. "Remittances and Inequality Reconsidered: Direct, Indirect, and Intertemporal Effects." *Journal of Policy Modeling* 14(2):187–208.

Taylor, J. Edward, and T. J. Wyatt. 1996. "The Shadow Value of Migrant Remittances, Income and Inequality in a Household-farm Economy." *Journal of Development Studies* 32(6):899–912.

Temple, Jonathan. 2001. "Growing into Trouble: Indonesia After 1966." London: C.E.P.R. Discussion Papers 2932.

Terry, Deborah J., Craig J. Carey, and Victor J. Callan. 2001. "Employee Adjustment to an Organizational Merger: An Intergroup Perspective." *Personality and Social Psychology Bulletin* 27(3):269–90.

Thailand's Ministry of Public Health, and World Bank. 2005. "Expanding Access to ART in Thailand: Achieving Treatment Benefits while Promoting Effective Prevention." Thailand's Ministry of Health and World Bank. Bangkok and Washington, DC. Processed.

Thomas, Duncan. 1990. "Intra-household Resource Allocation: An Influential Approach." *Journal of Human Resources* 29(4):635–64.

Thomas, Duncan, Elizabeth Frankenberg, Jed Friedman, Jean-Pierre Habitch, Mohamed Hakimi, Nathan Jones, Gretel Pelto, Bondan Sikoki, Teresa Seeman, James P. Smith, Cecep Sumantri, Wayan Suriastini, and Siswanto Wilopo. 2005. "Causal Effect of Health on Labor Market Outcomes: Experimental Evidence." University of California. Los Angeles, CA. Available on line at http://csde.washington.edu/downloads/thomas05.05.20.pdf. Processed.

Thomas, Duncan, Elizabeth Frankenburg, Katheleen Beegle, and Graciela Teruel. 1999. "Household Budgets, Household Composition and the Crisis in Indonesia: Evidence from Longitudinal Household Survey Data." Paper presented at the Population Association of America Meetings. March 25. New York.

Thomas, Vinod. 1987. "Differences in Income and Poverty within Brazil." *World Development* 15(2):263–73.

Thomas, Vinod, Yan Wang, and Xibo Fan. 2002. "A New Dataset on Inequality in Education: Gini and Theil Indices of Schooling for 140 Countries, 1960–2000." World Bank. Washington, DC. Processed.

Thompson, Edward P. 1963. *The Making of the English Working Class.* New York: Pantheon Books.

Thorbecke, Erik. 2005. "Economic Development, Income Distribution and Ethics," Ithaca, Cornell University. Processed.

Tien Dung, Luu. 2003. *Judicial Independence in Transitional Countries.* New York: United Nations Development Program. Available on line at http://www.undp.org/oslocentre/docsjuly03/DungTienLuu-v2.pdf.

Tilly, Charles. 1995. *Popular Contention in Britain.* Cambridge, MA: Harvard University Press.

———. 1998. *Durable Inequality.* Berkeley, CA: University of California Press.

Timmer, Peter. 2005. "Operationalizing Pro-poor Growth: Indonesia Country Study." Center for Global Development. Washington, DC. Available on line at http://siteresources.worldbank.org/INTPGI/Resources/342674-1115051237044/oppgindonesiaMay2005.pdf. Processed.

Topalova, Petia. 2004. "Factor Immobility and Regional Impacts of Trade Liberalization: Evidence on Poverty and Inequality from India." Ph.D thesis. Massachusetts Institute of Technology.

Toulmin, Camilla, and Julian Quan. 2000. *Evolving Land Rights, Policy and Tenure in Africa.* London, UK: International Institute for Environment and Development and Natural Resources Institute.

Townsend, Robert M. 1994. "Risk and Insurance in Village India." *Econometrica* 62(3):539–91.

———. 1995. "Financial Systems in Northern Thai Villages." *Quarterly Journal of Economics* 110(4):1011–46.

Tremblay, Richard E., and Wendy M. Craig. 1995. "Development Crime Prevention." *In* Michael Tonry and David P. Farrington, (ed.), *Building a Safer Society: Strategic Approaches to Crime Prevention.* Chicago, IL: Chicago University Press.

Udry, Christopher. 1996. "Gender, Agricultural Production and the Theory of Household." *Journal of Political Economy* 104(5):1010–46.

Ugaz, Cecilia, and Catherine Waddams Price, eds. 2003. *Utility Privatization and Regulation: A Fair Deal for Consumers?* Northampton, MA: Edward Elgar.

UNAIDS. 2002. *Report on the Global HIV/AIDS Epidemic 2002.* Geneva: UNAIDS.

UNCTAD. 2004. *World Investment Report 2004.* New York: United Nations Conference on Trade and Development. Available on line at http://www.unctad.org/Templates/WebFlyer.asp?intItemID=3235&lang=1.

UNESCO. 2005. *EFA Global Monitoring Report.* New York: UNESCO. Available on line at http://portal.unesco.org/education/.

UNICEF. 2003. *UNICEF Programs: Support for Families and Communities.* Paris: UNICEF.

United Kingdom's Commission for Africa. 2005. *Our Common Interest.* London: United Kingdom's Commission for Africa.

United Nations. 2002. *Population Ageing Report.* New York: United Nations.

———. 2003. *Human Security Now: Protecting and Empowering People.* New York: United Nations, Commission on Human Security.

United Nations Development Programme. 1995. *Human Development Report 1995.* New York: Oxford University Press.

———. 2003. *Human Development Report 2003: Millennium Development Goals: A Compact among Nations to End Human Poverty.* New York: Oxford University Press.

United Nations International Organization for Migration. 2000. *World Migration Report 2000*. Geneva: International Organization for Migration.

United Nations Research Institute for Social Development (UNRISD). 2005. *Policy Report on Gender and Development: 10 Years after Beijing*. New York: United Nations.

USAID, UNAIDS, and UNICEF. 2004. *Children on the Brink 2004: A Joint Report on Orphan Estimates and Program Strategies*. Paris: UNICEF. Available on line at http://www.unicef.org/publications/index_22212.html.

Vakis, Renos. 2003. "Livelihoods, Labor Markets and Rural Poverty." Washington, DC: World Bank, Guatemala Poverty Assesment (GUAPA) Program Technical Paper 1.

Valdés-Prieto, Salvador. 1992. "Financial Liberalization and the Capital Account: Chile 1974–1984." *In* Gerard Caprio, Izac Atiyas, and James A. Hanson, (ed.), *Financial Reform: Theory and Experience*. Cambridge, MA: Cambridge University Press.

Van de Walle, Dominique, and Dorothyjean Cratty. 2004. "Is the Emerging Non-Market Economy the Route out of Poverty in Vietnam?" *Economics of Transition* 12(2):237–75.

van den Brink, Rogier, Mike de Klerk, and Hans Binswanger. 1996. "Rural Livelihoods, Fiscal Costs and Financing Options: A First Attempt at Quantifying the Implications of Redistributive Land Reform." *In* Johan van Zyl, Johann Kirsten, and Hans Binswanger, (ed.), *Agricultural Land Reform in South Africa: Policies, Markets and Mechanisms*. Cape Town: Oxford University Press.

van der Berg, Servaas, and Caryn Brendenkamp. 2002. "Devising Social Security Interventions for Maximum Poverty Impact." Cape Town: CSSR Working Paper 13.

Van Niekerk, Gardiol. 2001. "State Initiatives to Incorporate Non-state Laws into the Official Legal Order: A Denial of Legal Pluralism?" *Comparative and International Law of Southern Africa* 34(3):349–61.

Velasco, Andrés. 1988. "Liberalization, Crisis, Intervention: The Chilean Financial System." Washington, DC: International Monetary Fund Working Paper Series 1988/66.

———. 1996. "Fixed Exchange Rates: Credibility, Flexibility and Multiplicity." *European Economic Review* 40(3-5):1023–35.

Voitchovsky, Sarah. 2004. "The Effect of Inequality on Growth: A Review of the Recent Empirical Literature." Oxford University. Oxford. Processed.

Wade, Robert. 1990. *Governing the Market: Economic Theory and the Role of Government in East Asian Industrialization*. Princeton, NJ: Princeton University Press.

Walder, Andrew G., and Jean C. Oi. 1999. "Property Rights in the Chinese Economy: Contours of the Process of Change." *In* Andrew G. Walder and Jean C. Oi, (ed.), *Property Rights and Economic Reform in China*. Stanford, CA: Stanford University Press.

Waller, Irving, and Daniel Sansfaçon. 2000. *Investing Wisely in Crime Prevention: International Experiences*. Washington, DC: Office of Justice Programs, Bureau of Justice Assistance. Available on line at http://www.ncjrs.org/pdffiles1/bja/182412.pdf.

Waller, Irwin, Brandon Welsh, and Daniel Sansfaçon. 1999. *Crime Prevention Digest II: Comparative Analysis of Successful Community Safety*. Quebec: International Center for the Prevention of Crime.

Walmsley, Terrie L., and L. Alan Winters. 2003. "Relaxing the Restrictions on the Temporary Movement of Natural Persons: A Simulation Analysis." London: CEPR Discussion Paper 3719.

Wan, Guanghua, Ming Lu, and Zhao Chen. 2004. "Globalization and Regional Income Inequality." Helsinki: United Nations University, World Institute for Development Economics Research, Discussion Paper 2004/10.

Washington Post. 2004. "Cambodia: Pinning Hope on Fair Labor Standards." *Washington Post,* November 17. Page: A19.

Widner, Jennifer A. 1993. "The Origins of Agricultural Policy in Ivory Coast: 1960-1986." *Journal of Development Studies* 29(4):25–60.

Wilkinson, Richard. 1992. "Income Distribution and Life Expectancy." *British Medical Journal* 304(6820):165–68.

———. 2000. *Mind the Gap: Hierarchies, Health and Human Evolution*. New Haven, CT: Yale University Press.

Willanakuy, Hatun. 2004. *Versión Abreviada del Informe Final de la Comisión de la Verdad y Reconciliación*. Lima, Peru: Comisión de la Verdad y Reconciliación.

Williamson, Jeffrey G. 1985. *Did British Capitalist Breed Inequality?* Boston, MA: Allen and Unwin.

Winters, L. Alan, Neil McCulloch, and Andrew McKay. 2004. "Trade Liberalization and Poverty: The Evidence so Far." *Journal of Economic Literature* 42(1):72–115.

Witte, John F. 2000. *The Market Approach to Education: An Analysis of America's First Voucher Program*. Princeton, NJ: Princeton University Press.

Wiwattanakantang, Yupana, Raja Kali, and Chutatong Charumilind. Forthcoming. "Connected Lending: Thailand Before the Financial Crisis." *Journal of Business.*

Wodon, Quentin. 2005. "Access to Basic Facilities in Africa." World Bank. Washington, DC. Processed.

Wodon, Quentin, Mohamed Ihsan Ajwad, and Corinne Siaens. 2005. "Targeting Utility Subsidies: Lifeline or Means-Testing?" World Bank. Washington, DC. Processed.

Women in Informal Employment Globalizing and Organizing. 2005. *The Importance of Organizing Informal and Casualized Women Workers: Findings of HomeNet Thailand's Recent Studies.* Cambridge, MA: Women in Informal Employment Globalizing and Organizing (WIEGO). Available on line at http://www.wiego.org/textonly/news.shtml.

Wood, Adrian. 1997. "Openness and Wage Inequality in Developing Countries: The Latin American Challenge to East Asian Conventional Wisdom." *World Bank Economic Review* 11(1):33–57.

World Bank. 1980. *World Development Report 1980*. New York: Oxford University Press.

———. 1990. *World Development Report 1990: Poverty*. New York: Oxford University Press.

———. 1993. *World Bank Policy Research Report 1993. The East Asian Miracle: Economic Growth and Public Policy*. New York: Oxford University Press.

———. 1994. *World Development Report 1994: Infrastructure for Development*. New York: Oxford University Press.

———. 1997a. *Hashemite Kingdom of Jordan: Health Sector Study* (World Bank Country Study). Washington, DC: World Bank.

————. 1997b. *Sharing Rising Incomes: Disparities in China.* Washington, DC: World Bank.

————. 1997c. *World Development Report 1997: The State in a Changing World.* New York: Oxford University Press.

————. 2000a. *Can Africa Claim the 21st Century?* Washington, DC: World Bank.

————. 2000b. *East Asia: Recovery and Beyond.* Washington, DC: World Bank.

————. 2000c. *Making Transition Work for Everyone: Poverty and Inequality in Europe and Central Asia.* Washington, DC: World Bank.

————. 2001a. *Colombia: Water Sector Reform Assistance Project.* Washington, DC: Project Appraisal Document Report No: 21868.

————. 2001b. *Coverage: The Scope of Protection in Retirement Incomes.* Washington, DC: World Bank Pension Reform Prime Note, Social Protection Unit.

————. 2001c. *Growing Health: A Review of Vietnam's Health Sector.* Washington, DC: World Bank.

————. 2001d. *Mexico—Land Policy: A Decade After the Ejido Reform.* Washington, DC: World Bank.

————. 2001e. *Social Protection Sector Strategy Paper—From Safety Nets to Spring Board.* Washington, DC: World Bank.

————. 2001f. *Thailand Social Monitor: Poverty and Public Policy.* Washington, DC: World Bank.

————. 2001g. *World Bank Policy Research Report 2001: Engendering Development Through Gender Equality In Rights, Resources And Voice.* New York: Oxford University Press.

————. 2001h. *World Development Report 2000/01: Attacking Poverty.* New York: Oxford University Press.

————. 2002a. *Bulgaria: Poverty Assessment Report 24516-BUL.* Washington, DC. World Bank.

————. 2002b. *World Development Report 2002: Building Institutions for Markets.* New York: Oxford University Press.

————. 2003a. *A Resource for Municipalities: Community Based Crime and Violence Prevention in Urban Latin America.* Washington, DC: World Bank, Department of Finance, Private Sector and Infrastructure, Latin American Region.

————. 2003b. *Global Economic Prospects.* Washington, DC: World Bank.

————. 2003c. *From Goats to Coats: Institutional Reform in Mongolia's Cashmere Sector.* Washington, DC: World Bank.

————. 2003d. *Kyrgyz Republic: Enhancing Pro-poor Growth Report 24638-KG.* Washington, DC: World Bank.

————. 2003e. *Romania: Poverty Assessment Report 26169-RO.* Washington, DC: World Bank.

————. 2003f. *The Contribution of Social Protection to the Millennium Development Goals.* Washington, DC: World Bank, Social Protection Unit.

————. 2003g. *The Impact of Legal Aid: Ecuador.* Washington, DC: World Bank, Legal Vice Presidency.

————. 2003h. *World Bank Policy Research Report 2003. Breaking the Conflict Trap: Civil War and Development Policy.* New York: Oxford University Press.

————. 2003i. *World Bank Policy Research Report 2003. Land Policies for Growth and Poverty Reduction.* New York: Oxford University Press.

————. 2003j. *World Development Report 2004: Making Services Work for Poor People.* New York: Oxford University Press.

————. 2004a. *A Fair Share for Women: Cambodia Gender Assessment.* Phnom Penh: UNIFEM, The World Bank, ADB, UNDP and DFID/UK in cooperation with the Ministry of Women's and Veteran's Affair.

————. 2004b. *Doing Business in 2004: Understanding Regulation.* Washington, DC: World Bank, IFC and Oxford University Press.

————. 2004c. "Gender Assessment of the Honduras Judicial Sector." World Bank. Washington, DC. Processed.

————. 2004d. *Implementation Completition Report: Improving Learning in Primary School Project (Report No. 27345).* Washington, DC: World Bank.

————. 2004e. *Kingdom of Morocco Poverty Report: Strengthening Policy by Identifying the Geographic Dimensions of Poverty.* Washington, DC: World Bank.

————. 2004f. "Private Participation in Infrastructure Project Database". Washington, DC, World Bank. Available on line at http://ppi.worldbank.org/.

————. 2004g. *Project Appraisal Document, Justice Services Improvement Project, Annexes 11 and 12.* Washington, DC: World Bank.

————. 2004h. *Reaching the Poor with Effective Health, Nutrition, and Population Services.* Washington, DC: World Bank.

————. 2004i. "Rural Poverty in Mexico." World Bank. Washington, DC. Processed.

————. 2004j. *Sierra Leone: Legal and Judicial Sector Assessment.* Washington, DC: World Bank, Legal Vice Presidency.

————. 2004k. *The Millennium Development Goals for Health: Rising to the Challenges.* Washington, DC: World Bank.

————. 2004l. *World Bank Policy Research Report 2004. Reforming Infrastructure: Privatization, Regulation, and Competition.* New York: Oxford University Press.

————. 2005a. "Growth, Poverty, and Inequality in Europe and Central Asia. Past, Present, and Future." World Bank. Washington, DC. Processed.

————. 2005b. *Pro-poor Growth in the 1990s: Lessons and Insight from 14 Countries.* Washington, DC: World Bank.

————. 2005c. *Pro-Poor Growth: Country Experiences in the 1990s.* Washington, DC: World Bank, Poverty Reduction Group.

————. 2005d. "Cambodia—Quality Basic Education for All." Washington, DC: World Bank.

————. 2005e. *Doing Business in 2005: Removing Obstacles to Growth.* Washington, DC: Oxford University Press for the International Finance Corporation (World Bank).

————. 2005f. *Global Monitoring Report. Millennium Development Goals: From Consensus to Momentum.* Washington, DC: World Bank.

————. 2005g. *World Development Indicators.* Washington, DC: World Bank.

————. 2005h. *World Development Report 2005: A Better Investment Climate for Everyone.* New York: Oxford University Press.

World Commission on the Social Dimensions of Globalization. 2004. *A Fair Globalization: Creating Opportunities for All.* Geneva. ILO.

World Health Organization. 2004. *World Report on Knowledge for Better Health.* Geneva: World Health Organization. Available on line at www.who.int/rpc/meetings/wr2004/en/.

Wößmann, Ludger. 2000. "Schooling Resources, Educational Institutions, and Student Performance: The International Evidence." Kiel Institute of Work Economics: Kiel Working Paper 983.

————. 2004. "How Equal are Educational Opportunities? Family Background and Student Achievement in the Europe and the US." Munich, Germany: Center for Economic Studies and Ifo Institute for Economic Research 1162.

Wrigley, E. A. 1998. *Continuity, Chance and Change: The Character of the Industrial Revolution in England.* Cambridge, UK: Cambridge University Press.

Yang, Dean. 2004. "International Migration, Human Capital, and Entrepreneurship: Evidence from Philippine Migrants' Exchange Rate Shocks." University of Michigan: Ford School of Public Policy Working Paper Series 02-011. Available on line at http://papers.ssrn.com/sol3/papers.cfm?abstract_id=546483.

Young, Mary Eming. 2002. "Early Child Development: A Stepping Stone to Success in School and Lifelong Learning." World Bank. Washington, DC. Processed.

Zaninka, Penninah. 2003. "Uganda." *In* J. Nelson and L. Hossack, (ed.), *Indigenous People and Protected Areas in Africa: From Principles to Practice.* Moreton-in-Marsh, UK: Forest People Programme.

Zeldes, Stephen. 1989. "Consumption and Liquidity Constraints: An Empirical Investigation." *Journal of Political Economy* 97(2):305–46.

Selected Indicators

Measuring equity

This report has concerned itself with equity, a concept which we have defined to mean equality of opportunities and the avoidance of absolute deprivation. As we made clear in the report, the focus is mostly on inequality of opportunity, and much less on overall inequality in a one-dimensional space, such as income or education. We might be quite sanguine about certain types of inequality across people if, for example, their outcomes varied for reasons that had to do mainly with their own efforts. But we are concerned with systematic differences in opportunities between individuals and groups of people due to different "circumstances" not under their control, i.e. when these groups are distinguishable from one another only in characteristics that in some sense can be argued to be "morally irrelevant" to their opportunities and outcomes in life.

To give the audience a sense of inequality of opportunities, we chose to present data on income/consumption, infant mortality, and years of education in a slightly different format than what we are normally used to seeing for as many countries in the world as possible. Table A1 presents poverty rates using national poverty lines as well as those using the international $1 and $2 per day poverty lines; information for the national poverty line is also presented for urban and rural breakdowns of the population. Table A2 presents alternative inequality measures to the commonly used Gini Index, followed by evidence on inequality of land. In Table A3, we present infant mortality rates for more than 50 countries by the sex of the infant, the education level of the mother, the location (urban or rural) of the family, and the ranking of the household by an asset index. Finally, in Table A4, we present educational attainment by location and gender, but also present measures of inequality in years of schooling, along with the share of this inequality that is attributable to gender and location.

Table A1. Poverty

	National poverty line								International poverty line				
		Population below the poverty line				Population below the poverty line				Population below $1 a day	Poverty gap at $1 a day	Population below $2 a day	Poverty gap at $2 a day
	Survey year	Rural %	Urban %	National %	Survey year	Rural %	Urban %	National %	Survey year	%	%	%	%
Albania	2002	29.6	19.8	25.4	..	..	..	..	2002 [a]	<2	<0.5	11.8	2.0
Algeria	1995	30.3	14.7	22.6	1998	16.6	7.3	12.2	1995 [a]	<2	<0.5	15.1	3.8
Angola	..	..	..	..	..	..	..	..	..	..	..	..	..
Argentina	1995	..	28.4	..	1998	..	29.9	..	2001 [b]	3.3	0.5	14.3	4.7
Armenia	1998–99	50.8	58.3	55.1	2001	48.7	51.9	50.9	2003 [a, c]	<2	<0.5	31.1	7.1
Australia	..	..	..	..	..	..	..	..	..	..	..	..	..
Austria	..	..	..	..	..	..	..	..	..	..	..	..	..
Azerbaijan	1995	..	..	68.1	2001	42.0	55.0	49.0	2001 [a]	3.7	0.6	33.4	9.1
Bangladesh	1995–96	55.2	29.4	51.0	2000	53.0	36.6	49.8	2000 [a]	36.0	8.1	82.8	36.3
Belarus	2000	..	..	41.9	..	..	..	..	2000 [a]	<2	<0.5	<2	<0.5
Belgium	..	..	..	..	..	..	..	..	..	..	..	..	..
Benin	1995	25.2	28.5	26.5	1999	33.0	23.3	29.0	..	..	..	..	..
Bolivia	1997	77.3	53.8	63.2	1999	81.7	50.6	62.7	1999 [a]	14.4	5.4	34.3	14.9
Bosnia & Herzegovina	2001–02	19.9	13.8	19.5	..	..	..	..	..	..	..	..	..
Brazil	1996	54.0	15.4	23.9	1998	51.4	14.7	22.0	2001 [b]	8.2	2.1	22.4	8.8
Bulgaria	1997	..	..	36.0	2001	..	..	12.8	2003 [a, c]	<2	<0.5	6.1	1.5
Burkina Faso	1994	51.0	10.4	44.5	1998	51.0	16.5	45.3	1998 [a]	44.9	14.4	81.0	40.6
Burundi	1990	36.0	43.0	36.4	..	..	..	..	1998 [a]	54.6	22.7	87.6	48.9
Cambodia	1997	40.1	21.1	36.1	1999	40.1	13.9	35.9	1997 [a]	(34.1)	9.7	77.7	34.5
Cameroon	1996	59.6	41.4	53.3	2001	49.9	22.1	40.2	2001 [a]	17.1	4.1	50.6	19.3
Canada	..	..	..	..	..	..	..	..	..	..	..	..	..
Central African Rep.	..	..	..	..	..	..	..	..	1993 [a]	66.6	38.1	84.0	58.4
Chad	1995–96	67.0	63.0	64.0	..	..	..	..	..	..	..	..	..
Chile	1996	..	..	19.9	1998	..	..	17.0	2000 [b]	<2	<0.5	9.6	2.5
China	1996	7.9	<2	6.0	1998	4.6	<2	4.6	2001 [a]	16.6	3.9	46.7	18.4
Hong Kong, China	..	..	..	..	..	..	..	..	..	..	..	..	..
Colombia	1995	79.0	48.0	60.0	1999	79.0	55.0	64.0	1999 [b]	8.2	2.2	22.6	8.8
Congo, Dem. Rep.	..	..	..	..	..	..	..	..	..	..	..	..	..
Congo, Rep.	..	..	..	..	..	..	..	..	..	..	..	..	..
Costa Rica	1992	25.5	19.2	22.0	..	..	..	..	2000 [b]	2.0	0.7	9.5	3.0
Côte d'Ivoire	..	..	..	..	..	..	..	..	2002 [a, c]	14.8	4.1	48.8	18.4
Croatia	..	..	..	..	..	..	..	..	2001 [a]	<2	<0.5	<2	<0.5
Czech Rep.	..	..	..	..	..	..	..	..	1996 [b]	<2	<0.5	<2	<0.5
Denmark	..	..	..	..	..	..	..	..	..	..	..	..	..
Dominican Rep.	1992	49.0	19.3	33.9	1998	42.1	20.5	28.6	1998 [b]	<2	<0.5	<2	<0.5
Ecuador	1994	47.0	25.0	35.0	..	..	..	..	1998 [b]	17.7	7.1	40.8	17.7
Egypt, Arab Rep.	1995–96	23.3	22.5	22.9	1999–00	..	..	16.7	1999–2000 [a]	3.1	<0.5	43.9	11.3
El Salvador	1992	55.7	43.1	48.3	..	..	..	..	2000 [b]	31.1	14.1	58.0	29.7
Eritrea	1993–94	..	..	53.0	..	..	..	..	..	..	..	..	..
Ethiopia	1995–96	47.0	33.3	45.5	1999–00	45.0	37.0	44.2	1999–2000 [a]	23.0	4.8	77.8	29.6
Finland	..	..	..	..	..	..	..	..	..	..	..	..	..
France	..	..	..	..	..	..	..	..	..	..	..	..	..
Georgia	1997	9.9	12.1	11.1	..	..	..	..	2001 [a]	2.7	0.9	15.7	4.6
Germany	..	..	..	..	..	..	..	..	..	..	..	..	..
Ghana	1992	..	..	50.0	1998–99	49.9	18.6	39.5	1998–99 [a]	44.8	17.3	78.5	40.8
Greece	..	..	..	..	..	..	..	..	..	..	..	..	..
Guatemala	1989	71.9	33.7	57.9	2000	74.5	27.1	56.2	2000 [b]	16.0	4.6	37.4	16.0
Guinea	1994	..	..	40.0	..	..	..	..	..	..	..	..	..
Haiti	1987	..	..	65.0	1995	66.0	..	..	2001 [a, c]	67.0	40.0	83.3	58.5
Honduras	1992	46.0	56.0	50.0	1993	51.0	57.0	53.0	1999 [b]	20.7	7.5	44.0	20.2
Hungary	1993	..	..	14.5	1997	..	..	17.3	2002 a	<2	<0.5	<2	<0.5
India	1993–94	37.3	32.4	36.0	1999–00	30.2	24.7	28.6	1999–2000 [a]	35.3	7.2	80.6	34.9
Indonesia	1996	..	..	15.7	1999	..	..	27.1	2002 [a]	7.5	0.9	52.4	15.7
Iran, Islamic Rep.	..	..	..	..	..	..	..	..	1998 [a]	<2	<0.5	7.3	1.5
Ireland	..	..	..	..	..	..	..	..	..	..	..	..	..
Israel	..	..	..	..	..	..	..	..	..	..	..	..	..
Italy	..	..	..	..	..	..	..	..	..	..	..	..	..
Jamaica	1995	37.0	18.7	27.5	2000	25.1	12.8	18.7	2000 [a]	<2	<0.5	13.3	2.7
Japan	..	..	..	..	..	..	..	..	..	..	..	..	..
Jordan	1991	..	..	15.0	1997	..	..	11.7	2002 [a, c]	<2	<0.5	6.5	1.4
Kazakhstan	1996	39.0	30.0	34.6	..	..	..	..	2003 [a]	<2	<0.5	24.9	6.3
Kenya	1994	47.0	29.0	40.0	1997	53.0	49.0	52.0	1997 [a]	22.8	5.9	58.3	23.9
Korea, Rep.	..	..	..	..	..	..	..	..	1998 [b]	<2	<0.5	<2	<0.5
Kuwait	..	..	..	..	..	..	..	..	..	..	..	..	..
Kyrgyz Rep.	2000	56.4	43.9	52.0	2001	51.0	41.2	47.6	2002 [a]	<2	<0.5	24.7	5.8
Lao PDR	1993	48.7	33.1	45.0	1997–98	41.0	26.9	38.6	1997–98 [a]	26.3	6.3	73.2	29.6

Table A1. Poverty—continued

	National poverty line								International poverty line				
		Population below the poverty line				Population below the poverty line				Population below $1 a day	Poverty gap at $1 a day	Population below $2 a day	Poverty gap at $2 a day
	Survey year	Rural %	Urban %	National %	Survey year	Rural %	Urban %	National %	Survey year	%	%	%	%
Latvia	..	..	..	..	..	..	..	..	1998 [a]	<2	<0.5	11.5	2.6
Lebanon	..	..	..	..	..	..	..	..	..	..	..	..	..
Lithuania	..	..	..	..	..	..	..	..	2000 [a]	<2	<0.5	6.9	1.5
Macedonia, FYR	..	..	..	..	..	..	..	..	2003 [a, c]	<2	<0.5	<2	<0.5
Madagascar	1997	76.0	63.2	73.3	1999	76.7	52.1	71.3	2001 [a]	61.0	27.9	85.1	51.8
Malawi	1990–91	..	..	54.0	1997–98	66.5	54.9	65.3	1997–98 [a]	41.7	14.8	76.1	38.3
Malaysia	1989	..	..	15.5	..	..	..	..	1997 [b]	<2	<0.5	9.3	2.0
Mali	1998	75.9	30.1	63.8	..	..	..	..	1994 [a]	72.3	37.4	90.6	60.5
Mauritania	1996	65.5	30.1	50.0	2000	61.2	25.4	46.3	2000 [a]	25.9	7.6	63.1	26.8
Mexico	1988	..	..	10.1	..	..	..	..	2000 [a]	9.9	3.7	26.3	10.9
Moldova	1997	26.7	19.3	23.3	..	..	..	..	2001 [a]	21.8	5.7	64.1	25.2
Mongolia	1995	33.1	38.5	36.3	1998	32.6	39.4	35.6	1998 [a]	27.0	8.1	74.9	30.6
Morocco	1990–91	18.0	7.6	13.1	1998–99	27.2	12.0	19.0	1999 [a]	<2	<0.5	14.3	3.1
Mozambique	1996–97	71.3	62.0	69.4	..	..	..	..	1996 [a]	37.9	12.0	78.4	36.8
Namibia	..	..	..	..	..	..	..	..	1993 [b]	34.9	14.0	55.8	30.4
Nepal	1995–96	44.0	23.0	42.0	..	..	..	..	1995–96 [a]	39.1	11.0	80.9	37.6
Netherlands	..	..	..	..	..	..	..	..	..	..	..	..	..
New Zealand	..	..	..	..	..	..	..	..	..	..	..	..	..
Nicaragua	1993	76.1	31.9	50.3	1998	68.5	30.5	47.9	2001 [a]	45.1	16.7	79.9	41.2
Niger	1989–93	66.0	52.0	63.0	..	..	..	..	1995 [a]	60.6	34.0	85.8	54.6
Nigeria	1985	49.5	31.7	43.0	1992–93	36.4	30.4	34.1	2003 [a, c]	70.8	34.5	92.4	59.5
Norway	..	..	..	..	..	..	..	..	..	..	..	..	..
Oman	..	..	..	..	..	..	..	..	..	..	..	..	..
Pakistan	1993	33.4	17.2	28.6	1998–99	35.9	24.2	32.6	2001 [a, c]	17.0	3.1	73.6	26.1
Panama	1997	64.9	15.3	37.3	..	..	..	..	2000 [b]	7.2	2.3	17.6	7.4
Papua New Guinea	1996	41.3	16.1	37.5	..	..	..	..	..	..	..	..	..
Paraguay	1991	28.5	19.7	21.8	..	..	..	..	2002 [b]	16.4	7.4	33.2	16.2
Peru	1994	67.0	46.1	53.5	1997	64.7	40.4	49.0	2000 [b]	18.1	9.1	37.7	18.5
Philippines	1994	53.1	28.0	40.6	1997	50.7	21.5	36.8	2000 [a, c]	15.5	3.0	47.5	17.8
Poland	1993	..	..	23.8	..	..	..	..	2002 [a, c]	<2	<0.5	<2	<0.5
Portugal	..	..	..	..	..	..	..	..	1994 [b]	<2	<0.5	<2	<0.5
Romania	1994	27.9	20.4	21.5	..	..	..	..	2002 [a]	<2	0.5	14.0	3.4
Russian Federation	1994	..	..	30.9	..	..	..	..	2002 [a]	<2	<0.5	7.5	1.3
Rwanda	1993	..	..	51.2	1999–00	65.7	14.3	60.3	1999–2000 [a]	51.7	20.0	83.7	45.5
Saudi Arabia	..	..	..	..	..	..	..	..	..	..	..	..	..
Senegal	1992	40.4	23.7	33.4	..	..	..	..	1995 [a]	22.3	5.7	63.0	25.2
Serbia & Montenegro	..	..	..	..	..	..	..	..	..	..	..	..	..
Sierra Leone	1989	..	..	82.8	2003–04	79.0	56.4	70.2	1989 [a]	57.0	39.5	74.5	51.8
Singapore	..	..	..	..	..	..	..	..	..	..	..	..	..
Slovak Rep.	..	..	..	..	..	..	..	..	1996 [b]	<2	<0.5	2.9	0.8
Slovenia	..	..	..	..	..	..	..	..	1998 [b]	<2	<0.5	<2	<0.5
South Africa	..	..	..	..	..	..	..	..	2000 [a]	10.7	1.7	34.1	12.6
Spain	..	..	..	..	..	..	..	..	..	..	..	..	..
Sri Lanka	1990–91	22.0	15.0	20.0	1995–96	27.0	15.0	25.0	2002 [a, c]	5.6	<0.5	41.6	11.9
Sudan	..	..	..	..	..	..	..	..	..	..	..	..	..
Sweden	..	..	..	..	..	..	..	..	..	..	..	..	..
Switzerland	..	..	..	..	..	..	..	..	..	..	..	..	..
Syrian Arab Rep.	..	..	..	..	..	..	..	..	..	..	..	..	..
Tajikistan	..	..	..	..	..	..	..	..	2003 [a]	7.4	1.3	42.8	13.0
Tanzania	1991	40.8	31.2	38.6	2000–01	38.7	29.5	35.7	1991 [a]	48.5	24.4	72.5	43.3
Thailand	1990	..	..	18.0	1992	15.5	10.2	13.1	2000 [a, c]	<2	<0.5	32.5	9.0
Togo	1987–89	..	..	32.3	..	..	..	..	..	..	..	..	..
Tunisia	1990	13.1	3.5	7.4	1995	13.9	3.6	7.6	2000 [a]	<2	<0.5	6.6	1.3
Turkey	..	..	..	..	..	..	..	..	2002 [a, c]	4.8	1.0	24.7	7.5
Turkmenistan	..	..	..	..	..	..	..	..	1998 [a]	12.1	2.6	44.0	15.4
Uganda	1993	..	..	55.0	1997	..	..	44.0	..	..	..	..	..
Ukraine	1995	..	..	31.7	..	..	..	..	1999 [b]	2.9	0.6	45.7	16.3
United Kingdom	..	..	..	..	..	..	..	..	..	..	..	..	..
United States	..	..	..	..	..	..	..	..	..	..	..	..	..
Uruguay	..	..	..	..	..	..	..	..	2000 [b]	<2	<0.5	3.9	0.8
Uzbekistan	2000	30.5	22.5	27.5	..	..	..	..	2000 [a]	17.3	4.3	71.7	25.2
Venezuela, RB de	1989	..	..	31.3	..	..	..	..	2000 [b, c]	9.9	3.6	32.1	12.2
Vietnam	1998	45.5	9.2	37.4	2002	35.6	6.6	28.9	..	..	..	..	..
West Bank & Gaza	..	..	..	..	..	..	..	..	..	..	..	..	..
Yemen, Rep.	1998	45.0	30.8	41.8	..	..	..	..	1998 [a]	15.7	4.5	45.2	15.0
Zambia	1996	82.8	46.0	69.2	1998	83.1	56.0	72.9	1998 [a]	63.7	32.7	87.4	55.4
Zimbabwe	1990–91	35.8	3.4	25.8	1995–96	48.0	7.9	34.9	1995–96 [a]	56.1	24.2	83.0	48.2

a = expenditure base; b = income base; c = preliminary data; .. denotes no data.

Table A2. Income/consumption inequality measures

	Survey year	y/c*	Income/consumption inequality			Survey year	Land inequality
			Gini index	GE (0)	90th/10th percentile ratio		Gini index
Albania	2002	c	0.31	0.15	3.95	1998	0.84
Algeria	1995	c	0.35	..	..	..	..
Argentina—urban	2001	y	0.51	0.49	13.71	1988	0.83
Armenia	2003	c	0.26	0.11	3.17	..	..
Australia	1994	y	0.32	0.20	4.88	..	..
Austria	1997	y	0.28	0.14	3.58	1999/2000	0.59
Azerbaijan	2001	c	0.36	0.22	4.62	..	..
Bangladesh	2000	c	0.31	0.16	3.85	1996	0.62
Belarus	2000	c	0.30	..	..	..	..
Belgium	2000	y	0.26	0.12	3.22	1999/2000	0.56
Benin	2003	c	0.36	0.22	4.93	..	..
Bolivia	2002	y	0.58	0.76	29.65	..	..
Bosnia & Herzegovina	2001	c	0.25	0.10	3.25	..	..
Botswana	1993.5	c	0.63	..	..	..	..
Brazil	2001	y	0.59	0.65	16.25	1996	0.85
Bulgaria	2003	c	0.28	0.12	3.56	..	..
Burkina Faso	2003	c	0.38	0.23	4.91	1993	0.42
Burundi	1998	c	0.42	0.31	6.49	..	..
Cambodia	1997	c	0.40	0.28	4.80	..	..
Cameroon	2001	c	0.45	..	..	..	..
Canada	2000	y	0.33	0.18	4.52	1991	0.64
Central African Rep.	1993	c	0.61	..	..	..	..
Chile	2000	y	0.51	0.47	10.72	..	..
China	2001	c	0.45	..	..	..	..
Colombia	1999	y	0.54	0.57	15.00	2001	0.8
Costa Rica	2000	y	0.46	0.39	9.65	..	..
Côte d'Ivoire	2002	c	0.45	0.33	6.75	..	..
Croatia	2001	c	0.29	0.17	..	..	..
Czech Rep.	1996	y	0.25	0.12	..	2000	0.92
Denmark	1997	y	0.27	0.14	..	1999/2000	0.51
Dominican Rep.	1997	y	0.47	0.40	9.17	..	..
East Timor	2001	c	0.37	0.22	5.42	..	..
Ecuador	1998	y	0.54	0.61	16.09	..	..
Egypt, Arab Rep.	2000	c	0.34	0.20	..	1990	0.65
El Salvador	2002	y	0.50	0.52	15.88	..	..
Estonia	1998	c	0.32	0.17	4.73	2001	0.79
Ethiopia	2000	c	0.30	0.15	3.34	2001	0.47
Finland	2000	y	0.25	0.10	3.12	1999/2000	0.27
France	1994	y	0.31	0.15	..	1999/2000	0.58
Gambia, The	1998	c	0.48	0.44	..	..	..
Georgia	2002	c	0.38	0.25	6.11	..	..
Germany	2000	y	0.28	0.12	3.58	1999/2000	0.63
Ghana	1999	c	0.41	0.28	7.30	..	..
Greece	1998	c	0.36	0.22	..	1999/2000	0.58
Guatemala	2000	y	0.58	0.66	16.81	..	..
Guinea	2003	c	0.39	0.24	5.09	..	..
Guinea-Bissau	1993	c	0.40	..	..	1988	0.62
Guyana	1998	y	0.45	..	..	..	..
Haiti	2001	y	0.68	0.98	45.43	..	..
Honduras	1999	y	0.52	0.51	11.72	1993	0.66
Hungary	2002	c	0.24	0.09	2.96	..	..
India	1999/2000	c	0.33	..	..	..	..
Indonesia	2000	c	0.34	..	..	1993	0.46
Iran	1998	c	0.43	0.33	..	..	..
Ireland	2000	y	0.31	0.16	4.27	1999/2000	0.44
Israel	2001	c	0.35	0.20	4.90	..	..
Italy	2000	c	0.31	0.16	4.26	1999/2000	0.73
Jamaica	2001	c	0.42	0.28	5.90	..	..
Japan	1993	y	0.25	0.10	..	1995	0.59
Jordan	2002	c	0.39	0.25	5.46	1997	0.78
Kazakhstan	2003	c	0.30	0.14	3.88	..	..
Kenya	1997	c	0.44	0.32	6.56	..	..
Korea, Rep.	1998	y	0.32	0.15	..	1990	0.34
Kyrgyzstan	2002	c	0.29	0.13	3.63	..	..
Lao PDR	1997/1998	c	0.35	0.20	4.10	1999	0.39

Table A2. Income/consumption inequality measures—continued

	Survey year	y/c*	Income/consumption inequality			Survey year	Land inequality
			Gini index	GE (0)	90th/10th percentile ratio		Gini index
Latvia	1998	c	0.34	0.19	..	2001	0.58
Lesotho	1995	c	0.63	..	..	1989/1990	0.49
Lithuania	2000	c	0.29	0.14	3.94	..	..
Luxembourg	2000	y	0.29	0.13	3.92	1999/2000	0.48
Macedonia, FDR	2003	c	0.36	0.21	5.60	..	..
Madagascar	2001	c	0.46	0.36	8.05	..	..
Malawi	1997/1998	c	0.50	0.44	..	1993	0.52
Malaysia	1997	y	0.49	0.43	..	..	..
Mali	2001	c	0.39	0.25	5.81	..	..
Mauritania	2000	c	0.38	0.24	5.92	..	..
Mexico	2002	y	0.49	0.47	11.87	..	..
Moldova	2001	c	0.36	..	..	..	..
Mongolia	1998	c	0.30	0.16	..	..	..
Morocco	1998	c	0.38	0.23	5.33	1996	0.62
Mozambique	1996/1997	c	39.60	0.27	..	..	..
Namibia	1993	c	70.70	..	..	1997	0.36
Nepal	1996	c	0.36	0.21	4.54	1992	0.45
Netherlands	1999	y	0.29	0.16	3.87	1999/2000	0.57
New Zealand	1997	y	0.37	0.23	..	..	..
Nicaragua	2001	c	0.40	0.27	6.52	2001	0.72
Niger	1995	c	0.51	..	..	..	..
Nigeria	2003	c	0.41	0.29	7.26	..	..
Norway	2000	y	0.27	0.14	2.95	1999	0.18
Pakistan	2001	c	0.27	0.12	3.09	1990	0.57
Panama	2000	c	0.55	0.60	18.65	2001	0.52
Paraguay	2001	y	0.55	0.61	18.26	1991	0.93
Peru	2000	c	0.48	0.51	14.60	1994	0.86
Philippines	2000	c	0.46	..	..	1991	0.55
Poland	2002	c	0.31	0.15	4.03	2002	0.69
Portugal	1997	y	0.39	0.27	..	1999/2000	0.74
Romania	2002	c	0.28	0.12	3.63	..	..
Russian Federation	2002	c	0.32	0.17	4.67	..	..
Senegal	1995	c	0.40	0.26	5.18	1998	0.5
Serbia & Montenegro	2003	c	0.28	0.12	3.60	..	..
Singapore	1998	y	0.43	0.33	..	..	..
Slovak Rep.	1996	y	0.26	0.12	..	..	..
Slovenia	1998	c	0.28	0.13	..	1991	0.62
South Africa	2000	c	0.58	0.61	16.91	..	..
Spain	2000	y	0.35	0.21	4.74	1999/2000	0.77
Sri Lanka	2002	c	0.38	0.23	4.98	..	..
St. Lucia	1995	c	0.44	0.37	9.38	..	..
Sweden	2000	y	0.25	0.11	3.18	1999/2000	0.32
Switzerland	1992	y	0.31	0.17	..	1990	0.5
Taiwan, China	2000	c	0.74	0.09	2.86	..	..
Tajikistan	2003	c	0.32	0.16	4.08	..	..
Tanzania	2001	c	0.35	0.20	4.89	..	..
Thailand	2002	c	0.40	0.25	5.56	1993	0.47
Trinidad & Tobago	1992	c	0.39	0.26	6.24	..	..
Tunisia	2000	c	0.40	0.28	..	1993	0.7
Turkey	2002	c	0.37	0.23	5.73	1991	0.61
Turkmenistan	1988	c	0.41	0.28	..	..	..
Uganda			..	..	..	1991	0.59
Ukraine	1999	y	0.29	..	..	..	..
United Kingdom	1999	y	0.34	0.20	5.00	1999/2000	0.66
United States	2000	y	0.38	0.26	6.30	1997	0.76
Uruguay—urban	2000	y	0.43	0.32	7.73	2000	0.79
Uzbekistan	2000	c	0.27	0.12	..	..	..
Venezuela, RB de	2000	y	0.42	0.33	7.94	1996/1997	0.88
Vietnam	2002	c	0.35	0.20	4.73	1994	0.53
Yemen, Rep.	1998	c	0.33	0.19	4.56	..	..
Zambia	1998	c	0.53	0.51	..	..	..
Zimbabwe	1995	c	0.57	..	..	..	..

Note: * c in this column indicates that the inequality measures refer to a distribution of consumption expenditures; y indicates that the inequality measures refer to a distribution of incomes; .. denotes no data.

Table A3. Health

| | | Infant mortality rate (deaths under age 12 months per 1,000 live births) | | | | | | | | | | | | |
| | | Overall | By gender | | By asset quintiles | | | | | By location | | By mother's education level | | |
	Survey year		Male	Female	Lowest	Second	Middle	Fourth	Highest	Urban	Rural	No education	Primary	Secondary or higher
Armenia	2000	44.1	46.1	41.9	52.3	50.0	36.8	49.6	27.3	35.9	52.7	..	..	44.3
Bangladesh	1993	100.5	107.3	93.4	..	..	..	..	..	80.9	102.6	113.3	89.0	57.5
Bangladesh	1996/1997	89.6	94.9	84.3	96.5	98.8	96.7	88.8	56.6	73.0	91.2	98.1	82.3	64.8
Bangladesh	1999/2000	79.7	82.3	76.9	92.9	93.6	78.1	62.8	57.9	74.2	80.7	91.9	74.5	54.7
Benin	1996	103.5	109.3	97.6	119.4	111.1	105.8	103.8	63.3	84.4	112.3	108.4	94.0	49.9
Benin	2001	94.8	97.6	92.0	111.5	108.2	106.3	78.1	50.0	72.9	104.5	100.2	87.5	53.1
Bolivia	1989	90.6	98.9	82.0	..	..	..	..	..	73.9	106.6	116.1	98.7	50.2
Bolivia	1994	86.6	90.8	82.3	..	..	..	..	..	68.8	105.8	122.2	99.5	48.2
Bolivia	1998	73.5	77.6	69.2	106.5	85.0	75.5	38.6	25.5	53.0	99.9	112.5	86.6	41.3
Brazil	1986	84.0	97.3	70.1	..	..	..	..	..	72.9	106.0	113.2	89.1	23.1
Brazil	1996	48.1	51.6	44.4	83.2	46.7	32.9	24.7	28.6	42.4	65.3	93.2	58.1	32.0
Botswana	1988	38.6	46.4	31.0	..	..	..	..	..	38.5	38.7	43.7	35.6	37.3
Burkina Faso	1992/1993	107.6	114.5	100.3	..	..	..	..	..	76.4	113.0	111.3	84.0	52.8
Burundi	1987	85.8	97.1	74.2	..	..	..	..	..	84.5	85.9	87.8	82.2	33.4
Cambodia	2000	92.7	102.8	82.2	109.7	108.2	88.2	88.7	50.3	72.3	95.7	102.5	93.6	59.7
Cameroon	1991	80.3	86.4	74.3	103.9	101.0	78.8	65.1	51.2	71.7	85.8	112.7	51.6	50.6
Cameroon	1998	79.8	85.1	74.6	108.4	86.3	72.6	58.7	55.8	61.0	86.9	103.9	74.1	49.9
Central African Rep.	1994/1995	101.8	109.2	94.1	132.3	116.8	99.2	97.6	53.7	79.9	116.3	114.2	100.2	52.0
Chad	1996/1997	109.8	119.6	100.0	79.8	136.7	120.2	115.0	89.3	99.3	112.8	112.7	101.6	74.9
Colombia	1986	38.7	40.8	36.4	..	..	..	..	..	37.5	40.7	49.3	42.0	28.6
Colombia	1990	27.0	27.6	26.4	..	..	..	..	..	28.9	23.4	60.5	27.3	20.4
Colombia	1995	30.8	34.9	26.5	40.8	31.4	27.0	31.5	16.2	28.3	35.2	26.9	36.5	25.6
Colombia	2000	24.4	28.5	20.1	32.0	31.6	22.0	11.9	17.6	21.3	31.1	42.3	28.2	19.6
Comoros	1996	83.7	92.5	74.8	87.2	108.5	83.7	62.6	64.6	63.8	90.0	87.4	78.5	67.1
Côte d'Ivoire	1994	91.3	99.1	83.2	117.2	97.3	88.9	78.8	63.3	74.7	99.7	98.8	78.1	61.0
Côte d'Ivoire	1998	111.5	130.3	92.5	..	..	..	..	..	84.7	123.9	123.5	94.7	61.8
Dominican Rep.	1986	70.1	79.0	61.0	..	..	..	..	..	71.9	67.9	96.1	73.7	47.5
Dominican Rep.	1991	44.4	53.3	34.9	..	..	..	..	..	37.2	54.4	46.8	54.1	25.9
Dominican Rep.	1996	48.6	51.0	46.1	66.7	54.5	52.3	33.5	23.4	45.8	52.6	84.7	53.8	29.3
Dominican Rep.	1999	36.8	38.8	34.9	..	..	..	..	..	35.3	39.1	34.7	50.6	17.9
Ecuador	1987	65.2	70.4	59.7	..	..	..	..	..	51.6	77.7	104.5	68.7	39.4
Egypt, Arab Rep.	1988	93.1	93.7	92.4	..	..	..	..	..	64.2	113.8	112.3	82.8	37.8
Egypt, Arab Rep.	1992	79.9	84.4	75.3	..	..	..	..	..	54.4	96.2	97.8	73.0	42.4
Egypt, Arab Rep.	1995	72.9	72.5	73.3	109.7	88.7	64.6	50.6	31.8	51.1	86.8	93.4	70.0	37.5
Egypt, Arab Rep.	2000	54.7	55.0	54.5	75.6	63.9	53.9	43.9	29.6	43.1	61.8	68.3	58.8	35.9
El Salvador	1985	70.9	81.1	59.7	..	..	..	..	..	57.6	82.4	99.7	64.2	24.9
Eritrea	1995	75.6	81.9	69.0	74.0	66.2	87.0	85.8	67.5	79.8	74.4	76.0	77.0	67.2
Ethiopia	2000	112.9	124.4	100.6	92.8	114.9	141.5	118.1	95.1	96.5	114.7	119.1	85.0	63.5
Gabon	2000	61.1	73.6	48.9	57.0	68.1	66.6	72.7	35.9	60.7	62.2	65.5	58.7	62.5
Ghana	1988	80.9	88.9	72.5	..	..	..	..	..	66.0	86.6	87.2	74.5	80.2
Ghana	1993	74.7	79.2	70.1	77.5	94.6	82.8	64.2	45.8	54.9	82.2	87.1	66.7	44.9
Ghana	1998	61.2	64.4	57.9	72.7	58.0	82.1	52.5	26.0	42.6	67.5	66.1	70.3	51.3
Guatemala	1987	79.2	89.5	68.5	..	..	..	..	..	66.6	84.2	82.9	80.1	41.8
Guatemala	1995	57.2	62.7	51.5	56.9	79.7	55.7	46.7	35.0	45.4	62.9	69.8	53.6	26.1
Guatemala	1998/1999	49.1	50.0	48.1	58.0	50.8	52.1	39.6	39.2	49.0	49.1	55.7	46.5	41.1
Guinea	1999	106.6	112.3	100.6	118.9	127.9	113.5	91.4	70.2	79.2	115.8	112.0	78.4	60.6
Haiti	1994	87.1	97.7	76.2	93.7	93.6	85.6	81.7	74.3	83.2	88.9	95.2	78.4	75.6
Haiti	2000	89.4	96.5	82.6	99.5	70.0	93.4	88.4	97.2	87.0	90.5	90.9	97.5	55.9
India	1992/1993	86.3	88.6	83.9	109.2	106.3	89.7	65.6	44.0	59.4	94.3	100.6	68.2	46.3
India	1998/1999	73.0	74.8	71.1	96.5	80.7	76.3	55.3	38.1	49.2	79.7	87.0	66.9	42.2
Indonesia	1987	..	84.1	63.8	..	..	..	..	..	49.9	83.3	100.9	75.0	36.2
Indonesia	1991	..	79.9	67.9	..	..	..	..	..	57.2	81.0	89.0	81.1	34.6
Indonesia	1994	..	73.5	58.8	..	..	..	..	..	43.1	75.2	90.5	70.4	39.5
Indonesia	1997	52.2	59.1	44.9	78.1	57.3	51.4	39.4	23.3	35.7	58.0	77.5	58.8	28.0
Jordan	1990	..	36.4	37.3	..	..	..	..	..	35.8	39.2	38.7	41.1	33.8
Jordan	1997	29.0	34.3	23.4	35.4	28.8	30.1	25.9	23.4	26.7	39.1	54.2	31.9	25.5
Kazakhstan	1995	40.7	46.7	34.6	39.2	43.1	36.6	48.9	35.1	39.2	42.1	..	..	40.9
Kazakhstan	1999	54.9	62.0	47.3	67.6	65.3	65.8	27.3	42.3	43.7	63.8	..	..	55.2
Kenya	1989	..	63.4	54.3	..	..	..	..	..	56.7	59.2	72.1	55.4	42.3
Kenya	1993	..	66.6	58.6	..	..	..	..	..	45.5	64.9	66.3	70.6	34.8
Kenya	1998	70.7	74.5	66.8	95.8	82.9	58.5	61.0	40.2	55.4	73.8	82.2	79.7	40.0
Kyrgyz Rep.	1997	66.2	71.9	60.2	83.3	73.3	67.5	49.6	45.8	54.3	70.4	..	255.6	66.0
Liberia	1986	..	168.9	135.4	..	..	..	..	..	140.4	160.7	162.7	146.3	112.5
Madagascar	1992	..	103.2	101.8	..	..	..	..	..	74.7	106.8	137.9	97.6	72.9
Madagascar	1997	99.3	108.7	89.5	119.1	118.3	103.2	76.2	57.5	77.9	105.0	124.2	102.0	63.5

Table A3. Health—continued

		Infant mortality rate (deaths under age 12 months per 1,000 live births)												
		Overall	By gender		By asset quintiles					By location		By mother's education level		
	Survey year	Overall	Male	Female	Lowest	Second	Middle	Fourth	Highest	Urban	Rural	No education	Primary	Secondary or higher
Malawi	1992	136.1	141.7	130.4	141.2	133.7	154.1	139.2	106.1	118.1	138.4	143.4	129.6	96.3
Malawi	2000	112.5	117.1	107.9	131.5	110.7	117.4	109.1	86.4	82.5	116.7	116.6	114.3	65.4
Mali	1987	..	136.6	125.5	..	..	..	..	..	89.8	144.1	139.1	74.6	74.1
Mali	1995	133.5	140.5	126.5	151.4	146.9	138.9	129.0	93.2	98.7	145.0	139.6	112.7	59.6
Mali	2001	126.2	136.4	115.6	137.2	125.2	140.6	128.7	89.9	105.9	131.9	130.0	122.4	51.7
Mauritania	2000/2001	66.8	..	..	60.8	59.4	78.0	72.8	62.3	..	..	..	..	..
Mexico	1987	..	60.4	52.4	..	..	..	..	..	41.6	79.2	27.6	..	83.9
Morocco	1987	..	82.8	80.6	..	..	..	..	..	64.1	90.9	85.6	52.8	62.5
Morocco	1992	63.1	68.6	57.4	79.7	67.7	62.4	58.5	35.1	51.9	69.3	67.7	53.2	20.9
Mozambique	1997	147.4	153.0	141.9	187.7	136.2	144.3	134.2	94.7	100.8	159.7	155.6	143.9	72.5
Namibia	1992	61.5	66.6	56.5	63.6	63.0	48.4	72.2	57.3	63.1	60.7	57.9	65.5	57.0
Nepal	1996	93.0	101.9	83.7	96.3	107.2	103.6	84.7	63.9	61.1	95.3	97.5	80.0	53.4
Nepal	2001	77.2	79.2	75.2	85.5	87.7	76.6	72.8	53.2	50.1	79.3	84.6	61.0	39.1
Nicaragua	1997/1998	45.2	50.2	40.2	50.7	53.7	45.7	40.2	25.8	40.0	51.1	62.1	45.3	31.0
Niger	1990	..	135.8	133.0	..	..	..	..	..	89.0	142.6	137.0	114.9	48.8
Niger	1998	135.8	140.9	130.5	131.1	152.3	157.2	142.0	85.8	79.9	146.7	140.9	99.6	70.1
Nigeria	1990	91.6	93.9	89.3	102.2	102.3	93.1	85.8	68.6	75.6	95.9	96.1	87.2	69.9
Nigeria	1999	..	73.3	68.0	..	..	..	..	..	59.3	74.9	76.9	70.8	55.7
Pakistan	1990	94.0	102.1	85.5	88.7	108.7	109.3	95.7	62.5	74.6	102.2	98.6	90.4	59.5
Paraguay	1990	35.9	39.0	32.6	42.9	36.5	46.1	33.5	15.7	32.6	38.7	52.2	39.1	22.9
Peru	1986	..	83.2	74.8	..	..	..	..	..	55.8	106.1	118.8	88.3	41.5
Peru	1992	..	68.1	59.2	..	..	..	..	..	47.5	89.9	100.0	83.2	33.9
Peru	1996	49.9	56.1	43.5	78.3	53.6	34.4	36.0	19.5	34.9	71.0	78.9	61.7	30.6
Peru	2000	43.2	46.0	40.2	63.5	53.9	32.6	26.5	13.9	28.4	60.3	73.4	53.5	27.4
Philippines	1993	..	43.5	32.9	..	..	..	..	..	31.9	44.3	76.7	46.6	28.9
Philippines	1998	36.0	39.4	32.3	48.8	39.2	33.7	24.9	20.9	30.9	40.2	78.5	45.1	28.3
Rwanda	1992	90.2	98.4	82.1	..	..	..	..	..	87.5	90.4	97.3	84.9	65.3
Rwanda	2000	117.4	123.2	111.6	138.7	120.2	123.4	118.9	87.9	77.9	123.5	134.8	113.9	59.5
Senegal	1986	90.9	98.6	82.9	..	..	..	..	..	70.1	101.9	96.2	67.2	51.4
Senegal	1992/1993	76.1	83.6	68.7	..	..	..	..	..	54.5	86.8	81.2	58.5	32.1
Senegal	1997	69.4	73.6	65.0	84.5	81.6	69.6	58.8	44.9	50.2	79.1	76.1	52.1	28.7
South Africa	1998	42.2	49.0	35.3	61.6	51.6	35.8	34.0	17.0	32.6	52.2	58.8	47.6	36.1
Sri Lanka	1987	..	39.6	24.9	..	..	..	..	..	34.4	32.2	52.2	34.0	27.9
Sudan	1990	77.1	83.7	70.3	..	..	..	..	..	74.0	78.6	82.4	70.1	62.5
Tanzania	1992	99.4	103.6	95.1	..	..	..	..	..	108.3	97.1	103.1	97.9	71.8
Tanzania	1996	94.1	100.8	87.1	87.3	118.0	95.6	102.1	64.8	81.7	96.8	105.9	89.3	63.9
Tanzania	1999	107.8	..	..	114.8	107.5	115.4	106.8	91.9	..	..	..	..	..
Thailand	1987	38.5	45.6	30.9	..	..	..	..	..	25.9	40.8	55.5	38.7	18.5
Togo	1988	84.0	88.5	79.3	..	..	..	..	..	74.7	87.3	88.2	79.3	54.3
Togo	1998	80.3	89.1	71.4	84.1	81.7	90.0	73.9	65.8	65.3	85.0	87.4	72.1	54.4
Trinidad & Tobago	1987	30.5	28.4	32.8	..	..	..	..	..	34.2	27.0	60.0	24.2	38.5
Tunisia	1988	55.5	56.3	54.7	..	..	..	..	..	49.6	61.8	61.8	49.6	34.4
Turkey	1993	68.3	70.5	66.0	99.9	72.7	72.1	54.4	25.4	58.1	82.6	92.2	63.4	25.4
Turkey	1998	48.4	51.0	45.5	68.3	54.6	42.1	37.5	29.8	42.2	58.6	66.3	46.2	27.9
Turkmenistan	2000	71.8	83.0	59.7	89.3	78.6	68.2	62.4	58.4	60.1	79.9	113.8	29.7	71.4
Uganda	1988	106.0	111.3	100.6	..	..	..	..	..	103.8	106.2	114.9	101.1	85.8
Uganda	1995	86.1	87.4	84.9	109.0	79.5	90.4	84.5	63.2	74.4	87.6	94.0	87.9	48.0
Uganda	2000/2001	89.4	93.3	85.5	105.7	98.3	94.5	81.0	60.2	54.5	93.7	106.7	88.4	52.6
Uzbekistan	1996	43.5	50.2	36.7	54.4	39.8	36.0	39.0	45.9	42.9	43.8	..	..	43.6
Vietnam	1997	34.8	42.0	26.9	42.8	43.2	35.2	27.2	16.9	23.2	36.6	48.8	43.3	29.0
Yemen, Rep.	1991/1992	100.3	108.1	92.1	..	..	..	..	..	90.9	102.2	102.4	77.5	43.7
Yemen, Rep.	1997	89.5	98.4	80.0	108.5	102.0	88.9	80.9	60.0	75.4	93.6	92.6	71.6	66.9
Zambia	1992	98.3	106.2	90.5	..	..	..	..	..	78.0	116.0	114.9	98.9	79.4
Zambia	1996	107.7	116.3	99.3	123.6	131.5	105.1	104.1	69.8	91.9	117.9	132.9	110.2	81.7
Zambia	2001/2002	93.9	95.1	92.7	115.2	93.1	113.8	80.8	56.7	76.7	102.6	108.1	98.8	70.3
Zimbabwe	1988	56.4	63.2	49.5	..	..	..	..	..	37.0	63.4	77.1	53.9	38.2
Zimbabwe	1994	51.2	56.9	45.5	52.0	49.5	47.4	64.2	41.6	44.3	53.6	61.6	53.9	38.6
Zimbabwe	1999	59.7	63.1	56.2	59.1	63.9	67.1	63.1	44.3	47.2	65.3	81.1	60.6	54.0

Note: Only countries for which some data are available are included in this table; .. denotes no data.

Table A4. Education

	Survey year	Share of total population by years of schooling				Mean years of schooling					Education inequality measures		Share of inequality attributable	
						Total	By location		By gender		Gini index	GE (0.5)	To location	To gender
		0	1–6 years	7–12 years	13 or above		Urban	Rural	Male	Female				
Afghanistan	..	..	..	..	..	..	..	..	..	..	..	..	..	..
Albania	2002	0.04	0.10	0.76	0.10	9.19	10.55	8.09	9.58	8.83	0.21	0.14	0.06	0.01
Angola	2000	0.33	0.47	0.20	0.00	3.65	..	..	..	..	..	..	..	..
Argentina	2001	0.01	0.08	0.65	0.26	10.33	..	..	10.26	10.40	0.22	0.09	..	0.00
Armenia	2000	0.01	0.02	0.61	0.36	11.44	11.98	10.60	11.50	11.38	0.13	0.04	0.05	0.00
Australia	1994	0.00	0.00	0.58	0.42	12.50	12.64	12.21	13.07	11.89	0.15	0.04	0.00	0.03
Austria	1995	0.00	0.01	0.89	0.10	10.64	11.10	10.35	10.97	10.30	0.14	0.03	0.02	0.02
Azerbaijan	1995	0.02	0.03	0.65	0.30	10.99	11.61	10.23	11.62	10.43	0.15	0.07	0.03	0.02
Bangladesh	1999/2000	0.46	0.26	0.24	0.04	3.92	6.31	3.29	4.94	2.90	0.62	1.18	0.04	0.03
Belarus	2002	0.02	0.28	0.27	0.44	11.27	..	..	10.84	11.61	0.25	0.13	..	0.00
Belgium	1997	0.03	0.12	0.47	0.38	11.52	..	..	11.65	11.39	0.22	0.12	..	0.00
Benin	2001	0.63	0.23	0.12	0.03	2.47	4.28	1.34	3.63	1.53	0.75	1.69	0.10	0.05
Bolivia	1998	0.10	0.35	0.35	0.20	7.63	9.28	4.07	8.48	6.84	0.38	0.38	0.16	0.02
Bosnia & Herzegovina	2001	0.06	0.16	0.69	0.10	9.32	11.03	8.71	10.29	8.39	0.24	0.18	0.03	0.03
Brazil	2001	0.20	0.21	0.23	0.36	8.38	8.67	6.61	8.44	8.32	0.39	0.53	0.01	0.00
Bulgaria	2003	0.06	0.22	0.24	0.48	10.85	12.22	7.50	10.76	10.94	0.19	0.26	0.05	0.04
Burkina Faso	1998/1999	0.86	0.08	0.04	0.02	1.00	4.28	0.33	1.48	0.63	0.90	2.63	0.27	0.03
Burundi	2000	0.61	0.32	0.05	0.02	2.13	..	..	..	..	..	..	..	..
Cambodia	1999	0.00	0.63	0.36	0.01	5.70	7.12	5.52	6.35	5.15	0.28	0.12	0.04	0.04
Cameroon	1998	0.32	0.29	0.30	0.08	5.32	7.58	4.14	6.54	4.27	0.50	0.84	0.05	0.03
Canada	2000	0.00	0.01	0.34	0.65	14.27	14.39	13.30	14.34	14.20	0.13	0.03	0.01	0.00
Central African Rep.	1994/1995	0.48	0.35	0.14	0.02	2.95	4.53	1.82	4.22	1.79	0.66	1.32	0.08	0.07
Chad	1996/1997	0.76	0.16	0.06	0.01	1.30	3.09	0.69	2.20	0.53	0.86	2.23	0.12	0.10
Chile	2000	0.02	0.19	0.54	0.24	10.27	10.83	6.77	10.42	10.14	0.23	0.13	0.08	0.00
China	2000	0.07	0.33	0.55	0.05	6.54	8.53	5.18	7.22	5.82	0.37	0.35	0.08	0.02
Colombia	2000	0.07	0.44	0.36	0.13	7.19	8.29	4.08	7.19	7.19	0.36	0.31	0.13	0.00
Comoros	1996	0.64	0.17	0.16	0.04	2.76	4.41	2.06	3.69	1.96	0.71	1.82	0.04	0.00
Congo, Dem. Rep.	2000	0.25	0.35	0.36	0.04	5.39	..	..	..	..	..	..	..	..
Costa Rica	2000	0.05	0.48	0.31	0.16	7.90	9.02	6.15	7.91	7.89	0.30	0.22	..	0.00
Côte d'Ivoire	1998/1999	0.56	0.24	0.14	0.06	3.43	5.30	2.16	4.40	2.52	0.68	1.48	0.07	0.03
Czech Rep.	1996	0.00	0.16	0.74	0.10	9.14	..	..	9.31	8.98	0.19	0.06	..	0.00
Denmark	1992	0.00	0.00	0.83	0.17	11.62	11.82	11.23	11.78	11.47	0.11	0.02	0.01	0.00
Dominican Rep.	2002	0.10	0.35	0.40	0.15	7.47	8.32	5.85	7.38	7.56	0.38	0.36	0.04	0.00
East Timor	2001	0.60	0.19	0.20	0.02	3.19	5.40	2.52	3.43	0.86	0.69	1.68	0.04	0.03
Ecuador	1998/1999	0.08	0.42	0.33	0.18	8.12	9.67	5.49	8.26	7.98	0.33	0.28	0.12	0.00
Egypt, Arab Rep.	2000	0.35	0.19	0.28	0.17	6.60	8.60	4.83	7.90	5.28	0.51	0.90	0.05	0.02
El Salvador	2000	0.18	0.38	0.32	0.12	6.56	8.32	3.53	6.98	6.22	0.45	0.56	0.13	0.00
Estonia	2000	0.00	0.02	0.58	0.40	12.49	..	..	12.13	12.80	0.16	0.04	..	0.01
Ethiopia	2000	0.74	0.16	0.09	0.01	1.56	5.16	0.88	2.21	0.94	0.83	2.14	0.15	0.04
Finland	2000	0.00	0.00	0.70	0.30	12.03	12.24	11.26	11.88	12.17	0.15	0.03	0.02	0.00
France	1994	0.20	0.12	0.48	0.20	8.26	8.58	7.36	8.24	8.28	0.37	0.49	0.00	0.00
Gabon	2000	0.19	0.32	0.38	0.11	6.71	7.45	4.55	7.62	5.78	0.39	0.52	0.04	0.02
Gambia, The	2000	0.58	0.14	0.19	0.09	3.82	..	..	..	..	..	..	..	..
Germany	2000	0.02	0.36	0.39	0.23	10.07	10.39	9.57	10.07	10.07	0.25	0.13	0.01	0.00
Ghana	1998/1999	0.31	0.14	0.41	0.14	6.62	8.79	5.39	8.31	5.22	0.46	0.78	0.04	0.04
Guatemala	1998/1999	0.29	0.45	0.21	0.05	4.58	6.28	3.10	5.14	4.07	0.54	0.83	0.07	0.01
Guinea	1999	0.77	0.09	0.09	0.05	1.97	4.44	0.86	3.06	1.08	0.84	2.22	0.14	0.06
Guinea-Bissau	2000	0.72	0.14	0.05	0.09	2.34	..	..	..	..	..	..	..	..
Guyana	2000	0.00	0.28	0.62	0.10	8.89	10.00	8.37	8.94	8.84	0.20	0.07	0.05	0.00
Haiti	2000	0.40	0.33	0.22	0.05	3.93	6.70	2.14	4.75	3.19	0.61	1.12	0.15	0.02
Honduras	2001	0.19	0.55	0.20	0.06	5.55	7.41	3.64	5.57	5.52	0.45	0.56	0.11	0.00
Hungary	1999	0.00	0.10	0.75	0.14	10.01	..	..	10.09	9.94	0.18	0.06	..	0.00
India	1998/2000	0.41	0.20	0.31	0.08	5.03	7.78	3.93	6.50	3.57	0.56	1.02	0.05	0.04
Indonesia	2002	0.09	0.50	0.34	0.07	7.38	9.04	5.85	7.99	6.77	0.32	0.29	0.08	0.01
Iraq	2000	0.26	0.33	0.27	0.14	6.36	..	..	..	..	..	..	..	..
Ireland	1996	0.00	0.03	0.79	0.18	11.00	..	..	11.14	10.86	0.11	0.04	..	0.00
Israel	2001	0.02	0.03	0.51	0.44	12.63	12.55	13.08	12.75	12.52	0.14	0.07	0.00	0.00
Italy	2000	0.03	0.19	0.68	0.10	9.05	9.49	8.56	9.32	8.79	0.23	0.12	0.01	0.00
Jamaica	2000	0.01	0.15	0.71	0.12	9.31	..	..	9.17	9.43	0.19	0.08	..	0.00
Japan	2000	0.00	0.11	0.53	0.36	11.74	11.99	10.79	11.95	11.52	0.17	0.08	0.01	0.00
Jordan	2002	0.00	0.19	0.54	0.26	10.42	10.70	9.55	10.74	10.13	0.21	0.07	0.01	0.01
Kazakhstan	1999	0.01	0.03	0.79	0.17	10.69	11.15	10.23	10.75	10.64	0.12	0.04	0.02	0.00
Kenya	1999	0.20	0.26	0.52	0.02	6.26	8.05	5.48	7.01	5.56	0.38	0.51	0.03	0.01
Kosovo	2000	0.07	0.12	0.63	0.18	9.35	10.46	8.61	10.85	7.93	0.46	0.21	0.03	0.15
Kyrgyz Rep.	1997	0.01	0.03	0.79	0.17	10.58	11.35	10.16	10.76	10.41	0.12	0.05	0.03	0.00

Table A4. Education—continued

	Survey year	Share of total population by years of schooling				Mean years of schooling					Education inequality measures		Share of inequality attributable	
						Total	By location		By gender		Gini index	GE (0.5)	To location	To gender
		0	1–6 years	7–12 years	13 or above		Urban	Rural	Male	Female				
Lao PDR	1997	0.32	0.44	0.20	0.04	4.08	7.32	3.36	5.38	2.85	0.53	0.84	0.07	0.06
Lesotho	2000	0.15	0.39	0.42	0.03	5.82	..	..	..	..	..	..	..	..
Luxembourg	2000	0.01	0.17	0.34	0.49	12.31	..	..	12.96	11.65	0.21	0.08	..	0.02
Madagascar	2001	0.00	0.65	0.26	0.09	6.34	8.02	5.65	6.38	6.30	0.31	0.16	0.08	0.00
Malawi	2000	0.30	0.40	0.30	0.01	4.23	7.67	3.60	5.46	3.08	0.52	0.80	0.06	0.05
Mali	2001	0.81	0.10	0.06	0.03	1.45	3.80	0.56	2.03	0.94	0.87	2.36	0.18	0.03
Mexico	1999	0.08	0.41	0.37	0.14	7.78	8.63	4.67	8.10	7.49	0.34	0.30	0.09	0.00
Moldova	2000	0.01	0.07	0.55	0.37	11.75	..	..	11.71	11.77	0.20	0.07	..	0.00
Mongolia	2000	0.02	0.08	0.63	0.27	10.05	..	..	..	..	..	..	..	..
Morocco	1992	0.63	0.18	0.15	0.04	2.84	4.70	0.94	3.92	1.90	0.74	1.72	0.03	0.04
Mozambique	1997	0.48	0.43	0.08	0.00	2.24	4.65	1.54	3.20	1.45	0.65	1.27	0.11	0.06
Myanmar	2000	0.26	0.47	0.27	0.00	4.32	..	..	..	..	..	..	..	..
Namibia	2000	0.20	0.23	0.53	0.04	6.65	8.29	5.35	6.73	6.57	0.38	0.52	0.05	0.00
Nepal	2001	0.64	0.17	0.17	0.02	2.46	5.38	2.09	3.88	1.22	0.74	1.76	0.04	0.09
Netherlands	1999	0.00	0.01	0.71	0.28	12.36	..	..	12.67	12.03	0.13	0.03	..	0.01
Nicaragua	2001	0.23	0.41	0.26	0.10	5.57	7.28	2.91	5.54	5.59	0.49	0.67	0.13	0.00
Niger	1998	0.85	0.09	0.05	0.02	1.12	3.49	0.52	1.57	0.75	0.88	2.56	0.16	0.03
Nigeria	1999	0.39	0.23	0.28	0.11	5.77	8.06	4.77	7.06	4.61	0.53	0.97	0.03	0.02
Norway	2000	0.00	0.00	0.70	0.30	12.70	12.97	12.36	12.75	12.65	0.11	0.03	0.01	0.00
Pakistan	2001	0.59	0.15	0.21	0.05	3.51	5.95	2.43	5.05	2.02	0.70	1.55	0.06	0.06
Panama	2000	0.04	0.32	0.43	0.21	9.52	10.84	7.04	9.29	9.74	0.27	0.17	0.11	0.00
Papua New Guinea	1996	0.48	0.33	0.11	0.08	3.90	..	..	4.98	2.79	0.62	1.25	..	0.03
Paraguay	2000	0.06	0.53	0.29	0.12	7.26	8.77	5.15	7.36	7.16	0.35	0.26	0.12	0.00
Peru	2000	0.08	0.32	0.39	0.21	8.76	10.24	5.56	9.51	8.03	0.30	0.26	0.14	0.01
Philippines	1998	0.03	0.32	0.46	0.19	8.77	9.94	7.41	8.71	8.84	0.24	0.14	0.07	0.00
Poland	1999	0.00	0.21	0.67	0.11	9.27	..	..	9.05	9.47	0.19	0.06	..	0.00
Romania	2002	0.01	0.14	0.70	0.15	9.73	..	..	10.14	9.33	0.21	0.09	..	0.01
Russian Federation	2000	0.00	0.01	0.40	0.59	13.70	..	..	13.60	13.79	0.14	0.04	..	0.00
Rwanda	2000	0.38	0.41	0.20	0.01	3.59	6.67	2.96	4.19	3.14	0.55	0.99	0.06	0.01
São Tomé & Principe	2000	0.17	0.42	0.27	0.15	6.54	..	..	..	..	..	..	..	..
Senegal	1992/1993	0.77	0.13	0.07	0.03	1.80	3.73	0.51	2.60	1.19	0.83	2.18	0.19	0.03
Sierra Leone	2000	0.74	0.04	0.19	0.03	2.44	..	..	..	..	..	..	..	..
Slovak Rep.	1992	0.01	0.14	0.74	0.11	10.36	..	..	10.74	9.99	0.15	0.05	..	0.01
Slovenia	1999	0.01	0.00	0.86	0.14	11.32	..	..	11.37	11.27	0.10	0.03	..	0.00
South Africa	1998	0.74	0.14	0.09	0.03	1.95	3.93	0.58	2.72	1.33	0.79	2.10	0.19	0.11
Spain	1990	0.13	0.22	0.43	0.22	9.12	..	..	9.48	8.77	0.31	0.33	..	0.00
Sri Lanka	2002	0.00	0.25	0.57	0.18	9.22	..	..	8.94	9.47	0.23	0.10	..	0.00
Sudan	2000	0.51	0.20	0.24	0.05	4.01	..	..	..	..	..	..	..	..
Suriname	2000	0.01	0.38	0.52	0.09	7.96	..	..	7.95	7.98	0.24	0.11	..	0.00
Swaziland	2000	0.20	0.24	0.52	0.04	6.78	..	..	..	..	..	..	..	..
Sweden	2000	0.00	0.09	0.61	0.30	12.00	12.53	11.46	11.84	12.15	0.16	0.04	0.02	0.00
Switzerland	1992	0.00	0.00	0.79	0.21	11.64	11.57	11.71	12.24	11.04	0.13	0.03	0.00	0.05
Taiwan, China	2000	0.05	0.22	0.47	0.26	9.48	9.74	7.03	10.15	8.84	0.30	0.24	0.02	0.01
Tajikistan	1999	0.00	0.05	0.63	0.32	11.96	11.33	12.18	11.94	11.97	0.20	0.07	0.01	0.00
Tanzania	1999	0.30	0.19	0.50	0.01	4.58	6.03	4.05	5.36	3.93	0.41	0.74	0.02	0.02
Thailand	2000	0.05	0.47	0.34	0.15	6.89	8.97	5.79	7.19	6.62	0.33	0.21	0.10	0.00
Togo	1998	0.47	0.32	0.19	0.02	3.15	5.03	2.12	4.57	1.98	0.62	1.25	0.08	0.07
Trinidad & Tobago	2000	0.01	0.12	0.78	0.09	9.17	..	..	9.19	9.14	0.19	0.09	..	0.00
Turkey	1998	0.17	0.50	0.23	0.09	6.14	6.93	4.61	7.23	5.08	0.38	0.47	0.04	0.03
Turkmenistan	1998	0.00	0.02	0.77	0.20	10.60	10.98	10.27	10.96	10.28	0.12	0.03	0.02	0.00
United Kingdom	1999	0.00	0.00	0.68	0.31	12.16	12.31	11.98	12.21	12.11	0.11	0.02	0.00	0.00
United States	2000	0.00	0.02	0.42	0.55	13.83	13.96	13.37	13.85	13.80	0.13	0.04	0.00	0.00
Uganda	1995	0.32	0.39	0.27	0.03	4.23	7.53	3.71	5.46	3.12	0.50	0.82	0.05	0.05
Uruguay	2000	0.01	0.34	0.45	0.20	9.41	..	..	9.32	9.49	0.24	0.10	..	0.00
Uzbekistan	1996	0.01	0.02	0.81	0.17	10.66	11.06	10.37	11.00	10.33	0.11	0.03	0.01	0.01
Venezuela, RB de	2000	0.08	0.34	0.42	0.17	8.29	9.92	7.96	8.08	8.51	0.30	0.26	0.01	0.00
Vietnam	2000	0.06	0.34	0.57	0.02	6.96	8.48	6.44	7.43	6.53	0.28	0.22	0.04	0.01
Yemen, Rep.	1999	0.65	0.11	0.17	0.07	3.34	5.95	2.27	5.35	1.54	0.73	1.81	0.06	0.10
Zambia	1992	0.16	0.30	0.49	0.06	6.26	8.45	4.91	7.41	5.14	0.37	0.44	0.08	0.04
Zimbabwe	1999	0.10	0.21	0.62	0.07	7.57	9.52	6.22	8.41	6.81	0.30	0.30	0.08	0.02

Technical notes

Table A1 Poverty

National poverty rate is the percentage of the population living below the national poverty line. **Rural (urban) poverty rate** is the percentage of the rural (urban) population living below the national rural (urban) poverty line. **Population below $1 a day** and **population below $2 a day** are the percentages of the population living on less than $1.08 a day and $2.15 a day at 1993 international prices. All above poverty indicators are also called headcount ratios. **Poverty gap** is the mean shortfall from the poverty line (counting the nonpoor as having zero shortfall), expressed as a percentage of the poverty line.

To measure poverty, one needs to define the relevant welfare measure, to select a poverty line, and to select a poverty indicator. The two most commonly used poverty indicators are the headcount ratio and the poverty gap, part of the FGT class of indexes from Foster, Greer, and Thorbecke (1984). The indexes are defined by

$$P_\alpha = \frac{1}{n} \sum_{i=1}^{J} \left[\frac{(Z - Y_i)}{Z} \right]^\alpha$$

where i is a subgroup of individuals with income below the poverty line Z; n is the total number of individuals in the sample; Y_i is the income of individual i; and α is a distinguishing parameter between FGT indexes. When α equals 0, the expression simplifies to J/n, or the headcount ratio. The poverty gap is given by α equal to 1.

The welfare measure can be income or consumption. Income is generally more difficult to measure accurately, and consumption comes closer to the notion of standard of living. And income can vary over time even if the standard of living does not. So whenever possible, consumption data are used to estimate poverty. But when consumption data are not available, income data are used.

Poverty line is a threshold below which a given household or individual will be regarded as poor. National poverty lines are established according to countries' own judgment of minimum acceptable living standards. Because countries have different definitions of poverty, consistent comparisons between countries can be difficult. Local poverty lines tend to have higher purchasing power in rich countries, where more generous standards are used than in poor countries. Is it reasonable to treat two people with the same standard of living—in terms of their command over commodities—differently because one happens to live in a better-off country?

Poverty measures based on an international poverty line attempt to hold the real value of the poverty line constant across countries, as is done when making comparisons over time. The commonly used $1 a day standard, an international poverty line measured in 1985 international prices and adjusted to local currency using purchasing power parities (PPP), was chosen because it is typical of the national poverty lines in low-income countries. Recalculated in 1993 consumption PPP terms in 1993 prices, the original $1 a day in 1985 PPP is now about $1.08 a day. PPP exchange rates are used because they take into account the local prices of goods and services not traded internationally. But PPP rates were designed for comparing aggregates from national accounts, not for making international poverty comparisons. As a result, there is no certainty that an international poverty line measures the same degree of need or deprivation across countries. Furthermore, any revisions in the PPP of a country to incorporate better price indexes can produce dramatically different poverty lines in local currency.

Since the World Bank produced its first global poverty estimates for *World Development Report 1990* using household survey data, the database has expanded considerably and now includes 440 surveys representing almost 100 developing countries. Some 1.1 million randomly sampled households were interviewed in these surveys, representing 93 percent of the population of developing countries. Along with improvements in data coverage and quality, the underlying methodology has also improved, resulting in better and more comprehensive estimates.

Data availability. Since 1979 there has been considerable expansion in the number of countries that field such surveys, in the frequency of the surveys, and in the quality of their data. The number of data sets rose dramatically from a mere 13 between 1979 and 1981, to 100 between 1997 and 1999. Sub-Saharan Africa continues to lag behind all other regions, with only 28 countries out of 48 having at least one data set available.

Data quality. A number of issues arise in measuring household living standards from survey data. As indicated above, one relates to the choice of income or consumption as a welfare indicator. Another issue is that household surveys can differ widely, for example, in the number of consumer goods they identify. And even similar surveys may not be strictly comparable because of differences in timing or the quality and training of survey enumerators.

Comparisons of countries at different levels of development pose a potential problem because of differences in the relative importance of consumption of nonmarket goods. The local market value of all consumption in kind (including own production, particularly important in underdeveloped rural economies) should be included in total consumption expenditure. Similarly, imputed profit from the production of nonmarket goods should be included in income. This is not always done, though such omissions were a far bigger problem in surveys before the 1980s. Most survey data now include valuations for consumption or income from own production. Nonetheless, valuation methods vary. For example, some surveys use the price in the nearest market, while others use the average farm-gate selling price.

In all cases the measures of poverty have been calculated from primary data sources (tabulations or household data) rather than existing estimates. Estimation from tabulations uses an interpolation method based on Lorenz curves with flexible functional forms, which have proved reliable in past work. Empirical Lorenz curves were weighted by household size, so they are based on percentiles of population, not households.

The Poverty Monitoring team in the World Bank's Development Research Group calculates the number of people living below various international poverty lines, as well as other poverty and inequality measures that are published in *World Development Indicators*. That database is updated annually as new survey data become available, and a major reassessment of progress against poverty is made about every three years.

Table A2 Income Distribution

The **Gini index** measures the extent to which the distribution of **income/consumption** (or **land**) among individuals or households within an economy deviates from a perfectly equal distribution. A Lorenz curve plots the cumulative percentage of total income received against the cumulative proportion of recipients, starting with the poorest individual or household. The Gini index measures the area between the Lorenz curve and a hypothetical line of absolute equality, expressed as the share of the maximum area under the line. Thus a Gini index of zero represents perfect equality, while an index of 1 implies perfect inequality. The Gini coefficient takes on values between 0 and 1 with zero interpreted as no inequality.

$$\text{Gini} = \frac{1}{2\,n^2\bar{y}}\sum_{i=1}^{n}\sum_{j=1}^{n}\left|y_i - y_j\right|$$

Generalized Entropy (or GE) indexes provide us with an alternative class of income/consumption (or other) inequality measures, given by

$$\text{GE}_c = \frac{1}{c^2 - c}\left[\frac{1}{n}\sum_{i=1}^{n}\left(\frac{y_i}{\bar{y}}\right)^c - 1\right].$$

The value of the measure GE ranges from 0 to infinity, with zero representing an equal distribution (all incomes identical) and higher values represent higher levels of inequality. The parameter c in the GE class represents the weight given to distances between incomes at different parts of the income distribution, and can take any real value. For lower values of c, GE is more sensitive to changes in the lower tail of the distribution, and for higher values GE is more sensitive to changes that affect the upper tail. The most

common values of c used are 0, 1 and 2: hence a value of $c = 0$ gives more weight to distances between incomes in the lower tail; $c = 1$ applies equal weights across the distribution; and a value of $c = 2$ give proportionately more weight to gaps in the upper tail. The GE measures with parameters 0 and 1 become, with l'Hopital's rule, two of Theil's measures of inequality (Theil, 1967), the mean log deviation and the Theil-T index respectively, as follows:

$$\text{GE}(0) = \frac{1}{n}\sum_{i=1}^{n}\log\frac{\bar{y}}{y_i}$$

$$\text{GE}(1) = \frac{1}{n}\sum_{i=1}^{n}\frac{y_i}{\bar{y}}\log\frac{y_i}{\bar{y}}$$

90th/10th percentile ratio is constructed by dividing the income (consumption) in the 90th percentile by the income (consumption) in the 10th percentile. A 90th/10th ratio of 5 means that the household in the 90th percentile earns (spends) five times as much as the household in the 10th percentile.

Survey year gives the year in which the country survey used to generate the reported data was completed.

Table A3 Health

To measure equity in health, we have only used data from 123 Demographic Health Surveys (DHS) collected in 67 countries between 1985 and 2002. In addition to breaking down infant mortality rates by "asset indices" created by Filmer and Pritchett (1998) (as documented in Gwatkin and others (2003, 2004), we compiled population breakdowns for different groupings using the interactive "STATcompiler" feature in the DHS website.

Infant mortality rate is the number of deaths to children under 12 months of age per 1,000 live births. Figures used in the table are based on births in the 10 years preceding the survey.

Asset quintiles are constructed using the Filmer-Pritchett method to create an index of wealth based on 20–30 household attributes—type of flooring and/or roof, source of water, availability of electricity, possession of such items as watches, radios, etc. Once the index is created it is applied to the country's household surveys to construct a distribution of assets that is then divided into fifths, each household belonging to one of these quintiles. Indicators for the quintiles are then formed as the average result for all families for that indicator (e.g. infant mortality rate) within each asset quintile.

Education is the number of years (or level) of formal education the child's mother has completed at the time of the survey.

Gender is the sex of the child (male or female) as reported by the child's mother (or household head if mother is not present).

Location is listed as urban if the surveyed household lives in a recognized city or surroundings, and listed as rural if otherwise.

Table A4 Education

For measuring educational attainment, we used a database that was put together by Araujo, Ferreira, and Schady. The data come from the individual-level records of various household surveys for 124 countries. The selection criteria were to choose a survey instrument that: (a) was nationally representative; (b) was collected on 2000 or on the closest year; and (c) included information on the actual number of years of education completed by the interviewees. The five-year cohorts group adults who were likely to have completed their education at the time of the survey. The cohorts are constructed based on *one survey* per country.

The measure **share of total population by years of schooling** gives the percent of the population having completed the reported number of years of schooling at the time the survey was taken.

Mean years of schooling gives the arithmetic mean for years of formal schooling for the **total** population, those living in **urban** areas, and those living in **rural** areas, as well as for **males** and **females.**

The Gini index and the Generalized Entropy indexes reported in this table are the same as those described in table A2, except for the fact that y now denotes years of schooling.

We report the **share of inequality** in education which is due to differences between urban and rural dwellers (**location**) and between males and females (**gender**).

The GE class of inequality measures can be decomposed into a between- and within-group component along the following lines:

$$\mathrm{GE}_c = \frac{1}{c(c-1)}\left[1-\sum_j g_j\left(\frac{\mu_j}{\mu}\right)^c\right] + \sum_j \mathrm{GE}_j g_j\left(\frac{\mu_j}{\mu}\right)^c \quad \text{if } c \neq 0,1$$

$$\mathrm{GE}_c = \left[\sum_j g_j \log\left(\frac{\mu}{\mu_j}\right)\right] + \sum_j \mathrm{GE}_j g_j \quad \text{if } c = 0$$

$$\mathrm{GE}_c = \left[\sum_j g_j\left(\frac{\mu_j}{\mu}\right)\log\left(\frac{\mu_j}{\mu}\right)\right] + \sum_j \mathrm{GE}_j g_j\left(\frac{\mu_j}{\mu}\right) \quad \text{if } c = 1$$

where μ is average per capita consumption, j refers to subgroups, g_j refers to the population share of group j, and GE_j refers to inequality in group j. The between-group component of inequality is captured by the first term to the right of the equal sign. It can be interpreted as measuring what would be the level of inequality in the population if everyone within the group had the same (group average) consumption level μ_j. The second term on the right reflects the within group inequality GE_j. Ratios of the respective components with the overall inequality level provide a measure of percentage contribution of between-group and within-group inequality to total inequality.

Selected world development indicators

In this year's edition, development data are presented in four tables presenting comparative socioeconomic data for more than 130 economies for the most recent year for which data are available and, for some indicators, for an earlier year. An additional table presents basic indicators for 75 economies with sparse data or with populations of less than 2 million.

The indicators presented here are a selection from more than 800 included in *World Development Indicators 2005*. Published annually, *World Development Indicators* reflects a comprehensive view of the development process. Its opening chapter reports on the Millennium Development Goals, which grew out of agreements and resolutions of world conferences organized by the United Nations (U.N.) in the past decade, and reaffirmed at the Millennium Summit in September 2000 by member countries of the U.N. The other five main sections recognize the contribution of a wide range of factors: human capital development, environmental sustainability, macroeconomic performance, private sector development and the investment climate, and the global links that influence the external environment for development. *World Development Indicators* is complemented by a separately published database that gives access to over 1,000 data tables and 800 time-series indicators for 222 economies and regions. This database is available through an electronic subscription (*WDI Online*) or as a CD-ROM.

Data sources and methodology

Socioeconomic and environmental data presented here are drawn from several sources: primary data collected by the World Bank, member country statistical publications, research institutes, and international organizations such as the U.N. and its specialized agencies, the International Monetary Fund (IMF), and the Organisation for Economic Co-operation and Development (OECD). Although international standards of coverage, definition, and classification apply to most statistics reported by countries and international agencies, there are inevitably differences in timeliness and reliability arising from differences in the capabilities and resources devoted to basic data collection and compilation. For some topics, competing sources of data require review by World Bank staff to ensure that the most reliable data available are presented. In some instances, where available data are deemed too weak to provide reliable measures of levels and trends or do not adequately adhere to international standards, the data are not shown.

The data presented are generally consistent with those in *World Development Indicators 2005*. However, data have been revised and updated wherever new information has become available. Differences may also reflect revisions to historical series and changes in methodology. Thus data of different vintages may be published in different editions of World Bank publications. Readers are advised not to compile data series from different publications or different editions of the same publication. Consistent time-series data are available on *World Development Indicators 2005* CD-ROM and through *WDI Online*.

All dollar figures are in current U.S. dollars unless otherwise stated. The various methods used to convert from national currency figures are described in the Technical notes.

Because the World Bank's primary business is providing lending and policy advice to its low- and middle-income members, the issues covered in these tables focus mainly on these economies. Where available, information on the high-income economies is also provided for comparison. Readers may wish to refer to national statistical publications and publications of the OECD and the European Union for more information on the high-income economies.

Classification of economies and summary measures

The summary measures at the bottom of each table include economies classified by income per capita and by region. GNI per capita is used to determine the following income classifications: low-income, $825 or less in 2004; middle-income, $826 to $10,065; and high-income, $10,066 and above. A further division at GNI per capita $3,255 is made between lower-middle-income and upper-middle-income economies. See the table on classification of economies on the next page for a list of economies in each group (including those with populations of less than 2 million).

Summary measures are either totals (indicated by **t** if the aggregates include estimates for missing data and nonreporting countries, or by an **s** for simple sums of the data available), weighted averages (**w**), or median values (**m**) calculated for groups of economies. Data for the countries excluded from the main tables (those presented in Table 5) have been included in the summary measures, where data are available, or by assuming that they follow the trend of reporting countries. This gives a more consistent aggregated measure by standardizing country coverage for each period shown. Where missing information accounts for a third or more of the overall estimate, however, the group measure is reported as not available. The section on *Statistical methods* in the *Technical notes* provides further information on aggregation methods. Weights used to construct the aggregates are listed in the technical notes for each table.

From time to time an economy's classification is revised because of changes in the above cutoff values or in the economy's measured level of GNI per capita. When such changes occur, aggregates based on those classifications are recalculated for the past period so that a consistent time series is maintained.

Terminology and country coverage

The term *country* does not imply political independence but may refer to any territory for which authorities report separate social or economic statistics. Data are shown for economies as they were constituted in 2003, and historical data are revised to reflect current political arrangements. Throughout the tables, exceptions are noted.

Technical notes

Because data quality and intercountry comparisons are often problematic, readers are encouraged to consult the Technical notes, the table on Classification of Economies by Region and Income (next page), and the footnotes to the tables. For more extensive documentation see *World Development Indicators 2005*.

Readers may find more information on the WDI 2005, and orders can be made online, by phone, or fax as follows:

For more information and to order online: **http://www. worldbank.org/data/wdi2005/index.htm.**

To order by phone or fax: **1-800-645-7247** or 703-661-1580; Fax 703-661-1501

To order by mail: The World Bank, P.O. Box 960, Herndon, VA 20172-0960, U.S.A.

Classification of economies by region and income, FY2006

East Asia and the Pacific		Latin America and the Caribbean		South Asia		High income OECD
American Samoa	UMC	Antigua & Barbuda	UMC	Afghanistan	LIC	Australia
Cambodia	LIC	Argentina	UMC	Bangladesh	LIC	Austria
China	LMC	Barbados	UMC	Bhutan	LIC	Belgium
Fiji	LMC	Belize	UMC	India	LIC	Canada
Indonesia	LMC	Bolivia	LMC	Maldives	LMC	Denmark
Kiribati	LMC	Brazil	LMC	Nepal	LIC	Finland
Korea, Dem. Rep.	LIC	Chile	UMC	Pakistan	LIC	France
Lao PDR	LIC	Colombia	LMC	Sri Lanka	LMC	Germany
Malaysia	UMC	Costa Rica	UMC			Greece
Marshall Islands	LMC	Cuba	LMC			Iceland
Micronesia, Fed. Sts.	LMC	Dominica	UMC	Sub-Saharan Africa		Ireland
Mongolia	LIC	Dominican Republic	LMC	Angola	LMC	Italy
Myanmar	LIC	Ecuador	LMC	Benin	LIC	Japan
Northern Mariana Islands	UMC	El Salvador	LMC	Botswana	UMC	Korea, Rep.
Palau	UMC	Grenada	UMC	Burkina Faso	LIC	Luxembourg
Papua New Guinea	LIC	Guatemala	LMC	Burundi	LIC	Netherlands
Philippines	LMC	Guyana	LMC	Cameroon	LIC	New Zealand
Samoa	LMC	Haiti	LIC	Cape Verde	LMC	Norway
Solomon Islands	LIC	Honduras	LMC	Central African Rep.	LIC	Portugal
Thailand	LMC	Jamaica	LMC	Chad	LIC	Spain
Timor-Leste	LIC	Mexico	UMC	Comoros	LIC	Sweden
Tonga	LMC	Nicaragua	LIC	Congo, Dem. Rep.	LIC	Switzerland
Vanuatu	LMC	Panama	UMC	Congo, Rep.	LIC	United Kingdom
Vietnam	LIC	Paraguay	LMC	Côte d'Ivoire	LIC	United States
		Peru	LMC	Equatorial Guinea	UMC	
Europe and Central Asia		St. Kitts and Nevis	UMC	Eritrea	LIC	
Albania	LMC	St. Lucia	UMC	Ethiopia	LIC	Other high-income
Armenia	LMC	St. Vincent & the		Gabon	UMC	Andorra
Azerbaijan	LMC	Grenadines	UMC	Gambia, The	LIC	Aruba
Belarus	LMC	Suriname	LMC	Ghana	LIC	Bahamas, The
Bosnia & Herzegovina	LMC	Trinidad & Tobago	UMC	Guinea	LIC	Bahrain
Bulgaria	LMC	Uruguay	UMC	Guinea-Bissau	LIC	Bermuda
Croatia	UMC	Venezuela, RB	UMC	Kenya	LIC	Brunei
Czech Rep.	UMC			Lesotho	LIC	Cayman Islands
Estonia	UMC	Middle East and North Africa		Liberia	LIC	Channel Islands
Georgia	LMC	Algeria	LMC	Madagascar	LIC	Cyprus
Hungary	UMC	Djibouti	LMC	Malawi	LIC	Faeroe Islands
Kazakhstan	LMC	Egypt, Arab Rep.	LMC	Mali	LIC	French Polynesia
Kyrgyz Rep.	LIC	Iran, Islamic Rep.	LMC	Mauritania	LIC	Greenland
Latvia	UMC	Iraq	LMC	Mauritius	UMC	Guam
Lithuania	UMC	Jordan	LMC	Mayotte	UMC	Hong Kong, China
Macedonia, FYR	LMC	Lebanon	UMC	Mozambique	LIC	Isle of Man
Moldova	LIC	Libya	UMC	Namibia	LMC	Israel
Poland	UMC	Morocco	LMC	Niger	LIC	Kuwait
Romania	LMC	Oman	UMC	Nigeria	LIC	Liechtenstein
Russian Federation	UMC	Syrian Arab Rep.	LMC	Rwanda	LIC	Macao, China
Serbia & Montenegro	LMC	Tunisia	LMC	São Tomé & Principe	LIC	Malta
Slovak Rep.	UMC	West Bank & Gaza	LMC	Senegal	LIC	Monaco
Tajikistan	LIC	Yemen, Rep.	LIC	Seychelles	UMC	Netherlands Antilles
Turkey	UMC			Sierra Leone	LIC	New Caledonia
Turkmenistan	LMC			Somalia	LIC	Puerto Rico
Ukraine	LMC			South Africa	UMC	Qatar
Uzbekistan	LIC			Sudan	LIC	San Marino
				Swaziland	LMC	Saudi Arabia
				Tanzania	LIC	Singapore
				Togo	LIC	Slovenia
				Uganda	LIC	Taiwan, China
				Zambia	LIC	United Arab Emirates
				Zimbabwe	LIC	Virgin Islands (U.S.)

Note: This table classifies all World Bank member economies, and all other economies with populations of more than 30,000. Economies are divided among income groups according to 2004 GNI per capita, calculated using the World Bank Atlas method. The groups are: low-income economies (LIC), $825 or less; lower-middle-income economies (LMC), $826–3,255; upper-middle-income economies (UMC), $3,256–10,065; and high-income economies, $10,066 or more.

Source: World Bank data.

Table 1. Key indicators of development

| | Population | | | Gross national income (GNI)[a] | | PPP gross national income (GNI)[b] | | Gross domestic product (GDP) per capita % growth | Life expectancy at birth | | Adult literacy rate % ages 15 and older | Carbon dioxide emissions per capita metric tons |
| | Millions | Average annual % growth | Density people per sq. km | $ billions | $ per capita | $ billions | $ per capita | | Male years | Female years | | |
	2004	2000–4	2004	2004	2004	2004	2004	2003–4	2003	2003	1998–2004	2000
Albania	3.2	0.6	116	6.6	2,080	16	5,070	5.6	72	77	99 [c]	0.9
Algeria	32.4	1.6	14	73.7	2,280	203 [d]	6,260 [d]	3.4	70	72	70 [e]	2.9
Angola	14.0	3.0	11	14.4	1,030	28 [d]	2,030 [d]	7.7	45	48	67 [e]	0.5
Argentina	38.2	1.0	14	142.3	3,720	476	12,460	8.0	71	78	97 [c]	3.8
Armenia	3.0	–0.5	108	3.4	1,120	13	4,270	10.3	71	79	99 [c]	1.1
Australia	20.1	1.2	3	541.2	26,900	588	29,200	1.8	77	83	..	18.0
Austria	8.1	0.3	98	262.1	32,300	258	31,790	1.9	76	82	..	7.6
Azerbaijan	8.3	0.7	100	7.8	950	32	3,830	10.6	..	..	99 [c]	3.6
Bangladesh	140.5	1.7	1,079	61.2	440	278	1,980	3.7	62	63	41	0.2
Belarus	9.8	–0.4	47	20.9	2,120	68	6,900	11.5	62	74	100 [c]	5.9
Belgium	10.4	0.4	344	322.8	31,030	326	31,360	2.6	75	81	..	10.0
Benin	6.9	2.6	62	3.7	530	8	1,120	0.2	51	55	34 [c]	0.3
Bolivia	9.0	1.9	8	8.7	960	23	2,590	1.6	62	66	87 [c]	1.3
Bosnia & Herzegovina	3.8	0.4	75	7.8	2,040	29	7,430	4.6	71	77	95 [e]	5.1
Brazil	178.7	1.2	21	552.1	3,090	1,433	8,020	3.9	65	73	88 [c]	1.8
Bulgaria	7.8	–0.9	70	21.3	2,740	61	7,870	6.1	69	76	98 [c]	5.3
Burkina Faso	12.4	2.4	45	4.4	360	15 [d]	1,220 [d]	1.6	42	43	..	0.1
Burundi	7.3	1.9	286	0.7	90	5 [d]	660 [d]	3.5	41	42	59 [e]	0.0
Cambodia	13.6	1.8	77	4.4	320	30 [d]	2,180 [d]	4.2	53	56	74 [e]	0.0
Cameroon	16.4	2.0	35	13.1	800	34	2,090	2.8	47	49	68 [e]	0.4
Canada	31.9	0.9	3	905.6	28,390	978	30,660	2.0	76	83	..	14.2
Central African Rep.	3.9	1.5	6	1.2	310	4 [d]	1,110 [d]	–0.8	41	42	49 [e]	0.1
Chad	8.8	2.9	7	2.3	260	13	1,420	27.4	47	50	26 [e]	0.0
Chile	16.0	1.2	21	78.4	4,910	168	10,500	4.9	73	80	96 [c]	3.9
China	1,296.5	0.7	139	1,676.8	1,290	7,170 [f]	5,530 [f]	8.8	69	73	91 [c]	2.2
Hong Kong, China	6.8	0.7	6,569	183.5	26,810	216	31,510	7.7	78	83	..	5.0
Colombia	45.3	1.7	44	90.6	2,000	309 [d]	6,820 [d]	2.3	69	75	94 [e]	1.4
Congo, Dem. Rep.	54.8	3.0	24	6.4	120	37 [d]	680 [d]	3.2	45	46	65 [e]	0.1
Congo, Rep.	3.9	2.8	11	3.0	770	3	750	1.4	50	54	83	0.5
Costa Rica	4.1	1.6	80	19.0	4,670	39 [d]	9,530 [d]	2.7	76	81	96	1.4
Côte d'Ivoire	17.1	2.0	54	13.3	770	24	1,390	–4.0	45	46	48 [c]	0.7
Croatia	4.5	0.7	81	29.7	6,590	53	11,670	2.2	70	78	98 [c]	4.5
Czech Republic	10.2	–0.2	132	93.2	9,150	187	18,400	4.2	72	79	..	11.6
Denmark	5.4	0.3	127	219.4	40,650	170	31,550	2.2	75	80	..	8.4
Dominican Rep.	8.9	1.5	183	18.4	2,080	60 [d]	6,750 [d]	0.6	64	70	88 [e]	3.0
Ecuador	13.2	1.5	48	28.8	2,180	49	3,690	5.0	69	74	91 [c]	2.0
Egypt, Arab Rep.	68.7	1.8	69	90.1	1,310	283	4,120	2.5	68	71	..	2.2
El Salvador	6.7	1.7	321	15.6	2,350	33 [d]	4,980 [d]	–0.2	67	74	80	1.1
Eritrea	4.5	2.2	44	0.8	180	5 [d]	1,050 [d]	–0.2	50	52	..	0.1
Ethiopia	70.0	2.1	70	7.7	110	57 [d]	810 [d]	11.2	41	43	42	0.1
Finland	5.2	0.2	17	171.0	32,790	154	29,560	3.6	75	82	..	10.3
France	60.0	0.5	109	1,858.7	30,090 [g]	1,759	29,320	1.9	76	83	..	6.2
Georgia	4.5	–1.1	65	4.7	1,040	13 [d]	2,930 [d]	9.6	69	78	..	1.3
Germany	82.6	0.1	237	2,489.0	30,120	2,310	27,950	1.5	76	81	..	9.6
Ghana	21.1	1.8	93	8.1	380	48 [d]	2,280 [d]	3.3	54	55	54 [c]	0.3
Greece	11.1	0.4	86	183.9	16,610	244	22,000	3.8	75	81	91 [e]	8.2
Guatemala	12.6	2.6	116	26.9	2,130	52 [d]	4,140 [d]	0.1	63	69	69 [c]	0.9
Guinea	8.1	2.1	33	3.7	460	17	2,130	0.5	46	47	..	0.2
Haiti	8.6	1.9	312	3.4	390	14 [d]	1,680 [d]	–5.5	50	54	52	0.2
Honduras	7.1	2.5	64	7.3	1,030	19 [d]	2,710 [d]	2.1	63	69	80 [c]	0.7
Hungary	10.1	0.1	109	83.3	8,270	157	15,620	4.6	69	77	99 [c]	5.4
India	1,079.7	1.5	363	674.6	620	3,347 [d]	3,100 [d]	5.4	63	64	61 [c]	1.1
Indonesia	217.6	1.3	120	248.0	1,140	753	3,460	3.7	65	69	88	1.3
Iran, Islamic Rep.	66.9	1.2	41	154.0	2,300	505	7,550	5.7	68	71	77 [e]	4.9
Ireland	4.0	1.3	58	137.8	34,280	133	33,170	4.2	75	80	..	11.1
Israel	6.8	1.9	313	118.1	17,380	160	23,510	2.6	77	81	97 [e]	10.0
Italy	57.6	–0.1	196	1,503.6	26,120	1,604	27,860	1.3	77	83	..	7.4
Jamaica	2.7	0.8	246	7.7	2,900	10	3,630	1.2	74	78	88	4.2
Japan	127.8	0.2	351	4,749.9	37,180	3,838	30,040	2.5	78	85	..	9.3
Jordan	5.4	2.7	61	11.6	2,140	25	4,640	4.9	71	74	90 [e]	3.2
Kazakhstan	15.0	–0.2	6	33.8	2,260	104	6,980	8.8	56	67	100 [c]	8.1
Kenya	32.4	1.9	57	15.0	460	34	1,050	0.4	45	46	74 [e]	0.3
Korea, Rep.	48.1	0.6	488	673.0	13,980	982	20,400	4.1	71	78	..	9.1
Kuwait	2.5	2.9	138	43.1	17,970	47 [d]	19,510 [d]	7.1	75	79	83	21.9
Kyrgyz Rep.	5.1	0.9	27	2.1	400	9	1,840	6.1	61	69	99 [c]	0.9
Lao PDR	5.8	2.3	25	2.2	390	11	1,850	3.6	54	56	69 [e]	0.1
Latvia	2.3	–0.7	37	12.6	5,460	27	11,850	9.4	66	76	100 [c]	2.5
Lebanon	4.6	1.3	445	22.7	4,980	25	5,380	5.0	69	73	..	3.5
Lithuania	3.4	–0.5	55	19.7	5,740	43	12,610	7.1	66	78	100 [c]	3.4
Macedonia, FYR	2.1	0.4	81	4.9	2,350	13	6,480	1.9	71	76	96 [c]	5.5
Madagascar	17.3	2.8	30	5.2	300	14	830	2.6	54	57	71 [e]	0.1
Malawi	11.2	2.0	119	1.9	170	7	620	1.8	37	38	64 [c]	0.1
Malaysia	25.2	2.0	77	117.1	4,650	243	9,630	5.2	71	76	89 [c]	6.2
Mali	11.9	2.4	10	4.3	360	12	980	–0.3	40	42	19 [c]	0.1
Mauritania	2.9	2.4	3	1.2	420	6 [d]	2,050 [d]	4.5	49	53	51 [c]	1.2

Note: For data comparability and coverage, see the technical notes. Figures in italics are for years other than those specified.

Table 1. Key indicators of development—continued

	Population			Gross national income (GNI)[a]		PPP gross national income (GNI)[b]		Gross domestic product (GDP) $ per capita % growth	Life expectancy at birth		Adult literacy rate % ages 15 and older	Carbon dioxide emissions per capita metric tons
	Millions	Average annual % growth	Density people per sq. km	$ billions	$ per capita	$ billions	$ per capita		Male years	Female years		
	2004	2000–4	2004	2004	2004	2004	2004	2003–4	2003	2003	1998–2004	2000
Mexico	103.8	1.4	54	703.1	6,770	995	9,590	2.9	71	77	90 [e]	4.3
Moldova	4.2	−0.4	128	2.6	710 [h]	8	1,930	7.8	63	71	96 [e]	1.5
Mongolia	2.5	1.2	2	1.5	590	5	2,020	9.1	64	68	98 [c]	3.1
Morocco	30.6	1.6	69	46.5	1,520	125	4,100	1.9	67	71	51	1.3
Mozambique	19.1	2.0	24	4.7	250	22 [d]	1,160 [d]	5.9	40	42	46	0.1
Namibia	2.0	1.8	2	4.8	2,370	14 [d]	6,960 [d]	3.2	41	40	85 [c]	1.0
Nepal	25.2	2.2	176	6.5	260	37	1,470	1.6	60	60	49 [c]	0.1
Netherlands	16.3	0.5	480	515.1	31,700	507	31,220	1.2	76	81	..	8.7
New Zealand	4.1	1.3	15	82.5	20,310	90	22,130	3.1	77	81	..	8.3
Nicaragua	5.6	2.5	46	4.5	790	18	3,300	1.4	67	71	77 [e]	0.7
Niger	12.1	3.0	10	2.8	230	10 [d]	830 [d]	−1.9	46	47	14 [c]	0.1
Nigeria	139.8	2.4	154	54.0	390	130 [d]	930 [d]	1.1	44	45	67	0.3
Norway	4.6	0.5	15	238.4	52,030	177	38,550	2.5	77	82	..	11.1
Oman	2.7	2.5	9	20.5	7,890	34	13,250	0.1	73	76	74	8.2
Pakistan	152.1	2.4	197	90.7	600	328	2,160	3.9	63	65	49 [e]	0.8
Panama	3.0	1.5	41	13.5	4,450	21 [d]	6,870 [d]	4.7	73	77	92 [c]	2.2
Papua New Guinea	5.6	2.3	12	3.3	580	13 [d]	2,300 [d]	0.5	56	58	57 [c]	0.5
Paraguay	5.8	2.3	15	6.8	1,170	28 [d]	4,870 [d]	0.4	69	73	92 [e]	0.7
Peru	27.5	1.5	22	65.0	2,360	148	5,370	3.5	68	72	88 [e]	1.1
Philippines	83.0	2.0	278	96.9	1,170	406	4,890	4.3	68	72	93 [c]	1.0
Poland	38.2	−0.3	125	232.4	6,090	482	12,640	5.4	71	79	..	7.8
Portugal	10.4	0.5	114	149.8	14,350	201	19,250	1.1	73	80	..	5.8
Romania	21.9	−0.7	95	63.9	2,920	179	8,190	7.7	66	74	97 [c]	3.8
Russian Federation	142.8	−0.5	8	487.3	3,410	1,374	9,620	7.7	60	72	99 [c]	9.9
Rwanda	8.4	2.2	341	1.9	220	11 [d]	1,300 [d]	3.5	39	40	64 [e]	0.1
Saudi Arabia	23.2	2.8	11	242.2	10,430	325 [d]	14,010 [d]	2.1	72	75	79 [e]	18.1
Senegal	10.5	2.3	54	7.0	670	18 [d]	1,720 [d]	3.8	51	54	39 [e]	0.4
Serbia & Montenegro	8.2	..	80	21.7	2,620 [i]	..	..	7.0	70	75	96 [c]	3.7
Sierra Leone	5.4	1.9	76	1.1	200	4	790	5.4	36	39	30 [e]	0.1
Singapore	4.3	1.9	6,470	105.0	24,220	115	26,590	6.3	76	80	93 [c]	14.7
Slovak Rep.	5.4	0.0	110	34.9	6,480	77	14,370	5.5	69	78	100 [c]	6.6
Slovenia	2.0	0.1	99	29.6	14,810	41	20,730	4.6	72	80	100	7.3
South Africa	45.6	0.9	38	165.3	3,630	500 [d]	10,960 [d]	4.3	45	46	..	7.4
Spain	41.3	0.5	83	875.8	21,210	1,035	25,070	2.6	76	84	..	7.0
Sri Lanka	19.4	1.3	301	19.6	1,010	78	4,000	4.8	72	76	90 [c]	0.6
Sudan	34.4	2.2	14	18.2	530	64	1,870	3.5	57	60	59 [e]	0.2
Sweden	9.0	0.3	22	321.4	35,770	267	29,770	3.3	78	82	..	5.3
Switzerland	7.4	0.7	187	356.1	48,230	261	35,370	1.3	78	83	..	5.4
Syrian Arab Rep.	17.8	2.3	97	21.1	1,190	63	3,550	1.3	68	73	83 [e]	3.3
Tajikistan	6.4	1.1	46	1.8	280	7	1,150	9.4	63	69	99 [c]	0.6
Tanzania	36.6	2.0	41	11.6 [j]	330 [j]	24	660	4.3	42	43	69 [c]	0.1
Thailand	62.4	0.7	122	158.7	2,540	500	8,020	5.4	67	72	93 [c]	3.3
Togo	5.0	2.1	91	1.9	380	8 [d]	1,690 [d]	0.8	49	51	53 [e]	0.4
Tunisia	10.0	1.1	64	28.3	2,630	73	7,310	4.5	71	75	74 [c]	1.9
Turkey	71.7	1.5	93	268.7	3,750	551	7,680	7.4	66	71	88 [c]	3.3
Turkmenistan	4.9	1.5	10	6.6	1,340	34	6,910	15.4	61	68	..	7.5
Uganda	25.9	2.7	132	6.9	270	39 [d]	1,520 [d]	3.1	43	44	69	0.1
Ukraine	48.0	−0.8	83	60.3	1,260	300	6,250	12.9	63	74	99 [c]	6.9
United Kingdom	59.4	0.2	247	2,016.4	33,940	1,869	31,460	3.0	75	80	..	9.6
United States	293.5	1.0	32	12,150.9	41,400	11,655	39,710	3.4	75	80	..	19.8
Uruguay	3.4	0.6	19	13.4	3,950	31	9,070	11.6	72	79	98	1.6
Uzbekistan	25.9	1.3	63	11.9	460	48	1,860	6.3	64	70	99	4.8
Venezuela, RB	26.1	1.8	30	105.0	4,020	150	5,760	15.3	71	77	93 [c]	6.5
Vietnam	82.2	1.1	252	45.1	550	222	2,700	6.4	68	72	90 [c]	0.7
West Bank & Gaza	3.5	4.2	564	3.8	1,120	..	..	−5.6	71	75	92 [c]	..
Yemen, Rep.	19.8	3.0	37	11.2	570	16	820	−0.4	57	58	49	0.5
Zambia	10.5	1.6	14	4.7	450	9	890	3.2	36	37	68 [e]	0.2
Zimbabwe	13.2	1.0	34	.. [k]	.. [k]	28	2,180	−6.7	39	38	90	1.2
World	6,345.1 s	1.2 w	49 w	39,833.6 t	6,280 w	55,584 t	8,760 w	2.9 w	65 w	69 w	82 w	3.8 w
Low income	2,338.1	1.8	80	1,184.3	510	5,279	2,260	4.4	57	59	64	0.8
Middle income	3,006.2	0.9	44	6,594.2	2,190	19,483	6,480	6.0	67	72	90	3.2
Lower middle income	2,430.3	0.9	63	3,846.9	1,580	13,709	5,640	6.2	68	72	89	2.9
Upper middle income	575.9	0.7	20	2,747.8	4,770	5,814	10,090	5.9	65	73	93	6.3
Low & middle income	5,344.3	1.3	55	7,777.5	1,460	24,753	4,630	5.5	63	66	81	2.2
East Asia & Pacific	1,870.2	0.9	118	2,389.4	1,280	9,488	5,070	7.6	68	71	85	2.1
Europe & Central Asia	472.1	−0.1	20	1,553.3	3,290	3,947	8,360	7.0	64	73	98	6.7
Latin America & Carib.	541.3	1.4	27	1,948.1	3,600	4,146	7,660	4.5	68	74	88	2.7
Middle East & N. Africa	294.0	1.8	33	588.6	2,000	1,693	5,760	3.3	67	70	74	4.2
South Asia	1,447.7	1.7	303	860.3	590	4,103	2,830	5.0	62	64	64	0.9
Sub-Saharan Africa	719.0	2.2	30	432.0	600	1,331	1,850	2.4	45	46	61	0.7
High income	1,000.8	0.7	30	32,064.0	32,040	31,000	30,970	2.8	75	81	91	12.4

Note: a. Calculated using the World Bank Atlas method. b. PPP is purchasing power parity; see definitions. c. National estimates based on census data. d. The estimate is based on regression; others are extrapolated from the latest International Comparison Programme benchmark estimates. e. National estimates based on survey data. f. Estimate based on bilateral comparison between China and the United States (Ruoen and Kai 1995). g. GNI and GNI per capita estimates include the French overseas departments of French Guiana, Guadeloupe, Martinique, and Réunion. h. Excludes data for Transnistria. i. Excludes data for Kosovo. j. Data refers to mainland Tanzania only. k. Estimated to be low income ($825 or less).

Table 2. Millennium Development Goals: eradicating poverty and improving lives

		Eradicate extreme poverty and hunger			Achieve universal primary education		Promote gender equality		Reduce child mortality		Combat HIV/AIDS and other diseases	Improve maternal health		
		Proportion of population below $1 (PPP) a day %	Prevalence of child malnutrition % of children under 5		Primary completion rate (%)		Gender parity ratio in primary and secondary school (%)		Under-five mortality rate per 1,000		HIV prevalence % of population ages 15–49	Maternal mortality rate per 100,000 live births Modeled estimates	Births attended by skilled health staff % of total	
	Survey year		1989–94[a]	2000–3[a]	1988/89–1993/94[b]	2000/01–2003/04[a]	1990/91	2002/03	1990	2003	2003	2000	1990–2[a]	2000–3[a]
Albania	2002 [c]	<2	..	13.6	..	101	96	100	45	21	..	55	..	94
Algeria	1995 [c]	<2	9.2	6.0	80	96	83	99	69	41	0.1	140	77	92
Angola		..	20.0	30.5	39	..	..	..	260	260	3.9	1,700	..	45
Argentina	2001 [d]	3.3	1.9	..	100	103	..	102	28	20	0.7	82	96	99
Armenia	2003 [c, e]	<2	..	2.6	91	110	..	101	60	33	..	55	..	97
Australia		..	..	..	..	..	101	98	10	6	0.1	8	100	..
Austria		..	..	..	..	101	95	97	10	6	0.3	4	..	..
Azerbaijan	2001 [c]	3.7	..	6.8	..	106	100	97	105	91	<0.1	94	..	84
Bangladesh	2000 [c]	36.0	68.3	52.2	46	73	77	107	144	69	..	380	..	14
Belarus	2000 [c]	<2	..	..	94	99	..	102	17	17	..	35	..	100
Belgium		..	..	..	..	..	101	106	9	5	0.2	10	..	..
Benin		..	35.0	22.9	22	51	48	66	185	154	1.9	850	..	66
Bolivia	1999 [c]	14.4	14.9	..	71	101	90	98	120	66	0.1	420	..	65
Bosnia & Herzegovina		..	..	4.1	..	..	..	..	22	17	<0.1	31	97	100
Brazil	2001 [d]	8.2	7.0	..	97	112	..	103	60	35	0.7	260	72	..
Bulgaria	2003 [c, e]	<2	..	..	90	97	99	97	19	17	0.1	32	..	..
Burkina Faso	1998 [c]	44.9	32.7	37.7	19	29	61	72	210	207	1.8 [f]	1,000	..	..
Burundi	1998 [c]	54.6	37.5	45.1	47	31	82	79	190	190	6.0	1,000	..	25
Cambodia	1997 [c]	34.1	..	45.2	..	81	73	85	115	140	2.6	450	..	32
Cameroon	2001 [c]	17.1	15.1	..	56	70	83	85	139	166	5.5 [g]	730	58	60
Canada		..	..	..	..	..	99	100	8	7	0.3	6	..	..
Central African Rep.	1993 [c]	66.6	..	..	27	..	60	..	180	180	13.5	1,100	..	44
Chad		..	..	28.0	19	25	41	59	203	200	4.8	1,100	..	16
Chile	2000 [d]	<2	1.0	0.8	..	104	101	100	19	9	0.3	31	..	100
China	2001 [c]	16.6	17.4	10.0	105	98	87	98	49	37	0.1	56	..	97
Hong Kong, China		..	..	..	102	101	103	101	..	..	0.1	..	..	..
Colombia	1999 [d]	8.2	10.1	6.7	71	88	114	104	36	21	0.7	130	82	86
Congo, Dem. Rep.		..	..	31.0	47	32	..	..	205	205	4.2	990	..	61
Congo, Rep.		..	23.9	..	54	59	85	87	110	108	4.9	510	..	..
Costa Rica	2000 [d]	2.0	2.2	..	72	94	100	101	17	10	0.6	43	98	98
Côte d'Ivoire	2002 [c, e]	14.8	23.8	..	46	51	66	69	157	192	7.0	690	..	63
Croatia	2001 [c]	<2	0.7	..	83	96	102	101	13	7	<0.1	8	..	..
Czech Rep.	1996 [d]	<2	1.0	..	..	106	98	101	13	5	0.1	9	..	..
Denmark		..	..	..	98	107	101	103	9	6	0.2	5	..	..
Dominican Rep.	1998 [d]	<2	10.3	5.3	62	93	..	108	65	35	1.7	150	93	98
Ecuador	1998 [d]	17.7	16.5	..	92	100	..	100	57	27	0.3	130	..	..
Egypt, Arab Rep.	1999–2000 [c]	3.1	9.9	8.6	..	91	81	94	104	39	<0.1	84	37	69
El Salvador	2000 [d]	31.1	11.2	10.3	59	89	101	96	60	36	0.7	150	..	69
Eritrea		..	41.0	39.6	19	40	..	76	147	85	2.7	630	..	28
Ethiopia	1999–2000 [c]	23.0	47.7	47.2	22	39	68	69	204	169	4.4	850	..	6
Finland		..	..	..	97	101	109	106	7	4	0.1	6	..	..
France		..	..	..	104	98	102	100	9	6	0.4	17	..	..
Georgia	2001 [c]	2.7	..	..	81	82	98	100	47	45	0.1	32	..	..
Germany		..	..	..	101	101	99	99	9	5	0.1	8	..	..
Ghana	1998–99 [c]	44.8	27.3	22.1	61	62	77	91	125	95	3.1	540	..	..
Greece		..	..	..	100	..	99	100	11	5	0.2	9	..	..
Guatemala	2000 [d]	16.0	33.2	22.7	..	66	..	93	82	47	1.1	240	..	41
Guinea		..	..	..	17	41	44	69	240	160	3.2	740	31	..
Haiti	2001 [c, e]	67.0	26.8	17.2	29	..	95	..	150	118	5.6	680	..	24
Honduras	1999 [c]	20.7	18.3	16.6	65	79	..	..	59	41	1.8	110	45	56
Hungary	2002 [c]	<2	2.2	..	82	102	100	100	17	7	0.1	16	..	..
India	1999–2000 [c]	35.3	53.2	..	78	81	70	88	123	87	0.9	540	..	43
Indonesia	2002 [c]	7.5	39.9	27.3	93	95	93	98	91	41	0.1	230	32	68
Iran, Islamic Rep.	1998 [c]	<2	..	..	101	107	85	95	72	39	0.1	76	..	90
Ireland		..	..	..	..	..	104	104	9	7	0.1	5	..	..
Israel		..	..	..	..	..	105	99	12	6	0.1	17	..	..
Italy		..	..	..	104	101	100	99	9	6	0.5	5	..	..
Jamaica	2000 [c]	<2	4.6	..	89	85	102	101	20	20	1.2	87	..	..
Japan		..	..	..	101	..	101	100	6	5	<0.1	10	100	..
Jordan	2002 [c]	<2	6.4	4.4	104	98	101	101	40	28	<0.1	41	87	100
Kazakhstan	2003 [c]	<2	..	..	..	110	102	100	63	73	0.2	210	..	..
Kenya	1997 [c]	22.8	22.5	19.9	86	73	92	94	97	123	6.7 [f]	1,000	..	41
Korea, Rep.	1998 [d]	<2	..	..	98	97	99	100	9	5	<0.1	20	98	..
Kuwait		..	..	..	53	96	97	104	16	9	..	5	..	..
Kyrgyz Rep.	2002 [c]	<2	..	5.8	..	93	..	100	80	68	0.1	110	..	..
Lao PDR	1997–98 [c]	26.3	40.0	40.0	46	74	75	83	163	91	0.1	650	..	19
Latvia	1998 [c]	<2	..	..	73	101	100	99	18	12	0.6	42	..	..
Lebanon		..	..	..	..	68	..	102	37	31	0.1	150	..	..
Lithuania	2000 [c]	<2	..	..	89	102	..	99	14	11	0.1	13	..	..
Macedonia, FYR	2003 [c]	<2	..	..	99	100	99	99	33	11	<0.1	23	..	98
Madagascar	2001 [c]	61.0	45.2	33.1	35	47	98	..	168	126	1.7	550	57	46
Malawi	1997–98 [c]	41.7	27.6	25.4	36	71	81	92	241	178	14.2	1,800	55	61
Malaysia	1997 [d]	<2	22.4	..	88	92	102	105	21	7	0.4	41	..	97
Mali	1994 [c]	72.3	30.6	33.2	12	40	58	71	250	220	1.7 [h]	1,200	..	41
Mauritania	2000 [c]	25.9	47.6	31.8	33	43	67	94	162	107	0.6	1,000	40	57

Note: For data comparability and coverage, see the technical notes. Figures in italics are for years other than those specified.

Table 2. Millennium Development Goals: eradicating poverty and improving lives—continued

		Eradicate extreme poverty and hunger			Achieve universal primary education		Promote gender equality		Reduce child mortality		Combat HIV/AIDS and other diseases	Improve maternal health		
		Proportion of population below $1 (PPP) a day %	Prevalence of child malnutrition % of children under 5		Primary completion rate (%)		Gender parity ratio in primary and secondary school (%)		Under-five mortality rate per 1,000		HIV prevalence % of population ages 15–49	Maternal mortality rate per 100,000 live births Modeled estimates	Births attended by skilled health staff % of total	
	Survey year		1989–94[a]	2000–3[a]	1988/89–1993/94[b]	2000/01–2003/04[b]	1990/91	2002/03	1990	2003	2003	2000	1990–2[a]	2000–3[a]
Mexico	2000 [c]	9.9	16.6	..	88	99	98	103	46	28	0.3	83	..	..
Moldova	2001 [c]	21.8		..	95	83	105	102	37	32	0.2	36	..	..
Mongolia	1998 [c]	27.0	12.3	12.7	..	108	109	110	104	68	<0.1	110	..	99
Morocco	1999 [c]	<2	9.5	..	47	75	70	88	85	39	0.1	220	31	..
Mozambique	1996 [c]	37.9		..	28	52	73	79	242	147	12.2	1,000	..	48
Namibia	1993 [d]	34.9	26.2	24.0	77	92	111	104	86	65	21.3	300	68	78
Nepal	1995–96 [c]	39.1	..	48.3	55	78	57	85	145	82	0.5	740	7	11
Netherlands		..	..	..	..	98	97	98	9	6	0.2	16	..	..
New Zealand		..	..	..	98	96	100	103	11	6	0.1	7	..	..
Nicaragua	2001 [c]	45.1	11.0	9.6	44	75	112	104	68	38	0.2	230	..	67
Niger	1995 [c]	60.6	42.6	40.1	18	26	56	69	320	262	1.2	1,600	15	16
Nigeria	2003 [c, e]	70.8	39.1	28.7	63	82	78	81	235	198	5.4	800	31	35
Norway		..	..	..	..	..	102	101	9	5	0.1	16	..	..
Oman		..	24.3	..	73	73	89	97	30	12	0.1	87	..	95
Pakistan	2001 [c, e]	17.0	40.0	35.0	..	..	..	71	138	98	0.1	500	19	23
Panama	2000 [d]	7.2	6.1	..	86	98	99	100	34	24	0.9	160	..	..
Papua New Guinea		..	..	..	51	53	79	87	101	93	0.6	300	..	..
Paraguay	2002 [d]	16.4	3.7	..	66	93	98	98	37	29	0.5	170	67	..
Peru	2000 [d]	18.1	10.7	7.1	..	102	..	97	80	34	0.5	410	..	59
Philippines	2000 [c]	15.5	29.6	..	87	95	100	102	63	36	<0.1	200	..	60
Poland	2001 [c]	<2	..	..	96	98	101	97	19	7	0.1	13	..	..
Portugal	1994 [d]	<2	..	..	98	..	103	102	15	5	0.4	5	..	..
Romania	2002 [c]	<2	5.7	3.2	96	89	99	100	32	20	<0.1	49	..	..
Russian Federation	2002 [c]	<2	4.2	5.5	95	93	104	..	21	21	1.1	67	..	99
Rwanda	1999–2000 [c]	51.7	29.4	24.3	44	37	96	95	173	203	5.1	1,400	26	31
Saudi Arabia		..	..	..	57	61	84	93	44	26	..	23	..	..
Senegal	1995 [c]	22.3	22.2	22.7	45	48	68	87	148	137	0.8	690	..	58
Serbia & Montenegro		..	..	1.9	71	96	103	101	26	14	0.2	11	..	99
Sierra Leone	1989 [c]	57.0	28.7	27.2	..	56	67	70	302	284	..	2,000	..	42
Singapore		..	..	3.4	..	..	95	..	8	5	0.2	30	..	..
Slovak Rep.	1996 [d]	<2	..	..	96	99	..	100	15	8	<0.1	3	..	..
Slovenia	1998 [c]	<2	..	..	97	95	..	99	9	4	<0.1	17	100	..
South Africa	2000 [c]	10.7	..	..	81	99	103	100	60	66	15.6 [i]	230	..	..
Spain		..	..	..	..	..	104	102	9	4	0.7	4	..	..
Sri Lanka	2002 [c, e]	5.6	37.7	..	103	113	102	103	32	15	<0.1	92	..	97
Sudan		..	33.9	40.7	44	49	77	86	120	93	2.3	590	69	..
Sweden		..	..	..	96	101	102	111	7	4	0.1	2	..	..
Switzerland		..	..	..	..	99	97	96	9	6	0.4	7	..	..
Syrian Arab Rep.		..	12.1	6.9	99	88	85	93	44	18	<0.1	160	..	..
Tajikistan	2003 [c]	7.4	..	..	100	100	..	88	119	95	<0.1	100	..	71
Tanzania	1991 [c]	48.5	28.9	..	46	58	96	..	163	165	8.8	1,500	44	..
Thailand	2000 [f]	<2	18.6	..	..	86	95	97	40	26	1.5	44	..	99
Togo		..	24.6	..	40	78	59	..	152	140	4.1	570	..	49
Tunisia	2000 [c]	<2	10.3	4.0	75	101	86	102	52	24	<0.1	120	..	90
Turkey	2002 [c, e]	4.8	10.4	..	..	95	81	85	78	39	..	70	..	..
Turkmenistan	1998 [c]	12.1	..	12.0	..	..	..	..	97	102	<0.1	31	..	97
Uganda		..	23.0	22.9	..	63	77	96	160	140	4.1	880	..	39
Ukraine	1999 [d]	2.9	..	3.2	93	98	..	99	22	20	1.4	35	..	..
United Kingdom		..	..	..	..	..	98	116	10	7	0.2	13	..	..
United States		..	1.4	..	..	..	100	100	11	8	0.6	17	..	..
Uruguay	2000 [d]	<2	4.4	..	95	92	..	105	24	14	0.3	27	..	..
Uzbekistan	2000 [c]	17.3	..	7.9	..	103	94	98	79	69	0.1	24	..	96
Venezuela, RB	2000 [d, e]	9.9	4.5	4.4	81	90	105	104	27	21	0.7	96	..	94
Vietnam	2000 [c]	..	44.9	33.8	..	95	..	93	53	23	0.4	130	..	85
West Bank & Gaza		..	..	..	..	106	..	1					..	97
Yemen, Rep.	1998 [c]	15.7	39.0	..	..	66	..	61	142	113	0.1	570	16	..
Zambia	1998 [c]	63.7	25.2	28.1	..	69	..	91	180	182	15.6 [j]	750	51	43
Zimbabwe	1995–96 [c]	56.1	15.5	..	96	81	96	95	80	126	24.6	1,100	..	..
World		29.3 t	.. w	.. w	.. w	87 w	95 w	95 w	84 w	1.1 w	407 w	.. w	57 w
Low income		46.8	..	65	71	74	87	148	119	2.1	689	..	38
Middle income		14.7	11.8	94	96	91	99	56	40	0.7	115	..	86
Lower middle income		15.9	12.3	95	96	89	99	60	42	0.7	121	..	85
Upper middle income		9.2	..	90	96	99	99	40	30	0.6	67	..	..
Low & middle income		30.6	..	81	84	84	94	103	85	1.2	444	..	57
East Asia & Pacific		20.6	15.3	97	97	89	98	59	41	0.2	116	..	87
Europe & Central Asia		..	..	94 [k]	95 [k]	98	..	46	36	0.7	58	97	..
Latin America & Carib.		9.7	..	88	96	..	102	53	33	0.7	193	..	..
Middle East & N. Africa		13.0	..	82	87	82	92	80	56	0.1	162	..	80
South Asia		53.2	..	74	80	71	89	130	86	0.8	567	..	36
Sub-Saharan Africa		33.2	31.4	50	59	79	83	187	171	7.2	916	..	39
High income		..	..	..	..	100	101	11	7	0.4	13	..	..

a. Data are for the most recent year available. b. Data are for 1990 or closest year. c. Expenditure base. d. income base. e. Preliminary data. f. Survey data, 2003. g. Survey data, 2004. h. Survey data, 2001. i. Survey data, 2002. j. Survey data, 2001/2002. k. Represent only 61% of the population.

Table 3. Economic activity

	Gross domestic product		Agricultural productivity Agr. Value added per agricultural worker 2000 dollars		Value added as % of GDP							
	$ millions 2004	Avg. annual % growth 2000–4	1989–91	2001–3	Agriculture 2004	Industry 2004	Services 2004	Household final cons. expenditure % of GDP 2004	General gov't. final cons. expenditure % of GDP 2004	Gross capital formation % of GDP 2004	External balance of goods and services % of GDP 2004	GDP implicit deflator Avg. annual % growth 2000–4
Albania	7,590	6.0	770	1,354	25	19	56	88	10	25	−23	3.6
Algeria	84,649	4.8	1,801	1,964	13	74	14	49	8	29	14	6.0
Angola	20,108	8.1	207	161	9	65	27	71	.. [a]	12	17	95.3
Argentina	151,501	−0.1	6,507	9,272	10	32	59	70	8	18	5	13.3
Armenia	3,549	12.0	..	2,646	25	39	36	83	10	25	−18	4.1
Australia	631,256	3.3	20,601	26,957	3	26	71	60	18	25	−2	2.9
Austria	290,109	1.2	11,153	24,456	2	32	66	57	19	23	2	1.8
Azerbaijan	8,523	10.7	..	1,026	13	54	32	63	12	49	−24	4.1
Bangladesh	56,844	5.1	239	309	21	27	53	78	5	23	−7	4.5
Belarus	22,849	6.7	..	2,259	16	38	46	77	11	14	−2	41.7
Belgium	349,830	1.2	19,687	38,431	1	26	72	55	23	20	3	1.9
Benin	4,075	4.5	360	583	36	14	50	77	14	20	−11	3.2
Bolivia	8,773	2.6	662	739	15	30	55	72	14	13	1	4.8
Bosnia & Herzegovina	8,121	3.8	..	..	15	32	53	91	23	21	−35	3.0
Brazil	604,855	2.0	1,658	3,004	5	17	78	61	14	19	5	10.6
Bulgaria	24,131	4.7	2,434	6,310	10	27	63	69	19	23	−11	4.0
Burkina Faso	4,824	5.2	140	163	31	20	49	82	13	19	−14	3.0
Burundi	657	2.7	119	104	51	20	29	98	8	11	−16	6.6
Cambodia	4,597	5.6	..	292	36	28	37	88	.. [a]	23	−11	1.5
Cameroon	14,733	4.6	725	1,143	44	16	40	71	11	18	0	2.7
Canada	979,764	2.5	27,739	36,702	..	..	..	56	19	20	4	2.2
Central African Rep.	1,331	−1.4	291	407	61	25	14	87	10	7	−4	2.0
Chad	4,285	14.3	164	220	61	9	30	53	5	25	18	5.7
Chile	94,105	3.4	4,775	6,177	9	34	57	58	12	23	7	5.5
China	1,649,329	8.7	242	357	15	51	35	42	12	45	1	2.0
Hong Kong, China	163,005	3.2	..	..	0	12	88	59	10	22	9	−3.9
Colombia	97,384	2.9	3,315	2,900	13	0	87	67	21	15	−2	7.0
Congo, Dem. Rep.	6,571	3.5	230	196	58	19	23	92	4	7	−3	55.5
Congo, Rep.	4,384	3.4	319	329	6	56	39	36	16	23	26	−2.9
Costa Rica	18,395	3.9	3,039	4,306	9	29	63	71	10	21	−2	9.0
Côte d'Ivoire	15,286	−1.5	610	806	25	19	55	73	9	8	10	3.3
Croatia	34,200	4.5	..	8,956	8	29	63	57	20	28	−5	3.3
Czech Rep.	107,047	2.9	..	4,300	3	39	57	50	23	28	0	3.1
Denmark	243,043	1.2	18,564	36,320	2	26	71	47	26	20	7	1.9
Dominican Rep.	18,673	2.4	2,273	4,076	11	31	58	73	5	21	1	20.6
Ecuador	30,282	4.2	1,969	1,441	7	30	63	64	11	22	3	12.0
Egypt, Arab Rep.	75,148	3.5	1,497	1,952	15	32	52	75	10	17	−2	4.3
El Salvador	15,824	1.9	1,571	1,613	9	33	58	86	12	17	−14	2.7
Eritrea	925	3.3	..	64	15	24	61	97	54	22	−73	15.8
Ethiopia	8,077	3.7	..	123	46	10	44	77	22	20	−19	2.3
Finland	186,597	2.2	16,056	30,391	3	31	66	52	22	18	7	1.3
France	2,002,582	1.4	20,265	38,647	3	24	73	55	24	19	1	1.7
Georgia	5,091	7.6	..	1,374	20	25	54	81	9	24	−15	5.0
Germany	2,714,418	0.5	10,963	22,127	1	29	69	59	19	18	4	1.2
Ghana	8,620	4.8	315	338	35	22	43	80	12	27	−19	24.4
Greece	203,401	4.1	7,579	9,226	7	24	69	67	15	26	−8	3.5
Guatemala	27,451	2.3	2,121	2,261	22	19	59	90	5	17	−12	7.2
Guinea	3,508	2.9	171	225	25	37	38	86	6	11	−2	8.6
Haiti	3,535	−1.0	802	469	28	17	55	98	5	23	−27	17.5
Honduras	7,371	3.3	950	1,133	14	31	55	74	14	29	−17	7.3
Hungary	99,712	3.5	2,247	4,041	4	31	65	69	11	24	−4	7.6
India	691,876	6.2	341	397	22	26	52	67	11	23	−1	3.9
Indonesia	257,641	4.6	477	556	17	46	38	65	8	23	4	7.9
Iran, Islamic Rep.	162,709	6.2	1,799	2,354	11	41	48	49	14	36	1	19.3
Ireland	183,560	5.4	..	..	3	42	55	44	15	22	19	3.8
Israel	117,548	0.9	..	..	..	..	..	59	29	18	−6	1.8
Italy	1,672,302	0.8	11,411	21,436	3	28	70	60	19	20	1	2.8
Jamaica	8,030	1.7	1,910	1,937	5	29	66	71	16	32	−20	9.9
Japan	4,623,398	1.3	19,163	25,339	1	30	68	57	18	24	2	−1.9
Jordan	11,196	5.1	1,456	960	2	25	73	81	20	21	−22	1.7
Kazakhstan	40,743	10.3	..	1,385	7	39	53	58	11	25	6	9.2
Kenya	15,600	1.5	184	148	16	19	65	79	17	12	−8	9.9
Korea, Rep.	679,674	4.7	5,312	9,888	3	35	62	55	13	29	3	2.9
Kuwait	41,748	2.4	..	..	..	..	..	50	26	9	16	0.6
Kyrgyz Rep.	2,205	4.5	..	929	39	23	38	71	17	16	−4	4.2
Lao PDR	2,412	5.7	351	459	49	26	25	84	5	19	−8	11.3
Latvia	13,629	7.5	..	2,385	4	25	71	63	21	29	−13	3.9
Lebanon	21,768	4.4	..	24,371	13	19	68	82	17	21	−20	2.7
Lithuania	22,263	7.5	..	4,071	7	33	60	67	16	23	−7	0.4
Macedonia, FYR	5,246	0.8	..	2,935	12	28	60	83	11	22	−17	2.3
Madagascar	4,364	0.9	187	176	29	16	55	81	9	24	−15	9.6
Malawi	1,813	1.8	77	130	39	15	46	88	15	11	−15	15.0
Malaysia	117,776	4.3	3,694	4,571	10	48	42	45	14	21	21	2.8
Mali	4,863	6.3	203	227	38	26	36	78	10	20	−8	4.7
Mauritania	1,357	5.3	244	278	19	30	51	85	18	17	−20	6.8

Note: For data comparability and coverage, see the technical notes. Figures in italics are for years other than those specified.

Table 3. Economic activity—continued

| | Gross domestic product | | Agricultural productivity Agr. Value added per agricultural worker 2000 dollars | | Value added as % of GDP | | | Household final cons. expenditure % of GDP | General gov't. final cons. expenditure % of GDP | Gross capital formation % of GDP | External balance of goods and services % of GDP | GDP implicit deflator Avg. annual % growth |
| | | | | | Agriculture | Industry | Services | | | | | |
	Millions of dollars 2004	Avg. annual % growth 2000–4	1989–91	2001–3	2004	2004	2004	2004	2004	2004	2004	2000–4
Mexico	676,497	1.5	2,224	2,708	4	25	71	68	12	22	−2	7.0
Moldova	2,595	6.9	..	726	23	21	55	97	15	21	−32	11.5
Mongolia	1,525	5.2	1,003	694	26	14	60	53	19	38	−10	9.5
Morocco	50,055	4.5	1,580	1,515	17	30	53	65	18	24	−6	1.0
Mozambique	5,548	8.5	117	136	26	31	43	76	11	22	−9	12.0
Namibia	5,456	3.2	792	1,003	11	26	64	56	29	23	−7	6.6
Nepal	6,707	2.6	196	208	40	23	37	76	10	26	−12	3.9
Netherlands	577,260	0.3	23,496	38,085	3	26	72	50	25	21	5	3.2
New Zealand	99,687	3.9	19,930	26,526	..	..	..	60	18	21	1	2.6
Nicaragua	4,353	2.3	1,167	1,934	18	25	57	74	16	36	−26	5.8
Niger	3,081	4.1	174	172	40	17	43	82	12	16	−10	1.9
Nigeria	72,106	4.9	576	836	26	49	24	40	22	21	17	15.7
Norway	250,168	1.7	19,055	30,854	1	38	61	46	23	18	14	1.4
Oman	21,698	3.5	..	..	..	..	..	44	22	16	18	−0.6
Pakistan	96,115	4.1	563	690	23	24	54	73	9	18	0	5.1
Panama	13,793	3.3	2,320	3,470	7	17	76	64	6	27	3	1.0
Papua New Guinea	3,909	0.6	390	434	26	39	35	56	14	18	12	7.3
Paraguay	7,127	1.2	2,201	2,380	27	24	49	79	7	18	−4	11.9
Peru	68,395	3.6	1,196	1,734	10	30	60	70	10	19	2	2.2
Philippines	86,429	4.2	910	1,016	14	32	54	73	10	17	0	5.0
Poland	241,833	2.8	..	1,358	3	31	66	64	18	20	−2	1.9
Portugal	168,281	0.3	3,807	5,444	4	29	68	61	21	25	−7	3.6
Romania	73,167	5.5	2,079	3,430	13	40	47	67	11	22	−1	23.7
Russian Federation	582,395	6.1	..	2,204	5	34	61	51	19	21	9	15.8
Rwanda	1,845	5.1	179	222	42	22	36	84	13	21	−18	5.1
Saudi Arabia	250,557	3.4	7,270	13,984	5	55	40	30	23	19	28	3.9
Senegal	7,665	4.6	270	260	17	21	62	76	14	21	−11	1.9
Serbia & Montenegro	23,996	4.5	..	..	..	..	..	92	18	18	−29	29.6
Sierra Leone	1,075	15.8	..	..	53	30	17	83	13	20	−16	4.7
Singapore	106,818	2.8	25,523	32,980	0	35	65	41	11	18	30	0.5
Slovak Rep.	41,092	4.6	..	..	3	29	68	56	20	26	−3	4.3
Slovenia	32,182	3.2	..	30,243	3	36	61	54	20	27	−1	6.4
South Africa	212,777	3.2	1,992	2,359	4	31	65	63	20	18	0	7.1
Spain	991,442	2.5	8,740	14,852	3	30	67	58	18	26	−2	4.3
Sri Lanka	20,055	3.8	696	737	17	25	58	76	8	25	−9	8.4
Sudan	19,559	6.0	308	613	39	18	43	71	12	20	−3	8.3
Sweden	346,404	2.0	20,416	30,469	2	28	70	49	28	16	7	1.7
Switzerland	359,465	0.5	..	..	..	..	..	61	12	20	7	1.2
Syrian Arab Rep.	23,133	3.1	2,065	2,799	24	28	47	60	10	23	7	3.2
Tajikistan	2,078	9.9	..	412	24	21	55	101	..[a]	9	−10	23.8
Tanzania [b]	10,851	6.8	246	283	45	16	39	78	13	19	−10	5.9
Thailand	163,491	5.3	493	588	10	44	46	57	11	27	5	2.1
Togo	2,061	2.6	356	404	41	23	36	86	10	18	−13	0.7
Tunisia	28,185	4.3	2,144	2,430	13	28	60	65	14	25	4	2.5
Turkey	301,950	4.2	1,749	1,764	12	27	61	65	13	26	−4	31.9
Turkmenistan	6,167	18.5	..	1,253	..	..	..	51	14	27	8	7.0
Uganda	6,833	5.8	187	230	32	21	47	76	16	22	−14	4.0
Ukraine	65,149	8.6	..	1,442	14	40	46	55	19	19	7	9.0
United Kingdom	2,140,898	2.2	21,655	25,609	1	27	72	66	21	16	−3	3.0
United States	11,667,515	2.6	26,105	47,566	..	..	..	71	15	18	−4	1.9
Uruguay	13,138	−1.2	5,346	6,632	13	27	60	71	12	15	2	13.4
Uzbekistan	11,960	4.8	..	1,520	35	22	43	55	18	18	8	33.1
Venezuela, RB	109,322	−1.3	5,016	6,153	4	41	54	50	13	21	16	27.7
Vietnam	45,210	7.2	212	290	22	40	38	66	7	35	−8	5.1
West Bank & Gaza	3,454	−13.3	..	..	6	12	82	84	53	3	−39	10.9
Yemen, Rep.	12,834	3.6	361	504	15	40	45	78	13	17	−8	8.0
Zambia	5,389	4.4	188	205	21	35	44	68	13	25	−6	20.8
Zimbabwe	11,750	−7.0	260	277	17	24	59	72	17	8	2	87.9
World	40,887,837 t	2.5 w	.. w	817 w	.. w	.. w	.. w	62 w	17 w	21 w	0 w	
Low income	1,253,353	5.4	320	375	23	25	52	69	12	22	−3	
Middle income	6,930,704	4.4	..	699	10	34	56	58	13	27	2	
Lower middle income	3,941,575	5.7	413	567	12	37	51	55	13	31	1	
Upper middle income	2,988,438	2.7	..	2,664	7	30	64	62	14	21	3	
Low & middle income	8,183,030	4.6	434	556	12	33	55	59	13	26	1	
East Asia & Pacific	2,367,508	7.5	..	398	15	49	36	47	12	39	2	
Europe & Central Asia	1,768,088	5.0	..	1,856	8	31	61	60	17	23	−1	
Latin America & Carib.	2,018,715	1.5	2,174	2,837	7	23	70	65	12	20	4	
Middle East & N. Africa	600,256	4.5	..	..	14	39	47	62	12	26	−1	
South Asia	878,785	5.8	344	406	22	26	52	69	10	22	−3	
Sub-Saharan Africa	543,990	3.9	312	326	13	28	58	65	18	19	0	
High income	32,715,777	2.0	..	..	..	..	..	63	18	20	0	

Note: a. Data on general government final consumption expenditure are not available; they are included in household final consumption expenditure. b. Data covers mainland Tanzania only.

Table 4. Trade, aid, and finance

	Merchandise trade Exports $ millions 2004	Merchandise trade Imports $ millions 2004	Manufactured exports % of total merchandise exports 2003	High technology exports % of manufactured exports 2003	Current account balance $ millions 2004	Net private capital flows $ millions 2003	Foreign direct investment $ millions 2003	Official development assistance or official aid[a] $ per capita 2003	External debt Total $ millions 2003	External debt Present value % of GNI 2003	Domestic credit provided by banking sector % of GDP 2004	Net migration thousands 1995–2000
Albania	580	2,150	84	1	−407	176	178	108	1,482	21	45.7	−267
Algeria	31,713	18,199	2	2	..	593	634	7	23,386	40	24.8	−185
Angola	14,440	4,960	..	..	1,178	1,903	1,415	37	9,698	100	4.5	−120
Argentina	34,320	22,309	27	9	3,029	1,169	1,020	3	166,207	115	45.4	−100
Armenia	715	1,351	62	1	−167	115	121	81	1,127	29	6.6	−225
Australia	86,582	107,763	30	14	−39,542	..	7,032		..	..	110.0	510
Austria	115,657	115,072	78	13	988	..	7,276		..	..	122.7	45
Azerbaijan	3,600	3,500	6	5	−2,021	3,235	3,285	36	1,680	23	11.2	−128
Bangladesh	8,150	12,100	89	0	132	86	102	10	18,778	25	40.7	−300
Belarus	11,093	16,343	62	4	−1,043	127	172	3	2,692	18	21.2	14
Belgium	308,854	287,236	80 [b]	8 [b]	..	..	125,060 [b]	..	..	..	112.2	99
Benin	600	770	8	2	−143	51	51	44	1,828	28 [c]	9.9	−29
Bolivia	2,092	1,772	17	8	36	295	167	105	5,684	37 [c]	52.2	−100
Bosnia & Herzegovina	1,784	5,890	..	..	−1,917	400	382	141	2,920	37	45.7	350
Brazil	96,474	65,904	52	12	11,669	13,432	10,144	2	235,431	54	80.9	−130
Bulgaria	9,888	14,378	66	4	−1,813	1,655	1,419	53	13,289	86	36.2	−50
Burkina Faso	380	1,150	17	2	−449	11	11	37	1,844	19 [c]	13.5	−121
Burundi	42	180	2	22	−100	8	0	31	1,310	150	36.6	−400
Cambodia	2,455	2,985	1	..	−125	87	87	38	3,139	71	8.7	100
Cameroon	2,630	2,100	7	2	..	154	215	55	9,189	52 [c]	14.9	0
Canada	321,967	275,799	61	14	25,870	..	6,273		..	..	96.8	733
Central African Rep.	115	145	37	0	..	4	4	13	1,328	155	16.4	11
Chad	1,820	780	..	..	..	837	837	29	1,499	45 [c]	7.7	99
Chile	32,000	24,823	16	3	1,390	3,844	2,982	5	43,231	67	70.2	60
China	593,369	561,423	91	27	45,875	59,455	53,505	1	193,567	15	166.9	−1,950
Hong Kong, China	265,670 [d]	273,010	93 [d]	13	16,039	..	13,624	1	..	..	149.3	300
Colombia	16,090	16,530	36	7	−1,110	−1,185	1,746	18	32,979	46	34.2	−200
Congo, Dem. Rep.	1,600	1,940	10	..	..	187	158	101	11,170	149	1.3	−1,410
Congo, Rep.	3,150	1,570	..	..	−3	201	201	19	5,516	368	11.8	42
Costa Rica	6,301	8,268	66	45	−967	842	577	7	5,424	36	42.5	128
Côte d'Ivoire	5,500	3,650	20	8	−305	69	180	15	12,187	89	18.8	150
Croatia	8,022	16,583	72	12	−1,668	8,031	1,998	27	23,452	102	68.4	−150
Czech Rep.	66,000	67,876	90	13	−5,661	5,342	2,514	26	34,630	48	45.7	52
Denmark	75,565	67,200	66	20	6,963	..	1,185		..	..	165.9	84
Dominican Rep.	5,660	7,660	34	1	867	1,112	310	8	6,291	33	36.2	−180
Ecuador	7,538	7,861	12	6	−455	2,143	1,555	14	16,864	82	20.1	−300
Egypt, Arab Rep.	7,682	12,831	31	0	3,743	−361	237	13	31,383	31	116.2	−500
El Salvador	3,295	6,269	57	5	−612	406	89	29	7,080	56	49.2	−38
Eritrea	20	670	..	..	−78	22	22	70	635	57	148.2	−9
Ethiopia	650	3,300	11	0	−65	54	60	22	7,151	24 [c]	4.0	−77
Finland	61,144	51,043	84	24	7,810	..	3,436		..	..	69.5	20
France	451,034	464,090	81	19	−4,833	..	43,068		..	..	107.2	219
Georgia	649	1,847	31	24	−349	320	338	48	1,935	44	18.8	−350
Germany	914,839	717,491	84	16	104,301	..	25,568		..	..	142.9	1,134
Ghana	2,830	3,910	16	3	352	−166	137	44	7,957	38 [c]	31.4	−51
Greece	14,760	53,082	58	12	−11,225	..	717		..	..	105.1	300
Guatemala	2,792	7,420	40	7	−1,051	68	116	20	4,981	21	15.1	−390
Guinea	640	700	25	0	−245	79	79	30	3,457	59 [c]	15.5	−227
Haiti	362	1,301	..	..	−13	8	8	24	1,308	29	31.7	−105
Honduras	1,560	3,890	21	0	−279	140	198	56	5,641	55	37.4	−20
Hungary	54,175	59,216	87	26	−8,819	5,149	2,506	25	45,785	70	59.6	100
India	72,530	95,156	77	5	6,853	10,651	4,269	1	113,467	19	59.9	−1,400
Indonesia	69,710	46,180	52	14	..	−3,685	−597	8	134,389	71	48.8	−900
Iran, Islamic Rep.	42,450	32,700	8	2	..	1,151	120	2	11,601	8	9.7	−456
Ireland	104,100	60,118	86	34	−748	..	26,599		..	..	118.4	89
Israel	36,874	43,425	93	18	504	..	3,880	66	..	..	82.8	276
Italy	346,060	349,049	87	8	−20,556	..	16,538		..	..	105.3	600
Jamaica	1,385	3,641	64	0	−761	513	721	1	5,584	86	31.3	−100
Japan	565,490	454,530	93	24	172,059	..	6,238		..	..	154.8	280
Jordan	3,970	7,892	69	2	−44	−161	376	233	8,337	82	94.1	35
Kazakhstan	20,251	13,300	18	9	533	5,674	2,088	18	22,835	94	18.5	−1,320
Kenya	2,650	4,660	24	4	−847	195	82	15	6,766	43	40.8	−21
Korea, Rep.	253,910	224,440	93	32	27,613	..	3,222	−10	..	..	100.8	−80
Kuwait	27,390	11,630	7	1	18,884	..	−67	2	..	..	106.0	347
Kyrgyz Rep.	719	941	39	2	−95	−12	46	39	2,021	98	8.4	−27
Lao PDR	455	655	..	..	..	19	19	53	2,846	91	9.6	−7
Latvia	3,882	6,898	60	4	−1,673	570	300	49	8,803	92	54.5	−56
Lebanon	1,749	9,338	68	2	−4,109	394	358	51	18,598	104	179.0	−30
Lithuania	9,111	12,362	63	5	−1,590	−141	179	108	8,342	58	30.0	−109
Macedonia, FYR	1,637	2,856	72	1	−279	90	95	114	1,837	40	22.1	−5
Madagascar	990	1,260	38	0	−309	13	13	32	4,958	31 [c]	15.0	−3
Malawi	470	745	12	1	−185	23	23	45	3,134	109 [c]	23.2	−50
Malaysia	126,497	105,176	77	58	13,381	2,207	2,473	4	49,074	56	134.3	390
Mali	1,140	1,200	40	8	−271	129	129	45	3,129	42 [c]	17.7	−284
Mauritania	365	400	21	..	..	218	214	85	2,360	73 [c]	−6.7	10

Note: For data comparability and coverage, see the technical notes. Figures in italics are for years other than those specified.

Table 4. Trade, aid, and finance—continued

	Merchandise trade Exports $ millions 2004	Imports $ millions 2004	Manufactured exports % of total merchandise exports 2003	High technology exports % of manufactured exports 2003	Current account balance $ millions 2004	Net private capital flows $ millions 2003	Foreign direct investment $ millions 2003	Official development assistance or official aid[a] $ per capita 2003	External debt Total $ millions 2003	Present value % of GNI 2003	Domestic credit provided by banking sector % of GDP 2004	Net migration thousands 1995–2000
Mexico	188,627	206,423	81	21	−7,798	9,541	10,783	1	140,004	25	34.9	−2,000
Moldova	986	1,774	32	3	−132	84	58	28	1,901	95	32.0	−70
Mongolia	858	988	38	0	−105	131	132	100	1,472	97	36.8	−90
Morocco	9,661	17,514	69	11	1,434	2,395	2,279	17	18,795	47	82.5	−300
Mozambique	1,390	1,765	8	3	−516	313	337	55	4,930	38 c	5.9	75
Namibia	1,830	2,450	41	3	337	..	..	73	..	..	55.8	20
Nepal	756	1,877	..	..	171	14	15	19	3,253	38	..	−99
Netherlands	358,781	319,864	71	31	16,403	..	15,695		..	..	166.9	161
New Zealand	20,358	23,186	29	10	−6,232	..	2,438		..	..	120.6	20
Nicaragua	771	1,884	13	4	−780	230	201	152	6,915	40 c	88.4	−155
Niger	430	560	8	3	..	..	23	31	39	2,116	26 c	11.4	−6
Nigeria	31,148	14,164	..	..	..	952	1,200	2	34,963	76	13.2	−95
Norway	82,018	48,203	21	19	34,445	..	2,055		..	..	11.1	67
Oman	14,236	7,865	14	2	1,446	−557	138	17	3,886	19	38.1	−40
Pakistan	13,326	17,908	85	1	−808	132	534	7	36,345	41	40.1	−41
Panama	950	3,466	11	1	−1,104	1,077	792	10	8,770	92	90.4	11
Papua New Guinea	2,460	1,670	6	39	..	2	101	40	2,463	81	23.4	0
Paraguay	1,626	2,916	14	6	76	121	91	9	3,210	51	18.5	−25
Peru	12,467	9,880	22	2	−72	2,562	1,377	18	29,857	60	17.4	−350
Philippines	39,598	42,635	90	74	3,347	1,350	319	9	62,663	81	54.0	−900
Poland	74,094	87,849	81	3	−3,585	7,118	4,123	31	95,219	48	34.6	−71
Portugal	34,983	53,776	86	9	−12,682	..	6,610		..	..	151.1	175
Romania	23,553	32,691	83	4	−3,311	3,880	1,844	28	21,280	46	15.3	−350
Russian Federation	183,185	94,834	21	19	60,109	15,784	7,958	9	175,257	52	26.0	2,300
Rwanda	80	250	10	25	−76	5	5	39	1,540	58 c	13.5	1,977
Saudi Arabia	119,550	42,954	10	0	51,488	..	−587	1	..	..	64.2	75
Senegal	1,530	2,680	34	9	−507	79	78	44	4,419	36 c	21.7	−100
Serbia & Montenegro	3,408	11,194	..	..	−3,148	1,462	1,360	162	14,885 e	84	..	−100
Sierra Leone	140	285	7	31	−65	3	3	56	1,612	100 c	30.3	−110
Singapore	179,547 d	163,820	85 d	59	28,183	..	11,431	2	..	..	80.2	368
Slovak Rep.	27,660	29,448	88	4	−282	1,525	571	30	18,379	69	44.0	9
Slovenia	15,805	17,297	90	6	−275	..	337	33	..	..	55.7	8
South Africa	45,929 f	55,200 f	58 f	5	−6,982	4,148	820	14	27,807	22	84.5	364
Spain	178,960	249,813	77	7	−49,225	..	25,513		..	..	138.7	676
Sri Lanka	5,800	7,950	74	1	−131	236	229	35	10,238	50	44.6	−160
Sudan	3,777	4,075	3	7	−818	1,349	1,349	19	17,496	120	11.5	−207
Sweden	121,012	97,644	81	15	22,844	..	3,268		..	..	113.1	60
Switzerland	118,384	111,468	93	22	50,568	..	17,547		..	..	175.2	80
Syrian Arab Rep.	6,435	5,320	11	1	752	146	150	9	21,566	113	30.1	−30
Tajikistan	915	1,375	..	..	−40	8	32	23	1,166	77	16.5	−345
Tanzania	1,440	2,535	18	2	−1,062	264	248	47	7,516	22 c,g	9.2	−206
Thailand	97,701	95,384	75	30	7,281	1,155	1,949	−16	51,793	41	105.4	−88
Togo	720	930	58	1	−140	20	20	9	1,707	91	16.7	128
Tunisia	9,685	12,738	81	4	−715	1,326	541	31	15,502	75	71.0	−20
Turkey	62,774	97,161	84	2	−15,451	2,849	1,562	2	145,662	81	0.0	135
Turkmenistan	3,870	3,320	..	..	444	..	100	6	..	0	..	50
Uganda	705	1,480	9	8	−250	202	194	38	4,553	33 c	11.0	−66
Ukraine	32,672	28,996	67	5	2,891	1,550	1,424	7	16,309	37	30.7	−700
United Kingdom	345,610	461,983	78	26	−46,879	..	20,696		..	..	157.9	574
United States	819,026	1,526,380	80	31	−665,939	..	39,889		..	..	270.8	6,200
Uruguay	2,905	3,072	34	2	103	37	275	5	11,764	91	53.3	−16
Uzbekistan	4,238	3,310	..	..	1,134	79	70	8	5,006	46	..	−400
Venezuela, RB	31,360	17,300	13	4	14,575	3,539	2,520	3	34,851	43	10.8	40
Vietnam	26,229	31,029	50	2	−604	1,192	1,450	22	15,817	39	61.0	−200
West Bank & Gaza	..	..	..	..	..	..	..	289	..	..	..	11
Yemen, Rep.	4,555	3,790	..	..	−296	−89	−89	13	5,377	40	5.2	−50
Zambia	1,410	1,670	14	2	..	91	100	54	6,425	121	35.3	86
Zimbabwe	1,250	2,990	38	3	..	−5	20	14	4,445	50	58.7	−125
World	9,122,837 t	9,338,667 t	77 w	18 w	.. s	572,774 s	12 w	.. s			171.1 w	.. w,i
Low income	215,695	251,818	60	4		18,208	13,283	14	414,454		47.1	−4,422
Middle income	2,244,720	2,138,024	64	20		181,237	138,493	9	2,139,684		76.4	−9,689
Lower middle income	1,223,079	1,170,291	68	22		103,824	90,627	8	1,053,736		104.4	−10,646
Upper middle income	1,021,641	967,734	61	19		77,412	47,867	10	1,085,948		40.7	957
Low & middle income	2,460,424	2,389,837	64	19		199,444	151,776	14	2,554,138		72.1	−14,111
East Asia & Pacific	964,989	895,174	81	33		62,049	59,612	4	525,535		140.7	−3,859
Europe & Central Asia	615,333 j	626,097 j	57	12		67,110	35,614	22	675,998		27.2	−1,858
Latin America & Carib.	458,500	437,379	57	14		41,087	36,533	12	779,632		49.7	−4,156
Middle East & N. Africa	170,996	153,367	20	3		4,848	4,756	26	158,827		49.0	−1,396
South Asia	101,332	138,464	79	4		11,143	5,163	4	182,785		56.1	−2,401
Sub-Saharan Africa	149,265	139,357	..	..		13,208	10,099	34	231,360		45.4	−439
High income	6,662,445	6,948,809	80	18		..	420,998				205.5	14,104

Note: a. Regional aggregates include data for economies that are not specified elsewhere. World and income group totals include aid not allocated by country or region. b. Includes Luxembourg. c. Data are from debt sustainability analysis undertaken as part of the Heavily Indebted Poor Countries (HIPC) initiative. d. Includes re-exports. e. Data are estimates and reflect borrowing by the former Socialist Federal Republic of Yugoslavia that are not yet allocated to the successor republics. f. Data on total exports and imports refer to South Africa only. Data on export commodity shares refer to the South African Customs Union (Botswana, Lesotho, Namibia, South Africa, and Swaziland). g. GNI refers to mainland Tanzania only. i. World totals computed by the UN sum to zero, but because the aggregates shown here refer to World Bank definitions, regional and income group totals do not equal zero. j. Data include the intratrade of the Baltic states and the Commonwealth of Independent States.

Table 5. Key indicators for other economies

	Population			Gross national income (GNI)[a]		PPP gross national income (GNI)[b]		Gross domestic product per capita % growth 2003–4	Life expectancy at birth		Adult literacy rate % ages 15 and older 1998–2004	Carbon dioxide emissions per capita metric tons 2000
	Thousands 2004	Avg. annual % growth 2000–4	Density people per sq. km 2004	$ millions 2004	$ per capita 2004	$ millions 2004	$ per capita 2004		Male years 2003	Female years 2003		
Afghanistan	..	..	..	5,543	..[c]	..	..	..	..	..	..	..
American Samoa	57	..	285	..	..[d]	..	..	..	..	..	..	..
Andorra	66	..	136	..	..[e]	..	..	..	..	..	..	..
Antigua and Barbuda	80	2.5	182	800	10,000	829	10,360	2.3	73	78	..	4.9
Aruba	99	..	521	..	..[e]	..	..	..	..	..	..	..
Bahamas, The	320	1.2	32	4,684	14,920	5,068	16,140	−0.6	66	74	..	5.9
Bahrain	725	2.0	1,022	8,834	12,410	12,860	18,070	4.7	71	76	88 [f]	29.1
Barbados	272	0.4	632	2,507	9,270	4,075	15,060	0.9	72	77	100	4.4
Belize	283	3.1	12	1,115	3,940	1,840	6,510	0.9	70	73	77 [f]	3.1
Bermuda	64	0.0	1,280	..	..[e]	..	..	..	75	80	..	7.2
Bhutan	896	2.7	19	677	760	..	..	2.3	62	65	..	0.5
Botswana	1,727	0.8	3	7,490	4,340	15,405	8,920	4.3	38	38	79	2.3
Brunei	361	1.7	69	..	..[e]	..	..	..	74	79	93 [f]	14.2
Cape Verde	481	2.5	119	852	1,770	2,720 [g]	5,650 [g]	2.9	66	72	76	0.3
Cayman Islands	44	..	745	..	..[e]	..	..	..	..	..	..	..
Channel Islands	149	0.0	745	..	..[e]	..	..	..	75	84	..	..
Comoros	614	2.4	276	328	530	1,131 [g]	1,840 [g]	−0.5	60	63	56	0.1
Cuba	11,365	0.4	103	..	..[h]	..	..	0.9	75	79	97	2.8
Cyprus	776	0.6	84	13,633	17,580	17,320 [g]	22,330 [g]	2.9	76	81	97 [f]	8.5
Djibouti	716	1.8	31	739	1,030	1,624 [g]	2,270 [g]	1.6	43	43	..	0.6
Dominica	71	0.0	95	261	3,650	375	5,250	1.6	75	79	..	1.4
Equatorial Guinea	506	2.5	18	..	..[d]	3,745	7,400	7.4	50	54	84 [i]	0.4
Estonia	1,345	−0.5	32	9,435	7,010	17,741	13,190	6.8	65	77	100 [f]	11.7
Faeroe Islands	48	..	34	..	..	..	..	..	..	..	..	..
Fiji	848	1.1	46	2,281	2,690	4,893 [g]	5,770 [g]	2.2	68	71	..	0.9
French Polynesia	246	1.1	67	..	..[e]	..	..	..	71	77	..	2.3
Gabon	1,374	2.2	5	5,415	3,940	7,692	5,600	−0.2	52	54	..	2.8
Gambia, The	1,449	2.5	145	414	290	2,753 [g]	1,900 [g]	6.2	52	55	..	0.2
Greenland	57	0.4	0	..	..[e]	..	..	..	65	73	..	9.9
Grenada	106	1.0	311	397	3,760	740	7,000	−3.8	70	76	..	2.1
Guam	164	1.5	298	..	..[e]	..	..	..	76	80	..	26.3
Guinea-Bissau	1,533	2.9	55	250	160	1,058	690	1.3	44	47	..	0.2
Guyana	772	0.4	4	765	990	3,173 [g]	4,110 [g]	1.1	58	67	..	2.1
Iceland	290	0.8	125	11,199	38,620	9,384	32,360	4.8	78	82	..	7.7
Iraq	25,261	2.1	58	..	..[h]	..	..	..	62	64	..	3.3
Isle of Man	77	..	135	..	..[e]	..	..	..	..	..	..	..
Kiribati	98	1.9	134	95	970	..	..	0.3	60	66	..	0.3
Korea, Dem. Rep.	22,745	0.5	189	..	..[c]	..	..	..	61	65	..	8.5
Lesotho	1,809	0.9	60	1,336	740	5,806	3,210	2.1	36	38	81 [i]	..
Liberia	3,449	2.4	171	391	110	..	..	−0.2	46	48	56	0.1
Libya	5,674	2.0	3	25,257	4,450	..	..	2.4	70	75	82	10.9
Liechtenstein	34	..	213	..	..[e]	..	..	..	..	..	..	..
Luxembourg	450	0.7	174	25,302	56,230	27,549	61,220	4.0	75	82	..	19.4
Macao, China	449	1.0	265	..	..[e]	9,605 [g]	21,880 [g]	8.9	77	82	91 [f]	3.8
Maldives	300	2.2	998	752	2,510	..	..	6.5	68	71	97	1.8
Malta	401	0.7	400	4,913	12,250	7,507	18,720	0.9	76	81	..	7.2
Marshall Islands	60	3.7	174	142	2,370	..	..	−3.6	..	..	..	..
Mauritius	1,234	1.0	16,842	5,730	4,640	14,650	11,870	3.2	69	76	84 [f]	2.4
Mayotte	172	..	460	..	..[d]	..	..	..	..	..	..	..
Micronesia, Fed. Sts.	127	1.8	181	252	1,990	..	..	−5.5	67	71	..	..
Monaco	33	..	159	..	..[e]	..	..	..	..	..	..	..
Myanmar	49,910	1.2	76	..	..[c]	..	..	..	55	60	90 [i]	0.2
Northern Mariana Islands	77	..	161	..	..[d]	..	..	..	..	..	..	..
Netherlands Antilles	222	0.8	277	..	..[e]	..	..	..	73	79	97	46.2
New Caledonia	229	1.8	13	..	..[e]	..	..	..	70	78	..	7.8
Palau	20	1.2	43	137	6,870	..	..	0.5	..	..	..	12.7
Puerto Rico	3,929	0.7	277	..	..[e]	..	..	..	72	82	94	2.3
Qatar	637	2.1	58	..	..[e]	..	..	..	75	75	89 [i]	69.6
Samoa	179	1.0	63	333	1,860	1,015 [g]	5,670 [g]	2.6	67	73	99	0.8
San Marino	28	..	463	653	..[e]	..	..	..	..	..	..	..
São Tomé & Principe	161	2.0	167	60	370	..	..	2.4	63	69	..	0.6
Seychelles	85	1.1	188	685	8,090	1,320	15,590	−3.2	69	77	92 [f]	2.8
Solomon Islands	471	2.9	17	260	550	829 [g]	1,760 [g]	0.7	68	71	..	0.4
Somalia	9,938	3.3	16	..	..[c]	..	..	..	46	49	..	..
St. Kitts and Nevis	47	1.5	131	357	7,600	526	11,190	3.3	69	74	..	2.4
St. Lucia	164	1.2	268	706	4,310	910	5,560	1.6	72	76	90 [f]	2.1
St. Vincent & the Grenadines	108	−0.8	278	396	3,650	677	6,250	4.8	70	76	..	1.4
Suriname	443	1.0	3	997	2,250	..	..	3.5	68	73	88 [i]	5.0
Swaziland	1,120	1.7	65	1,859	1,660	5,566	4,970	0.8	42	43	79 [i]	0.4
Timor-Leste	925	4.3	62	506	550	..	..	−3.5	60	64	..	..
Tonga	102	0.4	141	186	1,830	735 [g]	7,220 [g]	1.3	69	74	..	1.2
Trinidad & Tobago	1,323	0.7	258	11,360	8,580	14,795	11,180	5.3	70	74	98	20.5
United Arab Emirates	4,284	6.9	51	..	..[e]	78,834 [g]	21,000 [g]	−5.4	74	77	77	18.1
Vanuatu	215	2.2	18	287	1,340	600	2,790	0.7	67	70	74 [f]	0.4
Virgin Islands (U.S.)	113	1.0	333	..	..[e]	..	..	..	77	80	..	121.2

Note: For data comparability and coverage, see the technical notes. Figures in italics are for years other than those specified.
a. Calculated using the World Bank Atlas method. b. PPP is purchasing power parity; see Definitions. c. Estimated to be low income ($825 or less). d. Estimated to be upper middle income ($3,256–$10,065). e. Estimated to be high income ($10,066 or more). f. National estimate based on census data. g. The estimate is based on regression; others are extrapolated from the latest International Comparison Programme benchmark estimates. h. Estimated to be lower middle income ($826–$3,255). i. National estimates based on survey data.

Technical notes

These technical notes discuss the sources and methods used to compile the indicators included in this edition of Selected World Development Indicators. The notes follow the order in which the indicators appear in the tables. Note that the Selected World Development Indicators uses terminology in line with the 1993 System of National Accounts (SNA). For example, in the 1993 SNA *gross national income* replaces *gross national product*.

Sources

The data published in the Selected World Development Indicators are taken from *World Development Indicators 2005*. Where possible, however, revisions reported since the closing date of that edition have been incorporated. In addition, newly released estimates of population and gross national income (GNI) per capita for 2004 are included in table 1.

The World Bank draws on a variety of sources for the statistics published in the *World Development Indicators*. Data on external debt for developing countries are reported directly to the World Bank by developing member countries through the Debtor Reporting System. Other data are drawn mainly from the U.N. and its specialized agencies, from the IMF, and from country reports to the World Bank. Bank staff estimates are also used to improve currentness or consistency. For most countries, national accounts estimates are obtained from member governments through World Bank economic missions. In some instances these are adjusted by staff to ensure conformity with international definitions and concepts. Most social data from national sources are drawn from regular administrative files, special surveys, or periodic censuses.

For more detailed notes about the data, please refer to the World Bank's *World Development Indicators 2005*.

Data consistency and reliability

Considerable effort has been made to standardize the data, but full comparability cannot be assured, and care must be taken in interpreting the indicators. Many factors affect data availability, comparability, and reliability: statistical systems in many developing economies are still weak; statistical methods, coverage, practices, and definitions differ widely; and cross-country and intertemporal comparisons involve complex technical and conceptual problems that cannot be unequivocally resolved. Data coverage may not be complete because of special circumstances or for economies experiencing problems (such as those stemming from conflicts) affecting the collection and reporting of data. For these reasons, although the data are drawn from the sources thought to be most authoritative, they should be construed only as indicating trends and characterizing major differences among economies rather than offering precise quantitative measures of those differences. Discrepancies in data presented in different editions reflect updates by countries as well as revisions to historical series and changes in methodology. Thus readers are advised not to compare data series between editions or between different editions of World Bank publications. Consistent time series are available from the *World Development Indicators 2005* CD-ROM.

Ratios and growth rates

For ease of reference, the tables usually show ratios and rates of growth rather than the simple underlying values. Values in their original form are available from the *World Development Indicators 2005* CD-ROM. Unless otherwise noted, growth rates are computed using the least-squares regression method (see *statistical methods* on page 305). Because this method takes into account all available observations during a period, the resulting growth rates reflect general trends that are not unduly influenced by exceptional values. To exclude the effects of inflation, constant price economic indicators are used in calculating growth rates. Data in italics are for a year or period other than that specified in the column heading—up to two years before or after for economic indicators and up to three years for social indicators, because the latter tend to be collected less regularly and change less dramatically over short periods.

Constant price series

An economy's growth is measured by the increase in value added produced by the individuals and enterprises operating in that economy. Thus measuring real growth requires estimates of GDP and its components valued in constant prices. The World Bank collects constant price national accounts series in national currencies and recorded in the country's original base year. To obtain comparable series of constant price data, it rescales GDP and value added by industrial origin to a common reference year, currently 2000. This process gives rise to a discrepancy between the rescaled GDP and the sum of the rescaled components. Because allocating the discrepancy would give rise to distortions in the growth rate, it is left unallocated.

Summary measures

The summary measures for regions and income groups, presented at the end of most tables, are calculated by simple addition when they are expressed in levels. Aggregate growth rates and ratios are usually computed as weighted averages. The summary measures for social indicators are weighted by population or subgroups of population, except for infant mortality, which is weighted by the number of births. See the notes on specific indicators for more information.

For summary measures that cover many years, calculations are based on a uniform group of economies so that the composition of the aggregate does not change over time. Group measures are compiled only if the data available for a given year account for at least two-thirds of the full group, as defined for the 2000 benchmark year. As long as this criterion is met, economies for which data are missing are assumed to behave like those that provide estimates. Readers should keep in mind that the summary measures are estimates of representative aggregates for each topic and that nothing meaningful can be deduced about behavior at the country level by working back from group indicators. In addition, the estimation process may result in discrepancies between subgroup and overall totals.

Table 1. Key indicators of development

Population is based on the de facto definition, which counts all residents, regardless of legal status or citizenship, except for refugees not permanently settled in the country of asylum, who are generally considered part of the population of the country of origin.

Average annual population growth rate is the exponential rate of change for the period (see the section on statistical methods on page 305).

Population density is midyear population divided by land area. Land area is a country's total area excluding areas under inland bodies of water and coastal waterways. Density is calculated using the most recently available data on land area.

Gross national income (GNI—formerly gross national product or GNP), the broadest measure of national income, measures total value added from domestic and foreign sources claimed by residents. GNI comprises gross domestic product (GDP) plus net receipts of primary income from foreign sources. Data are converted from national currency to current U.S. dollars using the World Bank Atlas method. This involves using a three-year average of exchange rates to smooth the effects of transitory exchange rate fluctuations. See the section on statistical methods for discussion of the Atlas method.

GNI per capita is GNI divided by midyear population. It is converted into current U.S. dollars by the Atlas method. The World Bank uses GNI per capita in U.S dollars to classify economies for analytical purposes and to determine borrowing eligibility.

PPP gross national income, which is GNI converted into international dollars using purchasing power parity (PPP) conversion factors, is included because nominal exchange rates do not always reflect international differences in relative prices. At the PPP rate, one international dollar has the same purchasing power over domestic GNI that the U.S. dollar has over U.S. GNI. PPP rates allow a standard comparison of real price levels between countries, just as conventional price indexes allow comparison of real values over

time. The PPP conversion factors used here are derived from price surveys covering 118 countries conducted by the International Comparison Program. For Organisation for Economic Co-operation and Development (OECD) countries data come from the most recent round of surveys, completed in 1999; the rest are either from the 1996 survey, or data from the 1993 or earlier round and extrapolated to the 1996 benchmark. Estimates for countries not included in the surveys are derived from statistical models using available data.

PPP GNI per capita is PPP GNI divided by midyear population.

Gross domestic product (GDP) per capita growth is based on GDP measured in constant prices. Growth in GDP is considered a broad measure of the growth of an economy. GDP in constant prices can be estimated by measuring the total quantity of goods and services produced in a period, valuing them at an agreed set of base year prices, and subtracting the cost of intermediate inputs, also in constant prices. See the section on statistical methods for details of the least-squares growth rate.

Life expectancy at birth is the number of years a newborn infant would live if patterns of mortality prevailing at its birth were to stay the same throughout its life.

Adult literacy rate is the percentage of persons aged 15 and above who can, with understanding, read and write a short, simple statement about their everyday life.

Carbon dioxide (CO_2) emissions measures those emissions stemming from the burning of fossil fuels and the manufacture of cement. These include carbon dioxide produced during consumption of solid, liquid, and gas fuels and from gas flaring.

The Carbon Dioxide Information Analysis Center (CDIAC), sponsored by the U.S. Department of Energy, calculates annual anthropogenic emissions of CO_2. These calculations are derived from data on fossil fuel consumption, based on the World Energy Data Set maintained by the UNSD, and from data on world cement manufacturing, based on the Cement Manufacturing Data Set maintained by the U.S. Bureau of Mines. Each year the CDIAC recalculates the entire time series from 1950 to the present, incorporating its most recent findings and the latest corrections to its database. Fuels supplied to ships and aircraft engaged in international transportation are excluded in these estimates because of the difficulty of apportioning these fuels among the countries benefiting from that transport.

Table 2. Millennium Development Goals: eradicating poverty and improving lives

Proportion of population below $1 a day (PPP$) is the percentage of the population living on less than $1.08 a day at 1993 international prices. For further information on poverty data, see the technical note for Table A1.

Prevalence of child malnutrition is the percentage of children under five whose weight for age is less than minus two standard deviations from the median for the international reference population ages 0–59 months. The reference population, adopted by the World Health Organization (WHO) in 1983, is based on children from the United States, who are assumed to be well nourished. Estimates of child malnutrition are from national survey data. The proportion of children who are underweight is the most common indicator of malnutrition. Being underweight, even mildly, increases the risk of death and inhibits cognitive development in children. Moreover, it perpetuates the problem from one generation to the next, as malnourished women are more likely to have low-birth-weight babies.

Primary completion rate is the percentage of students completing the last year of primary school. It is calculated by taking the total number of students in the last grade of primary school, minus the number of repeaters in that grade, divided by the total number of children of official graduation age. The primary completion rate reflects the primary cycle as defined by the International Standard Classification of Education (ISCED), ranging from three or four years of primary education (in a very small number of countries) to five or six years (in most countries), and seven (in a small number of countries). Because curricula and standards for school completion vary across countries, a high rate of primary completion does not necessarily mean high levels of student learning.

Gender parity ratio in primary and secondary school is the ratio of female gross enrollment rate in primary and secondary school to the gross enrollment rate of males. Eliminating gender disparities in education would help to increase the status and capabilities of women. This indicator is an imperfect measure of the relative accessibility of schooling for girls. With a target date of 2005, this is the first of the targets to fall due. School enrollment data are reported to the UNESCO Institute for Statistics by national education authorities. Primary education provides children with basic reading, writing, and mathematics skills along with an elementary understanding of such subjects as history, geography, natural science, social science, art, and music. Secondary education completes the provision of basic education that began at the primary level, and aims at laying foundations for lifelong learning and human development, by offering more subject-or skill-oriented instruction using more specialized teachers.

Under-five mortality rate is the probability that a newborn baby will die before reaching age five, if subject to current age-specific mortality rates. The probability is expressed as a rate per 1,000. The main sources of mortality data are vital registration systems and direct or indirect estimates based on sample surveys or censuses. To produce harmonized estimates of under-five mortality rates that make use of all available information in a transparent way, a methodology that fits a regression line to the relationship between mortality rates and their reference dates using weighted least squares was developed and adopted by both UNICEF and the World Bank.

Prevalence of HIV is the percentage of people ages 15–49 who are infected with HIV. Adult HIV prevalence rates reflect the rate of HIV infection in each country's population. Low national prevalence rates can be very misleading, however. They often disguise serious epidemics that are initially concentrated in certain localities or among specific population groups and threaten to spill over into the wider population. In many parts of the developing world most new infections occur in young adults, with young women especially vulnerable. The estimates of HIV prevalence are based on extrapolations from data collected through surveys and from surveillance of small, nonrepresentative groups.

Maternal mortality rate is the number of women who die from pregnancy-related causes during pregnancy and childbirth, per 100,000 live births. The data shown here have been collected in various years and adjusted to a common 1995 base year. The values are modeled estimates based on an exercise carried out by the World Health Organization (WHO) and United Nations Children's Fund(UNICEF). In this exercise maternal mortality was estimated with a regression model using information on fertility, birth attendants, and HIV prevalence. This cannot be assumed to provide an accurate estimate of maternal mortality in any country in the table.

Births attended by skilled health staff are the percentage of deliveries attended by personnel trained to give the necessary supervision, care, and advice to women during pregnancy, labor, and the postpartum period, to conduct deliveries on their own, and to care for newborns. The share of births attended by skilled health staff is an indicator of a health system's ability to provide adequate care for a pregnant women. Good antenatal and postnatal care improves maternal health and reduces maternal and infant mortality. But data may not reflect such improvements because health information system are often weak, material deaths are underreported, and rates of maternal mortality are difficult to measure.

Table 3. Economic activity

Gross domestic product is gross value added, at purchasers' prices, by all resident producers in the economy plus any taxes and minus any subsidies not included in the value of the products. It is calculated without deducting for depreciation of fabricated assets or for depletion or degradation of natural resources. Value added is the net output of an industry after adding up all outputs and subtracting intermediate inputs. The industrial origin of value added is determined by the International Standard Industrial Classification (ISIC) revision 3. The World Bank conventionally uses the U.S. dollar and applies the average official exchange rate reported by the International Monetary Fund for the year shown. An alternative conversion factor is applied if the official exchange rate is judged to diverge by an exceptionally large margin from the rate effectively applied to transactions in foreign currencies and traded products.

Gross domestic product average annual growth rate is calculated from constant price GDP data in local currency.

Agricultural productivity refers to the ratio of agricultural value added, measured in constant 2000 U.S. dollars, to the number of workers in agriculture.

Value added is the net output of an industry after adding up all out-puts and subtracting intermediate inputs. The industrial origin of value added is determined by the International Standard Industrial Classification (ISIC) revision 3.

Agriculture value added corresponds to ISIC divisions 1–5 and includes forestry and fishing.

Industry value added comprises mining, manufacturing, construction, electricity, water, and gas (ISIC divisions 10–45).

Services value added correspond to ISIC divisions 50–99.

Household final consumption expenditure (private consumption in previous editions) is the market value of all goods and services, including durable products (such as cars, washing machines, and home computers), purchased by households. It excludes purchases of dwellings but includes imputed rent for owner-occupied dwellings. It also includes payments and fees to governments to obtain permits and licenses. Here, household consumption expenditure includes the expenditures of nonprofit institutions serving households, even when reported separately by the country. In practice, household consumption expenditure may include any statistical discrepancy in the use of resources relative to the supply of resources.

General government final consumption expenditure (general government consumption in previous editions) includes all government current expenditures for purchases of goods and services (including compensation of employees). It also includes most expenditures on national defense and security, but excludes government military expenditures that are part of government capital formation.

Gross capital formation (gross domestic investment in previous editions) consists of outlays on additions to the fixed assets of the economy plus net changes in the level of inventories and valuables. Fixed assets include land improvements (fences, ditches, drains, and so on); plant, machinery, and equipment purchases; and the construction of buildings, roads, railways, and the like, including commercial and industrial buildings, offices, schools, hospitals, and private dwellings. Inventories are stocks of goods held by firms to meet temporary or unexpected fluctuations in production or sales, and "work in progress". According to the 1993 SNA net acquisitions of valuables are also considered capital formation.

External balance of goods and services is exports of goods and services less imports of goods and services. Trade in goods and services comprise all transactions between residents of a country and the rest of the world involving a change in ownership of general merchandise, goods sent for processing and repairs, nonmonetary gold, and services.

The **GDP implicit deflator** reflects changes in prices for all final demand categories, such as government consumption, capital formation, and international trade, as well as the main component, private final consumption. It is derived as the ratio of current to constant price GDP. The GDP deflator may also be calculated explicitly as a Paasche price index in which the weights are the current period quantities of output.

National accounts indicators for most developing countries are collected from national statistical organizations and central banks by visiting and resident World Bank missions. Data for high-income economies come from the OECD data files.

Table 4. Trade, aid, and finance

Merchandise exports show the f.o.b. (free on board) value of goods provided to the rest of the world valued in U.S. dollars.

Merchandise imports show the c.i.f. value of goods (the cost of the goods including insurance and freight) purchased from the rest of the world valued in U.S. dollars. Data on merchandise trade come from the World Trade Organization (WTO) in its annual report.

Manufactured exports comprise the commodities in Standard Industrial Trade Classification (SITC) sections 5 (chemicals), 6 (basic manufactures), 7 (machinery and transport equipment), and 8 (miscellaneous manufactured goods), excluding division 68.

High technology exports are products with high R&D intensity. They include high-technology products such as in aerospace, computers, pharmaceuticals, scientific instruments, and electrical machinery.

Current account balance is the sum of net exports of goods and services, net income, and net current transfers.

Net private capital flows consist of private debt and nondebt flows. Private debt flows include commercial bank lending, bonds, and other private credits; nondebt private flows are foreign direct investment and portfolio equity investment.

Foreign direct investment is net inflows of investment to acquire a lasting management interest (10 percent or more of voting stock) in an enterprise operating in an economy other than that of the investor. It is the sum of equity capital, re-investment of earnings, other long-term capital, and short-term capital, as shown in the balance of payments. Data on the current account balance, private capital flows, and foreign direct investment are drawn from the IMF's *Balance of Payments Statistics Yearbook* and *International Financial Statistics*.

Official development assistance or official aid from the high-income members of the OECD are the main source of official external finance for developing countries, but official development assistance (ODA) is also disbursed by some important donor countries that are not members of OECD's Development Assistance Committee (DAC). DAC has three criteria for ODA: it is undertaken by the official sector; it promotes economic development or welfare as a main objective; and it is provided on concessional terms, with a grant element of at least 25 percent on loans.

Official development assistance comprises grants and loans, net of repayments, that meet the DAC definition of ODA and are made to countries and territories in part I of the DAC list of aid recipients. Official aid comprises grants and ODA-like loans, net of repayments, to countries and territories in part II of the DAC list of aid recipients. Bilateral grants are transfers in money or in kind for which no repayment is required. Bilateral loans are loans extended by governments or official agencies that have a grant element of at least 25 percent and for which repayment is required in convertible currencies or in kind.

Total external debt is debt owed to nonresidents repayable in foreign currency, goods, or services. It is the sum of public, publicly guaranteed, and private non-guaranteed long-term debt, use of IMF credit, and short-term debt. Short-term debt includes all debt having an original maturity of one year or less and interest in arrears on long-term debt.

Present value of debt is the sum of short-term external debt plus the discounted sum of total debt service payments due on public, publicly guaranteed, and private nonguaranteed long-term external debt over the life of existing loans.

The main sources of external debt information are reports to the World Bank through its Debtor Reporting System from member countries that have received World Bank loans. Additional information has been drawn from the files of the World Bank and the IMF. Summary tables of the external debt of developing countries are published annually in the World Bank's *Global Development Finance*.

Net migration is the total number of migrants during the period, that is, the number of immigrants less the number of emigrants, including both citizens and noncitizens. Data shown in the table are five-year estimates. Data are from the United Nations Population Division's *World Population Prospects: The 2004 Revision*.

Domestic credit provided by banking sector includes all credit to various sectors on a gross basis, with the exception of credit to the central government, which is net. The banking sector includes monetary authorities, deposit money banks, and other banking institutions for which data are available (including institutions that do not accept transferable deposits but do incur such liabilities as time and savings deposits). Examples of other banking institutions include savings and mortgage loan institutions and building and

loan associations. Data are from the IMF's *International Finance Statistics*.

Statistical methods

This section describes the calculation of the least-squares growth rate, the exponential (endpoint) growth rate, and the World Bank's Atlas methodology for calculating the conversion factor used to estimate GNI and GNI per capita in U.S. dollars.

Least-squares growth rate

Least-squares growth rates are used wherever there is a sufficiently long time series to permit a reliable calculation. No growth rate is calculated if more than half the observations in a period are missing.

The least-squares growth rate, r, is estimated by fitting a linear regression trendline to the logarithmic annual values of the variable in the relevant period. The regression equation takes the form

$$\ln X_t = a + bt,$$

which is equivalent to the logarithmic transformation of the compound growth equation,

$$X_t = X_o (1 + r)^t.$$

In this equation, X is the variable, t is time, and $a = \log X_o$ and $b - \ln (1 + r)$ are the parameters to be estimated. If b^* is the least-squares estimate of b, the average annual growth rate, r, is obtained as $[\exp(b^*) - 1]$ and is multiplied by 100 to express it as a percentage.

The calculated growth rate is an average rate that is representative of the available observations over the entire period. It does not necessarily match the actual growth rate between any two periods.

Exponential growth rate

The growth rate between two points in time for certain demographic data, notably labor force and population, is calculated from the equation

$$r = \ln (p_n /p_1)/n,$$

where p_n and p_1 are the last and first observations in the period, n is the number of years in the period, and ln is the natural logarithm operator. This growth rate is based on a model of continuous, exponential growth between two points in time. It does not take into account the intermediate values of the series. Note also that the exponential growth rate does not correspond to the annual rate of change measured at a one-year interval which is given by

$$(p_n - p_{n-1})/p_{n-1}.$$

World Bank Atlas method

In calculating GNI and GNI per capita in U.S. dollars for certain operational purposes, the World Bank uses the Atlas conversion factor. The purpose of the Atlas conversion factor is to reduce the impact of exchange rate fluctuations in the cross-country comparison of national incomes. The Atlas conversion factor for any year is the average of a country's exchange rate (or alternative conversion factor) for that year and its exchange rates for the two preceding years, adjusted for the difference between the rate of inflation in the country and that in Japan, the United Kingdom, the United States, and the Euro Zone. A country's inflation rate is measured by the change in its GDP deflator. The inflation rate for Japan, the United Kingdom, the United States, and the Euro Zone, representing international inflation, is measured by the change in the SDR deflator. (Special drawing rights, or SDRs, are the IMF's unit of account.) The SDR deflator is calculated as a weighted average of these countries' GDP deflators in SDR terms, the weights being the amount of each country's currency in one SDR unit. Weights vary over time because both the composition of the SDR and the relative exchange rates for each currency change. The SDR deflator is calculated in SDR terms first and then converted to U.S. dollars using the SDR to dollar Atlas conversion factor. The Atlas conversion factor is then applied to a country's GNI. The resulting GNI in U.S. dollars is divided by the midyear population to derive GNI per capita.

When official exchange rates are deemed to be unreliable or unrepresentative of the effective exchange rate during a period, an alternative estimate of the exchange rate is used in the Atlas formula (see below).

The following formulas describe the calculation of the Atlas conversion factor for year t:

$$e_t^* = \frac{1}{3}[e_{t-2}\left(\frac{p_t}{p_{t-2}} / \frac{p_t^{S\$}}{p_{t-2}^{S\$}}\right) + e_{t-1}\left(\frac{p_t}{p_{t-1}} / \frac{p_t^{S\$}}{p_{t-1}^{S\$}}\right) + e_t]$$

and the calculation of GNI per capita in U.S. dollars for year t:

$$Y_t^\$ = (Y_t/N_t)/e_t^*$$

where e_t^* is the Atlas conversion factor (national currency to the U.S. dollar) for year t, e_t is the average annual exchange rate (national currency to the U.S. dollar) for year t, p_t is the GDP deflator for year t, $p_t^{S\$}$ is the SDR deflator in U.S. dollar terms for year t, $Y_t^\$$ is the Atlas GNI per capita in U.S. dollars in year t, Y_t is current GNI (local currency) for year t, and N_t is the midyear population for year t.

Alternative conversion factors

The World Bank systematically assesses the appropriateness of official exchange rates as conversion factors. An alternative conversion factor is used when the official exchange rate is judged to diverge by an exceptionally large margin from the rate effectively applied to domestic transactions of foreign currencies and traded products. This applies to only a small number of countries, as shown in Primary data documentation table in World Development Indicators 2005. Alternative conversion factors are used in the Atlas methodology and elsewhere in the Selected World Development Indicators as single-year conversion factors.

Table 5. Key indicators for other economies

Population is based on the de facto definition, which counts all residents, regardless of legal status or citizenship, except for refugees not permanently settled in the country of asylum, who are generally considered part of the population of the country of origin.

Average annual population growth rate is the exponential rate of change for the period (see the section on statistical methods below).

Population density is midyear population divided by land area. Land area is a country's total area excluding areas under inland bodies of water and coastal waterways. Density is calculated using the most recently available data on land area.

Gross national income (GNI—formerly gross national product or GNP), the broadest measure of national income, measures total value added from domestic and foreign sources claimed by residents. GNI comprises gross domestic product (GDP) plus net receipts of primary income from foreign sources. Data are converted from national currency to current U.S. dollars using the World Bank Atlas method. This involves using a three-year average of exchange rates to smooth the effects of transitory exchange rate fluctuations. (See the section on statistical methods below for further discussion of the Atlas method.)

GNI per capita is GNI divided by midyear population. It is converted into current U.S. dollars by the Atlas method. The World Bank uses GNI per capita in U.S dollars to classify economies for analytical purposes and to determine borrowing eligibility.

PPP Gross national income, which is GNI converted into international dollars using purchasing power parity (PPP) conversion factors, is included because nominal exchange rates do not always reflect international differences in relative prices. At the PPP rate, one international dollar has the same purchasing power over domestic GNI that the U.S. dollar has over U.S. GNI. PPP rates allow a standard comparison of real price levels between countries, just as conventional price indexes allow comparison of real values over time. The PPP conversion factors used here are derived from price surveys covering 118 countries conducted by the International Comparison Program. For Organisation for Economic Co-operation and Development (OECD) countries data come from the most recent round of surveys, completed in 1999; the rest are either from the 1996 survey, or data from the 1993 or earlier round and extrapolated to the 1996 benchmark. Estimates for countries not included in the surveys are derived from statistical models using available data.

PPP GNI per capita is PPP GNI divided by midyear population.

Gross domestic product (GDP) per capita growth is based on GDP measured in constant prices. Growth in GDP is considered a broad measure of the growth of an economy. GDP in constant prices can be estimated by measuring the total quantity of goods and services produced in a period, valuing them at an agreed set of base year prices, and subtracting the cost of intermediate inputs, also in constant prices. See the section on statistical methods for details of the least-squares growth rate.

Life expectancy at birth is the number of years a newborn infant would live if patterns of mortality prevailing at its birth were to stay the same throughout its life.

Adult literacy rate is the percentage of persons aged 15 and above who can, with understanding, read and write a short, simple statement about their everyday life.

Carbon dioxide (CO_2) emissions measures those emissions stemming from the burning of fossil fuels and the manufacture of cement. These include carbon dioxide produced during consumption of solid, liquid, and gas fuels and from gas flaring.

The Carbon Dioxide Information Analysis Center (CDIAC), sponsored by the U.S. Department of Energy, calculates annual anthropogenic emissions of CO_2. These calculations are derived from data on fossil fuel consumption, based on the World Energy Data Set maintained by the UNSD, and from data on world cement manufacturing, based on the Cement Manufacturing Data Set maintained by the U.S. Bureau of Mines. Each year the CDIAC recalculates the entire time series from 1950 to the present, incorporating its most recent findings and the latest corrections to its database. Estimates exclude fuels supplied to ships and aircraft engaged in international transportation because of the difficulty of apportioning these fuels among the countries benefiting from that transport.

Index